TREES & SHRUBS
A complete guide

By the same author:

TREES & SHRUBS
A complete guide

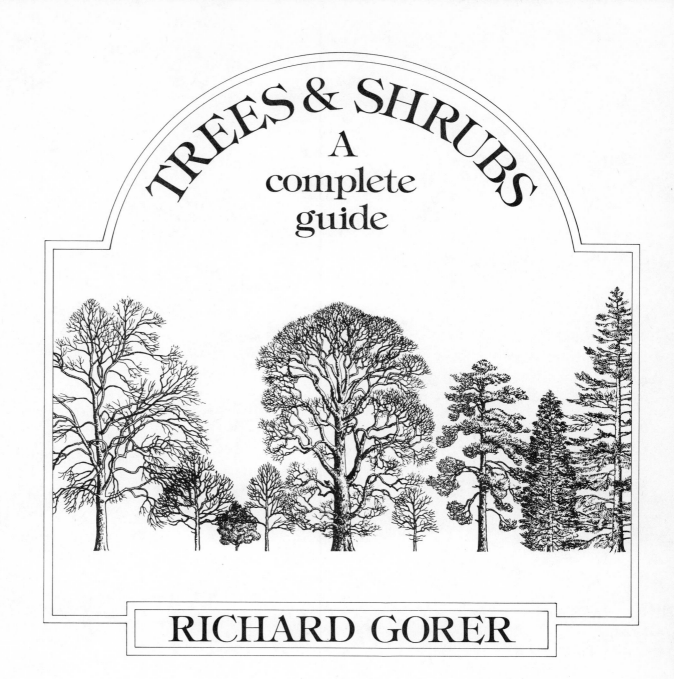

RICHARD GORER

DAVID & CHARLES
NEWTON ABBOT   LONDON
NORTH POMFRET (VT)   VANCOUVER

ISBN 0 7153 6850 8

Library of Congress Catalog Card Number
76–4364

Set by Trade Linotype Ltd in 10pt Times New Roman
and printed in Great Britain by Redwood Burn Limited for
David & Charles (Publishers) Limited   Brunel House
Newton Abbot   Devon

Published in the United States of America by David &
Charles Inc   North Pomfret   Vermont 05053   USA

Published in Canada by Douglas David & Charles
Limited   1875 Welch Street   North Vancouver   BC

Contents

Introduction

Assuming, in spite of so much evidence to the contrary, that honesty really is the best policy, we should, perhaps, start by defining our terms of reference. This book is intended to give capsulated descriptions and information regarding the trees and shrubs that are generally hardy in the United Kingdom. Since the number of these is very large indeed, it has been necessary to be extremely selective in the choice of subjects, and it is only fair that the reader should know the principles that have guided this selection.

Availability

The first principle is that the plant should be available. If you read W. J. Bean's masterly *Trees and Shrubs Hardy in the British Isles* (originally in three volumes, now in process of revision in four volumes), you are liable to be infected with his enthusiasm for the genus *Carya*, only to find that very few species are commercially available. In the same way visitors to the rhododendron shows at the RHS may be attracted by *Rhododendron nakotiltum,* but since there are very few plants in cultivation, none of which are in nurseries, there would seem little point in recommending it.

Hardiness

Our second criterion is that the plant should be capable of being grown without protection in an insular climate with winter temperatures that may frequently fall as low as $-8°C$, but where such frosts are not often unduly prolonged; the summer temperature will rarely rise above $25°C$, but will fluctuate quite considerably, while prolonged dry spells are comparatively infrequent. The average rainfall will be 30–40in a year, fairly evenly distributed throughout the twelve months.

This means that many plants which are adapted to a Continental climate, where the winters may be much more severe than anything liable to be experienced in Great Britain, but where the hotter drier summers enable wood to be ripened more satisfactorily, may grow less satisfactorily in the UK than they will in parts of Europe. We may cite *Cornus florida* and *Pseudolarix* as examples. On the other hand, our insular winters may mean that certain Mediterranean plants will survive here, whereas further south they will succumb to a Continental winter. This applies not only to plants from the Mediterranean, but also to some from western China, the Himalaya, New Zealand and the milder parts of the Americas.

In countries other than the British Isles the following points should be borne in mind. In the northern United States and in Canada it is unlikely that many plants of Mediterranean origin will succeed and plants from the lower portions of the Sino-Himalaya may be somewhat doubtful. Fortunately the plants grown in the Arnold Arboretum at Boston will provide a good guide. Shrubs and trees from Siberia, Manchuria and northern Japan will do extremely well. In the southern parts of Australia and in Tasmania there will probably be difficulty in growing plants from the north and from parts of the Sino-Himalaya owing to the somewhat scanty rainfall, although there should be no difficulty as regards temperature, while in New Zealand there should be no difficulty experienced in growing any of the plants to be described below.

This has meant the exclusion of all those plants that will only thrive in such districts as Cornwall and western Scotland and other parts affected by the Gulf Stream. I have, however, included a few subjects that should survive anywhere in the UK with wall protection, noting this essential in the description.

In any case it should be borne in mind that hardiness tends to be somewhat relative and the exceptional winter may damage plants that under normal circumstances would survive without trouble. For example *Hoheria lyallii* will survive most winters happily, but in the exceptional 1962 winter many plants were cut to the ground, although most regenerated. Where I know such phenomena are probable I have mentioned it. It should also be borne in mind that hardiness is not entirely a matter of winter temperatures. Many plants are intolerant of prolonged drought, so that some plants, such as most of the *Abies,* will not thrive in the eastern part of the country, although they are unmoved by the severest winters and grow magnificently in the colder parts of the North-West and in Scotland. Here again this information will be reflected in the text, where I have such information, although there may be lacunae, owing to ignorance.

Selection

For the most part descriptions will be confined to species with hybrids and cultivars receiving the most perfunctory mention and, in such cases as *Rosa* and *Rhododendron*, where the number of hybrids is very large, they have been completely disregarded. This is regrettable but, for reasons of space, essential.

Similarly regrettable has been the exclusion of all plants whose dimensions do not attain a metre either vertically or horizontally. Such plants are usually either planted in the alpine garden or treated as herbaceous subjects, but it is only the wish to keep the book of a reasonable length that can be pleaded in justification.

Rate of Growth

Where possible I have indicated the probable rate of growth, dividing the subjects under three categories: rapid, moderate and slow. Rapid growers can be expected to make at least 30cm of new growth each year, moderate growers will make 15–30, while slow growers will rarely elongate by more than 15cm each year. This rate of growth is calculated for what I imagine are average conditions, but it should be emphasised that such rates are liable to considerable variations according to local conditions and microclimates and the terms should probably only be regarded as indicative. For example, if conditions are very dry when the new growths of a rapid grower are elongating, they may well fall below the expectation that such a description would suggest. Unsuitable soils, continuous wind, insect pests, excessive drought or precipitation or bad drainage will all affect the plant's growth, quite apart from such physical conditions as the state of the plant's roots. Newly-planted subjects, if their roots have been damaged in the lifting, may well take a year or longer to get back to their original condition, so it will be that period before the plant starts to grow at the expected rate.

Another point to be borne in mind is that many plants grow at different rates at different ages. For example, most of the berberis and mahonias will make practically no growth from seed for the first two or three years, but after that will start growing rapidly; and all plants, once they have attained certain dimensions will grow more slowly.

With all these qualifications you will appreciate that the terms rapid, moderate and slow are to be regarded with some scepticism, although they will hold good for comparative rates of growth.

The main difference between a shrub and a tree is that the tree radiates from a central growth, the trunk, which is capable of almost indefinite expansion, while a shrub will have a number of growths ascending from the rootstock, which are short-lived compared to a tree trunk and which frequently die back and are renewed. Sometimes the distinction is tenuous. *Erica arborea* is a somewhat low shrub around the Mediterranean, but makes a tree with a long trunk in the Canary Islands and the Ethiopian mountains. Moreover some trees have two or more trunks. Ordinarily trees tend to be considerably taller than shrubs.

Symbols and abbreviations

In the effort to save space a number of symbols and abbreviations have been employed. The figures in bold type before the descriptions may be interpreted as follows:

1. The plant has attractive mature bark.
2. The year-old wood is attractively coloured.
3. The emerging leaves are attractively coloured.
4. The plant has attractive flowers.
5. The plant has attractive fruit.
6. The plant may be expected to colour well in the autumn.
7. The plant will make a specimen or shade tree.

If the figures are in parentheses it means that the qualities indicated are of rare or uncertain occurrence. For example, *Idesia polycarpa* has very attractive fruits, but these will only be produced if both a male and a female plant are planted in proximity; if only a single tree is present no fruits will be set.

It may be observed that the numbers follow the seasons, starting in winter when the bare bark or the coloured young wood will be the feature most in evidence; in spring the emerging young leaves will display their charms; in spring or summer the flowers appear; the fruits appear later, while autumn tints will close the display. Trees that exist purely for their beauty of habit also merit mention. Beauty of foliage being a rather nebulous quality has not been included, although mentioned in the text.

Autumnal colour is not a constant factor, being dependent on a number of variables, of which the weather during the summer would seem to be the main influence, but which is also influenced by the soil, in some cases, by age (liquidambar never seems to colour before it has become fairly sizeable), and sometimes by genetic factors; some clones of *Cercidiphyllum* never seem to colour, whereas others are extremely brilliant. Where results are known to be doubtful you will find **(6).** The figure without the brackets indicates that the plant colours well in most districts.

The fact that a species has no symbol in front of it does not mean that it is necessarily unattractive. For example the Box has no beauty of flower or fruit, yet it is a most useful adjunct in the garden. Similarly plants such as *Eleagnus pungens* may not, in themselves, be particularly attractive, but may have variegated forms which are highly desirable.

In the descriptions the following abbreviations are used:

sp   a single species; spp   more than one
brs   branches
bts   branchlets
lv   leaves
fl   flowers
fr   fruit
cv   cultivar
var   variant

Measurements

Metric measurements are employed as well as temperatures in centigrade. The measurements can roughly be translated into feet and inches if you reckon two and a half centimetres to the inch and forty inches to the metre.

Introductions

The dates of introduction to cultivation of the various plants and the name of the collector responsible for their introduction, if known, is given at the close of the description. In many cases it will be found that these differ from those given in other reference books. This is because I have done a large amount of research on this subject, although I have only given the results here without my substantiating reasons.

English Names

Where English names are of general application, such as beech or lilac, they are inserted next to the latin name. Where they are somewhat recondite, such as clammy locust or farkleberry they have been omitted.

Technical Terms

It is extremely difficult to give satisfactory and precise descriptions of plants without employing technical terms, and this might be a suitable place to insert some of the more usually employed ones. There is a glossary in alphabetic order at the end of the book, but here I am considering the parts of the plant separately.

Framework

A tree consists of a central stem or *trunk* from which radiate *branches*. These continue both to elongate and to ramify each year and the growths of the current year are referred to as *branchlets*. Both trunk, branches and branchlets are covered with *bark*, a thick skin which may be differently coloured on the branchlets from other parts of the plant. In some plants, notably in birches, the bark peels off at regular intervals to reveal fresh bark, often of a very attractive texture, underneath. This is known as *exfoliation*. Sometimes the wood is armed with sharp, pointed outgrowths which are known as *spines* or *thorns*. In theory the term 'thorn' should be reserved for pointed outgrowths tipping the branches and branchlets, but in practice both terms are used as though they were synonymous. In the case of the rose family, the outgrowths are termed *prickles*.

The Leaf

Evergreen leaves persist throughout the winter and in some cases for several years, although with broad-leaved trees they tend to fall after the current year's leaves have unfurled. Deciduous leaves fall in the latter part of the year. Semi-evergreen plants will keep much of their foliage through a mild winter, but lose them all under severe conditions.

The leaf consists of the leaf-stalk or *petiole* and the blade or *lamina*. Sometimes there are small leaf-like appendages on, or at the base of, the petiole; these are known as *stipules*. Leaves can either be *simple* as in lilac or *compound*, consisting of a number of separate *leaflets*, as in laburnum. If leaves spring direct from the stem without a petiole, they are termed *sessile*. The surface of the leaf (and of the branchlets) may be quite smooth or *glabrous*, downy or *pubescent*, hairy or *villous*. Sometimes the branchlets and young leaves (and also many fruits) are covered with a fine bloom, which is easily removed; they are known as *pruinose*. If one or both sides of the leaf is covered with a felty or woolly covering, this is referred to as an *indumentum*. This can be persistent or only temporary. Small hard lumps on the leaves or at the base of the petiole are referred to as *glands* and these are also occasionally found at the tips of hairs, when they are generally rather sticky. Leaves that are rough to the touch are referred to as *hispid* or *scabrid*.

The shape of leaves is described both generally and in detail. The end of the leaf furthest from the petiole is the *apex*, the part nearest is the *base*, the edge of the leaf is the *margin*. If the margin is unbroken the leaf is *entire*, if the margin is very finely toothed it is *serrate*; if more coarsely toothed it is *dentate*; if shallowly edged with rounded incisions it is *crenate* or *crenulate*, while if the leaf is regularly and quite deeply divided it is *lobed* and the divisions are referred to as *lobes*. If the apex is blunt it is *obtuse*, if it comes gradually to a point it is *acuminate* or *acute*, while if the point is prolonged it is *cuspidate* or *long-acuminate*. If the apex is obtuse apart from a small abrupt point, this point is known as a *mucro* and the apex is described as *mucronate*. Most leaves are provided with a central vein (or nerve) from which the other veins radiate. This is known as the *midrib*. Some plants such as many *Viburnum* species have three or more main veins, while most conifers lack the regular venation of broad-leaved trees.

The simplest leaf shape is *linear*, where the leaf is long, narrow and of equal width throughout; if it is somewhat wider at the centre it should be termed *ensiform*. If, apart from some narrowing at the base and apex, the leaf is the same width throughout, it is termed *oblong*. If the leaf at first broadens out from the base and then contracts towards the apex it is *lanceolate*, while if the reverse takes place and the broader portion is towards the apex it is *oblanceolate*.

The prefix ob- is used to designate a reversal of the usual form; thus *ovate* means that the leaf is egg-shaped with the broadest portion at the base, *obovate* has the broadest portion near the apex. Usually the petiole joins the leaf at the base, but occasionally it joins the leaf towards its centre. Such leaves are known as *peltate* (eg, *Tropaeolum*). The other simple leaf-shapes most often to be met with are *elliptic,* where the leaf tapers to a point at each end, *orbicular* or round, *cordate* or heart-shaped, *sagittate* or shaped like an arrow-head, *hastate* or shaped like a halberd, *rhomboid* or diamond-shaped, *reniform* or kidney-shaped, *deltoid* or triangular and *pandurate* (or panduriform), shaped like the body of a violin.

Compound leaves are named from the way that the leaflets are arranged. If three leaflets arise from a central point, the leaf is *ternate* or *trifoliate,* if more than three leaflets arise, the leaf is *digitate*. If the leaflets are arranged in pairs along a central midrib or stalk (*Rachis*), possibly with a single terminal leaflet, the leaf is *pinnate,* and the leaflets are sometimes referred to as *pinnae*. The shape can be compounded still further, as each of the pinnae could be replaced by a smaller pinnate leaf to give a *bipinnate* leaf, or each leaflet of a ternate leaf could itself divide into three leaflets, giving nine leaflets in all or a *biternate* leaf.

There are a number of leaves that are so deeply lobed that they are intermediate between simple and compound leaves. If these lobes reach practically to the midrib, the leaves are termed *pinnatisect,* or *palmatisect* if the basic shape is pinnate or palmate. If the lobing stops quite a distance from the midrib, the leaves are *pinnatifid* or *palmatifid*.

The way the leaves are situated on the stem is often of importance in determining genera and species. They may be *opposite*; if more than two leaves arise from the same point on the stem the leaves are said to be in *whorls*. If the leaves are not opposite, they are *alternate*.

The place where the leaf or petiole joins the stem is known as a *node* and as an *axil*, so that any growth or inflorescence arising from the space between the stem and the petiole is known as *axillary*.

The Inflorescence

Like leaves, inflorescences may be simple, with a solitary flower, or compound, with many flowers. If the inflorescence comes at the end of a branch it is known as *terminal*; if it arises from the axil of a leaf it is axillary.

Among compound inflorescences the simplest is the *raceme*. Here there is a central stem or rachis, which elongates as the flowers open; these spring from the rachis, each on a *pedicel*, usually starting at the bottom. Should the pedicels be branched the inflorescence is no longer a raceme but a *panicle*. In some cases the pedicels of a raceme are of varying length, so that all the flowers open at the same level, those on the outside having much longer pedicels than those higher up the raceme. This is known as a *corymb*. Sometimes an inflorescence consists of a number of small branches, arranged rather haphazardly, each with a single terminal flower. This is known as a *cyme*. Where all the pedicels radiate from a single point at the top of the stem, the inflorescence is an *umbel*. Sometimes a number of single flowers or small racemes emerge from a single point, and the resultant cluster of flowers is known as a *fascicle*.

Sometimes leaf-like appendages are found beneath the flowers. These are known as *bracts* and on occasion, as in the flowering dogwood (*Cornus florida*) they are coloured and take the place of petals, in which case they can be described as petaloid bracts.

The flower is usually composed of a number of, generally green, *sepals* known collectively as the *calyx,* and a number of coloured *petals,* known collectively as the *corolla*. These surround the sexual organs; the male *stamens,* consisting of filaments and pollen-bearing anthers, and the female *pistil,* comprising the *stigma, style* and *ovary*. Sometimes the petals are lacking or inconspicuous and their place taken by the sepals becoming coloured, as in clematis. Such coloured, petaloid sepals are often referred to as *tepals*. In some plants the sexes occur in different flowers, which may also differ in appearance. The staminate flowers are male, and the pistillate are female. If they occur on different plants, as in hollies, they are called *dioecious*, if, as in hazel, they are both found on the same plant, the plants are called *monoecious*. The majority of flowers are either called *perfect* or *hermaphrodite*. On some occasions both perfect and unisexual flowers are found on the same plant. These are termed *polygamous*.

Sometimes flowers are abnormal and the stamens and/or the stigma and style may be converted into organs resembling petals. Such flowers are termed *double* (latinised as *flore pleno*). Such flowers are usually unable to set seed and must be propagated asexually (layering, cuttings or grafting). Races of plants that all descend by asexual propagation from one single plant are referred to as *clones*.

The shape of the flower is referred to as *patulate* or saucer-shaped (as in a single rose), *cupular* or cup-shaped, *campanulate* or bell-shaped (but if the body of the bell is elongated, it may be termed *funnel-campanulate*), *rotate*, if the flower is circular with the petals resembling the spokes of a wheel, or *urceolate* if it is urn-shaped with an elliptical form constricted at the mouth. Pea-shaped flowers are termed *papilionaceous*. Tubular flowers may expand at the mouth; if the expanded portions are small they are often termed *lobes* but if sizeable they may be termed a *limb*. In a pea-shaped flower the wide back petal is referred to as the *standard*, while the two conjoined petals in the centre are referred to as the *keel*. Flowers of the daisy family, the *Compositae,* are composed of a number of small flowers, of which the centre ones usually lack conspicuous petals and are called *disk florets,* while the outer ring often have at least one large showy petal and are composed of *ray florets.* Symmetrical flowers are sometimes termed *actinomorphic,* while flowers that are symmetrical in only one plane (such as many azaleas) are sometimes termed *zygomorphic.*

The Fruit

A plant's main function is to set seed to obtain an increase in population, and the containers of the seeds are termed fruits. They can be dry and hard or they can be fleshy and coloured. Dry, hard fruits are generally termed *capsules* and various capsules are given different names, of which the *pod* is the best known. If the capsule splits open to release the seeds it is known as *dehiscent,* while a dry, hard, indehiscent fruit is often called a *nut.* Winged fruits that depend on the wind for distribution are termed *samaras,* although in the case of the ashes and maples the samaras are popularly known as keys. A small, dry, indehiscent fruit is termed an *achene*, while the enlarged part of the stem that includes the fruit is termed the *receptacle*. Thus the botanical description of a strawberry is a number of achenes based on a fleshy coloured receptacle.

Fleshy fruits are named according to the way that the seeds are protected. If they are enclosed in a stony or woody substance, as in the case of the plum, the fruits are known as *drupes*, or, if small, *drupelets*. Thus a raspberry is botanically an aggregate fruit composed of several drupelets. Drupes are usually single-seeded, but not invariably; the fruits of ivy may contain five seeds. In pears and apples the seeds are protected by a hard layer, but this is neither stony nor woody and they are surrounded by a fleshy receptacle. Such fruits are known as *pomes*. If the seeds lie in the flesh of the fruit without any protection, the fruit is termed a *berry*. True berries are found in the blueberry and black currant. In common parlance any small, coloured fruit is termed a berry, which may be incorrect botanically, but causes no difficulty to gardeners. Some genera have specialised names for their fruits; the fleshy receptacles around the fruit of roses are termed *heps* or *hips,* while the pome-like fruits of the hawthorns are known as *haws.* Fruits may be round, egg-shaped, *pyriform* (pear-shaped) or *turbinate* (top-shaped).

Profiles

Shrubs may have erect or arching branches. Trees are usually basically either round-headed or pyramidal; often changing shape as they age. Thus the cedar starts by being pyramidal, but becomes flat-topped when old. If trees have a columnar habit, with the branches erect and nearly parallel to the trunk they are termed *fastigiate.* If, on the other hand, the branches arch or hang down to give a weeping effect, the form is referred to as *pendulous.* Trees such as the cedar where the main branches and their side-growths are all on the same horizontal plane are termed *tabular.*

ABELIA ROBERT BROWN *Caprifoliaceae*

Named in honour of Dr Clarke Abel, who accompanied Lord Amherst's embassy to China in 1816. A genus of shrubs, the majority of which are somewhat tender. The genus is concentrated on the Sino-Himalaya but there are outliers in Mexico. They are useful shrubs for their late-flowering propensities and are moderate growers. Tolerant as regards soil reaction.

Abelia X grandiflora (ANDRE) REHDER

4. An evergreen shrub of 1–2m; a hybrid between the evergreen and hardy *A. uniflora,* which seems to be no longer in cultivation, and the tender and deciduous *A. chinensis.* The hybrid was first described in 1886. Lv dark green, ovate, pointed, 2–6m long, and 1–3cm wide, shallowly toothed, glabrous. Fl funnel-shaped, pale pink, fragrant, 1·5cm long, terminal and axiliary. Fl 7–10. Moderate grower. May be cut to the ground in severe winters but regenerates.

Abelia 'Edward Groucher'

4. A cross between *A. X grandiflora* and *A. schumannii.* Similar to *A. X grandiflora* but fl dark purple-pink. Lv in whorls of three on non-flowering shoots.

Abelia schumannii

Abelia schumannii (GRAEBNER) REHDER

4. A deciduous shrub, to 2m. Shoots slender, arching, downy and purplish when young. Lv ovate, rounded at apex, 1–3cm long and half as wide. Fl funnel-shaped, rosy pink, to 3cm long, singly from axils of lateral shoots. Fl 6–10. Moderate grower; damaged in severe winters but regenerates. Native of central China. Introduced by Wilson in 1910.

Abelia triflora R. BROWN

4. A deciduous shrub or small tree, to 5m or, occasionally, much more. Bts bristly; lv lanceolate, to 7cm long and 2cm wide, hairy; dull dark green. Fl in terminal clusters, 5cm across, on lateral · shoots; pale pink, fragrant. Corolla tubular with reflexed circular lobes 1cm long and 1·3cm across. Sepals 5, reddish, silky and persistent. Fl 6. Probably the hardiest species. Introduced in 1847 by Major Edward Madden.

ABELIOPHYLLUM *Oleaceae*

A monotypic genus related to *Forsythia.* It is slow-growing and never seems to attain any great height but is valuable for its early flowers.

Abeliophyllum distichum NAKAI

4. Deciduous shrub, of up to 3m against a wall but rarely more than 2m otherwise. Lv ovate, 5–9cm long, inconspicuously hairy. Fl in short racemes, opening before lv, axillary. Fl funnel-shaped, 4-petalled, 1cm long, white or very pale pink. Fl 2–3. Can be pruned quite hard after flowering. Propagated by cuttings of half-ripe wood or by layers. Introduced from Korea in 1924.

ABIES MILLER *Pinaceae* Silver Fir

A genus of some fifty species, found throughout the north temperate zone, forming evergreen trees, often of considerable dimensions and usually of pyramidal habit. The branches are formed in whorls, a fresh whorl being produced each year. The needles are comparatively broad and are usually white beneath, giving the genus the common name of silver fir. Male and female flowers are produced on separate branches; the male inflorescence always on the underside of the branches, the female cones always erect – a feature which serves to distinguish *Abies* from the related genera of *Picea* and *Tsuga.* If a needle is pulled off *Picea* it brings a portion of the bark away with it.

Most species require cool, moist conditions, but *A. concolor* and the two Mediterranean species, *pinsapo* and *cephalonica,* will tolerate drier conditions. Generally, therefore, they do best in the north and west of the UK. They are deep-rooting and are unlikely to succeed in shallow soils. Seed appears the best method of propagation, but cuttings of leading shoots can often be induced to root; cuttings of lateral shoots tend to preserve their horizontal mode of growth and rarely make satisfactory trees. All the species will tolerate severe winter conditions but may be damaged by late spring frosts, and so should not be planted where these occur frequently.

Abies alba MILLER

7. (*A. pectinata* DE CANDOLLE) Evergreen tree of up to 50m. Lv to 3cm long and 3mm wide, with two white bands beneath. Cones up to 15cm long and 5cm across, at first green and then reddish-brown. Both pendulous and fastigiate forms of this occur and have been given the cv names 'Pendula' and 'Pyramidalis'. The plant only succeeds in high-rainfall areas and is of little use in southern England. The plant is native to the European mountains.

Abies amabilis FORBES

5.7. Evergreen tree, up to 80m in the wild but less than 30m in cultivation. Whitish bark and long needles up to 3cm, although only 3mm across, with a rich, dark and glossy green upper surface and a vivid, bluish underside. The cones are spectacular, being bright purple in colour, 15cm long and 6cm across. The plant requires an acid soil but is still an uncertain grower, although where it does do well it is one of the most attractive trees. It seems to be short-lived in cultivation, although in its native regions of western Canada and the USA it survives for 250 years.

Abies bracteata (D. DON) NUTTALL

5.7. (*Pinus venusta* DOUGLAS) Evergreen tree, to 50m in the wild but rarely more than 38m in cultivation. Pyramidal in profile, but with a curious steeple-like top. Lv flat, spine-tipped; dark green above, blue-white below, 5·5cm long and 2mm wide. Cones to 10cm long and 6cm across; purplish-brown and surrounded by spines, to 5cm long, emanating from the bracts. A very remarkable tree both in its shape and extraordinary cones, but somewhat tender, very susceptible to spring frosts, so requiring a well-protected situation. Confined to the Santa Lucia Mountains in California, whence it was introduced by William Lobb in 1853.

Abies cephalonica LOUDON

7. Evergreen tree of up to 40m. Lv to 2·8cm long and 2mm wide; dark, glossy green. Cones to 15cm long but only 4cm across, dark brown. A native of Greece, introduced by Sir Charles Napier in 1824, and one of the few of the genus that will tolerate chalky soils and comparatively low rainfall, so that it succeeds in southern and eastern areas of the UK. It starts to make its growth in late April and so can be damaged by late spring frosts. The manner in which the lv stand out all round the stem makes this sp comparatively easy to recognise.

Abies concolor (GORDON) HILDEBRAND

3.7. (*Pinus concolor* GORDON) Evergreen tree, to 45m in cultivation but less in the wild, with attractive glaucous foliage (more marked in the form 'Violacea'). Lv to 7·5cm long and 3mm wide. Cones purplish in colour, 19cm long and 4cm across. The cv 'Wattezii' has the young lv silvery-yellow. This plant manages to thrive in quite dry conditions and is one of the best of the genus for southern Britain. The plant is

native to many of the western states of the USA, farther west it is replaced by var *lowiana* (*A. lowiana* [GORDON] A. MURRAY), which has the lv differently arranged on the brs and often the trunk of a mature tree forks, so that the apex is more or less square.

Abies delavayi FRANCHET

5.7. Apparently an extremely variable sp, which now includes under varietal status the plants formerly known as *A. fabri* CRAIB, *A. faxoniana* REHDER, *A. forrestii* ROGERS and *A. georgei* ORR. *A. delavayi* in its typical form seems never to have been received in cultivation. All the var are rare in cultivation, although they include some of the most beautiful plants of the genus. The form most likely to be obtainable is var *forrestii*, and this is described here. Lv dark green above, vivid milk-white on the underside; notched at the apex, up to 3·5cm long (5cm on young trees), 5mm wide. The cones are about 10cm long, 6cm wide and are a remarkable blue in colour. The plant is very intolerant of prolonged drought and, although a rapid grower in the young stages, does not appear to be very long-lived. First sent back from Yunnan by Forrest in 1910, the largest plants in cultivation are around 20m in height. Var *georgei* is similar, but differs in the cones having long, protruding bracts which form a remarkable tail-like appendage at the apex; this was first discovered by Forrest in 1922 and further sendings were made in 1931.

Abies firma SIEBOLD AND ZUCCARINI

7. A vigorous-growing tree, up to 50m in the wild and 30m in cultivation so far. Lv 3cm long, 4mm wide, notched at the apex, particularly in young trees, and arranged in two V-shaped ranks; dark, shining green above, pale below. Cones to 12cm long, 5cm across, brown in colour. An attractive tree requiring acid soil and ample rainfall. Native of Japan. Introduced by J. G. Veitch in 1861.

Abies grandis LINDLEY

7. The largest and most rapid-growing in the genus, capable of reaching 95m in the wild and already 60m in cultivation. When put in deep soil with a good rainfall it will increase at the rate of 50cm or more each year. The lv are set horizontally in ranks of two, with the lower rank greatly exceeding the upper in length. The largest are up to 3cm long and 3mm wide, shining green above, white beneath. The cones are up to 10cm long, 5cm wide, and bright green before they ripen. Native of western N America from Vancouver to California, first introduced in 1832 by Douglas.

Abeliophyllum distichum

Abies homolepis SIEBOLD AND ZUCCARINI

5.7. A tree of up to 30m in height. Lv to 3cm long and 1·5mm wide, slightly notched at the apex; dark green above, blue-white beneath. Cones to 10cm long, 4cm wide, rich purple at first, finally brown and very striking when produced abundantly, which does not happen regularly. Although ample moisture is required for the best results, there are some tolerable specimens in southern England. The plant is a native of Japan and does not seem to have been introduced before 1870.

Abies koreana WILSON

5. Although it can reach 20m in the wild, this plant has proved very slow growing in cultivation and the largest trees in Britain, which are around 50 or 60 years old, are about 10m. Lv are small, to 2cm long, 2mm wide, somewhat glaucous and white beneath. Cones to 7·5cm long, 2·5cm wide, a brilliant violet-purple and produced when the trees are 1m high. A useful plant for small gardens where it makes a bushy, pyramidal plant, while its cones are very beautiful. It is native to S Korea, where it was first collected by Père Faurié in 1908, but most plants come from seed collected by Wilson in 1917.

Abies magnifica MURRAY

1.5.7. Known as the red fir, owing to its conspicuous red bark, this is a native of western N America, whence it was introduced by Jeffrey in 1851. In the wild it reaches heights between 60 and 70m, but the highest cultivated tree in the UK is about 35m. Lv to 4cm long and 2mm wide, glaucous and found on the top of the bts as well as on the sides. Cones to 20cm long and 10cm across, purple while immature, finally brown. A rapid growing tree, but somewhat short-lived in cultivation compared with the 250 years it will survive in the wild. It does best in cool, moist districts and will not tolerate atmospheric pollution.

Abies nordmanniana SPACH

5.7. A large tree, up to 65m in the wild, and tolerant of quite chalky conditions. Lv densely arranged on the upper side of the bts, to 3cm long and 2mm wide; glossy green above, whitish beneath. Cones to 15cm long, 5cm wide, reddish-brown with bracts extruded and bent downwards. In some districts it is badly attacked by aphis, which cause distortion of the brs, but otherwise it is one of the easiest of the genus to satisfy. Native of the Caucasus mountains, first introduced about 1848.

Abies numidica CARRIÈRE

7. A tree of up to 20m in the wild but over 30m in cultivation. Lv arranged all round the shoots (except the weaker ones where they are arranged in two ranks with a V-shaped gap), 2cm long and 2mm wide, rounded or notched at the apex; dark green above, white beneath. Cones to 18cm long, 2cm across, cylindric, brown. The upper sides of the lv often have a greyish patch near the apex, which makes the plant easy to distinguish. Like *A. cephalonica* and *A. pinsapo,* this will tolerate chalky or alkaline soil and will also tolerate dry conditions. It is thus particularly suitable for the south and east of the UK. Pendulous and glaucous forms occur occasionally. Native to Algeria, where it is found with *Cedrus atlanticus.*

Abies pindrow ROYLE

5.7. A slender, pyramidal tree, up to 70m in the wild but rarely more than 30m in cultivation. Lv on all sides of the shoot, except below, horizontal at the sides, pointing forwards at the top; 7cm long, 2mm wide; in young plants they are pointed, in older plants bifid at the apex. Cones an attractive deep purple at first, later brown; 18cm long, 8cm across. In var *brevifolia* DALLIMORE AND JACKSON (*A. gamblei* HICKELL) the bts are reddish not grey as in the type, and the lv do not exceed 3cm in length. This tree requires rather mild, moist conditions. Native of the western Himalaya east to Kumaon, introduced 1837, probably by Wallich.

Abies pinsapo BOISSIER

7. A tree, to 33m, with the lv very densely arranged all round the bts, more symmetrically than in any other sp; dark green on both surfaces, very rigid, 2cm long and 2mm wide. Cones to 7cm long and 3cm wide, purplish-brown. Native to SE Spain, around Ronda, always on limestone and so suitable for chalk and limestone districts; it will also tolerate prolonged drought. Glaucous forms occur and are very handsome. Young trees grow very rapidly but slow down as they age. Introduced 1839.

Abies procera REHDER

5.7. Probably better known as *A. nobilis* ([D. DON] LINDLEY), a name that had to be discarded owing to an earlier use of *A. nobilis.* A very large tree, up to 80m in the wild and already 50m in cultivation. Lv very glaucous (exceptionally so in cv "Glauca"), 3·5cm long and 1·5mm wide, very densely arranged at the sides and the top of the bts. Cones very conspicuous, to 30cm long and 9cm across, bright green when immature but finally purplish-brown. The plant requires a moist climate and deep soil, but this need not be particularly rich. It thrives in exposed positions and is seen at its best in Scotland. Native to the western USA. Introduced by Douglas in 1831.

Abies spectabilis (D. DON) G. DON

5.7. (*Abies webbiana* LINDLEY) A tree of up to 50m in the wild and about 33m in cultivation, and most attractive as a young tree. Lv in two sets, leaving a V-shaped gap at the top, to 5cm long, and 3mm broad; dark green above, blue-white beneath, notched at the apex. Cones to 15cm long, 6cm across, violet-purple when immature, later brown. Remarkable for its long lv with their vivid blue-white undersides. It requires a rather mild climate, where there is no risk of late spring frosts, and ample moisture at all times. Native to the Himalaya from Afghanistan to Assam, where it occurs higher than *A. pindrow*, where their habitats overlap. Introduced 1822, presumably through Wallich.

Abies veitchii LINDLEY

7. A rapid-growing but rather short-lived tree, to 25m, with remarkably smooth bark. Lv to 3cm long and 1·5mm wide; dark green above, shining white beneath; arranged all around the bts, pointing forwards and curving upwards, the apex is abruptly cut off (truncate). Cones to 6cm long, 2·5cm across, bluish-purple when immature, finally brown. The plant requires acid soil, but is more tolerant of atmospheric pollution than the majority of the genus, although somewhat intolerant of drought. Native of the island of Honshu, Japan, where it was first found by J. G. Veitch on Mt Fuji in 1860, but not apparently brought to W Europe until Charles Maries sent it in 1879.

ABUTILON KUNTHEL *Malvaceae*

A genus of mainly-tropical, woody and herbaceous plants. About 100 species have been distinguished, the majority of tropical or subtropical origin, but one species and one hybrid are normally hardy in most parts of the British Isles, although often short-lived. The species comes readily and rapidly from seed, usually flowering two years after sowing. The hybrid comes equally rapidly, but may not reproduce itself truly and is best propagated by tip cuttings of half-ripe wood. The plants require full sunshine and are usually very intolerant of strong winds, which appear to damage the roots owing to the plants swaying. If plants are pruned reasonably hard after flowering, this seems to prevent them becoming leggy and top-heavy. Most writers suggest that the plants are more tender than they have proved to be.

Abutilon vitifolium (CAVANILLES) PRESL

4. A semi-evergreen shrub, up to 10m, but usually around 5 or 6. Lv greyish, hairy on both surfaces, most markedly below, basically heart-shaped but deeply 3- or 5-lobed; lobes pointed,

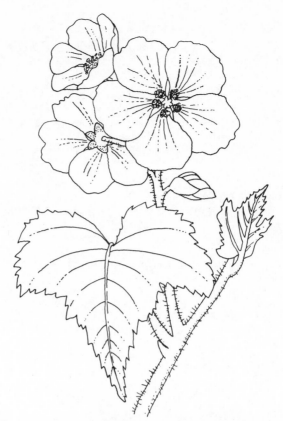

Abutilon vitifolium

coarsely toothed, arranged alternately on petioles up to 7cm long. Lv up to 15cm long and 7cm across. Fl in few-flowered, axillary corymbs; each flower circular, patulate, to 15cm diameter, lavender- blue. A white-flowered form frequently occurs. Fl 6-7. Native of Chile, introduced by Captain Cottingham of Dublin who imported seed in 1836.

Abutilon X suntense BRICKELL

4. A hybrid between the last sp and the rather tender violet-flowered *A. ochsenii,* a plant of weak straggling habit. It is an extremely rapid and vigorous grower, but, at the time of writing, has only been known for about 3 years, during which it has attained 5m, so its ultimate height is as yet unknown. Lv bright green, 3-lobed, the central lobe much longer and thinner than the two lateral ones, which are obscurely lobed in their turn; up to 17·5cm long and 15cm wide, on 10cm petioles; the lamina obscurely hairy on both surfaces. Fl usually violet, but sometimes lavender, 5cm in diameter, appearing before *A. vitifolium*. Fl. 5-6.

ACANTHOPANAX MIQUEL *Araliaceae*

A genus of some 50 species, only two of which are reliably hardy and commercially obtainable.

They have no beauty of flower or fruit and are grown for the sake of their elegant foliage. They require rich, loamy soil and shelter from strong winds.

Acanthopanax sieboldianus MAKINO

(*A. pentaphyllus* [SIEBOLD AND ZUCCARINI] MARCHALL). A deciduous shrub, to 3m with arching brs, often with a spine at the base of each petiole or leaf cluster. Lv palmate, leaflets obovate, to 6cm long, 2·5cm wide, dentate. Fl small, greenish, in an umbel to 2·5cm in diameter, followed by black 2–5 seeded drupes. The white-edged cv 'Variegatus' is more elegant. Fl 6–8. Native to China and Japan. Introduced 1874.

Acanthopanax simonii SCHNEIDER

Deciduous shrub, to 3m; brs armed with downward-pointing spines. Lv composed of 5 leaflets, at the end of a petiole 5–7cm long, sometimes prickly. Leaflets varying in size, the largest in the centre, lanceolate, up to 15cm long and 2·5cm across, the outermost the smallest; dark green above, lighter below; bristly-hairy on both surfaces. Fl in a cluster of umbels, each on a stalk to 5cm long. Fl 7–8. Fr black. Introduced from China 1900, but main introduction by Wilson in 1901.

ACER LINNAEUS *Aceraceae* Maple

A genus of about 200 species distributed throughout the north temperate zone; ranging from lofty trees to dwarf shrubs, usually deciduous. Leaves opposite, generally more or less deeply 5-lobed, but the lv are sometimes entire and, in the sections Trifoliata and Negundo, palmate and composed of 3 or 5 leaflets. Perhaps the most characteristic feature of the genus is the fruit, composed of a pair of winged samaras, consisting of a nutlet, which may be one or two-seeded, and a membranous wing, which assists in wind dispersal of the seeds. The flowers are often inconspicuous and the plants are mainly grown for the sake of their foliage, which often colours well in the autumn. One group, known as the snakebark maples, are characterised by attractive striped bark, which makes them conspicuous in the garden in winter. Seed appears to be the best method of propagation, but germination is very uncertain with some species, notably *A. griseum*. Cuttings are very difficult to root. The genus was divided into fourteen sections by Pax, dependent on various characters, but they are of little assistance to the gardener and are not used here. With some few exceptions the plants are rapid growers, but sometimes appear to be short-lived and die suddenly without any previous signs of weakness.

Acer argutum MAXIMOWICZ

2.7. A small tree, rarely more than 8m, with reddish bts and 5-lobed (rarely 7-lobed), broadly ovate lv, with the lobes deeply incised and with a toothed margin. Rather exceptionally for the genus, the plant is dioecious. In male plants the fl comes before the lv in clusters of racemes. In female plants the racemes are single and axillary. Lv are about 10cm long and 8cm across. A very handsome foliage tree, native to Japan. Introduced by Charles Maries in 1881.

Acer buergerianum MIQUEL

7. (*A. trifidum* HOOKER AND ARNOTT) A deciduous tree, to 12m. Lv are markedly 3-lobed, to 8cm long and wide, slightly glaucous on the underside. Fl in a few-flowered corymb. Fl 5. Fr with wings to 2·5cm long. A rapid grower, but otherwise of slight interest. Presumably first sent from Japan by Buerger, an assistant of Siebold, but native of China.

Acer campestre LINNAEUS

6.7. The common maple of British hedgerows. Can make a tree of 20m, but usually around 8m and can be grown as a bush. Lv obscurely 5-lobed, usually around 7cm long and wide, but very variable in size, with milky sap in the petioles. Fl green, inconspicuous in erect corymbs. Fl 4–5. Fr sometimes reddish, about 5cm across. Frequently turns golden or occasionally crimson in the autumn, but this seems dependent on the soil.
3. cv 'Schwerinii'. In this cv the expanding lv are purple in colour.

Acer capillipes MAXIMOWICZ

1.3.6.7. A deciduous tree, to 12m, with handsome striated bark. The first year growth is reddish-brown in colour, which serves to distinguish this sp from the not dissimilar *A. rufinerve*. Lv basically deltoid, 3-lobed to 8cm long, 6cm across, petioles and main veins reddish. Fl very minute in slender pendulous racemes, fr also small with wings less than 1cm. Fl 5. The leaves usually crimson very effectively in the autumn. A splendid tree but with no beauty of flower or fruit; native of Japan. Introduced by Professor Sargent in 1892.

Acer cappadocicum GLEDITSCH

7. (*A. laetum* C. MEYER, *A. pictum colchicum* hort) Deciduous tree, to 23m. Lv green, 5–7-lobed, the ends of the lobes drawn out to a fine point, as much as 15cm wide and nearly as long. Fl yellow in small corymbs; fr with wings 2cm long. Native to the Caucasus, and eastward to Persia and Afghanistan. The type is rare in cultivation and its place is usually taken by 3. 'Rubrum' in which the young lv are dark red as

they unfurl. Another cv **3.6.** 'Aureum', has the lv yellow when they emerge, they then turn green, but turn golden before falling. The lv have long petioles, up to 20cm long, which contain a milky sap.

Acer circinatum PURSH

4.5.6. Generally a thicket-forming shrub to 3m, but can be induced to form a tree to 10 or 12m. Lv almost circular, obscurely 7–9-lobed, often turning crimson and orange in the autumn. Fl slightly before the leaves in small corymbs, to 1·2cm across, with purple sepals and white petals, conspicuous. Fr red while still unripe, wings about 3·5cm long. Fl 4, fr to 9. A useful garden plant. Native to western N America. Introduced by Douglas in 1826.

Acer cissifolium (SIEBOLD AND ZUCCARINI) K. KOCH

6.7. (*Negundo cissifolium* SIEB AND ZUCC). A small deciduous tree, to 10m, with a rounded head. Lv trifoliate, each leaflet to 8cm long, 3cm across, ovate, on a common petiole to 8cm long. Fl very small in pendulous racemes, which subsequently elongate, so that the fruiting racemes may be up to 20cm long and quite conspicuous. Samaras to 2·5cm long. The plant is dioecious. The lv colour well red and yellow in the autumn. Native of Japan. Introduced before 1870, but the exact date and the introducer seem unknown.

Acer crataegifolium SIEBOLD AND ZUCCARINI

1.7. A small tree, to 10m, with attractive white-striped bark. Lv small, to 7·5cm long, half as wide, basically ovate but shallowly 3–5-lobed, with a toothed margin, somewhat glaucous. Bts purplish. Fl inconspicuous in small, erect racemes. The plant is obviously very close to *A. capillipes,* but lacks the brilliant autumn colour and has smaller lv. Introduced from Japan by Maries in 1879.

Acer davidii FRANCHET

1.6.7. A very variable tree, to 15m, with handsome striated bark. It is widespread in China and the plants collected by Maries and Wilson in Hupeh and Szechwan differ markedly from those collected by Forrest and Kingdon Ward in Yunnan. The more northerly forms have lv to 11cm long and 7.5cm wide, the Forrest sendings have lv to 18cm long and 11cm across and the whole tree is of a more open habit, with the lv widely separated. Lv usually unlobed, ovate, heart-shaped at base, toothed, often colouring well in the autumn. The plant is either monoecious or dioecious. Fl on racemes to 6cm long for males, 9cm long for females, yellowish. Samaras to 3cm long. Introduced by Maries in 1879.

Acer diabolicum K. KOCH

7. A round-topped, deciduous tree, to 10m; dioecious. Lv up to 16cm long and wide, 5-lobed with large-toothed margin. Fl yellow, before the leaves, petal-less, in short drooping corymbs. Fl 4. Samaras to 3cm long, with two horn-like remains of the style between the wings. Lv and petioles woolly when young, petioles and main veins remain bristly throughout. One of the largest-leaved sp but otherwise of little importance. On the other hand, f *purpurascens,* **3.4.5.6.** with purple flowers, young leaves and young fruits, is an attractive tree, that often colours well in the autumn. Native to Japan, introduced by Maries in 1880, but f *purpurascens,* presumably of Japanese garden origin was introduced in 1878.

Acer distylum SIEBOLD AND ZUCCARINI

7. Deciduous tree, to 15m, but so far less in cultivation. Lv ovate, with heart-shaped base, unlobed, to 16cm long, 12cm across, slender-pointed at the apex, margin serrate. Fl yellow in panicles up to 6cm long on long pedicels. Samaras about 3cm long held erect. Native of Japan. Introduced by Maries in 1879.

Acer ginnala MAXIMOWICZ

4.5.6. A deciduous shrub or small tree, to 7m. Lv 3-lobed, to 8cm long and 6cm wide, turning bright red in the autumn but then soon falling. Fl yellowish-white in long-stemmed panicles, very fragrant. Fr bright red while immature, wing 2·5cm long. An elegant shrub with attractive foliage, closely related to *A. tataricum.* Introduced in 1880 from St Petersburg Botanic Garden. Native of Manchuria, N China and Japan.

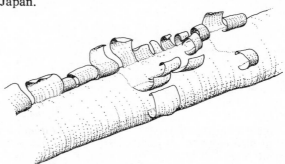

Acer griseum

Acer griseum (FRANCHET) PAX

1.6. (*A. nikoense* var *griseum* FRANCHET) Slow-growing tree, as high as 20m in the wild but not more than 15m so far in cultivation. Trifoliate lv terminal leaflet to 6cm long, 3cm wide, oval-lanceolate, side leaflets smaller. The bark peels off yearly disclosing orange-coloured newer bark beneath. Lv turn red or orange in the autumn. Fl in few-fld clusters or solitary, dioecious; fr 3cm long. Seeds show only 5 per

Acer macrophyllum

cent germination. Native of China, introduced by Wilson in 1901.

Acer grosseri PAX

1.6.7. Small deciduous tree or many-stemmed shrub, up to 15m. Bark attractively striped. Lv roundish, obscurely 3-lobed, to 6cm long, 5cm across, usually, although not invariably, turning brilliant red in the autumn. In gardens it is usually replaced by var *hersii* REHDER (*A. hersii* REHDER) which is a more vigorous plant, more regularly tree-like and has lv more pronouncedly lobed. Fl. and fr inconspicuous. Plants sometimes collapse suddenly after 15–20 years, usually in soils with a high water-table. Some trees of var *hersii* have attained a height of 13m, but 10m or less is more usual. Both the type and the var are native to central China and both were introduced in the 1920s.

Acer heldreichii BOISSIER

7. Deciduous tree, to 30m, with remarkable and unique lv. These are up to 18cm wide, slightly less in length, 5-lobed, the three terminal lobes extremely long and reaching almost to the base; these lobes are narrowly oblong-lanceolate, dark-green above, slightly glaucous below. Fl yellow in erect panicles. An elegant tree. Native to SE Europe. Introduced 1879.

Acer japonicum THUNBERG

4.6. A large shrub or small tree, to 10m (occasionally to 15m). Lv basically roundish but 7–11-lobed, 5–12cm long. Fl purplish-red before the lv emerge. The type is rare in cultivation but several cvs are grown including: 'Aconitifolium' a small shrub with lv palmatisect and lobes themselves divided, turning crimson in autumn; 'Aureum' with lv always pale gold; and 'Vitifolium' with lv to 15cm long and wide, colouring very brilliantly. Native of Japan. Introduced 1864.

Acer lobelii TENORE

4.7. Deciduous tree, to 20m, with erect brs, giving a columnar form. Lv 5-lobed to 17cm wide, and slightly less long; fl yellow before the lv. According to Loudon a variety of *A. platanoides,* but also close to *A. cappadocicum.* Bts glaucous. Native to S Italy. Introduced in 1826 according to Sweet's *Hortus Britannicus.* Rehder gives 1838 and Bean 1683, but this is probably a misreading of Loudon.

Acer macrophyllum PURSH   Oregon Maple

4.5.7. Deciduous tree, to 30m. Young trees fastigiate, later developing a rounded top. Lv 3 or 5-lobed, as much as 15cm across; the central lobe is itself divided. In the USA the lv colour orange in the autumn, but this rarely happens in Great Britain. Fl yellow in dense pendulous racemes, fragrant. Samaras up to 3cm long, brown-bristly, sometimes in threes. The largest-leaved maple, doing best in neutral or acid soil. Native to western N America; introduced by Douglas in 1826.

Acer maximowiczii PAX

1.2. Small tree, to 6m, with striated bark and purple bts, which are conspicuous on young plants, less so in mature ones. Lv very variable, 3- or 5-lobed, sometimes both on the same tree, oblong-ovate to 7cm long. Fl reddish. Native of Central China. Introduced by Wilson,

Acer mono MAXIMOWICZ

7. (*A. pictum* THUNBERG) Tree, to 20m. Lv 5- or 7-lobed, to 16cm long, 15cm wide. Fl opening with the emerging lv greenish-yellow in corymbs, to 7cm long. Fr nearly 3cm long. A variable plant of which var *tricuspis* REHDER is very distinct, with its small 3-lobed lv, each on a slender petiole up to 7cm long, so that the lv are always agitated. The type is native to Japan, Manchuria, N China and Siberia and was introduced from Japan by Maries in 1881. Var *tricuspis* comes from Szechwan and was introduced by Wilson in 1901.

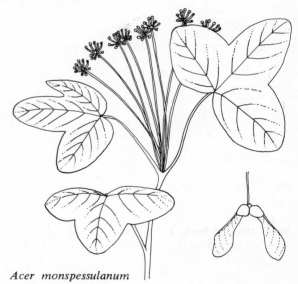

Acer monspessulanum

Acer monspessulanum LINNAEUS

5.7. A small, deciduous tree, usually to 9m, but occasionally to 15m or more. Lv 3-lobed, to 5cm long, slightly wider, dark green; similar to *A. campestris,* but without milky sap in the petioles and lv 3- not 5-lobed. Fl greenish-yellow in few-flowered corymbs. Fr reddish; samaras up to 3cm long, often quite showy. Native of Mediterranean regions and parts of central Europe. Introduced 1739.

Acer negundo LINNAEUS   Box Elder

7. Tree, to 20m, but usually around 13m. Lv pinnate, although appearing palmate, each leaflet to 10cm long, elliptic. Lv composed usually of 5 leaflets, sometimes only 3, occasionally 7 or 9. The plant is dioecious. Fl inconspicuous. A number of variegated cvs exist. Native to N America from New York to the Mississippi and west to California. Cultivated by Bishop Compton in 1688, so probably introduced by John Banister.

Acer nikoense MAXIMOWICZ

6.7. A moderately-sized, slow-growing tree, rarely over 10m, but up to 15m in the wild. Lv trifoliate, central leaflet elliptic, to 12cm long, 6cm wide, lateral ones slightly smaller, petiole very hairy and stout. The lv usually colour very brilliantly in the autumn. The fl are yellow, usually in threes, and are quite large for the genus, up to 1cm across, but not very conspicuous. Fr large, the wings to 5cm long. A very useful and ornamental tree for small gardens. Native of Japan and central China. Introduced by Maries in 1881.

Acer opalus MILLER

4.7. A tree, sometimes to 20m, but usually rather less. Lv shallowly 5-lobed, to 10cm long, slightly wider. Fl before lv in March or April, bright yellow and very showy; arguably the best maple for floral display. In the var *tomentosum* and *obtusatum,* the lv are larger than those of the typical form, and woolly below. Native of South and Central Europe. Introduced 1752.

Acer palmatum THUNBERG   Japanese Maple

3.5.6. Known chiefly through cv, as it has long been cultivated in Japan and many different forms are known, from low dome-shaped bushes, barely 1m high, to small trees to 7m. Lv generally 5-lobed, but 7-lobed in the Heptalobum group. In the Dissectum group, the lv are palmatifid, with 7, 9, or 11 linear lobes to each leaf. Several purple-leaved forms exist both in the typical form, the Dissectum group, and even the Heptalobum section. The samaras are usually pink when immature and the unfolding leaves are also often pink. Outstanding clones are: **3.5.6.** 'Heptalobum Osakazuki' – young lv pink, mature lv to 12cm long, deeply 7-lobed, autumn colour brilliant scarlet; **2.3.6.** 'Heptalobum Senkaki' – bts brilliant coral-pink, lv very finely dissected, turning gold in autumn; slow growing to start with, but more rapid when established, up to 10m high.

The plants need a neutral or slightly acid soil and are badly affected by strong winds or late spring frosts, so that they cannot be grown everywhere. Severe winter cold seems to do no damage. First introduced in 1820; from China, according to Sweet, from Japan according to Loudon.

Acer pensylvanicum LINNAEUS Snakebark Maple

1.3.6.7. A small, deciduous tree, rarely more than 7m, with a rather erect habit. Bark beautifully striated. Lv pinkish on emergence, when mature 3-lobed, up to 18cm long, slightly less wide, usually turning golden yellow before they fall. In the cv 'Erythrocladum', the bts are bright red. A fairly rapid-growing tree and highly desirable. Native to the eastern USA. Introduced 1755, probably by John Bartram.

Acer platanoides LINNAEUS   Norway Maple

4.6.7. Deciduous tree, to 23m or, rarely, higher. Lv 5-lobed, to 17cm wide, 13cm long on adult trees, larger on young ones, often colouring well in the autumn. Fl before leaves, greenish-yellow in erect corymbose panicles, showy. A rapid-growing tree that will thrive in any soil. Native of most of Europe. A large number of variants are in cultivation, with purple or variegated lv. The purple-lv usually have reddish flowers. The cv 'Columnare' has a fastigiate habit and comparatively small lv. The cv 'Dissectum' and 'Lorbergii' have deeply dissected lv.

Acer pseudoplatanus LINNAEUS   Sycamore

7. Deciduous tree, to 30m or more. Lv 3- or 5-lobed, to 17cm wide on established trees, larger on young ones. Fl in drooping racemes, yellowish-green. Comes very rapidly from seed, which can be a nuisance in many gardens. A number of variants have arisen, of which the most outstanding is **3.** 'Brilliantissimum', a slow-growing tree with the emerging lv a brilliant peach colour, although these fade to a rather blotchy green. Other variants have purple undersides to the lv or yellow lv ('Corstorphinense', 'Worleei'). Native of Europe.

Acer rubrum LINNAEUS   Red Maple

4.5.7. Deciduous tree, to 35m. Lv 3- or 5-lobed with the lobes markedly triangular, to 15cm long, 13cm across; dark green above, blue-white and somewhat downy below. The lv colour well in the USA but are unreliable in the UK, although the clone known as 'Schlesingeri' was selected for its brilliant autumn hues. Fl before the lv red, in clusters. Fr about 2cm long, dull red. The plant requires acid soil and is somewhat slow growing. Native of eastern N America, introduced 1656, but by whom is not known.

Acer rufinerve SIEBOLD AND ZUCCARINI

1.2.6.7. A tree, to 12m, with bluish bts and green bark with grey-brown striations. Lv usually 3-lobed, with reddish down along the main veins on the underside; to 12cm long, dark green, often turning crimson in the autumn, but not invariably. Allied to *A. capillipes,* but distinguished by its glaucous bts. In the var *albolimbatum*

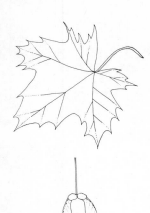

Acer saccharinum

(HOOKER F) the margin of the lv is covered with white dots and this character is transmitted by seed, although the extent and area of the dots varies considerably from plant to plant. Native to Japan. Var *albolimbatum* was exhibited by Standish and Noble in 1869, which rather suggests that the seed may have been sent back by Fortune in 1860, as this firm received most of his sendings. The type was collected by Maries in 1879.

Acer saccharinum LINNAEUS   Silver Maple

4.6.7. (*A. dasycarpum* EHRHART, *A. eriocarpum* MICHAUX). A fast-growing deciduous tree, to 35m, with a rounded head but pendulous young brs (most marked in the cv 'Pendulum'). Lv 5-lobed, to 15cm long and wide, light green above, silvery below and slightly downy, usually turning yellow or red before falling. Fl greenish-white, before the lv and usually very early in the year. Seeds are ripe by June, but rarely ripen in the UK. Very ornamental with the silvery undersides of the lv exposed by every slight breeze. Introduced from eastern N America in 1725.

Acer saccharum HUMPHREY MARSHALL
                                                    Sugar Maple

4.7. (*A. barbatum* MICHAUX) A slow-growing tree, to 30m in America but somewhat less in Britain, forming a round-headed tree. Lv deeply 5-lobed, to 15cm long and wide. Fl before lv, greenish-yellow in clusters. In the northern USA the lv colour marvellously in the autumn, but rarely do so in the UK where the tree is of little interest. It is the main source of maple syrup. Introduced 1735, probably by Bartram.

Acer sempervirens LINNAEUS

(*A. orientale* auct *A. creticum* LINNAEUS) A slow-growing plant, usually a smallish bush, but capable of making a tree to 10m. Lv leathery, very variable in shape from simply ovate to 3-lobed, to 5cm long and 4cm across. Fl and fr inconspicuous. Lv are retained on the tree until January. *A. syriacum* BOISSIER AND GAILLARDOT, from the near East, is distinguished by its evergreen habit and usually has slightly larger lv (to 7cm), but the two are best regarded as conspecific. *A. sempervirens* comes from SE Europe and was introduced in 1752.

Acer spicatum LAMARCK

5.6. Deciduous shrub or small tree, to 8m. Lv generally 3-lobed, to 7cm long and wide, covered below with grey down, turning red and yellow in the autumn. Fl in June on slender erect racemes to 15cm long, greenish-yellow. Fr small, about 1cm long but bright red. Rare in cultivation, but desirable and suitable for small gardens. Introduced in 1750 by Bartram for the Duke of Argyll.

Acer tataricum LINNAEUS

5.6. Deciduous shrub or small tree to 10m. Lv unlobed on adult trees, obscurely 3- or 5-lobed in younger plants. Adult lv broadly ovate to 8cm long, 6cm wide, usually turning yellow just before falling. Fl in erect panicles, to 7cm long, greenish-white. Fr to 3cm long, red when ripe and quite conspicuous. Allied to *A. ginnala*, but fl not fragrant and the fr of *A. ginnala* is not red. Native of SE Europe and western Asia. Introduced 1759.

Acer tetramerum PAX

1.2.7. Elegant, deciduous, dioecious tree, to 7–10m. Bts reddish-purple, bark striated. Lv to 9cm long, 6cm wide, ovate, usually unlobed, toothed. Often produces more than one trunk. Fl yellow, males in few-flowered corymbs, females in short racemes, opening with the lv in spring. Native of Tibet, N Burma and western China. Introduced by Wilson, 1901, with a subsequent sending in 1910 and 4 Forrest sendings.

Acer trautvetteri MEDWEDEW

3.7. Deciduous tree, to 16m; bts dark red. Very brilliant in early spring when the crimson bud scales elongate. Lv deeply 5-lobed, to 15cm long and 20cm wide. Fl in May in erect cormbs. Fr reddish in late summer, wings to 5cm long, sometimes overlapping, not spread, which distinguishes it from the allied *A. velutinum* in which the wings are spread horizontally. Native of the Caucasus and Persian mountains. Introduced 1866.

Acer tschonoskii MAXIMOWICZ

1.6. Large shrub or small tree, to 7m. Bark striated, but not so markedly as its allies. Lv deeply 5-lobed, to 10cm long and wide, turning a very brilliant yellow in the autumn. Fl inconspicuous in short racemes. Native of Japan. Introduced 1902. In N Korea and N China it is represented by the var *rubripes* KOMAR with reddish bts and petioles.

Acer velutinum BOISSIER

7. Large deciduous tree, to 25m or more, represented in gardens by the var *vanvolxemii* (MASTERS) REHDER. Lv very large, 3–5-lobed, to 20cm wide and slightly longer, somewhat glaucous beneath and downy on the veins (in the typical form, the lv are covered with dense pale brown velvety down below). Fl in erect panicles, yellowish, to 10cm long, appearing in early June. Native of the Caucasus. Introduced by Van Volxem in 1873.

ACTINIDIA LINDLEY *Actinidiaceae*
A genus of deciduous, twining shrubs containing

19

about twenty-five species. The plants must be treated as dioecious, although hermaphrodite flowers do occasionally occur. The pith in the centre of the branches is sometimes useful in determining the species, as in some it is solid, while in others it is chambered (lamellate). The flowers are sometimes showy, but the best known species are grown for their variegated leaves. Fruit usually a berry. Cuttings of half-ripened wood will generally root readily.

Actinidia arguta (SIEBOLD AND ZUCCARINI)
MIQUEL

4. A very vigorous twiner, to 20m or more, capable of reaching the tops of large trees. Lv nearly circular, dark green, to 10cm long and 8cm wide, petiole pinkish to 7cm long, sometimes bristly. Fl in few-flowered, axillary clusters, yellow, fragrant, 2cm in diameter, patulate. Fr a greenish-yellow berry. Native of Japan, China and the Amur regions of Manchuria and Siberia. Introduced about 1874. A variable plant, of which the Chinese form with broader lv is sometimes given specific rank as *A. giraldii* DIELS. A closely allied sp is *A. purpurea* REHDER, with darker lv, white fl and purple fr. This is less vigorous, not exceeding 8m. Fl 6.

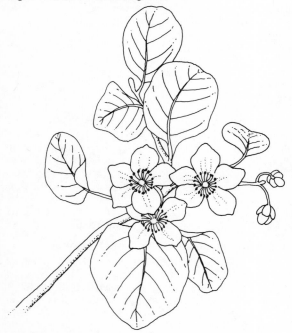

Actinidia chinensis

Actinidia chinensis PLANCHON
Chinese Gooseberry

4. Vigorous twiner, to 8m, bts covered with red-purple hairs. Lv on non-flowering shoots, heart-shaped, to 20cm long and 18cm across, on flowering shoots smaller and rounder, to 8cm long and 10cm across. Fl patulate, 3cm in diameter, opening white fading to buff. Fl. 6. Fr. about 3cm long, covered with red-brown hairs. The most attractive sp for its flowers. The fr is edible. Although the plant has been known since 1874, it does not seem to have reached cultivation until Wilson sent seeds in 1900.

Actinidia kolomikta (RUPRECHT) MAXIMOWICZ

A rather weak climber, to 7m but usually considerably less, throwing up a large number of shoots. Lv ovate with a heart-shaped base, to 15cm long and 10cm across, purplish when young and later in the season many of the lv become conspicuously blotched with pink and white. According to Rehder only the male plant shows this variegation and it is shown neither on young plants nor on those in shaded situations. Fl in axillary clusters of 2–3, white, fragrant, 1·3cm across. Fl 6. Pith brown and lamellate, while that of the similar *A. polygama* (see below) is white and solid. Extensively grown for its curiously variegated lv. Native of China, Manchuria and Japan. Introduced about 1855, but by whom is not known.

Actinidia melanandra FRANCHET

A tall, vigorous twiner, to 20m. Lv elliptic, abruptly pointed, to 10cm long and 4cm across, glaucous below. Fl white to 2·5cm wide, females borne singly, males in a short raceme of from 3 to 7 fl. Fr ovoid, 2·5cm long, reddish-brown, pruinose. Native of western China. Introduced by Wilson in 1910.

Actinidia polygama (SIEBOLD AND ZUCCARINI)
MAXIMOWICZ

(*Trochostigma polygama* SIEB AND ZUCC) Slender climber, to 7m, forming almost a thicket in the wild. Lv elliptic, to 14cm long and half as wide. Often most of the leaf becomes silvery-white or pale yellow as the season advances (only the male plant according to Rehder) and this variegation is the main reason for the plant being in cultivation. Fl white, fragrant, usually in threes, 2cm across. Fr a yellow berry 3cm long. The plant is very attractive to cats, who delight to roll on the young shoots, so that some protection is necessary; the same applies in a lesser degree to *A. kolomikta*. Native to Japan, as well as Manchuria and central China. Introduced 1861, presumably by Siebold.

AESCULUS LINNAEUS *Hippocastanaceae*
A genus of deciduous trees and shrubs distributed throughout the northern temperate zone. The leaves are large, palmate, usually composed of 5 or 7 leaflets. The flowers are in terminal panicles,

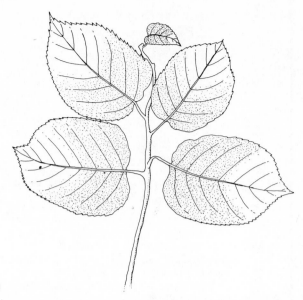

Actinidia kolomikta

Aesculus californica

4 or 5 petalled, while the fruit is a large capsule, sometimes prickly, containing one or two large seeds, known as conkers or horse chestnuts. Most species are perfectly hardy, although some of those from California are unreliable in their flowering in Britain.

Aesculus arguta BUCKLEY

4. A shrub, occasionally a small tree, to 10m, with lv of 7 to 9 leaflets, each elliptic, to 15cm long (but usually 7–9cm). Fl in pyramidal panicles to 20cm long, pale yellow. Fl 5–6. Capsule, rounded, 1–3-seeded. Seed, shining brown 2·5cm across. Allied to *A. glabra* (qv), but dwarfer and with longer, slenderer lv. Native of eastern Texas, not introduced to cultivation until 1909.

Aesculus californica (SPACH) NUTTALL

3.4. (*Calothyrsus californica* SPACH) Bush or small, spreading tree, to 5m (rarely a tree to 12m in the wild). Lv small, blue-green when young, usually 5 leaflets, narrowly ovate to 10cm long. Fl fragrant in dense, cylindrical panicles to 20cm long, 6cm across, white or pale pink. Often the terminal fl opens long before the others and may have set a small fr before the rest open. Fl 6–8. Very attractive plant, but not a regular flowerer in the UK needing a warm and dry summer to ripen its wood well. Native of California. Introduced by William Lobb in 1850.

Aesculus X carnea HAYNE Red Horse Chestnut

4.7. Tree to 18m. Lv of 5 or 7 leaflets, obovate, dark green to 15cm long. Fl in panicles to 20cm long, red or pink. Fr rounded, slightly prickly. Originally a chance garden hybrid between the horse chestnut, *A. hippocastanum*,

and the red buckeye *A. pavia,* which occurred about 1818. At some period this turned into an amphidiploid, capable of setting seed which would breed more or less true. (*A. hippocastanum* and *A. pavia* each have 40 chromosomes *A. X. carnea* has 80). *A. hippocastanum* has been pollinated by *A. X carnea* to give the plant known as *A. X plantierensis,* with larger panicles and soft pink fl. This is a triploid and sterile. Fl 5–6.

Aesculus flava SOLANDER

4.6.7. (*A. octandra* MARSHALL). Tree to 25m or slightly more with lv of 5–7 leaflets, obovate, to 17cm long, 7cm across, often colouring well in the autumn. Fl in rather slender panicles to 18cm long, 7cm across. Pale yellow. Fl 5–6. Hardy, but in England does best in the south. Native to central USA. Introduced 1764, probably by Bartram.

Aesculus glabra WILLDENOW

4.6.7. A tree, usually around 10m, but occasionally to 20m. Lv of 5 leaflets, obovate, to 15cm long and 5cm across, often colouring brilliantly before falling. Fl in erect panicles, to 17cm long, 7cm across, greenish-yellow and not particularly ornamental. Fl 5–6. Native of SE and central USA. Introduced 1812, which suggests either Nuttall or Bradbury as the introducer.

Aesculus hippocastanum LINNAEUS
Horse Chestnut

3.4.7. Tree to 30m, rapid growing. Lv of 5 or 7 obovate leaflets to 30cm long and 12cm wide; very attractive when first unfurling, covered with down. Fl in panicles to 30cm high and 10cm through, white with a central blotch, at first yellow, later pink. One of the most attractive of large trees for its fl. Fl 5–6. 'Baumannii' has double fl and is accordingly sterile. The cv known as 'Pyramidalis' has a fastigiate habit. Native of SE Europe. Introduced by Busbecq to Clusius from Constantinople in 1576.

Aesculus indica (CAMBESSEDES) HOOKER

3.4.7. Tree, around 17m in cultivation, over 30m in the wild. Lv usually with 7 leaflets, bronzy when young; lanceolate up to 30cm long and 50cm across. Fl in long panicles up to 40cm long, 10 or 12cm across, white flushed yellow and pink. Fl 6–7, a month later than the common horse chestnut. Growth is fairly rapid to start with, but slows down, so that plants known to be eighty years old are 17m high. Perfectly winter hardy, but can be damaged by late spring frosts. The cv 'Sydney Pearce' is a selected, very free-flowering form, with fl which are richer coloured in a denser panicle. Plants start to flower when quite young, sometimes after only seven years. Native to the NW Himalaya. Introduced 1851 by Colonel Henry Bunbury.

Aesculus neglecta LINDLEY

4. A large shrub or small tree of uncertain affinities, possibly of hybrid origin. Lv with five leaflets, obovate to 16cm long. Fl in panicles to 15cm long, yellow streaked with red, or yellow or red without variants (var *georgiana* SARGENT) Fl 5–6. The cv known as **3.** 'Erythroblastos' has extremely brilliant young growth, shrimp-pink in colour with bright carmine petioles; all these shades eventually fade out. The plant is very slow-growing. *A. neglecta* was first described in 1826, from a plant imported from France as *A. glabra,* probably native to the south-east USA.

Aesculus parviflora WALTER

4. (*A. macrostachya* MICHAUX) Suckering shrub, to 5m, but usually about 3m. Lv of 5 or 7 leaflets, to 20cm long, 9cm wide, usually somewhat less. Fl in cylindrical panicles to 30cm long, 10cm across, white with reddish anthers and filaments. Fl 8. Very useful for its late flowering. Hardy but susceptible to late spring frosts. Native to the south-east USA from Carolina to Florida. Introduced by John Fraser in 1785.

Aesculus pavia LINNAEUS   Red Buckeye

4. A shrub to 3 or 4m. Lv with 5 leaflets, to 12cm long, lanceolate, toothed. Fl in panicles to 15cm long, usually 10cm. Each fl is tubular, about 3cm long and bright red, but barely opening and so less attractive than it sounds. Fl 6. Native to the south-east USA from Virginia to Florida and Louisiana. Introduced 1711.

Aesculus turbinata BLUME

4.7. Tree, to 30m in the wild, somewhat slow-growing. Very similar to the common horse chestnut, but lv to 40cm long, 15cm across. Fl in erect panicles to 20cm high, creamy-white, opening about three weeks later than *A. hippocastanum.* Fl 6. Fr without spines. Native of Honshu and Hokkaido in Japan, where it is the sole representative of the genus. Introduced in 1880.

AILANTHUS DESFONTAINES *Simaroubaceae*
A genus of nine species from SE Asia and N Australia, only one of which is in general cultivation. This is generally dioecious, but monoecious forms do occur. *A. altissima* is a useful plant for growing in towns and cities, as it tolerates a polluted atmosphere. If possible the female plant should be obtained, as not only does it bear attractive fruits, but the flower of the male plant smells disagreeably. Propagated by suckers or by root cuttings.

Ailanthus altissima (MILLER) SWINGLE

6.7. (*Toxicodendron altissimum* MILLER) Tree, to 20m, with greyish bark. Lv pinnate, composed of from 15–30 elliptic leaflets to 15cm individually. The whole lv may be as long as 40 cm on adult trees and over 1m in length on young plants. There are a few glandular teeth at the base of each leaflet. Fl in terminal panicles, inconspicuous, but the fr, composed of numerous red samaras in a panicle up to 30cm tall and wide, are often very striking, although it is chiefly for its foliage that the plant is grown. It appears to do best in the south of the UK. Native of N China. Introduced through Peter Collinson, probably from Père d'Incarville, in 1751.

Ailanthus altissima

AKEBIA DECAISNE *Lardizabalaceae*
A genus of two species of twining shrubs, with handsome leaves and monoecious flowers which are fragrant, but not particularly showy. The fruits are ornamental, but are rarely produced in the UK. Propagated by layers or cuttings.

Akebia quinata (HOUTTUYN) DECAISNE

4.5. (*Rajania quinata* HOUTTUYN) A rapid-growing, semi-evergreen, twining shrub. Lv palmate on slender petioles to 12cm long, with five leaflets; leaflets stalked, obovate, to 8cm long, 3cm across, of a very fresh, soft green. Fl in slender hanging racemes; male fl small, pale purple, at the ends of the racemes; female fl much larger, 3cm across, usually two at the start of the raceme, dark chocolate, very fragrant. Fl 5. Fr sausage-shaped, to 10cm long, purplish. Fr rarely produced and it is suggested that cross-pollination may be necessary. Native of China, Japan and Korea. Introduced by Robert Fortune in 1847.

Akebia trifoliata (THUNBERG) KOIDZUMI

4.5. (*Clematis trifoliata* THUNBERG, *A. lobata* DECAISNE) Deciduous twining shrub of vigorous habit, although less so than *A. quinata.* Lv trifoliate, each leaflet stalked, rounded, to 10cm long. Fl in a pendulous raceme to 12cm long. Male fl minute, numerous, pale purple; female fl at base of raceme, to 1·8cm across, purple. Fl 3–4. Fr sausage-shaped, to 12cm long, pale violet, later splitting open. Native to China and Japan. Introduced about 1890.

ALANGIUM LAMARCK *Alangiaceae*
A genus of seventeen species of shrubs and trees, mainly from southern Asia. At one time the hardier species were put in a separate genus *Marlea.* Propagation by seed.

Alangium platanifolium (SIEBOLD AND ZUCCARINI) HARMS

4. Slow-growing, deciduous shrub, rarely more than 2m high in cultivation, although a small tree in the wild. Lv alternate, roundish, 3–5-lobed, to 20cm long and wide; dark green above, faintly downy below, on petioles to 7cm long. Fl in cymes of 2–4, arising from axils of the current year's growth. They are tubular at first, and up to 3cm long; later the petals recurve; somewhat fragrant and a rather dull white. Fl 6–7. Fr an egg-shaped drupe about 1cm long or less. After poor summers the wood does not ripen sufficiently and much of the current year's growth dies back, making this a rather unsatisfactory garden plant. Native of China and Japan. Introduced from Japan by Maries in 1879. Rehder gives a date of 1867.

ALNUS B. EHRHART *Betulaceae* Alder
A genus of about thirty species of deciduous trees and shrubs of rather moderate ornamental value. Flower monoecious. The male catkins long and slender usually in clusters, the female catkins, much shorter, sometimes solitary sometimes clustered; flowering in the early spring either before or with the expanding leaves (there are three autumn-flowering species not in general cultivation). Distributed throughout the north temperate zone and extending to Peru in S America. The trees are most useful for their tolerance of very wet soils and will often survive where other trees will not. The fruits are cone-like, correctly described as strobiles, and contain minute flattened nutlets. Propagated by seeds or hard-wood cuttings.

Alnus cordata DESFONTAINES

7. (*A. cordifolia* TENORE) Tree, to 25m, of pyramidal shape. Lv more or less heart-shaped, to 10cm long, 7cm across; finely toothed, dark green on slender petioles to 7cm long. Male catkins in threes or sixes, terminal, to 7cm long, opening in March; female catkins usually in threes, erect. One of the better sp which will grow in any soil, either a dry chalky soil or one that is waterlogged. Native to Corsica and Italy. Introduced 1820.

Alnus glutinosa (LINNAEUS) GAERTNER
Common Alder

7. (*Betula glutinosa* LINNAEUS) Tree, to 30m, usually not more than 15m, of narrow pyramidal habit. Bts covered with minute glutinous glands. Lv orbicular, to 10cm long, about 7cm across, dark green. Male catkins in March, usually in tufts of 3 or 5, to 10cm long. Fr in clusters, 1·6cm long. Native of Europe, western Asia and North Africa. Forms with

golden lv ('Aurea') and lobed lv ('Imperialis' and 'Laciniata') are less vigorous than the type, although more desirable.

Alnus incana (LINNAEUS) MOENCH Grey Alder

7. (*Betula alnus* var *incana* LINNAEUS) Tree, to 22m, pyramidal in habit. Bts covered with grey down. Lv ovate to 10cm long, 5cm across; dull green above, covered with grey down below at first. Male catkins open in February, in clusters of 3–4, to 10cm long. Fr in clusters, to 1·5cm long. The type is rarely seen in gardens but various cv are not infrequent. Of these the best, but the rarest, is **2.4.** 'Ramulis coccineis', in which the bts and male catkins are red in colour and very attractive in February. Easier to obtain is **2.4.** 'Aurea', with reddish-yellow bts, orange catkins and yellowish lv. 'Laciniata' has the lv deeply lobed. Native to most of Europe, but not the UK.

Alnus japonica SIEBOLD AND ZUCCARINI

Pyramidal tree, to 25m. Lv lanceolate or elliptic, to 12cm long, 5cm across, dark shining green. Male catkins erect, in large clusters, to 9cm long. Fr oval, 2cm long. Native to Japan and NE Asia. Date of introduction unknown. A hybrid between this sp and *A. subcordata,* called **3.** *A. X spaethii,* has the young lv violet-purple in colour.

Alnus rubra BONGARD (*A. oregana* NUTTALL)

4.7. Tree, to 17m, with a pyramidal head and slightly pendulous brs. Bts dark red, winter buds bright red. Lv oval, to 15cm long, 10cm across, shallowly lobed; dark green above, pale green or grey below. Petioles and main veins reddish or yellowish. Male catkins in clusters to 15cm long. Fr on orange coloured stalks, 2cm long. Often

Akebia quinata

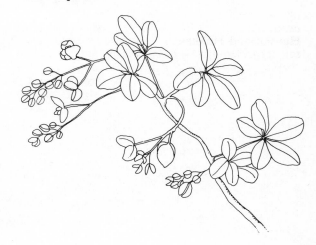

sold under the name of *A. rhombifolia,* which is a distinct, although not dissimilar, sp. Native to western N America. Introduced about 1880.

Alnus viridis (CHAIX) DE CANDOLLE

Shrub of 1–2m. Lv rather sticky, roundish, to 9cm long, 8cm across; dark green above, usually glabrous, slightly hairy below. Male fl opening with lv, to 8cm long. Fr in lax racemes, 1·5cm long. Native of mountains of central Europe and the USA where it is sometimes given specific rank as *A. crispa.* Neither sp is particularly ornamental, but they are useful for planting in cold, waterlogged positions, where little else will grow.

AMELANCHIER F. MEDICUS *Rosaceae*

A genus of about twenty-five species, mainly N American, but species exist also in Europe and E Asia. Deciduous trees or shrubs with alternate simple leaves; flowers in racemes, composed of 5 strap-shaped petals, to give a slightly starry corolla. Fruit a berry-like pome, containing one seed per cell and from 8–10 cells per pome. The species most commonly met with is usually sold under the name *A. canadensis,* but this is practically meaningless, as plants under this name may be *A. arborea, A. laevis* or, most likely, *A. X lamarckii.* The true *A. canadensis,* better known as *A. oblongifolia,* is a rather rare plant. All the *Amelanchiers* are desirable garden plants, with their attractive flowers and often gorgeous autumn tints. Propagated by seed or by layers.

Amelanchier arborea (MICHAUX THE YOUNGER) FERNALD

4.6. (*Mespilus arborea* MICHAUX, *A. canadensis* AUCT) Tree, to 10m, usually less, with a rounded head. Lv with white hairs on each surface when young, later hairless; ovate, to 7cm long, 3cm wide, colouring brilliantly in the autumn. Fl white, in erect racemes, about 2cm long. Fl 4. Fr ripening in June, black-purple, dry. Native to eastern and central states of USA. Introduced 1746, presumably through Bartram.

Amelanchier asiatica (SIEBOLD AND ZUCCARINI) WALPERS

4.6. Deciduous tree, to 12m, of graceful, somewhat pendulous habit. Lv ovate-elliptic, to 7cm long, 3·5cm across, covered with loose floss when young, later glabrous; usually, but not invariably, turning red in the autumn. Fl in erect racemes, to 6cm long, slightly larger than *A. arborea* and always later. Fl 5. Fr black-purple like a currant. Native to China, Korea and Japan, whence it was introduced in 1865.

Amelanchier canadensis (LINNAEUS) MEDICUS

4.6. (*Mespilus canadensis* LINNAEUS, *A. oblongifolia* ROEMER). Suckering shrub, to 6m, with upright, rather fastigiate habit. Lv elliptic, to 5cm long, 3cm across, hairy when young, later glabrous. Fl in erect racemes, also covered with floss at first, to 7cm long; petals shorter than in *A. arborea* or *A. laevis.* Fl 5. Fr black and juicy. Lv often colour well. Can be increased by division. Native to eastern N America, where it colonises boggy ground, so may well thrive in unsuitable positions in gardens.

Amelanchier cusickii FERNALD

4.6. Shrub from 1–3m with the largest fl of the genus. Lv always glabrous, roundish, to 5cm long, 3·5cm across. Fl in erect racemes, as much as 5cm across. Fl 5. Native to a small part of the Rocky Mountains.

Amelanchier florida LINDLEY

4.6. Shrub, to 3m, sometimes small tree to 10m, with numerous upright stems. Lv roundish, to 5cm long, 3·5cm wide, either glabrous or slightly tomentose when young. Fl white in erect racemes, of 5–15 in number; fl about 5cm across. Fl 5. Fr dark purple, edible. Native to western America from Alaska to NW California. Introduced by Douglas in 1826.

Amelanchier laevis WIEGAND

3.4.6. (*A. canadensis* HORT) Small tree, to 12m, with rounded head. Young lv *bronzy-purple, hairless.* Lv elliptic, to 7cm long, 3cm wide. Fl in lax racemes, generally longer than those of *A. arborea.* Fr purplish-black, juicy. Very similar to *A. arborea,* but distinct through the italicised characters. Native to eastern USA and as far north as Newfoundland.

Amelanchier X lamarckii SCHRÖDER

3.4.6. (*A. X grandiflora* REHDER, *A. X confusa* HYLANDER, *A. lancifolia* AUCT) The sp most frequently met with in gardens, usually as *A. canadensis,* and apparently a hybrid between *A. arborea* and *A. laevis.* Similar to *A. laevis,* but young lv both purple-bronze *and* hairy. Fl slightly larger than either sp, reddish in bud. In the cv 'Rubescens' the fl are very pale pink. Fl 4–5.

Amelanchier ovalis MEDICUS Snowy Mespilus

3.4. (*A. vulgaris* MOENCH) Small tree, to 6m or large shrub. Lv roundish, covered with white wool on the underside, and appearing glistening white when unfurling to 3cm long, 2·5cm across. Fl in few-flowered erect racemes, each fl up to 3cm across, making the sp one of the largest-flowered. Fl 5. Fr black, pruinose. Native to the mountains of Europe, usually growing in rocky gorges and more floriferous in the wild than in cultivation. The lv do not usually colour in the autumn.

Amelanchier stolonifera WIEGAND

4. Suckering shrub, only slightly over 1m high, although it can reach 2m. Lv oval, finely toothed to 5cm long and 3cm across, with white down on the underside when young, later glabrous. Fl white, rather small, in short erect racemes. Fl 5. Fr purplish, edible. Found on acid soils in eastern N America, apparently not introduced before 1883, although the plant known as *A. X spicata* (LAMARCK) K. KOCH, which is thought to be a hybrid between *A. stolonifera* and *A. canadensis,* has been known since 1800. This makes a large suckering shrub from 2–4m tall, with obovate lv to 5·5cm long, 3cm across. Fl on erect woolly-stalked racemes to 5cm long. Fl 4–5. Fr blackish.

AMPELOPSIS MICHAUX *Vitidaceae*

Deciduous climbers, supporting themselves by tendrils and very close to the true vines (*Vitis* species) from which they are distinguished solely by the flower. In *Ampelopsis* the petals spread outwards as in most plants, whereas in *Vitis* they are united at the tips to form a sort of cap, which falls off when the stamens are ripe. Some *Ampelopsis* species have a compound leaf which is not found in *Vitis,* but all the plants have been known as *Vitis,* before *Ampelopsis* was generally accepted. They are all vigorous plants and require a warm climate and the attractive blue grapes of some species are usually only seen after hot summers. The Virginian creepers (*Parthenocissus* species) are sometimes incorrectly referred to *Ampelopsis.* Most species are reasonably hardy, but in cold districts will require wall protection. There are about twenty species, mostly from E Asia.

Ampelopsis aconitifolia BUNGE

Handsome and vigorous foliage climber and one of the hardiest spp. Lv palmate, usually with 5 leaflets, each leaflet pinnatifidly lobed, to 7cm long, 3cm across. Fl inconspicuous. Fr orange or yellow. Native of China. Introduced 1868.

Ampelopsis bodinieri (LÉVEILLÉ AND VANIOT) REHDER

5. *Vitis bodinieri* LEV AND VAN, *A. micans* REHDER Climber, to 7m, with purplish young growth and petioles. Lv triangular-ovate or broad ovate and slightly 3-lobed, to 12cm long; velvety, dark green above, somewhat glaucous below. Fl in panicles, in May to June. Fr dark blue, in October. Native to central China. Introduced by Wilson in 1900.

Ampelopsis brevipedunculata (MAXIMOWICZ) TRAUTVETTER

5. (*Vitis heterophylla* THUNBERG) A vigorous climber with roughly-hairy young shoots, but glabrous in var *maximowiczii,* which is the form most commonly seen. Lv very variable, from heart-shaped and unlobed to deeply 3- or 5-lobed with intermediate shapes, often several on the same plant. Fr bright, almost gentian-blue, in October. Lv to 15cm long, usually about 12cm. The form known as 'Citrulloides' has the lv very deeply 5-lobed, while the cv 'Elegans' has pinkish young growth and the lv variegated white and very pale green. This cv is delicate and a slow grower. The handsome fr are only produced after hot summers and it is recommended that the root run should be restricted in some way. Native of E Asia and Japan. Introduced 1868.

Ampelopsis chaffanjonii (LÉVEILLÉ) REHDER

(*A. watsoniana* WILSON) Handsome foliage climber, succeeding best on a south wall. Lv pinnate with 5–7 leaflets. The whole leaf up to 30cm long, individual leaflets oblong-oval to 11cm long, 5cm across, purple on the underside. Native of Hupeh, China. Introduced by Wilson in 1900.

Ampelopsis megalophylla DIELS AND GILG

Vigorous climber with quite extraordinarily large lv. These are pinnate, with the lower leaflets often pinnately divided themselves, as long as 60cm and nearly as wide. Leaflets 7 or 9, usually ovate, to 15cm long, and 7·5cm across; coarsely toothed, deep green above, glaucous beneath. Young growths somewhat glaucous. Can make as much as 3m of growth in a season. Probably not suitable for cold districts, but not very well-known. Fr. black. Native of W China. Introduced by Père Farges in 1894 and by Wilson in 1900.

Ampelopsis orientalis (LAMARCK) PLANCHON

6. (*Cissus orientalis* LAMARCK) Sometimes a climber, sometimes a sprawling bush, with very variable lv. These are usually pinnate, but can also be bipinnate or biternate. In pinnate forms there are usually 9 leaflets, but not invariably, and these are usually ovate or diamond-shaped to 8cm long and 5cm across; dull green above, slightly glaucous below. Distinguished from the other spp described by the fl having 4 not 5 petals. Fr like red currants. Native of the near East, where it grows on the mountains to 1600m, so tolerant of cold winters. Introduced in 1818.

ARALIA LINNAEUS *Araliaceae*

Formerly the genus *Aralia* contained numerous species which have now been assigned to other genera leaving comparatively few in *Aralia* itself. Only one species is commonly found in gardens, where it is noteworthy for its fantastically large leaves. Propagated by suckers or root cuttings.

Aralia elata (MIQUEL) SEEMANN

4. Usually a suckering shrub to 6m but occasionally a deciduous tree. Young growths very thick and spiny. Lv bipinnate, to over 1m long, 70cm across, composed of numerous oval,. short-stalked leaflets, each to 12cm long, 7cm across; dark green above, pale green and hairy below. Fl individually small, whitish-green, in a huge umbellate panicle to 60cm long and 30cm wide. Native of Japan and NE Asia. Introduced in 1830, presumably through Siebold. *A. chinensis,* under which name this is sometimes sold, is barely distinct. Fl 8–9. Lv are larger in good, rich soil, but the plant seems longer-lived in rather poor soil. Forms with white or yellow variegated lv exist.

ARAUCARIA JUSSIEU *Araucariaceae*

A small genus of about ten species from S America and Australasia. Coniferous, leaves evergreen and persisting for many years. Only one species is hardy in the UK. Propagated by seed.

Araucaria araucana (MOLINA) K. KOCH
Monkey Puzzle

7. (*Pinus araucana* MOLINA, *A. imbricata* PAVON) Tree, to 25m, of pyramidal form, with br produced in tiers of 5–7, a fresh tier each year. Lv leathery and hard, ovate with a spiny apex, to 5cm long and 2·5cm across, arranged spirally and very densely on the stems and persisting for 10–15 years. Plants either monoecious or dioecious. Male fl in catkins to 12cm long, shedding their pollen in July. Female cones globose, to 17cm thick, spine covered, taking 2 years to ripen their seed. Native to Chile. A few plants were introduced by Archibald Menzies in 1795, but the main introduction was by William Lobb in 1843, although there seems to have been an importation of seed in 1839, for which no collector has been named.

ARBUTUS LINNAEUS *Ericaceae*

A small genus of evergreen trees or shrubs, with white urceolate flowers and ornamental fruit, which are drupes but superficially resemble strawberries. Unlike most of the *Ericaceae,* *Arbutus* species will generally thrive in alkaline soils. They grow fairly rapidly to start with, subsequently slowing down.

Arbutus X andrachnoides LINK

1.4.5.7. (*A. hybrida* KER-GAWLER) A hybrid between the hardy, lime-loving *A. unedo* and the rather tender, acid-loving *A. andrachne.* Evergreen tree, to 12m, with peeling reddish-brown bark, which is conspicuous on older trees. Lv oval, toothed, to 10cm long, 4cm across, glossy green above, rather glaucous below. Fl in some forms in March and April, as in *A. andrachne,* in others from October to November, as in *A. unedo.* Fr globose, red, fairly smooth, about 1cm across. The hybrid was first made in 1800, but has been found in the wild in Greece.

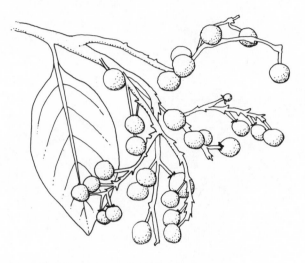

Arbutus menziesii

Arbutus menziesii PURSH MADRONA

1.4.5.7. Tree, to 30m in the wild, but rarely more than 15m in cultivation. Bark peels yearly and a striking, smooth terra-cotta trunk is disclosed. Lv oval, to 15cm long, 7cm across; dark green above, whitish below. Fl in a terminal panicle, pyramidal in shape, to 20cm long and 15cm across; small, urn-shaped, white to 6mm long. Fl 5. Fr about 1cm across, orange-red. Fr 10. Raised from seed it proves a rapid grower, but older plants may take a year or so to settle down after moving. Native of California. Introduced by Douglas in 1827. Hardy in most parts of the UK and should be more often seen.

Arbutus unedo LINNAEUS Strawberry Tree

1.4.5.7. Small tree, to 10m but usually 5–6m with attractive reddish bark, which sheds yearly. Lv oval, to 10cm long, 4cm across, dark green and rather leathery. Fl in small panicles, urceolate, white (occasionally pink). Fr round, rather rough, 2cm in diameter. Fl and Fr 10–12. Native to W Ireland and the Mediterranean. The form known as 'Rubra' has quite deep pink fl but never makes more than a large shrub.

Arbutus unedo

ARISTOLOCHIA LINNAEUS *Aristolochiaceae*

A large genus of some 180 species from both temperate and tropical regions. For our purposes the genus consists of two species of vigorous, twining deciduous shrubs with large cordate leaves. The flowers are curiously shaped, tubular and bent in the centre with an expanded mouth. They tend to be hidden beneath the leaves. Useful plants for screens, but not particularly showy.

Aristolochia macrophylla LAMARCK
Dutchman's Pipe

(*A. durior* HILL, *A. sipho* L'HERITIER) Vigorous, deciduous climber with smooth, twining stems. Lv kidney- or heart-shaped, to 25cm long and nearly as wide, but usually about 15cm; dark green above, pale below, petiole to 7cm. Fl tubular, bent, yellow-green outside, purple within at the orifice; to 3cm long, partly concealed by the lv, axillary. Fl 6. Native to eastern USA. Introduced by John Bartram in 1763. Both Rehder and the latest edition of Bean give 1783, by which time John Bartram was dead. *Hortus kewensis* gives the date of 1763 and Bartram as the introducer.

Aristolochia tomentosa SIMS

Vigorous climber, similar to the last sp but with very woolly bts, lv rounder and smaller, to 20cm long and a rather dull green. Petiole and fl scape both woolly. Fl similar to the last sp, 6–7. Native to the south-eastern USA. Introduced 1799, introducer unknown.

ARONIA MEDICUS *Rosaceae*
A small genus of three N American shrubs, in-

cluded by Linnaeus in *Pyrus*. They are mainly distinguished by the colour of the fruit. Normally they are easily grown and quite handsome.

Aronia arbutifolia (LINNAEUS) PERSOON
4.5.6. Rapid-growing shrub, to 3m, bts covered with down. Lv elliptic, to 9cm long, 2cm across; dark green above, grey-felty below, usually colouring brilliant red in the autumn. Fl in corymbs about 4cm across, each fl about 1cm across, white or pale pink. Fl 5–6. Fr red, 6mm wide, hanging until the new year. Fr 9–10. Native to eastern USA. Introduced about 1700.

Aronia melanocarpa (MICHAUX) ELLIOTT
4.5. Suckering shrub, usually only 1m, but occasionally nearly 2m. Bts glabrous. Lv obovate, to 7·5cm long, 5cm across; shining green above, pale green below, lacking the felty underside of the last sp. Fl white, to 1cm across, in corymbs of up to 12 fl. Fl 4–5. Fr to 1cm across, blackish-purple, soon falling. Fr 9. Native to eastern N America. Introduced about 1700.

Aronia prunifolia (MARSHALL) REHDER
4.5. Shrub, to 4m, barely distinguishable from *A. arbutifolia,* except for its dark purple fr, which persist for longer than those of *A. melanocarpa.* The plant comes from the same habitats as the two last spp, but is not a hybrid between them, as appearances would suggest.

Aristolochia macrophylla

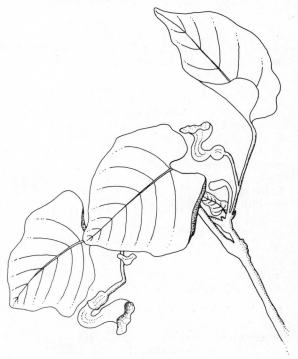

ASIMINA ADANSON *Annonaceae*

The family is confined to tropical subjects, including the custard apple, and only one species is hardy in temperate climes.

Asimina triloba (LINNAEUS) DUNAL

4. (*Annona triloba* LINNAEUS) Although a small tree in its native land, in the UK this only makes a large deciduous shrub to 3m. Bts covered with reddish down when young, later glabrous. Lv alternate, obovate, to 20cm long, 7cm wide. Fl produced on the second year wood, purple, about 5cm across, enclosed in 3 large, green sepals. Fl 6. Fr, which is rarely produced in the UK, is flask-shaped, to 10cm long, yellow, edible. Fr 10. Native to eastern USA. Introduced by Bartram to Collinson in 1736. In the USA known, rather confusingly, as the pawpaw. Propagated by seed.

ATRIPLEX LINNAEUS *Chenopodiaceae*

A genus of about 120 species of which a few are grown for the sake of their grey or silvery leaves and their tolerance of sea spray; most of the species are littoral in habitat. They may be either monoecious or dioecious. They rarely flower or fruit in cultivation, but can be propagated by cuttings.

Atriplex canescens JAMES

Evergreen shrub of lax, spreading habit, to 2m tall, but considerably wider. Lv alternate, linear lanceolate, to 5cm long, 8mm wide; light grey, almost white in colour, as are the bts. Generally dioecious. Fl 7; inconspicuous. Native to the Rocky Mountains from British Columbia to Nebraska, usually in dry and salty localities. Introduced 1870.

Atriplex halimus LINNAEUS Tree Purslane

A semi-evergreen shrub, to 2·5m, of rather loose habit. Lv alternate, ovate or diamond-shaped, to 6cm long and 2·5cm across; smooth, silvery grey on each surface; the bts are covered with silvery down. Fl 7, inconspicuous and rarely produced. Native of southern Europe, usually by the sea. Can be cut to the ground in severe winters, but it will always spring again from the base.

AUCUBA THUNBERG *Cornaceae*

A genus of about three dioecious, evergreen shrubs, of which only one is in general cultivation. Easily propagated by cuttings.

Aucuba japonica THUNBERG

5. Rounded shrub, to 3m (5m according to Rehder) with leathery oval lv usually variegated with yellow spots or blotches; lv to 20cm long,

Atriplex halimus

7cm across, glossy, toothed towards the apex. Fl small, purplish in terminal panicles. Fr a bright-red, oval drupe, about 1cm or more in diameter. An extremely tolerant plant, growing happily in deep shade, although not fruiting readily in such positions. Male and female plants must be planted close to each other in the ratio of one male to five females to secure the ornamental fruits. Native of Japan. A variegated female form was introduced by a Mr John Graeffer in 1783. Male plants were not received until 1860, when Fortune, J. G. Veitch and Siebold all sent plants back.

BERBERIS LINNAEUS *Berberidaceae*

A genus of 450 deciduous or evergreen shrub species. Leaves originally pinnate, but only the terminal leaflet now survives, the other pinnae either suppressed or metamorphosed into spines. Plants with terminal inflorescences and pinnate leaves are put in the separate genus *Mahonia* (qv). The wood of *Berberis* is always yellow and the flowers are either yellow or some shade of orange and axillary. Fruit a berry, often very ornamental. The flowers are usually small and produced in racemes or panicles, and are composed of six sepals, which are often coloured like the petals, and six petals, which are often smaller than the sepals. Most of the species are hardy and about 300 have been described. They also hybridise very readily and seed from a garden where many species are grown close together is unlikely to come true. Plants can be propagated by means of cuttings of fairly-ripened wood or by layers. Usually the plants are rapid growers, but seedlings are slow for the first year or so and then accelerate. The genus has been arranged in fifteen series, which are perhaps worth reproducing, as this will save much space in the descriptions:

1 *Buxifoliae* Lv evergreen, small. Fl solitary or in fascicles. Fr black.
2 *Actinacanthae* Lv evergreen or deciduous. Fl solitary or few-flowered clusters. Fr black.
3 *Ilicifoliae* Lv evergreen, small, toothed. Fl racemose. Fr blue-black.
4 *Wallichianae* Lv evergreen, elliptic. Fl solitary or fascicled.
5 *Angulosae* Lv deciduous. Fl solitary or few-flowered clusters. Fr red or pink.
6 *Polyanthae* Lv usually deciduous. Fl paniculate or racemose. Fr red.
7 *Tinctoriae* Lv deciduous or semi-evergreen. Fl in racemes. Fr red or purple, often pruinose.
8 *Asiaticae* Lv evergreen or semi-evergreen. Fl in racemes or panicles. Fr black, often pruinose.
9 *Integerrimae* Lv deciduous, petioled. Fl racemose or spicate. Fr red.
10 *Heteropodae* and 11 *Tchonoskyanae* contain no plants in cultivation at the moment.
12 *Sinenses* Bts purplish or red-brown. Lv deciduous, usually obovate. Fl usually in racemes, sometimes fascicled or solitary. Fr red.
13 *Dasystachyae* is not in cultivation at the moment.
14 *Brachypodae* Bts pubescent. Inflorescence spicate.
15 *Vulgares* Bts grey or yellowish-grey. Lv deciduous, serrate. Fl racemose, pendulous. Fr red or purple, usually pruinose.

Berberis aggregata SCHNEIDER
(*B. geraldii* VEITCH) *Polyanthae*
4.5.6. Shrub, to 2m. Lv clustered, obovate, to 2cm long, glaucous beneath. Fl in dense panicles to 3cm long. Fl 5–6. Fr red, slightly pruinose. Fr 9–10. Lv often colour red in autumn. Native of west China. Introduced by Wilson in 1908.

Berberis angulosa WALLICH *Angulosae*
4.5. Shrub, to 1·5m high and considerably wider. Lv dark green, shining, rather leathery;

obovate, to 3cm long. Spines stiff, usually in threes or fives. Fl solitary or in few-flowered racemes, each on a pedicel, to 2·5cm long and 1·6cm across; orange-yellow, globose. Fl 5–6. Fr elliptic, scarlet, to 1·6cm long. Notable for the size of its fl and fr, although not one of the showiest species. Native to northern India. Introduced about 1850, possibly by Madden, possibly by Joseph Hooker.

Berberis aristata DE CANDOLLE
Probably not in cultivation. Plants sold as *B. aristata* or as *B. chitria* are usually *B. glaucocarpa*, see below.

Berberis bergmanniae SCHNEIDER *Wallichianae*
4.6. Evergreen shrub, to 3m, of dense, somewhat pyramidal habit. Lv in clusters of up to 5, spiny, obovate, leathery, to 5cm long. Fl in clusters, on pedicels to 1cm long. Fl 5–6. Fr oval, black with bluish bloom on reddish stalks. Fr 9–10. Native of W China. Introduced by Wilson in 1908.

Berberis buxifolia LAMARCK *Buxifoliae*
4. (*B. dulcis* SWEET) Shrub, to 3m, usually evergreen, but losing its lv in exceptionally severe winters. Lv leathery, spine-tipped, obovate, to 2·5cm long, tapered at the base into a short petiole. Fl solitary, orange-yellow; fr dark purple. Fl 3–4. Fr 8–9. The earliest-flowering sp. Native to Chile. Introduced by Anderson in 1826.

Berberis calliantha MULLIGAN *Wallichianae*
4. Dwarf evergreen shrub, rarely exceeding 1m in height, but spreading quite considerably. Lv elliptic but spiny-toothed, giving a holly-like appearance; to 6cm long, 2cm across, dark, shining green above, white beneath. Fl solitary or up to 3, pale yellow, to 2·5cm across. Fl 5. Fr ovoid, to 1·5cm long, black covered with greyish bloom. Native to Tibet. Introduced by Kingdon Ward in 1924.

Berberis candidula SCHNEIDER *Wallichianae*
4. Dwarf, spreading evergreen shrub, barely over 1m high, making a dome-shaped bush. Lv oblong, spiny, dark green and shining above, shining white beneath. Fl solitary, globose, bright yellow. Fl 5–6. Fr purplish, bloomy. Native of China. Introduced by Père Farges in 1895 to Messrs Vilmorin.

Berberis X carminea AHRENDT
4.5.6. A name given to a series of hybrids with *B. aggregata* as one parent, while the other is not certainly known, but thought to be members of the *Angulosae*. They all make vigorous shrubs of varying height with paniculate inflorescences of pale yellow flowers in June and

July, and bright red fruits and vivid red leaf colour in the autumn. Various clones have been named as 'Barbarossa', 'Buccaneer' and 'Fire King', while plants of rather smaller dimensions, little more than 1m high, are 'Bountiful' and 'Sparkler'. They are all deciduous and appear to have arisen through chance hybridization.

Berberis chillanensis (SCHNEIDER) SPRAGUE
Actinacanthae

4. (*B. montana* var *chillanensis* SCHNEIDER) Deciduous shrub, to 3m, usually less. Bts greyish. Lv narrowly obovate, to 1·2cm long, 5mm across. Fl in fascicles, sepals pale yellow, petals pale orange, rather like a small 'Soleil d'Or' Narcissus, about 1cm across. Fl 4–5. Fr about 8mm long, black with purple bloom. Native to Chilean and Argentine Andes. Introduced by H. F. Comber in 1926. The plant is similar to *B. montana,* but smaller-flowered.[1]

Berberis concinna JOSEPH HOOKER *Angulosae*

4.5. Low deciduous or semi-evergreen bush, to 1m. Lv spiny, obovate, to 2·5cm long, bright green above, white below. Fl on pedicels to 3cm long, globose, bright yellow, 1·3cm across. Fl 5–6. Fr oblong, fleshy, red, to 2cm long. Attractive for its rounded, compact habit and bright yellow, large fl. Best propagated by seed. Native to central Himalaya at 4,000m and over. Introduced by Joseph Hooker in 1850.

Berberis darwinii WILLIAM HOOKER *Ilicifoliae*

4.5. Evergreen shrub, usually to 4m, but in mild, rainy districts considerably more, although the plant tends to spread horizontally rather than vertically. Lv spiny, leathery, very dark green, obovate, to 3cm long. Fl in drooping racemes to 10cm long, orange-yellow tinged with red. Fl 4–5. Fr about 8mm long, bluish-purple. There is often a second flowering in the autumn. One of the most splendid garden shrubs; well established plants flower very profusely. Perfectly hardy, but resents drought and strong winds. Native of Chile; discovered by Charles Darwin on his voyage in the *Beagle* in 1835. Introduced by William Lobb in 1849.

Berberis diaphana MAXIMOWICZ *Angulosae*

4.5.6. Low deciduous shrub, rarely over 1m high. Lv obovate, to 2·5cm long, grey-green above, grey below. Fl solitary or in a few-flowered cluster, bright yellow, on pedicels to 2cm long, 1·5cm across. Fr pink or red, about 1·5cm long, slightly pruinose. Lv colour well in the autumn. Native of NW China. Introduced from Kansu by Przewalski about 1894.

Berberis dictyophylla FRANCHET *Angulosae*

4.5.6. Graceful, deciduous bush with arching stems, to 2m. Bts covered with white bloom at

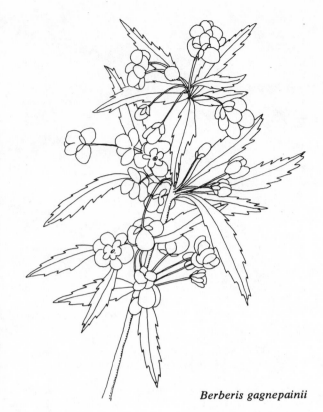

Berberis gagnepainii

first. Lv obovate, to 2cm long, bright green above, white beneath. Fl yellow, usually single, 1·5cm across. Fl 6. Fr red with white bloom. Lv colour red and gold in the autumn. A very desirable sp with flowers that are large for the genus. Native of Yunnan and Szechuan. Introduced by George Forrest in 1916 (Rehder gives date of introduction as 1890).

Berberis francisci-ferdinandii SCHNEIDER
Tinctoriae

4.5. Deciduous shrub of rounded habit, to 3m. Bts purplish. Lv on a petiole to 1cm long, oval or obovate, to 7cm long, faintly spiny-toothed. Fl yellow; 8mm across, on long, drooping, slender panicles to 12cm long. Fl 6. Fr usually thickly on the panicle, bright scarlet, to 1cm long. Extremely showy when well-fruited. Native to W China. Introduced by Wilson in 1900.

Berberis gagnepainii SCHNEIDER *Wallichianae*

4. Evergreen, very spiny shrub, to 2m or more. Lv linear lanceolate, apex acute, to 10cm

[1] In his monograph *Berberis and Mahonia* published in 1961 by the Linnean Society, Dr L. Ahrendt has considerably increased the number of series. In his classification, *B. chillanensis* and *B. montana* go into the series Montanae, while *B. valdiviana* is in the series Laurinae.

long, 8mm across; rather leathery, dull dark green. Fl in fascicles of 6–10 on pedicels 2cm long; bright yellow, 1·2cm across. Fl 5–6. Fr black, bloomy. Native of Szechuan. Introduced by Wilson in 1904.

Berberis glaucocarpa STAPF *Asiaticae*

4.5. (*B. coriacea* BRANDIS) It is this plant that usually usurps the name of *B. aristata*. Deciduous or semi-evergreen shrub of suckering habit to 4m. Bts pale yellow. Lv oblanceolate, to 6cm long, 2·5cm across; green on both surfaces, entire or slightly toothed. Fl in a raceme to 3cm long, yellow. Fl 5–6. Fr blackish, thickly covered with white bloom. Native of western Himalayas. Introduced 1832, presumably through Wallich.

Berberis gyalaica AHRENDT *Asiaticae*

4.5.6. Deciduous shrub with arching stems, to 3m. Bts dark red, spines yellow. Lv sessile, elliptic, to 1·2cm long; green above, greyish below, turning bright red in the autumn. Fl in dense panicles to 5cm long. Fl 7. Fr black with a blue bloom. Unusual in its combination of black fr and red autumn coloration. Native to SE Tibet. Introduced by Kingdon Ward in 1924.

Barely distinct are two other spp. *B. sheriffii* AHRENDT and *B. taylori* AHRENDT, introduced in 1938 by the Ludlow, Sherriff and Taylor expedition. *B. sheriffii* seems to be the hardiest of the three.

Berberis hookeri LEMAIRE *Wallichianae*

4. (*B. wallichiana* of WILLIAM HOOKER but not of DE CANDOLLE). Evergreen shrub, to 2m, with very crowded stems. Lv lanceolate to obovate, to 7cm long, 2·5cm wide; leathery, spine-toothed, dark green above, glaucous below (but green below in the var *viridis*). Fl in fascicles of 3–6, 1·6cm across, pale yellow, but sepals sometimes tinged with red. Fl 4–5. Fr long and narrow, to 1·2cm, black, persistent. Native of the Himalaya. A plant known as *B. wallichiana* was introduced, presumably by Wallich himself, in 1820. It was also sent back in 1849 by Thomas Lobb.

Berberis hypokerina AIRY-SHAW *Wallichianae*

4. Kingdon Ward's Silver Holly, apparently very striking in its native Burma. Evergreen, rather gawky, shrub, little more than 1m high, with purple stems. Lv oblong-oval, to 15cm long, 6cm across, margins spiny, dark green above, shining silver below. Fl in fascicles, up to 15, to 9mm across, pale yellow. Fl 5–6. Fr blue-purple. Notable for its very large and strikingly coloured lv. Introduced by Kingdon Ward in 1926. It apparently grows in shade in its native N Burma.

Berberis insignis J. D. HOOKER AND T. THOMSON *Wallichianae*

4. Frequently without spines, although this character is not constant. Evergreen shrub, to 2m. Lv single or in threes, lanceolate, to 12cm long, 4cm wide; spiny-toothed, shining green above, pale below with conspicuous veins. Fl in clusters of up to 25, pale yellow, globular. Fl 4–5. Fr black, oval, 8mm in diameter. Has a reputation for tenderness, but survives most winters, although sometimes damaged. Native of Sikkim, Nepal and Bhutan. Introduced by Joseph Hooker in 1850.

Berberis jamesiana FORREST AND W. W. SMITH *Tinctoriae*

4.5.6. Deciduous shrub, to 3m, bts purple. Lv in clusters of 2–6, obovate or rounded, spine-tipped, to 5cm long, 4cm across, turning red in autumn. Fl yellow in racemes to 19cm. Fl 6–7. Fr globose, scarlet, like red currants. Fr 10. Native of Yunnan, discovered and introduced by Forrest in 1913.

Berberis julianae SCHNEIDER *Wallichianae*

4. Tall, evergreen shrub, to 3m and more. Lv elliptic to oblanceolate, short-stalked, spiny-toothed, to 7cm long, 1cm across. Fl in clusters of up to 15, yellow. Fl 4–5. Fr black with blue bloom. Easy and quick-growing sp. Native of Central China. Introduced by Wilson in 1900.

Berberis kawakamii HAYATA *Wallichianae*

3.4. Evergreen shrub, to 2m. Lv copper-coloured when young, later narrowly oval, to 5cm long and 2cm across, glossy green, sharp-toothed. Fl bright yellow in clusters of up to 12. Fl 3–4. Fr dark blue. One of the better evergreen asiatic sp with fl of a brighter yellow than most of the Wallichianae. Native of Taiwan. Introduced by Wilson in 1918.

Berberis koreana PALABIN *Sinenses*

4.5.6. Deciduous shrub, to 2m. Bts reddish. Spines on vigorous shoots, to 1cm long, sometimes flattened at base. Lv to 7cm long, oval, colouring in autumn. Fl in drooping racemes to 10cm. Fr ovoid, red, long-persistent. Native of Korea. Introduced in 1905, by whom is not recorded.

Berberis linearifolia PHILIPPI *Buxifoliae*

4. Evergreen shrub, to nearly 3m. Lv in clusters of 3–6, linear, to 4·5cm long; dark green above, glaucous beneath. Fl in fascicles of 4 or 6, each on a red pedicel to 3cm long; rich orange inside, red or apricot without; each fl about 2cm across. Fl 4–5. Fr black with blue bloom. The most strikingly coloured sp in cultivation. Plants that are not well established seem rather tender,

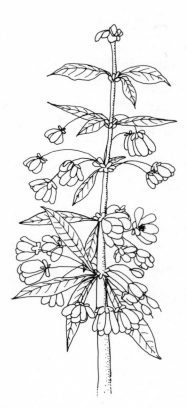

Berberis linearifolia

but once established they appear to withstand the coldest winters without injury.

In the wild it hybridises with *B. darwinii* and the resultant hybrid has been called *B. X lologensis* SANDWITH. The plant resembles *B. darwinii,* but with larger and better coloured fl and narrower leaves. Both this plant and *B. linearifolia* will grow well on chalky soils.

Native of Chile. Introduced by Harold Comber in 1927.

Berberis lycium ROYLE *Asiaticae*

4.5. Deciduous or semi-evergreen shrub, wide-spreading, to 3m. Lv oblanceolate to 5cm long, light green above, glaucous below, spine-tipped. Fl bright yellow in racemes to 7cm. Fl 5–6. Fr blackish with bluish bloom. Often confused with *B. lycioides* STAPF, one of the plants usually sold as *B. aristata*, which has slightly larger lv, longer racemes and fr with a blue-white bloom, while the lv are not spine-tipped. *B. lycium* is known to have been brought back by Joseph Hooker from the Himalaya in 1850, but may well have been brought in before as *B. aristata*.

Berberis mitifolia STAPF *Brachypodae*

4.5.6. (*B. brachypoda gibbsii* HORT) Deciduous shrub, to 3m, with downy bts, which are grey. Lv obovate, to 7cm long and 2·5cm across,

tapering to a stalk of 1cm; downy on both sides turning red in autumn. Fl pale yellow, in spike-like pendulous racemes to 10cm long. Fl 5. Fr dark red. Native of Hupeh, collected by Wilson in 1901. An excellent plant.

Berberis montana GAY *Actinacanthae*

4. Deciduous, rather fastigiate, shrub, to 5m. Lv in clusters of 2–7, oblanceolate, to 3·5cm long and 1cm wide; untoothed. Fl in few-flowered clusters, at least 2cm wide; sepals yellow, petals orange, much resembling a 'Soleil d'Or' narcissus. Fl 4–5. Fr black, with purple bloom. Native of Chile. Introduced by H. Comber in 1927. This has the largest fl of any sp in cultivation, but is of no interest when out of flower.

Berberis morrisonensis HAYATA *Angulosae*

4.5.6. Shrub, to 2m; bts reddish. Lv in clusters of 3–8, obovate, rounded at the apex, to 2·5cm long, lv colour red very late in the season, usually November and December and persist until the New Year. Fl pale yellow, in few-fld clusters. Fl 6. Fr bright red and transparent. The fl are inconspicuous, but the fr, when formed, is attractive; but the main interest is in the very late autumn colour. Native of Taiwan on Mt Morrison. Introduced originally by W. R. Price in 1912; again by Wilson in 1918.

Berberis orthobotrys SCHNEIDER *Vulgares*

4.5. (*B. vulgaris* var *brachybotrys* J. HOOKER) Deciduous shrub, to 1m or slightly more. Lv oblanceolate, to 2·8cm long, 1cm wide. Fl yellow, in small corymbose racemes to 3cm. Fr red, long-persisting. The plant tends to cover itself with fl so that the lv are practically invisible and the fr are also produced in quantity. A form with smaller lv with grey bloom below is sometimes known as var *canescens* and sometimes as 'Unique'. Native of Kashmir and Afghanistan. Introduced in 1879.

Berberis prattii SCHNEIDER *Polyanthae*

4.5. (*B. aggregata* var *prattii* SCHNEIDER) Deciduous shrub, to 3m and more, with pale yellow bts, which are red at first. Lv in clusters of up to 10, oblong, to 3cm long; green above, greyish beneath. Fl small, pale yellow, in *erect* panicles up to 25cm long, although more usually about 15cm long. Fl 6–7. Fr bright pink. Sometimes sold under the name *B. polyantha*, which is usually semi-evergreen with dark red fruits and is not in commerce. A form with rather smaller *pendulous* panicles has been given the name var *laxipendula* AHRENDT. The fruits do not colour until late in the year and are very persistent. Native of China, collected by Wilson in 1904.

Berberis pruinosa FRANCHET *Wallichianae*

4.5. Evergreen shrub, to 4m. Lv in tufts of 3–5; leathery, shining green above, grey-white below, spiny-toothed. Fl usually in clusters, occasionally in umbels, lemon yellow. Fl 4–5. Fr black with silvery bloom. Native of Yunnan. Introduced by Père Delavay in 1894.

Berberis replicata w. w. SMITH *Wallichianae*

4.5. Evergreen shrub, slightly less than 2m, with arching branches. Bts yellowish. Lv in clusters of 3–5, linear-oblong with recurved margins, so that they appear linear; spine-tipped, to 5cm long, dull, dark green above, white beneath. Fl in clusters of up to 10, bright yellow. Fl 4–5, earlier in mild years. Fr red at first finally dark purple. Native of Yunnan. Introduced by Forrest in 1917.

Berberis X rubrostilla CHITTENDEN

4.5.6. Thought to be a hybrid of *B. wilsonae* pollinated by *B. aggregata.* Lv oblanceolate about 2·5cm long. Fl in pendulous racemes, pale yellow. Fl 6–7. Fr coral-red, translucent, about 1cm long. It is chiefly as a fruiting shrub that this is grown, as the fl are not remarkably showy, although useful in appearing late in the season. 'Cherry Ripe' with fr which are creamy-white when young, later cerise, is a seedling from *B. X rubrostilla.* The shrub will eventually reach nearly 2m.

Berberis sargentiana SCHNEIDER *Wallichianae*

4. Evergreen shrub, to 2m, with reddish bts. Lv oblong lanceolate, to 12cm long and 3cm across; dark green above, pale below. Fl in sessile clusters of 2–6, pale yellow. Fl 4–5. Fr black. Quite unmoved by the severest winters, but otherwise not very exciting. Native of W. China. Introduced by Wilson in 1907.

Berberis soulieana SCHNEIDER *Wallichianae*

4. (*B. stenophylla* HANCE) Evergreen shrub, to 2m, rather stiff and upright. Lv linear-oblong, to 10cm long, 1·5cm across. Fl yellow and quite large, in clusters of about 8 on short pedicels. Fl 5. Fr black with greyish bloom. Native of central China. Introduced (by Père Soulié?) in 1897.

Berberis X stenophylla LINDLEY

4. Perhaps the most popular berberis in cultivation. A hybrid between *B. darwinii* and the dwarf *B. empetrifolia,* which appeared in a Sheffield nursery in 1860. There are numerous dwarf forms, but the form most usually seen can reach up to 3m and has graceful arching stems. Lv in tufts, linear, spine-tipped, to 2·5cm long; dark green and dull above, glaucous beneath. Fl in short, few-fld racemes, yellow-orange. Fl 4–5 and often again in the autumn. Fr globose, black with bluish bloom.

A number of dwarf forms are sometimes offered under the name *B. X irwinii* BYHOUWER. These seem to be of the same parentage, but with *B. empetriformis* as the seed-parent, and rarely exceed 1m in height, with foliage similar to that of *B. darwinii. B. X. stenophylla* is best propagated by cuttings, as seedlings tend to resemble *B. darwinii.*

Berberis temolaica AHRENDT *Angulosae*

2.4.5. A striking foliage shrub, deciduous, to somewhat over 2m, with arching stems which are bluish-white when young. Lv also glaucous when young, obovate, to 4·5cm long, white beneath. Fl solitary, pale yellow. Fl 5. Fr red with white bloom. Plants are often very slow to get away, but patience is usually rewarded. Neither fl nor fr are very conspicuous. Native of Tibet, discovered and introduced by Kingdon Ward in 1924.

Berberis thunbergii DE CANDOLLE *Sinenses*

4.5.6. Deciduous shrub, to nearly 3m, with stiff, upright branches and reddish-brown bark. Lv in tufts, spathulate, to 3cm long, usually rounded at the apex, occasionally spine-toothed, usually colouring red in the autumn. Fl usually single but sometimes in pairs, reddish. Fr bright red, persisting for much of the winter. A very ornamental shrub for autumn colour and fruit. The form known as 'Atropurpurea' has purplish lv but these do not colour so well in the autumn. 'Rose Glow' has purple lv with pink and white variegation. Native to Japan. Introduced about 1864.

Berberis valdiviana PHILIPPI *Ilicifoliae*

4. Evergreen shrub, to 4m. Lv oblong-oval, to 7·5cm long and 3cm wide, usually entire, sometimes spiny-toothed. Fl bright yellow in pendulous racemes of about 30 fl. Fl 5. Fr purplish, covered with bloom. May be cut to the ground in severe winters, but generally regenerates. Native to Chile. Introduced 1902 and subsequently in 1929.

Berberis veitchii SCHNEIDER *Wallichianae*

4. (*B. acuminata* VEITCH) Evergreen shrub of spreading habit to 2m. Bts bright red. Lv 2–4, narrowly lanceolate, spiny-toothed, to 15cm long. Fl in clusters of 4–8, from second-year wood, each fl on a slender pedicel to 3cm; 2cm across, bronzy-yellow. Fl 4–5. Fr black with bluish bloom. Notable for its reddish young wood and unusually coloured, rather large fl. Native to Central China. Introduced from Hupeh by Wilson in 1900.

Berberis vernae SCHNEIDER *Integerrimae*

4.5. (*B. caroli* var *hoanghensis* SCHNEIDER).
Deciduous shrub, to 2 or 3m, of graceful spreading habit. Lv in largish clusters of up to 8,
spathulate, to 4·5cm long with a petiole 1cm
long. Fl small, bright yellow, crowded on a
pendulous raceme to 5cm long. Fl 5. Fr salmon-
pink. Fr 9–10. The only member of the series in
general cultivation and not easy to obtain,
although a handsome and very hardy shrub.
Native of western and central China. Introduced
by Wilson from Szechuan in 1910.

Berberis verruculosa HEMSLEY AND WILSON
Wallichianae

4. Evergreen shrub, to 2m, with bts covered
with small, dark brown excrescences, giving a
wrinkled appearance which is characteristic. Lv
oval, dark green above, glaucous beneath, spiny-
toothed, leathery, to 3cm long. Fl bright, golden
yellow, solitary or in few-fld clusters, large to
2cm across. Fl 4–5. Fr black with bluish bloom.
Native to W China. Introduced by Wilson in
1904.

Berberis vulgaris LINNAEUS *Vulgares*
Barberry

4.5. Deciduous shrub, rarely over 2m. Lv in
tufts, to 5cm long, obovate or elliptic, grey-green.
Fl in pendulous racemes to 8cm long, yellow.
Fl 5–6. Fr ovoid, bright red. Fr 9–10. Native of
Europe (incl the UK), N Africa and W Asia;
naturalised in USA. Handsome both in fl and,
even more, in fr. 'Atropurpurea' has deep purple
lv.
Var *amurensis* REGEL (*B. amurensis* RUPRECHT)
has lv up to 10cm long, 5cm across, and racemes
to 9cm with larger fl and fr. Flowering slightly
earlier. *B. X ottawensis* SCHNEIDER is the name
for hybrids between *B. vulgaris* and *B. thunbergii*.
These add good autumn colour to their virtues,
but the infl is clustered rather than racemose.
'Superba' has bronzy red lv turning crimson in
the autumn.

Berberis wilsoniae HEMSLEY *Polyanthae*

4.5.6. Deciduous or semi-evergreen shrub, of
spreading habit, usually only 1m high, but to
nearly 2m in var *stapfiana*. Bts slightly pubescent
at first, reddish. Lv to 2cm, oblanceolate, grey-
green above, glaucous below. Fl pale yellow in
fascicles or very short racemes. Fl 6–7. Fr roundish, coral pink, transparent. Fr 9–11. Var
subcaulialata has larger lv and fr ripening in
November.
All the various forms seem good garden
shrubs, although the amount of autumn colour
in the lv varies greatly from plant to plant. Both
var *stapfiana* and var *subcaulialata* seem to have
been introduced before *B. wilsoniae* itself. Var

stapfiana, collected by Potanin and grown at St
Petersburg; var *subcaulialata* collected by Père
Soulié and grown by Vilmorin. Both these introductions date from 1894, while Wilson did not
introduce *B. wilsoniae* until 1904. The type and
the various var come from W China.

Berberis yunnanensis FRANCHET *Angulosae*

4.5.6. Deciduous shrub, to 2m. Lv rounded,
to 3·5cm long and 2cm across, medium green.
Fl in clusters of 3–8, pale yellow, 2cm across on
pedicels to 3cm long. Fl 5. Fr oval, bright red,
to 1·2cm long. Lv turn bright crimson in autumn.
One of the best sp for its large fl and fr and
showy autumn colour. Native of Yunnan; discovered by Delavay in 1885 and probably introduced to France about ten years later.

BERCHEMIA NECKER *Rhamnaceae*

A small genus of deciduous twining shrubs. They
are not of great interest as the flowers are small
and inconspicuous, while the fruit, which may
be ornamental, is not very frequently produced
in the UK. The main interest lies in the leaves
with their conspicuous and attractive veining.
There are probably about fifteen species in all
from Asia, E Africa and N America.

Berchemia lineata DE CANDOLLE

5. Deciduous twiner, to 7m. Lv oval to 3cm
long, 2cm across; dark green above, pale below,
with 4–6 parallel veins running from the midrib
to the margin. Fl white, very small, in terminal
clusters and also from terminal axils. Fl 6. Fr a
small drupe, blue-black. Fr 10–11. Native to
China, Taiwan and N India. Introduction
before 1774.

Berchemia racemosa SIEBOLD AND ZUCCARINI

5. Deciduous twiner, to 13m, often a spreading tangled shrub. Lv ovate with cordate base,
to 7cm long, half as wide, glaucous beneath with
7–9 pairs of parallel veins radiating from the
midrib to the margin. Fl in terminal, pyramidal
panicle, to 15cm long, greenish. Fl 7–8. Fr first
red, later black. Fr 7–9 the year following
flowering. There is a cream, variegated form in
cultivation. Native of Japan and Taiwan. Introduced in 1880.

BETULA LINNAEUS *Betulaceae* Birch

A rather confused genus of trees and shrubs,
mainly grown for the sake of their ornamental
bark in winter. Leaves alternate, generally ovate
with toothed margins on a petiole. Flower
monoecious. The male catkins formed in the
autumn and expanding the following spring;
female catkins shorter and stiffer, disintegrating

when the seeds are ripe. Most species require good rich soil, but the common silver birch, *B. pendula,* thrives on the poorest soils, while *B. nigra* thrives happily in waterlogged positions. They tend to be very strong feeders and to throw out roots well beyond the canopy, so that they are not really suitable for small gardens. Propagation is best by seed, which usually germinates readily. Growth is fairly rapid, but larger plants usually remain quiescent for a year or so after being moved. The bark on the trunk tends to peel yearly and is often different in colour from that on the branches and branchlets. The genus comprises about forty species distributed throughout the northern temperate and Arctic zones, but the differences between some species are extremely slight.

Betula albo-sinensis BURKILL

1.7. (*B. bhojpattra* var *sinensis* FRANCHET) A tree, to 30m in the wild, but so far not more than 16m in cultivation. The trunk is bright orange to orange-red, peeling off to show a glaucous bloom beneath. In the var *septentrionalis* SCHNEIDER, which appears to do rather better in the UK, the bark is orange-brown to orange-grey. Lv ovate, slender-pointed, to 7cm long and 3cm across. Male catkins to 6cm long, female to 3cm. Branches dark brown. Native to W China. Introduced by Wilson in 1901.

Betula coerulea-grandis BLANCHARD

1.7. Small tree, to 12m, with white bark and brown brs. Lv triangular-ovate, to 7cm long; bluish-green above, paler below. Not particularly striking, but a useful small tree. Native to eastern N America. Introduced 1905, according to Rehder.

Betula costata TRAUTVETTER

1.7. Tree, to 30m. Bark greyish-brown, peeling in papery flakes, brs brown. Lv oblong-ovate with long point, to 8cm long. Female catkins almost globular. Very similar to the next sp, mainly differentiated by its long narrow lv and the shape of the fr, although the lv are usually 10–14 veined, while most forms of *B. ermanii* have 7–11, but its specific distinction is hard to maintain. Native of NE Asia. Introduced 1880.

Betula ermanii CHAMISSO

1.2.7. (*B. ulmifolia* REGEL) Tree, to 30m in the wild, but rarely more than 20m in cultivation. The trunk is creamy or pinkish-white and peels yearly; brs orange-brown. Lv broadly ovate, with long point and cordate base, to 7 or 8cm long, 5cm across. Female catkins barrel-shaped, to 3cm long. Very handsome with its contrasting trunk and brs. Native to NE Asia and Japan, somewhat liable to damage from late spring frosts, but otherwise quite hardy. Apparently introduced about 1890, but the exact date seems uncertain. The var *subcordata* KOIDZUMI (*nipponica* MAXIMOWICZ) is said to be less liable to spring frost damage and may also produce more than one trunk.

Betula grossa SIEBOLD AND ZUCCARINI

7. (*B. ulmifolia* SIEB AND ZUCC) Tree, to 25m in cultivation, rather more in the wild. Bark dark grey or blackish, fissured on old trees. Brs yellow-brown at first, later chestnut-brown. Lv oblong-ovate, heart-shaped at base, to 10cm long. Female catkins ellipsoid. Bark and young wood aromatic. Native of Japan. Introduced in 1896.

Betula jacquemontii SPACH

Probably a form of *B. utilis* (qv).

Betula lenta LINNAEUS

7. Tree, to 25m, with non-peeling, almost black, bark, fissured on old trees. Brs chestnut-brown. Lv ovate-oblong, to 15cm long and 8cm across, heart-shaped at the base, short-petioled. Young bark aromatic and pleasant tasting. Male catkins to 7cm long, female catkins, cylindrical, to 3cm long. Not a particularly good doer. Very similar to *B. grossa,* but native to eastern N America from Maine to Alabama. Introduced 1759, presumably through Bartram or Humphrey Marshall.

Betula luminifera WINKLER

3.7. Tree, to 20m. Trunks yellowish-grey, not peeling, brs brown. Young lv reddish. Mature lv ovate, to 12cm long and 9cm across; dull green above, shining green below with shining resin-glands. Lv persist well into November. Female catkins cylindrical, to 8cm long. Native of W China and introduced by Wilson in 1901. Possibly conspecific with the Himalayan *B. alnoides* D. DON, which has peeling bark, but is otherwise not easily distinguished. *B. alnoides* is somewhat tender, while *B. luminifera* appears perfectly hardy although not long-lived.

Betula lutea MICHAUX

1.7. Tree, to 30m in the wild, but rarely more than 15m in cultivation. Trunk peeling to show yellowish-brown bark, brs reddish-brown. Lv ovate, to 10cm long and 5cm across, dull green. Young bark aromatic but bitter. Allied to *B. lenta,* but distinct in its yellowish peeling bark. Native to eastern N America from Newfoundland to Georgia (only on mountains so far south). Introduced in 1816 according to Sweet's *Hortus Britannicus,* 1800 according to Rehder. Certainly introduced by Fraser before 1811.

Betula maximowicziana REGEL

1.7. Tree, to 30m in the wild, but 17m in cultivation. Trunk and brs orange-brown; trunk later becoming greyish; bts warty. Lv cordate, to 15cm long and 11cm wide, downy at first, later glabrous. Male catkins to 7cm long, female catkins in racemes, each to 6cm long. The largest leaved sp in cultivation. Said to be a vigorous grower, but a 65-year-old plant at Kew was only 13m high. Native of Japan. Introduced in 1888 by James H. Veitch.

Betula medwediewii REGEL

2.6. Spreading shrub with pale brown young wood and bright green winter buds, which may be 1cm long. Lv roundish, resembling an alder, to 10cm long and 7cm across; veins sunken to give a slightly rugose effect; usually turning golden before falling. Mature shrubs may be 5m high, but nearly twice as wide. Of striking appearance in autumn and winter. Native to the Caucasus. Introduced in 1897.

Betula nigra LINNAEUS

7. (*B. rubra* MICHAUX) Pyramidal tree, to 30m. Bark white to start with, later turning black and peeling off in large flakes. Brs whitish or reddish-brown; bts warty and downy. Lv diamond-shaped, to 8cm long and 6cm across, glossy green above, glaucous below. Male catkins to 7cm long, female, erect, to 3cm long. A very useful tree for planting in districts with a high water table or by streams or ponds. Native to the eastern USA and among the first plants sent by Bartram to Peter Collinson in 1736.

Betula papyrifera MARSHALL

1.7. (*B. papyracea* AITON). Tree, to 30m or more, and the provider of the bark for birch-bark canoes. Trunk gleaming white, coming away in thin paper-like layers. Bts warty. Lv ovate, to 7cm long and 5cm across, dark green. Male catkins to 10cm long, female catkins, drooping, to 3cm long. Several variants have been named, among which the most conspicuous are: Var *commutata* (REGEL) FERNALD, from British Columbia, with reddish-brown bark on the trunk and yellowish bts; lv ovate to 7cm long on young trees. This fine var has no objection to wet situations. Var *humilis* (REGEL) FERNALD AND RAUP (var *neoalaskana* (SARGENT) RAUP) has the bark varying in colour from red-brown to dull white. It is native to Alaska and makes a somewhat smaller tree. Var *kenaica* (EVANS) HENRY is smaller still, rarely exceeding 10m, with orange-tinged bark and lv not more than 5cm long. A good sp for small gardens.

The type is native to N America as far south as Nebraska. Introduced in 1750 by Bartram.

Betula pendula ROTH · Silver Birch

1.7. (*B. verrucosa* EHRHART, *B. alba* in part LINNAEUS). Tree, to 20m, with silvery-white trunk and purple-brown bts, which are warty and not downy in any way, thereby distinguishing the plant more easily from *B. pubescens*, with which Linnaeus confused this plant, describing them both as *B. alba*. Bts tend to be pendulous. Lv ovate to diamond-shaped, to 6cm long and 3cm across. Male catkins to 6cm long, female to 3cm. The common silver birch of British woodlands, thriving in the poorest soils. A number of variants have been propagated of which the most spectacular is 'Dalecarlica' with long, pinnatifidly-lobed lv. The original plant was observed in 1767 and named by Linnaeus' son in 1781, and most of the plants sold under this name have been propagated by grafts from the original tree, which was found in Dalecarlia. One other tree has since been found in Sweden with these extraordinary lv. It is not always as vigorous as the type.

The plant known as 'Tristis' or 'Elegans' has a more pronounced weeping habit, while 'Youngii' weeps very profusely, but makes no central trunk; it has to be grafted on to a trunk of *B. pendula*, when it makes a very attractive small mushroom-topped tree. 'Purpurea' has deep purple lv. 'Fastigiata' has the habit of a Lombardy poplar.

Betula platyphylla SUKATCHEV

1.3.7. (*B. mandschurica* (REGEL) NAKAI). The type is propably not in cultivation but is represented by the Japanese var *japonica* (MIQUEL) HARA (*B. japonica* MIQUEL). Tree, to 25m, with pure white bark and reddish bts. Young lv expand tinged with red. Lv ovate, to 7cm long and 6cm across. Female catkins to 8cm long. Resembles the silver birch, but has larger lv, which are attractive when unfurling. Known in cultivation since 1887.

Betula populifolia MARSHALL

1.7. Small, short-lived tree, to 15m. Bark ash-white, bts warty and glabrous. Lv more or less triangular, with a long tapering point, to 9cm long and 6cm across, petiole to 2·5cm long. Male catkins to 9cm long, female to 3cm. Quite a useful small tree with its elegant lv and thriving in very poor soil, but not as handsome as *B. pendula* and rather short-lived (30–40 years). Native of eastern N America from Nova Scotia to Delaware. Introduced in 1750, possibly through Humphrey Marshall, but more probably from Bartram.

Betula pubescens EHRHART

1.7. Tree, to 20m. Bark sometimes white, but more usually brownish or greyish, trunk often

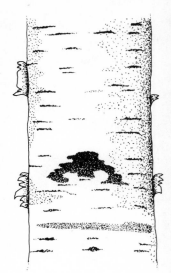

Betula papyrifera

turning dark and rugose at the base. Brs ascending more than those of *B. pendula,* bts downy with no warts. Otherwise scarcely to be differentiated from *B. pendula,* although it never makes as large a tree. Curiously it is a tetraploid, having twice as many chromosomes as *B. pendula* in each cell (*B. pendula* has 28, *B. pubescens* 56). It is not as attractive a plant as *B. pendula,* and like it is native of most of northern and central Europe.

Betula utilis   D. DON

1.7. (*Betula bhojpattra* WALLICH) Included in this confusing species is *B. jacquemontii* SPACH. Tree, to 20m in the Indian Himalaya but up to 30m in China (var *prattii* BURKILL). The sequence appears to be that the most westerly sp is *B. jacquemontii,* which merges into *B. utilis* in Kumaon and this, in turn merges into var *prattii* in Kansu and Szechuan. Trees of *B. jacquemontii* in cultivation have the most lovely white bark, but this is not, apparently, the most usual colour in the wild. The bark of *B. utilis* and var *prattii* varies in colour from dark chocolate, through mahogany-brown to creamy-white, flushed pink. Some of the Himalayan forms proved rather tender, but the Chinese plants appear perfectly hardy.

The bts are covered with grey down and eventually become reddish-brown. Lv ovate, rounded at base and pointed at apex, to 7cm long and 5cm wide, dark green, slightly downy. The lv of *B. utilis* and var *prattii* have 9–12 pairs of lateral veins, those of *B. jacquemontii* have 7–9, but the differences are all very slight and there seems no good reason to give *B. jacquemontii* more than varietal distinction. *B. utilis* was introduced from the Himalayas by Joseph Hooker in 1849. *B. jacquemontii* was sent from St Petersburg by Regel in 1880 and var *prattii* was first sent by Wilson in 1908 and subsequently by Forrest.

BROUSSONETIA   VENTENAT   *Moraceae*

A small genus of deciduous, dioecious trees and shrubs, allied to the mulberry. Male flowers in catkins, female flowers in heads, which later swell to make fleshy syncarps, composed of a head of drupelets. About three species only in eastern Asia. Easily propagated by cuttings of half-ripe wood.

Broussonetia kazinoki   SIEBOLD AND ZUCCARINI

(*B. kaempferi* of gardens, not of SIEB AND ZUCC). Deciduous shrub, to 5m, of spreading habit. Bts purplish-red, slightly downy at first. Lv usually ovate, sometimes 2–3-lobed, up to 25cm long and 12cm across on vigorous shoots, much smaller on weak ones. Male fl in clusters,

each 1cm long, female flowers in a globular head. Fr globular, woolly. Native of Japan and Korea. Introduced about 1844, possibly through one of Siebold's correspondents.

Broussonetia papyrifera   (LINNAEUS)   VENTENAT
Paper Mulberry

4.5.7. (*Morus papyrifera* LINNAEUS) Vigorous shrub or small tree to 16m. Bts very downy. Lv of different shapes, often on the same branch; in general lv on younger plants are lobed, often shaped like a sycamore, on older trees ovate. Lv to 20cm long on petioles that may be 10cm long, dull green above, grey and downy below. Male catkins, often curly, to 7cm long, yellowish. Fr 1cm across, orange-red. Native of China and Japan. Received by Peter Collinson before 1751, probably from Père d'Incarville, who was his principal Chinese correspondent.

There is a curious cv 'Lanciniata' in which the lv is reduced to the petiole and the three main veins, each with a small lamina at the end. The plant is always rather dwarf and is very curious.

BUDDLEIA   LINNAEUS   *Loganiaceae*

A genus of deciduous and evergreen shrubs, usually of moderate dimensions, with opposite leaves which are often woolly. Flowers tubular with expanded limb in terminal and/or axillary racemes or panicles, usually small but very numerous. Propagated by seed or by cuttings of half-ripe young wood. Native of temperate and subtropical S America, S Africa and central and eastern Asia. A large number of species are in cultivation, but few are reliably hardy. There are about 100 species known altogether.

Buddleia albiflora   HEMSLEY

4. (*B. hemsleyana* KOEHNE) Vigorous deciduous shrub, to 4m, with erect branches. Lv lanceolate with long, tapered point, to 22cm long and 6cm wide; dark green above, silvery-grey and woolly below. Fl in slender terminal and axillary panicles, to 50 cm long (usually not more than 20cm), composed of small fragrant lilac fl with orange centres. Fl 7–9. Native of China. Introduced by Wilson in 1900. Differs little from the well-known *B. davidii.*

Buddleia alternifolia   MAXIMOWICZ

4. Normally a spreading deciduous shrub with arching brs, but can be trained to make a very attractive small, weeping tree. Unique in the genus with its alternate lv. Lv lanceolate, to 10cm long and 1cm wide; dark green above, greyish, downy below. Fl in axillary clusters on year-old wood, often so profuse as to hide the stem completely; bright lilac-purple. Fl 6–7.

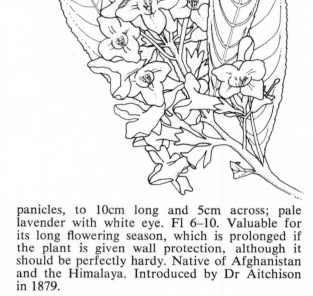

Buddleia alternifolia

Buddleia colvilei

Native of Kansu. Introduced by Purdom and Farrer in 1915. A very attractive and long-lived garden plant.

Buddleia colvilei JOSEPH HOOKER AND THOMSON

4. Large deciduous shrub, to 10m, with long, arching shoots. All parts of the new growths covered at first with reddish-brown wool, which soon vanishes. Lv lanceolate-ovate to 25cm long and 6cm across, shallowly-toothed, downy at first, later glabrous on both surfaces. Fl in terminal hanging panicles, to 20cm long and 8cm across. Each fl is up to 2·5cm long and wide, deep pink or crimson. Fl 6. Has a reputation for tenderness, but once established seems to withstand very severe frost without injury. Often given wall protection, but it is rather large for most walls. It is certainly the most handsome of the genus and should be tried in more places.

Native of the Sikkim Himalaya. Apparently introduced by Joseph Hooker in 1849, but nothing seems to have come of this introduction. From a subsequent one, it first flowered in 1892.

Buddleia crispa BENTHAM

4. (*B. paniculata* WALLICH) Deciduous, very woolly shrub, to 4m but spreading further. Bts and lv covered with a white or tawny tomentum. Lv lanceolate, to 12cm long and 4·5cm wide. Fl fragrant, in small terminal panicles, to 10cm long and 5cm across; pale lavender with white eye. Fl 6–10. Valuable for its long flowering season, which is prolonged if the plant is given wall protection, although it should be perfectly hardy. Native of Afghanistan and the Himalaya. Introduced by Dr Aitchison in 1879.

Buddleia davidii FRANCHET

4. (*B. variabilis* HEMSLEY) The best-known sp. Deciduous shrub, to 5m, with downy bts. Lv lanceolate, to 30cm long (usually around 15cm) and to 7cm wide; dark green above, white tomentose below. Fl in long terminal panicles, sometimes as long as 70cm, strong-smelling; usually lilac or purple, always with orange eye. Fl 7–9. A number of named cv exist with flowers ranging from dark violet and reddish-purple to white. Var *nanhoensis* (CHITTENDEN) REHDER is a dwarf form never more than 2m high, which is more compact in all its parts. Native of China. Apparently first introduced from Russia about 1890, but all modern forms descend from seed collected by Wilson between 1900 and 1908.

Buddleia globosa HOPE

4. Semi-evergreen shrub, to 5m, of rather sparse erect habit, particularly when old. Bts covered with yellowish tomentum. Lv lanceolate, tapered at both ends, to 20cm long and 5cm wide;

38

dark green and wrinkled above, yellowish tomentose below. Fl fragrant, in globular masses about 2cm across, many of which are arranged in terminal panicles, orange-yellow in colour. This is, indeed, the only hardy orange-flowered sp. Fl 5–6. Native to Peru and Chile. Obtained by the nursery firm of Lee and Kennedy in 1774, but from whom is not known. The plant can sustain damage during very severe winters, but is rarely destroyed.

Buddleia nivea DUTHIE

3.4. Deciduous shrub, to 3m. Bts covered in thick white tomentum, which becomes somewhat tawny later, as does the tomentum on the underside of the lv. Lv lanceolate, toothed, to 20cm long and 10cm wide; dark green above eventually. Fl in terminal and axillary branched panicles, to 15cm long; corolla-tube and calyx densely coated with white tomentum, so that only the expanded limb shows lavender. Fl 8. Rather striking in its intense woolliness, but of little floral beauty. Native of China. Introduced by Wilson in 1901.

Buddleia X weyerana WEYER

4. A hybrid between *B. globosa* and *B. davidii,* but fl arranged in globose masses along terminal panicles. 'Golden Glow' has fl orange and yellow shaded with mauve; 'Moonlight' has pale cream fl with deep orange tube. Mr van de Weyer raised these in 1914.

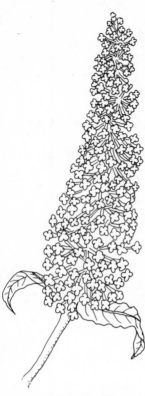

Buddleia davidii

Buddleia globosa

BUPLEURUM LINNAEUS *Umbelliferae*

A genus of about seventy-five species most of which are herbaceous; indeed very few umbellifers are shrubby. Propagated by cuttings.

Bupleurum fruticosum LINNAEUS

4. Evergreen shrub, to 3m, with purplish bts. Lv alternate, elliptic, to 9cm long and 3cm across, bluish-green. Fl in terminal umbels up to 10cm across, yellowish-green, the fl enclosed in an involucre. Fl 7–8. Very suitable for exposed and windy situations, particularly along the coast, but can be damaged in very severe winters. Native of the Mediterranean region and in cultivation since 1600.

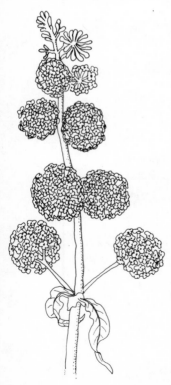

BUXUS LINNAEUS *Buxaceae*

A genus of about thirty species of evergreen shrubs or trees from Europe, Asia and N. Africa, as well as species in the West Indies and central America. The plants are monoecious and the flowers have no beauty, but the plants have a certain charm with their neat, round leaves which are very closely set on the branches. The plants are slow growing and are sometimes used for hedging, while the form of *B. sempervirens,* known as 'Suffruticosa' has been used as an edging for beds, etc., for centuries. Most species are easily propagated by cuttings.

Buxus balearica LAMARCK

Shrub or small tree, to 8m. Lv roundish-oval, to 3cm long and 2cm across, notched at the apex; glossy green above, pale green below. Distinguished from the common box by its larger lv and more robust shoots. Native of the Balearics and SW Spain. Introduced by Dr Fothergill before 1780.

Buxus microphylla SIEBOLD AND ZUCCARINI

Usually a dwarf shrub, to 1m high, but up to 2m in var *japonica* and up to 5m in var *sinica.* Other var are dwarf plants about 60cm high. Lv rather thin, oblanceolate, to 2cm long and 8mm across, bts glabrous, thereby distinguishing the plant from *B. sempervirens* where the brs are minutely hairy. Native to Japan, Korea, and China. Introduced from Japan about 1860, probably by Siebold.

Buxus sempervirens LINNAEUS   Box

Spreading bush or small tree, to 7m, bts faintly pubescent. Lv ovate, notched at the apex, to 2.5cm long and half as wide, liable to turn bronze during severe winters. A very large number of cv exist, some with variegated lv, others with long narrow lv, and some of prostrate or spreading habit. The plant has a wide distribution in the wild over most of Europe, N Africa and western Asia.

Buxus wallichiana BAILLON

Shrub, not more than 3m in cultivation, with very downy bts. Lv elliptic, to 5cm long and 1.5cm across, midrib and petiole downy. Dark green, but less shining than those of *B. sempervirens.* An exceptionally slow grower, reaching only 2m in fifty years. Cuttings are very reluctant to root. Native to the NW Himalaya. Introduced about 1880.

CALLICARPA LINNAEUS *Verbenaceae*

A small genus of about forty species of shrubs, noted for their handsome fruits, which are, however, only freely produced when a number of plants are placed close together. Most of the species are subtropical and only two can be regarded as satisfactory, although even they may be damaged in severe winters, but will usually spring again from the root.

Callicarpa bodinieri LÉVEILLÉ

4.5.6. (*C. giraldiana* SCHNEIDER) Deciduous

Callicarpa giraldiana

shrub, to 3m, bts downy at first. Lv wide-elliptic, to 12cm long and 5cm across, often turning pink before they fall, downy on the under side. Fl in axillary cymes, small, pinkish-lilac. Fl 7. Fr lavender or purple, each about 4mm in diameter. Fr 10–11. Native of China. Introduced to Germany by Padre Giraldi about 1899.

Callicarpa japonica THUNBERG

4.5.6. Deciduous shrub, to 2·5m. Bts at first tomentose, later glabrous. Lv narrowly ovate, taper-pointed, to 12cm long and 5cm wide; glabrous on both surfaces. Fl in axillary cymes, 3cm across, pale pink. Fl 8. Fr violet. Fr 10–11. Native of Japan. Introduced about 1845.

CALYCANTHUS LINNAEUS *Calycanthaceae*

A small genus of deciduous N American shrubs of three or four species. Leaves opposite, flower with numerous strap-shaped petals and sepals on short lateral branches, where they are terminal or from nodes of last year's wood. The wood is fragrant and so are the leaves except in the case of *C. fertilis.* The species are hardy so far as winter cold is concerned, but only flower freely where the summers are fairly sunny and warm. Seeds are rarely set in this country. They can be

propagated by layers or, occasionally, by detaching sucker growths.

Calycanthus fertilis WALTER

4. Shrub, to 2m. Lv ovate, acuminate, to 12cm long; dark green above, faintly downy and glaucous below. Fl to 6cm across, greenish purple to reddish-brown, without fragrance. Fl 6–9. Native to the south-eastern USA. Introduced by John Lyon in 1806. Often confused with the next sp.

Calycanthus floridus LINNAEUS

Carolina Allspice

4. Straggling shrub, to 3m. Lv oval, to 12cm long; dark green above, densely pubescent below, aromatic. Fl 5cm across, fragrant reddish purple. Fl 6–8. Native to SE USA overlapping the range of the last sp. Introduced by Mark Catesby in 1726.

Calycanthus occidentalis

WILLIAM HOOKER AND ARNOTT

4. Straggling shrub, to 4m. Lv cordate to oval-lanceolate, up to 20cm long; dark green above, glabrous or only slightly pubescent beneath, pale green. Fl to 7cm across, purplish-red with brownish tips to the petals. Larger in all its parts than the preceding spp but less floriferous and of ungainly habit. Native of California. Introduced by Douglas in 1831.

CAMELLIA LINNAEUS *Theaceae*

A genus of evergreen trees or shrubs, more or less confined to eastern Asia. The leaves are alternate, on short petioles and are usually faintly toothed. The flowers are terminal or axillary, usually singly, with numerous stamens, patulate. The fruits are fleshy, containing large oily seeds, which do not retain their vitality for very long. Propagated by seed, by stem or leaf cuttings, or by grafting. Owing to their flowering early in the year there is a risk of damage from spring frosts and, if possible, plants should be situated where they do not receive early morning sun. Acid soil is essential for their success and they appear to thrive best in a humus-rich soil. Only a few species are sufficiently hardy to merit inclusion in this handbook, but a larger number of species can be grown in sheltered areas.

Camellia cuspidata VEITCH

3.4. Shrub, to 4m, of rather slender, erect habit. Young lv copper-coloured, mature lv elliptic, taper-pointed, to 7·5cm long and 2·5cm across, dark or purplish-green above, shining, pale below. Fl terminal and axillary, generally single, white, to 3cm across. The plants known as 'Cornish Snow', 'Michael' and 'Winton' are

Camellia cuspidata

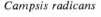

Campsis radicans

crosses between this sp and *C. saluenensis.* They all closely resemble *C. cuspidata* but with fl up to 5cm across, sometimes pink-flushed. Fl 4–5. Introduced from western China by Wilson in 1900.

Camellia japonica LINNAEUS

4. Shrub or tree, to 14m. The true sp is rarely seen, but there are an enormous number of cv, ranging in colour from white to deep crimson, while single, semi-double and fully double fl occur. The lv are ovate, deep, shining green, to 10cm long and half as wide. The fl are terminal, up to 10cm in diameter, occasionally more, with a very conspicuous mass of golden stamens in the single cv. Fl 3–5 according to the season. Native of Japan and Korea, and has long been a garden plant in China. Introduced for Lord Petre in 1742 with many subsequent sendings of various cv.

Camellia saluenensis STAPF

4. Shrub, to 5m, of erect, bushy habit. Lv elliptic, to 6cm long and 3cm across; dark, glossy green above, paler below. Bts slightly hairy at first. Fl singly or in pairs, terminal, somewhat funnel-shaped, rose-madder, each petal to 3cm long. Fl 3–5. Although mature plants appear perfectly hardy, young plants require protection in severe winters, and in cold districts one would do better with the hybrid *C. X williamsii* (qv). Native of Yunnan between the Salween and Shweli rivers. Introduced by Forrest about 1917.

Camellia X williamsii W. W. SMITH

4. A series of hybrids between *C. japonica* and *C. saluenensis,* of which a number of named clones are in cultivation. Most have not been very long in existence, so the ultimate height of the plants is not known, but most plants seem to be about 7m at the most and some have a rather straggly and decumbent habit. Lv generally up to 9.5cm long and 5.5cm across; dark green above, pale below, with both surfaces shining. Fl of various colours and shapes, usually some shade of pink, single or semi-double and varying in size from 5 to 12cm in diameter. 'November Pink' may start to flower in November and continue off and on until May, but most flower 3–5. Arguably these are the best camellias for garden decoration, being hardy, very floriferous and less liable to be damaged by wind and rain than the larger fl of *C. japonica.*

CAMPSIS LOUREIRO *Bignoniaceae*

A genus of only two species of climbing, deciduous shrubs, with opposite pinnate leaves, supporting themselves by aerial roots, and large trumpet-shaped flowers in terminal panicles. Included in *Bignonia* by older botanists and sometimes still met with under this name. Propagated by layers or, occasionally, sucker growths can be detached with roots attached.

Campsis radicans (LINNAEUS) SEEMANN

4. (*Bignonia radicans* LINNAEUS) Vigorous deciduous climber, to 12m or more, supporting itself by aerial roots. Lv pinnate, to 37cm long, composed of 7–11 ovate leaflets, to 10cm long and 5cm across; dark green and glabrous above, downy beneath. Fl in terminal panicles of 4–12 fl, brick-red, to 7cm long and 3·5cm across. Fl 8–9. Most satisfactory after a hot summer. Native of south-eastern USA. Introduced in 1640.

Campsis X tagliabuana (VISIANI) REHDER

4. (*Tecoma tagliabuana* VISIANI). A hybrid between the last sp and the more attractive, but tenderer *C. grandiflora* from China. Lv as in the last sp (the lv of *C. grandiflora* are glabrous beneath). Fl more brilliant and wider, to 7cm long and wide. The best-known cv, and probably the only one available commercially, is 'Mme Galen'. Fl 8–9.

CARAGANA LAMARCK *Leguminosae*

A genus of deciduous shrubs with pinnate leaves and pea-shaped flowers. There are stipules, often spiny, at the base of the leaves and often the terminal leaflet is replaced by a spine. The plants are confined to central and eastern Asia, chiefly the more northerly part. Easily propagated by seed.

Caragana arborescens LAMARCK

4. Deciduous shrub, to 7m, which can be trained as a small tree. Bts slightly winged. Lv spine-tipped with from 4–6 pairs of leaflets (or more on young plants). Stipules spine-tipped and eventually hardening into spines. Fl yellow, in clusters from the buds of the previous year's growth, to 2cm long. Fl 5. Pod to 5cm long. The cv 'Lorbergii' has very thin linear leaflets. Native of Siberia and Mongolia. Grown at Chelsea by Philip Miller in 1752. Possibly one of the '3 different species of Siberian Cytisuses' sent to Peter Collinson by Dr Gmelin in 1748.

Caragana decorticans HEMSLEY

4. Deciduous shrub, to 6m, with spiny stipules 6mm long. Lv to 3·5cm long, with 3–6 pairs of oval leaflets to 1cm long, leaflets and rachis spine-tipped. Fl pale yellow, 2·5cm long. Fl 5–6. Pod to 5cm long. Native of Afghanistan. Introduced by Aitchison in 1879.

Caragana frutex (LINNAEUS) K. KOCH

4. Unarmed, deciduous shrub, to 3m, with

erect brs, slightly pendulous at the extremity. Lv of only 2 pairs of leaflets, obovate, to 2·5cm long, glabrous. Fl bright yellow, to 2·5cm long. Fl 5. Pod cylindrical to 3·5cm long. Native of southern Russia and central Asia. Cultivated in 1752, perhaps from the same source as *C. arborescens*.

Caragana maximowicziana KOMAROV

4. Spreading, deciduous shrub, to 2m. Bts slightly downy at first, armed with slender spines to 2cm long, formed from the rachis of the lv. Lv in 4–6 pairs of linear, downy leaflets, bright green. Fl solitary, short-stalked, bright yellow, to 2·5cm long. Fl 5–6. Pod to 2cm long, downy. Native of western China and eastern Tibet. Introduced by Wilson in 1910.

Caragana microphylla LAMARCK

4. Wide-spreading arching deciduous shrub, to 3m, with greyish young wood. Stipules spiny, lv composed of up to 9 pairs of leaflets, to 7cm long, rachis spine-tipped. Leaflets oval, to 8mm long, silky at first, later glabrous, grey-green. Fl to 2cm long, bright yellow. Fl 5–6. Pod to 3cm long. Native of northern central Asia from Siberia to China. Sent from Siberia to Peter Collinson by Mr Demidoff, a Siberian mine owner, in 1750. The date of 1789 given by Aiton and copied thereafter is incorrect.

Caragana sinica (BUCHHOLZ) REHDER

4. (*C. chamlagu* LAMARCK) Probably better known under the synonym. Shrub of rounded bushy habit, to 1m 60cm, with spiny stipules. Lv composed of 2 pairs of leaflets only, of which the top pair is much larger than the lower one, rachis spine-tipped. Leaflets obovate, as long as 3·5cm on young plants and half as wide, only to 1·7cm on older plants. Dark green, glossy. Fl reddish-yellow to 3cm long. Fl 5–6. Pod to 3·5cm long. Notable for its large lv and fl. Native of northern China, sent to Peter Collinson by Père Héberstein in August 1752. Again the date in *Hortus Kewensis* of 1773 is incorrect.

CARPENTERIA TORREY *Philadelphaceae*

(*Saxifragaceae* before *Philadelphaceae* family was founded.) A genus of one species only.

Carpenteria californica TORREY

4. Evergreen shrub, to 5m. Lv opposite, elliptic-lanceolate, to 11cm long and 2·5cm across; bright green and glabrous above, softly downy below and glaucous. Fl in terminal clusters, fragrant, patulate, white with a large cluster of golden anthers in the centre, to 7cm across. Fl 6–8. Requires wall protection in most districts, but if given this is fairly persistent. Best increased by cuttings or layers, as some forms from seed are inferior. Native to California. Introduced in 1880.

CARPINUS LINNAEUS *Carpinaceae*

Formerly in *Betulaceae*. A genus of deciduous trees scattered over the north temperate zone. The plants are monoecious, the male catkins occurring on the old wood, the female ones are terminal on year-old wood. The female flowers are enclosed in large bracts, which are unequally lobed at the base. The female catkin is generally erect to start with, but later elongates and becomes pendulous. The leaves are alternate and conspicuously veined. About forty species are known, but they do not differ much among themselves so few are in cultivation. Generally they are fairly rapid growers. The seed is a small nut, which is partly exposed in the section *Carpinus,* but enclosed in the bracts in the section *Distegocarpus*, which has sometimes been treated as a separate genus. Seed is the best method of propagation, but cultivars must be grafted on to the common hornbeam, *C. betulus* and this can also be done with the rarer species.

Carpinus betulus LINNAEUS Hornbeam

7. A tree up to 25m, first pyramidal, later round-headed. Trunk grey and sometimes fluted attractively. Bts slightly pubescent at first, later glabrous. Lv elongated-oval, to 8cm long and 5cm across, toothed, slightly downy on the underside; dark green, often turning yellow before falling. Male catkins 3cm long, female to 7cm long, with conspicuous green bracts, each of which may be 2·5cm long, turning brown before falling. Fl 4. The plant is extremely useful for hedging.

A number of cv exist: 'Asplenifolia' has shallowly-lobed lv; 'Columnaris' is fastigiate and slow-growing; 'Fastigiata' is also fastigiate, but quicker-growing. A weeping form, 'Pendula' and cvs with purple and variegated lv also exist. Native of Europe including the UK.

Carpinus caroliniana WALTER

6.7. (*Carpinus americana* MICHAUX) Small tree, to 12m, usually less. Bts slightly hairy at first, bark grey, fluted. Winter buds very small, 3mm long (those of *C. betulus* are 7mm long or more). Rather slow-growing. Fl similar to those of *C. betulus*, but bracts slightly larger and wider. Lv turn orange or scarlet in the autumn. Native to eastern N America. Introduced in 1812 by Frederick Pursh according to *Hortus Kewensis*.

Carpinus henryana WINKLER

7. Deciduous tree, to 20m, bts silky-hairy. Lv ovate-lanceolate, to 9cm long and 3cm across, toothed, glabrous above, midrib and veins hairy

Carpinus caroliniana

Carya cordiformis

beneath. Fr in clusters, to 5cm long, bracts to 1·5cm long. A vigorous, leafy tree. Native to central and western China. Introduced by Wilson in 1907.

Carpinus japonica BLUME

5.7. (*Distegocarpus carpinus* SIEBOLD AND ZUCCARINI) Usually a small tree but up to 17m in the wild. Lv oblong-ovate, to 11cm long and 4cm across, with deeply impressed veins; unevenly toothed, dark green above and glabrous, paler below, with hairs on midrib and veins. Male catkins to 5cm long, female to 6cm, turning bronzy-pink at midsummer. Native of Japan, introduced in 1895.

Carpinus laxiflora (SIEBOLD AND ZUCCARINI) BLUME

5.7. (*Distegocarpus laxiflorus* SIEB AND ZUCC) Deciduous tree, to 16m, with oval lv, acuminate, to 7cm long and 3cm across. Usually represented in gardens by the var *macrostachya* OLIVER (*C. fargesii* FRANCHET) with lv to 10cm long and 5cm across and fr 12cm long and 5cm across, which makes a fruiting plant showy, although the fr are only green. The variety comes from China and was introduced by Wilson in 1900. The type is native to Japan and was not introduced until 1914.

Carpinus turczaninowii HANCE

6.7. Spreading tree, to 7m in the wild and somewhat more in cultivation. Bts slightly hairy. Lv ovate, to only 5cm long; dark green and glabrous above, downy on veins and midrib below. Fr in clusters only 5cm long. Lv colour orange and orange-brown before falling. The var *ovalifolia* WINKLER appears a larger tree, with more elongated lv. Native of N China. Introduced by Farrer & Purdom in 1914. The var *ovalifolia* is found in W China and was sent to Kew by Augustine Henry in 1889.

CARYA NUTTALL *Juglandaceae* Hickory

A genus of large, deciduous trees with pinnate leaves, monoecious, the pith solid, thereby distinguishing the genus from the others in the *Juglandaceae,* where the pith is laminated. Male catkins are produced either at the base of the previous year's growth or at the base of the branchlets. The female inflorescence is terminal, subsequently becoming like a walnut. They are stately and long-lived trees of fairly rapid growth, but with a great dislike of root disturbance. Ideally they should be grown from seed and put almost immediately in their final position as this enables the large taproot to descend undisturbed. However, young plants can be established, although it takes a year or so for them to settle

down. The leaves start to unfurl very late in the year, usually towards the end of May, and in wet seasons the wood may not ripen satisfactorily, so that some of the new growth each year will die off in the winter. This restricts the rate of growth in some districts, but, even so, the rate of increase is moderate and in the south of the country reasonably rapid. The leaves usually turn a good, clear yellow before falling, which increases the attraction of the plant, although the display is not, perhaps, sufficiently spectacular to warrant a **6** before the descriptions. Similarly the bark of fairly established trees is by no means lacking in attractiveness.

Carya cordiformis (WANGENHEIN) K. KOCH

7. (*Juglans cordiformis* WANGENHEIM, *Carya amara* NUTTALL) The most satisfactory of the spp available. Tree up to 33m, with smooth bark on young trees, later becoming shallowly furrowed. Winter buds bright yellow. Leaves to 20cm long (sometimes more) composed usually

Carya cordiformis

of 7 leaflets, of which the lowest pair are much smaller than the others; leaflets narrowly ovate or elliptic, to 15cm long and 6cm across, glabrous above, slightly downy below at first, petiole downy. Male catkins in threes to 7cm long. Nuts pear-shaped, to 3cm long. Native of eastern N America. Introduced, probably by Bartram, in 1766.

Carya laciniosa (F. A. MICHAUX) LOUDON

7. (*Juglans laciniosa* MICHAUX, *Carya sulcata*

NUTTALL) Tree, to 40m in the wild, although the largest specimen in England is only about 20m. Bark detaching itself in large plates, often 1m long. Bts pubescent at first, later glabrous and orange-coloured. Lv to 30cm long, leaflets usually 7, occasionally 5 or 9; the lowest pair are much smaller than the others, which are obovate, to 20cm long and 6cm across, although usually somewhat less, glabrous above and somewhat shining, downy below, toothed. Male catkins to 10cm long, roundish, to 6cm long. Native of the eastern USA. Introduced in 1804, possibly by the younger Michaux.

Carya ovata (MILLER) K. KOCH

7. (*Juglans ovata* MILLER, *Carya alba* NUTTALL) Tree, to 30m, with loose, grey bark detaching itself in flakes up to 30cm long. Bts glabrous at first, later smooth and reddish-brown. Lv composed of 5 leaflets, the whole lv to 35cm long (more on young trees) and the largest leaflet, which is narrowly obovate, to 17cm long and 7cm across, eventually glabrous on both surfaces, turning a good clear yellow in the autumn. As always, the lowest pair of leaflets is much smaller than the upper ones. Male catkins in threes to 12cm long. Fr roundish, to 5cm long. Native of eastern N America. Introduced in 1629 according to *Hortus Kewensis,* in 1730 according to Sweet.

CARYOPTERIS BUNGE *Verbenaceae*

A small genus of about six deciduous shrubs, with opposite leaves, valuable for their late flowering, but of rather dubious hardiness, coming as they do from parts of eastern Asia, where the winters may be cold, but the summers are hot and dry, so that it often fails to ripen its wood properly. Fairly easily propagated by cuttings of half-ripe wood or, in the case of *C. incana,* by soft cuttings, which, however, should be rooted in heat.

Caryopteris X clandonensis SIMMONDS

4. A shrub, barely reaching 1m. A hybrid between *C. incana* and *C. mongolica* and more vigorous and hardier than either parent. Lv lanceolate, acuminate, to 5cm long; dull green above and somewhat wrinkled, silvery and downy below. Fl in roundish cymes, bright blue, from the upper lv axils. Fl 8–9. Best pruned back each winter.

Caryopteris incana (HOUTTUYN) MIQUEL

7. (*C. mastacanthus* SCHAUER, *C. tangutica* MAXIMOWICZ) Spreading bush to 2m. Bts covered with grey indumentum. Lv scented, ovate, to 7cm long and 3cm across, deeply toothed; dull green above, grey-tomentose below, as are the petioles. Fl in cymes from upper lv axils, violet-blue. Fl tubular, about 6mm long,

with a 5-lobed mouth. Fl 9–10. May be lost in very severe winters, but generally hardy. Native to China and Japan. Originally introduced by Fortune in 1844, later by Maries and by Farrer.

CASSINIA R. BROWN *Compositae*

A small genus of evergreen shrubs of rather heath-like appearance. The leaves are alternate, but so numerous and so closely appressed to the stems, that this is not apparent. Most species are doubtfully hardy, but *C. fulvida* will succeed in most places. The flowers have only disc florets and are crowded in terminal panicles, but the plants are grown mainly for their ornamental foliage. The genus is distributed over Australasia and southern Africa, but all the cultivated species are native to New Zealand.

Cassinia fulvida JOSEPH HOOKER

3. (*Diplopappus chrysophyllus* KOEHNE) Evergreen shrub, to 2m, with a rather erect habit. Young lv and bts covered with a golden down, which persists on the underside of the lv. The lv are very crowded on the brs, closely appressed and overlapping, only about 8mm long; dark green above. Fl in terminal corymbs, up to 7cm across, composed of numerous small, white disc florets. Fl 7. May succumb in exceptionally severe winters. Native to New Zealand and, as with so many plants from there, the introducer does not seem to be known. It was in cultivation in 1880.

Cassinia vauvilliersii (DECAISNE) J. HOOKER

3. (*Orothamnus vauvilliersii* DECAISNE) Shrub, to 2m, but usually half that size, very similar to the last sp but the tomentum may be bright or pale yellow. Lv rather larger, to 8cm long and 3cm across. Fl rather rarely produced in the UK, white, in terminal corymbs 5cm across. Fl 7. Native to New Zealand; in cultivation in 1902.

CASTANEA MILLER *Fagaceae*

A genus of deciduous trees or shrubs; monoecious, the male flower in long catkins, the female in spiny burs which enclose edible nuts. The leaves are large, alternate, toothed, oblong, and rather similar in all species, of which there are only about ten distributed through the north temperate zone. They will thrive in most soils and will survive prolonged drought. They are fairly rapid growers, but do not fruit until fairly mature.

Castanea henryi (SKAN) REHDER AND WILSON

4.7. Unlike most of the spp this is rather slow-growing. A tree, to 25m in the wild, with dark, glabrous bts. Lv oblong, to 20cm long and 6cm across; green on both surfaces, on a petiole 2·5cm long. Male catkins to 10cm long, creamy-yellow; fr to 2·5cm across bearing a single nut. Fl 7. Native of China. Introduced by Wilson in 1900.

Castanea mollissima BLUME

4.7. Another rather slow-growing Chinese sp, up to 20m in the wild. Bts thinly hairy or downy. Lv oblong, to 20cm long and 4cm across, sometimes glabrous below, sometimes covered with white down. Male catkins to 10cm long, nuts about the size of those of *C. sativa,* from which it is barely distinct. Fl 7. Native of China. Introduced from Pekin by Dr Sargent in 1903 but, according to Rehder, before then in 1853.

Castanea pumila (LINNAEUS) MILLER
Chinquapin

4. (*Fagus pumila* LINNAEUS) Deciduous shrub or small tree, usually a shrub, to 2m, spreading by means of suckers. Lv oblong, to 12cm long and 5cm across; dark green above, white tomentose below. Male catkins 10cm long, fr 3.5cm across, usually containing a single nut. Fruit rarely ripens in the UK. In the northern part of the Mississippi basin it is replaced by **4.7.** *Castanea ozarkensis* ASHE, which differs only in its tree-like habit (it can attain 20m) and also in its larger lv (to 20cm long). Fl 7. Although rare in cultivation, *C. pumila* was introduced as long ago as 1699 according to *Hortus Kewensis* and was often sent by Bartram. *C. ozarkensis* was only introduced in 1891. Both spp are native to the USA, *C. pumila* from Pennsylvania south to Florida and Texas, *C. ozarkensis* mainly in Arkansas.

Castanea sativa MILLER
Sweet Chestnut

4.7. Tree to 33m or more, with a very wide trunk. Bts soon glabrous. Lv to 22cm long, 7cm across; with yellowish tomentum below at first, but soon glabrous. Male catkins to 12cm long, burs to 5 cm across. Forms with variegated and with irregularly-shaped lv are known. Native to Europe, north Africa and the near East.

CATALPA SCOPOLI *Bignoniaceae*
A genus of about ten species of trees, usually deciduous (all those in cultivation are) with opposite leaves and showy flowers in terminal panicles. The branches have no terminal bud, so that the plants branch very frequently and some training is necessary to obtain a trunk, before the plants can be left to branch without interference. The plants grow rapidly, but do not appear to be very long-lived. According to W. J. Bean they tend to deteriorate after forty or fifty years, which is rapid for a large tree. The fruits are long, narrow pods. Seed is the best method of propagation, but cuttings of young, firm shoots root fairly readily with a little heat. The leaves are also large and ornamental.

Catalpa bignonioides WALTER   Indian Bean

4.5.7. Deciduous tree, to 16m, with a rounded head. Lv in young trees very large, in adult trees to 25cm long and 20cm across, oval to heart-shaped on long petioles (to 18cm); light green above and glabrous, hairy below. Fl tubular-campanulate, about 3·5cm long and wide, in a terminal panicle to 25cm long and wide; white with yellow and purple spots. Fl 7–8. Fr to 35cm long, but narrow, only produced in hot seasons. The cv 'Aurea' has very attractive golden-yellow lv which retain their colour throughout the season. Although the plant is more floriferous in the south of Britain, it is always hardy. It should have an open, sunny situation and fairly deep soil. It is ineffective in shallow, chalky soils, although it tolerates alkalinity as such. Native of the eastern USA. Introduced by Mark Catesby about 1726.

Catalpa X erubescens CARRIÈRE

4.7. A hybrid between the last sp and the Chinese *C. ovata* (qv). Lv purplish when unfurling, later more or less heart-shaped, sometimes slightly 3-lobed, to 30cm long. Fl smaller than those of *C. bignonioides,* more numerous, but produced with less abandon. It appears to be a larger tree than *C. bignonioides,* plants up to 30m are known. The cv 'Purpurea' has the young lv and bts so dark a purple that they appear nearly black, although this gradually fades. The hybrid was originally made in 1874, but not introduced into Britain until 1891.

Catalpa ovata GEORGE DON

4.5.7. (*C. kaempferi* SIEBOLD) A small tree, usually not more than 8m, occasionally to 15m, but with a wide-spreading head that can be as wide as the height. Lv to 25cm long, basically oval, but often 3-lobed, on a petiole to 15cm long. Panicles to 25cm long, the fl tubular with expanded mouth, dull yellow with red spots and a yellow flush at the base of the tube, about 2·5cm long and wide. Fl 7–8. Fr to 30cm long. Native of China, but long cultivated in Japan and first obtained from there in 1849 by Siebold, although he could not have collected it himself, as he left Japan in 1829 and did not return until 1860.

Catalpa speciosa ENGELMANN

4.5.7. The largest sp with trees of up to 33m in the wild and apparently long-lived. Lv ovate-cordate, to 30cm long and 20cm across, pale brown tomentose below. Panicles to 20cm long, rather wider, fewer-flowered than *C. bignonioides,* but fl larger, to 5cm long and wide, white with yellow spots and a very few purple ones. Fl 7, before *C. bignonioides.* Fr to 50cm long. Native of central USA. Introduced 1754 according to Rehder, not until 1880 according to Bean.

CEANOTHUS LINNAEUS *Rhamnaceae*

A genus of about fifty species of shrubs, native to northern and central America, both evergreen and deciduous, with leaves either opposite or alternate. The flowers are small but numerous, in umbels or fascicles which often amalgamate into quite sizeable panicles, which are very decorative. The majority of species and hybrids are too tender for most parts of the UK and require to be given wall protection, although occasionally plants are seen thriving in the open in what would appear very unsuitable conditions. Propagation is by semi-hard stem cuttings with a heel which are usually ready in late July. Cuttings of this kind root easily and grow away rapidly. Although the plants will thrive in most soils, they appear to do rather better when the reaction is acid.

Ceanothus americanus LINNAEUS

4. A small, deciduous, white-flowered hardy shrub from the east coast of N America. It is not particularly ornamental in itself, but is valuable for being the parent of the hybrids known as *C. X delilianus,* which is this sp crossed with the tender, deciduous, bright blue *C. coeruleus* from Mexico. These all form small deciduous shrubs with terminal panicles of fl in varying shades of blue and pink. The best-known is the powder blue 'Gloire de Versailles' but there are also the deep blue 'Indigo', which seems somewhat more tender, and the bright pink 'Marie Simon'. These are generally hardy in all but the most exposed situations. Since they flower on the current year's growth, they can be hard pruned in the spring if this is considered desirable. Fl 7–10.

A further hybrid is *C. X burkwoodii,* in which the cv 'Indigo' has been crossed with *C. dentatus,* while 'Autumnal Blue' has *C. thyrsiflorus* as the other parent. These are both evergreens, to some 2m, with oval lv to 3cm long and fl in terminal panicles to 6cm long, bright blue in 'Burkwoodii', somewhat paler in 'Autumnal Blue', which also has larger lv. Both plants are frost-tolerant when well established. Fl 7–10. *C. americanus* introduced in 1713, *C. X delilianus* raised about 1830, *C. X burkwoodii* raised before 1929.

Ceanothus dentatus TORREY AND GRAY

4. An evergreen shrub, to 4m, with alternate lv which are elliptic, to 1cm long, shiny green above, with a grey tomentum below, toothed. Fl in round clusters on short lateral growths, bright blue. Fl 5. One of the hardiest of the sp. In California it tends to grade into **4** *C. papillosus,* which, typically, has the upper surface of the lv furnished with small, wart-like excrescences, known as *papillae.* The fl are blue but vary in intensity, the most vivid probably being the plant known as *C. X veitchianus,* although other authorities assign this to *C. thyrsiflorus.*

Closely related, also, is *C. impressus,* a spreading shrub, distinguished by the impressed veins on the upper surface of the lv and with deep blue fl (4–5). *C. papillosus* crossed with the tender *C. rigidus* gave rise to the very attractive and reasonably hardy hybrid 'Delight', which makes a large plant trained against a wall and is covered with brilliant blue panicles up to 5cm long (4–5).

C. dentatus introduced by Lobb from California in 1848, *C. papillosus* by the same collector in 1850, *C. impressus* was introduced about 1935.

Ceanothus thyrsiflorus ESCHSCHOLZ

4. Evergreen shrub, sometimes a small tree, to 10m. Lv alternate, ovate, to 3cm long, stalked. Probably the hardiest of the evergreen spp. Fl pale blue in panicles to 7cm long. Fl 5–6. The var *griseus* TRELEASE, sometimes given specific status as *C. griseus,* is similar but with lv grey-silky beneath.

C. X lobbianus is a natural hybrid between var *griseus* and *dentatus* with bright blue fl *C. X veitchianus* is another natural hybrid sent back by W. Lobb, for which *rigidus* is suggested as one parent and either *dentatus* or *thyrsiflorus* as the other. The vigorous powder-blue 'Cascade' is probably a good form of *griseus.* Native of California. *C. thyrsiflorus* introduced 1837 by a ship's surgeon, *C. X lobbianus* and *C. X veitchianus* sent by W. Lobb about 1853.

CEDRELA LINNAEUS *Meliaceae*

A genus of about eighteen species of deciduous or evergreen trees, mostly from the tropics. The one hardy species is of interest as being the only hardy member of the mahogany family, although it seems to thrive best in the southern part of Britain. In appearance it much resembles *Ailanthus,* from which it is distinguished by the leaflets being entire, not toothed. Propagated by seed or by root cuttings.

Cedrela sinensis JUSSIEU

4.7. (*Ailanthus flavescens* CARRIÈRE) Deciduous tree, to 25m, with downy bts. Lv pinnate, to 60cm long, with 5–12 pairs of ovate, acuminate leaflets, each to 10cm long. Fl small, campanulate, fragrant and white, in terminal panicles up to 30cm long. Fl 6. Fr a woody capsule about 2·5cm long. Native of northern and western China. First introduced in 1862.

CEDRUS TREW *Pinaceae* Cedar

Authorities differ as to whether there are one, two, three or four species of cedar, but for garden purposes it seems best to recognise three. All are slow-growing, evergreen conifers of the largest size, characterised by their pyramidal, tabular habit when young and adolescent, becoming flat-topped when aged. There are two main types of growth, one which elongates a few inches each year and carries the needles spirally, and short spur-like growths, which barely elongate and have a thick tuft of needles at the end. The plants are monoecious, both male and female flowers are erect; the males in finger-like catkins to 7cm long, the females in stout cones, which are flat at the top and may reach a length of 11cm and a width of 7cm. The cones are purplish at first and quite ornamental. Propagation by seed is the most satisfactory method, but cultivars may have to be grafted and cuttings are possible. All the species are generally hardy, although young plants of *C. deodara* may be damaged by prolonged severe frosts, but mature plants appear to be as hardy as the other species.

Cedrus atlantica

Cedrus atlantica MANETTI

7. Evergreen tree, to 40m or more, pyramidal when young, becoming flat-topped when full grown. Bts downy, more so than those of *C. libani*. Needles to 2·5cm long, usually a silvery green. Cones to 7cm long, 5cm across, cylindrical.

The form known as **3** *glauca* has lv of a very

attractive blue-grey, which is most brilliant when the younger needles are elongating. There is also a yellowish-leaved form, 'Aurea', which is slow-growing and a pendulous form, 'Pendula'. Native of the Atlas Mountains. Introduced about 1840.

Cedrus deodara (ROXBURGH) GEORGE DON
Deodar

7. (*Pinus deodara* ROXBG) Evergreen tree, to 80m in the wild, but so far not more than 40m in cultivation, with a graceful pyramidal habit when young with the bts pendulous and the leading shoot arching. Bts downy. Lv to 4 or 5cm long, grey-green or occasionally glaucous on young trees, dark green on more mature specimens. Cones egg-shaped, to 10cm long and 7cm across. Native of the western Himalaya. Introduced by Nathaniel Wallich, in 1822.

Cedrus libani A. RICHARD[1] Cedar of Lebanon

7. Tree up to 40m, pyramidal when young, ultimately flat-topped, with a very wide spread. Lv to 3cm long, usually dark green, but glaucous forms occur occasionally. Cones to 12cm long, 5cm across. A smaller form is found in Cyprus, reaching to 15m in the wild, with lv only to 1cm long and smaller cones. Joseph Hooker regarded this as a subspecies of *C. libani*, while Henry treats it as a separate sp, *C. brevifolia*.

The cedar of Lebanon itself is one of the grandest of specimen trees any garden can boast. Native of extreme western Asia, most common in Turkey. Introduced before 1659.

CELASTRUS LINNAEUS *Celastraceae*

A small genus of clambering shrubs, not supporting themselves by any means, but laying themselves over shrubs and small trees. The leaves are deciduous in all cultivated species. The flowers are in terminal or axillary clusters, sometimes dioecious, small and inconspicuous. The fruits are handsome; a woody capsule, usually 3-lobed, which splits open to reveal the yellow inside walls and the seeds which are surrounded by a red, fleshy substance known as an aril. The plants spread vigorously in deep soil and can take up a considerable amount of room, particularly with the dioecious species where two plants are necessary. A considerable number of species have been introduced to cultivation, but only a few are obtainable nowadays. More than thirty species are known from America, Australia and eastern Asia. Propagation by seed or by layers.

Celastrus hypoleucus (OLIVER) LOESENER

5. Deciduous climber, to 7m, bts covered with a purple, waxy bloom. Lv oblong, mucronate,

1 Most writers give Loudon as the authority for this name.

Celastrus orbiculatus

to 15cm long and 6cm across; dark green above, blue-white beneath. Fl usually hermaphrodite, so that a single plant should bear fruit. Fl in a long terminal raceme and in axillary racemes, yellowish, inconspicuous. By the time the fr is ripe the raceme may be as much as 20cm long. Fr about the size of a pea, green outside, yellow inside with a red aril attached to the seeds. Like all the spp these are liable to remain attractive from November to January, being at their most brilliant after the lv have fallen. This sp seems less vigorous than most of the others in cultivation and with its attractive lv is arguably the best sp to obtain, but it is not very common. Native of Hupeh and Szechuan. Introduced by Wilson in 1900.

Celastrus orbiculatus THUNBERG

5. (*C. articulatus* THUNBERG) Vigorous, twining, deciduous climber, to 14m; usually dioecious, although some hermaphrodite plants occur occasionally. Bts armed with spines, which later disappear. Lv toothed, orbicular or obovate, sometimes acuminate, sometimes mucronate, to 12cm long on a 2cm petiole. Fl in few-flowered axillary cymes, green and inconspicuous. Fr green without, golden yellow within and the seeds have a scarlet aril. A well-fruited plant covered with these brilliant capsules is one of the most striking plants for winter ornament. Native of Japan and China. Introduced 1869 according to Rehder, but not received in this country until 1870 according to Bean.

Celastrus rosthornianus LOESENER

5. Deciduous climber, to 7m, bts very slender and often pendulous. The plant is generally hermaphrodite. Lv shining, oval-lanceolate, finely toothed; to 7cm long and 3cm across, tapered at base and apex. Fl and fr in small axillary cymes. Fr rather smaller than a pea, golden yellow with scarlet aril and long persisting. Native of western China. Introduced by Wilson in 1910.

CELTIS LINNAEUS *Ulmaceae*

A genus of deciduous and evergreen trees, of which all the cultivated species are deciduous. In appearance the plants resemble elms, but can always be distinguished by their drupaceous fruits, quite unlike the dry samaras of the true elms. The leaves are alternate, generally toothed with three main veins. The flowers are monoecious, although the female flowers, which are usually singly or in pairs in the axils, may also have a few stamens; the purely staminate flowers are in clusters at the base of the new growth. Like the elms the leaves often turn a good, clear yellow before falling. The European *C. australis*, although obtainable, never seems to do well in the UK, presumably because the summers are not hot enough for the wood to ripen satisfactorily, as it does perfectly well in places such as Madrid, where the winters may be as cold as anything liable to be experienced in Britain.

Celtis laevigata WILLDENOW

5.7. (*C. mississippiensis* DE CANDOLLE, *C. integrifolia* NUTTALL) Deciduous tree, to 20m or more in the wild, but so far less in Britain, where it is probably not very long-lived, although trees nearly 100 years old are known. Lv oval-lanceolate, to 7cm long and 3cm across, acuminate, margins usually not toothed; dark green and glabrous above, slightly downy below. Fr ovoid, 6mm long, orange red. Native of the southern USA. Introduced in 1812, probably by Bradbury.

Celtis occidentalis

48

Celtis occidentalis

Celtis occidentalis LINNAEUS

5.7. Tree, to 15m, but usually less, with rough, grey, warty bark. Bts either glabrous or downy. Lv varying in shape from elliptic to wide-ovate, rounded at the base, acuminate, toothed, to 11cm long; slightly downy below, slightly scurfy above. Fr round, 8mm across, yellowish at first, finally nearly black.

The plant most often seen in cultivation is var *cordata* (PERSOON) WILLDENOW (var *crassifolia* LAMARCK), with much larger heart-shaped lv to 15cm long and 7·5cm across. This is also more vigorous, making long pendulous growths each season of 1m or more in length.

The typical plant is found throughout the USA and was first introduced by the younger Tradescant in 1656. Var *cordata* is found only west of the Appalachians, and was first introduced, so far as is known, in 1812.

Celtis sinensis PERSOON

5.7. A small, fairly rapid-growing tree, to 10m and more with a rounded head. Lv ovate, toothed at the apex, dark glossy green; to 7cm long and 4cm across. Fr ovoid, black. Handsome on account of its glossy lv. Native of China and Japan. Introduced in 1820 according to Loudon, 'about 1793' according to Rehder, and 1910 according to the latest edition of Bean. The 1820 date would seem the most probable, as it is not in *Hortus Kewensis*, which one would have expected if the 1793 introduction occurred.

CEPHALANTHUS LINNAEUS *Rubiaceae*

A small genus of deciduous and evergreen shrubs, of which only one species is hardy. The leaves are opposite, sometimes whorled, the flowers are tubular with four rounded lobes at the apex, very small.

Cephalanthus occidentalis LINNAEUS
Button Bush

4. Deciduous shrub, to 2m usually, occasionally becoming tree-like and attaining 5m. Lv oval-elliptic, to 12cm long and 6cm wide; glossy dark green above, paler below with down along the midrib. Fl in axillary, globular button-like clusters to 3cm across, pale cream. Fl 8. Requires acid soil and rather moist conditions. Useful for its late flowering, but not particularly brilliant. Native to eastern N America. Introduced in 1735 by John Bartram.

CEPHALOTAXUS SIEBOLD AND ZUCCARINI
Cephalotaxaceae

Formerly included in *Taxaceae*. A small genus of evergreen, east-Asian shrubs, generally monoecious. The leaves are spirally arranged, but disposed in two ranks; dark green above, somewhat glaucous below and linear. The male flowers are in globular clusters in the axils of the second-year wood, the female flowers eventually make a small, plum-like fruit, which is greenish-purple and takes two years to ripen. The shrubs resemble yews very closely.

Cephalotaxus fortunei WILLIAM HOOKER

Evergreen shrub or small tree to about 7m, with brs in whorls. Lv linear, acuminate, to 9cm long and 3mm wide. Fr brownish, to 3cm long and 2cm wide. Native of northern China. Introduced by Robert Fortune in 1849.

Cephalotaxus harringtonia (FORBES) K. KOCH

(*C. drupacea* SIEBOLD AND ZUCCARINI, *Taxus harringtonia* FORBES) Shrub or small tree, to 10m, with grey bark. Lv less symmetrically disposed than in the last sp, less slenderly pointed and shorter; to 6cm long and 3mm wide. Fr green, to 3cm long. There is a handsome fastigiate form, known as 'Fastigiata'. The plant has long been known as *C. drupacea*. Native of Japan and China. Introduced from Japan by Siebold in 1829.

Cephalotaxus harringtonia (fastigiata)

CERCIDIPHYLLUM SIEBOLD AND ZUCCARINI
Cercidiphyllaceae

A genus of either one or three species according to different authorities. Here the entities are regarded as a single species and its varieties.

Cercidiphyllum japonicum
SIEBOLD AND ZUCCARINI

3.6.(7). In the wild a deciduous tree up to 30m, but in cultivation either a tree of up to 20m or a large bush, with several potential trunks. The tree is dioecious, but in both cases the fl are inconspicuous. Lv purplish when unfolding in the spring and usually (but by no means invariably) colouring in the autumn. The colour may be golden, orange, red, pale pink or mauve. Lv bluish-green when fully developed,

49

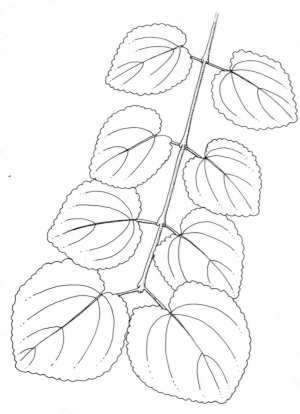

Cercidiphyllum japonicum

nearly circular, to 10cm long and broad. Perfectly hardy as regards winter frost, but very susceptible to spring frosts and requires a long summer to ripen its wood adequately. The Chinese form, var *sinense* REHDER AND WILSON, which is characterised by its single trunk, seems a somewhat better garden plant, while var *magnificum* NAKAI makes a smaller tree in the wild, but has larger, more rounded lv and also seems, in cultivation, to be a better doer than the type.

The type was introduced in 1865, var *sinense* was introduced by Wilson in 1907, while var *magnificum*, which is found on the Japanese island of Honshu, was not received before 1920.

CERCIS LINNAEUS *Leguminosae*

A small genus of about seven species of deciduous trees scattered throughout the northern temperate zone. The leaves are alternate, rounded and entire, with a heart-shaped base. The flowers spring in fascicles from the old wood, usually appearing slightly before the leaves. They are pea-shaped and purplish-pink or white. The attractive Chinese species are, unfortunately, doubtfully hardy in most parts of the UK,

although *C. chinensis* must experience winters far more severe than anything we can produce. Indeed it is not, usually, winter cold that makes these trees unsatisfactory, as the lack of a good hot summer to ripen the wood adequately. The most reliable is the European species *C. siliquastrum*.

Cercis canadensis LINNAEUS

4.5. Small tree or tall shrub, usually not more than 7m in the UK. Lv cordate to orbicular, pointed, to 12cm wide and 11cm long. Fl bright red in bud, pale pink when open, each about 1cm long. Fl 5–6. Fr a pod, quite a distinct pink in colour. Although it grows well it is shy to flower in this country. Native to eastern and central N America. Introduced in 1641 according to Rehder, 1731 according to Aiton.

Cercis racemosa OLIVER

4. Tree of up to 13m, with downy bts. Lv cordate, to 12cm long and 10cm wide; dark green and glabrous above, downy below. Fl in racemes springing from year-old or older wood, each raceme up to 10cm long and carrying up to 40 fl; appearing in May before the lv. Possibly not very hardy, but little seems to be known about this lovely tree and it is evidently worth trying. Like all the genus it can only be moved as a small plant and, ideally, should be grown from seed and planted out almost at once. Native of Hupeh and Szechuan. Introduced by Wilson in 1907.

Cercis siliquastrum LINNAEUS   Judas Tree

4.7. Usually a rather tall bush, but on occasions a small tree to 12m. Lv roundish, cordate at the base, up to 10cm across and a little less in length. Fl before the lv in clusters from most wood over a year old, rosy-purple (there is a white form). Fl 5. Native to the eastern Mediterranean and in cultivation at least since the sixteenth century. It does better in the dry, eastern part of the country, particularly East Anglia, and comes very readily from seed; young plants grow rather rapidly.

CERCOCARPUS KUNTH *Rosaceae*

A curious genus, native to western N America, of evergreen shrubs or small trees, grown, mainly as curiosities, for their curious plumed fruit. The flowers, which are axillary, have no petals, only a cluster of stamens. The elongated fruit is surmounted by the plumed style and if present in sufficient numbers is quite conspicuous. A number of species are hardy, but few are now obtainable.

Cercis siliquastrum

Cerlocarpus betuldides

Cercocarpus betuloides J. TORREY AND A. GRAY

5. (*C. betulifolius* NUTTALL) Shrub or small tree, to 7m, with smooth grey bark. Lv elliptic, to 2·5cm long, dark green, margins toothed at the apex. Fl petalless, in axillary clusters of 2–4. Fr a slender capsule terminated with the plume-like style, which may be as much as 10cm long.

CHAENOMELES LINDLEY *Rosaceae*

A small genus of only three species which have, however, been hybridised amongst themselves, so that it is somewhat doubtful if the true species are at all common in cultivation, although they are all listed in many catalogues. The plants were also for long included in the genus *Cydonia,* in which only one species is now left. Further confusion has been caused by the fact that the plant that Thunberg called *Pyrus japonica* and which later became *Chaenomeles japonica* proved not to be the plant which everyone had assumed it to be and which had received the common name of japonica. The species are deciduous, with alternate leaves with large stipules at their base. The leaves are toothed, which is regarded as one of the characters sufficient to distinguish *Chaenomeles* from *Cydonia* (the other characters are the deciduous calyx and the styles being united at their base). The flowers are patulate, appearing before or with the leaves. The fruit is a five-celled pome. Propagation is by seeds, by layers or by cuttings. The plants are all quite hardy, but are often trained against a wall, as they are of rather sprawling habit if left to themselves. Flowering can be encouraged by spur pruning.

Chaenomeles cathayensis (HEMSLEY) SCHNEIDER

4.5. Thorny, deciduous shrub, to 5m or more, with zig-zag brs. Lv on a short petiole, lanceolate, to 12cm long; glabrous above, with reddish down beneath when young. Fl in clusters of 2–3, 3·5cm across; white, pale pink, or in var *wilsonii* REHDER, salmon-pink. Fl 3–4. Fr very large, ovoid, to 15cm long and 9cm across; green or greenish-yellow, makes an agreeable conserve as do all the fr of this genus. Almost certainly a native of China, but never found convincingly wild. The date of its introduction is unrecorded, except for the fact that it was before 1900, but probably not much before.

Chaenomeles X californica WEBER

4.5. Hybrids of *C. cathayensis* with *C. X. superba* (see below) and therefore including all three known spp of the genus. They make erect, rather spiny shrubs with lanceolate lv, and large fl, up to 5cm across, of pink or rose. The fr is bright yellow. *C. X clarkiana* WEBER was the name for crosses between *C. cathayensis* and *C. japonica,* but these do not seem to be available in the UK and are said to have been surpassed by *C. X californica.*

Chaenomeles japonica (THUNBERG) SPACH

4.5. (*Pyrus japonica* THUNBERG, *Cydonia maulei* T. MOORE) Low, spreading, spiny shrub, rarely as much as 1m high, but considerably more in width. Bts downy at first. Lv ovate or rounded, tapering to a short petiole, to 5cm long, coarsely toothed, with stipules which are ovate and up to 2cm across. Fl from axils of year-old wood, orange-red to scarlet and dark ruby, 3·5cm across. Fl 3–5. Fr round, 3·5cm across, yellow with red flush. Native of Japan. Introduced in 1869 to the nurserymen Maule of Bristol, where it was not recognised as Thunberg's plant and called *C. maulei.*

Chaenomeles speciosa (SWEET) NAKAI Japonica

4.5. (*Cydonia lagenaria* LOISELEUR, *Pyrus japonica* of the Bot Mag t 692) Deciduous, spreading spiny shrub to 3m high but up to 7m across. Bts glabrous or very slightly pubescent when young. Lv elliptic, to 9cm long, finely toothed; shining green above, glabrous, stipules reniform and toothed, up to 3·5cm across. Fl in clusters of 2–4 on the bare wood, up to 4·5cm across, scarlet or blood red. Fl 2–6. Fr pear-shaped, greenish-yellow, to 6cm long and broad. One of the most popular of spring-flowering shrubs and deservedly so. Native of China, but long cultivated in Japan. In 1796 Sir Joseph

Banks received a plant from one of his Chinese correspondents and in 1830 Siebold brought a number of cv from Japan.

C. X vilmoriniana WEBER is the name given to hybrids between *C. speciosa* and *C. cathayensis,* two of which have been in commerce as 'Mount Everest' and 'Afterglow'. They are very spiny shrubs, to 3m, with lanceolate, coarsely toothed lv to 10cm and pink-flushed white fl.

Chaenomeles X superba (RAHM) REHDER

4. A series of hybrids between *C. speciosa* and *C. japonica* and most of the smaller japonicas will be included under this name. In general they make shrubs to 2m with lv either ovate or oblong, which may be either finely or coarsely toothed. Bts generally downy. Colours range from white to pink, all shades of red to orange-scarlet. Among the best known cv are 'Boule de Feu', 'Knaphill Scarlet' and 'Rowallane'.

CHAMAECYPARIS SPACH *Cupressaceae*

A small genus of six species of evergreen trees, all but one of which come from countries bordering on the Pacific. Closely related to the true cypresses, they can be distinguished by their flattened branchlets and the fewer seeds in each cone, which is itself smaller than most in *cupressus*. They are also, by and large, much hardier and more suitable trees for the UK. They require reasonably moist conditions and are not particularly suitable for shallow soils, particularly where chalk forms the subsoil. The leaves of mature plants are flattened and scale-like, closely appressed to the stem, but in seedlings the leaves are awl-shaped and radiate around the stem. Some plants, like 'Peter Pan', never grow up and maintain their juvenile foliage all their lives; before this was recognised, such plants were regarded as belonging to a separate genus *Retinispora* (or *Retinospora*). Such forms are very attractive with their wiry foliage. The American species are fairly rapid growers, the Asian ones somewhat less so, although they are not slow. Most of the forms in cultivation are columnar in habit, although the usual shape of wild trees is narrowly pyramidal. Propagation is easiest by cuttings taken in late summer, but seeds are also a possibility and cultivars can be grafted on to young plants of the type. The plants are monoecious.

Chamaecyparis lawsoniana (A. MURRAY) PARLATORE

7. (*Cupressus lawsoniana* A. MURRAY) Tree, to 65m in the wild and about half that in cultivation. The tree appears infinitely variable and a very large number of forms have been named. What appears the typical form is a slenderly pyramidal tree, clothed to the ground, with the brs in two ranks and the bts slightly pendulous. Lv scale-like, very small and numerous, in colours ranging from dark green to glaucous blue-grey. Cones small, round, about 8mm across, composed of 8 scales. The male fl are crimson, borne in small clusters on the edges of the bts. The number of cv is very large, up to 80, and can be roughly divided into those with glaucous lv and a columnar habit, of which 'Allumii' is probably the best known, forms with yellowish young growth, such as 'Aurea' and 'Elegantissima', and forms with pendulous growths, of which 'Filiformis' is arguably the most outstanding. Native to the western USA in Oregon and California. Received at Lawson's nursery at Edinburgh in 1854.

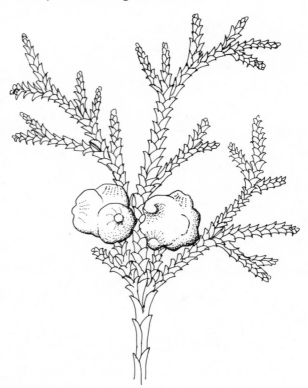

Chamaecyparis nootkatensis

Chamaecyparis nootkatensis (D. DON) SPACH

7. (*Cupressus nootkatensis* D. DON) Tree, to 30m in cultivation, of narrow pyramidal form, spreading somewhat in aged specimens. The bts are always somewhat pendulous and remarkably so in the very handsome cv 'Pendula'. It resembles the last sp in many ways and is best distinguished by the strong scent of the lv when crushed. The male fl are yellow, while those of *C. lawsoniana* are crimson. There are also a golden-leaved cv 'Lutea' and a white variegated form. A splendid evergreen for reasonably deep soils. Native of NW America from Oregon to Alaska. Introduced in 1853, possibly by W. Lobb.

Chamaecyparis obtusa (SIEBOLD AND ZUCCARINI) ENDLICHER

7. (*Retinispora obtusa* SIEB AND ZUCC) A rather slow-growing tree which reaches 40m in the wild but has yet to reach 30m in cultivation. If the lower brs are cut off, they reveal attractive reddish bark. The tree is pyramidal in habit, with very thin bts. The lv are of two different sizes, the lateral pair being larger than the top and bottom lv, which they partially envelop. The lv also have round ends, which distinguishes them from most other spp which have the lv pointed. The plant has been much cultivated in Japan and a number of variants are in cultivation, of which the most notable are 'Aurea', with bright yellow young lv, 'Crippsii', which makes a short, thick pyramid of gold, and 'Lycopodioides' with sprawling brs that somewhat resemble a club moss. Native of Japan. Introduced both by Fortune and J. G. Veitch in 1860–1.

Chamaecyparis pisifera (SIEBOLD AND ZUCCARINI) ENDLICHER

7. (*Retinispora pisifera* SIEB AND ZUCC) Nearly as variable a plant as *C. lawsoniana* and the typical plant is rarely seen. This is a pyramidal tree, up to 50m in the wild, but so far not more than 25m in cultivation. The lv are sharply pointed and are all about the same length. The cones are also somewhat smaller in this sp than in *C. obtusa*. There are numerous dwarf forms and a cv with golden lv. In the form known as 'Filifera', which is very slow-growing, the brs are much reduced and elongated to become somewhat cord-like. They are pendulous. 'Filifera aurea' with yellow lv is rarely more than a shrub to 4m.

In the forms ranged under the varietal name *plumosa*, the lv are all of the juvenile, awl-like type, which are arranged in pairs along the brs and semi-erect. This can, in time, make as large a plant as typical *C. pisifera* and bear cones. There is also a golden-leaved form of this.

The variety *squarrosa*, regarded as a separate sp by Siebold and Zuccarini, has even more juvenile foliage, which is soft to the touch and an attractive silver-grey in colour (and blue-white beneath in the cv 'Boulevard'). These lv are densely packed along the brs, up to 6mm long. 'Squarrosa sulphurea' has lv of a yellowish hue.

Native of Japan and introduced by Fortune, J. G. Veitch and Siebold in 1860–1.

Chamaecyparis thyoides (LINNAEUS) BRITTON, STERNS AND POGGENBERG

7. (*Cupressus thyoides* LINNAEUS) Tree, to 15m in cultivation of elegant columnar form. Like *C. obtusa* the lateral lv are longer than those above and below, but unlike the Japanese sp the lv are pointed. The lv are normally grey-green, but an attractive blue-green in the cv 'Glauca'. In the wild the tree tends to grow in bogs and ground liable to be flooded and would probably thrive well in similar situations here and is in any case intolerant of prolonged drought. Native of eastern N America and one of the first plants sent by Bartram to Peter Collinson in 1736.

Chimonanthus praecox

CHIMONANTHUS LINDLEY *Calycanthaceae*
So far as gardens are concerned only a single species is in cultivation, although three species are known, all native to China.

Chimonanthus praecox (LINNAEUS) LINK
Winter Sweet

4. (*Calycanthus praecox* LINNAEUS, *Chimonanthus fragrans* LINDLEY) Deciduous shrub, to 3m, but taller if trained against a wall. Lv opposite, lanceolate, to 12cm long, acuminate, rough to the touch, shining green. Fl after the lv have fallen, axillary, solitary, on the current year's wood. Greenish-yellow with purplish inner tepals. In the cv 'Grandiflorus' the fl are a purer yellow, larger (up to 4cm across as opposed to the 2·5cm of the type), but less fragrant. Propagated by seeds or by layers. Hardy, but in very cold districts best trained against a wall, in which case it should be pruned at the end of February. Several years are required to arrive at flowering stage. Fl 11–3. Attractive owing to its winter flowering, although not showy. Native of China. Sent to the Earl of Coventry in 1766.

CHIONANTHUS LINNAEUS *Oleaceae*

A genus of only two species of deciduous shrubs or small trees with opposite leaves and panicles of white flowers composed of 4 or 5 long, narrow petals. The fruit is a small, dark blue, one-seeded drupe. The plants are either dioecious, or, if they bear perfect flowers, still require cross-fertilisation to produce fruits. Propagated by seed or by layers.

Chionanthus retusus LINDLEY

4.5. In cultivation a shrub of spreading habit to 6m high, but often a small tree of up to 13m in the wild. Lv oval or obovate, to 10cm long and 5cm across, rounded at the apex; shining green above, slightly downy below. Fl in terminal panicles on the current year's growth, each panicle to 7cm long and 10cm across. Fl 6–7. A very striking and attractive shrub thriving best in deep loamy soil. Native of China. Introduced by Fortune in 1845, but all the plants seem to have been lost. Introduced again by Maries in 1879.

Chionanthus virginicus LINNAEUS Fringe Tree

4.5. Shrub or small tree up to 10m. Lv oblong or elliptic, to 20cm long and nearly half as wide; dark green above and slightly downy along the midrib, paler below and more pubescent. Fl in axillary panicles from the top of the previous year's growth; each panicle rather narrow but to 20cm long, pure white and slightly fragrant, 4- or 5-petalled. Male plants have larger fl and longer panicles. A more vigorous grower than the Chinese sp but less floriferous, except after a very good summer. Fl 5–6. Distinguished from the Chinese sp by the larger lv, the fl on the year-old wood and by its earlier flowering. Native of the eastern USA from Pennsylvania southwards. Introduced through John Bartram in 1736.

CHOISYA KUNTH *Rutaceae*

A small genus of which only one species is hardy in the UK. Propagated by cuttings.

Choisya ternata KUNTH

4. Evergreen shrub to 3m, with downy bts. Lv opposite, ternate, each leaflet elliptic, to 7cm long and 2cm across, at the end of a longish petiole up to 5cm. Fl in a cluster of axillary corymbs at the end of the shoots. Each fl white, fragrant patulate, to 3cm across. Fl 4–5. Sometimes damaged after very severe winters, but rarely killed. Native of Mexico. Introduced in 1866.

Choisya ternata

CHORDOSPARTIUM CHEESEMAN *Leguminosae*

A monotypic genus.

Chordospartium stevensonii CHEESEMAN

4. A shrub, rarely more than 2m in cultivation, although in the wild occasionally a small tree to 9m. Bts thin, pendulous, much like those of the common broom. Lv fugacious and only seen on young plants. Fl in racemes from the places where the leaf-axils might be expected; occasionally the raceme is solitary, sometimes they are in clusters of up to 5. Each raceme to 8cm long, densely set with small pea-shaped flowers, lilac-purple in colour. Each fl about 8mm long. Fl 7. Pods single-seeded.

Not very long-lived, like so many of the brooms and their relatives. Needs perfect drainage and full light, but even so may be killed in very severe winters. It is very attractive when in full flower and this is the more welcome for coming in July. Propagation by seed. Native to the foothills of the Kaikura range, S Island, New Zealand. Introduced in 1923.

CHRYSOLEPIS HJELMQVIST *Fagaceae*

A genus of two species of evergreen trees; formerly included in the genus *Castanopsis*, but reasonably distinct therefrom. The plants are monoecious, both sexes being borne on the same catkin.

Chrysolepis chysophylla (W. HOOKER)
HJELMQVIST

3. (*Castanopsis chrysophylla* (W. HOOKER) DE CANDOLLE) Evergreen bush or small tree, only about 10m in cultivation, although occasionally up to 30m in the wild. Bts thickly covered with a golden indumentum, which persists on the underside of the lv. Lv ovate-lanceolate, to 10cm long and 2·5cm across, acuminate, dark glossy green above. Fl in catkins, the males at the top the females at the base, terminal. Sometimes male and female fl are borne on separate inflorescences. Fr a spiny burr, taking two years to ripen. The plant is a reasonably rapid grower and is propagated by seed. It is suggested that the lower brs should not be cut away, so that the trunk is exposed to sunlight. The plant thrives in many parts of the UK although by no means everywhere. Native of Oregon and California. Introduced by Hartweg in 1846, although there would seem to have been an earlier introduction in 1844 or 1845 according to Bean and Rehder. It was also sent back in 1849 by W. Lobb and the next year by Jeffrey.

CISTUS LINNAEUS *Cistaceae*

A genus of about twenty species from the Mediterranean region and the Atlantic seaboard of SW Europe. As such they may well succumb during severe winters and only *C. laurifolius* can be expected to survive these. However, they come so readily from seed or cuttings that they can easily be replaced and usually start to flower in their second year. They are not in any case particularly long-lived. Their flowers are large, patulate but ephemeral, opening in the morning and falling by the late afternoon. The leaves are opposite, evergreen, usually oblong and acuminate, often aromatic. The *Cistus* are remarkably useful for clothing very dry situations. A number of natural and artificial hybrids exist.

Cistus albidus LINNAEUS

4. Bushy shrub to 2m, with bts, underside of lv, flower stalks and sepals all covered with white down. Lv sessile, oblong-ovate, to 5cm long and 2cm across. Fl in terminal clusters, each on a peduncle to 2cm long, about 6cm across, purple-pink with yellow blotch in the centre. Fl 6–7. A native of SW Europe and N Africa and usually rather tender.

Cistus X corbariensis POURRET

4. A hybrid, which has been found in the wild, between *C. laurifolius* and *C. salviifolius.* A spreading shrub, rarely more than 1m high, with lv on short petioles to 1cm long. Lv ovate, dull dark green, pointed, to 5cm long and 2·5cm across, dark green above, paler below, pubescent on both sides. Fl on short, axillary shoots, in clusters of up to 3, but flowering singly. Fl to 3·5cm across, white with yellow at the base of the petals. Fl 6–7. One of the hardier and more reliable plants, first observed around Corbières in SW Mediterranean France.

Cistus crispus LINNAEUS

4. Low, spreading shrub, not more than 60cm high, with white hairy bts. Lv sessile, lanceolate, 3·5cm long and 1cm across, markedly undulate and covered with starry down on both surfaces. Fl in terminal and axillary heads, about 4cm across and, in the best forms, a rich crimson, making this the richest-coloured sp available. Fl 6–7. All authorities say that this is a reasonably hardy sp, although it is rarely found much above sea level in the SW Mediterranean.

Cistus X cyprius LAMARCK

4. A hybrid between *C. ladanifer* and *C. laurifolius,* so presumably not originating in Cyprus where *C. ladanifer* does not occur. A vigorous shrub, to 3m, with sticky bts, which exude a fragrant gum. Lv shortly-stalked, lanceolate, to 10cm long and 3cm across; dark green above in summer, but becoming metallic grey and very attractive in the winter, sticky. Fl in cluster of 3–6 on axillary shoots, up to 7cm across, white with a crimson blotch. Fl 6–7. One of the more reliable *Cistus* and particularly useful for its showy winter lv.

Cistus hirsutus LAMARCK

4. Much-branched shrub, to 1m. Bts very downy with white hairs. Lv sessile, oblong-ovate, to 6cm long and 2cm across, very hairy with white hairs on the upper surface. Fl in terminal clusters, 4cm across, white with a slight yellow stain at the base. Fl 6. Native of Spain and Portugal, but naturalised in Brittany and so reasonably hardy, more so than the allied *C. salviifolius.*

Cistus ladanifer LINNAEUS

4. A rather leggy shrub of up to 2m, with resinous brs. Lv sticky, virtually sessile, elliptic, to 10cm long and 2cm wide; dark green and glabrous above but with grey tomentum beneath. Fl solitary, from axillary shoots, large – up to 10cm across – white or white with a deep crimson blotch. Fl 6–8. Although less hardy than *C. laurifolius,* this plant has often withstood very severe frosts without injury and it has almost the largest fl in the genus.

Cistus laurifolius LINNAEUS

4. A rather stiff shrub, to 3m, with hairy, glutinous bts. Lv ovate-lanceolate, shortly-

Cistus ladanifer

stalked, to 7cm long and 3·5cm across; dull green above, downy beneath and sticky on both surfaces, turning metallic-grey in the winter. Fl in cymose panicles borne on axillary shoots, to 7cm across, pure white. Fl 6–8. Can be confused with the last sp but distinct in its stalked lv and fl in clusters. Easily the hardiest sp and can be planted with confidence in any dry open situation.

Cistus parviflorus LAMARCK

4. Rounded shrub, to 1m with downy bts. Lv nearly heart-shaped, glaucous, to 6cm long and 3cm across, downy. Fl in terminal and axillary heads, several opening simultaneously, rose-pink, about 2·5cm across. Fl 6. A native of the eastern Mediterranean and unexpectedly hardy, while the fl are of a unique colour, only otherwise found in its hybrid with *C. monspeliensis,* known as *C. X skanbergii.* It is as hardy or hardier than this hybrid and has more attractive foliage. Unfortunately the fl are over rather soon.

Cistus populifolius LINNAEUS

4. Shrub, to 2m or more, with sticky bts. Lv long-stalked, heart-shaped, to 8cm long and 6cm across, the petiole may be 2·5cm long. Fl enclosed in crimson sepals, in terminal and axillary heads, 5cm across, white with a yellow blotch. Fl 6–8. Distinct in its long-stalked lv and its crimson sepals, which do not, however, occur in all forms. Generally a hardy sp. The var *lasiocalyx,* with much larger fl, is more tender as it comes from the most southerly part of its range.

CLADOTHAMNUS BONGARD *Ericaceae*
A monotypic genus, confined to western N America, requiring acid soil.

Cladothamnus pyrolaeflorus BONGARD

4. (The specific epithet is also spelt *pyroliflorus.*) Deciduous shrub, to 2m (rarely to 3m), with many upright brs. Lv alternate, obovate-oblong, to 5cm across and 12 mm wide, sessile, glabrous. Fl solitary, from upper axils, to 2·5cm across, patulate; pink with yellow tips to the petals. The plant requires acid soil which does not dry out. Not a suitable plant for districts where late spring frosts occur frequently, but easily tolerating the worst the winter can do in the UK. Native of western N America from Alaska to Oregon.

CLADRASTIS RAFINESQUE *Leguminosae*
A small genus of about four species of deciduous trees, one American, the others E Asian. The leaves are alternate, pinnate, the base of the petiole swollen to enclose the leaf-buds of the next year. The flowers are pea-shaped in long panicles. Propagated by seed, or root cuttings.

Cladrastis lutea (MICHAUX) K. KOCH

4.6.7. (*Virgilia lutea* MICHAUX) Tree, usually to 13m, with smooth, pale grey trunk and brs and a rounded head. Lv to 30cm long, composed usually of 7–9 leaflets of which the terminal one is much the largest, being ovate and up to 11cm long and 7cm across, while the smallest basal ones are 3·5cm long and 1cm across. The lv are a brilliant green and turn golden before falling. Fl in terminal pendulous panicles, to 35cm long and up to 15cm across at the base, composed of white, pea-shaped fl each about 3cm long, with a yellow blotch at the base of the standard. They are slightly fragrant but not produced with much freedom. Fl 6. Native to the eastern USA. Introduced both by Lyon and by Fraser 1802.

Cladrastis sinensis HEMSLEY

4.7. Deciduous tree, so far to 13m in cultivation. Bts with rust-coloured tomentum. Lv composed usually of 11–13 leaflets, sometimes more, which are arranged alternately, each one elliptic, to 12cm long and 3cm wide; bright green above, glaucous beneath with rust-coloured tomentum on the rachis. Fl in an erect panicle, up to 30cm long and 22cm wide, composed of pale pink, pea-shaped fl, 12mm long. Fl 7–8. An attractive tree and useful for its late flowering. It flowers with more freedom than *C. lutea.* The lv do not start to unfurl before June. The plant is apparently perfectly hardy, although the best

Cladrastris lutea

trees are in the more sheltered parts of the UK. Native of China. Introduced by Wilson in 1901.

CLEMATIS LINNAEUS *Ranunculaceae*

A fairly large genus of over 200 species of climbing or herbaceous plants, mainly, although not invariably, deciduous. The climbing species with which we are concerned here obtain their support by twisting their petioles around twigs or whatever support is given in the garden. The flowers lack true petals, their place being taken by coloured sepals and, in the section *Atragene*, some of the stamens are petaloid. The fruit is an achene and the seeds are sometimes topped with hairs, which make them very ornamental, particularly in the case of *C. tangutica*. The large-flowered hybrids are based on three Asian species *CC. florida, lanuginosa* and *patens*; the latter two species are not in general cultivation and are said to be slightly tender. Hybrids with *C. patens* in their make-up tend to flower in June and July and should be pruned as soon as flowering is finished; plants with *C. lanuginosa* as a hybrid, flower on the current year's growth and may well be hard pruned in February. 'Nelly Moser' is an exemplar of the *patens* hybrid and 'Jackmannii' of the *lanuginosa* group. The species can be propagated by seed. and both species and hybrids can be propagated by internodal cuttings of fairly firm new growth or by layers. All *Clematis* thrive best with their roots in the shade. The genus is divided into a number of sections as follows:

Viorna Tepals making an urn-shaped fl. Often growths only annual, dying back to a woody base.

Connatae Lv pinnate or bipinnate. Fl campanulate in axillary panicles.

Cirrhosae Lv simple or ternate. Fl campanulate, singly from axils of year-old wood.

Atragene Lv ternate to biternate. Fl solitary from axils of year-old wood, with petaloid stamens, fairly open.

Viticella Lv simple to bipinnate, sometimes ternate. Fl axillary or terminal on the current year's growth, often large.

Flammula Divided into several series:

1 *Montanae* Lv ternate or pinnate. Fl large, patulate, from axillary buds of year-old wood, usually fl in fascicles.

2 *Rectae* Lv simple to bipinnate. Fl on current year's growth in terminal and axillary panicles.

3 *Vitalbae* Lv always compound. Fl small, sometimes dioecious.

4 *Orientales* Lv biternate or pinnate. Fl yellow, often with plumose fr.

Clematis alpina (LINNAEUS) MILLER *Atragene*

4. (*Atragene alpina* LINNAEUS) Deciduous climber up to 3m. Lv biternate, composed of 9 leaflets, ovate, up to 5cm long and 1·5cm across. The whole lv may be 15cm long. Fl solitary, nodding, half open, to 3·5cm long; petaloid stamina white, sepals blue, achenes with a silky tuft of hairs on each seed. Fl 4–5. A charming plant that in nature tends to scramble over rocks rather than to ascend into trees. Native of Europe and N Asia and barely distinct from the E Asian *C. macropetala* (qv).

Clematis armandii FRANCHET *Montanae*

4. Evergreen, vigorous climber, to 10m. Lv ternate, oblong-lanceolate, up to 15cm long and 6cm wide; glossy green and rather leathery. Fl in dense, axillary clusters, to 6cm across with 4–7 sepals which are white, or pink in the cv 'Apple Blossom'. Fl 4. The plant should never be more than very lightly pruned. Doubts have been cast on its hardiness, but it is rarely killed by frost if happy in other ways. Native of China. Introduced by Wilson in 1900.

Clematis campaniflora BROTERO *Viticella*

4. Vigorous, deciduous climber, to 7m or more. Lv pinnate, composed of 15 or 21 leaflets (really 5 or 7 sets of 3 leaflets). The leaflets are narrow-lanceolate, up to 7cm long and 2cm across. Fl usually solitary, produced from the axils of the current growth, on a stem up to 7cm long. Four sepals, white tinged with violet. The fl is patulate rather than campanulate and is about 2·5cm across. Native of Portugal. Introduced in 1816.

Clematis chrysocoma FRANCHET *Montanae*

4. Includes *C. spooneri* REHDER AND WILSON (*C. chrysocoma* var *sericea* SCHNEIDER). It is the variety which is most often met with and which is described here. Moderate, deciduous climber, to 6m but usually only half that height. Bts, young lv, petioles and peduncles all covered with yellowish-brown tomentum. Lv trifoliolate, eventually glabrous on the upper side. Each leaflet is more or less ovate, to 4cm long and wide, somewhat 3-lobed. Fl composed of 4 white sepals, tinged with purple-pink, to 9cm across, produced singly from the axils of the year-old wood, occasionally 2 or more flowers coming from the same axil. Each fl is on a stem some 7cm long. Fl 6.

The typical *C. chrysocoma* has smaller fl and often produces further ones on the current year's growth. It does not seem to be a true climber, but a rather weak shrub to 2m high and less hardy. *C. chrysocoma* is native to China. The type was introduced to Vilmorin, possibly by Père Farges, about 1890. Var *sericea* was introduced by Wilson in 1909.

Clematis cirrhosa LINNAEUS *Cirrhosae*

4. Evergreen climber, to 3m, with silky bts. Lv ovate or 3-lobed, toothed, to 5cm long and 4cm across. Fl solitary or in pairs, from axils of the year-old wood, patulate, on a peduncle up to 5cm long and about 6cm in diameter; greenish-white, sometimes speckled or flushed with reddish-purple. Fl 1–3. Fr surmounted by attractive silky tassels. The var *balearica* WILLKOMM AND LANGE (*C. balearica* RICHARD) is characterised by the lv being deeply dissected to give a ferny appearance. They turn a delightful bronzy-purple in the winter. It is somewhat less hardy than the type and does best on a south-facing wall, which can be recommended for the type as well, owing to its flowering in mid-winter. Var *balearica* seems to flower more freely than the type. Native of the Mediterranean; var *balearica* confined to the Balearic Islands, Corsica and Sardinia.

Clematis fargesii FRANCHET *Rectae*

4. Represented in cultivation by the var *souliei* FINET AND GAGNEPAIN, which is barely distinct from the type. Deciduous climber, to 7m, with purplish, downy bts. Lv 5-ternate, appearing bipinnate, up to 22cm long. Leaflets ovate, toothed or rarely 3-lobed, to 5cm long and 4cm across, downy on both surfaces. Fl with 6 sepals, produced usually in 3-flowered cymes but sometimes singly from the axils, on a stalk up to 15cm long; each fl pure white, to 6cm across. Fl 6–9. Seed vessels with feathery styles persisting. Useful for its long flowering season, although this means that it is never very showy at any one time. Native of W China. Introduced by Wilson in 1911.

Clematis flammula LINNAEUS *Rectae*

4.5. Deciduous climber to 3 or 4m. Lv variable, but usually pinnate with from 3 to 7 leaflets, which may be trifoliate themselves. Bright green, usually lanceolate to 4cm long 2cm across. Fl in large panicles up to 30cm long (usually much less) composed of numerous 4-sepalled starry fl which are up to 2·5cm across, pure white and very fragrant. Fl 8–10. Native of southern Europe, but perfectly hardy and naturalised in a few places in the UK.

The hybrid with *C. viticella* known as X *triternata* 'Rubro-marginata' (or X *violacea* 'Rubro-marginata') has slightly larger fl up to 3cm across, which are reddish-violet with a white centre. They are equally fragrant.

Clematis florida THUNBERG *Viticella*

4. Deciduous climber (sometimes semi-ever-green), to 4m, with ternate or biternate lv. Leaflets ovate-lanceolate, to 5cm long and 3cm across; shining dark green above, rather downy below. Fl axillary and solitary on a downy stalk up to 10cm long, with a pair of leaf-like bracts at the centre. The fl are up to 7cm across, white with a greenish stripe down the back of each sepal. There may be 4 or 6 sepals to each fl. The stamens are a very dark purple.

The type may not be in cultivation now, and in gardens the plant is represented by the cv 'Sieboldii' ('Bicolor') in which the stamens have become petaloid. The cv 'Fortunei', a double pure white form, introduced by Fortune from Japan in 1860, was much used by breeders in the nineteenth century but is probably now lost to cultivation. Native of China and much cultivated in Japan. The type was obtained by Dr. Fothergill in 1776, while 'Sieboldii' was grown by Siebold in the 1830s and was received in England in 1836. The plant has a reputation of being slightly tender, but this is not borne out by experience.

Clematis grata WALLICH *Vitalbae*

4.5. Strong-growing, deciduous climber, to 10m, with downy bts. Lv composed of 3 or 5 leaflets, of which the terminal one may be as much as 12cm long and wide and is roundish in shape, somewhat shining and silvery. Fl in terminal and axillary, few-flowered panicles, each fl being 4–5 sepalled and a dull white, about 2cm across. Fl 8–10. Seeds with long silky tails.

The Chinese var *grandidentata* REHDER AND WILSON, introduced by Wilson from Hupeh in 1904, differs from the tender Himalayan *C. grata* in its usually trifoliate lv. It is perfectly hardy, but in no way outstanding.

Clematis flammula

58

Clematis X jackmanii T. MOORE

4. The founder member of a whole race of hybrids built on *C. lanuginosa*, a rather weak-growing Chinese clematis, which has flowers up to 15cm across, but which is probably no longer in cultivation. Jackman's original cross is said to be *C. lanuginosa* X *C. viticella* and is still in cultivation after 112 years. Hybrids of this race flower on the current year's growth, usually late in the season and are generally pruned hard in very early spring, but can be left unpruned if required to get up high into trees.

Clematis macropetala LEDEBOUR *Atragene*

4. Deciduous climber, to 3m or more, with downy bts and biternate lv, each lv being up to 15cm long; the leaflets ovate-lanceolate, to 3cm long and 2cm across. Fl from upper axils of the previous year's growth, 4-sepalled, up to 10cm across; the sepals blue, violet, or pink, the centre filled with petal-like segments, giving the impression of a double fl. These segments are more or less white in colour, shading on the outside to meet the colour of the sepals. Fl 5–6. Seeds fairly woolly and ornamental. Often considered one of the most delightful spp in the whole genus. Native of Kansu in China and Siberia. Introduced by Purdom in 1910 and later by Farrer in 1914. Very close to *C. alpina*, but with larger fl and a later flowering season.

Clematis maximowicziana FRANCHET ET SAVATIER *Rectae*

4. Much better known as *C. paniculata* THUNBERG, but unfortunately Gmelin had previously used this name for the plant known as *C. indivisa* WILLDENOW, so *maximowicziana* must stand. Vigorous, deciduous climber, to 10m, with pinnate lv having either 3 or 5 leaflets. Each leaflet is ovate-cordate, to 7cm long, stalked, dark green. Fl in panicles from axils of the current year's growth, each panicle about 10cm long, each fl 4-sepalled, starry, white, fragrant, about 3cm across. Fl 8–10. Seed with grey plumes. Resembles a very vigorous *C. flammula*, but is not as satisfactory a plant, being a shy flowerer in this country, although excellent on the continent. Native of Japan. Date of introduction uncertain. Rehder suggests 1864.

Clematis montana DE CANDOLLE *Montanae*

4. Vigorous, deciduous climber, to 8m or more. Lv trifoliolate, each leaflet ovate-lanceolate, but deeply toothed to give an irregular outline, up to 10cm long, 5cm wide, but usually less. Fl long-stalked, 4-sepalled, white, to 6cm across, produced with the young lv from axils of the previous year's growth. Fl 5.

Var *rubens* KUNTZE is a Chinese form with purplish bts, bronzy young lv and purplish-pink fl usually not opening before June. Another var, *wilsonii* SPRAGUE, is also a Chinese plant with fl up to 7·5cm across, white, not opening until July and August.

The type is native to the Himalaya and was brought back by Lady Amherst in 1831, although the plants were probably produced by Wallich. Var *rubens* was brought back by Wilson in 1900 and var *wilsonii* in 1904. All the forms are excellent, very floriferous, garden plants.

Clematis orientalis LINNAEUS *Orientales*

4. Including *C. glauca* WILLDENOW and *C. graveolens* LINDLEY. A fairly vigorous, deciduous climber to 7m or slightly more, with a large range over most of Asia and thus highly variable. Lv up to 20cm long, pinnate, but often the lower pinnae are trifoliate. Leaflets, ovate-lanceolate lobed, to 6cm long, more or less glaucous. Fl solitary from axils of current year's growth, on peduncles up to 10cm long; slightly urn-shaped but opening wide later, yellow in various shades from pale lemon to nearly orange (*C. glauca* var *akebioides*). The plant collected by Ludlow and Sheriff under number LSE 13372 has extraordinarily thick tepals of a pale lemon shade. Other forms are less thick-tepalled but may be more brilliantly coloured; some forms have purple stamens, which increases the attractiveness. Fl 8–9. The date of introduction is not known but Miller was growing it in 1731.

Clematis patens MORREN AND DECAISNE *Viticella*

4. Deciduous climber, to 4m. Lv composed of 3 or 5 leaflets, each ovate-lanceolate, to 10cm long and 5cm across. Fl solitary on long-stalks, up to 15cm across, white or pale blue, 6–8-sepalled. Fl 6–7. Close to *C. florida* from which it differs in having no bracts on the flower stalk and in its lv which are ternate or biternate in *C. florida*. Recently re-introduced to cultivation, once a main influence in early-flowering, large-flowered hybrids of which 'Nelly Moser' is one of the best known. The main ancestor in these hybrids is a plant brought back by Fortune from Japan in 1861 and known as 'Standishii', with pale blue fl. This was a Japanese garden plant and may have been a hybrid of *patens* and *florida*. The plant is probably native to Japan and was certainly brought thence by Siebold in 1836. Plants from the *patens* hybrids flower considerably earlier than the *jackmanii-lanuginosa* group.

Clematis rehderiana CRAIB *Connatae*

4. Deciduous climber, to 8m, with downy stems. Lv pinnate, to 20cm long, made up of 7 or 9 leaflets; these ovate, coarsely toothed, to 7cm long and 4cm across, faintly downy above and

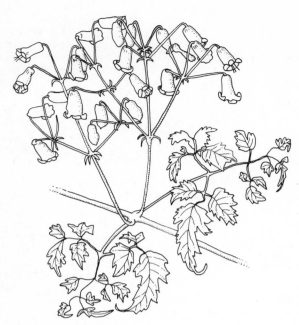

Clematis rehderiana

thickly below. Fl campanulate, nodding in erect panicles carrying numerous fl; these about 2cm long, yellowish-white, fragrant. Seeds plumose, but not very conspicuous. Native of W China. Introduced in 1898 by Père Aubert. When introduced it was mistaken first for *C. nutans* ROYLE and then for *C. buchananii* DE CANDOLLE, both Himalayan plants, neither of which appear to be in cultivation, but it is still occasionally met with in catalogues under either of these names.

Clematis serratifolia REHDER *Orientales*

4.5. Deciduous climber, to 3m. Lv biternate, the leaflets ovate-lanceolate, to 7cm long, glabrous, bright green. Fl produced singly, or up to 3 from the axils, sepals half expanded to 2·5cm long, 4, yellow with purple filaments to the stamens. Seeds with feathery styles some 5cm long. Fl 8–9. Distinct from most of the orientales by its biternate lv. Very close to *C. tangutica* (qv) but with smaller, more numerous fl and flowering 2 months later. Native of Korea. In cultivation in 1908.

Clematis tangutica (MAXIMOWICZ) KORSHINSKY *Orientale*

4.5. (*C. orientalis* var *tangutica* MAXIMOWICZ) Maximowicz would seem justified, as the plant is not easily separated from other forms of *C. orientalis*. Deciduous climber, to 5m, with downy bts and young lv. Lv pinnate or bipinnate, grey-green, to 20cm long, the leaflets coarsely toothed, to 8cm long. Fl solitary on downy stalks, which are up to 15cm long, campanulate at first, later opening wider, bright yellow; some fl may be as

much as 10cm across and they are followed by very ornamental fr; the seeds being crowned with very long, silky styles. Fl 6. There is often a second, later flowering. One of the most ornamental of the genus, both for its yellow fl and its handsome fr. Only differentiated from *C. orientalis* by its downy stems and young lv and by its earlier flowering season, although the fl are larger.

Native of western China, first found at Tengeh, hence its name. Sent by Potanin to St Petersburg, whence it was sent to Kew in 1898. It was collected again by Purdom in 1911 and most plants in cultivation come from this sending.

Clematis texensis BUCKLEY *Viorna*

4. (*C. coccinea* ENGELMANN) In Britain a semi-herbaceous climber, the growths dying back to a woody stock each year. Lv pinnate, with a tendril in place of the final leaflet. Leaflets 4–8, each on a stalk somewhat longer than the lamina, ovate, to 7cm long and wide. Fl solitary, axillary, urn-shaped, up to 3cm long (4cm in the cv 'Major'), purplish to scarlet. Seeds with feathery styles. Fl 7–9. Needs a south wall, but is unique in its fl colour. The true sp is not frequently seen in cultivation, but there are hybrids such as 'Gravetye Beauty' and 'Etoile Rose' which have much the colour of *texensis* but with more open fl and a similar semi-herbaceous habit. The sp has also been bred into the *Jackmanii* group to give such plants as 'Ville de Lyon' and 'Ernest Markham' with pink and red-purple colouring. The sp is, as its name implies, native to Texas and was first introduced in 1868.

Clematis tangutica

Clematis veitchiana CRAIB

4. Differs from *C. rehderiana* mainly in its bipinnate lv which may have as many as 21 leaflets.

Clematis viticella LINNAEUS *Viticella*

4. Vigorous climber, to 4m or more, with much of the current year's growth dying back each year, so that winter pruning will enhance the appearance of the plant. Lv pinnate, the lower leaflets often trifoliate, to 12cm long; leaflets to 5cm long, ovate, sometimes lobed. Fl 1–3 from upper lv axils, with 4 spreading sepals; fl somewhat nodding, deep violet, reddish or white, up to 4cm across. Fl 7–9.

There are a number of agreeable hybrids which are close to the sp but have slightly larger fl, among which are 'Alba Luxurians' with white fl and purple anthers, and 'Kermesina' with claret-coloured tepals. The seeds lack any feathery styles. Native of S Europe and cultivated since 1597.

CLERODENDRON LINNAEUS *Verbenaceae*

Also spelt *Clerodendrum*. A genus of about 100 species, mainly tropical. The leaves are opposite, the flowers are in terminal cymes, usually tubular, and the fruit is a drupe. Propagated by suckers or root cuttings.

Clerodendron bungei STEUDEL

4. (*C. foetidum* BUNGE) In Britain herbaceous rather than shrubby, dying down each year to a woody rootstock, but throwing up growths to 2m. Lv cordate, to 20cm long and 18cm across, fetid when crushed, coarsely toothed. Fl in terminal, rounded corymbs, which are 12cm across; each fl tubular, with reflexed lobes, 2cm across, reddish-purple, fragrant. Fl 8–9. Native of China. Introduced by Fortune in 1844 and valuable for its late-flowering, reddish fl.

Clerodendron trichotomum THUNBERG

4.5. Shrub or small tree, to 6m, deciduous. Lv of variable size and shape, ovate to elliptic, entire, toothed or lobed. They are usually oval, to 21cm long and 7cm across, with downy underside. Fl in axillary cymes, which coalesce to give the appearance of a large terminal inflorescence up to 22cm across. Calyx crimson, later spreading and somewhat fleshy. Fl tubular, with 5 spreading lobes, fragrant, white, up to 3cm across. Fr the size of a pea, blue, later black. Fruits are usually only produced after a hot, dry summer. There is always a risk of much of the growth dying back in the winter, but this does not happen with the **3.** var *fargesii* REHDER (*C. fargesii* DODE). In this variant the lv are purple as they unfurl, the shoots are more slender, the calyx is

Clerodendron trichotomum

green not crimson (although it becomes pinkish eventually), and the fr is a much lighter blue. Fl 7–8. Fr 10.

C. trichotomum is native to China and Japan and was in cultivation in 1880. Var *fargesii* was sent to Vilmorin by Père Farges in 1898. Both forms are very valuable for their late, fragrant fl and, when they are produced, their striking fr.

CLETHRA LINNAEUS *Clethraceae*

The family contains only this single genus. Shrubs or small trees, deciduous or evergreen. The leaves are alternate, short-petioled, usually finely toothed. The flowers are in terminal racemes or panicles and five-petalled while the fruit is a three-valved capsule. Propagated by seeds, layers or cuttings of half-ripe wood in August. A number of Chinese species are hardy in southern England, but doubtful farther north and have all, with the exception of *C. delavayi*, been excluded. Acid soil seems essential.

Clethra alnifolia LINNAEUS

4. Deciduous shrub, to 3m, with erect brs and finely pubescent bts. Often suckering, which provides a means of increase. Lv obovate, to 10cm long and 5cm across, nearly glabrous. Fl in terminal and axillary erect racemes, to 15cm long and to 9mm across, white, fragrant. Fl 8. In the form known as 'Paniculata' (*Clethra paniculata* AITON), the inflorescence is densely paniculate. There is also a pink-flowered form 'Rosea' with glossy lv. Native of eastern N America. In cultivation before 1731. 'Paniculata' sent over by William Young in 1770.

Clethra delavayi FRANCHET

4. Deciduous shrub, making, on occasion, a tree to 12m in the wild. Bts downy, sometimes reddish. Lv lanceolate-elliptic, to 15cm long and 6cm across, deep green above. Fl in a single, terminal raceme to 15cm long and 3cm across, one-sided; each fl is white with a yellow tinge, about 2cm across. The raceme is rarely erect. Fl 7–8. Regarded as the handsomest of the hardy clethras, it seems curiously temperamental in its habits, thriving in Northumberland but unsuccessful at Kew. It appears that it requires a rather wet climate, as all the clethras are somewhat intolerant of drought and its success must be regarded as hazardous in inclement districts, although not necessarily impossible. Native of Yunnan. Introduced by Forrest in 1913.

Clethra tomentosa LAMARCK

4. (*C. alnifolia* var *pubescens* AITON) Shrub, to nearly 3m, with very woolly bts. Lv obovate, toothed at the apex, to 10cm long, 5cm across, nearly glabrous above, white-woolly below. Fl in erect, terminal and axillary racemes, up to 15cm long, woolly, each fl to 1cm across, white, fragrant. Fl 9. Distinguished from the similar *C. alnifolia* by its very woolly stems and undersides of lv, by its larger fl and by flowering a month later. Native of the eastern USA as far north as North Carolina, so somewhat more tender than *C. alnifolia*, which extends as far north as Maine. Introduced possibly in 1731, but probably somewhat later.

CLEYERA DE CANDOLLE *Theaceae*

A small genus of evergreen shrubs from Eastern Asia with alternate leaves and perfect flowers, which serves to distinguish them from the related genus *Eurya,* where the plants are dioecious. Propagated by cuttings.

Cleyera japonica THUNBERG

4.5. Evergreen shrub or small tree, to about 4m in cultivation. Lv alternate, coriaceous, ovate-oblong, to 10cm long and 4cm wide; deep green above and glossy, paler below, glabrous. Fl axillary on year-old wood, 1–3 in number, flat, about 1cm wide; fragrant, yellowish-white or ivory. Fl 6–7. Fr a drupe about the size of a pea, bright red, eventually turning black.

C. japonica 'Tricolor', sometimes given specific rank as *C. fortunei,* is a shrub, to 2m, with lv to 15cm long and 3·5cm wide which are deep green in the centre, but have a wide yellow margin. This is more tender than the type and requires some protection in most districts. It also flowers rarely.

C. japonica is found from Nepal to Japan; the Japanese forms have smaller lv than those from Nepal and seem somewhat hardier. 'Tricolor' was brought back from Japan by Fortune in 1860. The type seems to have arrived about ten years later.

COLLETIA JUSSIEU *Rhamnaceae*

A genus of around ten species of S American, deciduous shrubs, of which the hardy members are of very curious appearance. Resembling gorse bushes, they have very small leaves which soon fall, their function being usurped by the spine-like small branches. In addition the flowers lack petals, or, if present, they are minute, being replaced by tubular sepals. The plant flowers extremely late in the year and is of value on that account alone. Propagated by means of cuttings.

Colletia armata MIERS

4. Spiny shrub, to 4m, the younger parts composed of greyish-green, cylindrical spines, slightly downy, to 3cm long. Fl tubular, waxy, fragrant, produced in clusters of 2–3 along the base of the spines; 5mm long, white generally, but pale pink in the cv 'Rosea', which is a much deeper pink in the bud. The plant is very floriferous once established. Fl 9–11. A very valuable plant on account of its late flowering and delicious perfume. Native of Chile. Apparently introduced by Messrs Veitch about 1880, but the collector is not known. Veitch themselves had no collector in Chile in those years.

Colletia cruciata GILLIES AND WILLIAM HOOKER

4. Shrub, to 3m, with two kinds of spines. The most frequent are broadly-triangular, up to 4cm across at the base; another form, found most frequently on juvenile plants, is a needle-shape with a flattened base and up to 4cm long, but slender. Fl at the base of the spines in pairs or larger clusters, tubular, with 5 reflexed lobes at the mouth. Yellowish-white, fragrant, only some 7mm long. Fl 9–10. Only flowers well after a hot summer. Native of Uruguay and N Brazil. Introduced by Dr Gillies in 1824.

COLQUHOUNIA WALLICH *Labiatae*

A small genus of about five species of shrubs from India and Malaysia. Propagated by seed or by cuttings.

Colquhounia coccinea WALLICH

4. Straggling, deciduous, shrub, to 3m, with downy bts and lv variable in size and in shape. They may be any shape from lanceolate to cordate and up to 20cm long and 12cm across; dull green and downy above, grey tomentose below. Fl in whorls at the end of the current year's growths, the whole inflorescence sometimes 30cm long. Fl funnel-shaped with a two-lipped mouth, up to 2·5cm long, lower lip 3-lobed and yellowish inside, otherwise fl scarlet. Fl 8–10. A reasonably hardy plant, but does better with some protection during very cold spells and is most suitable for growing against a wall. The leaves, when crushed, have a fragrance of apples. Native of the Himalaya and China. Introduced about 1850.

COLUTEA LINNAEUS *Leguminosae*

Deciduous, unarmed shrubs, with pinnate leaves and axillary racemes of pea-shaped flowers followed by pods which are usually inflated and which do not split down the centre, but open at one end only when ripe. Propagated readily by seeds, but cuttings of half-ripened wood are also used.

Colutea arborescens

Colutea arborescens LINNAEUS   Bladder Senna

4.5. Vigorous shrub, to 4m. Lv to 15cm long, leaflets 9–13, obovate, up to 2·5cm long, notched at the apex, hairy below when young, later glabrous or nearly so. Fl yellow, in racemes to 10cm long, each fl about 2cm long. Fl 6–9. Fr a large, often red flushed, inflated pod, up to 7cm long and 3cm across. Although it flowers over a long period, it never makes a very brilliant display. Native to SE Europe, naturalised in Britain.

Colutea X media WILLDENOW

4.5. A hybrid between the last sp and *C. orientalis*, first observed in 1790. A vigorous

shrub, to 4m. Lv somewhat glaucous, with 11–13 leaflets which are obovate and usually about 12mm long. Fl coppery or brownish-red. Pod inflated, often suffused with purple of the same dimensions as that of *C. arborescens*.

Colutea orientalis MILLER

4. (*C. cruenta* AITON) Deciduous shrub, to 2m, with very attractive, glaucous, grey-white lv. These up to 10cm long with 7–9 leaflets. The leaflets are roundish, up to 1·5cm long. Fl, 2–5, in axillary racemes, reddish-brown, small (about 1·5cm long). Fl 6–9, but never very showy. Pod not markedly inflated, suffused with purple, up to 3cm long. Native of the near East. Introduced, according to Aiton, in 1710, possibly by Sherard.

COMPTONIA L'HERITIER *Myricaceae*

A monotypic genus containing a single, deciduous, monoecious shrub with alternate leaves. Propagated by seed, layers or cuttings.

Comptonia peregrina (LINNAEUS) COULTER
Sweet Fern

(*Liquidambar peregrina* LINNAEUS) A deciduous shrub, rarely over 1m high, with alternate, pinnatifid lv, which are sweetly aromatic. The lv are up to 10cm long, but only 1·5cm across, pinnatifidly-lobed into more or less rounded lobes. Male catkins cylindrical, to 2·5cm long; female fl globular, surrounded by downy scales to give a burr-like look. The bts are very hairy, except in the var *asplenifolia* FERNALD when they are almost glabrous and the lv are somewhat smaller than in the type. Grown for its attractively shaped and fragrant lv. Must have acid soil. Native of eastern N America from Nova Scotia to North Carolina. Introduced 1714.

CORIARIA LINNAEUS *Coriariaceae*

A family of only one genus, which comprises both shrubs and herbaceous plants in about ten species with a very wide distribution from the Mediterranean to the Sino-Himalaya and Japan to the east, Chile and Mexico to the west, and New Zealand to the south. The leaves are opposite or whorled, and often so closely set on the branchlets as to give them a fern-like appearance. In general the leaves and fruits are poisonous, although there are reports of the fruits of *C. sinica* being used as a foodstuff and people have been known to eat the fruits of *C. terminalis* without ill-effect. The flowers are small and some species are monoecious, but after fertilisation the small green petals enlarge, becoming fleshy and coloured, so that the fruits resemble berries. Most of the species are somewhat tender and may be killed to the ground in severe winters, although they usually regenerate from the base. The most ornamental species, *C. terminalis*, tends to behave like a herbaceous plant in any case and can be planted with confidence in most areas, although they do not relish dry, chalky soils. Propagated by seed or by cuttings of half-ripened wood.

Coriaria japonica ASA GRAY

5. Deciduous shrub to 1m or occasionally more, but often less, as in the UK the wood rarely ripens adequately. The plant renews itself by strong sucker growths from the base. Lv nearly sessile, ovate-lanceolate, to 9cm long on

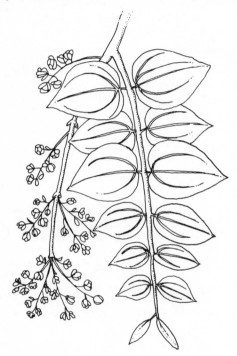

Coriaria terminalis

the main shoots but up to 13cm on sucker growths. Brilliant green in colour. Fl, monoecious, produced in axillary racemes from year-old wood, the racemes grouped in twos or threes; male racemes more slender than the pistillate ones, petals greenish, becoming fleshy and bright red, later black on the female fl. The fr are about 5mm across. Normally a rather short-lived plant. Native of Japan. Introduced to the USA in 1892.

Coriaria myrtifolia LINNAEUS

5. Suckering shrub, to 2m, with the suckers branching the second year. Lv emerging late in the season, sessile or nearly so, attractively glaucous, opposite or in threes, ovate, to 6cm long. Fl in short racemes from axils on the year-old wood, each raceme not more than 2.5cm long. Fr eventually black. The whole plant is extremely poisonous. Native of the western Mediterranean and liable to be killed in very severe winters.

Coriaria terminalis HEMSLEY

5. A subshrub, sending annual stems up to 1m or slightly more from a woody rootstock. The stems branch as they elongate and they are thickly clothed with opposite, sessile, ovate lv to 7cm long and over half as wide. Fl on terminal racemes, up to 22cm long, both sexes on the same raceme. Female fl eventually forming fr up to 12mm across, which are black in the type, red in the cv 'Fructu-rubro' and yellow in the var *xanthocarpa* REHDER, which appears to be the most widespread form in the wild and is the most attractive form for garden ornament. The yellow-fruited var is native from Sikkim to Yunnan and was introduced about 1895, while the black-fruited form was brought by Wilson from Szechuan in 1907.

CORNUS LINNAEUS *Cornaceae*

A genus of mainly deciduous trees and shrubs. The leaves are generally opposite, but, in a few species, alternate, petioled and entire. The flowers are small, four-petalled, in terminal corymbs or clustered into heads; the fruit is a drupe. The genus has been divided into three or four sections as follows:

1 *Thelycrania* ENDLICHER Fl white in cymes or panicles without an involucre. Fr berry-like.
2 *Macrocarpium* SPACH Fl in dense umbels, yellow, with an involucre. Fr large.
3 *Benthamidia* SPACH Fl yellowish in clusters subtended by large showy bracts.

Thelycrania is also known as *Swida*; *Benthamidia* has been subdivided to put the spp with fleshy fruits (*C. kousa* and *C. capitata*) into the sub-section *Benthamia*, but here we are only dealing with three sections. Propagation is by means of seeds, layers, offsets for the stoloniferous species, or cuttings, which are not very easy to root.

Cornus alba LINNAEUS *Thelycrania*

2.5. (*C. sibirica* RAFINESQUE). Deciduous, wide-spreading shrub, to 3m, with erect stems and bright red bts. Lv opposite, oval, on petioles to 2·5cm long, lamina to 11cm long, and more than half as wide; dark green but glaucous below. Fl in terminal cymes, whitish-yellow. Fr white or bluish. A number of forms with variegated lv exist of which 'Elegantissima', with a creamy-white margin, and 'Spaethii', with much yellow variegation, are the most conspicuous. 'Sibirica' has rather brighter-red young wood. Native of Siberia and northern China. Introduced about 1741, possible from one of Collinson's correspondents.

Cornus alternifolius LINNAEUS THE YOUNGER
Thelycrania

Deciduous shrub or small tree, to 7m. The shrub tends to have erect brs, but in tree form the brs are tabular, giving an attractive flat-topped appearance. Lv, unusually for the genus, alternate, oval-elliptic, to 12cm long and 6cm across; pale green above, glaucous below. Fl in cymes up to 6cm across, small, crowded, yellowish-white. Fl 6. Fr black with blue bloom. There is an attractive variegated form 'Argentea' with white variegation.

The plant is not usually very successful in Britain, presumably requiring a continental type summer as winter cold will not affect it at all. This is not surprising since it comes from as far north as Nova Scotia, although it is also found as far south as Georgia and Alabama. Introduced to James Gordon in 1760, which suggests a sending from John Bartram.

Cornus amomum MILLER *Thelycrania*

2.5. Spreading shrub, to 3m, with purple bts, which are downy at first. Lv ovate, to 10cm long and 5cm across; dark green and glabrous above, paler and reddish tomentose below. Fl in cymes to 6cm across, yellowish-white. Fl 7. Fr 6mm in diameter, pale blue. *Cornus obliqua* RAFINESQUE is similar but with glaucous, narrower lv, with a white tomentum below. Native of the eastern USA. Introduced about 1683 by John Banister.

Cornus controversa HEMSLEY *Thelycrania*

2.7. (Originally confused with *C. brachypoda* MEYER and *C. macrophylla* WALLICH). Deciduous tree, to 16m, with tabular brs and red bts. Lv *alternate,* ovate, acuminate, to 15cm long and 7cm across, on a petiole to 5cm long, sometimes turning purple in the autumn. Fl white, in large cymes up to 17cm across. Fl 6–7. Fr. blue-black. The form known as 'Variegata' has narrower, rather distorted, white-variegated lv and is very slow-growing but striking in appearance. The plain-leaved type is one of the most elegant of moderately-sized trees and grows quite fast, although not flowering until fairly sizeable. Native of the Himalaya, China and Japan. Introduced from the latter in 1880, while the variegated form arrived about ten years later.

Cornus florida LINNAEUS *Benthamidia*
Flowering Dogwood

4.6. Spreading shrub or small tree, not more than 7m high in cultivation, although taller in the wild. Lv opposite, ovate-elliptic, to 15cm long and 7·5cm across, often turning crimson in the autumn. Fl very small in a tight head, greenish, but subtended by four obcordate, petal-like bracts to give the appearance of a large, open flower; 10cm in diameter. Normally the bracts are white, but various shades of red are not uncommon and the form known as *rubra* tends to be rather more floriferous than the white form. Fl 5–6. Acid soil appears to be preferred by this plant.

Although a beautiful shrub when in full blossom, it only seems to flower freely in southern England from Sussex westwards, as it needs a warm summer to ripen its wood properly. It is never damaged by cold winters, but is somewhat susceptible to late spring frosts. Native of the eastern USA from Massachusetts to Florida. Introduced about 1731.

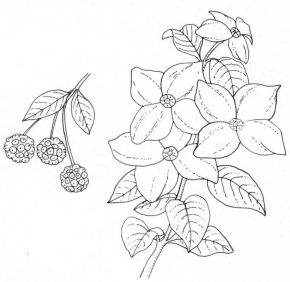

Cornus kousa

Cornus kousa HANCE *Benthamidia*

4.5.6. Deciduous shrub or small tree, to 7m. Lv ovate, acuminate, to 7cm long and 4·5cm across, with undulant margins.Lv often turn red before falling. Fl very small, but subtended by four oblong-ovate, white petal-like bracts to 5cm long and 2cm wide, which persist for some time. Fl 6. Fr fleshy, to 3cm wide, resembling a strawberry.

The var *chinensis* OSBORN is very similar, but seems a better garden plant as it has larger fl and grows more rapidly; it also flowers about a fortnight later than the type.

This is one of the very best of all garden shrubs, well-established plants covering themselves with fl. Fr are rarely produced unless more than one plant is present, but they too are very showy. As the plant matures, the bracts appear to get larger and rounder. The plant seems to require a deep, loamy soil, preferably acid or neutral, but it will survive with greater or less success in most soils. The type comes from Japan and Korea, the var, as its name suggests, from China. The type was introduced from Japan in 1875, the var by Wilson in 1907.

Cornus macrophylla WALLICH *Thelycrania*

4.5.7. Deciduous tree, to 15m, with yellowish or reddish-brown bts. Lv opposite, ovate-elliptic, acuminate, to 17cm long and 8cm across; bright green and glabrous above, glaucous and slightly hairy below on petioles to 3cm long. Fl in terminal, rounded cymes, to 15cm diameter; yellowish-white, each fl 1cm across. Fl 7–8. Fr 6mm in diameter, blue-black. A very handsome foliage tree; the fl are not very conspicuous owing to their nondescript colour. Native of the Himalaya, China and Japan. Introduced from India through Wallich in 1827.

Cornus mas LINNAEUS *Macrocarpium*
Cornelian Cherry

4.(6). Deciduous, spreading shrub or small tree, to 8m. Lv ovate or elliptic, to 10cm long and 3cm across; dark green, turning purple in the autumn on some soils. Fl yellow, in umbels from axils of the year-old wood, produced before the lv. The individual fl are small but the umbels are about 2cm in diameter and produced with profusion on mature trees. Fl 2–3. Fr red, cherry-like, 1·5cm long and nearly as wide, edible, but produced rather sparingly and hidden beneath the lv. Very useful for its early flowering and indifference to frost at this period. Some variegated cv exist, of which 'Elegantissima', with yellow and pink variegation, makes a handsome, but slow-growing, foliage shrub. 'Aurea' has a wide yellow margin to the lv and 'Variegata' a creamy-white one. Native to much of Europe and cultivated since time immemorial.

Cornus nuttallii AUDUBON *Benthamidia*

4.(6). Deciduous tree, up to 17m in the wild, but in cultivation usually a large bush not more than 6m. Lv elliptic-ovate, to 12cm long and 7cm across. Fl very small, in a dense head, purplish; subtended by a number of petal-like bracts, usually 6 but occasionally less or more, which are roundish, up to 7cm long and 5cm across and make a wide open 'flower' up to 15cm across. The bracts are white, becoming pink-flushed before they fade. Fl 5–6. Probably requires acid soil. A very attractive plant, but doing best in the south of the UK and sometimes short-lived even there. The lv often turn yellow

and red before they fall. Distinct from the other cultivated *Benthamidia* in that the bracts, which, like all in this group, are formed and visible in the autumn, are not folded over the fl buds but already spreading. Native of western N America from British Columbia to Southern California. Discovered by Thomas Nuttall and introduced by him in 1835.

Cornus officinalis SIEBOLD AND ZUCCARINI
Macrocarpium

4. A rather leggy shrub or small tree to 10m in the wild, very close to *C. mas*, but with rather deeper yellow fl and patches of rusty hairs on the underside of the lv, along the midrib. Fl 2–3.

Cornus paucinervis HANCE *Thelycrania*

4. Deciduous shrub to 2m with reddish-brown branchlets. Leaves narrowly elliptic, to 10cm long, 4·5cm across, with few veins. Fl in rounded terminal cymes up to 4cm across, white, each fl 8mm across. Fl 7–8. Fr sparingly produced, black, 7mm across. Useful for its late flowering. Native of China, introduced by Wilson in 1907.

Cornus racemosa LAMARCK *Thelycrania*

4.5. (*C candidissima* MARSHALL, *C. paniculata* L'HÉRITIER) Spreading, deciduous shrub, to 3m or more, with greyish bark. Lv opposite, ovate-lanceolate, to 9cm long and half as wide; dark green above, whitish below. Fl in numerous terminal cymes, up to 5cm in diameter, white. Fl 6–7. Fr white, 6mm across, on bright red stalks, but, unfortunately, not produced with much freedom. Native to eastern and central USA. Introduced in 1758 either by Bartram or Humphrey Marshall. Allied to *C. alba* and *C. stolonifera* but less rampant.

Cornus rugosa LAMARCK *Thelycrania*

4.5. (*C. circinata* L'HÉRITIER) Upright shrub or small tree, to 3m, with purplish bts. Lv orbicular with a mucronate apex, to 12cm long and wide; dark green and nearly glabrous above, covered with dense white hairs below. Fl in cymes, to 7cm across, white. Fr pale blue. Fl 6–7. Native of eastern N America from Nova Scotia to Virginia. Introduced in 1784 by the well-known nursery firm of Loddiges. Both Michaux and William Bartram supplied them with shrubs and trees from N America.

Cornus sanguinea LINNAEUS *Thelycrania*
Dogwood

4.6. Deciduous, erect shrub, to 4m, with purplish bts. Lv ovate-elliptic, to 7cm long and 4cm across, colouring in the autumn reddish-purple (sometimes a brilliant red). Fl scented, in terminal cymes, to 5cm across, greenish-white. Fr blackish, 6mm wide. Native of Europe including Britain.

Cornus stolonifera MICHAUX Thelycrania

2.4.5. Stoloniferous, spreading, suckering shrub, to 3m with purplish-red bts (yellowish-green in the cv 'Flaviramea'). Lv elliptic, to 12cm long and 6cm across; dark green above, glaucous below. Fl in cymes, to 5cm wide, yellowish-white. Fl 5–6. Fr white, 5mm across. Native of most of N America. Introduced about 1656 according to Rehder, but the exact date seems lacking as the plant was long considered a form of *C. alba*.

COROKIA ALAN CUNNINGHAM Cornaceae

A small genus of four or five species of evergreen shrubs with alternate leaves and five-petalled and five-stamened yellow, rather starry, flowers. The genus is endemic to New Zealand. Two species are reasonably hardy, although they do better with wall protection. Propagated by seed and by cuttings.

Corokia cotoneaster RAOUL

4.(5). A somewhat curious, rounded bush, to nearly 3m, with downy, white bts and shining black, very thin, interlaced, wiry brs. Lv sparingly produced at long intervals from each other, alternate, spathulate, only 2cm long and 8mm across; dark green above, white tomentose below. Fl yellow, starry, 1·2cm across, axillary. Fl 5. Fr orange to red, to 8mm long, not commonly produced in Britain. A very curious plant with its sparse lv and wiry, dark brs. Usually grown against a wall, but generally satisfactory without this protection if sheltered from excessive wind. If it should be cut down in very severe winters it generally regenerates in the spring. Native of New Zealand. Introduced about 1875.

Corokia X virgata TURRILL

4.5. Originally described as a sp, this is now thought to be a natural hybrid between the last sp, *C. cotoneaster*, and the tender *C. buddleoides*. Plants raised from seed show a certain amount of variation. Shrub of up to 2m or slightly more in cultivation, but possibly taller eventually. Bts covered with white down. Brs are thin and somewhat zig-zag, but not interlaced as in the last sp. Lv spathulate, to 4cm across; dark green above, white tomentose below. Fl in groups of 3 from the upper lv axils, yellow, starry, only about 1cm across. Fl 5. Fr orange-yellow, fairly freely produced. A moderately hardy shrub, sometimes damaged after severe frost but usually regenerating. First observed in 1907.

CORONILLA LINNAEUS Leguminosae

A genus of evergreen and deciduous shrubs and herbaceous plants, about twenty in number, from central Europe and the Mediterranean. It has pinnate leaves and the flowers are in long-stalked umbels. The pods are pea-shaped, long, thin and jointed, with a single seed in each joint. They are easily satisfied with regard to soil, and thrive well in chalky conditions.

Coronilla emerus LINNAEUS Scorpion Senna

4. Deciduous shrub, to 3m, of spreading habit. Lv alternate, to 6cm long, composed of 7–9 leaflets, which are rounded and up to 2cm long. Fl borne on axillary umbels, usually only 3-flowered, on a peduncle to 5cm long. Fl yellow, 2cm long, with a reddish line down the back of the standard. Fl 5–8.

The var *emeroides* WOHLFART (*C. emeroides* BOISSIER) is perhaps slightly preferable. It only reaches to 1·5m, has opposite lv and the fl are borne in umbels of from 4–8 on peduncles of up to 7cm long. Native of central and southern Europe, with var *emeroides* confined to the eastern Mediterranean region. Both the sp and the var have a very long flowering season.

Coronilla glauca LINNAEUS

4. An evergreen shrub, to 3m, needing wall protection in most districts. Lv to 3·5cm long, composed of 5 or 7 leaflets, very glaucous; they are obovate to 1·5cm long. Fl fragrant, each one to 1·2cm long, golden yellow, borne in dense umbels of up to 10 fl on a peduncle to 5cm long. Pod jointed, ending in a slender tail. Fl 4–6 and possibly again in the autumn. The plant is reasonably hardy with wall protection but may be lost during very severe winters. There is a variegated-leaved form which is more tender. Easily propagated from seed. Native of southern Europe. Introduced in 1722.

CORYLOPSIS SIEBOLD AND ZUCCARINI Hamamelidaceae

A small genus of about twelve species of deciduous shrubs, with alternate, toothed leaves resembling those of the hazel (*Corylus*). The flowers appear before the leaves in catkin-like, pendulous racemes, which are really modified branches, and after flowering produce leaves at the base. The flowers are always primrose yellow and five-petalled. The plants are propagated by seed or, with some difficulty, by cuttings. Almost all the species are hardy, but the flowers are often damaged by spring frosts and should be kept away from known frost pockets.

Corylopsis glabrescens FRANCHET AND SAVATIER

4. Including *C. gotoana* MAKINO, which differs in a few minor particulars. Deciduous shrub, or small tree, to 6m. Bts glabrous. Lv round-ovate, bristle-toothed, up to 10cm long and 7cm across, on short petioles, slightly glaucous

Coronilla emerus

below. Fl fragrant, in drooping catkin-like racemes up to 3·5cm long, primrose yellow. Fl 3–4. Native of Japan. First introduced to the USA in 1905 and not received in Britain until 1916.

Corylopsis pauciflora   SIEBOLD AND ZUCCARINI

4. Spreading shrub, rarely more than 1m high. Lv ovate, cordate at the base, to 7cm long and 5cm across, pinkish when emerging. Fl large for the genus, up to 2cm across, but produced in few-flowered spikes of only 2 or 3. Requires a shady situation and the foliage is intolerant of strong winds. Fl 3. Native of Japan. Introduced to America in 1862 and to the UK by Maries in 1874.

Corylopsis platypetala   REHDER AND WILSON

4. Although a small shrub in the wild, this has reached 7m in cultivation. Bts glandular-hairy at first, later glabrous. Lv broadly ovate, to 10cm long and 7cm across; dark green when grown in the shade, glaucous and waxy if grown in the sun. Fl in catkin-like racemes, to 5cm long; many-flowered, the individual fl small. Fl 3–4. Does best on acid soil. *C. yunnanensis* DIELS, sent back by Forrest in 1906, is barely separate. Native of western China. Introduced by Wilson in 1907.

Corylopsis sinensis   HEMSLEY

4. Shrub, to 5m, with pubescent bts and petioles. Lv oblong-ovate, to 9cm long and 6cm across, somewhat tomentose below. Fl fragrant, in drooping catkin-like racemes to 5cm long, consisting of up to 18 fl, each about 8mm long. Fl 4. Native of western and central China. Introduced by Wilson in 1900.

Corylopsis spicata   SIEBOLD AND ZUCCARINI

4. Spreading bush to 2m, with silky bts which tend to be somewhat zig-zag. Lv cordate, to 10cm long and 7cm across, finely-toothed; pale green above, downy-glaucous below. Raceme to 4cm long, containing up to 10 fl which are yellow and have the fragrance of cowslips. Fl 3–4. Native of Japan. Introduced by John Gould Veitch in 1861, making this the first sp to be introduced into the UK.

Corylopsis veitchiana   BEAN

4. Rounded shrub, to 2m, with glabrous, reddish bts. Lv ovate, acuminate, cordate at the base; purplish when young, glaucous and glabrous eventually. Fl fragrant, primrose-yellow, in a drooping, catkin-like raceme to 5cm long, with conspicuous, reddish, protruding anthers. Fl 3–4. *C. wilsonii* HEMSLEY is similar but has larger lv, bts at first pubescent, and the floral bracts are villous on both surfaces, unlike any other sp.

Both spp are native to central China and introduced by Wilson in 1900.

Corylopsis willmottiae   REHDER AND WILSON

4. Upright shrub, to 4m, with warty bts and conspicuous pale green winter buds. Lv roundish-ovate, to 10cm long and 7cm across; dark green and glabrous above, glaucescent and pubescent below. Fl in dense catkin-like racemes, up to 7cm long; greenish yellow, fragrant. Fl 3. Arguably the most attractive sp with its long, catkin-like racemes and its great freedom of flowering, while the green buds make the plant interesting during the winter. Native to Szechuan. Introduced by Wilson in 1909.

CORYLUS   LINNAEUS   *Corylaceae*

A small genus of some fifteen species of deciduous shrubs or trees distributed throughout the north temperate zone. The leaves are alternate, usually ovate and toothed. The plants are monoecious, the male flowers being in long catkins, without petals, but with conspicuous anthers, and the female flowers very small and enclosed in green scales from which only the crimson stigmas emerge. Both male and female flowers emerge in early spring before the leaves. The fruit is a nut, enclosed in a leafy involucre usually known as the husk. Most species produce numerous sucker growths from the roots, which can be detached and used for propagation, but which should always be removed. Plants can also be propagated by layers and by seed. The plants do excellently on chalky soils.

Corylus avellana   LINNAEUS   Hazel Nut

4. Deciduous shrub, to 6m, which can be trained as a small tree, but is naturally thicket-forming with numerous sucker growths. Lv roundish, to 10cm long and 7cm across, sometimes lobed in the upper part (notably in the cv 'Heterophylla'), and toothed in the lower part. Dark green and slightly downy above and below. Male catkins to 6cm long, the nut is about 2cm long, in a husk, with a lobed end, about the same length as the nut. The lv usually turn yellow before falling, but are not outstandingly showy. Fl 2–3. A number of cvs exist, of which the most extraordinary is 'Contorta' in which all the growths are curled like a corkscrew. There are also yellow and purple leaved cv and a pendulous form. Distributed throughout Europe, also in N Africa and the near East.

Corylus colurna   LINNAEUS

4.7. A tree, to 20m in the UK but up to 30m elsewhere, with pale scaling bark on the trunk and furrowed on the brs. Bts yellowish, downy. Lv ovate, shallowly lobed, to 15cm long and 11cm across, dark green and slightly downy. Male catkins to 7cm long. Nuts to 1·5cm across set in a husk to 3cm across, with long narrow lobes up to 2·5cm long. The nuts in clusters. Unusual in its tree-like habit, but it is necessary to remove all sucker growths and the lower brs to get a tree-like specimen. Closely allied spp are *C. chinensis* FRANCHET and *C. jacquemontii* DECAISNE. *C. colurna* itself is native to SE Europe and western Asia, most notably Turkey, where it is grown commercially. Introduced about 1582.

Corylus maxima MILLER   Filbert

4. Shrub or small tree, to 7m, very similar to *C. avellana* but larger in all its parts. Lv more or less orbicular, mucronate, toothed, to 12cm long and 10cm wide. Male catkins to 7 cm long. Nut to 3cm long, with the husk considerably longer to 5 or 6cm, cut into numerous narrow lobes. The cv 'Purpurea' has the lv so dark a purple as to appear almost black and the catkins are also purple. Fl 2–3. Native of southern Europe. Introduced in 1759.

Corylus tibetica BATALIN

4.(7). A tree, to 7m in the wild but occasionally twice that in cultivation, with dark brown, glabrous bts. Lv broadly ovate to 12cm long and 7cm across, apex mucronate, slightly hairy on both surfaces, toothed, on a hairy petiole to 2·5cm long. Male catkins to 7cm long. Nuts in clusters of 3–6, the husks covered with slender spines, so that the cluster resembles a sweet chestnut burr. Native to China and Tibet. Introduced to Vilmorin (by Père Farges?) in 1898 and subsequently by Wilson in 1901.

COTINUS ADANSON *Anacardiaceae*

A small genus of only two species of deciduous shrubs; one European the other American, one with perfect flowers, the other dioecious. The leaves are alternate, entire, oval or orbicular. The flowers are in panicles with numerous sterile flowers later developing thread-like, feathery elongations, which make the fruits of *C. coggygria* very attractive. Formerly included in *Rhus*, from which it can be distinguished by its simple leaves and characteristic inflorescence. Propagated by seed and by cuttings.

Cotinus coggygria SCOPOLI

Smoke Tree, Wig Tree

4.5.6. (*Rhus cotinus* LINNAEUS) Rounded deciduous shrub, to 5m but often wider than high. Lv glabrous, orbicular, to 7cm diameter, on a petiole about half as long. Fl in terminal panicles, which are large, to 20cm long and wide, but which contain comparatively few fertile fl, the barren pedicels being elongated into long

threads, which are pinkish at first and later smoky-grey, when the silky hairs elongate. In the autumn the lv usually turn various shades of orange and red. Fl 6–7. There are purple-leaved cv such as 'Royal Purple'. In the strain known as **2.** 'Foliis Purpureis' the lv are purple as they unfurl and later turn green, while in the cv known as 'Purpureus' the lv are green, but the inflorescence is purple. The nomenclature of the various forms is somewhat confusing. The plant does excellently on chalky soils and seems to do best in rather poor conditions. Native of S. Europe, extending eastwards to the Himalaya and China.

Cotinus obovatus RAFINESQUE

2.6. Much better known as *C. americanus* NUTTALL (*Rhus cotinoides* NUTTALL). Deciduous, dioecious shrub to 5m in cultivation, up to 10m in the wild. Bts and young lv pinkish-bronze. Lv spatulate, downy beneath at first, to 12cm long, 6cm across, usually colouring very brilliantly, scarlet and orange in the autumn. Fl in a pyramidal terminal panicle to 30cm long, 21cm across, with numerous thread-like sterile pedicels, which are pale purple and by no means as attractive or conspicuous as those of *C. coggygria*. Fl 6–7. Requires acid soil and rather poor conditions. A rare native of some of the southern states of the USA. Introduced in 1882.

COTONEASTER MEDICUS[1] *Rosaceae*

A genus of deciduous or evergreen shrubs, occasionally small trees, distributed throughout Europe, N Africa and N Asia, but lacking in Japan. About 50 species are generally recognised, but owing to the plants' ability to form fertile seeds without pollination (apomixis) a number of microspecies can be determined, but these need not deter the gardener and are not discussed here. The general characteristics of the genus are alternate leaves, entire; solitary flowers or in corymbs, usually on short lateral branches, with white or pink petals, five in number. The fruit is a small pome. Although a few species have attractive flowers, the majority are grown for the sake of their brilliant fruits, and where there is a large bird population, these may prove unsatisfactory subjects. On the other hand they will thrive in any well-drained soil, be it acid or alkaline, and they grow rapidly. They are propagated by means of cuttings of half-ripe wood or by seed, which may take two years to germinate. The genus has been divided into two sections: *Chaenopetalum* KOEHNE, in which the flowers have spreading petals, and *Cotoneaster* (*Orthopetalum* KOEHNE) in which the petals are upright, often small and tinged with red.

1 There would appear to be some doubt as to who first published the generic name. Most authorities agree on MEDICUS, but Rehder gives BALTHASAR EHRHART as the authority and Wills gives RUPP. For naming purposes some older botanists treated the genus as feminine, thus altering the ending of specific names.

Cotoneaster acutifolius TURCZANINOW
Cotoneaster

6. Represented in gardens by the var *villosulus* REHDER AND WILSON. Vigorous deciduous shrub, to 4m, with spreading, slightly pendulous brs. Bts clothed with yellowish tomentum. Lv ovate-lanceolate to 10cm long and 5cm across, dull green above, hairy beneath. Fl in few-flowered corymbs, pinkish-white. Fl 5–6. Fr pyriform, woolly at first, later black. The lv often colour well in the autumn. Native of western China. Introduced by Wilson in 1900.

Cotoneaster amoenus WILSON *Cotoneaster*

4.6. Evergreen shrub of spreading habit, to 2m, bts with grey tomentum. Lv ovate-elliptic, to 2cm long 1cm across, glossy green above, with grey tomentum below. Fl white, in corymbs of 6–10, fr bright red, 6mm long. Native of Yunnan and among the first plants to be sent back by Wilson in 1899.

Cotoneaster apiculatus REHDER AND WILSON
Cotoneaster

6. Deciduous spreading shrub, to 2m, with brs arranged in a herring-bone fashion. Bts yellow-tomentose. Lv nearly orbicular, to 1cm in diameter. Fl solitary, white or pink, fr red. Closely allied to *C. horizontalis*. Native of Szechuan. Introduced by Wilson in 1910.

Cotoneaster bullatus BOIS *Cotoneaster*

5.6. Deciduous shrub, to 2m or more, with upright brs, which are comparatively few in number. Lv practically sessile, ovate-oblong, to 9cm long, half as wide, dark green and quilted (bullate) above, pale and slightly tomentose below. Fl in 10–30 flowered corymbs, each corymb to 5cm across, only a few fl opening at any one time and the pink petals soon falling. Fl 6. The lv often turn orange and scarlet before falling. Fr shining, sealing-wax red, each pome pyriform and about 8mm wide. Native of western China and Tibet. Introduced to Vilmorin about 1898.

Cotoneaster conspicuus MARQUAND
Chaenopetalum

4.5. Semi-evergreen shrub, to 3m high or else of low spreading habit, very suitable to be trained to trail down walls or banks. Lv narrow-obovate, to 1cm long and 6mm across, dull green above, grey-tomentose below. Fl solitary, white with purple anthers, up to 1·2cm across and densely scattered over the brs. Fr, scarlet, globose 1cm across. Fl 5. The fl are among the largest in the genus and the plant is highly attractive both in fl and fr. The fr have the advantage of not being particularly attractive to birds. Some authorities refer to the spreading form as var *decorus*

RUSSELL. Native of SE Tibet. First introduced by Kingdon Ward in 1925.

Cotoneaster dielsianus PRITZ *Cotoneaster*

5.6. (*C. applanatus* DUTHIE) Deciduous shrub, to 2m, with long, slender arching brs and the lateral brs arranged in a herring-bone fashion. Bts very downy. Lv ovate to 3cm long, 2·5 across, dark green and slightly hairy above, brown tomentose below. Fl in clusters of up to 7, pinkish, but soon falling. Fr scarlet, round, 7mm in diameter. The lv usually colour well before falling.

The var *elegans* REHDER AND WILSON, is characterised by narrower and smaller lv, which persist for longer and finally become glabrous and shining, and by the orange-red fr. Both the type and its var make extremely elegant and showy shrubs in September and October, when the arching brs are covered with the red fr. Native of Central China. Introduced by Wilson in 1900, who also introduced the var *elegans* from Szechuan in 1908.

Cotoneaster distichus LANGE *Cotoneaster*

5. (*C. rotundifolius* WALLICH?) Semi-evergreen shrub, to 2·5m, with stiff brs, often arranged in herring-bone fashion. Lv nearly orbicular, mucronate, to 1·2cm long and wide, shining green above. Fl solitary or in pairs, pinkish-white. Fr bright scarlet, top-shaped, 12mm long. An excellent fruiting shrub, the more so as the birds do not seem to attack the fr for some time. Native of the Himalaya. Introduced through Wallich in 1825.

Cotoneaster divaricatus REHDER AND WILSON
Cotoneaster

5.6. Deciduous shrub, to 2m, with greyish-hairy bts. Lv oval-elliptic, to 2·5cm long and 1·5cm across, dark glossy green above, paler and slightly hairy below, often colouring orange in the autumn. Fl in clusters of 3 and singly, deep pink. Fr red, ovoid, 8mm long. A good plant for autumn foliage and fr and useful for hedging. Native of western China. Introduced by Wilson in 1904.

Cotoneaster foveolatus REHDER AND WILSON
Cotoneaster

5.6. Deciduous shrub, to 4m, with yellowish-tomentose bts, later becoming grey. Lv ovate-elliptic, to 10cm long and 4·5cm across, dull green and glabrous above, slightly bullate, paler and sparsely hairy below, turning bright scarlet and orange before falling. Fl in 3–7-flowered corymbs, white with pink flush. Fr roundish red at first, finally black.

4. *C. moupinensis* FRANCHET is closely allied, but distinguished by its corymbs, which

Cotoneaster conspicuus

carry up to 18 fl, and its more bullate lv, which are very strongly veined beneath.

Native of Hupeh, China. Introduced by Wilson in 1908. *C. moupinensis* was introduced to France in 1900.

Cotoneaster franchetii BOIS *Cotoneaster*

5. Evergreen shrub, with tan pubescent bts and a gracefully arching habit. Lv elliptic, to 3cm long and 1·5cm across, hairy on both surfaces at first, later shining green above, pale brown tomentose below. Fl in corymbs of 5 to 15 fl, white flushed pink. Fr orange-scarlet oblong, covered with greyish tomentum, to 8mm long. Preferable to the type is **5.6.** var *sternianus* TURRILL, which is often catalogued as *C. wardii*, a sp which is rare in cultivation. The var has orange-red fr which are round rather than oblong, and which lack the tomentum which detracts from the beauty of the fr in the type. In addition the older lv turn orange at the time the fr are ripe. Native of Tibet and western China. Introduced by Père Soulié about 1894; var *sternianus* introduced from Burma by Cox and Farrer in 1919.

Cotoneaster frigidus WALLICH *Chaenopetalum*

4.5. Large shrub, to 6m or small tree to 13m, bts slightly downy at first. Lv narrowly oval, to 12cm long and 5cm across, dull green and glabrous above, woolly beneath at first, later nearly glabrous. Fl in flat corymbs, to 10cm or more across, each fl about 8mm across, white. Fr bright red, about the size of a pea, produced in great profusion. One of the best of fruiting trees, but possibly surpassed by some of its hybrids. The form *fructu-luteo* has pale yellow or white fr. Native of the Himalaya. Introduced through Wallich in 1824.

It has hybridised with various other members of the section, most notably *salicifolius* and *henryanus*, to give rise to such plants as 'Cornubia', with lv to 12cm long; 'Exburiensis', an evergreen plant with pale yellow fr; 'St Monica', a semi-evergreen with lv colouring before they fall; and 'John Waterer', a semi-evergreen shrub with elliptic lv and scarlet fr. All these hybrids are very prolific with their ornamental fr and all show great vigour.

Cotoneaster glaucophyllus FRANCHET *Chaenopetalum*

4.5. The type, which is a deciduous shrub, is not in cultivation, but is represented by two evergreen var, of which the most frequently seen is f *serotinus* (HUTCHINSON) STAPF (*C. serotinus* HUTCHINSON). This makes a spreading shrub, to 10m, bts, petioles and peduncles, white tomentose. Lv oval-elliptic, dark green above, paler below and eventually glabrous, to 7cm long and

3·5cm across. Fl in corymbs to 7cm across, white with reddish anthers. Fl 7–8. Fr bright red, ovoid, 6mm across. Fr 11–3. Useful for its late flowering and the length of time the fr persist on the shrub.

Var *vestitus* W. W. SMITH has lv to 6cm long, which are densely downy beneath. Fl 7. Fr 12–3. The type and its var are all native to China. *F. serotinus* was introduced by Forrest from Yunnan in 1907. Var *vestitus*, also from Yunnan, arrived in 1912.

Cotoneaster harrovianus WILSON *Chaenopetalum*

4.5. Spreading evergreen shrub, to 2m high and through, bts slightly downy at first. Lv obovate, mucronate, dark green above, slightly downy at first, later glabrous, pale-yellow tomentose below; to 6cm long and 2·5cm across. Fl in axillary and terminal corymbs, to 3·5cm across, white. Fl 6–7. Fr red, not fully coloured before November. Native of Yunnan and sent back by Wilson with *C. amoenus* in 1899.

Cotoneaster hebephyllus DIELS *Chaenopetalum*

4.5. Deciduous shrub, to 3m or small tree to 4m, with slender brs. Bts downy at first, later glabrous and purplish. Lv orbicular, mucronate, to 3cm long and wide, glabrous and dark green above, slightly downy below. Fl in clusters of from 3–12 fl, white with violet anthers. Fl 5. Fr ovoid, very dark red, to 8mm across. One of the most handsome sp for flowers. Native of eastern Himalaya and Yunnan. Introduced thence by Forrest in 1910.

Cotoneaster henryanus (SCHNEIDER) REHDER AND WILSON *Chaenopetalum*

4.5. (*C. rugosus* var *henryanus* SCHNEIDER). Loosely growing evergreen shrub, to 4m, with arching brs and pendulous bts, which are hairy at first. Lv oblong-lanceolate, to 11cm long and 4cm across, dark green above, with greyish tomentum below, which does not persist for more than a year. Fl white, in corymbs up to 7cm across, from short axillary twigs, anthers purple. Fl 6–7. Fr reddish-brown. The largest-leaved evergreen sp. Native of central China. Introduced by Wilson in 1901.

Cotoneaster horizontalis DECAISNE *Cotoneaster*

4.5.6. Deciduous shrub of usually prostrate habit, but up to 3m or more if growing against a wall. Brs arranged in a herring-bone (distichous) fashion. Bts densely brown, tomentose. Lv suborbicular, dark glossy green above, paler below, to 1·2cm long and very little less in width. Fl singly, or in pairs, pinkish, small. Fr round, bright red, 5mm across. The lv remain green until November, when they start to turn orange

71

and red, but the brs are usually not bare until January. An excellent shrub for north or east-facing walls or for training down banks. A white-variegated form exists.

The var *perpusillus* SCHNEIDER is character-ised by its very small lv not more than 7mm long. Native of China. The type was introduced by Père David in 1870; the var *perpusillus* by Wilson in 1908.

Cotoneaster integerrimus MEDICUS *Cotoneaster*

Deciduous shrub, to 2m, of rounded habit. Bts tomentose, grey. Lv broadly ovate, sometimes pointed at the apex, dull green above, grey-tomentose below; to 3·5cm long and 2cm across. Fl in small clusters of 2–4, white flushed pink. Fl 4–5. Fr dull red. Native of Europe and one locality in Wales. Not particularly ornamental.

Cotoneaster lacteus WILLIAM WRIGHT SMITH
Chaenopetalum

4.5. Evergreen shrub, to 4m. Bts tomentose, at first white, later pale yellow. Lv obovate, pointed, to 6cm long and 3cm across; dark green above, tomentose below, first white, later yellow-ish. Fl in corymbs, to 7cm across, milk-white. Fl 6–7. Useful for its late flowering. Fr ovoid, red, 4mm wide. Native of Yunnan. Introduced by Forrest in 1913.

Cotoneaster lindleyi STEUDEL *Chaenopetalum*

4. (*C. nummularius* of LINDLEY, not of FISCHER) Tall, deciduous shrub, to 4m, with long, arching brs. Bts grey-downy at first, later glabrous. Lv suborbicular, mucronate, to 6cm long and 4·5cm wide; dark green above, grey-tomentose below. Fl in corymbs of 5–12 fl, white. Fl 5–6. Fr black, round, 7mm across. The only sp in the section with black fr. Native to NW Himalaya. Introduced through Wallich in 1824.

Cotoneaster lucidus SCHLECHTENDAL
Cotoneaster

4.6. Deciduous shrub, to 3m, bts slightly hairy. Lv oval, to 5cm long and half as wide, shining green above, paler and slightly hairy below, usually colouring well in the autumn. Fl in clusters of 3–10, pinkish-white. Fl 5–6. Fr black. Native of Siberia and the Altai mountains. Introduced about 1840.

Cotoneaster microphyllus LINDLEY
Chaenopetalum

4.5. Evergreen shrub of generally prostrate habit, but occasionally reaching a height of 1m or much more if trained against a wall. Bts woolly, very rigid. Lv ovate, to 12mm long and 6mm across, dark, shining green above, grey-tomentose beneath. Fl usually solitary, 9mm across, white. Fr bright red, round, 7mm across.

Var *cochleatus* (FRANCHET) REHDER AND WILSON is more prostrate and compact, while var *thymifolius* (LINDLEY) KOEHNE (*C. thymi-folius* LINDLEY) is a very small-leaved, high montane form, suitable for rock gardens.

Native of the Himalaya, eastwards to China. Introduced through Wallich in 1824; var *thymi-folius* introduced by Joseph Hooker in 1852.

Cotoneaster multiflorus BUNGE *Chaenopetalum*

4.5. (*C. reflexus* CARRIÈRE) Deciduous shrub or small tree, to 4m, with pendulous and arching brs. Lv oval, to 6cm long and 3·5cm across, at first hairy, later glabrous, medium green above, paler below. Fl white, in many-flowered corymbs. Fl 5–6. A very attractive plant for its abundant fl. Fr roundish, red 8mm across. Var *calocarpus* REHDER AND WILSON is a Chinese form with longer, narrower lv and larger fr.

A plant with a very wide distribution from the Caucasus to China, with an outlying colony (var *granatensis* WENZIG) from the Sierra Nevada in Spain. First introduced from the Altai mountains in 1837, according to Bean and Rehder, but not mentioned by Loudon in 1840.

Cotoneaster nitens REHDER AND WILSON
Cotoneaster

6. Deciduous shrub, to 2m, with pale brown, tomentose bts. Lv dense, roundish, to 2cm long and 1·2cm across, tapered at both ends; dark glossy green above, slightly downy beneath at first, colouring well in the autumn. Fl in clusters of 3, pink. Fl 6. Fr egg-shaped, to 9mm long, black.

C. harrysmithii FLINCK AND HYLMO is very similar, of weaker growth, with indumentum on both surfaces of the lv, which are elliptic and not more than 1·5cm long.

Native of China. Introduced by Wilson from Szechuan in 1910; *C. harrysmithii* introduced by Dr Harry Smith in 1934.

Cotoneaster nitidifolius MARQUAND *Cotoneaster*

4.5. Deciduous spreading shrub with densely grey-hairy brs, later glabrous and brown. Lv elliptic to 6cm long and 2·5cm across, pale, glittering green on the upper surface, slightly tomentose below. Fl white in cymes of 4–9 fl. Fl 6. Fr top-shaped (turbinate) to 6mm long, dark crimson. Very distinct in its glittering lv. Native of Yunnan. Introduced by Forrest in 1924.

Cotoneaster obscurus REHDER AND WILSON
Cotoneaster

5. Spreading, deciduous shrub, to 3m, with pubescent bts. Lv ovate-elliptic, to 5cm long and half as wide, dull green above, brown-tomentose below. Fl pink, in cymes of 3–7 flowers. Fl 6. Fr pyriform, very dark red. Usually represented in gardens by the var *cornifolius* REHDER AND WILSON with lv of up to 7cm long and larger fr. Native of China. Introduced from Szechuan in 1910 by Wilson.

Cotoneaster pannosus FRANCHET *Chaenopetalum*

4.5. Evergreen shrub, to 3m or more, with slender, arching brs. Bts white-tomentose. Lv elliptic, to 2·5cm long and half as wide, dull green and glabrous above, white-tomentose below. Fl in corymbs of 15–20, white. Fl 6. Fr globose, 6mm in diameter, dull red. Very similar in appearance to *C. franchetii* (qv), but with smaller lv, which are glabrous above, smaller fr, and white, not pink, fl. Native of China. Introduced by the Abbé Delavay to France in 1888.

Cotoneaster racemiflorus (DESFONTAINES) K. KOCH *Chaenopetalum*

4.5. (*Mespilus racemiflora* DESFONTAINES) This plant has a very wide ranging habitat from north Africa and western Asia to China and Tibet, and numerous slight variants have been given varietal or specific names.

Deciduous shrub, to 3m but usually less, with grey-tomentose bts. Lv obovate, to 3cm long, dark green above and eventually glabrous, grey-tomentose below. Fl in clusters of 4–12, white. Fl 5–6. Fr round, scarlet, about 8mm across. Var *microcarpa* REHDER AND WILSON has smaller lv and fr; var *veitchii* REHDER AND WILSON has elliptic lv, larger fl (to 1·5cm across) and larger fr (to 1·2cm in diameter). The type was in cultivation in Paris in 1829; var *microcarpa* was introduced by Wilson in 1910 and var *veitchii* in 1900.

Cotoneaster salicifolius FRANCHET *Chaenopetalum*

4.5. Spreading, evergreen shrub, to 5 or 6m. Bts white-tomentose. Lv oval-lanceolate, to 8cm long and 2cm across, somewhat wrinkled above and glabrous, white-tomentose beneath. Fl in corymbs of up to 5cm across, dirty white. Fl 6. Fr small, 5mm across bright red and very freely produced. The type is comparatively rarely seen but in cultivation are var *floccosus* REHDER AND WILSON, with lv to 6cm long and 2cm across, and corymbs only about 2·5cm across. Fr very bright red; and var *rugosus* (PRITZ) REHDER AND WILSON (*C. rugosus* PRITZ), with larger lv (to 7cm long and 3cm across) and larger fr. 'Fructu-luteo' has yellow fr. Native of western China. Wilson introduced var *rugosus* in 1907 and var *floccosus* the following year.

Cotoneaster simonsii BAKER *Cotoneaster*

5.6. Deciduous or semi-evergreen, erect shrub to 3 or 4m. Bts brown-tomentose. Lv ovate-elliptic, to 2·5cm long and 1·5cm across, dark green and eventually glabrous above, pubescent below. Fl in clusters of 2–4, white. Fl 6–7. Fr scarlet, ovoid, to 1cm long. The lv often colour fairly effectively. The plant is often used for hedging. Native of the Khasia Hills in Assam and, presumably, collected by the free-lance collector Mr Simons. Date of introduction not known, but he was active in the later 1850s and early '60s and the plant is known to have been in cultivation in 1869.

Cotoneaster turbinatus CRAIB *Chaenopetalum*

4.5. Vigorous evergreen shrub, to 4m, with grey-tomentose bts. Lv elliptic, to 6cm long and 2·5cm across, dull green above, white-tomentose below. Fl in rounded corymbs to 6cm across, white with pink anthers. Fl 7–8. Fr top-shaped (turbinate), deep red and rather downy, 7mm long. Notable for its very late flowering. The downy fr is coloured in October. Native of western China. Introduced to Vilmorin by one of the French missionaries in 1897.

Cotoneaster zabelii SCHNEIDER *Cotoneaster*

5. Deciduous shrub, to 3m, bts grey-hairy. Lv ovate, to 3·5cm long and 1·2cm across, dull green and slightly hairy above, yellowish-tomentose below. Fl in clusters of 4–10, pink. Fl 5. Fr globular, red-purple to 8mm long. A shrub of graceful habit with arching brs, but not otherwise particularly distinguished. Native of western China. Introduced from Hupeh by Wilson in 1907.

CRATAEGUS LINNAEUS *Rosaceae*

A large genus of deciduous, or rarely semi-evergreen shrubs and trees, distributed throughout the north temperate zone but with a preponderance of species in N America. At one time over 1,000 species were described, many differing from each other only in the most minute details, and the number has now been considerably reduced. Even so, many botanists would recognise a hundred species from N America to this day, although the number in cultivation is considerably less. Normally the plants are armed with spines, but occasionally these are lacking. They all have alternate leaves which in Old World species are more or less deeply lobed, while those from America tend to be ovate and toothed at the margin. The leaves are petioled and usually have stipules at their base. The flowers are usually in flattish corymbs, rarely solitary, white, with the exception of some cultivars of *C. oxyacantha*. The fruit is a berry-like pome, referred to as a haw. They are very useful garden trees and shrubs with attractive flowers and fruit and often the leaves colour brilliantly before they fall. They appear to thrive in any soil that is not water-logged and, for the most part, are hardy anywhere in the UK. Large plants do not move very easily, but small plants do and generally grow away very rapidly, so that it is much the best to start with small plants.

Propagation is best by seed, although this may take two years (occasionally three) to germinate. There is also some trouble with seeds from cultivated plants, in that the various species hybridise easily, and there is always a risk that seed from cultivated plants may not produce the true species. Failing seed, the plants are usually propagated by grafting on to stocks of *C. monogyna*, although this is not usually as satisfactory. The genus has been divided into some twenty-nine series, but these are not used here.

Crataegus altaica LANGE

4.5. (*C. korolkowii* LOUIS HENRY) Small tree, to 8m, with reddish bts and practically unarmed. Lv basically ovate, but very deeply 3 or 5-lobed, to 10cm long and wide. Fl in compound cymes to 7cm across, white with yellow anthers. Fl 5–6. Fr yellow. Fr 8–9. The handsome yellow fruit does not persist long on the tree. *C. wattiana* HEMSLEY AND LACE is very similar, with slightly less deeply-lobed lv, and the fr is orange rather than yellow. Both spp are native to central Asia from the Altai to Baluchistan and Turkestan. Probably introduced through Dr Regel, *C. altaica* arriving in 1876 and *C. wattiana* in 1888.

Loudon mentions a *C. purpurea* var *altaica*, for which he gives *C. altaica* LEDEBOUR as a synonym. This had blackish fr, but would seem to have preceded Lange's name which may, therefore, need to be changed. It may be the plant now known as *C. dsungarica*.

Crataegus azarolus LINNAEUS

4.5. Tree, to 10m but usually less, slightly spiny. Bts finely downy. Lv deeply 3 or 5-lobed, to 7cm long and wide, bright green above, downy below. Fl large for the genus, up to 1·3cm across in heads up to 7cm across, white with purple anthers. Fl 6. Fr also large, to 2·5cm in diameter, edible, white, yellow, orange or red.

The form most usually seen is var *sinaica* (BOISSIER) LANGE (*C. sinaica* BOISSIER), which is characterised by the lv being quite glabrous and the fr yellow or orange. Native of the Mediterranean basin and the near East. In cultivation since the seventeenth century; var *sinaica* introduced in 1822 as *C. maroccana* PERSOON.

Crataegus chlorosarca MAXIMOWICZ

4.5.(6). Small, pyramidal, unarmed tree, to 8m. Bts slightly hairy at first, later deep purple. Lv to 5cm long and wide, shallowly 7–9-lobed, hairy on both surfaces at first, the upper later becoming glabrous. Fl 1·2cm wide, white, with

20 stamens and 5 styles, in corymbs to 5cm across. Fl 5. Fr purple-black. Closely allied is *C. dsungarica* ZABEL (*C. purpurea* BOSC?), which is spiny, lv to 8cm long and wide, 3–7-lobed. Fl white, 1·5cm across, 20 stamens, 3–5 styles. Fl 5. Fr purple-black. Thought to be a natural hybrid of *C. altaica* with *C. songorica* K. KOCH, which is barely distinguishable except in its hairy, not glabrous, flower stalks and the fl having only 2–3 styles.

C. chlorosarca is native to Manchuria and Japan and was in cultivation in 1880. *C. dsungarica* is native to Russian central Asia and, if it is synonymous with *C. purpurea* BOSC, was introduced in 1822. As *C. dsungarica* it was in cultivation in 1885.

Crataegus coccinioides ASHE

4.5. (*C. speciosa* SARGENT) Round-headed tree, to 8m or large shrub, with stout thorns to 5cm long, which are purplish in colour. Lv broadly ovate, toothed and shallowly lobed, tinged reddish when unfurling, to 6cm long and broad. Fl in clusters of 4–7, 2cm across, white with red anthers, 20 stamens and 5 styles. Fl 5. Fr roundish, 1·5cm wide, falling rather rapidly. Fr 10. On some soils the lv colour brilliantly in the autumn. Native of the Mississippi basin. Introduced in 1883.

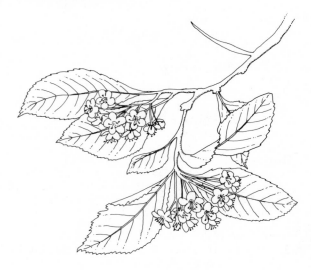

Crataegus crus-galli

Crataegus crus-galli LINNAEUS Cockspur Thorn

4.5.6. Tree, to 12m, with horizontal brs and a flat top, with thorns up to 7cm long at first, but increasing in length and branching. Lv obovate, toothed only in the upper half, to 10cm long and 3cm across, glabrous and dark green, turning scarlet in autumn. Fl in corymbs to 7cm across, each fl white, to 1·6cm across with ten pink-anthered stamens. Fl 6. Fr globose, red,

74

1·2cm across hanging for a long time. One of the best thorns for the garden. Native of eastern N America. Introduced, probably by John Banister, in 1691.

C. persistens SARGENT, is very close to *C. crus-galli*, but has 20 stamens and the lv remain green until November and do not colour. Possibly of hybrid origin.

Crataegus dahurica KOEHNE

4.5. Small, unarmed tree, to 7m, with dark purple bts. Lv ovate, toothed, but barely lobed, to 5cm long and 3cm across, nearly glabrous. Fl in dense corymbs to 7cm across, each fl white, 1·5cm wide, with 20 purple-anthered stamens and usually 3 styles. Fl 4–5. Fr globose 8mm wide, orange-red. With brilliant fruit and coming into leaf very early in the year, it is unsuitable for known frost-pockets. Native of SE Siberia. In cultivation in 1895, probably via St Petersburg.

Crataegus douglasii LINDLEY

4. Tree, to 10m or more, often unarmed but sometimes with thorns to 2cm long. Lv obovate, tapered at the base, double-toothed in the upper half, sometimes lobed at the base, to 10cm long and 7cm across. Fl in corymbs 5cm across, each fl 1·2cm across, white with 20 stamens and 2 styles. Fl 5. Fr black, soon falling. Native of central and western N America. Introduced by Douglas in 1828.

Crataegus durobrivensis SARGENT

4.5. Shrub, to 6m, with glabrous bts and thorns to 5cm long. Lv broadly ovate, sharply toothed in the upper part, some of the dentations being almost lobular, to 7cm long and 6cm wide. Fl in compact clusters, each fl as much as 2·5cm across, white, with 20 pink-anthered stamens and 5 styles. Fl 6. Fr round, brilliant crimson 1·6cm across. Notable for its large fl and fr; the latter not falling before January. Apparently confined to the banks of the Genesee river at Rochester, New York and, incredibly, not noticed before 1900 and introduced to cultivation the following year.

Crataegus flabellata (SPACH) K. KOCH

4.5. Tree, to 7m, with glabrous bts. The brs have slightly curved thorns to 10cm long. Lv fan-shaped (flabellate), to 7cm long and wide, downy when young, later glabrous, sharply toothed at the top of the fan. Fl in small corymbs, each fl to 2cm across, with 5–10 stamens (20 in var *grayana* (EGGLESTON) PALMER), with 3–5 styles. Fl 5. Fr rounded or ellipsoid, to 1·3cm across. Closely related and differing only in minor particulars is *C. macrosperma* ASHE, sometimes met with under the synonym of *C. coccinea indentata*. Notable for

its elegant lv. Native of eastern N America, mainly Canada. Introduced in 1823 according to Sweet.

Crataegus flava AITON

5.6. Tree, to 7m, with thin spines to 3·5cm long. Lv obovate or rhombic, finely toothed, slightly hairy at first, glossy green eventually, to 6cm long, and 3cm across. Fl white, with 10–20 purple-anthered stamens and 3–5 styles, about 2cm across in clusters of 3–7. Fl 5–6. Fr yellowish-orange, pyriform, about 1·5cm long. Neither fl nor fr particularly showy. Native of eastern North America. Introduced by Mark Catesby in 1724.

Crataegus intricata LANGE

4.5. (*C. coccinea* LINNAEUS in part. He also gave this name to *C. pedicellata*) A shrub, to 4m, with spreading or upright brs with slender spines to 3·5cm long. Lv ovate, to 5·5cm long and half as wide. Fl in clusters of 3–7, to 1·5cm across, 10 stamens with yellow or pink anthers and 3–5 styles. Fl 5–6. Fr reddish brown. Native to eastern N America. Introduced in 1730 according to Rehder, but no *crataegus* is recorded as introduced in that year in Aiton, Sweet or Loudon.

Crataegus jackii SARGENT

4.5. Shrub or small tree, to 3m. Lv oval, toothed, to 3·5cm long and half as wide, occasionally colouring well in the autumn. Fl in clusters to 5cm across, each fl to 1·5cm across with 5–10 stamens with yellow anthers. Fl 5–6. Fr red, ovoid, to 1·3cm long. Native of Quebec province.

Crataegus jonesiae SARGENT

4.5. Tree, to 7m. Bts downy at first, later orange-brown and glabrous. Thorns to 7cm long. Lv broadly ovate, to 10cm long and half as wide, toothed in the upper half. Sometimes colouring well in the autumn. Fl up to 2·5cm across in corymbs of 7–10, white, with 10 pink-anthered stamens and 2–3 styles. Fr large, bright red, to 1·5cm long. A showy and attractive sp. Native to Canada and New England.

Crataegus laciniata BERNARDINO DA UCRIA

4.5. (*C. orientalis* BIEBERSTEIN) Much better known under the synonym. Tree, to 7m, practically unarmed, bts often pendulous, grey-hairy. Lv basically triangular or rhombic, to 5cm long and broad, deeply cut into 5–9 narrow lobes, which are themselves toothed; dark green with greyish hairs above, grey-tomentose below. Fl in corymbs of 12 or more fl, each fl up to 2cm across, white, with purple anthers and 2–4 styles. Fl 6. An extremely elegant, small tree with attractive fl and fr as well as the greyish foliage. Native to SE Europe and western Asia. Introduced in 1810.

Crataegus X lavallei HERINCQ

4.5. (*C. X carrierei* VAUVEL) A hybrid, thought to be between *C. crus-galli* and *C. stipulacea* LOUDON (*C. mexicana* DE CANDOLLE). The cv in cultivation is known as 'Carrierei'. Semi-evergreen tree, to 7m, with downy bts. Thorns infrequent, but up to 3·5cm long. Lv elliptic-ovate, to 11cm long and 6cm across, coarsely toothed, persisting until December. Fl in erect corymbs, 7cm across, each fl 2·5cm wide, with 20 stamens and 1–3 styles. Fl 6. Fr pyriform, orange red with brown flecks, also long persisting. A similar hybrid is *C. X grignonensis* MOUILLEFERT. *C. X lavallei* was first described in 1880; *C. X grignonensis* in 1873. Both occurred in France.

Crataegus macracantha LOUDON

4.5.6. Shrub or small tree of up to 5m, with reddish-brown, glabrous bts and extremely large thorns, sometimes to 12cm long. Lv round-oval, to 10cm long and 7cm across, toothed, dark green, colouring red and orange in the autumn. Fl in corymbs to 7cm across, each fl 1·8cm across, white with 8–10 yellow-anthered stamens and 5 styles. Fl 6. Fr bright crimson, globose, to 1·2cm across. A handsome sp very distinct in its enormous thorns.

Native of the eastern USA. If it is the *C. glandulosa* of *Hortus Kewensis* it was introduced, probably by John Bartram, in 1750. As *C. macracantha,* it was obtained by the firm of Loddiges in 1819, either from Michaux or William Bartram.

Crataegus mollis (TORREY-GREY) SCHEELE

4.5.6. (Includes *C. arkansana* SARGENT) Tree, to 13m, with greyish-hairy bts, grey wood and thorns to 5cm long. Lv broad-ovate, deeply toothed, to 12cm long and nearly as broad, downy on both surfaces, petiole to 5cm long. Fl in corymbs to 7cm across, each fl up to 2·5cm across, with about 20 stamens and 4–5 styles. Fl on very downy pedicels. Fl 4–5. Fr large, round, red, to 2·5cm in diameter and falling by the end of September. Closely allied is *C. arnoldiana* SARGENT, a tree of up to 7m with densely zig-zag brs and thorns to 7cm long. Fl has only 10 stamens; fr ripe in August. *C. mollis* is native to most of the central USA. Introduced in 1683 (presumably as *C. coccinea*) according to Rehder. *C. arnoldiana* is confined to Massachusetts and Connecticut and was only introduced in 1901.

Crataegus monogyna JACQUIN   May, Hawthorn

4.5.(6). Shrub or tree, to 12m, with spreading brs and stout thorns to 2·5cm long. Lv basically oblong-ovate, but deeply 3–7-lobed, the lobing being generally more pronounced in established plants. Lv to 6cm long and 4cm across, glossy green and often colouring well in the autumn. Fl in corymbs to 7cm across, each fl about 1·5cm wide with 20 stamens and 1 style. Fl 5–6. Fr ellipsoid, dull crimson.

The cv 'Biflora', the Glastonbury Thorn, starts to produce young foliage again in November or December and may flower as early as mid-January, although usually later unless the winter is very mild. The type is the common hawthorn of so many hedgerows in Britain which make the countryside so enchanting in early summer. There are a number of cv with pendulous and fastigiate brs and with extra dissected lv.

Crataegus oxyacantha LINNAEUS

May, Hawthorn

4.5.(6). Only distinguishable from the last sp by having shallowly lobed lv, 2 styles (and 2 nutlets in each fr), and being generally somewhat smaller, not more than 7m high. Lv 3–5-lobed, to 5·5cm long and 3·5cm across. Although the two spp are so similar that one would have thought the last sp were best described as var *monogyna* JACQUIN of Linnaeus's *C. oxyacantha,* it is this sp which has sported considerably. Pink and red forms occur, as well as plants with double pink, red or white fl and a form with yellow fr. All are attractive trees. The double forms do not usually colour well in the autumn and, of course, do not bear fr, but the single pink and red forms can have good autumn colour.

Crataegus pedicellata SARGENT

4.5.6. (*C. coccinea* LINNAEUS, but see also under *C. intricata*) Tree, to 7m, with brs spreading and ascending slightly. Bts sparsely hairy at first, later glabrous. Spines to 5cm long. Lv broadly-ovate, to 10cm long and 7cm across, coarsely toothed. Fl in loose corymbs to 5cm across, each fl to 2cm across with ten pink-anthered stamens and 4–5 styles. Fl 5. Fr pyriform, ripe in September, scarlet, 2cm long.

The var *ellwangeriana* EGGLESTON (*C. ellwangeriana* SARGENT) has larger fl and fr, to 2·5cm across and long respectively, while the petioles and pedicels are slightly more hairy than in *C. pedicellata.* This is probably the best form to obtain. *C. holmesiana* ASHE has a rather fastigiate habit and reaches 10m, while the lv are slightly narrower, but these differences are hardly sufficient to give it specific identity. Native to eastern N America. Grown by Bishop Compton in 1683, which suggests an introduction by John Banister.

Crateagus phaenopyrum (LINNAEUS THE YOUNGER) MEDICUS Washington Thorn

4.5.6. (*C. cordata* AITON) Tree, to 10m, with a rounded head. Thorns, slender, to 7cm long, sometimes branched. Lv basically triangular, cordate at the base, sharply toothed, to 7cm long and 5·5cm across, shining green, colouring brilliantly in the autumn. Fl in corymbs to 7cm across, each fl small, to 1cm across, cream with 20 pink-anthered stamens and 2–5 styles. Fl 7. Fr sealing-wax scarlet, round, 7mm across, hanging until the spring. Notable for its very late flowering, the latest of all the thorns, as well as for its brilliant autumn display. Native of the south-eastern USA. Introduced, presumably by John Bartram, in 1738.

Crateagus pinnatifida BUNGE

4.5.(6). The form to obtain is the var *major* N. E. BROWN. Tree, to 8m, with a dense, rounded head. Spines short, but usually absent. Lv basically oblong, but pinnatifidly lobed, to 15cm long and wide, deep green with reddish veins and midrib at first, on a petiole up to 7cm long. Fl in corymbs to 7cm across, each fl white, 2cm across, with 20 pink-anthered stamens and 3–4 styles. Fl 5–6. Fr pendulous, ellipsoid, to 2.5cm long, red with minute dots. The lv turn purple rather late in the autumn. Very distinct in its very large lv and long petioles; a striking tree. The type is native to NE Asia and arrived, via Russia, in 1860. Var *major* comes from N China, where it is used as a fruit tree, and arrived in 1880, possibly sent by Bretschneider.

Crateagus prunifolia (LAMARCK) PERSOON

4.5.6. A tree of uncertain origin, as it does not appear to be truly wild in any situation. Widely spreading tree, to 7m, with sharp, stiff straight thorns to 7 cm long. Lv roundish-ovate to 8cm long and 6cm wide, turning brilliant crimson in the autumn. Fl in corymbs to 6cm across, creamy-white, 2cm across, with 10–15 pink-anthered stamens and 2–3 styles. Fl 6. Fr round, bright red, 1·5cm long, falling with the lv in October. Thought to be a possible hybrid between *C. crus-galli* and *C. macracantha*; a very ornamental tree. Native to North America. Introduced in 1812, according to Sweet, 1818 according to Loudon, but in cultivation in 1760.

Crateagus punctata JACQUIN

4.5. Tree, to 11m, with horizontal brs spreading considerably. Bts grey-hairy at first. Spines infrequent, but to 7cm long. Lv broadly ovate, sometimes mucronate, tapered at the base, to 10cm long and 7cm across. Fl in large corymbs to 10cm across, each fl to 2cm across, white with 20 stamens and 5 styles. Fl 6. Fr deep crimson,

speckled with brownish dots, falling in October. The form 'Aurea' has yellow fr and is probably the best yellow-fruited thorn available. Conspicuous for its abundant fl and fr. Native of eastern N America. Introduced by John Bartram in 1746.

Crateagus saligna GREENE

4.5. Tree, to 7m, with reddish, glabrous bts. Thorns to 2cm long. Lv oval, to 5cm long and half as wide, shining dark green. Fl small, in corymbs 4–5cm across, with 15–20 stamens and 3–5 styles; white, turning orange as they fade. Fl 5. Fr round, 7mm across, red at first, finally blue-black. Occasionally the lv colour well in the autumn. Native of Colorado. Introduced 1902.

Crateagus stipulacea LOUDON

4.5. (*C. pubescens stipulacea* STAPF, *C. mexicana* DE CANDOLLE Semi-evergreen tree, to 10m in the wild, but probably less in cultivation, sparingly armed with spines to 4cm long or quite unarmed. Bts tomentose at first. Lv more or less rhombic, to 10cm long, 5cm across, double-toothed in the upper half; dark green above, grey-downy below, persisting until January or sometimes later and occasionally colouring before they fall. Fl in corymbs to 7cm across, each fl to 2cm across, with 15–20 pink-anthered stamens and 2–3 styles. Fl 6. Fr greenish yellow or orange. *C. X lavallei* is a better garden plant. Native of the mountains of Mexico. Introduced by A. B. Lambert in 1824, but it is not known who sent the material to him.

Crateagus tanacetifolia (LAMARCK) PERSOON

3.4.5. Small tree, to 11m, with grey-tomentose bts, usually without thorns. Lv silvery as they unfurl, basically obovate but 5–7 pinnatifidly lobed, with grey-silver pubescence on both surfaces, to 5cm long and 3cm across. Fl large and fragrant in 6–8-flowered clusters, each fl to 2·5cm across, with 20 red-anthered stamens and 5 styles. Fl 6–7. Fr large, edible, orange, more or less round and downy to 2·5cm across, always with mossy bracts at the base, which serve to distinguish the sp from the similar *C. laciniata*. A very attractive small tree, but slow-growing.

Slightly more rapid in growth, but not otherwise very dissimilar, is its hybrid *C. X dippeliana* LANGE (*C. X leeana* (LOUDON) BEAN), with larger lv up to 7cm long, and smaller, red fr. Its other parent has never been satisfactorily established, although *C. punctata* has been suggested. It occurred spontaneously in the famous Vineyard nursery of Lee and Kennedy and first flowered in 1836. The sp is native to western Asia and was introduced in 1789.

Crateagus tomentosa LINNAEUS

3.4.5.6. (*C. calpodendron* (EHRHART) MEDICUS,

C. pyrifolia AITON) Small tree, to 5m, with very zig-zag brs and few thorns and practically invisible winter buds. Bts slightly downy. Lv reddish-bronze when unfurling, obovate, toothed in the upper half, to 12cm long and 7cm across, downy on both surfaces at first, later nearly glabrous below and quite so above. The lv colour very brilliantly in the autumn. Fl in rather lax corymbs to 12cm across, each fl about 1·5cm across, white with 16–20 pink-anthered stamens and 2–5 styles. Fl 6. Fr always held erect, oval or pyriform, orange-red. *C. succulenta* SCHRADER is barely distinct, but has glabrous bts, smaller lv and corymbs, is rather thorny and has fr which are red rather than orange-red.

According to Rehder, Linnaeus's *C. tomentosa* refers in part to *C. uniflora* and *C. calpodendron* would be the first correct name. Native of eastern N America. Introduced by Lee and Kennedy in 1765, but it is not known from whom they received it. *C. succulenta* is also native to eastern N America and was in cultivation before 1830.

Crataegus uniflora MOENCH

(*C. parvifolia* AITON) Shrub, to under 3m, with hairy bts. Spines to 3cm long. Lv obovate, tapered at the base, to 5cm long and half as wide, shining green above with a few hairs, slightly hairier below. Fl solitary or up to 3 in a cluster, cream, to 2cm across with 20 cream-anthered stamens and 3–5 styles. Fl 5–6. Fr pyriform, about 1·2cm long, greenish-yellow. An unusual, but not very showy sp. Native of eastern N America. Grown by Bishop Compton before 1704, so possibly a John Banister introduction.

Crataegus wilsonii REHDER

4.5. Tree or large shrub to 7m, with stout thorns to 2·5cm long, and sparsely hairy bts. Lv of two forms, those on vigorous new extension growths basically ovate but deeply 3 or 5-lobed; those on flowering growths and weak new growths basically ovate and toothed, to 10cm long and 6cm across, shining dark green above, sparsely hairy along the veins below. Fl in corymbs to 6cm across, each fl about 1cm across with 15–20 pink-anthered stamens and 2–3 styles. Fl 6. Fr shining red, about 1cm long, less across.

Interesting botanically as showing a link between the lobed-leaved European and Asiatic spp and the unlobed spp from N America, but also an attractive tree in its own right. Native of Hupeh, whence Wilson introduced it in 1907.

CRYPTOMERIA DAVID DON *Taxodiaceae*

A monotypic genus confined to Japan and China.

Cryptomeria japonica (LINNAEUS THE YOUNGER)
D. DON

7. (*Cupressus japonica* LINNAEUS THE YOUNGER)

An evergreen, pyramidal tree, to 60m in the wild but not more than 35m in cultivation and usually less. It is very variable, some forms have the juvenile foliage persisting into the adult stage and the form, known as 'Elegans', is so distinct from the adult form that it is hard to believe they belong to the same species. The typical form is a tree with reddish, peeling bark, needles awl-shaped, curving inwards, arranged spirally in 5 ranks, to 2cm long, bright green. Male fl in short terminal spikes, female fl globular, about 1·5cm in diameter, forming a cone of 20–30 scales, each scale holding 2–3 seeds. The cone ripens in the first year, but persists after the seeds have been shed. The plant does best in mild moist districts and requires a fairly deep soil. It seems to have no dislike of alkalinity as such, but is of no use on shallow chalky soils unless liberally dressed with humus.

There are a large number of eccentric forms. 'Elegans', mentioned above, has longer, softer needles which turn bronze during the winter, and is usually seen as a large shrub to 10m. 'Araucarioides' has long thin pendulous brs, densely set with rather wide, awl-shaped lv. 'Spiralis' is usually a rather dwarf form in which the lv are spirally twisted round the bts.

Originally obtained about 1840. Fortune collected it in quantity in Shanghai in 1844; Siebold had collected it about 1824 and sent it to Java, whence Thomas Lobb collected seeds in 1853. 'Elegans' was brought back from Japan by J. G. Veitch in 1861, but, so far as can be ascertained, no seeds of wild Japanese plants were collected until Charles Maries sent back seeds in 1879.

CUDRANIA TRÉC *Moraceae*

A small genus of five or six species of evergreen or deciduous trees or shrubs, usually armed with thorns and all dioecious. The leaves are alternate, the flowers are in axillary, globular heads, inconspicuous. Only the male plant is in cultivation in the UK. It is propagated by cuttings.

Cudrania tricuspidata (CARRIÈRE) LAVALLÉE

(*Maclura tricuspidata* CARRIÈRE) Deciduous shrub or small tree, to 7m, with a rounded head of thorny brs. Lv ovate or obovate, occasionally with 3 shallow lobes at the apex, to 10cm long, half as wide. Fl in pairs of round balls, 8mm across, from the axils of the current year's growth. Fl 7. Acid soil seems to be required. Native of China. Introduced in 1862.

CUNNINGHAMIA ROBERT BROWN *Pinaceae*

A small genus of two or three species from eastern Asia. It is an evergreen, with spreading branches and pendulous branchlets. The leaves

Cryptomeria japonica

Cryptomeria japonica

are densely and spirally arranged, but so twisted as to appear in two spreading, horizontal ranks. The leaves persist for some five years. It is propagated by seeds or by cuttings.

Cunninghamia lanceolata (LAMBERT) W. HOOKER

7. (*Pinus lanceolata* LAMBERT) Evergreen tree, to 30m in cultivation, but somewhat slow-growing. Bark brownish, scaling off yearly to reveal the reddish inner bark. Needles linear lanceolate, to 5cm long, pointed at the ends, dark bluish-green above, with 2 broad, white bands beneath. Male fl in cylindrical terminal clusters. The cones are nearly globular, about 3·5cm across. A handsome tree, doing best in rather mild districts, although never seriously damaged by winter cold and requiring plenty of moisture during the summer. Native of China. Introduced by William Kerr in 1804.

X CUPRESSOCYPARIS

M. L. GREEN *Cupressaceae*

The name of hybrids between *Cupressus* and *Chamaecyparis* of which only one is commonly grown.

X *Cupressocyparis leylandii* DALLIMORE

7. An evergreen columnar tree of very rapid growth, reaching to higher than 30m. It makes a tall, columnar specimen, similar in lv and general appearance to *Chamaecyparis nootkatensis,* which is the seed parent for most forms, while the pollen parent is *Capressus macrocarpa* (qv); the reverse cross has also been made. It does occasionally bear cones, which are only 2cm across with 5 seeds to each scale. The plant is unsurpassed for windbreaks or hedging, and is tolerant of chalky conditions and withstands sea spray. Its average increase is 60cm each year, but it is best planted as a young specimen. It is also, unlike *Cupressus macrocarpa,* completely hardy to low temperatures. A number of named clones are in existence, differing little from each other with the exception of 'Naylor's Blue' which has rather glaucous lv. Propagated by cuttings taken either in early spring or in late summer. The hybrid first occurred in 1888, although its hybrid origin was not realised before 1925.

CUPRESSUS LINNAEUS *Cupressaceae*

A small genus of twelve or more species of evergreen coniferous trees, or somewhat rarely, shrubs, with scale-like leaves very densely appressed to the stems, which are arranged in plume-like sprays. The plants are monoecious, the male flowers being composed of short-stalked stamens, while the female flowers are globular and eventually make quite a sizeable cone, composed of rounded scales with a boss in the centre and usually with a mucro at the top. Each scale contains numerous seeds, more than those in the related *Chamaecyparis*, and the cones are usually considerably larger than those of that genus. The foliage is generally somewhat aromatic. Most of the species in cultivation are on the borderline of hardiness and are liable to be more or less seriously damaged in severe winters. They usually make handsome, spire-like, columnar trees.

Cupressus bakeri JEPSON

7. Represented in commerce by the ssp *matthewsii* C. B. WOLF, which tends to be larger in all its parts than typical *C. bakeri.* Tree, to 20m, with reddish-brown bark, later turning grey. Lv dark grey-green, scale-like, bts arranged all round the shoot. Cones to 2cm across. Both the sp and the ssp are closely allied to *C. macnabiana* ANDREW MURRAY, which has been in cultivation longer, but appears to be rather short-lived. They all have a somewhat spreading habit, but also prove the hardiest among the genus. They are all native to California, although *C. bakeri* reaches as far as Oregon. Ssp *mathewsii* is confined to the Siskiyou mountains. *C. macnabiana* was introduced by Jeffery in 1854. *C. bakeri* was not in cultivation before 1917.

Cupressus glabra SUDWORTH

7. (*C. arizonica* of gardens, but probably not *C. arizonica* of GREENE) A dense, bushy tree to 25m, with a spreading crown. Bark reddish, smooth, and on young trees is shed in strips. Lv glaucous, grey-green. Cone 2·5cm across, composed of 6–8 scales. The form known as 'Pyramidalis' or 'Conica' makes a beautiful spire-like tree. Native of western Arizona. Probably introduced in 1882.

Cupressus macrocarpa GORDON
Monterey Cypress

7. (*C. lambertiana* GORDON) Tree, to 30m, with a narrow pyramidal habit when young, later becoming flat-topped with horizontal brs. Lv deep, rich green. Cones to 3·5cm long and 2·5cm across. 'Lutea' has attractive yellow lv. A very rapid-growing tree, but liable to be seriously damaged or killed in exceptionally severe winters. Native of California, where it is confined to only 2 coastal localities. Introduced by Hartweg in 1838.

Cupressus sempervirens LINNAEUS
Italian Cypress

7. Tree of up to 20m in the UK, although up to 50m in the Mediterranean regions. Lv very dark green. The form most usually seen makes a tall, spire-like tree with upright brs, but in the wild it tends to make a pyramidal tree with horizontal brs. Old trees seem reasonably hardy, but young ones are winter tender and should be placed in sheltered situations. Probably native to the eastern Mediterranean, but widespread in cultivation throughout the whole region.

CYDONIA MILLER *Rosaceae* Quince

Now a monotypic genus; the scarlet-flowered plants, formerly known as *Cydonia*, are now in *Chaenomeles*, while a Chinese plant, formerly known as *C. sinensis*, has been given a genus of its own – *Pseudocydonia*. Most forms can be propagated by detaching suckers, but they can also be propagated by cuttings.

Cydonia oblonga MILLER   Quince

4.(5).(6). (*Pyrus cydonia* LINNAEUS) Deciduous, suckering shrub or small tree, to 6m. Bts grey-tomentose. Lv ovate-elliptic, to 10cm long and 6cm across, dull green above, grey-tomentose below. Fl solitary, like a small, wild rose, pale pink or white, 5cm across. Fl 5. Fr pyriform, yellow, varying in size but in the form known as 'Lusitanica' it is up to 10cm long and 9cm across. Much used for preserves on the continent. The lv often turn a good clear yellow before falling. Probably native to SE Europe, but so long in cultivation for its fr that no very convincing wild populations are known.

CYTISUS LINNAEUS *Leguminosae*

A genus of mainly deciduous shrubs, with alternate leaves but these are not always present. When they are, they are usually either simple or trifoliate, but in many species they do not persist for long on adult plants, and most of the necessary photosynthesis is performed by the green branchlets. The genus is not easily separated from *Genista,* the most notable difference between the two genera being that the seed of *Cytisus* has a small wart-like appendage, close to where it is attached to the pod. This strophiole, as it is called, is lacking in the seeds of *Genista*. Many species of *Genista* are spiny, whereas *Cytisus* is unarmed. Both genera may have the flower in terminal racemes, but in *Cytisus* they are also often axillary, which they are not in *Genista*. Species with a more or less spiral style (of which *C. scoparius* is the best known) were put by Wimmer into a separate genus, *Sarothamnus,* but this is not generally accepted. By some the genus is divided into seven sections, but this is scarcely necessary.

The species are best propagated by seed, which usually germinates readily. Seedlings should be potted up separately as soon as possible and then put in their permanent positions, as they cannot usually be moved without risk of damaging the tap root and so killing the plant. Cultivars and hybrids must be propagated by cuttings of firm, young wood, which are usually ready about August. They are not long-lived plants, so are best renewed every five years or so. Many of the species tend to become leggy and are usually kept in shape by fairly severe pruning directly after the flowering is finished. There are probably about fifty species, mainly around the western Mediterranean but with some species in the Canaries, while others go as far north as the British Isles.

Cytisus albus LINK

The well-known *C. albus* LINK must now be known as *C. multiflorus* qv. The epithet *albus* was first used by Hacquet for a prostrate plant from the Balkans.

Cytisus battandieri MAIRE

3.4. Deciduous or semi-evergreen shrub, to 5m. Bts covered with silver down. Young lv beautifully silver. Lv trifoliate, on a petiole to 6cm long, each leaflet obovate to 9cm long and 3·5cm across, covered with silvery hairs on both surfaces. Fl in a cone-shaped, tightly-packed, raceme, with a fragrance of pineapple, about 12cm long. The individual pea-shaped florets are golden-yellow and about 1cm long. Fl 6. Pods, ripening rarely in the UK, erect to 5cm long. Unique in the genus for its very large lv. Hardy in most places, but best with some wall protection. Native of the middle Atlas Mountains of Morocco. Introduced in 1922.

Cytisus X dallimorei ROLFE

4. Shrub, to 3m, of erect habit, like that of the seed parent *C. scoparius*. Lv trifoliate, downy, small, soon falling. Fl about 1·5cm long, solitary or in pairs from the axils, rosy-pink with crimson wing petals. Fl 5–6. Raised in 1900 by pollinating *C. scoparius* 'Andreanus' by *C. multiflorus*. An attractive shrub in itself and a parent of many modern pink and red hybrids.

Cytisus grandiflorus (BROTERO) DE CANDOLLE

4. (*Spartium grandiflorum* BROTERO) Deciduous shrub, to 3m, scarcely distinguishable from *C. scoparius*. Bts silvery, villous. Lv simple or trifoliate, each leaflet to 1cm long. Fl from axils of year-old wood, solitary or in pairs, about 2·5cm long, 2cm across, bright yellow. Fl 5. Pods to 2·5cm long, covered in thick, grey wool. Distinct from *C. scoparius* in its woolly pods. Native of Spain and Portugal. Introduced in 1816.

Cytisus ingramii BLAKELOCK

4. Densely-branched, deciduous shrub, to 2m or slightly more. Bts hairy at first, later glabrous. Lv sessile, simple or trifoliate, leaflets elliptic-oblong, to 2·5cm long and 2cm across. Fl axillary, single, to 2·5cm long and 2cm across; the standard cream with a brown blotch, the wings and keel yellow. Fl 6. Pods hairy to 3cm long. May be damaged in very severe winters. Native of NW Spain. Discovered and introduced by Collingwood Ingram in 1936.

Cytisus multiflorus (AITON) SWEET   White Broom

4. (*C. albus* LINK *Spartium multiflorum* AITON) Deciduous shrub, to 3m or more, with very slender, but numerous arching brs. Bts downy. Lv trifoliate or simple, leaflets linear, not more than 1cm long, soon falling. Fl white, axillary, up to 3 from each axil, 9mm long. Fl 5. Pods 2·5cm long, hairy. Native of Spain and Portugal. In cultivation in 1752.

Cytisus nigricans LINNAEUS

4. Deciduous shrub, between 1–2m high, with downy bts. Lv trifoliate, on petioles to 2cm long; the leaflets obovate to 2·5cm long. Fl in erect, terminal racemes at the end of the current year's growth. The racemes can be 30cm long, each fl yellow, to 1cm long. Fl 7–8. Pod to 3cm long, hairy. Attractive with its long, late-flowering racemes, but often short-lived. It is good policy to remove the racemes after flowering to prevent excessive seed-setting, while pruning should be done in early spring. Native to central and SE Europe. Introduced in 1730.

Cytisus X praecox WHEELER

4. A hybrid between *C. purgans* (qv) and *C. multiflorus,* which was first observed about 1867. Plants from seed do not come true and it is best propagated by cuttings. Shrub, to 3m, with a dense mass of slender, arching brs. Bts silky. Lv generally simple, about 1cm long, soon falling. Fl axillary, produced in great profusion, sulphur yellow with a rather heavy scent. Fl 4–5.

Cytisus purgans (LINNAEUS) SPACH

4. (*Genista purgans* LINNAEUS) Rather dense, deciduous shrub, usually not more than 1m high and as wide or wider. Lv sessile, usually simple and soon falling, linear-obovate to 1cm long. Fl axillary, deep yellow, singly or in pairs, to 12mm long. Fl 4–5. Pod to 2·5cm long, hairy. Requires a very sunny position. Useful for its early flowering and rich golden colour. Native of central France and south to central Spain. In cultivation in 1750.

Cytisus ratisbonensis SCHAEFFER

4. Includes *C. elongatus* WALDSTEIN AND KITAIBEL Deciduous shrub, some forms erect to 2m, others procumbent and only 30cm high. Bts grey-hairy. Lv trifoliate, on petioles to 2cm long. Leaflets ovate, to 3cm long and 1cm across, glabrous above, silky beneath. Fl axillary, in pairs or in fours, to 2·5cm long, bright yellow with the standard sometimes dotted with red. Fl 5. Pod to 2·5cm long with a few hairs. Native of central Europe from Germany to western Russia and south to the Balkans. Introduced about 1800.

Cytisus scoparius (LINNAEUS) LINK   Broom

4. (*Spartium scoparium* LINNAEUS *Sarothamnus scoparius* (L) WIMMER) Deciduous shrub, to 2m, with slightly downy bts. Lv trifoliate and simple. The trifoliate lv with a short petiole, the simple lv usually sessile. Leaflets linear-obovate, to 1·5cm long, soon falling. Fl golden-yellow, axillary, single or in pairs, to 2·5cm long with the rounded standard 2cm across. Fl 5–6. Pod to 5cm long, hairy until it ripens.

A number of colour variants occur, of which the most notable is 'Andreanus', the bacon and eggs broom, where the wing petals are brownish-crimson. The true cv is best grafted on to laburnum, but seedlings may produce improved forms, as well as inferior ones. 'Sulphureus' has pale yellow fl. There is also a prostrate form. Native of western Europe including the UK.

Cytisus sessilifolius LINNAEUS

4. Deciduous, rather bushy shrub, to 2m. Lv trifoliate, sessile, or with a short petiole; leaflets obovate or roundish, acuminate, glabrous, to 2cm long, bright green. Fl in terminal racemes on side-shoots of the current year's growth, bright yellow, 12mm long. The racemes hold up to 12 blooms. Fl 6. Pod to 3cm long, glabrous. Native of southern Europe and N Africa. In cultivation since 1600.

Cytisus supinus LINNAEUS

4. (*C. capitatus* SCOPOLI) Shrub, to 1m or more, occasionally procumbent. Bts hairy. Lv trifoliolate on a petiole to 1cm long. Leaflets elliptic, or obovate, glabrous above, hairy beneath, to 2·5cm long. Fl in terminal umbels to 5cm across, each fl bright yellow, to 2·5cm long, from a very hairy, tubular calyx 1cm long. Fl 7–8. Pod, hairy to 3cm long. Useful for its late flowering, so pruning should be done in early spring. Native of central and southern Europe. Introduced in 1755.

DANAE MEDICUS *Liliaceae*

A monotypic genus, which lacks leaves but instead has leaf-like stems known as cladodes.

Danae racemosa (LINNAEUS) MOENCH
                              Alexandrian Laurel

5. (*Ruscus racemosus* LINNAEUS, *D. laurus* MEDICUS) Evergreen shrub, to 1m or slightly more, with one-branched erect or spreading woody stems. Cladodes alternate, ovate-lanceolate, acuminate, practically sessile, bright green, glabrous. Fl small, greenish-yellow, in terminal racemes of 4–6 fl. Fr a red globular berry, about 7mm across. Is tolerant of very shady positions, but not of prolonged drought. Propagated by seed or by division. Native of western Asia. Introduced in 1713.

DAPHNE LINNAEUS *Thymelaeaceae*

A small genus of rather low-growing shrubs, both evergreen and deciduous, confined to the temperate regions of Europe and Asia. The leaves are alternate (except in the case of *D. genkwa*), sessile or nearly so. The flowers are tubular with reflexed lobes, the coloured portion being sepals, not petals, which are lacking. The fruit is in the form of a drupe, often colourful. Most of the species are too low-growing to be included in this account. They can be increased by seed, by cuttings, by layering and by grafting on to plants of *D. laureola*. Some species are slow-growing and all are liable to die suddenly for no obvious reason. Most of the species are found wild on limestone formations and will accordingly do well in limy soils, although this is not strictly necessary. *D. pontica* is found on acid soil in the wild. The species all resent being moved and should be put into their permanent positions while still young plants, and are best kept in pots until they are large enough to plant out. They are probably not very long-lived plants even in the wild.

Daphne X burkwoodii TURRILL

4. Semi-evergreen shrub, to 1m, with thin branching stems, clothed with lanceolate dark green lv about 2·5cm long. Fl in terminal clusters to 3cm across, with red buds and pale pink fl which are very fragrant. Fl 5–6. A hybrid of *D. cneorum* and *D. caucasica*, which first flowered in 1935. It is sometimes met with as *Daphne* 'Somerset', a practically identical plant of the same parentage.

Daphne caucasica PALLAS

4.5. An upright shrub, to 2m, with oblanceolate lv to 4cm long and 1cm across; pale green above and glaucous below. Fl in terminal clusters to 5cm across, each fl shining white and fragrant. Fl 5–6. Fr reddish-yellow. *D. altaica* PALLAS and *D. sophia* KALENICZENKO are probably nothing more than geographical forms of *D. caucasica*, although they are usually lower. *D. caucasica*, as its name suggests, is found in the Caucasus, *D. altaica* in the Altai mountains and *D. sophia* in various parts of central Russia. The first of these to be introduced was, apparently, *D. altaica*, about 1796 – presumably by Pallas.

Daphne collina SMITH

4. An evergreen shrub making a rounded bush, to 1m, with silky bts. Lv obovate, to 4cm long and 1·5cm across, dark green above and glabrous, paler and hairy below. Fl in a terminal cluster up to 5cm across, each fl about 1cm across, rosy purple and fragrant. Fl 5–6.

Closely related, and a much better garden plant, is *D. neapolitana* LODDIGES, which is thought to be a natural hybrid between *D. collina* and *D. cneorum*. They are, however, not very likely to meet in the wild and it is probably better regarded as a variety of *D. collina*. It differs in its shorter and narrower lv, which are less hairy below, and in its smaller fl, but these are produced with great freedom from March until June. A very vigorous shrub, not exceeding 1m in height, but spreading very widely. *D. collina* is native to the central and eastern Mediterranean and was introduced in 1752. *D. neapolitana* arrived in 1822, presumably from near Naples.

Daphne genkwa SIEBOLD AND ZUCCARINI

4. Deciduous shrub to 1m with erect brs; bts silky-pubescent. Lv elliptic-oblong, opposite, to 5cm long and 1·5cm across, with silky hairs on the veins below. Fl axillary, before the lv, in clusters of 3–7; the fl up to 1cm long and wide, lilac-blue. Fl 5. One of the loveliest sp but easily the most difficult to establish. It would appear to require acid soil, and plants on their own roots thrive much better than grafted ones. It seems rarely to be killed by low winter temperatures. Plants also do best when placed in dappled shade. Native of China, it was long cultivated both there and in Japan. First introduced by Fortune in 1843 in a special form, with larger fl and shorter lv, which is sometimes given specific rank as *D. fortunei* and sometimes varietal status.

Daphne gnidium LINNAEUS

4.5. Evergreen shrub of very upright growth, occasionally to 2m, but usually less. Lv linear, to 4cm long. Fl in terminal heads about 2cm across, white. Fl 6–8. Fr red. Useful for its late flowering, but otherwise not a very attractive shrub. Native to the Mediterranean and usually not very hardy.

Daphne laureola LINNAEUS   Spurge Laurel

4. Evergreen bushy shrub, to 1m or slightly more. Lv elliptic, to 12cm long and 3cm across, shining green. Fl from upper axils in clusters of 3–8, usually (but not invariably) fragrant, yellowish-green, each fl about 8mm long and 6mm across. Fl 3–4. Fr blue-black. Native to most of Europe, including the UK where it grows on the chalk. Will thrive in quite dense shade.

Daphne mezereum

Daphne mezereum LINNAEUS   Mezereon

4.5. Deciduous shrub, occasionally to 2m, usually less, with erect brs. Lv oblanceolate, to 8cm long and 2cm across, bright green above, greyish below. Fl axillary, before the lv in clusters of 2–3 all along the previous year's growth, pale or dark purple, very fragrant. Fl 2–4. Fr red, about 8mm across. *D. m.* 'Alba' has white fl and yellow fr and seems slightly more vigorous, while 'Grandiflora' has larger, deeper fl which often start to open in October.

One of the most attractive shrubs for late winter decoration. It has proved very susceptible to cucumber virus, which damages many plants. Large plants become very leggy, but resent the old wood being cut out. Native of most of Europe, including the UK, growing in rather shady situations with ample water during the summer.

Daphne odora THUNBERG

4. (*D. indica* of gardens) Evergreen shrub, to 2m, although it rarely achieves this height in the UK. Lv elliptic, to 9cm long and 2·5cm wide, dark green. Fl in terminal clusters, reddish-purple, fragrant; each fl to 1cm long and 1·5cm across. Appears to do best in acid or neutral soil. Fl 3–5. This plant is not entirely hardy; oddly enough the form with variegated lv seems to be hardier than the green-leaved type, which is the reverse of normal experience. However, the plant will tolerate a good many degrees of frost and, given a sheltered situation, can usually be expected to survive in most parts of the UK. Native to China and Japan. Introduced in 1771 by a Mr Benjamin Torin.

Daphne pontica LINNAEUS

4. Evergreen shrub, to 1m or slightly more. Lv elliptic-obovate, to 7cm long and 3cm across. Fl in pairs from the axils of the previous year's growth, fragrant, yellowish-green, on long peduncles, opening just as the new growth is starting to elongate. Fl 4–5. Very close to *D. laureola,* but preferring an acid soil and more attractive. Native of western Asia. Grown by Miller in 1752.

Daphne retusa HEMSLEY

4.5. Evergreen shrub, to 1m, although usually somewhat less. Lv leathery, oblong-ovate, to 5cm long and 2cm across, very densely set on the brs. Fl in quite large terminal heads, to 7cm across, each fl to 2cm across and 1·5cm long; purple outside, nearly white inside, fragrant. Fl 5. Fr a translucent red, about 12mm across. Native of China. Introduced by Wilson in 1901.

Daphne tangutica MAXIMOWICZ

4.5. Shrub, to 1m, scarcely to be distinguished from the last sp but with longer lv (to 8cm long) and slightly smaller fl. Probably only a geographical variety of *D. retusa* (or rather, since Maximowicz's name has priority, the other way round). Native of NW China. Introduced by Wilson in 1910 and by Farrer in 1914.

Daphne odora

DAPHNIPHYLLUM BLUME *Euphorbiaceae*

A genus of some twenty-five species of evergreen shrubs or small trees, only one of which is usually obtainable in commerce. The plants are dioecious and the species below is chiefly grown in a somewhat jocular manner, as its leaves greatly resemble those of *Rhododendron decorum*.

Daphniphyllum macropodum

Daphniphyllum macropodum   MIQUEL

Evergreen shrub, to about 3m in cultivation, but sometimes a small tree to 15m in the wild. In the best forms the bts are reddish, and so are the petioles and midribs, but this is not universal. Lv oblong, acuminate, to 20cm long and 9cm across, dark green above, glaucous below. Male fl without petals, female fl with pinkish bracts. Fr a black drupe. Native to China, Japan and Korea. Introduced from Japan by Maries in 1879.

DAVIDIA BAILLON *Davidiaceae*

A monotypic genus (some authorities recognise two species) of a single deciduous tree, with alternate leaves.

Davidia involucrata BAILLON
Handkerchief Tree

4.(6).7. A rapid-growing, deciduous tree, to 20m, with somewhat ascending br. Lv much resembling those of the lime tree, cordate or broadly ovate, to 15cm long and 12cm across, with a toothed margin. Under surface either hairy or glabrous (var *vilmoriniana*). On some soils the lv turn yellow before falling. Fl apetalous in a globular cluster, comparatively inconspicuous, but subtended by two very large white bracts, of which the lower may by 15cm long and 7cm across, while the upper is somewhat smaller. Fl 5–6. The fr is green, containing a single large nut. In spite of its exotic appearance, this appears to be perfectly hardy and tolerant of most soils. It flowers in about 10 years from seed, which usually takes 2–3 years to germinate.

It can also be propagated by layering. Native of China. Of the first sending by the Abbé Farges in 1897, only one seed germinated. In 1901 Wilson sent back a large quantity of seeds, most of which germinated, while in 1904 he sent back the first seeds of David's type form with the hairy underside to the lv.

DECAISNEA JOSEPH HOOKER AND THOMSON
Lardizabalaceae

A small genus of only two species.

Decaisnea fargesii FRANCHET   Blue Bean

4.5. Deciduous shrub, to 5m in the wild and rarely more than 3m in cultivation, with thick, erect stems. Lv pinnate, to 80cm long, with anything from 13 to 25 leaflets. These are ovate, acuminate, to 15cm long, half as wide, dark green above, glaucous beneath. Fl in terminal, drooping panicles on the lateral brs, the panicles to 45cm long. The fl lack petals, but are formed of campanulate, yellowish-green sepals, each fl to 3cm long on a pedicel to 2cm long. Male and female fl occur on the same panicle. Fl 6. The fr is a carpel, resembling a broad bean pod, which is up to 10cm long and 2cm wide, and a dull blue in colour. Fr 10. Liable to be damaged by late spring frosts, but otherwise hardy. The blue fr are remarkable, but it is not a very

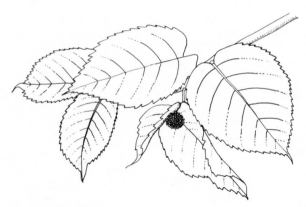

Davidia involucrata

handsome shrub. Native to China. Introduced by the Abbé Farges in 1895 (1893 according to Rehder).

DESMODIUM DESVAUX *Leguminosae*

A mainly tropical genus of herbs and shrubs, distinguished from the allied *Lespedeza* by their jointed several-seeded pods; the pods of *Lespedeza* being single-seeded.

Desmodium tiliifolium (DAVID DON) GEORGE DON

4. Deciduous sub-shrub, throwing up annually erect stems to 130cm, which are pubescent. Lv trifoliate, on petioles to 7cm long. The terminal leaflet is the largest, sometimes almost diamond-shaped, to 10cm long and 7cm wide, the other two leaflets more or less ovate and around half as large; glabrous above, glabrous, sparingly or fully pubescent beneath. Those of the form most commonly seen are sparingly pubescent. Fl in terminal panicles, the lower brs of which spring from the topmost lv axils. Fl pea-shaped, about 12mm long, varying in colour from lilac to deep pink. The fl are produced in very large numbers, although individually small. Fl 8–10. Pods up to 7cm long. A useful plant for its late flowering, but in cold, wet summers the flowers may not develop. Propagated by seed or careful division. Native of the Himalaya. Introduced in 1879.

DEUTZIA THUNBERG *Philadelphaceae*

A genus of mainly deciduous shrubs, native to the Himalaya and eastern Asia, with a few species in Mexico, a curious case of discontinuous distribution. The branches are hollow, the leaves are opposite, short-petioled, the flowers have their parts in fives, with ten stamens and three to five styles. The filaments of the stamens are winged (in *Philadelphus* the parts are in fours). The flowers are either in panicles or in cymes, very rarely solitary. The genus has been divided into two sections, based upon the arrangement of the petals in the unopened bud. The majority have the petals only touching at their margins (sect *Eudeutzia*), the others have the petals overlapping (sect *Mesodeutzia*). The first section has in turn been divided into four series dependent on the type of inflorescence (paniculate, cymose, corymbose or solitary). These series are not referred to here.

Deutzia is characterised by hairs on the branchlets and other parts of the plant, which reveal themselves as star-shaped under magnification. The species mostly flower in June and only exceptions will be noted below. The fruit is a hard capsule, containing numerous small seeds which germinate readily. However, propagation is usually by semi-hard or hard wood cuttings which root fairly readily. At the end of the last century and in the early years of this one considerable hybridisation took place, mostly by the firm of Lemoine. All species are hardy but the young shoots can be affected by late spring frosts.

Deutzia chunii HU

4. Shrub, to 2m. Lv oblong-lanceolate, to 7cm long, serrate, dull green above, grey and woolly beneath. Fl in terminal panicles on the lateral brs, each panicle to 8cm long. The fl are flushed pink outside, white within and slightly reflexed. Fl 7. Useful for its late flowering and pink-flushed fl. Native of E China, only introduced in 1935.

Deutzia compacta CRAIB

4. Shrub, to 2m. Lv oblong-lanceolate, acuminate, minutely serrate, up to 7cm long and 2·5cm across; much smaller on flowering shoots. Fl in compact corymbs to 5cm across, each fl small, not more than 8mm wide, pink in bud, white when open, with a hawthorn-like scent and reddish anthers. Fl 7. Native of western China, whence it was obtained by the firm of Vilmorin in 1905.

Deutzia corymbosa R. BROWN

4. Vigorous shrub, to 3m, appearing quite glabrous, although a lens will reveal minute hairs on the lv and bts. Lv ovate, acuminate, to 12cm long and 6cm across. Fl in a flat corymb to 7cm across, white with yellow anthers. Fl 6–7. Native of the Himalaya. Introduced through Royle in 1830.

Deutzia discolor HEMSLEY

4. Erect shrub, to 2m. Lv oblong-lanceolate, to 11cm long and 3cm across, dull green above, grey beneath. Fl large for the genus, in corymbs to 7cm across, each fl to 2·5cm across, largest in the form known as 'Major'. Most forms are white within, pink or purple outside, but there can be some variation and all white forms occur. Native of central and western China. Introduced by Wilson in 1901.

Deutzia glomeruliflora FRANCHET

4. Shrub, to 2m but usually somewhat less. Lv ovate-oblong or lanceolate, to 7cm long, acuminate, dull green above, grey and woolly below. Fl with purple sepals, in corymbs to 5cm across; each fl to 2cm across, pure white. Fl 5–6. Valuable for its early flowering and large fl. Native of western China. Introduced by Wilson in 1908.

Deutzia gracilis SIEBOLD AND ZUCCARINI

4. Rather slow-growing shrub, to 2m but usually little more than 1m. Lv oblong-lanceolate, acuminate, to 7cm long and 1·5cm across, quite a bright green above. Fl in erect racemes or panicles, to 7cm long, each fl pure white, campanulate, to 2cm long. Fl 5–6. Golden-leaved and variegated-leaved forms have existed. *Deutzia X lemoinei* is a hybrid between this sp and *D.parviflora*, which is more vigorous, up to 2½m with panicles to 8cm. The hybrid was raised in 1891. The sp is native to Japan, whence it was introduced about 1840.

85

Deutzia hypoglauca REHDER

4. (*D. rubens* REHDER) Shrub, to 2m, with glabrous bts. Lv oblong-lanceolate, to 9cm long and 4cm across, quite glabrous below and nearly white. Fl in corymbs to 6cm wide, each fl pure white, 2cm across. Distinct in the glabrous underside to the lv. Native of central China. Introduced by Purdom in 1910.

Deutzia longifolia

Deutzia longifolia FRANCHET

4. Vigorous shrub, to 2m but spreading widely. Lv lanceolate or oblong-lanceolate, acuminate, rounded at the base; grey-green above, white hairy below, to 12cm long but barely 1cm across. Fl in flattish panicles, to 7cm long and wide, each fl to 2·5cm across, rather starry, rosy-purple. Fairly close to *D. discolor,* but distinct with its long narrow lv and deeper purple fl. Hybridised with this sp, it has given rise to such cv as 'Mont Rose' and 'Contraste', with showy purple fl. The sp is native to western China and was introduced by Wilson in 1901.

Deutzia mollis DUTHIE

4. Shrub of up to 2m, with reddish-brown bts. Lv ovate-elliptic, to 11cm long and 5cm across, and, like most spp, larger on the vigorous new shoots. Lv dull green above, grey-hairy below. Fl in corymbs to 8cm across, each fl to 1cm across, hawthorn-shaped, white. Not, apparently, a very showy shrub, but unusual in the genus with its rounded petals. Native of Hupeh. Introduced by Wilson in 1901.

Deutzia monbeigii W. W. SMITH

4. Shrub, to 2m. Lv small, ovate, to 2cm long and half as wide, dull green above, white woolly below. Fl in corymbs of 5–12 fl, starry, about 2·5cm across, shining white. Fl 6–7. A graceful shrub with its small, white-felted lv and late flowering. Native of western China. Introduced by Forrest in 1917.

Deutzia pulchra VIDAL

4. Shrub, to nearly 3m. Lv ovate-lanceolate, to 10cm long and 5cm across, scaly on both surfaces, although more so beneath. Fl pendulous, in long, drooping panicles to 10cm and occasionally to 17cm, the individual fl only 1cm long, white with a pink tinge. Fl 5–6. One of the showiest sp. Native of Formosa. Introduced by Wilson in 1918.

Deutzia purpurascens REHDER

4. A shrub probably more important as a parent than in its own right. To 2m or slightly more, spreading widely. Lv elliptic-ovate, somewhat acuminate, dull green above, slightly hairy below. Fl with purple sepals, in rounded corymbs to 5cm across, each fl to 2cm across, starry, purple outside, white within. Fl 5–6. Native of Yunnan. Introduced by the Abbé Delavay to Vilmorin in 1888.

D. gracilis X *D. purpurascens* is *D. X rosea* (LEMOINE) REHDER, a shrub usually little over 1m, with small panicles of campanulate pink fl. A number of forms have been clonally propagated, such as 'Campanulata', 'Carminea' and 'Venusta'. *D. X lemoinei* (see under *D. gracilis*) pollinated by *D. purpurascens* gave the hybrid known as *D. X maliflora* REHDER, with rather starry pink fl in 'Fleur de Pommier' and in 'Boule de Rose'. On the other hand 'Avalanche' is pure white. *D. purpurascens* pollinated by *D. parviflora* (which appears to have dropped out of cultivation) gave the hybrid known as *D. X kalmiiflora* LEMOINE, with large, spreading fl to 2cm across, carmine outside and white within. *D. X elegantissima* REHDER (*D. purpurascens* X *D. sieboldiana*) is very similar to *D. purpurascens*, but the fl are pinkish within as well as outside.

Deutzia scabra THUNBERG

4. (*D. crenata* SIEBOLD AND ZUCCARINI) Vigorous shrub, to 3m or more, with erect brs. Lv ovate or ovate-lanceolate, to 10cm long and 5cm across, somewhat scurfy on both surfaces. Fl in erect, rounded panicles to 15cm long, each fl to 2cm long and wide, somewhat starry, white or white inside, pink-flushed outside. Fl 6–7. A number of double-flowered forms exist, of which 'Candidissima' with fl 2·5cm across, is the best known. 'Watereri' has large fl to 2·5cm across, single, flushed outside with pink.

Native of Japan and China. Introduced from Japan in 1833, according to Loudon, which would suggest a slightly earlier importation by Siebold. Bean and Rehder both give a date of 1822. It is not mentioned in Sweet's *Hortus Britannicus* of 1830.

Pollinated by *D. vilmoriniae* (qv) the resultant hybrid is called *D. X magnifica* REHDER. The original had double fl, but the form known as 'Latiflora' has spreading petals, to 4cm across, while 'Superba' and 'Eburnea' both have campanulate fl.

Deutzia schneideriana. REHDER

4. Shrub, to 2m. Lv elliptic-ovate to 7cm long, acuminate, grey-green above, grey-tomentose below. Fl in panicles to 6cm long (8cm long in var *laxiflora*) pure white; each fl to 2cm across, starry. Fl 6–7. Usually flowering late in the season. Native of central China. Introduced by Wilson in 1907.

Deutzia setchuenensis FRANCHET

4. Shrub, to 2cm, of graceful but rather straggling habit. Lv oval-lanceolate, acuminate, to 10cm long (in the var *corymbiflora* REHDER, which is the only form in cultivation), dull green and rough above, grey-downy below. Fl in loose corymbs to 10cm across, each fl to 1·5cm across. Fl 5–6. Native of China. Introduced (by Farges?) in 1893.

Deutzia sieboldiana MAXIMOWICZ

4. (*D. scabra* of SIEBOLD AND ZUCCARINI but not THUNBERG) Shrub, to 1·5m, lv oval, to 7cm long and 3cm across, somewhat wrinkled above and dull green, slightly paler and more hairy below. Fl in erect, rather lax, panicles to 6cm long, each fl starry, pure white to 1·5cm across. Native of Japan. Introduced in 1885. Crossed with *D. X rosea* (see under *D. purpurascens*) the resultant hybrid was named *D. X carnea* REHDER. This has purple sepals, and fl in erect panicles to 2cm across, pink outside, white within.

Deutzia vilmoriniae LEMOINE

4. Shrub, to nearly 3m, growing rapidly and of graceful habit. Lv elliptic to oblong-lanceolate, dull green and rough above, grey-hairy below; to 14cm long and 5cm across. Fl in lax corymbs up to 7cm long and wide, each fl white, starry to 2·5cm across. Native of Szechuan. Introduced by Père Farges in 1897.

Deutzia wilsonii DUTHIE

4. Considered to be a natural hybrid between *D. discolor* and *D. mollis*. Shrub, to 2m, usually somewhat less, with reddish-brown bts. Lv elliptic or oblong-lanceolate, to 12cm long and 3·5cm across, rough and slightly wrinkled above, grey-hairy below. Fl in panicles, about 7–10cm across, each fl white, starry, to 2·5cm across. Apparently sets good seed, which comes true. Native of China. Introduced by Wilson in 1901.

DIERVILLA ADANSON *Caprifoliaceae*

A genus of only three species of low deciduous, suckering shrubs, native to N America. Leaves opposite, flowers in axillary and terminal cymes. At one time the genus *Weigela* was included in *Diervilla*. Propagation is by seed, by cuttings or by removing rooted suckers.

Diervilla lonicera MILLER

4. (*D. canadensis* WILLDENOW, *D. lutea* PHILIPPI) Spreading shrub, to 1m or slightly over. Brs round and smooth. Lv oval to ovate-oblong, to 12cm long and 6cm across, toothed, on a short petiole not above 1cm long. Fl funnel-shaped with reflexed mouth, yellow, in 1cm-long terminal and axillary few-flowered cymes on the current year's growths. Fl 6–7. Native of N America from Newfoundland to North Carolina. The date of introduction seems somewhat dubious. It is said to have been brought to France by Dr Dierville in 1720, but it was in 1700 that he travelled in Canada. In England Miller was growing it in 1739, possibly from Bartram. The plant will thrive in shade.

Diervilla sessilifolia BUCKLEY

3.4. Tufted deciduous shrub, to 1m. Brs four-angled. Lv bronzy-purple when first unfurling and keeping this colour for much of the season in some forms. Lv practically stalkless, ovate-lanceolate, to 17cm long and half as wide, toothed, glabrous, except for the midrib, which is pubescent. Fl in quite large terminal and axillary cymes, pale yellow, to 12mm long; the terminal cymes may be as much as 7cm across. Fl 6–8. The most ornamental sp. Native of the south eastern USA from N Carolina to Alabama. Introduced in 1844, but possibly previously as a superior form of the last sp.

Diervilla rivularis GATTINGER

4. Shrub, to 2m. Very close to *D. sessilifolia*, with the same habitat but brs smooth and round and faintly downy. Lv downy on both surfaces and not more than 8cm long. Fl 7–8. Introduced in 1898.

DIOSPYROS LINNAEUS *Ebenaceae*

The only hardy genus in the ebony family, and of the 200 existing species only four are hardy in the UK. They include deciduous and evergreen trees or shrubs with alternate leaves and dioecious flowers. The fruit is a berry, sometimes, as in the case of the persimmon, very large. They have no beauty of flower, but often the leaves colour well in the autumn and they make quite attractive trees at all times. The male flowers are usually in clusters, while the female flowers are solitary. Seed appears the best method of increase.

Diospyros armata HEMSLEY

Evergreen or semi-evergreen bush in Britain, but apparently a small tree to 8m in the wild, with spreading, spiny brs. The bts are faintly hairy at first. Lv elliptic-oval to 6cm long and half as wide, dark glossy green with a few obscure dots. Male fl in small corymbs, very small but fragrant. Fr a small yellowish berry about 2cm across. Native of China. Introduced by Wilson in 1904.

Diospyros kaki LINNAEUS   Persimmon

5.6. Large shrub or small deciduous tree, which can reach 12m. Lv elliptic-ovate, to 20cm long and 9cm across, glossy green above, somewhat downy below, usually colouring orange and purple in the autumn. Male fl yellowish-white in clusters of 3, about 1cm long. Fl 6. Fr ·tomato-like, to 7cm across. Fr is only produced in temperate countries with wall protection, but the plant seems hardy enough. Native of China. Obtained by Sir Joseph Banks in 1789.

Diospyros lotus LINNAEUS   Date Plum

7. Deciduous tree, to 10m in the UK. Lv ovate-elliptic, to 12cm long and 5cm across, dark shining green above, glaucous below. Male fl in axillary clusters of 1–3, reddish-green. Female fl solitary. Fl 7. Fr roundish, to 2cm across, purple or yellow. Probably native of China, but long cultivated for its rather unpleasing fr. Grown in the UK in 1597.

Diospyros virginiana LINNAEUS

1.6.7. Deciduous tree, to 20m, with very attractive and picturesque fissured bark on older specimens. Lv elliptic or ovate-acuminate, to 12cm long and 5cm across, glossy green above, paler below, often colouring well in the autumn. Fl in axillary clusters of 1–3, about 1cm long. The female fl solitary and slightly larger. Fr

Dipelta floribunda

round, to 4cm across, edible, yellowish with a red flush. Fl 5–6. Young plants are said to be somewhat tender, but older plants are completely hardy. Native of the eastern USA from Connecticut to Florida. Introduced about 1629.

DIOSTEA MIERS *Verbenaceae*

A small genus of Andean shrubs. *D. juncea* is propagated by seed or by cuttings taken in July and August.

Diostea juncea MIERS

4. Slender, deciduous shrub or small tree, to 5m. Bts rush-like, sparsely downy at first, later glabrous. Lv opposite, in pairs at long intervals along the brs, sessile, oblong-ovate, to 2cm long and 6mm across, toothed and slightly downy. Fl in short, spicate racemes, terminal on lateral twigs. The fl are tubular, about 8mm long, pale lilac. Fr a drupe containing 2 seeds. Fl 6. Native of the Andes of Chile and Argentina. Introduced about 1890.

DIPELTA MAXIMOWICZ *Caprifoliaceae*

A small genus of ornamental deciduous shrubs with opposite leaves and flowers, which resemble those of *Weigela,* being funnel-campanulate with five lobes at the mouth. They are distinct in the number of bracts at the base of the flower, of which two continue to grow after flowering and eventually enclose the ovary, looking rather like the fruit of the elm. Propagated easily by seed or by cuttings.

Dipelta floribunda MAXIMOWICZ

4. Deciduous shrub, to 5m, but usually less, with downy bts. Lv oval-elliptic, to 10cm long and 4cm across, downy on both surfaces at first but soon glabrous, on short petioles. Fl in terminal and axillary clusters of 1–6, funnel-shaped, 5-lobed, to 3cm long, fragrant, pale pink with a yellow throat. Bracts peltate, eventually 2cm long and 1·5cm across. Fl 5–6. Native of western and central China. Introduced by Wilson in 1902.

Dipelta ventricosa HEMSLEY

4. Deciduous shrub, usually not more than 2m but able to reach 5m. Lv ovate, acuminate, to 15cm long and 4cm across, sometimes slightly toothed. Fl usually solitary from the axils and in a terminal cluster of 3 on side-shoots, campanulate, verging towards urceolate, to 3cm long and 2cm across, deep pink with an orange mark in the throat, 5-lobed. Bracts heart-shaped, eventually to 1·6cm long and 8mm wide. Fl 5–6. Native of western China. Introduced by Wilson in 1904.

Dipelta yunnanensis FRANCHET

4. Similar to *D. floribunda* but with cream-coloured fl with orange markings in the throat. Fl 6. Introduced by Forrest in 1910.

DIPTERONIA OLIVER *Aceraceae*

The only other genus, after *Acer*, in the family, of which only two species, both Chinese, are known.

Dipteronia sinensis OLIVER

5. Small tree, to 8m, or large bush. Lv pinnate, opposite, to 30cm long, composed of 7–11 leaflets, each leaflet lanceolate-ovate, 4–10cm long, 1–3cm across, toothed, slightly hairy when young. Fl very small, greenish-white in upright panicles to 30cm long. Fr similar to those of a Wych-elm, to 2·5cm long, winged and flat, soft red when mature. Fl 6. Attractive for its pinnate leaves and coloured fr. Introduced by Wilson in 1900.

DISANTHUS MAXIMOWICZ *Hamamelidaceae*

A monotypic genus, requiring acid soil and slightly frost tender when young.

Disanthus cercidifolia MAXIMOWICZ

6. Shrub, to 3m or rarely 5, with round, glabrous bts. Lv orbicular-cordate, to 12cm long and broad, colouring very vividly in the autumn.

Disanthus cercidifolia

Fl small, red-purple, borne as the lv fall. Fl 10. Remarkable for its brilliant autumnal lv. Introduced from Japan 1892.

DISELMA JOSEPH HOOKER *Cupressaceae*

A monotypic, evergreen genus from Tasmania.

Diselma archeri J. D. HOOKER

(*Fitzroya archeri* BENTHAM AND HOOKER) A dioecious shrub or small tree from 2–6m, either compact, in wind-swept situations, or straggling. Lv scale-like, closely appressed and overlapping, alternate or whorled. Fl insignificant; male fl terminal in clusters, female fl solitary. Cone very small, composed of only two pairs of scales, of which only the upper pair contain 2 seeds each. The plant is so rare in cultivation that little is known about it, but in general Tasmanian plants tend to be hardy only in the milder parts of the UK. It does, however, come from heights of 1,000m and more, so must be used to severe weather conditions. There seems to be no record as to when it was first introduced.

DISTYLIUM SIEBOLD AND ZUCCARINI
Hamamelidaceae

A small genus of evergreen trees or shrubs, of slight ornamental value.

Distylium racemosum SIEBOLD AND ZUCCARINI

Evergreen shrub of restricted size in cultivation, although apparently a tree to 25m in Japan. Lv alternate, narrow-obovate, to 7·5cm long and half as wide, shining dark green. Fl either polygamous or unisexual, petalless, with reddish-purple stamens, which are quite conspicuous, in erect racemes to 3cm long. Fl 3–4. A variegated form has been in commerce. Introduced from Japan in 1876.

EDGWORTHIA MEISSNER *Thymelaceae*

(Sometimes spelt *Edgeworthia.*) A small genus with only one species in cultivation. Often regarded as tender, but grows successfully against a north wall.

Edgworthia chrysantha LINDLEY

4. (*Edgworthia papyrifera* SIEBOLD AND ZUCCARINI) Straggling shrub, to 2m, with thin, wiry stems. Lv narrow-elliptic to 15cm long and 3cm across, silky when young. Fl in terminal nodding corymbs, which open a rank at a time over two weeks or so; pale yellow at first, fading to nearly white, fragrant. The exterior of the fl are covered with silky hairs. Fl 3–4. Fr not set in cultivation. Introduced from China in 1845.

ELAEAGNUS LINNAEUS *Elaeagnaceae*

A genus of some forty-five species distributed in Asia and N America, both evergreen and deciduous, usually shrubs, but occasionally trees. The young growths are densely covered with scales, which are also found on most other parts. The flowers are small, tubular, often fragrant; the fruit is drupe-like (the calyx tube becomes fleshy after fertilisation). The fruit is set more easily if cross fertilisation is possible. The plants will thrive in almost any soil. The young wood of some species is spiny. Propagation is by semi-hard cuttings with a heel, which usually root readily. The genus contains some of the most handsome foliage shrubs in cultivation, *E. angustifolia* and *E. commutata* being particularly fine.

Elaeagnus angustifolia LINNAEUS   Oleaster

1. Deciduous shrub or small tree, to 6m. Mature plants have a dark brown smooth bark, which is attractive. The young growths tend to be thorny. Bts covered with grey-silver scales as are the surfaces of the lv. Lv lanceolate, to 8cm long and 2·5cm across, much resembling those of *Pyrus salicifolia.* Fl in fascicles of 3 in lower leaf axils, tubular, yellow, fragrant, to 1cm long. Fl 6. Fr elliptic, yellow with silvery scales, about 1cm long; said to be edible, but not often produced in cultivation. Var *orientalis* (LINNAEUS)

KUNTZE is spineless with slightly larger lv. A handsome and striking foliage shrub, which appears much whiter under Mediterranean conditions. Native of western Asia and possibly SE Europe. Cultivated since the sixteenth century.

Elaeagnus commutata BERNHARDI   Silver Berry

(*E. argentea* PURSH.) Deciduous suckering shrub, to 4m, but usually rather less. Bts with reddish-brown scales. Lv ovate to 6cm long and 3cm across, covered with silver scales on both surfaces, these scales persisting throughout the season. Fl in groups of 1–3, to 1·5cm long, yellow within silvery without, fragrant. Fl 5–6. Fr elliptic, 1cm long, silvery. One of the most striking foliage shrubs with its metallic-looking leaves, which preserve their beauty throughout the season. Easily propagated by detaching the suckering growths. Sometimes confused with *Shepherdia argentea*, which has opposite lv while those of this sp are alternate. Native to eastern N America and probably introduced in 1813.

Elaeagnus X ebbingei BOOM

Evergreen shrub with the parentage *E. macrophylla X E. pungens,* to 4 or 5m. Bts reddish-brown. Lv covered with rusty scales when emerging, wide-elliptic, to 10cm long and 6cm wide, glossy-green with a few silver scales on the upper surface, shining silver below. Fl in late autumn, white, fragrant to 1cm long. Fl 9–10. Fr round, orange in following spring but rarely seen in cultivation. Useful for its rapid growth and resistance to wind and salt spray. Raised in 1929.

Elaeagnus glabra THUNBERG

Evergreen climbing or sprawling shrub to 7m, unarmed. Bts brown, shining. Lv elliptic-ovate, shining green above, covered with lustrous brown and yellow scales below, to 7cm long and half as wide. Fl white within, brownish outside, very fragrant, 1cm long. Fl 10–11. Useful for its late flowering, but one of the least attractive of the genus. Native of Japan introduced about 1888.

Elaeagnus macrophylla THUNBERG

3. Evergreen, wide-spreading shrub, to 4m, but spreading more widely. Bts silvery as are also the young lv; later they become dull green above, but remain silvery below. The lv are orbicular, to 11cm long and 6cm wide. Fl in small clusters in the leaf axils, very fragrant, white with a few silvery scales on the exterior. Fl 10–11. Fr ellipsoid, reddish. An attractive shrub, flowering freely when well-established. Native of Japan, brought back by Maries in 1879, but, according to Rehder, originally introduced in 1843.

Elaeagnus multiflora THUNBERG

5. (*E. longipes* GRAY) Spreading, deciduous shrub to 3m, usually wider. Bts red-brown, lv elliptic to 6cm long, light green above, silvery below. Fl either singly or in pairs, yellowish, about 1·5cm long. Fl 4–5. Fr on pedicels 2cm long, about 1·5cm long, ovoid, orange-red. Fr 7–8. The only species which fruits consistently in cultivation and it is for its fr that it is cultivated. Native of China and Japan. Introduced 1862.

Elaeagnus pungens THUNBERG

Evergreen, spreading shrub to 4m high, but generally less in height and more in width, usually somewhat spiny. Bts brown, lv elliptic-oblong, with slightly waved margins, shining green above, dull white beneath. Fl 1–3, about 1cm long, smelling like the gardenia. Fl 10–11. Fr apparently red, but very rarely seen.

The type is rarely seen but *E. p.* 'Aurea', with yellow margined lv, 'Maculata' with a golden centre to the lv, and 'Variegata' with cream-margined lv, are among the most popular of variegated-leaved shrubs, giving much winter cheer to the garden, but shy to flower. *E. p. reflexa* SERVETTAZ (*E. reflexa* MORREN AND DECAISNE) is thought to be a hybrid of this sp with *E. glabra*, but is not very desirable with its semi-climbing habit. Native of Japan. Introduced, presumably through Siebold, in 1830.

Elaeagnus umbellata THUNBERG

Deciduous shrub or small tree, to 6m, but often 10m wide. Bts yellowish-brown (but silvery in the var *parvifolia* (ROYLE) SERVETTAZ). Lv lanceolate on short petioles, 9cm long and 3cm across, mid-green above, silvery below. Fl in clusters of 1–3, silvery without, creamy within. Fl normally 5–6, but often a second flowering takes place in August. Fr round, reddish-brown. A plant with a wide range from the Himalayas where var *parvifolia* predominates, to China, Korea and Japan. Introduced 1829 from Nepal.

EMBOTHRIUM FORSTER *Proteaceae*

A small genus of only about five species from S. America and Australia. They are evergreen or semi-evergreen tall shrubs or small trees. One species, *E. coccineum*, is in cultivation mainly represented by its hardy variety *E. c. lanceolatum* O. KUNTZE. The plant prefers acid or neutral soil, plenty of moisture throughout the year, which makes it unsuitable for eastern parts of Great Britain, and to have its roots in the shade and its lv in the sun. Propagation is by seed or by suckers, when they occur. Normally a rather short-lived plant in the UK.

Embothrium coccineum

Embothrium coccineum lanceolatum O. KUNTZE
Chilean Fire Bush

4. Semi-evergreen, erect shrub to about 7m, occasionally much larger. Lv linear, lanceolate, dark green, to 10cm long and 3cm across. Fl in short, axillary racemes, brilliant scarlet, tubular at first, to 3cm long; later the petals curl back to reveal the anthers. In a well-flowered specimen the stems are practically invisible when the plant is in flower. Fl 5–6. The hardiest form is sometimes known as 'Norquinco Valley'. 'Longifolium' has longer and more persistent lv. Introduced by H. Comber from Chile in 1925.

ENKIANTHUS LOUREIRO *Ericaceae*

A small genus of deciduous and evergreen shrubs, with very characteristic whorled branches, from the Himalaya and SE Asia. Most of the species in cultivation colour well in the autumn. The flowers are campanulate or urceolate. Acid soil is essential. Best propagated from seed.

Enkianthus campanulatus (MIQUEL) NICHOLSON

4.6. (*Andromeda campanulata* MIQUEL) Deciduous shrub, usually not more than 3m but occasionally a small tree to 10m. Lv in a terminal cluster or alternate, obovate, to 6cm long and 3cm across, dull green, often turning yellow and red in the autumn. Fl campanulate, creamy

Enkianthus campanulatus

yellow with red veining, about 8mm long. Fl 5–6. The var *palibinii* BEAN has deep red fl. Native of Japan. Introduced by Maries in 1880.

Enkianthus cernuus MAKINO

4.6. Only the var *rubens* appears to be in cultivation. Deciduous shrub, to 5m occasionally but usually not more than 2 or 3. Lv obovate, to 2cm long and half as wide, slightly toothed, colouring red in the autumn. Fl 10–12 in a pendulous raceme, campanulate, about 1cm long, slightly fringed, deep red. Fl 5. Native of Japan, in cultivation in 1900.

Enkianthus chinensis FRANCHET

4.(6). (*E. himalaicus* HOOKER, *E. sinohimalaicus* CRAIB) Tall shrub or small tree, to 7m, with red bts. Lv with red petioles, elliptic to 7cm long, nearly or quite glabrous. Fl in umbel-like racemes, broad-campanulate, 1.5cm wide, reddish-yellow with darker veins. Lv occasionally colour well in the autumn, but not invariably. Fl 5. Found in the Himalaya, Burma and China, whence came the hardiest forms, introduced by Wilson in 1900 and 1904.

Enkianthus perulatus (MIQUEL) SCHNEIDER

4.6. (*E. japonicus* HOOKER, *Andromeda perulata* MIQUEL) A small deciduous shrub, not exceeding 2m and slow-growing. Lv elliptic, to 3cm long and half as wide, turning bright red in the autumn. Fl urceolate, white, appearing with the lv in April. Native of Japan. Obtained by Standish and Noble in 1870.

ERICA LINNAEUS *Ericaceae*

A large genus of some 500 species of evergreen shrubs or, occasionally, trees, with the bulk of the species in S Africa, otherwise confined to Europe and the Mediterranean basin. The lv are usually whorled and linear, the fl in terminal spikes or panicles. Most of the hardy species are too small to be included here. As a general rule ericas need an acid soil, although the dwarf *E. carnea* thrives on alkaline soil, while *E. erigena* and *E. terminalis* are lime-tolerant. Propagation is by seed, which is very minute and should be sown on the surface of a peaty mixture, or by cuttings of semi-hard shoots which can be taken between July and September.

Erica arborea LINNAEUS

4. Evergreen shrub, to 3m, occasionally (mainly in the Canaries and Abyssinia) a tree to 8m. Bts covered with branched hairs. Lv in whorls of 3, densely covering all the twigs and an attractive soft green. Fl globular, fragrant, white in terminal clusters, about 3mm long, produced in great profusion. Fl 3–5. The plant is somewhat liable to damage with prolonged frosts and where these are expected it is best replaced by var *alpina* DIECK, a form found on the mountains of central Spain. This makes a smaller, rather stiffer shrub, which appears completely impervious to the worst frosts. It rarely exceeds 1·5m in height. Native of the mountains of Abyssinia, peak of Teneriffe, Iberian peninsula and Mediterranean region. Its roots serve to make the Bruyère (Briar) pipes.

Erica australis LINNAEUS

4. Evergreen shrub, to 2m, with downy bts and linear lv in whorls of 4, about 7mm long. Fl in dense clusters at ends of the rather lax shoots; tubular with reflexed lobes, about 1cm long, reddish-purple. Fl 4–6. The most attractive of the shrubby ericas, but most forms in cultivation appear to be somewhat frost-tender, although in some places in Spain (eg near the Laguna Negre, Soria), it is found high in the mountains and plants from there should prove frost tolerant. The albino 'Mr Robert' is said to be hardier. Native of the Iberian peninsula. Introduced in 1769.

Erica erigena ROSS

4. Long known as *E. mediterranea*, recent investigation of Linnaeus's herbarium shows that he applied the name to a species different from this plant. Evergreen shrub to 2m with dark green lv in whorls of 4, the linear lv to 8mm long. Fl in terminal racemes, fl cylindrical, pink, about 7mm long. Fl 3–5. The hybrid with the dwarf *E. herbacea* (*E. carnea*) known as *E. X darleyensis* is too low for inclusion here, but well worth growing. Native of the Atlantic coast of Spain, Portugal, France and Ireland, but penetrating to eastern Spain, at least near Ronda.

Erica lusitanica RUDOLPHI

4. Evergreen shrub, to 4m, with difficulty distinguished from *E. arborea.* The main distinctions are the hairs on the bts are unbranched, the lv are slightly longer, the fl are also slightly larger and are pink in the bud. The principal distinction is that the fl open about a month earlier than those of *E. arborea,* sometimes as early as January in mild winters. When juxtaposed, the lv of *E. lusitanica* are a much paler green and the plant is somewhat more attractive. Native of Portugal, W Spain and SW France; slightly frost tender.

Erica terminalis SALISBURY

4. (*E. stricta* DONN) Shrub, to 3m, with erect, but rather weak twigs. Lv usually in whorls of 4, but 5 and 6 have been noted, dark green, to 8mm long. Fl in terminal umbels of 4–8 blooms, urceolate, to 7mm long, bright pink. Fl 6–9. Fairly lime-tolerant. The most reliably hardy of the tall heaths and the only summer flowerer. Native of Sardinia, Corsica, southern Italy and eastern Spain. Introduced in 1765.

E. X veitchii BEAN

4. A chance hybrid, noted at Veitch's nursery in 1905, between *E. arborea* and *E. lusitanica;* which grows more vigorously than the parents, but is somewhat tender.

ESCALLONIA MUTIS *Escalloniaceae*

Formerly included in *Saxifragaceae.* A genus of between fifty and sixty, usually evergreen, South American shrubs, with alternate leaves and flowers in terminal panicles or racemes, five-petalled. Most of the species are only hardy near the coast, but the white-flowered *E. virgata,* the only deciduous species in cultivation, appears perfectly hardy and this has been used as a seed parent with some of the more attractive red-flowered species to produce a number of hybrids which are reasonably hardy; although liable to be damaged in very severe winters they are rarely killed. There are very many of these and they are not dealt with here. They all require sunlight, and they prefer acid or neutral soil; although they will tolerate a little lime, they are not of much use in dry chalky soils. They have a long flowering season throughout the summer, usually attain a height of some 3m eventually, although with their sprawling habit they tend to spread outwards rather than upwards, and are extremely valuable for the shrub garden in late summer and early autumn. Those with large leaves probably have *E. punctata* or *E. macrantha* as the main red-flowered parent, those with smaller leaves either *E. rubra* or *E. rosea.*

Escallonia illinita PRESL

4. Evergreen shrub of spreading character, to 4m, with sticky bts. Lv oval, to 6cm long and half as wide, shining green above, somewhat sticky beneath when young. Fl in terminal panicles to 10cm long and 4cm across, white, each fl about 8mm across, tubular with reflexed lobes. Fl 6–8. One of the hardiest spp, but rather fetid. Native of Chile. Introduced about 1830.

Escallonia macrantha W. HOOKER AND ARNOTT

4. Evergreen shrub, to 3m or more, of spreading habit. Bts covered with down and glutinous. Lv broad-oval, to 8cm long and 5cm across, toothed, shining green above, dotted with aromatic glands beneath. Fl in terminal racemes or panicles up to 10cm long, bright rose-red, about 1·5cm long and wide. Fl 6. Very resistant to sea-salt, so an excellent seaside plant, where it is sometimes employed for hedging. Somewhat tender inland. Now regarded as a var of *E. rubra.* Native of Chile. Introduced by W. Lobb in 1846.

Escallonia punctata DE CANDOLLE

4. Evergreen shrub, to 4m, with sticky bts. Lv obovate, to 5cm long and 2cm across but usually smaller, slightly toothed, short-petioled, glossy green above, resinous below. Fl in panicles to 5cm long and wide, deep crimson. Fl 6–8. Slightly tender and closely allied to *E. rubra* (qv) of which Joseph Hooker considered it a variety. Native of Chile.

Escallonia rosea GRISEBACH

4. (*E. pterocladon* W. HOOKER) Evergreen shrub, to 5m occasionally, but usually not more than 3m. Lv narrow-ovate, to 2·5cm long and 6mm wide, dark glossy green above, pale below, but glabrous. Fl in racemes to 8cm long at the ends of main and lateral brs, fragrant, white (rarely pink). Fl 6–8. Native of Patagonia. Introduced by W. Lobb in 1847. Generally hardy.

Escallonia rubra PERSOON

4. (*E. microphylla*) Vigorous evergreen, to 5m, of loose sprawling habit. Bts reddish and downy. Lv generally rather small, lanceolate, up to 5cm long and half as wide, aromatic. Fl in terminal panicles to 8cm long, red, 8mm across and 12mm long. Fl 7–9. Perfectly hardy. Native of Chile. Introduced in 1827.

Escallonia virgata (RUIZ AND PAVON) PERSOON

4. (*E. philippiana* MASTERS) Deciduous shrub, to 3m, with arching brs. Lv obovate, to 2cm long and 4mm wide, glabrous. Fl in leaf axils and in a small terminal raceme, patulate, not tubular, white, about 1cm wide. The growths form many small lateral twigs that are covered in flowers. The hardiest member of the genus. Fl 6–8. Introduced from Valdivia by Pearce in the 1860s.

Escallonia viscosa FORBES

4. Closely allied to *E. illinita*. Evergreen shrub, to 4m, with sticky bts. Lv obovate, to 8cm long and 3cm across, dark glossy green above, sticky below. Fl in pendulous panicles to 15cm long, white, about 8mm wide and 1cm long. Fl 6–8. Somewhat fetid. Native of Chile. Date of introduction uncertain.

EUCALYPTUS L'HÉRITIER *Myrtaceae*

A genus of some 500 trees and shrubs, mainly native to Australia. Most species show a characteristic change in the foliage between young plants up to two or three years old and adult plants. They usually grow extremely rapidly; seedlings often attain a height of 60 or even 90cm in the first year. They tend to elongate rapidly without producing side growths, and quite severe pruning is necessary to encourage branching. Only young plants should be moved and, indeed, it is best to grow them from seed, pricking them out into deep, narrow pots as soon as two pairs of leaves have been produced and putting them in their permanent quarters in the autumn. During the first winter or so, the plants should be protected from severe frost by piling bracken or straw around the stems. Subsequently they should prove hardy, although prolonged icy winds can cause considerable damage. Only one species is reliably hardy in the UK, although other species, if seed is collected from high altitudes, may be expected to be satisfactory in all but the coldest, most exposed sites. The leaves have inconspicuous petals, but have a very conspicuous boss of stamens which are white in the hardy species, although some of the greenhouse species have handsome red flowers. Seed is the only ready means of propagation. Not suitable for shallow soils.

Eucalyptus gunnii JOSEPH HOOKER

7. (*E. Whittinghamensis* hort) Evergreen tree, to 25m. Juvenile lv opposite, orbicular, glaucous, to 5cm across; adult lv sickle-shaped, sage green, to 10cm long and 2cm across. Fl in small, axillary clusters, with a mass of conspicuous cream stamens. Fl 10. Fr a capsule with a characteristic 'lid'. A somewhat variable plant as regards leaf dimensions. Native of Tasmania and S Australia. Introduced about 1850.

Eucalyptus niphophila MAIDEN AND BLAKELY

1. Small evergreen tree and comparatively slow-growing, to 7m, with very attractive grey and white-streaked bark, which peels off every 2 or 3 years; bts glaucous. Juvenile lv opposite and sessile, more or less ovate, light green, to 3cm long and 2cm across. Adult lv sickle-shaped, glaucous, leathery, to 9cm long and 2·5cm wide. Fl in umbels of 3 to 7 from upper lv axils, white, about 2cm across. Fl 9–10. An attractive tree for its bark and foliage and generally hardy. Native of Victoria, Australia; possibly an alpine form of *E. pauciflora*.

EUCRYPHIA CAVANILLES *Eucryphiaceae*

A small genus of evergreen shrubs and trees from Chile, Tasmania and Australia. Unfortunately only one species is generally hardy, but this has been crossed with two of the more tender species to produce reasonably hardy hybrids. Reproduction is by cuttings or layers and is not easy, although rooting hormones and mist propagation have made it less difficult. Seed is admirable for the species, but with the hybrids the results would be uncertain. Lime-free soil is essential and the plants, like so many Chileans, like their roots shaded and ample moisture. They are remarkably attractive late-flowering plants.

Eucryphia glutinosa BAILLON

4.6. (*E. pinnatifolia* GAY) Deciduous or semi-evergreen shrub or, rarely, a small tree, to 5m. Lv in terminal clusters, pinnate, composed

Eucalyptus gunnii

Eucryphia glutinosa

of 3 or 5 leaflets, each ovate, toothed, to 5cm long, half as wide; often colouring well in the autumn. Fl white, somewhat like a wild rose in appearance, but with conspicuous stamens, to 6cm across. Fl 7–8. Native of Chile. Introduced by Pearce in 1859.

Eucryphia X intermedia BAUSCH

4. A hybrid between *E. glutinosa* and the Tasmanian *E. lucida* (which was the first sp to be introduced to cultivation), making a columnar evergreen tree to 7m. Lv either simple or trifoliate, sometimes both shapes on the same tree, shining green above, glaucous beneath. Fl to 5cm across but usually rather less, white with yellow stamens, not produced until the plant is fairly large, fragrant. Fl 8–9. The clone in cultivation is known as 'Rostrevor'. Raised by Sir John Ross at Rostrevor and first flowered in 1936.

Eucryphia X nymansensis BAUSCH

4. A hybrid between the tall evergreen *E. cordifolia* and *E. glutinosa*. Tall, evergreen, columnar tree, to 10m or more. Lv simple or trifoliate, occasionally pinnate, with 5 leaflets, dull green, to 7cm long. Fl white, 6cm across, not appearing on young plants. Fl 8–9. Although the plant grows rapidly in congenial conditions, it is slow in coming to flowering size. 2 clones are in cultivation, 'Mount Usher' and 'Nymansay'. The latter was the first to be raised, at Nymans in Sussex, in 1915.

EUONYMUS LINNAEUS *Celastraceae*
Spindle Tree

A genus of 176 deciduous and evergreen shrubs, or rarely, small trees with opposite leaves and inconspicuous flowers. The majority of cultivated species have attractive coloured fruits, which usually open to disclose the seeds enclosed in a coloured aril. Many species also have brilliant autumn foliage. Most of the species will grow in any soil, although calcareous conditions are usual for the European species. The genus is found in all continents except Africa and S America.

Euonymus alatus SIEBOLD

6. Slow growing, spreading, deciduous shrub, to 3m but usually little more than 1m. Bts square at first, later developing two corky wings on opposite angles (these are lacking in var *apterus* REGEL). Fl and fr inconspicuous, the former dull purple, the latter scarlet, but small and hidden beneath the foliage. This latter turns a curious puce colour in the autumn, quite unlike any other autumn tint and the plant is then very brilliant. The plant is native to NE Asia and Japan and was introduced in 1860.

Euonymus cornutus HEMSLEY

5. Deciduous or evergreen shrub, to 3m, with thin, arching brs. Lv lanceolate, acuminate, rather like a willow, to 5cm long and 1cm across. Fl in small panicles in May. Fr a large, pink capsule from which emerge 4–6 long, thin, hornlike extensions. These fr are very singular, but tend to hide underneath the leaves somewhat. Native of China. Introduced by Wilson in 1908.

Euonymus latifolius

Euonymus europaeus LINNAEUS Spindle Tree

5.6. Deciduous shrub or small tree, to 8m. Lv elliptic-ovate, to 7cm long and 4cm wide, often colouring brilliantly in the autumn. Fl yellowish-green, inconspicuous. Fr red, about 2cm wide, later opening to reveal the seeds coated with their orange arils. There are some variants known, of which 'Albus' has white fr; 'Atropurpureus' has the bts and young lv dull purple (this form usually colours more brilliantly); and 'Aucubaefolius', which has the lv mottled with yellow and cream. Native of Europe, including the UK where it is often abundant on the chalk. Very attractive for autumnal decoration.

Euonymus fortunei HANDEL-MAZZETTI

(*E. radicans* SIEBOLD) Evergreen creeping or climbing shrub, attaching itself by means of roots in much the same way as ivy. It can attain a height of 7m if trained on a wall or up a tree. Juvenile lv oval, to 3cm long and 1cm across, adult lv to 5cm long and half as wide. Fl and fr inconspicuous. A number of different forms have been named, including 'Carrierei', which only bears adult lv and can make an independent shrub; 'Coloratus', in which the lv turn purple over winter; and also a number of forms with silver or cream variegation. The plants are tolerant of deep shade. Native of China, Korea and Japan. Introduced from 1865 onwards.

Euonymus japonicus THUNBERG

Evergreen shrub, usually little more than 2m high, but apparently capable of making a small tree to 8m. Lv obovate or oval-elliptic, to 7cm long and 5cm across, rather leathery, dark, shining green, slightly toothed. Fl inconspicuous, greenish-white. Fr rarely produced, whitish, 8mm across. There are a number of variants with silver and gold variegation and a form 'Microphyllus' with very small lv of slow growth. This also has cream and yellow-variegated forms. The dark green form will grow in sun or in shade; the variegated forms require full light to maintain the variegation. Popular in the nineteenth century as a hedging plant, particularly in coastal areas. Native of southern Japan. Introduced in 1804.

Euonymus latifolius MILLER

5.6. Shrub, usually to 3m but occasionally more, often spreading by means of sucker growths. Lv elliptic or obovate, to 12cm long and 5cm across, finely-toothed, often colouring well in the autumn. Fl in May, inconspicuous, but fr large, 2cm across before opening, 4–5-winged, rosy-pink; arils orange. The fr is ripe in September and falls before the lv colour, whereas in *E. europaeus* fr and lv are coloured at the same time. Native of Europe. In cultivation since 1730.

Euonymus sachalinensis MAXIMOWICZ

5.6. (*E. planipes* KOEHNE) Scarcely to be differentiated from the last sp, but lv more coarsely toothed and the petiole is not grooved above, as it is with *E. latifolius*. Native of Japan. Introduced about 1892.

Euonymus yedoensis KOEHNE

5.6. Strong-growing, deciduous shrub to 4m. Lv obovate to obovate-oblong or elliptic, to 12cm long and 7cm wide, turning yellow and crimson in the autumn. Fl inconspicuous, but with purple anthers, thereby distinguishing the plant from *E. europaeus* with yellow anthers. Fr pink (or bright crimson in the form known as 'Calocarpa'), arils orange. Close to *E. europaeus,* but with larger lv and fr ripening earlier. Now regarded as synonymous with *E. hamiltonianus* WALLICH var *Sieboldianus* (BLUME) KOMAR. Native of Japan

and Korea. Introduced 1865 by Parsons, but not named before 1904.

EVODIA FORSTER *Rutaceae*

A genus of about fifty evergreen and deciduous, dioecious shrubs and trees. Most of the species are tropical, but Wilson brought back a number of hardy species from China, of which only one is in commerce. The genus is also spelt *Euodia.*

Evodia hupehensis DODE

4.(5). Deciduous tree, to 20m, with smooth purple-brown bts. Lv pinnate, usually with 7–9 leaflets, each leaflet ovate, to 12cm long and 2cm across, medium green and smooth above, paler beneath. Fl in pyramidal panicles, up to 16cm across, whitish. Fl 6–7. If trees of both sexes are present the female will later produce handsome heads of red fruits. The plant thrives in poor and shallow soils and seems to do better on chalk. Native of central China. Introduced by Wilson in 1908.

EXOCHORDA LINDLEY *Rosaceae*

A small genus of deciduous shrubs from Asia with alternate leaves and large white flowers in terminal racemes. Generally they are plants of the easiest culture, but they will not thrive on very shallow soils. Two species seem to have no objection to chalk, *E. korolkowii* and *E. serratifolia*; the other species seem to do better on neutral or slightly acid soil. Propagation seems best by seed, although occasionally sucker growths appear and semi-hard stem cuttings with a heel are also possible.

Exochorda giraldii HESSE

4. Deciduous, spreading shrub, to 3 or 4m, with pinkish bts, as well as petioles and midribs. Lv elliptic, usually without serration. Fl in terminal racemes of 6–8 fl, generally 4cm across, but 5cm in the var *wilsonii* REHDER. Fl 5. Var *wilsonii*, although barely distinct, is the best form to obtain as it is more floriferous, as well as having larger fl. Introduced by Padre Giraldi from NW China before 1897; var *wilsonii* introduced by Wilson from central China in 1907.

Exochorda korolkowii LAVALLÉE

4. (*E. albertii* REGEL) Deciduous, erect-growing shrub, to 5m. Lv obovate, to 8cm long on non-flowering shoots, but only 2cm long on flowering shoots. The larger lv are slightly toothed in the upper half. The lv are among the first to appear in the spring. Fl in 5–8-flowered racemes, each fl about 3–4cm across. Fl 4–5. Less floriferous than the Chinese spp, but crossed with *E. racemosa* has formed the attractive hybrid *E. X macrantha* SCHNEIDER, which is a

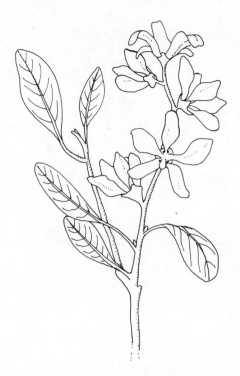

Exochorda giraldii

very effective shrub. Native of Turkestan at 1,500–2,000m. Introduced 1878.

Exochorda racemosa (LINDLEY) REHDER

4. (*Spiraea grandiflora* W. HOOKER) Deciduous, spreading shrub, to 3m. Lv narrowly obovate, to 7cm long and 2cm across, usually entire, sometimes toothed at the apex. Fl in erect racemes, to 4cm across, 6–10 in each raceme. Fl 5. Thrives best in acid soils. Native of eastern China. Introduced by Fortune in 1849.

Exochorda serratifolia S. MOORE

4. Allied to *E. giraldii* but a more compact shrub, to 2m. Lv elliptic, to 9cm long and 5cm across, margins serrate. Fl in erect racemes of 6–8, each fl about 4cm across. Fl 5. Does well on chalk. Native of Manchuria and Korea. Introduced in 1918.

FAGUS LINNAEUS *Fagaceae*

Although some ten species of beech are known, it is really only the native *F. sylvatica* which thrives in the UK. The plants are monoecious; the male flower in catkins, female flowers in clusters of two to three. The fruit is the well-known beech nut, but fertile seeds are by no means set every year. The plant seems to reach its largest dimensions over chalk, but appears to grow quite satisfactorily in any well-drained soil. Propagation is best by seed, but variegated and other eccentric forms are usually grafted. Cuttings are possible, but not easy.

Fagus sylvatica LINNAEUS   Beech

6.7. Large, deciduous tree, to 30m or more, with a smooth, grey trunk. Bts covered with silky hairs at first, later smooth. Lv oval, a very brilliant green when first unfurled, to 10cm long and 6cm wide, usually turning golden before falling.

A very large number of different forms have been isolated, of which var *heterophylla* LOUDON – the cut-leaved beech – with the lv deeply incised and lobed, is one of the most attractive. Several weeping forms are grouped under the name 'Pendula' while various purple and copper-leaved forms are now grouped under var *purpurea* AITON. There is also a pendulous form of the purple beech, and a cut-leaved form, known as 'Rohanii'. There are also forms with white and with yellow variegation, a purple form with a pink margin and a golden-leaved form, although the gold does not usually persist throughout the whole season; moreover the lv tend to scorch in hot sun, but do not develop their gold in the shade. 'Dawyck' is a fastigiate tree, giving a poplar-like effect, and so is more suitable for smaller gardens, although no beeches will ever suit very small spaces. However, the beech is also an excellent subject for hedging, and inside the hedge the withered leaves adhere throughout the winter, giving additional protection against winds.

Fagus sylvatica

97

Fatsia japonica

FATSIA DECAISNE AND PLANCHET *Araliaceae*

A monotypic genus.

Fatsia japonica DECAISNE AND PLANCHET

(*Aralia japonica* THUNBERG, *A. sieboldii* HORT) Sometimes known as the castor oil bush. Evergreen, spreading bush, to 5m, with very large, palmate lv often as much as 40cm across. The lv are 7–9-lobed, and on a long petiole, up to 15cm and occasionally more. The fl are in large, terminal panicles to 7cm across, greenish-white. Fl 10–11. Fr (rarely seen) a blackish berry. There is a variegated form with the lobe-tips white. *X Fatshedera* is a hybrid between this plant and the ivy *Hedera helix*, and is a semi-scandent shrub with lv similar to *Fatsia* but smaller. *F. japonica* itself is mainly grown for the sake of its lv and requires a sheltered, semi-shady position. The late fl are valuable and are produced on young bushes. Native of Japan. Introduced, presumably through Siebold, in 1838.

FITZROYA J. D. HOOKER *Cupressaceae*

A monotypic genus, indigenous to Chile. Propagated by seed (but this is rarely set in the UK), or by cuttings.

Fitzroya cupressoides (MOLINA) JOHNSTON

(*Pinus cupressoides* MOLINA, *Fitzroya patagonica* J. D. HOOKER) Evergreen tree or large bush, usually dioecious, occasionally monoecious. Growing up to 50m in Chile, but rarely to as much as 10m in the UK. Bark reddish, bts pendulous, green when young, later reddish. Lv in alternate whorls of 3, linear oblong, to 3mm long; green on the upper surface, whitish below.

Male fl small, solitary, in upper leaf axils; female fl solitary, on short side-shoots. Cone about 8mm across, composed of 3 whorls of 3 woody scales, of which only the topmost whorl usually bears seed. The lowest whorl is minute. The cones are fragrant.

An elegant foliage shrub, which does not survive everywhere and is probably not suited to chalky soils. In Chile it is found in a wide range of differing habitats, including marshy country. Said to have been discovered by Captain Fitzroy of the *Beagle* in 1834, but had previously been named by Molina (who died in 1829). Introduced by William Lobb in 1849.

FONTANESIA LABILLARDIÈRE *Oleaceae*

A genus of two species remarkably similar in appearance, but one from China and the other from western Asia, with no known intermediates. They are deciduous shrubs, resembling privet, but more akin to the ashes, with winged fruit. Succeeding in all soils and easily propagated by cuttings.

Fontanesia phillyreoides LABILLARDIÈRE

4. Deciduous, twiggy shrub, to 3m. Lv ovate-lanceolate, glabrous, to 6cm long and 1·5cm wide. Fl small but numerous, in terminal and axillary panicles, up to 3cm long. Fl 6. Fr a winged disk. *F. fortunei* CARRIÈRE is taller (up to 5m), the lv lanceolate and the fl panicles up to 5cm long; this may well be only a geographic form of *F. phillyreoides*. *F. phillyreoides* is native to western Asia, around the Mediterranean and Black Sea. Introduced in 1787. *F. fortunei* is found in eastern China and was brought back by Fortune from Shanghai in 1845.

FORSYTHIA VAHL *Oleaceae*

A genus of yellow-flowered, deciduous shrubs all from eastern Asia with one exception in SE Europe. The flowers emerge before the leaves early in the year and often wreathe the branches, to make them one of the showiest and most popular subjects for spring decoration. The flowers form on the year-old wood, so it is advisable to prune the plant as soon as flowering is complete. Birds often attack the unopened buds, sometimes stripping bushes completely. A number of hybrids are also in cultivation, mainly based on *F. X intermedia*, which is *F. suspensa X viridissima*. Hard wood cuttings root very readily.

Forsythia europaea DEGEN AND BALDACCHI

4. Deciduous shrub, to 2m, with upright growths. Lv ovate, to 7·5cm long and half as wide. Fl yellow, about 3cm across and 2cm long.

Fl 3–4. The least attractive sp, but interesting for its European habitat (Albania, Jugoslavia, Bulgaria). Only detected in 1897 and introduced in 1899.

Forsythia giraldiana LINGELSHEIM

4. Deciduous shrub, to 2m. Lv lanceolate or elliptic, to 10cm long, slightly hairy beneath. Fl about 2cm across, rather pale yellow. Fl 2–4. The earliest sp to flower and one that should be seen more often. Native to NW China. Introduced in 1910.

Forsythia ovata NAKAI

4. Probably *F. japonica* MAKINO should also come here. Spreading, rather low shrub, to 1·5m high. Lv ovate to 7cm long and half as wide (to 12cm in *F. japonica*). Fl deep yellow, to 2cm long and slightly wider. Fl 3–4. Another early flowerer. Native to Korea. Introduced in 1917 by Wilson.

Forsythia suspensa VAHL

4. Shrub, to 3m, but the trailing form, var *sieboldii* ZABEL, can be trained up a wall for 10m. Var *atrocaulis* REHDER has purple-black bts and is thus more attractive; the fl are a rather pale yellow.

The best form for growing as an upright shrub is var *fortunei* REHDER (*F. fortunei* LINDLEY). Lv ovate, but on strong shoots, sometimes 2 or 3-lobed, to 10cm long and half as wide. Fl in clusters, sometimes as many as 6, deep yellow, except in var *atrocaulis* and a sport therefrom known as 'Nymans' with pale yellow fl. Fl 3–4. Native of China, long cultivated in Japan and introduced thence to Holland by Pistorius, presumably a correspondent of Siebold, in 1833. This was var *sieboldii*; var *fortunei* was collected by Fortune in 1860 and var *atrocaulis* by Wilson in 1908.

Forsythia viridissima LINDLEY

4. Deciduous shrub, to 3m, with square stems and lanceolate lv to 15cm long and 4cm across, tapering at both ends. Possibly toothed or with entire margins. Fl in clusters of up to 3, bright yellow, to 3cm across. Fl 4–5. The last sp to flower and easily distinguished with its long lanceolate lv and square stems. Native of China. Introduced by Fortune in 1844.

FOTHERGILLA LINNAEUS *Hamamelidaceae*

A small genus of deciduous shrubs from the south-eastern USA. The flowers are produced in terminal spikes before the leaves and have no petals but a mass of conspicuous white stamens. The leaves usually colour very brilliantly in the autumn. The plants require acid or neutral soil and can be propagated by seed, layers or by cuttings.

Fothergilla gardenii MURRAY

4.6. (*F. alnifolius* LINNAEUS THE YOUNGER) The smallest sp, not exceeding 1m, with slender brs both erect and spreading. Lv either oval or obovate, blunt or slender pointed, turning crimson in autumn. Fl before lv in spikes to 3cm long and 2·5cm across of white, yellow-anthered stamens, fragrant. Fl 4–5. Found from Virginia to Georgia. Introduced in 1765; probably one of the last sendings of John Bartram.

Fothergilla major LODDIGES

4.6. Slow-growing, spreading, deciduous shrub to 3m. Lv orbicular or ovate to 10cm long and wide, wrinkled above when young and dark green, glaucous and slightly hairy below, turning orange-yellow in the autumn. Fl opening as the lv unfurl, in spikes to 5cm long, with pinkish-white stamens. Fl 4–5. Native to Georgia. Introduced in 1765, but subsequently lost and reintroduced as recently as 1902.

Fothergilla monticola ASHE

4.6. Dubiously distinct from *F. major*, but only to 2m high with a more spreading habit. Lv green below, not glabrous, turning red in autumn. Fl spikes to 6cm long, slightly larger than those of *F. major*. Probably included among the 1765 introductions, but not diagnosed as a separate sp before 1899. Native from N Carolina to Alabama.

FRAXINUS LINNAEUS *Oleaceae*

The ashes are distributed throughout the northern hemisphere and comprise a genus of some seventy species of deciduous trees, rarely shrubs, with opposite pinnate leaves and winged seeds known as keys. The genus divides fairly happily into two sections: *Ornus*, with the flowers possessing petals produced in terminal and lateral panicles after the leaves; and *Fraxinaster*, with the flowers produced before the leaves and devoid of petals. This section is sometimes divided into two subsections: *Sciadanthus*, with the flowers possessing a calyx; and *Bumelioides,* where the calyx is lacking. Intermediate between the two sections is the Chinese *F. chinensis*, with the habit of the *Ornus* section, but the petals lacking, and *F. dipetala*, with the habit of *Fraxinaster* but with petals. *F. chinensis* is thus given a section all to itself – *Ornaster*, and *F. dipetala* is given a subsection, Dipetalae. *F. dipetala*, although attractive, is not generally hardy.

Fraxinus americana LINNAEUS *Fraxinaster*
White Ash

7. (*F. alba* MARSHALL) Deciduous tree, to 40m, of rapid growth. Lv pinnate, to 37cm overall, with 7–9 oblong-lanceolate leaflets, each to 15cm long and half as wide. In the USA these colour well deep purple or yellow in autumn. Fl with calyx, sometimes unisexual, in lateral panicles. Fr to 5cm long. Native to eastern N America. Introduced in 1724.

Fraxinus angustifolia VAHL *Fraxinaster*

7. Tree, to 25m but occasionally more, with glabrous bts and lv. Lv to 25cm long with 7–13 leaflets, to 7cm long but only 2cm across. Fl polygamous, but lacking either petals or calyx. Fr to 3cm long. Var *lentiscifolia* HENRY has the leaflets more spreading, while 'Pendula' has slender pendulous brs. Distinguished only by down along the midrib and main veins is *F. oxycarpa* WILLDENOW, of which there is a clone **6.** 'Raywood' in which the lv turn purple in autumn. *F. angustifolia* is native to western S. Europe and N. Africa. *F. oxycarpa* to eastern S. Europe and western Asia extending to the Caucasus and Iran.

Fraxinus bungeana DE CANDOLLE *Ornus*

4. Shrub to 5m, rarely a small tree. Winter buds nearly black. Lv usually of 5 leaflets, to 15cm overall, each leaflet obovate, to 5cm long and half as wide. Fl small, white, in dense panicles to 8 cm. Fl 5–6. Fr to 3cm long. Notable for its shrubby habit and conspicuous fl. Native to north China. Introduced in 1881.

Fraxinus chinensis ROXBURGH
Ornus ss Ornaster

6. Tree, to 15m, with grey buds and bts. Lv very large on young trees and on mature trees each leaflet may be up to 10cm long and about half as wide, while the terminal leaflet is often as much as 13cm long. The lv is usually made up of 7–9 leaflets. In some districts they turn purple in the autumn. Fl in lax, terminal panicles to 15cm long, lacking petals, but fragrant. Fl 5–6. Fr to 4cm long. Native of China. Introduced in 1891.

Fraxinus excelsior LINNAEUS *Fraxinaster* Ash

7. Tree, to 45m, with nearly black buds. Lv up to 30cm long with 9–11 leaflets, each oblong-lanceolate, to 11cm long and 3cm across. Fl lacking petals or calyx in lateral clusters. Keys to 3cm long, 8mm wide. Fl 4–5. Formerly forms with yellow and white variegated lv existed, but these seem to be lost. The weeping ash, 'Pendula', makes an impressive tent, while 'Jaspidea' has yellow bts and the lv turn gold before falling. Other aberrant forms are in cultivation but not

very attractive. Native of Europe including Britain.

Fraxinus latifolia BENTHAM *Fraxinaster*

7. (*F. oregona* NUTTALL) Tree, to 25m, bts usually downy. Lv to 30cm, usually with 7 leaflets, which are oblong-oval to 12cm long and 5cm across; dark green above, pale and downy below. Winter buds brown. Fl without petals but with a calyx. Fr. to 5cm long and 9mm across. Native to the western USA from Washington southwards to California. Detected by Douglas, but not apparently in cultivation before 1870.

Fraxinus mariesii JOSEPH HOOKER *Ornus*

4.5. Slow-growing shrub or small tree to 8m, usually rather less. Lv purplish when unfurling, up to 17cm long, composed of 3 or 5 leaflets; petiole is purplish, turning dark green later. The leaflets are ovate, to 7cm long and 4·5cm across. Fl white or creamy white, very small but numerous in axillary and terminal panicles to 15cm long. Fl 6–7. Fr to 2·5cm long, deep purple. Arguably the most attractive member of the genus and very suitable for small gardens owing to its modest dimensions and slow rate of growth. Native of central China. Introduced by Charles Maries in 1878, one of the few plants he collected in that neighbourhood.

Fraxinus ornus LINNAEUS *Ornus* Manna Ash

4.7. Round-headed, very leafy tree, to 20m; winter buds grey. Lv to 20 cm long, with 5–9 leaflets, ovate or oblong, shining green. Leaflets usually about 5cm long and 2cm across. Fl whitish, in terminal panicles to 10cm long, produced with new lv. Fl 5. Fr about 2·5cm long. Native to south-eastern Europe and western Asia. Handsome when well-grown as a specimen tree; when younger could be mistaken for a *Sambucus*.

Fraxinus paxiana LINGELSHEIM *Ornus*

4.7. Tree, to 20m; winter buds covered with rusty down. Lv large, to 30cm long, with 7–9 leaflets, the largest of which can reach a length of 18cm. Fl in terminal and axillary panicles to 15cm long, white. Fl 5–6. Fr to 3cm long. A handsome tree which should be more often planted where spring frosts are not frequent. Native to western and central China and the Himalaya. Introduced by Wilson in 1901.

Fraxinus pennsylvanica MARSHALL *Fraxinaster*

7. (*F. pubescens* LAMARCK) and including *F. lanceolata* BORKHAUSEN Tree, to 20m, with downy young shoots (glabrous in var *lanceolata* SARGENT) and brown winter buds. Lv to 30cm long, with 7–9 leaflets, each oblong-lanceolate to 15cm long and 5cm across, dull green. Fl with calyx. Fr to 5cm long. In var *aucubaefolia* REHDER, the lv are mottled with yellow, while *lanceolata* 'Variegata' has greyish lv with a whitish margin. Native to the north-eastern USA. Introduced in 1783.

Fraxinus sieboldiana BLUME *Ornus*

4.6. (*F. longicuspis* SIEBOLD AND ZUCCARINI) A small tree, to about 12m in cultivation but up to 17m in the wild, with grey bts and rusty downy winter buds. Lv to about 15cm overall with five leaflets to 10cm long and 4cm across. Sometimes turning purple in the autumn. Fl in terminal and axillary panicles to 12cm long. Fl 5–6 white. Fr to 4cm long. Fairly close to *F. ornus,* but a smaller tree, usually with not more than 5 leaflets. Native to Japan and Korea. Introduced in 1894.

Fraxinus sogdiana BUNGE *Fraxinaster*

(*F. potamophila* HERDER) Small tree, to 10m, with green, smooth bts. Lv to 30cm long with, usually, 9–11 leaflets, although up to 13 have been noted; the leaflets are distinctly stalked, up to 7cm long and 3cm across. Fl lacking petals and calyx. Fr to 5cm long. Native of Turkestan, in cultivation about 1890. An elegant small tree.

Fraxinus spaethiana LINGELSHEIM *Fraxinaster*

4. (*F. serratifolia* HORT) Small tree, to 15m, with glabrous grey bts. Lv to 45cm long, usually with 7 or 9 leaflets, oblong, the largest to 20cm long and 7cm across, the smallest to 10cm long and half as wide, oblong. The main petiole is much swollen where it clasps the bt and is tinged reddish-brown. Fl in lateral panicles. Fr to 3·5cm long. With its enormous lv, a very conspicuous tree. Native of Japan. Introduced about 1873.

Fraxinus tomentosa F. MICHAUX *Fraxinaster*

7. Tree, to 40m, with hairy bts and petioles. Lv to 30cm or more; leaflets 7–9, elliptic, to 25cm long; smooth above, downy below. Fl with calyx. Fr to 7cm long. Notable for its large lv. Native to the eastern USA from New York to Florida. Only introduced in 1913.

Fraxinus velutina TORREY *Fraxinaster*

7. A medium-sized tree, to 15m, with velvety bts, while the petioles and the immature lv are also clothed with this velvety down (but this character does not apply to var *glabra* REHDER). Lv to 15cm, with 5–7 leaflets usually, lanceolate, to 6cm long and 1·8cm across. Fl lacking a calyx. Fr to 2cm. Var. *coriacea* REHDER has less pubescence and rather leathery lv. Var *toumeyi* (BRITTON) REHDER has smaller lv, with 3–5 leaflets and a less open habit. Native to Arizona and New Mexico. Introduced to Kew in 1891.

Fraxinus xanthoxyloides (DON) DE CANDOLLE *Fraxinaster*

Shrub, or occasionally small tree, to 7m. Bts covered with dense, dark brown down at first, later purplish on upper surface. Lv with 5–9 leaflets, the whole lv not more than 7cm long, leaflets ovate to 2·8cm long and 1cm wide. Fr to 5cm long. Var *dimorpha* (COSSON AND DURIEU) WENZIG has the bts glabrous. Var *dumosa* (CARRIÈRE) LINGELSHEIM makes a dense bush, only to 2m, and the leaflets are not more than 1·5cm long. *F. xanthoxyloides* comes from Afghanistan and the Himalaya and entered cultivation in 1870; the two var come from N Africa, mainly Algeria, and arrived in 1855 and 1865.

FUCHSIA LINNAEUS *Onagraceae*

A genus of some seventy species mainly from central and S America, but with a couple of outliers in New Zealand. Deciduous in the UK, with the leaves usually in whorls. The flowers are notable for their waxy coloured tubular calyx, with reflexed lobes which may be more conspicuous than the bell-like corolla. In colder districts the hardy species may be cut down to the ground in severe winters, but they can be relied on to regenerate. There are a number of hybrids between *F. magellanica* and larger flowered tender species, some of which are hardy ('Exoniensis', 'Mme Cornelissen', 'Mrs Popple' etc) and which are not described here as they do not generally exceed 1m high. The same applies to the small-flowered species in the section *Encliandra*, where the sepals and petals are the same length and the sepals lack a tube. Propagation is usually by soft wood cuttings, which root readily with a little heat or outside in the summer.

Fuchsia magellanica LAMARCK

4. Deciduous shrub, to 3m or more in suitable districts. Lv opposite or in whorls of 3 or 4, elliptic-ovate, to 5cm long; dark green with reddish petioles. Fl purple with red sepals. Tube to 1cm long (which serves to distinguish this plant from the similar *F. coccinea*, with which in early days it was often confused). In *F. coccinea* the tube does not exceed 6mm with stamens and style protruding. The fl are borne in pairs, on peduncles 5cm long, from June or July until the frosts come. Fr a purplish berry about 2cm long, but rarely produced. There is an albino with white sepals and pink corolla, known correctly as var *molinae* but usually met with as *F. magellanica alba*. In the early 1830s hybrids between this sp and *F. coccinea* were raised, whether or not intentionally is not clear, and from one of these hybrids it is thought an

F2 seedling gave rise to the plant known as 'Riccartonii', with more globose fl and a shorter tube, which is the most floriferous and hardiest of fuchsias.

Native of Chile and Argentina. Probably first introduced by Cruckshank in 1822, but the plant became so confused with *F. coccinea*, introduced from Brazil in 1788 by a Captain Firth, that early introductions are not easy to confirm.

GARRYA LINDLEY *Garryaceae*

A family with only the one genus of about fifteen species of dioecious evergreen shrubs or small trees. The leaves are opposite, short-petioled, and the flowers are in axillary and terminal catkin-like racemes, without petals. The male flower has four sepals and so is more conspicuous than the females, which lack sepals, although they do have two bracts which serve to give a sepal-like appearance. Only one species is reliably hardy, and this can be damaged in exceptionally severe winters and does best with wall protection in cold areas. Propagation by cuttings of half-ripe wood, or by seed.

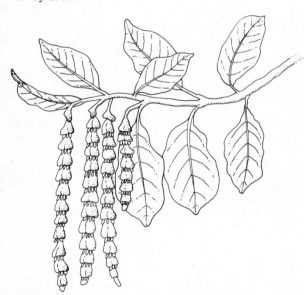

Garrya elliptica

Garrya elliptica LINDLEY

4. Evergreen shrub, to 4m or more in mild districts or against a wall. Bts downy. Lv oval or round, to 7cm long and half as wide, dark green and glabrous above, grey-woolly below. Male catkins to 30cm long in mild districts or with selected clones, female catkins never more than 10cm long and usually less. Catkins fully formed 11–2, the stamens usually producing their pollen in the latter month. Plants dislike moving and should be obtained ex-pots. Native of the western USA. Introduced by Douglas in 1828.

GAULTHERIA LINNAEUS *Ericaceae*

A large genus of over 200 species with a very wide distribution, only Africa apparently lacking any representative. The leaves are alternate and have very short petioles. The urn-shaped flowers are usually five-lobed, the fruit is a dry capsule enclosed by the enlarged fleshy calyx, which gives a berry-like appearance. The flowers are usually in terminal or axillary panicles. There are not many hardy species and many of these are prostrate shrubs, which will not be treated here. The genus can easily be confused with *Vaccinium*, which has a true berry, but in flower the ovary is uppermost in *Gaultheria*, while in *Vaccinium* the ovary is inside the flower. The species here described requires acid soil, which should always be somewhat damp; it also requires shady conditions.

Gaultheria shallon PURSH

4.5. Evergreen, suckering shrub, up to 2m but usually considerably less, with reddish bristly bts. Lv rather leathery, ovate, to 10cm long and slightly more than half as wide. Fl in terminal and axillary racemes to 12cm long, pinkish, to 9mm long. Fl 5–6. Fr a dark purple 'berry', edible. A good ground cover in shady situations, otherwise not outstandingly ornamental. Native to NW America. Introduced by Douglas in 1826.

GENISTA LINNAEUS

A genus of mainly deciduous shrubs, closely allied to *Cytisus* from which it is distinguished chiefly by the absence of a wart-like swelling at the base of the seed known as a strophiole. In *Genista* the upper lip of the calyx is deeply two-lobed, while that of *Cytisus* is only shortly-toothed. For most species the leaves of *Genista* are simple, while those of *Cytisus* are trifoliate, but there are exceptions and there are also a number of anomalous species agreeing with neither, which some botanists put into separate genera. Most *Genista* species are low or prostrate shrubs and not mentioned here. The species which are discussed are best raised from seed, although cuttings are possible, and should be planted in their permanent positions from pots, as they do not transplant at all readily. They like sunny positions and are happy in any soil.

Genista aetnensis (BIVONA) DE CANDOLLE

4. (*Spartium aetnense* BIVONA) Tall shrub or small tree, to 7m. Lv usually absent, narrow-linear in seedlings, the pendulous bts doing service for them. Fl along the ends of the present year's growth, golden-yellow, each about 1cm long. Fl 7–8. Valuable for its late flowering, a very floriferous shrub, usually becoming tree-like as it ages. Native to Sicily and Sardinia.

Genista cinerea (VILLARS) DE CANDOLLE

4. (*Spartium cinereum* VILLARS) Deciduous shrub, to 3m, with bts covered with silky hairs when young. Lv often absent, grey-green, linear, to 12mm long with silky hairs below. Fl in clusters of 2–4, about 1·5cm long, bright yellow. Fl 6–7. Native to the western Mediterranean region.

Genista tenera (JACQUIN) O. KUNTZE

4. (*Spartium virgatum* AITON) Bushy shrub, to 4m. Lv linear, grey-green, to 1·7cm long. Fl in terminal racemes to 5cm long, each fl about 12mm long, bright yellow. Fl 6–7 and sporadically to 10. One of the few spp which will thrive in partial shade. Native to Madeira and Teneriffe and possibly a geographical form of *G. cinerea*, although fairly distinct. Introduced by Masson from Madeira in 1777.

GINKGO LINNAEUS *Ginkgoaceae*

Both the family and the genus now consist of a single species, although from fossil evidence other species are known to have existed in the past. Moreover, although the plant is commonly found around Chinese temples, it has never been found convincingly wild and would appear to have been preserved from extinction on account of its ornamental character.

Ginkgo biloba LINNAEUS   Maidenhair Tree

6.7. (*Salisburia adiantifolia* SMITH) Deciduous tree, to 30m or more, although the largest in the UK is little more than 25m. The plants are dioecious and slow-growing. Lv fan-shaped, like the frond of a maidenhair fern, to 7cm long and wide, yellowish-green turning golden before falling. Male fl in short, cylindrical catkins to 2cm long; female fl on short stalks, eventually becoming like a plum, with yellowish-green flesh, each fr to 3cm long and with an unpleasing odour. Male trees are much more common in cultivation. Seeds are rarely set in the UK, although seed is the only reliable method of increase; they are set freely in warmer parts of Europe and the USA. The tree is perfectly hardy and appears to thrive in all soils. It is found in both pendulous and fastigiate forms, as well as intermediates. Brought from Japan to Europe in 1728 and obtained by the nurseryman James Gordon in 1754.

GLEDITSIA LINNAEUS *Leguminosae*

(Sometimes spelt *Gleditschia*). A genus of eleven species of deciduous trees with very attractive leaves, which are pinnate or bipinnate. Trunk and branches usually fiercely spiny, the spines often being branched. The flowers are either perfect or unisexual, inconspicuous and in small racemes. The fruit is a pod, which is sometimes very large. The plants come late into growth and in very cold districts may not ripen their growth satisfactorily, which has been found to cause damage to seedlings. Mature plants are usually perfectly hardy in the species described below. *G. delavayi*, with reddish young growths, is liable to damage in very severe winters and so has been omitted. Any soil seems to suit these plants and seed appears the best method of propagation.

Gleditsia aquatica MARSHALL

Deciduous, shrubby tree in the UK, but a tree to 20m in the USA. Trunk and brs armed with spines that can reach 10cm and are often branched. Lv to 20cm long, pinnate or bipinnate, with 12–24 leaflets; each oblong to 2cm long and 1cm wide, glossy green. Fl in racemes to 10cm long. Fl 6. Pods not more than 4cm long, single-seeded, but not produced in the UK. A slow-growing plant. Native to the south-east USA. Introduced by Mark Catesby in 1723.

Gleditsia caspica DESFONTAINES

7. Deciduous tree, to 13m, with trunk and brs armed with somewhat flat spines up to 15cm long. Bts green, glabrous. Lv pinnate or bipinnate, to 25cm long, with up to 20 leaflets which are ovate, up to 5cm long and 2cm wide; lamina glabrous and shining green, midribs and rachis downy. Fl greenish, in racemes to 10cm. Pods sickle-shaped to 20cm long and 3cm wide.

This plant seems invariably to have been confused with *G. sinensis*, but seeds of a *Gleditsia* were received by Peter Collinson in 1747 from Persia, and in 1759 he noted 'a three-thorned Acacia I raised from seed sent from Persia, that puts forth monstrous long thorns from the solid stem of the tree, without shoots or leaves'. Whether this was also the source of the plants offered by Kennedy and Lee in 1774, which have been assigned to *G. sinensis*, is not clear, although it is not easy to see why *G. sinensis* should have been brought so early into cultivation. Almost certainly Collinson's plant was *G. caspica*, so that Loudon's date of introduction of 1822 is incorrect.

Gleditsia japonica MIQUEL

7. Tree, to 20m or more in the wild but slow-growing in the UK and so far not more than 10m. Trunk and brs armed with flattened, branched spines; bts purple-brown. Lv pinnate or bipinnate, to 30cm, with 14–24 leaflets which are ovate or lanceolate, to 1·5cm long (larger on mature trees in the wild). Pods to 25cm long, 3cm wide, scimitar-shaped and later twisted. Evidently fairly closely allied to *G. caspica*. Native to Japan. In cultivation by 1800 according to Rehder, but not received at Kew before 1894.

Gleditsia sinensis LAMARCK

7. (*G. horrida* WILLDENOW) Deciduous tree, to 15m in the wild, with conical (not flattened) spines which are often branched. Bts green. Lv pinnate, to 20cm long, with 8–14 leaflets which are ovate, to 8cm long and 2·8cm wide, stalks and rachis downy, lv glabrous. Fl in racemes, greenish-white, to 9cm long. Pods nearly straight, to 25cm long and 3cm wide, purplish. Native of China from the Pekin region and in Szechuan. Probably introduced around 1774, but see note to *G. caspica*.

Gleditsia triacanthos

Gleditsia triacanthos

Gleditsia triacanthos LINNAEUS   Honey Locust

6.7. Tree of up to about 20m in cultivation but over 40m in the wild. Trunk and brs usually armed with thick spines to 10cm long according to Rehder, as much as 30cm according to Bean; the spines are often three-branched, as its name would imply. Lv to 20cm long, bipinnate in young plants, often only pinnate on established trees, with 14–32 leaflets 1–3cm long, ovate or oblong; glossy green, turning clear yellow before falling. This plant is usually dioecious. Pods as long as 45cm, falcate and twisted. In the forma *inermis* the spines are lacking; 'Inermis aurea' is not only spineless but has yellow young lv. 'Bujotii' is a pendulous form, while 'Elegantissima' makes a small shrub of not more than 5m after many years. Native to central N America. Introduced by John Banister to Bishop Compton about 1699.

GRISELINIA G. FORSTER   *Cornaceae*

A small genus of evergreen trees and shrubs from New Zealand, Chile and southern Brazil, of which only one species is reliably hardy. The plants are dioecious, but neither sex has any floral beauty. They propagate reasonably easily from soft or hard wood cuttings.

Griselinia littoralis RAOUL

Large shrub, or, in mild districts, a small tree to 15m. Bts yellowish-green. Lv coriaceous, oval, to 11cm long and 6–11cm wide; glossy, yellowish-green at first, later bright green. Fl in axillary racemes to 7cm long, yellowish-green and inconspicuous. Fl 5. There are two variegated cv; one with a margin golden at first, fading to whitish, the other with a green margin and coloured centre. Some clones of this plant appear far hardier than others. It is excellent as a seaside shrub, but flourishes inland in some normally cold districts; thus plants should preferably be purchased from local nurseries. Native. of New Zealand. Introduced about 1850.

GYMNOCLADUS LINNAEUS   *Leguminosae*

A small genus of only four species, one from N America, the others from E Asia. Of these only one species is hardy in the UK.

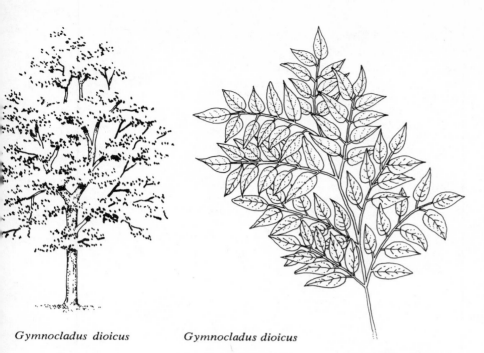

Gymnocladus dioicus

Gymnocladus dioicus

Gymnocladus dioicus (LINNAEUS) K. KOCH
Kentucky Coffee Tree

6.7. (*G. canadensis* LAMARCK) Deciduous tree, to 35m in the wild but rarely above 15m in the UK. Bts very pale grey and conspicuous in winter. Lv pinnate below, bipinnate towards the apex, very large, sometimes to 1m long and 60cm wide, but more usually to 45cm long. Leaflets are pinkish-purple when unfurling, ovate, to 6cm long and half as wide, downy below when young, later glabrous, turning a good clear yellow in the autumn before falling. The main rachis remains on the tree long after the leaflets have fallen. The plant is dioecious, with the fl in terminal panicles but rarely seen in cultivation, as are the pods, which are said to be up to 25cm long and 5cm wide. (Once used as an additive to coffee.) The plant is not affected by any winter cold, but it comes very late into leaf, so that in cold, wet summers the wood may not ripen properly, and the plant is a slow grower in any case. It is well worth growing for its spectacular leaves. Native of eastern and central USA. Introduced by Bartram before 1748.

HALESIA LINNAEUS *Styracaceae*

A small genus of five species of deciduous trees or shrubs; four from N America and one from China. The leaves are alternate, the flowers pendulous, in clusters from joints of year-old wood. Acid or neutral soil is essential for these plants, but otherwise they present no difficulty. They are propagated by seed or by layers.

Halesia carolina LINNAEUS Snowdrop Tree

4. (*H. tetraptera* ELLIS) Large shrub or small tree, to 10m in cultivation but occasionally larger in the wild; probably not very long-lived. Bts downy at first, later glabrous. Lv ovate-elliptic, to 12cm long, glabrous above, downy below, with a short petiole. Fl pendulous, white, 4-lobed, to 2cm long and wide in clusters of 3–5 from the nodes of the year-old wood. Fl 5. Fr pyriform, with 4 wings to 3cm long. Native of south-eastern USA. Introduced in 1756 by J. E. Ellis.

Halesia diptera ELLIS

4. Shrub, to 5m, with downy bts which later become glabrous. Lv elliptic, to 13cm long and 7cm across, downy on both surfaces at first, later nearly glabrous, petiole to 2cm long. Fl pendulous, white, to 2cm long. Fl 5. Fr oblong, to 5cm long with only two wings. Less hardy and less floriferous than *H. carolina*. Native to USA from South Carolina to Florida and Texas. Introduced by Ellis in 1758.

Halesia monticola (REHDER) SARGENT

4.(7). (*H. carolina var monticola* REHDER) Deciduous tree, to 30m in the wild; ultimate dimension in cultivation in the UK not yet known. Very close to *H. carolina* but larger in all its parts, and in mature trees the bark is very distinct, separating from the trunk in large scales, while in *H. carolina* the scales are very small and do not detach themselves. Lv only slightly larger than those of *H. carolina* but in the western forms (var *vestita* SARGENT) the young lv are densely white woolly below, and always somewhat downy. Fl to 3cm long, white, although there is a pale pink form of var *vestita*. Fl 5–6. Fr 4-winged as in *H. carolina*, to 5cm long.

First distinguished as a var of *H. carolina* in 1913 and given specific rank in 1922, although apparently in cultivation in 1897. Native from N Carolina south to Tennessee and Georgia, while var *vestita* spreads westward from N Carolina to Arkansas and Oklahoma. Var *vestita* does not necessarily have larger fl, although those in commerce appear to be better than the type.

HALIMODENDRON FISCHER *Leguminosae*
A monotypic genus of a single shrub, related to *Caragana*.

Halimodendron halodendron (PALLAS) SCHNEIDER

4. (*Robinia halodendron* PALLAS, *H. argenteum* FISCHER) Deciduous shrub, to 2m, with spiny greyish brs. Lv pinnate, usually with only 2 pairs of leaflets and a terminal spine. Leaflets lanceolate, to 3cm long and 6mm wide, silvery

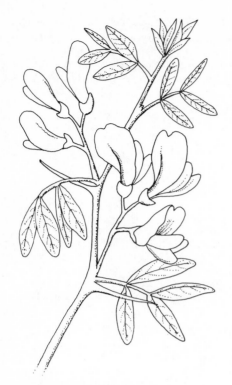

Halimodendron halodendron

grey in colour. Fl in racemes to 5cm long, each fl about 1·5cm long, pinkish-purple (darker in the cv 'Purpureum'). Pods inflated to 2·5cm long and half as wide. Fl 6–7. Native of much of central Asia, where it is often found in salt marshes, so very suitable for maritime situations; otherwise it likes full sunshine and appears indifferent to the type of soil. Often grafted on to standards of *Caragana arborescens* or of *Laburnum*. Introduced by Dr Pitcairn in 1779, presumably from seed collected by Pallas.

HAMAMELIS LINNAEUS *Hamamelidaceae*

A small genus of six deciduous shrubs. The leaves are alternate and like the hazel in appearance, hence the name witch hazel, applied first to the American species. The flower consists of four long, very narrow petals, which give the flower a spidery appearance. Most soils will suit the species but they do not like it too shallow nor too heavy. Seed is the best method of increase, but it may take two years for seeds to germinate and then the plants are slow-growing. Cultivars are usually grafted on to *H. virginiana*. The Asian species open their flowers very early in the year, and these are quite unaffected by the severest frosts, so they are among the most valuable of all shrubs for winter ornament. In addition, the leaves often colour quite attractively in the autumn.

Hamamelis japonica SIEBOLD AND ZUCCARINI

4.6. Shrub or small tree, which in the rather indeterminate form known as var *arborea* (MASTERS) GUMBLETON can reach 10m, but which is usually a spreading bush of about 5m. Lv oval, to 9cm long and 6cm across, often colouring well in the autumn. Fl yellow, scented, the inside of the calyx reddish, in clusters before the lv. Fl 1–2. Var *flavopurpurascens* (MAKINO) REHDER (sometimes known as *H. japonica rubra*) has the petals suffused with red, while the interior of the calyx is deep purple. Not particularly attractive but a valuable parent of hybrids. 'Zuccariniana' is a pale yellow form flowering a month later than the type. Native of Japan. Introduced 1862.

Hamamelis X intermedia REHDER

4.6. The collective name for hybrids between *H. japonica* and *H. mollis*. The most spectacular of these have been raised in the Kalmthout arboretum where the presence of *H. japonica* var *flavopurpurascens* has given rise to plants with orange and red fl. Among these are 'Diane', with coppery fl, and 'Jelena', which is orange. Probably the pale sulphur plant known as *H. mollis* 'Pallida' belongs here. The darker coloured cv also have red or orange in their autumn colour.

Hamamelis mollis OLIVER

4.6. Deciduous shrub or small tree, either of spreading habit or, in the clone known as 'Goldcrest', fairly upright. Lv roundish, heart-shaped at base, hairy below, to 12cm long and 9cm wide, turning yellow before falling. Fl in numerous clusters, large, about 3cm across, petals not wavy as in *H. japonica*; golden-yellow, very fragrant. Fl 12–2, although 'Goldcrest' may be a month later. Calyx lobes reddish-brown inside. Native of China. Originally introduced by Maries in 1879 but long thought to be a superior form of *H. japonica*. The distinctness of the sp was recognised in 1888, but it was not until 1898 that Veitch started propagating the only plant that had emerged from Maries's seeds. This form is now known as 'Coombe Wood'. Further sendings were made to the Arnold arboretum by Wilson in 1907–8. The most floriferous of the spp.

Hamamelis vernalis SARGENT

4.6. Suckering shrub, usually little more than 2m. Lv obovate, to 12cm long and 8cm across, downy below when young (or always in the form *tomentella*). Fl rather small, closing up in cold weather and unfurling the petals when the temperature rises; generally yellow, but forms with red bases to the petals and even with quite red petals occur from time to time. The calyx is

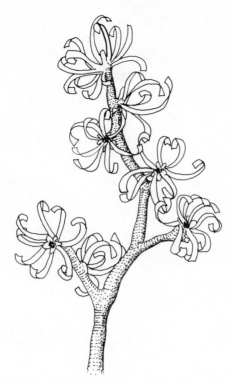

Hamamelis mollis

yellowish-brown inside. Fl 12–3. The cv **3.4.6.** 'Sandra' has the young lv plum purple and they remain purple-flushed throughout the year, turning orange and red in the autumn. Certainly known since 1845, it was only diagnosed as a distinct sp in 1913, although it was in cultivation in 1908. Native to Missouri, Louisiana and Oklahoma.

Hamamelis virginiana LINNAEUS   Witch Hazel

4.6. Shrub or small tree, to 5m or more in the wild. Bts downy at first. Lv to 12cm long and 9cm across, broad-ovate, turning clear yellow in the autumn. Fl pale yellow, small, mainly produced before the lv fall. Calyx pale brown within. Fl 9–11. Less attractive than the other spp as the fl tend to be hidden beneath the lv. Native of eastern N America. Introduced, probably by Bartram, in 1736.

HEBE COMMERSON *Scrophulariaceae*

A genus of 100 species or more of evergreen shrubs and small trees, mainly confined to New Zealand but with outliers in S America and Australia. The leaves are opposite, the upper ones enclosed in the pair not yet open, but in a few dwarf forms the leaves are reduced to small scale-like processes, much resembling the scales of cupressus or chamaecyparis. The flowers are in axillary racemes, patulate, four-lobed and with

a long season. Most of the species are on the borderline of hardiness and all seem to do best in maritime districts. They appear to thrive in all types of soil, including chalky ones. Besides the species, there are a number of hybrids, most of which will not be discussed here. Indeed only the hardiest species and hybrids are mentioned and all the dwarf species are omitted. Propagation by cuttings of half-ripened wood is not difficult, and seed germinates readily, although owing to the plants' propensity for hybridising it cannot always be assumed to come true. In floral character, the plants are scarcely distinguishable from the herbaceous *Veronicas* of the northern hemisphere, but their shrubby character is unique to them, although at one time they were included in that genus.

Hebe brachysiphon SUMMERHAYES

4. (*H. traversii* of gardens) Evergreen shrub, to 2m, wide-spreading and rounded. Lv densely arranged, narrow-oval, to 2·5cm long and 6mm wide, glabrous, dark green. Fl in axillary racemes from end of shoots, about 7cm long, each fl about 8mm across, white; anthers purplish. Fl 7–8. One of the hardiest spp. Introduced from New Zealand about 1868.

Hebe buxifolia (BENTHAM) COCKAYNE AND ALLAN

4. Probably only a scentless form of *H. odora* (J. HOOKER) COCKAYNE, which is preferable, owing to its perfume. Evergreen shrub to 1·5m, lv ovate-oblong, 1cm long and 5mm wide, dark shining green, glabrous. Fl in clusters which combine to form a corymb to 5cm wide, each fl to 8mm wide, white (sometimes pink in the plant known in gardens as *H. anomala*). Fl 6–8. Hardy, not very free flowering, but a neat shrub. Introduced from New Zealand about 1885.

Hebe cupressoides (J. HOOKER)

COCKAYNE AND ALLAN

4. Evergreen shrub, usually about 1m but occasionally to 2m and more. The plant looks remarkably like a cypress or juniper with much divided brs which are closely covered with imbricated scale-like lv, only about 2mm long, grey-green. Fl in small terminal clusters, pale blue, about 4mm wide. Fl 6–7. Reasonably hardy and worth growing for its curious foliage. Native of New Zealand.

Hebe elliptica (G. FORSTER) PENNELL

4. (*Veronica decussata* AITON) Large shrub or small tree to 6m. Lv oval-elliptic, to 3cm long and 1·5cm wide, pale green, shortly petioled. Fl in erect axillary racemes at ends of shoots. Racemes to 3cm long; fl 1·5cm wide, white or bluish. Fl 7–9. Originally obtained by Dr Fothergill from the Falkland Islands in 1776.

Native to these as well as Tierra del Fuego, Chile and New Zealand. The true sp is hardy, but most plants in cultivation are forms of the hybrid with *H. speciosa*, known as *H. X franciscana* (EASTWOOD) SOUSTER, which is only reliably hardy in maritime districts.

Hebe hulkeana (VON MULLER) COCKAYNE AND ALLAN

4. Shrub, to 2m with wall protection, but about 1m otherwise, with a loose, straggling habit. Lv in widely separated pairs, ovate, to 5cm long and 3cm wide, dark glossy green. Fl in large terminal panicles, sometimes as much as 30cm long, each fl about 8mm across, lavender. Fl 5–6. *H. lavaudiana* (RAOUL) COCKAYNE AND ALLAN is barely distinct, but has smaller lv and fl white or pinkish. The most spectacular of the genus for fl. Long regarded as tender, but apparently reasonably hardy if given rather poor, stony soil. In one garden in Scotland it sows itself in walls. Introduced about 1860.

Hebe matthewsii (CHEESEMAN) COCKAYNE

4. Erect shrub, to 1m and more, with reddish bts. Lv coriaceous, oblong-oval, to 3cm long and 2cm wide. Fl in axillary racemes from ends of brs, racemes to 10cm long, cylindrical, fl to 8mm wide, white or purplish. Fl 7–8. A hardy sp but rare in cultivation. Probably from South Island, New Zealand, but possibly a natural hybrid.

Hebe salicifolia (G. FORSTER) PENNEL

4. Evergreen shrub, to 5m. Lv lanceolate, to 15cm long (usually not more than 10) and 2cm across, grey-green. Fl in axillary racemes from ends of shoots, each raceme up to 15cm long. Fl small but numerous, about 6mm wide, white or pale lilac. One of the hardier spp and much used in hybridising. Native of New Zealand and Chile.

Hebe speciosa (RICHARD CUNNINGHAM) COCKAYNE AND ALLAN

4. Evergreen shrub, to 1·5m, with stout brs. Lv fleshy, obovate, to 10cm long and 4cm wide, bright green and shining. Fl in axillary racemes in upper axils of the shoots, to 7cm long and half as wide; fl 8mm wide, violet or reddish purple. Fl 7–10. The main parent of the larger hybrids, although only reliably hardy in maritime districts. The true sp is probably rare in cultivation, although introduced in the late 1830s. Most of the hybrids are *H. speciosa X salicifolia* or *H. speciosa X elliptica* (with further hybrids between these hybrids) and they tend to absorb much of *H. speciosa*'s tenderness, although generally hardier than this sp. Since cuttings root easily they can be kept from year to year. Native of New Zealand. Discovered by R. Cunningham in 1833; introduced by Allan Cunningham subsequently.

HEDERA LINNAEUS *Araliaceae* Ivy

A small genus of evergreen climbing shrubs, attaching themselves by means of aerial rootlets. The number of species depends on which authority is followed, as all the species are superficially very similar and specific differences may depend on the number of rays on the stellate hairs which are found at the tips of young growths and around the inflorescence. The leaves of sterile shoots are basically heart-shaped, but either shallowly or deeply three or five-lobed; extremely variable, and differing leaf shapes have been given varietal names. Fruiting branches, which are produced as soon as the plant emerges into full light, have the leaves unlobed and ovate with a sinuous margin. If portions of these fruiting branches, which do not bear aerial rootlets, are rooted, the resultant ·plants preserve the adult leaves and also have an arborescent, rather than a climbing habit and were once popular for garden ornament as tree ivies. All the species appear reasonably hardy in the UK. Propagation by cuttings of young shoots is quite easy. The fruit is a three to five-seeded, berry-like drupe and seeds germinate fairly easily, but are, of course, of no use with the various variegated or otherwise aberrant forms.

Hedera canariensis WILLDENOW

Vigorous climber with green or reddish stems and petioles. Lv shallowly 3–5-lobed, up to 15cm across, rounded and smaller on fruiting branches. Stellate hairs with 12–16 rays, joined for quarter of their length. The form known as 'Azorica' has the young wood and lv thickly covered with light brown down, and the lv may be as much as 7-lobed. 'Gloire de Marengo' (also known as *foliis variegatis*) has the lv grey-green with a creamy-white margin and blotches; the petioles are pinkish. Fl in an umbel, greenish-white. Fl 10–11. Fr blue-black.

Hedera colchica K. KOCH

(*H. regneriana* HIBBERD, *H. coriacea* HIBBERD) Very vigorous climber with very large, generally unlobed lv to 25cm long and 18cm wide, dark green and leathery. Young growths covered with yellowish scurf, of which the stellate hairs have 15–25 rays, joined together except at the tips. Fruiting lv barely distinct from juvenile lv, but narrower and oblong-ovate. Generally represented in cultivation by the cultivar 'Dentata', which has larger, often toothed leaves. Fl greenish. Fl 10–11. Fr black. Native of regions from the Black Sea to the Caspian; mainly centered on the Caucasus. There are various variegated forms with creamy and yellowish variegation. Sent to Britain by Dr Roegner, director of the botanic garden at Odessa in 1851, but may have been received previously.

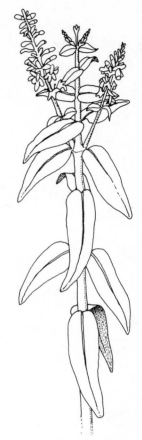

Hebe salicifolia

Hedera helix LINNAEUS English Ivy

An extremely variable plant as regards leaf-shape, with numerous cv with variegated and oddly-shaped lv, so that it is by no means easy to give a description of the type. Lv alternate, basically triangular, very dark green on sterile shoots, lighter and shining green on fruiting brs; usually 3–5-lobed, but the depth of the lobes varies greatly and occasionally forms with almost unlobed lv occur, while the fruiting brs bear unlobed, oblong lv. The stellate hairs have 5–8 rays. Fl greenish-yellow; fl 10–11. Fr black.

Ivy can be trained up established trees without damaging them, but it can strangle young trees. On buildings it appears to do no harm whilst growing. It is when ivy is removed from walls that damage may result. The number of named cv is very large, but they can be divided basically into plants with white or with yellow variegation (which is only effective if the plant is in a reasonably well-lit situation) or plants with unusually lobed lv. 'Hibernica', the Irish ivy, is a tetraploid with large lv to 15cm wide, usually 5-lobed, while **6.** var *poetica* WEST has yellow fruits and replaces *H. helix* in SE Europe and Asia Minor.

Hedera nepalensis K. KOCH

6. Slightly less vigorous plant with basically triangular lv with two lobes at the base and a number of small lobules towards the apex, grey-green, to 11cm long and 6cm wide. Fruiting lv entire, ovate-lanceolate to 7 cm long. Hairs with 12–15 rays. Fl greenish. Fl 10. Fr yellow or orange. Does best on a wall. Distinct from *H. helix* var *poetica* with its greyish lv with lobules. Native of the Himalayas.

Hedera rhombea (MIQUEL) BEAN

Lv not actually diamond-shaped (rhombic), rather more triangular and shallowly 3-lobed. Adult lv rhombic-ovate. Juvenile lv to 5cm long, fruiting lv to 10cm long. Hairs with 15–20 rays. Fr black. A variegated form is known. Native of Japan and Korea. Hardy and vigorous.

HEDYSARUM LINNAEUS *Leguminosae*
A genus of some 150 species in the northern temperate zone, mainly herbaceous. *H. multijugum* is usually propagated by cuttings or layers as seeds are of uncertain germination.

Hedysarum multijugum MAXIMOWICZ

4. Low, rather leggy shrub, to 1·5cm, bts downy. Lv pinnate, alternate, to 15cm long, with 17–27 leaflets to 2cm long and 8mm wide, pointed, glabrous. Fl in terminal axillary racemes, produced over a long period. The racemes to 30cm long, though generally less, erect. Fl pea-shaped, to 2cm long, magenta with patch of yellow at base of standard. Fl 6–9. Pod flat, circular, one-seeded. Requires a sunny position and rather sandy soil. The plant in cultivation has been given the name of var *apiculatum* SPRAGUE, differing from the typical form in its lv. In the typical form the lv have up to 41 leaflets, rounded at the apex not pointed, and hairy not glabrous. Our plant was probably collected in Kansu by Przewalski and sent to St Petersburg Botanic Garden, whence it was distributed by Regel about 1880.

HIBISCUS LINNAEUS *Malvaceae*
A genus of about 200 species of herbaceous plants and shrubs, mainly tropical. The leaves are alternate and the floral parts in fives.

Hibiscus syriacus LINNAEUS

4. Deciduous shrub, to 3m or more, with erect brs; rarely a small tree. Lv basically ovate but 3-lobed and toothed, to 10cm long and half as wide. Fl produced singly from terminal leaf axils; trumpet-shaped with 5 petals, as much as 10cm wide; white, mauve, reddish and violet. Fl 9–10. Quite hardy as regards low winter temperatures, but in cold districts may need some shelter owing to its late flowering. A large number of named cv exist, both single and double. Propagation is by cuttings or layers and plants benefit by being pruned at the end of March. Native of China and India, but in European gardens since 1600. *H. sinosyriacus* L. H. BAILEY has broader leaves and larger flowers. A native of central China, it needs a sunny, sheltered site to flower well. Several fine cv are available.

HIPPOPHAE LINNAEUS *Eleagnaceae*
A genus of only two species of deciduous, dioecious shrubs; one from Europe and the other from the Himalaya. The latter is less attractive, but, growing naturally at a considerable height, is perfectly hardy. Propagated by seed or by layers.

Hippophae rhamnoides LINNAEUS

Sea Buckthorn

6. Deciduous shrub, sometimes a small tree to 12m. Bts covered with silvery scales, which also occur on both sides of the lv at first, later the upper surface becomes less scaly. Lv with a very short petiole, linear, to 7cm long but only 6mm wide. Both male and female fl are inconspicuous, produced as the lv are emerging, in clusters from the lv axils. Fr orange, round, about 1cm in diameter, persisting until February

Hippophae rhamnoides

and not touched by birds. The plant is best planted in groups of 6 or 7, with the male plant in the middle of the females as pollination is effected by the wind. The winter buds of male plants are large and conical or ovoid, while those of female plants are rounded and smaller.

Native of Europe, including the UK where it grows near the sea. *H. salicifolia* D. DON from the Himalayas lacks the attractive silvery lv and the berries are pale yellow. It was introduced in 1822; probably not in commerce.

HOHERIA ALLAN CUNNINGHAM *Malvaceae*

A genus of five or six species of evergreen and deciduous shrubs and small trees native to New Zealand. They have alternate leaves and flowers either solitary or in fascicles in upper axils. The evergreen species are somewhat tender, but the two deciduous species appear normally hardy, although they may be damaged in exceptional winters.

Hoheria glabrata SPRAGUE AND SUMMERHAYES

4. A rapid-growing, deciduous shrub, to 10m but usually not more than 6m. Juvenile lv nearly round, but deeply-lobed, adult lv heart-shaped, hairy when young, glabrous when mature, to 10cm long and 5cm across. Fl wide-campanulate, to 4cm across, stalked, in fascicles of up to 5 in upper axils. Fl 7–8. A very attractive shrub, formerly confused with the next sp, from which it is distinguished only by small botanical characters.

Hoheria lyallii JOSEPH HOOKER

4. (*Plagianthus lyallii Gaya lyallii*) Very similar to the last sp but, as far as gardeners are concerned, distinguished by the grey down persisting on the lv and bts. Somewhat slower growing and possibly less liable to be injured in severe frosts.

HOLBOELLIA WALLICH *Lardizabalaceae*

A genus of five species of evergreen, twining shrubs, native to China and the Himalayas. The leaves are palmate or ternate, opposite, the flowers monoecious, not very showy. Only one species appears reliably hardy.

Holboellia coriacea DIELS

(5). Evergreen twiner, to 7m in the wild but apparently more in cultivation. Lv composed of three-stalked leaflets, the middle one the largest, oblong-oval, to 15cm long and half as wide, the lateral leaflets somewhat smaller and narrower; dark green and rather leathery. Male fl in terminal and axillary corymbs, white, female fl in axillary corymbs from base of young shoots, greenish-white and rather larger. In some forms the fl are fragrant. Fl 4–5. Fr rarely produced, but handsome, purple, sausage-shaped, fleshy, to 6cm long and 2·5cm across. Introduced from Hupeh by Wilson in 1907.

HOLODISCUS MAXIMOWICZ *Rosaceae*

A small genus of American shrubs, related to *Spiraea*, from which they are chiefly distinguished by their seeds which are in achenes, each achene single-seeded, while the capsule of *Spiraea* is a many-seeded follicle.

Holodiscus discolor (PURSH) MAXIMOWICZ

4. (*Spiraea discolor* PURSH, *S. ariaefolia* SMITH) Large, spreading deciduous shrub, to 4m high but spreading more widely with arching brs. Lv alternate, ovate, with deep toothing or shallow lobes, to 9cm long and 7cm wide on vigorous young growths, smaller on flowering brs, slightly hairy above, densely covered with grey felt below (some forms are white woolly below). Fl in pendulous panicles to 30cm long, although usually half this; white. Fl 7. Native of western N America. Introduced by Douglas in 1827 and for long a favourite garden shrub.

HYDRANGEA LINNAEUS *Hydrangeaceae*

A small genus of shrubs from all over America, eastern Asia and the Philippines. Those from central and S America are evergreen, the others deciduous. The leaves are opposite, the flowers in corymbs or in panicles, typically with large, sterile florets around the outside and numerous rather small fertile flowers within, but in many species there are cultivars with all the flowers sterile. The showy parts of the sterile flowers are actually sepals. Most species are on the border-line of hardiness; although they are comparatively rarely killed by severe frosts, they are often badly damaged. Propagation is by layers or by cuttings of half-ripe wood.

Hydrangea arborescens LINNAEUS

4. (Including *H. cinerea* SMALL and *H. radiata* WALTER). Deciduous, rather slow-growing shrub of 1–3m. Bts downy at first, later glabrous. Lv more or less heart-shaped, to 17cm long and 15cm across, toothed, dark green, glabrous on both surfaces. Fl white in a corymb to 15cm wide with few sterile fl. Fl 7–9. In the cv 'Grandiflora' all the florets are sterile and the plant is very decorative and easily the hardiest all sterile-flowered *Hydrangea* available.

H. cinerea SMALL differs in the underside of the lv being covered with a greyish indumentum. Here again there is an all sterile-flowered cv known as 'Sterilis'. *H. radiata* WALTER has the undersides of the lv densely covered with white indumentum, which induced Michaux to name the plant *H. nivea*. *H. arborescens* was sent by Bartram in 1736 and is native to the eastern USA but may have been in cultivation before according to *Hortus Kewensis*. 'Grandiflora' was found in the wild in Ohio in 1890. *H. cinerea* did not enter cultivation before 1908. *H. radiata* was introduced by Fraser in 1786.

Hydrangea aspera D. DON

4. (Includes *H. villosa* REHDER) Deciduous, rather spreading shrub, to 4m high and rather wider, of moderate growth. Bts hairy. Lv narrow-ovate, to 25cm long and 10cm wide, hairy above, thickly coated with white hairs below. Fl in terminal and upper axillary corymbs to 25cm across. Sterile fl to 2·5cm wide, varying in colour from dirty white to mauve, purple and pale pink. Fertile fl usually pinkish purple with blue stamens, small but numerous. The plant can fl at any time from 7 to 9 according to the actual plant. Ssp *strigosa* MCCLINTOCK (*H. strigosa* REHDER) differs only in the underside of the lv having a covering of short, stiff hairs. Old plants are winter hardy, but susceptible to spring frosts. Young plants are slightly tenderer and should be protected during the winter. The plant will only grow where there is very good drainage. The plant is found from Nepal through China to Taiwan and also appears in Java and Sumatra. Most plants in cultivation come from Wilson's collecting in 1907 and 1910.

Hydrangea heteromalla D. DON

4. (Includes *H. bretschneideri* DIPPEL) Shrub to 3m. Bts hairy, later glabrous. Lv variable, but generally more or less heart-shaped, to 20cm long and 14cm wide. The most usual form in cultivation is often known as *H. bretschneideri* and has ovate lv to 12cm long, with reddish petioles and bark peeling off yearly, while typical *H. heteromalla*, although it may well have the red petioles, has close bark. Fl in corymbs, with a number of sterile fl to 15cm wide, white fading to purple. Fl 7–8. The sp is resistant to drought and in mild districts can reach 6m.

H. bretschneideri is the hardiest form, seed having been sent by Dr Bretschneider from the area around Pekin about 1882. Other forms have come from China and Nepal, whence the first plants were introduced in 1821, presumably through the agency of Wallich.

Hydrangea macrophylla (THUNBERG) SERINGE

4. (*Hydrangea hortensia* SIEBOLD) The species from which the garden hydrangeas have derived is native to Japan, but probably not in cultivation, although Wilson collected seeds in 1917. The garden forms are shrubs up to 3m, rarely more, but spreading widely. Lv rather thick, obovate or elliptic, to 15cm long and half as wide, shining green, glabrous. Fl in terminal corymbs which may be rounded in the cv with mainly sterile fl (Hortensia group) or flat in the so-called Lace-cap group, with mainly fertile fl. These corymbs may be very large, while the individual sterile florets may be only 3cm across. Fl are white, pink or blue, but this latter colour only occurs on acid soil, where pink and crimson cv may turn blue or purple. Fl 7–9.

A number of cv are generally hardy and established plants are rarely killed even in the worst winters, as new shoots are frequently sent up from the base. All the Lace-caps have been bred for growing outdoors, where they seem happiest in a semi-shaded position, while the more conventional Hortensias prefer full sun, although they will generally grow in semi-shade but flower less freely. The plants are deep rooting and not suitable for shallow soils, particularly if chalk is near the surface. The first European importation was from China whence Sir Joseph Banks received it in 1789. This plant still exists under the name 'Joseph Banks' and is cream fading to pink or blue, but is not particularly hardy.

Hydrangea paniculata SIEBOLD

4. Shrub or small tree usually around 4m, but occasionally 7–10. Lv occasionally in whorls of 3, ovate-elliptic, toothed, to 15cm long and half as wide, slightly bristly above and below. Fl in pyramidal panicles to 20cm long, 14cm wide at base. The plant most commonly seen is the cv

'Grandiflora' in which nearly all the fl are sterile and, if severely pruned, mature plants can produce panicles as long as 45cm. 'Praecox' is a quick-growing form, with sterile fl only at the base of the panicle, and flowers in mid-July, whereas 'Grandiflora' is open at the end of August. The plant needs good, rich loam, but is generally hardy. 'Grandiflora' was sent back by Siebold in 1862. 'Praecox' was collected by Dr Sargent in 1893.

Hydrangea petiolaris SIEBOLD AND ZUCCARINI

4. Vigorous, deciduous climber to 25m, attaching itself by means of aerial roots, much like an ivy. Year-old wood often peeling. Lv ovate, toothed, bright green, to 11cm long and half as wide. Fl in flat corymbs, to 25cm wide, with large white sterile fl to 4cm wide, stalked separately from the small, dull white, fertile fl. Fl 6. Flowers earlier if grown as a bush than when trained into a tree. Perfectly hardy. Native of Japan, Sachalin and Korea. Introduced in 1878. *H. anomala* D. DON (*H. altissima* WALLICH) is barely distinct, although it has smaller corymbs and may be less hardy. It comes from the Himalayas and was introduced in 1839.

Hydrangea quercifolia WILLIAM BARTRAM

4.(6). Shrub, to 2m in the wild but rarely more than 1m in cultivation in the UK. Bts reddish-hairy. Lv basically ovate but 5–7-lobed, much like a large oak leaf, to 20cm long and 14cm across, often colouring well in the autumn but not invariably. Fl in large, erect, pyramidal panicles to 25cm long. Sterile fl to 3cm wide, white fading to purple, fertile fl white. Fl 7–9. Young plants somewhat tender but older plants appear quite hardy; a fine summer is necessary to ripen the wood and if this does not take place fl will not be produced. The plant seems to thrive in acid soil and likes a well-lit situation. Native to south-eastern USA from Florida to Missouri. Introduced 1803 by John Fraser, although *Hortus Kewensis* credits William Hamilton.

Hydrangea sargentiana REHDER

4. Deciduous shrub, to 3m, with very stout bts, covered with stiff bristles which give them a moss-covered appearance. The plant, when well established, throws up numerous suckers. Lv on non-flowering shoots very large, ovate with a heart-shaped base, to 25cm long and 18cm across, dull green and somewhat hairy above, covered with pale bristles below; lv on flowering shoots, smaller and narrower, to 12cm long and 7cm wide. Fl in a flat corymb; sterile fl to 3cm wide, pale purplish-pink, fertile fl pale violet. Fl 7–8.

Requires a well-lit, but not too sun-drenched, situation and should be given ample space; plants in shade or crowded become leggy. Now

regarded as a ssp of *H. aspera*. Extremely hardy, and even if damaged by May frosts, will quickly recover. Native of Hupeh, China. Introduced by Wilson in 1908.

Hydrangea serrata   (THUNBERG) SERINGE

4. (*Viburnum serratum* THUNBERG) Rather dwarf shrub rarely exceeding 1m. Lv elliptic to lanceolate with an acute apex, to 15cm long and 6cm wide, usually considerably less. The margins serrate, usually glabrous above and sparsely hairy below along the veins. Fl in flat corymbs to 10cm wide with a number of sterile fl to 2cm across, which may be white, pink or blue. In some cv the bts are almost black. 'Preziosa' has only sterile fl which open pink and fade to deep crimson. Fl 7–8. Native of Japan. First introduced about 1843, in a cv close to 'Rosalba'. Long cultivated in Japanese gardens and only known in garden forms. Closely allied to *H. macrophylla*, but always smaller and hardier, although it can be damaged in severe winters.

Hydrangea serratifolia   (W. HOOKER AND ARNOTT) PHILIPPI

4. (*H. integerrima* (HOOKER AND ARNOTT) ENGLER) Better known under its synonym, this makes an evergreen climbing shrub, the stems adhering by means of aerial roots. Lv generally entire, but sometimes slightly serrate, leathery, elliptic, conspicuously veined, to 15cm long and half as wide. On young plants the lv are not more than 5cm long. Fl in terminal and axillary corymbs, uniting to make a panicle which can attain a length of 15cm. The buds are enclosed in 4 papery bracts. Fl usually all fertile, creamy-white. Fl 7–8. Not particularly showy, but interesting as being the only one of the evergreen S American hydrangeas to be hardy in the UK. Rare in commerce. Native of Chile and Argentina. Introduced by Harold Comber in 1925–7.

HYMENANTHERA ROBERT BROWN *Violaceae*

A small genus of four or five species from Australasia, remarkable for their family alliance with violets and pansies; they are evergreen or semi-evergreen with alternate leaves. The flowers are axillary, solitary or clustered, very small. The fruit is a berry, somewhat ornamental. Propagated by seeds or cuttings.

Hymenanthera angustifolia R. BROWN

5. (Includes *H. dentata* R. BROWN) Evergreen or semi-evergreen shrub, to 2m, with warty bts. Lv glabrous, linear, oblanceolate, to 3cm long and 3mm wide (but larger and conspicuously toothed in *H. dentata*), dark green, turning purplish in winter. Fl solitary or in pairs, in axils, yellowish, 6mm across. Fl 5. Fr a round berry, white with purple markings, 8mm in diameter. Fruit ripe by August or September. Native of Tasmania, southern Australia and New Zealand, whence some plants are unisexual, while Tasmanian plants appear to be perfect. *H. dentata*, from New South Wales and Victoria was introduced by Allan Cunningham in 1820.

Hymenanthera crassifolia JOSEPH HOOKER

5. Spreading, semi-evergreen shrub of 1–2m but much more across. Lv obovate, glabrous, to 2·5cm long and 8mm wide, somewhat leathery; dark green. Fl crowded in axils, only 3mm across, yellowish-brown. Fr a round berry, 6mm in diameter, white, sometimes stained purple and borne very freely. Native of New Zealand and in cultivation about 1875.

HYPERICUM LINNAEUS *Guttiferae*
St John's Wort

A genus of herbaceous plants, shrubs and trees (only in the tropics are they tree-like), with leaves opposite or whorled. The flowers are generally patulate and yellow in colour with five petals and numerous stamens. Most of the species in cultivation in the UK are not sufficiently tall to figure here, and of those that remain the nomenclature has become somewhat involved. Until recently they were mainly regarded as forms of *H. patulum*, a somewhat tender species probably not in cultivation at all. The genus has been revised by Dr N. K. B. Robson and, after examining these so-called varieties of *H. patulum*, he has given most of them new specific names. This makes admirable sense, but it does mean that plants formerly sold as *H. patulum* var *henryi* may be any one of four species or more. The various specific differences are generally confined to the shape of the stems and of the sepals and all the species have large golden flowers and some also have good autumn tints.

Hypericum acmosepalum ROBSON

4.6. Semi-evergreen shrub, to 1·5m, with arching brs and reddish bts, which are flattened and four-angled below the fl. Lv narrow, elliptic or oblanceolate, to 6cm long and 2cm across, very shortly petioled. The older lv tend to turn red in the autumn. Fl in clusters of 1–3 (rarely to 6), to 5cm wide, deep yellow. They are followed by conical capsules which are red-flushed. Fl 7–9. Has appeared as *H. patulum* var *henryi*, *H. kouytchense* and *H. oblongifolium*. Originally sent back by Maire in 1906; most plants come from Forrest sendings.

Hypericum forrestii (CHITTENDEN) ROBSON

4.5.6. (*H. patulum* var *forrestii* CHITTENDEN) This was usually sold under the name of *H.*

patulum henryi. Deciduous shrub, to 2m, with erect stems. Lv very shortly petioled, ovate or lanceolate, to 4cm long and 1·5cm wide. Lv turn orange and red in autumn. Fl patulate, to 6cm wide, singly or in threes. Fl 8. Fr bronzy-red when young, conical.

Probably here should come the plant known as 'Hidcote', which it is thought may well be a hybrid of *H. forrestii* and the popular evergreen creeping *H. calycinum*, the Rose of Sharon. 'Hidcote' makes an almost-evergreen shrub, to 2m but spreading more widely. Lv ovate, dark green above, pale below, to 4cm long. Fl to 7cm across in few-flowered cymes. Fl 7–10. Fr usually not set. *H. forrestii* was sent back by Forrest in 1906 and subsequently.

Hypericum frondosum MICHAUX

4. (*H. aureum* BARTRAM) Deciduous, rounded shrub, to slightly over 1m, sometimes coming from a single stem with many brs. Bark reddish and exfoliating yearly. Lv glaucous, oblong, to 5cm long. Fl in terminal clusters, orange-yellow, about 3·5cm across. Fl 7–8. Fr cone shaped with large, leaflike sepals. Native of the south-eastern USA, discovered by William Bartram in 1776 but apparently not in cultivation until late in the nineteenth century. Rehder's date of 1747 must be an error.

Hypericum kouytchense LÉVEILLÉ

4.5. Generally known as *H. patulum* var *grandiflorum* or as *H. penduliflorum*. Spreading, semi-evergreen shrub, rarely over 1m high. Lv ovate, to 6cm long and 2cm wide, medium green above, pale below. Fl single, to 6cm or more wide with very long stamens. Fl 7–9. Fr conical, turning red shortly after the petals fall. Collected in Kweichow by the missionaries Bodinier and Esquirol and sent to Vilmorin about 1900.

Hypericum prolificum LINNAEUS

4. Evergreen shrub, to 1·5m, with mainly unbranched stems and peeling light brown bark. Lv narrowly oblong, to 6cm long and 1cm wide, tapering to a short petiole, dark shining green. Fl in terminal and axillary clusters, bright yellow, each fl to 2·5cm wide. Fl 7–9. A vigorous and showy plant, rarely seen nowadays but available in commerce. Native of eastern and central USA from New Jersey to Georgia. Introduced 1758, according to *Hortus Kewensis*, presumably by Bartram.

Hypericum uralum D. DON

4. (*H. patulum* var *uralum* KOEHNE) Evergreen shrub, to 1m, with ovate lv to 4cm long and half as wide, fragrant when crushed. Fl solitary or in few-flowered clusters, about 2·5cm across, somewhat cup-shaped and one cv is

Hypericum forrestii

Idesia polycarpa

known as 'Buttercup'. Fl 8–9. Very close to the true *H. patulum,* but lv and fl smaller. Native of eastern and central Himalaya, also Indo-China and Sumatra. Introduced from Nepal, presumably through Wallich, in 1820.

IDESIA   MAXIMOWICZ   *Flacourtiaceae*

A monotypic genus.

Idesia polycarpa   MAXIMOWICZ

5.7.   Deciduous, dioecious tree, to 15m with horizontal brs; a reasonably rapid grower. Lv heart-shaped, like a poplar but somewhat toothed on the margin, dark green above, glaucous beneath, to 15cm long and 13cm wide on a petiole to 11cm long. Fl in terminal panicles, yellowish; male fl in panicles to 15cm long, female panicles somewhat longer. Fl 6–7. Fr in large clusters of berries, each about the size of a pea, dark red. Sometimes not ripening properly in bad summers. In the var *vestita* DIELS the underside of the lv is covered with a dense white tomentum, and the fr are said to be almost scarlet. Fruiting trees are attractive, but since plants of both sexes are needed for this, the species is only suitable for large gardens. Native of Japan and China. The Japanese plant was introduced via St Petersburg in 1864. Var *vestita* first collected by Wilson in 1908, also sent back by Forrest and by Farrer and Purdom.

ILEX   LINNAEUS   *Aquifoliaceae*   Holly

A large genus of some 300 species with evergreen or deciduous leaves. The flowers are either unisexual or perfect and the fruit, which are correctly drupes, are small and are always referred to as berries. Many of the species have very spiny leaves and they are generally slow-growing. Very often, once a certain size has been attained, the leaves lose their spines. Propagation is by seeds or, for the various cultivars and hybrids, by cuttings or by grafting. Cuttings are slow to root and seeds only germinate the second year. The common holly, *I. aquifolium,* is dioecious and plants of both sexes are necessary for berries to be produced. The hollies do best in rich, deep soil, but they will grow practically anywhere, although they dislike drought.

If berries are required it is necessary with most species, including the most popular *I. X altaclarense* and *I. aquifolium,* to have both male and female plants, and in this connection it may be noted that some of the cultivar names are misleading; thus 'Golden Queen' is a male clone, while 'Golden King' is female. If the plants are only being grown for their foliage this will not matter. Plants with coloured leaves in the centre are liable to revert to an all-green leaf, while those with the margins coloured maintain their variegation. A very large number of species have been brought into cultivation, but comparatively few are described here.

Ilex X altaclarensis   (LOUDON)   DALLIMORE

4.5.   This name covers a complex group of hybrids, probably of several generations, between the common holly, *I. aquifolium,* and the tender *I. perado* from Madeira and the Canaries. They are slow to moderate-growing trees, eventually to 13m high, making a dense pyramidal mass. The plants differ from *I. aquifolium* chiefly in the larger lv, which may be 12cm long, whereas those of *I. aquifolium* rarely exceed 7cm. The bts tend to be purplish. The female 'Camelliifolia', with large handsome fr, has very large lv which are usually spineless. 'Hodginsii' is a good male form to serve as pollinator. 'Golden King' is a good female, while 'Maderensis' and 'Maderensis Variegata' are handsome males.

Ilex aquifolium   LINNAEUS   Common Holly

4.5.   Evergreen tree, to 25m occasionally, making a dense, leafy pyramid from the ground up, although the lower brs can be cut off to display a handsome smooth trunk. Lv basically oblong, but with undulate margins thickly beset with prickles, although these become less as the tree gets taller, and in tall specimens the upper lv may lack spines completely. Usually the lv are up to 7cm long, but vary in width from 2–5cm. Fl small, white, fragrant, in clusters in

Ilex cornuta

the axils, sometimes produced with great freedom and then reasonably showy. Fl 5–6. Fr generally red, but bronze in 'Amber', yellow in 'Bacciflava'. There are an immense number of cv, mainly with gold or cream variegation, but in 'Ferox' the surface of the lv is covered with spines, while others have unusually shaped lv. Native of most of Europe, including the UK.

Ilex cornuta LINDLEY

Slow-growing, evergreen shrub, to 3m, of rounded habit, usually spreading more widely horizontally than vertically. Lv coriaceous, basically rectangular, with a large spine at each corner and a curved spine at the apex; there may also be additional spines. Lv to 10cm long and 7·5cm across. Fl dull white. Fl 4–5. Fr larger than those of *I. aquifolium*, but sparingly produced except in the cv 'Burfordii' which fruits readily, is a very dwarf plant, and has lv usually with only the apical spine. Native of China and Korea. Introduced by Fortune from Shanghai in 1846 and another form in 1853. 'Burfordii' was raised in the USA about 1895.

Ilex crenata THUNBERG

Very slow-growing, dense, evergreen shrub, apparently occasionally to 7m in the wild but rarely more than 1–2m in cultivation. Lv elliptic, obovate or oblong, to barely 2cm long and 6mm wide, densely set on the brs. Male fl in small clusters, female fl solitary, often both on the same plant. Fr black. The form known as 'Latifolia', introduced by Fortune in 1860, has a more vigorous habit; to 4–5m and elliptic lv to 3cm long and half as wide. Other cv are very dwarf plants for the rock garden. Native to Japan and Korea. The typical plant is said to have been introduced in 1864.

Ilex latifolia THUNBERG

4.5. Evergreen tree, to 7–8m in the UK, although up to 20cm in the wild, with stout angular bts. Lv thick, shining green, to 20cm long and 7cm wide, oblong, toothed but not spiny. Fl yellowish, often both sexes on the same plant. Fl 6. Fr red, 8mm in diameter. Native of Japan and apparently doing best in the southern part of the UK. Obtained from Japan by Siebold in 1840.

Ilex opaca AITON

4.5. Evergreen tree or large shrub to 10m, much like *I. aquifolium*, with rather dull lv to 9cm long and half as wide. Male fl in stalked cymes, female fl solitary. Fr red, about 6mm in diameter. Less attractive than *I. aquifolium*. Requires acid soil. Native to the eastern USA. Introduced, probably by Bartram, in 1744.

Ilex pedunculosa MIQUEL

4.5. Evergreen shrub or small tree, from 6–10m. Lv ovate, acuminate, unarmed, to 8cm long and nearly half as wide, dark shining green. Fl borne on the current season's growth, the males in clusters, the females usually solitary. Fl 6. Fr bright red, about 6mm in diameter, borne on a slender peduncle to 4cm long. Very distinct in its long-stalked fr. Fr 10–11. The plant is monoecious, with both sexes on the same plant. Native of Japan and China. Introduced by Sargent in 1893 from Japan. Wilson introduced forms from China in 1901 and 1907 with somewhat larger lv.

Ilex pernyi FRANCHET

4.5. Evergreen shrub or small tree, to about 4m in cultivation, but up to 10m in the wild. Lv basically square, but with a long triangular apex, spine-tipped, with spines also at the corners of the square base, to 5cm long and half as wide. Fl yellow, in small axillary clusters, hermaphrodite. Fl 5. Fr red, 6mm in diameter. An elegant, slow-growing, pyramidal bush. Native of central China. Introduced by Wilson in 1900.

Ilex serrata THUNBERG

5. Deciduous shrub, to 5m, slow-growing. Lv oval, but tapered at both ends, sometimes colouring in the autumn, to 7cm long and 2·5cm wide. Fl in axillary clusters, inconspicuous. Fl 6. Fr red, 4mm in diameter. Female plants fruit well when mature, but are less ornamental than *I. verticillata*. Native of Japan. Introduced to cultivation in 1866, but not received in the UK before 1893.

Ilex verticillata (LINNAEUS) ASA GRAY

4.5. (*Prinos verticillatus* LINNAEUS) Deciduous shrub, to 3m, of rather spreading habit. Lv lanceolate, purplish when young, tapered at both ends, glabrous above, downy beneath, to 7cm long and 2·5cm wide. Male fl in axillary clusters, female fl solitary or in few-flowered clusters. Often both sexes on the same plant, but not invariably. Fl 6–7. Fr red (or yellow in 'Chrysocarpa' and 'Aurantiaca') about 6mm in diameter, hanging for a long time. 'Christmas Cheer' is a free-fruiting, rather dwarf, female clone. This plant seems to do best on acid or neutral soils. Native of the eastern USA. Introduced by Bartram in 1736.

INDIGOFERA LINNAEUS *Leguminosae*

A genus of some 300 species of shrubs and herbaceous plants, mainly from the tropics. A number of shrubby species from eastern Asia are hardy in the UK; although they may be cut down yearly in cold districts, they invariably spring vigorously again from ground level and, since they flower in axillary racemes from the ends of the current year's growth, the floral display is not affected. All the plants are deciduous, with pinnate leaves and racemes of many pea-shaped flowers, pinkish or purple in colour, rather small, of typical pea shape. The plants seem to be indifferent to soil conditions, but require a warm, sunlit situation. Propagation is by seed or by cuttings of half-ripe wood. Valuable for their late flowering.

Indigofera amblyantha CRAIB

4. Deciduous shrub, to 2m, with hairy young shoots. Lv of 7–11 leaflets, to 12cm long on a petiole to 4cm long. Fl in slender erect racemes, to 10cm long, each fl only 6mm long, pale pink to lilac-purple. Pods to 4cm long. Fl 6–10. *I. potaninii* CRAIB and *I. pseudotinctoria* of gardens differ very slightly, if at all, from *I. amblyantha*, except that *I. pseudotinctoria* starts to flower at the end of May. All are natives of China. *I. pseudotinctoria* sent to Kew by Henry in 1897, *I. amblyantha* introduced by Wilson in 1908 and by Purdom and Farrer in 1913.

Indigofera gerardiana WALLICH EX BAKER

4. Apparently the correct name is *I. heterantha* WALLICH EX BRANDIS. A deciduous shrub, to 1m in cold districts but 2–3m in mild situations. Lv to 10cm long, of 13–21 leaflets, oval to 1·5cm long, grey-hairy on both surfaces. Fl in axillary racemes to 12cm long, each containing about 24 rosy-purple fl about 1cm long. Fl 6–9. Starts late into growth. Native of the NW Himalaya. Introduced about 1840, possibly through Hugh Falconer or perhaps an early Madden sending.

Indigofera hebepetala BENTHAM

4. Shrub, to 3m but in cold districts not much more than 1m. Lv to 22cm with 7–9 leaflets, broadly oval, to 5cm long and half as wide. Fl in racemes up to 22cm long, each fl about 1·5cm long with crimson standard and pink wings and keel. Fl 8–9. Very distinct with its large lv with comparatively few leaflets. In cultivation before 1881, but date of introduction unknown. Native to NW Himalaya.

Indigofera kirilowii PALIBIN

4. (*I. macrostachya* BUNGE) Small shrub, to little over 1m. Lv to 15cm long with 7–11 leaflets slightly hairy on both surfaces. Fl in erect racemes to 10cm long, somewhat concealed by the lv. Fl bright pink, about 2cm long. Fl 6–7. Native of China, Korea and southern Japan. Introduced to Vilmorin in 1899.

ITEA LINNAEUS *Iteaceae*

A small genus of about ten species of evergreen and deciduous shrubs, all Asian, with one exception in eastern North America. Two or three species are in cultivation, but only the American plant is reliably hardy, although the evergreen *I. ilicifolia* is admirable in mild districts or growing against a wall in colder ones. Propagation is by cuttings or by division of the plant, as it sends up fresh shoots from the rootstock yearly.

Itea ilicifolia

Itea virginica LINNAEUS

4.(6). Deciduous shrub from 1–3m, usually not very tall. Single stems are thrown up yearly from the base, branching the second year and then producing terminal racemes of fl. Lv oblong, tapered at each end to 9cm long and 3cm wide, often remaining until December and sometimes colouring bright red. Fl in terminal, erect racemes up to 15cm long, composed of numerous fragrant, white fl each to 8mm wide. Fl 7–8. The plant requires moist, acid soil and the old growths should be regularly removed. Native of the eastern USA. Introduced by Bartram in 1744.

JASMINUM LINNAEUS *Oleaceae*

A somewhat confusing genus of some 200 species mainly from the tropics. The only constant features would appear to be the saucer-shaped flower at the end of a slender tube and the black berry-like fruit. Otherwise the leaves may be opposite or alternate, evergreen or deciduous, simple or pinnate. Propagation by cuttings is usually easy and some species will layer themselves if allowed to trail. Most species require a sunny position to flower well.

Jasminum beesianum FORREST AND DIELS

4.6. Deciduous climber or sprawling shrub, apparently sometimes an erect shrub in the wild. Lv opposite, ovate to lanceolate, to 5cm long and 2cm wide, dark green above, greyish below. Fl in axillary clusters, usually of threes, to 1cm wide, pink to deep carmine. Fl 5–6. Fr shining black. Unique in the genus for its red fl, but not very showy. Introduced by Forrest from Yunnan in 1906.

J. X stephanense LEMOINE is a hybrid between this sp and *J. officinale* (qv). Lv simple or pinnate, with up to 5 leaflets. The plant is a twiner up to 7m and the emerging lv are often cream or yellow variegated. Fl in terminal clusters, much like those of *J. officinale,* but smaller and pale pink in colour. Fl 6–7. The cultivated clone was raised in France about 1921, but similar plants have been seen in the wild by Delavay in Yunnan and later by Rock.

Jasminum fruticans LINNAEUS

4.6. Semi-evergreen shrub in the UK, evergreen in the wild, up to 2m but usually little more than 1m. Lv alternate with one or three leaflets, linear-ovate, to 2cm long and 7mm wide, deep green and glabrous. Fl in terminal clusters of 3–5, about 1·5cm wide, deep yellow. Fl 6–8. Fr black, pea-size. Native of the Mediterranean region, but quite hardy.

Jasminum humile LINNAEUS

4. (Includes *J. farreri* GILMOUR, *J. revolutum* SIMS and *J. wallichianum* LINDLEY, all now reduced to forms of this polymorphous species.) Evergreen or semi-evergreen shrub, to 1·5m in the typical form but to 3m in f *farreri*. Lv alternate, pinnate, with up to 9 leaflets. Fl in terminal clusters of up to 10, to 1·5cm wide (but up to 2·5cm across in f *revolutum*), yellow; some forms are fragrant, others lack scent. The most desirable form, *revolutum*, is unfortunately the least hardy. Fl 6–7. *J. humile* has been known as the Italian yellow jasmine since 1650 and was probably introduced from Turkey, although native from Afghanistan to central China.

Jasminum nudiflorum LINDLEY Winter Jasmine

4. Sprawling, deciduous shrub, which can be trained against a wall but prefers to fall down a slope. The growths can extend to 5m, but much of this is in horizontal spread. Lv opposite, trifoliate, each leaflet to 7mm long, elliptic, deep shining green. Fl produced after the lv, solitary in the axils, bright yellow with short tube, six-limbed, to 2·5cm across. Fl 11–3. Fr rarely set, but a black berry. One of the best and most reliable winter-flowering shrubs. 'Aureum' has the lv blotched with yellow, but is not very attractive. Native of China. Introduced by Fortune in 1844.

Jasminum officinale LINNAEUS Jasmine

4. Deciduous, twining shrub, to 15m. Lv pinnate with 5–9 leaflets, which are elliptic, the terminal leaflet the largest, sometimes to 6cm long and half as wide. Fl in a cluster of terminal cymes, white and very fragrant. Each fl to 2·5cm long with a tube of the same length. Fl 6–10. Fr small, black. The form known as 'Affine' (or sometimes as *grandiflorum*) has larger fl which are flushed pink on the outside. 'Aureum' has the lv blotched with yellow. Native of mountains from the Caucasus to China. 'Affine' was sent from the Himalayas by Dr Royle in the 1830s, but the plant has been in cultivation from time immemorial, owing to its fragrant fl which are much employed in the making of perfumes.

JUGLANS LINNAEUS *Juglandaceae*

A small genus of about fifteen species of deciduous trees, occasionally shrubs, with pinnate, alternate leaves which are often aromatic. The plants are monoecious, the male flower in pendulous catkins borne towards the ends of the main shoots, the female flower small, in clusters at ends of short shoots of the current year. Flowers usually appearing with the leaves which unfurl late in the season. The fruit, of which the common walnut is best known, are drupes, with the stone enclosed in a green, fleshy husk. Distinguished from the related *Carya* in its simple, not branched, catkins and in the pith of the branchlets being lamellate, not continuous. Best grown from seed and put in permanent positions as early as possible. The plants are moderate or slow growers, although the common walnut, *J. regia*, is somewhat more rapid. The plants can be damaged by late spring frosts, although usually they do not start to unfurl before most risk has gone.

Juglans ailantifolia CARRIÈRE

7. (*J. sieboldiana* MAXIMOWICZ) Rather slow-growing, deciduous tree, not more than 17m after a century of cultivation. Bts and petioles glandular-hairy. Lv pinnate, to 60cm (occasionally to 90cm) long, made up of 11–17 leaflets, oblong-acuminate, heart-shaped at base, to 15cm long and 5cm wide. Male catkins to 30cm long. Female fl in long racemes, but nuts very rarely set. Notable for its very large lv. Native of Japan. Introduced by Siebold in 1860.

Juglans mandshurica MAXIMOWICZ

7. Similar to the last sp, but to 25m. Bts covered with brown hairs. Lv to 60cm with 11–19 leaflets, with down on both surfaces when young. Male catkins usually only about 10cm, but occasionally up to 25cm. Fr clustered. *J. cathayensis* DODE is barely distinct, with larger lv and male catkins to 35cm long, but succeeds better in cultivation if it can be obtained. *J. mandshurica* is native to Siberia and N China, introduced by Maximowicz to St Petersburg in 1859. *J. cathayensis* is native to central and western China. Introduced by Wilson in 1903.

Juglans nigra LINNAEUS

7. Tree, to 33m, with furrowed bark. Bts downy. Lv to 60cm long with 11–23 leaflets, the terminal one often lacking. Lv ovate, acuminate, to 12cm long and 5cm across. Male catkins to 10cm. Fr solitary or in pairs. A splendid specimen tree doing better than the common walnut. Native to eastern and central USA. Introduced in 1629, probably from France.

Juglans regia

Juglans regia LINNAEUS   Walnut

7. Tree, to 33m, with glabrous bts. Lv to 30cm, usually with 5–7 leaflets, but up to 13 have been noted. The leaflets oval, to 15cm long and half as wide. In 'Laciniata' the leaflets are deeply and narrowly lobed. Male catkins to 10cm. Fr to 5cm wide. Apparently native from SE Europe to SW China. Cultivated since the sixteenth century in the UK.

JUNIPERUS LINNAEUS *Cupressaceae*

A genus of from thirty-five to forty species of evergreen shrubs and trees, distributed throughout the northern hemisphere from the Arctic Circle to tropical mountains in east Africa. The leaves are always awl-shaped on young plants, while on adult plants they may be awl-shaped (acicular) or scale-like, as in most of the *Cupressaceae*. The leaves are opposite, or in whorls of three. Plants are either monoecious or dioecious. The flowers are terminal and axillary, the male flower making a small catkin, the female flower eventually turning into a berry-like fruit. The fruit is a cone in which the scales have become fleshy and which contains from one to twelve seeds. The fruit sometimes take two or three years to ripen. Propagation is by seed, which may take a year to germinate, although soaking the seeds in hot water just before sowing is said to hasten germination. They can also be propagated by stem cuttings with a heel which are taken in July and August. Most of the species do excellently on chalky or alkaline soils, although this is not essential.

Juniperus chinensis LINNAEUS

7. A very variable plant, usually a narrowly pyramidal or columnar tree to 20m, but some forms are prostrate, while others make small conical bushes. The plant is dioecious. Juvenile lv are acicular, and sometimes the only form present. Adult lv scale-like, but usually both forms are to be found on mature trees. Male fl in small, bright yellow catkins, which are quite conspicuous as they are produced so plentifully. Fr ripening in the second year, about 8mm across, brown, with a glaucous bloom. 'Aurea' has yellow young lv, 'Pyramidalis' has glaucous lv and so has 'Fortunei' (= *J. sphaerica* LINDLEY). 'Variegata' is a decumbent form with some white lv. Native to China, Mongolia and Japan. Usually thought to have been introduced by William Kerr in 1804, but Rehder says that it was in cultivation before 1767.

Juniperus communis LINNAEUS   Juniper

7. Typically a rather lax bush, from 1–3m but occasionally (in the forms known as 'Hibernica' and 'Suecica') columnar trees to 10m or even more, while the form known as 'Oblonga Pendula' makes a columnar plant with pendulous bts and is most attractive. The bts are triangular and the awl-shaped lv are in whorls of 3 and persist on the brs for 3 years. They are up to 15mm long, rather grey-green in colour. Young plants make quite rapid growth, but mature plants remain practically stationary. The plants are generally, although not invariably, dioecious. The fr take 2 or 3 years to ripen and eventually make a blackish berry with a blue bloom, which is up to 12mm across. There are a number of very dwarf cv known. The plant has probably the widest distribution of any shrub from Canada and the USA through northern and central Europe (including the UK) to much of Asia and as far as the western Himalaya.

Juniperus drupacea LABILLARDIÈRE

7. Tree, to 20m in the wild but not more than about 12m in cultivation, usually columnar, but fairly widely pyramidal in the wild. Bts triangular. Lv acicular or narrow-lanceolate, up to 2cm long and 5mm across, the largest in the genus. The plants are dioecious and only the male plant appears to be in cultivation. The berry is the largest in the genus, up to 2·5cm across, brown, with a glaucous bloom. It is also distinct in that the lv are firmly attached to the stem and extend downwards to the lower whorl. Native of SE Mediterranean from Greece to Syria. Introduced about 1820.

Juniperus excelsa BIEBERSTEIN

7. Columnar tree, to 13m in cultivation although up to 30m in the wild. Bts extremely slender. Adult lv scale-like, appressed, in opposite pairs. Juvenile, awl-shaped lv occasionally also present. The plants are either monoecious or dioecious and the berry is about 12mm across, purplish-brown with a glaucous bloom. An attractive columnar tree, 'Perkinsii', which appears to be hard to obtain, has glaucous juvenile foliage. 'Stricta' is now regarded as the same as *J. chinensis* 'Pyramidalis'. Native of the Caucasus, SE Asia and the Balkans. Introduced, possibly through Bieberstein, in 1806 according to Loudon. *Hortus Kewensis* says it was obtained from Siberia by Sir Joseph Banks in that year.

Juniperus horizontalis MOENCH

A spreading, low shrub, usually well under 1m in height but spreading for 2m or more. In the wild both scale-like and awl-shaped lv are present, but in cultivation the plants usually only show juvenile lv. The stems root as they extend, so that propagation is very easy. The fr is a berry which is blue-black, but not, apparently, ever produced in cultivation. A number of selected forms exist of which 'Douglasii' has steel-blue lv which turn bronzy in winter. Almost all the forms are more or less glaucous. It is found on acid soils in the wild and will thrive on them in cultivation. Native of the eastern parts of N America. For long thought to be a form of *J. sabina*, so the exact date of introduction is dubious.

Juniperus X media VAN MELLE

Hybrids raised accidentally between *J. chinensis* and *J. sabina*, the resultant plants may be found in some catalogues under either of the two spp. The plants are not usually very tall but widely spreading, giving the impression of a pyramidal tree that has lost its leader. The lv are awl-shaped, closely appressed and the bts are pendulous. The best-known cv, 'Pfitzeriana', has rather glaucous lv, while there are forms with yellowish lv and 'Armstrongii' has apple-green lv. All are very decorative, low, wide-spreading evergreens. The cv 'Plumosa' is sometimes met with as *J. japonica* and has scale lv rather than acicular ones.

Juniperus recurva BUCHANAN-HAMILTON

7. A small tree or large shrub, to 10m, of pyramidal habit, clothed to the ground with gracefully drooping brs. It can be either monoecious or dioecious. The lv are acicular, but overlapping and in whorls of 3, up to 7mm long, dull grey-green (but attractively glaucous in the var *coxii*). Fr ripening in the second year, rather small, not more than 9mm long, purplish-brown. The var *coxii* (*J. coxii* A. B. JACKSON) is to be preferred to the type in its more vigorous growth and glaucous lv. The plant appears to be somewhat variable as its range extends from the eastern Himalaya to Burma and China. In favoured localities the tree can get as high as 15m. Although generally hardy, the plant only seems to thrive well in fairly mild localities. Introduced originally from the Himalaya in 1830, presumably through Wallich.

Juniperus sabina LINNAEUS — Savin

Usually a shrub from 1–2m high, which is capable of extending itself horizontally almost indefinitely; the brs rooting themselves and so, eventually, a single plant can become a large thicket. The extension takes place mathematically; first the main brs elongate and thence laterals emerge, so that the ground is covered in rectangles, and eventually these laterals provide further laterals, so that the whole area is covered. Occasionally the shrub is more upright, reaching to 5m, and then it does not extend so far horizontally. Plants are both monoecious and dioecious. The whole shrub has a rather unpleasant smell when bruised in any way. The bts are 4-cornered and the lv on mature plants are scale-like, dull green and persist for 3 or 4 years. Occasionally the juvenile acicular lv are seen on mature plants, particularly in the var *tamariscifolia* AITON, a spreading form with erect brs. The brownish berry ripens in about 12 months, is about 5mm across and brownish in colour. The

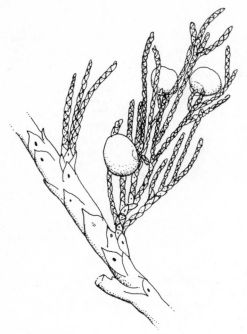

Juniperus sabina

juvenile awl-shaped lv are in opposite pairs about 4mm long. The plant is native to much of Europe, the Caucasus and parts of N America.

Juniperus squamata BUCHANAN-HAMILTON

A shrub with very variable characters. The typical form is prostrate with erect lateral brs, but the var *fargesii* REHDER AND WILSON makes a tree to 13m, while var *meyeri* REHDER makes an upright shrub to about 8m. The lv are always awl-shaped, closely-set in whorls of 3, are about 4mm long in the type, somewhat longer in var *fargesii,* and more or less glaucous; var *meyeri* being the most conspicuous from the foliage point of view. The type is sometimes found under the name of *J. pseudosabina*, a name that has been applied to so many species as to be now meaningless. In fact its closest ally seems to be *J. recurva*. The fr ripens in the second year, is blackish, ellipsoid, about 8mm long. The type was introduced from Nepal through Wallich in 1824, var *fargesii* from China by Wilson in 1907 and var *meyeri* by Meyer from China in 1914.

Juniperus thurifera LINNAEUS

Spanish or Incense Juniper
In the wild this makes a tree to 12m, but in cultivation this is somewhat rare and it tends to make an elegant, pyramidal shrub to 7m. The juvenile awl-shaped lv tend to persist even on aged specimens, which will, however, also bear the tightly-appressed, scale-like lv, as well as some intermediate in form. The plants are dioecious. The fr takes 2 years to ripen. The wood burns with fragrance and is used for making incense. The plants may well be damaged during severe winters, although they are rarely destroyed. Native of SW Europe and N Africa. Introduced in 1752.

Juniperus virginiana LINNAEUS   Pencil Cedar

7. A handsome, pyramidal tree, usually to 15m in cultivation but occasionally twice as high, bearing both acicular and scale lv. The bark peels off in long strips and is reddish-brown in colour. The acicular lv are glaucous, up to 6mm long, the scale lv are barely 1mm long. The plants are dioecious. The fr, which ripens in 1 year, is glaucous-blue and about 6mm long. A large number of cv have been isolated, of which 'Hillii', with greyish foliage turning purple in winter and a very slender erect habit, is outstanding, while 'Pendula', with spreading brs and hanging bts, is another attractive form. At one time yellow and white variegated forms existed, but they appear to have been lost or allowed to disappear as they were not, apparently, very attractive. *J. dealbata* LOUDON (*J. scopulorum* SARGENT) is a closely allied sp from the western USA. Native to eastern N America from Canada to Texas. Said to have been introduced by Evelyn in 1664, but one would have thought that the younger Tradescant might have been the original introducer. In spite of its natural habitat, it thrives on chalky soils as well as acid ones.

Juniperus wallichiana J. D. HOOKER

A rare and slow-growing, dioecious tree, which can reach 20m in the Himalaya but is barely half that height in cultivation. Both adult and juvenile lv occur at the same time. The juvenile lv acicular, in whorls of 3, about 6mm long, scale-leaves in 4 ranks. The juvenile lv are glaucous, the scale leaves are bright green. Introduced by Joseph Hooker in 1849.

KALMIA LINNAEUS *Ericaceae*

A small genus of mainly evergreen shrubs from the eastern USA and the West Indies, requiring acid soil and a sunny, well-drained situation, although *K. angustifolia* and the dwarf *K. polifolia* grow in boggy situations in the wild. Seed or layering are the easiest methods of propagation, except in the case of *K. angustifolia,* where sucker growths can be detached. Cuttings for exceptionally good forms of *K. latifolia* are slow and not easy to root. The flowers are bowl-shaped, with rather a starry outline and the anthers characteristically held in little cavities, whence they spring forward when ripe and when the stamen is touched. Most of the species are rather too dwarf for inclusion here.

Kalmia angustifolia LINNAEUS

4. Dwarf, evergreen shrub, rarely more than 1m high and often considerably less. Lv in opposite pairs or whorls of 3, ovate, to 5cm long and 2cm wide, bright green above, glaucous below. Fl in terminal panicles to 5cm wide, each fl 5-lobed, saucer shaped, 8mm wide, deep red. Fl 6. Can be propagated by detaching sucker-growths. Easily grown, sometimes rather leggy. Native of eastern N America. Introduced 1736, possibly by Bartram.

Kalmia latifolia LINNAEUS   Mountain Laurel

4. Also known in the USA as calico bush. Spreading evergreen shrub to over 3m (apparently up to 10m in the wild) but usually wider than high and somewhat slow-growing. Lv alternate, oval-elliptic to 10 cm long and 3cm wide, dark green and rather coriaceous. Fl in terminal clusters up to 10cm wide; each fl 5-lobed, to 2·5cm wide, varying in colour from nearly white to deep pink. Fl 6–7. An exceptionally lovely shrub, which is perfectly hardy but which does not always do well in cultivation. Probably it requires full sun to ripen the wood, but should never dry out at the root. Native of eastern N America. Introduced in 1734.

Kalmia latifolia

KERRIA DE CANDOLLE *Rosaceae*

A monotypic genus, allied to *Rhodotypos* (qv). Propagated by cuttings, division, or detaching suckers.

Kerria japonica 'pleniflora'

Kerria japonica DE CANDOLLE

4. A rather sprawling, deciduous, bushy shrub, to 2m high but considerably taller if trained against a wall, with slender, pendulous bts. Lv alternate, ovate-lanceolate with toothed margins, smooth above, hairy below, to 10cm long on non-flowering shoots and only about 3cm long on flowering brs. Fl yellow, 5-petalled, patulate, to 4·5cm wide, singly on short, lateral twigs from the previous year's growth. Fl 4–5. Fr not usually produced. The double-flowered form 'Pleniflora' is much more commonly seen in gardens. The white-variegated 'Variegata' is less robust but has a long flowering season. Native of China, but long cultivated in Japan. 'Pleniflora' was introduced by William Kerr, after whom the genus is named, in 1804. The single form was sent back by Reeves in 1834.

KOELREUTERIA LAXMANN *Sapindaceae*

A genus of eight species, only one of which is hardy in the UK. Propagated by seed, root cuttings or sometimes by suckers.

Koelreuteria paniculata LAXMANN

Golden Rain Tree
3.4.5.6.(7.) Deciduous tree, to 20m occasionally but usually about half that height; growing

Koelreuteria paniculata

rapidly when young, later more slowly. Lv alternate, bright pink when first unfurling, later bronze and subsequently medium green, turning golden (sometimes scarlet) before falling; pinnate, up to 45cm long, with 9–15 leaflets, each leaflet ovate but lobed, sometimes deeply, to 10cm long. Fl in terminal panicles, pyramidal, up to 30cm long, each fl four-petalled and about 1cm wide, bright yellow. Fl 7–8. Fr an inflated capsule to 5cm long, bronzy. Var *apiculata* REHDER differs in its bipinnate lv but seems to come more rapidly to a flowering size, so is probably to be preferred. Young plants look rather gaunt but the tree has so many attractions that it is worth growing everywhere. Native of China. Introduced in 1763, probably through one of Collinson's correspondents. Var *apiculata* introduced by Wilson in 1904 from Szechuan.

KOLKWITZIA GRAEBNER *Caprifoliaceae*
A monotypic genus allied to *Abelia*. Propagated by cuttings, or by suckers.

Kolkwitzia amabilis GRAEBNER Beauty Bush
4. Spreading, deciduous bush, to 3 or 4m, of twiggy habit. Bts hairy at first, later glabrous, but rough to the touch. Lv opposite, ovate, acuminate, shallowly toothed, to 7cm long and 5cm wide, dull green and hairy above, paler and bristly below, on a very short petiole. Fl in pairs forming profuse terminal corymbs to 7cm across. Each fl is tubular with 5 rounded lobes at the mouth about 1·5cm long and wide, clear pink with yellow in the throat and hairy within. Fl

5–6. Fr covered with brown bristles. The plant varies in the colour and size of fl and it is worth while obtaining named clones such as 'Rosea' and 'Pink Cloud'. The plant will grow on any soil, but requires a sunny position and flowers better after hot summers. Native of Hupeh, China. Introduced by Wilson in 1901.

X LABURNOCYTISUS SCHNEIDER
Leguminosae
A curious graft hybrid.

X Laburnocytisus adamii (POITEAU) SCHNEIDER
4. (*Cytisus adamii* POITEAU) Deciduous tree of up to 8m. Lv like those of *Laburnum anagyroides* (qv), trifoliolate but somewhat smaller, to 5cm long. Fl in pendulous racemes, to 15cm long, yellow suffused with purple. Fl 6. Some brs will be pure *L. anagyroides* while others, making small faggots, will be *Cytisus purpureus*. Raised by J. L. Adam at Vitry-le-Francois in 1825, when he attempted to graft *Cytisus purpureus* on a standard of *Laburnum anagyroides*. The result was a graft chimaera, with elements of both parents in the tissues. Not a beautiful tree, but interesting.

LABURNUM MEDICUS *Leguminosae*
A small genus of only three species, of which two are in general cultivation. With attractive racemes of yellow flowers, rapid growing and tolerant of air pollution, their worth in the garden is outstanding. However, all parts of the plants, particularly the seeds, are very poisonous, and so children should be kept away from the pods. Easily raised from seed, but cultivars require to be grafted.

Laburnum alpinum (MILLER)
BERCHTOLD AND PRESL
4. (*Cytisus alpinus* MILLER) Deciduous tree of up to 7m. Bts glabrous. Lv trifoliolate, the leaflets obovate to 10cm long, petiole to 5cm. Lv glabrous above, slightly downy below. Fl in pendulous racemes to 30cm long. Each fl 1·8cm long, bright golden-yellow. Fl 6. The best of the species. Native of the Alps, Apennines, Yugoslavia and Czechoslovakia. In cultivation in 1596, probably earlier.

Laburnum anagyroides MEDICUS
4. (*L. vulgare* BERCHTOLD AND PRESL) Differs from the last sp in its pubescent greyish-green bts. Lv with a petiole to 7cm long, but leaflets smaller, not more than 7cm long. Racemes shorter, usually 15cm, occasionally to 25cm. The shape of the pods also differs and they are slightly hairy. It comes into flower earlier, usually late May. 'Aureum' has soft

Kolkwitzia amabilis

yellow lv in the earlier part of the year and 'Autumnale' flowers a second time later in the year; 'Pendulum' has an attractive weeping habit. Native of central and southern Europe.

Laburnum X watereri DIPPEL

4. The name for hybrids between *L. alpinum* and *L. anagyroides,* of which the cv known as 'Vossii' is outstanding, with slightly hairy bts and pendulous racemes which occasionally reach 60cm. Raised in Holland at the end of the nineteenth century.

LARIX MILLER *Pinaceae* Larch

A genus of about twelve species of deciduous trees with horizontal branches to give a pyramidal habit. They bear two types of branchlets. Those that extend considerably have the leaves spirally arranged, the others are short, spur-like lateral growths, which barely increase in length and bear terminal clusters of leaves of unequal length. The leaves are linear, needle-like. The plants are monoecious. The male flowers are usually globular or cylindric, composed of numerous yellow stamens emerging from brown scales. The female flowers are erect, usually subtended by coloured bracts (the so-called larch roses), eventually making a short-stalked cone, consisting of a number of thin, woody scales which persist almost indefinitely, although the seeds are shed after the first year. These persistent cones are the main distinction between this genus and the allied *Pseudolarix* where the cones soon disintegrate.

Larches are among the loveliest of conifers with their brilliant spring green, their attractive female flowers and the gold colour which the leaves assume before falling. They are essentially montane plants, but will grow in most situations in the UK, although they will not tolerate bad drainage. A possible exception would be *L. laricina,* which is often found in marshy ground in the wild. Propagation is best done by seed.

Larix decidua MILLER

4.6.7. (*Larix europaea* DE CANDOLLE) Tree, to 50m, with fissured, scaling bark, greyish in young trees, brown in older ones. Bts yellowish. Lv linear, brilliant green, to 3·5cm long. Lv turn gold before falling. Female fl with rosy bracts and cones remaining reddish for some time. Cones egg-shaped, to 3·5cm long and 2·5cm across. Fl 3–4. Both fastigiate and pendulous forms exist. Native to much of northern Europe. Introduced by the elder Tradescant in 1629.

Larix gmelinii (RUPRECHT) LITVINOV

4.6.7. (*L. dahurica* TURCZANINOW, *L. davurica* TRAUTVETTER) A very variable sp of east Asian larches of which the type has usually hairless, yellowish bts and makes a tree to 25m or more, but is sometimes only a large bush. Lv to 2·5cm long. Male fl small, not more than 4mm long, female fl pale pink. Fl 3. Cones to 2·5cm long.

Besides the type there are two distinct var in cultivation. Var *japonica* (REGEL) PILGER is usually little more than a bush in cultivation, although it can make a smallish tree. Otherwise it differs from the type in its shorter lv and smaller cones. The bts are reddish-brown and somewhat pubescent at first. Var *principis-rupprechtii* (MAYR) PILGER is the most vigorous form and may well make a very large tree in time. The bts are a bright red-brown, making them conspicuous in winter. The lv, which are an exceptionally brilliant green when first unfurled, may reach a length of 10cm, and the fl and cones are also larger.

L. gmelinii was introduced in 1827, var *japonica* was introduced by Mayr in 1888 and var *principis-rupprechtii* was introduced in 1903.

Larix laricina (DUROI) K. KOCH

6.7. (*L. americana* MICHAUX) Tree, to 20m or more, with reddish-brown bark. Bts covered with glaucous bloom. Lv triangular, very narrow, to 3cm long. Male and female fl both small, the bracts around the female fl are green with a red margin. Cones small, to 1·8cm long and 1cm across. In its native N America it often grows in marshy ground, so it might well prove successful in situations where other larches would fail. *L. laricina* was sent by Bartram about 1760.

This would appear to be an appropriate place to mention another putative N American larch, *L. pendula* (AITON) SALISBURY This is a rather mysterious plant that was first sent by Bartram, in 1739, to Lambert, Collinson and Miller, who were all more or less contemporaries. The botanist Pursh also mentions it as growing in swamps from Canada to New Jersey, but it has not been seen since in a wild state. Augustine Henry maintained that *L. pendula* was a hybrid between *L. decidua* and *L. laricina,* but, given the date of introduction, this seems unlikely and it is more satisfactory to regard the plant as a good sp which has become extinct in the wild and only persists in cultivation. It makes a tree to 30m, with pinkish branchlets, lv not triangular, to 3cm long, cones to 3cm long and 2·5cm across.

Larix leptolepis (SIEBOLD AND ZUCCARINI) MURRAY

2.6.7. (*L. japonica* CARRIÈRE, *L. kaempferi* (LAMBERT) CARRIÈRE) Tree, to 30m, with reddish bts which are at first very downy. The plant is somewhat more densely branched than *L. decidua.* Lv up to 3·5cm long, rather glaucous green in colour. The female fl are greenish, although the bracts have a narrow pink margin. The cones are practically globular, to 2·5cm long and wide, and when expanded look very much like wooden roses. Native of Japan. Introduced by J. G. Veitch in 1861 and extensively planted in forestry. *L. X eurolepis* HENRY is a hybrid between *L. decidua* and *L. leptolepis*. It has yellow bts, lv to 3·5cm long and pink female fl. It grows with greater rapidity than either of the parents. It was first noticed in 1885 and has already made trees of over 20m.

LAURUS LINNAEUS *Lauraceae*

Formerly a number of trees were included in *Laurus*, but now it is confined to two species of evergreen dioecious trees.

Laurus nobilis LINNAEUS   Bay Tree

(7). Dioecious, evergreen tree or shrub to 20m occasionally but more usually 10–15m. Lv alternate, oval-elliptic, dark green, coriaceous to 10cm long and 3cm wide, aromatic. Fl small, yellowish, in small umbels from the upper leaf axils, each fl to 1cm across. Fl 5–6. Fr a round black berry, 1cm in diameter. Liable to have lv browned during really severe winters, but rarely destroyed. Native of the eastern Mediterranean region. Cultivated since time immemorial.

LAVATERA LINNAEUS *Malvaceae*

A genus of about twenty-five species of herb-aceous and sub-shrubby plants; most of the latter are found in littoral districts in the wild and are thus excellent for planting near the sea; inland they may prove slightly tender. They come read-ily from seed or from cuttings.

Lavatera olbia LINNAEUS

4. Deciduous sub-shrub, to 2m, branching from the woody stock. Bts and young lv covered with white hairs. Lv rounded, 3–5-lobed, to 15cm long and wide, upper lv more lanceolate and either 3-lobed or unlobed. Fl saucer-shaped, to 5·5cm wide, borne singly or in pairs from lv axils. Purplish red, but pink in 'Rosea'. Fl 6–10. Useful for its long flowering. *L. maritima,* with pale pink, crimson centred fl up to 6cm wide, is pre-ferable but somewhat tender away from the coast. Both spp are native to the western Medi-terranean and have long been in cultivation.

LEDUM LINNAEUS *Ericaceae*

A small genus of evergreen shrubs with alternate leaves and terminal clusters of white flowers, not easily distinguished from each other. They require acid soil and inhabit rather boggy situ-ations in the wild. Propagated by seed, layers and cuttings.

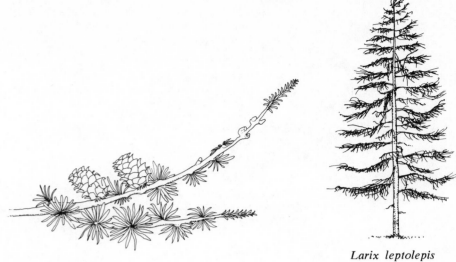

Larix leptolepis

Larix leptolepis

Ledum glandulosum NUTTALL

4. Evergreen shrub, to 2m in the wild but so far less in cultivation. Bts glabrous. Lv ovate, to 5cm long and 2cm wide, dark green above, white and scaly beneath. Fl in terminal clusters about 5cm across, white, each fl about 1cm wide. Fl 5. Distinguished from the other spp by its greater height and glabrous lv and bts. Native to western N America. Introduced in 1894.

Ledum groenlandicum OEDER   Labrador Tea

4. Evergreen shrub, to 1m high and wide. Bts rusty-tomentose as are also the underside of the lv. Lv narrow-oblong, to 5cm long and 1cm across, aromatic, margins recurved, dark green above. Fl in rounded corymbs to 5cm wide, each fl to 2cm across. Fl 4–6. The best sp for cultiva-tion in the UK. Native to eastern N America and Greenland. Introduced (by Bartram?) 1763.

Ledum palustre LINNAEUS

4. Evergreen shrub to 1m 30cm. Distinguished from the last sp only by the smaller, linear lv to 3cm long and 6mm wide. Fl 4–5. Not as satis-factory as *L. groenlandicum*. Native to arctic and subarctic regions in Europe, Asia and western America. Grown by Parkinson in 1629.

LESPEDEZA MICHAUX *Leguminosae*

A genus of about fifty species of shrubs, sub-shrubs and herbaceous plants; all the species described below are Asiatic and are similar in superficial appearance to *Indigofera*, but the leaves are trifoliate not pinnate, and the pods one-seeded. They will thrive in any soil, but require as much sunlight as possible.

Lespedeza bicolor TURCZANINOW

4. Deciduous sub-shrub in the UK with annual stems to 2m and more, but in warmer climes a shrub to 3m. Lv trifoliolate with leaflets broadly oval, to 5cm long and 3–4cm wide; dark green above, paler beneath, slightly hairy on both surfaces. Fl in racemes to 12cm long from upper axils, pea-shaped but not more than 1cm long. Fl 8–9. Like all the spp useful for its late flowering. Native of Manchuria, northern China and Japan, from whence it was introduced by Maximowicz in 1856.

Lespedeza buergeri MIQUEL

4. Shrub, to 6m in the wild but less in cultivation. Leaflets elliptic-ovate, to 4cm long and 2cm across, finely pubescent at first, later glabrous. Fl in axillary racemes to 10cm long, purple and white, to 1cm long. Fl 7–9. Native of Japan. Introduced in 1894.

Lespedeza thunbergii (DE CANDOLLE) NAKAI

4. (*Desmodium thunbergii* DE CANDOLLE) Deciduous sub-shrub, to 3m, with arching stems which start late in the season. Stems at first with greyish hairs. Lv trifoliolate, leaflets to 5cm long and 2cm wide, glabrous above, grey-hairy below. Fl in axillary racemes to 15cm long, rosy purple, each fl to 2cm long, very profuse after a hot summer. Fl 9–10. Very striking in a good season, but may not flower at all in cold seasons. Native of northern China and Japan. Obtained by Siebold in 1837.

LEUCOTHOE DAVID DON *Ericaceae*

A genus of some forty-five evergreen or deciduous shrubs, mainly from the Americas, but also found in Asia and Madagascar. The leaves are alternate and the flowers in axillary and terminal racemes, urn-shaped. The capsules are round and hard, not fleshy as in *Gaultheria*. The plants require moisture-retentive, acid soil and semi-shaded conditions. Propagation by seed, cuttings, suckers or division.

Leucothoe davisiae TORREY

4. (*L. lobbii* VEITCH) Evergreen shrub to 1m with sturdy, erect brs. Lv oblong-ovate, to 6cm long and 2·5cm wide, dark green, glabrous, shallowly toothed. Fl in a compound of axillary and terminal racemes, each to 10cm long; corolla urceolate, about 6mm long, white. Fl 6–7. The most handsome sp for flowering. Native of western N America. Introduced by William Lobb in 1853.

Leucothoe fontanesiana (STEUDEL) SLEUMER

4. (*L. catesbaei* of gardens, but not of WALTER) Evergreen shrub, to 2m, with reddish,

downy bts. Lv lanceolate, acuminate, to 12cm long and 3cm wide, toothed; dark green above, paler below. The lv often turn bronze in the winter. Fl in axillary racemes to 5cm long, occasionally also in terminal panicles to 7cm; each fl urn-shaped, white, 6mm long. The fl are all produced on the underside of the brs and so are not very showy. Fl 5. 'Rainbow' is a cv with lv variegated pink at first, later white, and very striking in the early part of the year. Native of the south-eastern USA; first obtained by Messrs Loddiges in 1793, either from William Bartram or Francois Michaux.

LIBOCEDRUS ENDLICHER *Cupressaceae*

As originally conceived, the genus consisted of some thirteen species of evergreen trees, with flattened branches, scale-like leaves and cones with four or six scales. The genus has been much reduced by Florin and, according to him, our plant, *L. decurrens*, should be in a separate genus, which he has called *Calocedrus*. Another rare hardy species, *L. chilensis*, is now *Austrocedrus*.

Libocedrus decurrens

Libocedrus decurrens TORREY

7. (*Calocedrus decurrens* FLORIN) Slow-growing, evergreen tree, columnar in gardens, pyramidal in the wild, usually to about 22m in cultivation but up to 50m in the wild. Brs erect, with bts and lv set edgewise so that both surfaces are exposed to the light, giving the tree a very characteristic appearance. Lv scale-like, closely

appressed, so that only the sharp points are separate; dark green on both surfaces. Cones with six scales, only 2cm long and 8mm wide, containing 4 seeds. 'Aureo-variegata' has parts of the shoots yellow in colour and is not very attractive, while the type is very striking and desirable. Native of Oregon and California. Introduced by Jeffrey in 1853.

LIGUSTRUM LINNAEUS *Oleaceae*

The privets comprise about fifty species, of which sixteen or more have been in cultivation, but they are not usually among the most attractive shrubs, owing to their rather displeasing perfume. They are shrubs or, rarely, trees with opposite leaves. The flowers are in terminal panicles and the fruit is a berry-like drupe. The flowers are small, tubular, with four spreading lobes, white or cream. One or two species are useful for their late flowering and a couple of species are also handsome foliage plants. Cuttings usually root easily.

Ligustrum compactum BRANDIS

4.5. (*L. yunnanense* HENRY, *L. chenaultii* HICKEL) Deciduous or semi-evergreen shrub, to 5m high and as wide or wider, with spreading, pendent brs. Lv lanceolate-elliptic, to 15cm long (to 25cm long in the form known as *L. chenaultii*) and 5cm wide, glabrous. Fl in pyramidal, terminal panicles to 16cm long and wide, creamy-white. Fl 7. Fr purple at first, later black. Native of the north-western Himalaya and SW China. First introduced from the Himalaya in 1874. The first importation from Yunnan was by Delavay in 1888.

Ligustrum delavayanum HARIOT

4.5. (*L. ionandrum* DIELS, *L. prattii* KOEHNE) Evergreen shrub, to 2m or more. Bts grey-pubescent. Lv ovate, to 3cm long and 1cm wide, dark green above, glabrous. Fl in small, terminal panicles to 3·5cm long, white with conspicuous violet anthers. Fl 6–7. Fr black. Liable to be damaged in severe winters, but not fatally. Introduced by Delavay in 1890.

Ligustrum japonicum THUNBERG

4. Evergreen shrub to 4m. Lv very dark green, glabrous, ovate, to 10cm long and half as wide, short-petioled. Fl in terminal, pyramidal panicles to 20cm long and wide. Fl 7–9. Fr black, but rarely produced in the UK. Similar to *L. lucidum* but less vigorous and with darker green foliage. 'Macrophyllum' is a form with extremely large lv. Native of N China, Korea and Japan. Obtained by Siebold in 1845.

Ligustrum lucidum AITON

4. Evergreen shrub to 6m or small tree to 15m. Lv ovate-elliptic, to 15cm long and about a third as wide, glossy green and glabrous. Fl in erect, terminal, pyramidal panicles to 20cm high and wide. Fl 8–9. Fr blue-black. Native of China. Obtained by Sir Joseph Banks in 1794.

Ligustrum ovalifolium HASSKARL

The well-known hedging plant. Evergreen or semi-evergreen shrub to 5m. Lv glossy green, oval, to 6 cm long and half as wide, glabrous. Fl in terminal panicles to 10cm long and wide, rather fetid. Fl 7. Fr black. 'Aureum' has attractive golden lv, 'Argenteum' has the lv with a white margin. Lv are often damaged after prolonged severe frost. Native of Japan. In cultivation in 1847.

Ligustrum quihoui CARRIÈRE

4.(5). Deciduous or semi-evergreen shrub, from 2 to 4m but spreading horizontally rather than vertically, with rather pendent brs. Lv narrowly obovate to 3cm long and 1cm wide, dark shining green. Fl in large, compound, terminal panicles to 20cm long and about half as wide. Fl 9–10. Fr purplish but rarely produced. One of the most attractive sp, particularly valuable for its late flowering, but in cold, wet seasons the buds may not open. Native of China and introduced into France in 1862.

Ligustrum sinense

126

Ligustrum sinense LOUREIRO

4.5. Deciduous or semi-evergreen shrub or small tree, to 7m. Lv pale green, elliptic, to 7cm long and 2cm across. Fl very freely produced in panicles to 10cm long and half as wide. Fl 7. Fr purplish-black. 'Variegatum' has the lv white and grey-green. The most floriferous and effective sp. Native of China. Introduced by Fortune in 1852.

Ligustrum vulgare LINNAEUS   Common Privet

Evergreen or semi-evergreen shrub, to 3m, now rarely seen in cultivation but formerly much used for topiary work and for hedging. Lv oval-lanceolate, to 6cm long and 1·5cm wide. Fl in erect panicles, dirty white and rather fetid, to 5cm long. Fl 6–7. Fr black. 'Aureum' has yellow lv and 'Xanthocarpum' has yellow fr. Native of most of Europe including the UK.

LINDERA THUNBERG *Lauraceae*

A genus of some eighty species of shrubs and trees with alternate leaves which are usually aromatic. The flowers are unisexual, in clusters, and usually produced before the leaves. The fruit is a drupe, usually berry-like, but only produced when both sexes are present.

Lindera benzoin (LINNAEUS) BLUME

6. (*Laurus benzoin* LINNAEUS) Rounded shrub, to 4m high and wide. Lv obovate, tapered at both ends, to 12cm long and 6cm wide, aromatic when crushed, turning golden in autumn. Fl small, produced from joints of the previous year's growth before the lv emerge. Fl 4. Fr red, oval to 8mm long. Native of the eastern USA. Introduced, perhaps by Banister, in 1683.

Lindera cercidifolia HEMSLEY

4.(5).6. Deciduous shrub or small tree, to 7–10m, with brown bts. Lv roundish, to 12cm long and 10cm wide, turning clear yellow in the autumn. Fl in clusters, bright yellow, before the lv. Fl 3–4. Fr dark red. Native of China. Introduced by Wilson in 1908 and later by Forrest. Barely distinct from the next sp.

Lindera obtusiloba BLUME

4.(5).6. (*L. triloba* of gardens) Distinguished from the last sp by its lv being usually 3-lobed, very brilliant green when young, the autumn tints yellow and pink and the fr black. A very attractive sp, native of China, Korea and Japan. First introduced by Maries in 1880.

LIQUIDAMBAR LINNAEUS *Hamamelidaceae*

A small genus of four species (or possibly only three) of deciduous trees with a curious disjunct distribution; one species is from eastern N America, one from the Near East and one or more from the Far East. The monoecious flowers lack petals and have no beauty. The leaves are lobed, resembling some *Acer* species, but alternate not opposite, generally colouring brilliantly in the autumn, although this does not always occur with young trees. They require a moist acid or neutral soil. Propagated by seeds – which take two years to germinate – or by layers.

Liquidambar formosana HANCE

3.6.7. Tree to 40m in the wild; not, so far, very tall in cultivation. Bts hairy or, in var *monticola* REHDER AND WILSON, glabrous. Lv palmately 3–5-lobed, plum-purple when young, later bronze and later still green, but turning crimson before falling. Plants from Taiwan are slightly tender, but plants sold as var *monticola*, from Wilson's collecting in 1907, appear to be perfectly hardy, although, since young plants grow continuously throughout most of the summer, the soft tip of the current year's growth may die back in cold or wet seasons. Originally introduced from Taiwan in 1884.

Liquidambar styraciflua LINNAEUS

6.7. Deciduous tree, to about 30m in cultivation in the UK but up to 50m in the wild, of narrow, pyramidal habit. Bts glabrous, young wood usually covered by corky wings. Lv basically heart-shaped but deeply 5–7-lobed, to 18cm wide and slightly less long, turning purple, crimson and orange in the autumn, although on some soils this does not always happen. In the wild it is found in rather swampy situations; in cultivation it likes ample moisture, but the soil should be reasonably drained. 'Variegata' has the lv margined white, later turning pinkish. Native of eastern N America. Possibly acquired by Tradescant early in the seventeenth century and certainly grown by Bishop Compton in 1686.

LIRIODENDRON LINNAEUS *Magnoliaceae*

A small genus of only two species of deciduous trees, remarkably similar in appearance. It has alternate leaves of very characteristic shape. Moist, fertile soil is necessary for these rapid-growing trees and they are best propagated by seed. These are produced in large numbers, but most will prove infertile.

Liriodendron tulipifera LINNAEUS   Tulip Tree

4.6.7. Large, deciduous tree, to 33m in the UK and up to 50m in the wild. Lv alternate, on petioles to 10cm long, shaped rather like a maple leaf with the apex snipped off. This apex is slightly rounded, with the nearest end at the

Liquidambar styraciflua

Liriodendron tulipifera

Liriodendron tulipifera

midrib, and the whole lv is somewhat the shape of a saddle; up to 20cm long and about 26cm wide, turning butter-yellow in the autumn. Fl shaped somewhat like a tulip, greenish, with an orange blotch at the base of the petals, solitary at the ends of twigs. Fl 6–7. Fl are only produced on mature trees. 'Aureomarginatum' has the lv with a yellow margin, while 'Fastigiatum' makes a columnar tree. Native of eastern N America from Nova Scotia southwards. Obtained by Tradescant about 1636.

LITHOCARPUS BLUME *Fagaceae*

A genus of about 100 species of evergreen trees, related to the oaks, from which they are most readily distinguished by their erect, not pendulous, male catkins. Most of the species, which come from eastern Asia, are somewhat tender or extremely so, but the solitary American species is usually hardy. The plant is best raised from seed and is not a very rapid grower.

Lithocarpus densiflorus (HOOKER AND ARNOTT) REHDER

3.(7). (*Quercus densiflorus* HOOKER AND ARNOTT) Evergreen tree, to 25m in the wild. Bts covered with thick, whitish wool. Lv alternate, at first covered with milky down, falling from the upper surface in the autumn, persisting longer below, ultimately dark glossy green above, somewhat glaucous below. Lv oval, acuminate, coriaceous, toothed, to 10cm long and half as wide, petiole to 2cm long. The lv persist for 2 or 3 years. Male fl in erect catkins to 10cm long, female fl at base forming acorns, either solitary or in pairs, to 2·5cm long in a shallow cup. Striking in the spring with its young white shoots. Native of Oregon and California. Introduced either 1865 or 1874.

LONICERA LINNAEUS *Caprifoliaceae*

A genus of about 200 species of shrubs and twining climbers, with opposite leaves, tubular flowers and berries as fruits. The genus has been divided into two subgenera: *Chamaecerasus*, in which the flowers are axillary and borne usually in pairs, and *Periclymenum*, in which the flowers are terminal in whorls or clusters. Most of *Chamaecerasus* are shrubs, but the section *Nintooa* consists of evergreen twiners. All the *Periclymenum* section are deciduous twiners and it includes the popular woodbine or honeysuckle. Propagation is by seed or by cuttings, which usually root readily, although internodal cuttings seem to do best for the *Periclymenum* section. Few of the shrubby species are of much garden value, but there are a few exceptions, while *L. nitida* is much used for hedging.

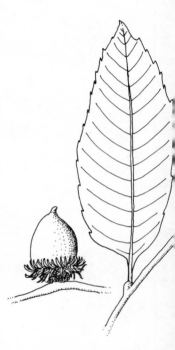

Lithocarpus densiflorus

Lonicera albertii REGEL

4. Deciduous shrub, to 130cm high and spreading more widely. Lv linear, to 3cm long and 3mm wide, glaucous blue-green. Fl fragrant, in pairs from the axils, rosy-pink, about 1cm long, on stalks about 6mm long. Fl 6. Fr purplish-red or nearly white. Native of Turkestan. Introduced by Regel about 1880.

Lonicera alseuosmoides GRAEBNER

4. Vigorous evergreen twiner. Lv narrowly elliptic, to 5cm long and 8mm wide. Fl in double pairs from the terminal lv axils giving a panicular effect, 1cm long, yellow outside, purple inside. Fl 7–10. Fr black with purple bloom. Native of China. Introduced by Wilson in 1904.

Lonicera X americana (MILLER) K. KOCH

4. An extremely showy, deciduous twiner of vigorous growth with purple bts. The plant is a hybrid between L. caprifolium and L. etrusca and seems originally to have occurred in the wild. Lv oval, glaucous, to 10cm long and 5cm wide, uniting before the fl to form a cup. Fl in numerous whorls to form a panicle up to 30cm long and 20cm wide; fragrant, two-lipped, the tube 5cm long and the lips 3cm wide, yellow flushed purple. Fl 6–7. One of the showiest and most floriferous honeysuckles and, like all these, doing best with the roots in the shade and the top in the sun. Certainly grown by Miller about 1730.

Lonicera X brownii (REGEL) CARRIÈRE

4. The name covering hybrids between L. sempervirens and L. hirsuta. Various clones are known under the names 'Fuchsioides', 'Plantier-ensis' and 'Dropmore Scarlet'. They are semi-evergreen, rather weak climbers with oval lv up to 8cm long and half as wide, uniting below the fl. Fl in whorls, two-lipped, various shades of orange-scarlet, up to 4cm long. Usually flowering 5–6 and 8–10, but 'Dropmore Scarlet' is a more vigorous plant, without the marked two lips, and flowers 7–10. The first cross is said to have been made before 1850.

Lonicera caprifolium LINNAEUS Woodbine

4.5. Deciduous climber to 7m or more, glabrous in all its parts. Lv obovate, glaucous, to 10cm long and half as wide, shortly stalked in the lower portions, joined to form a cup and sessile below the fl. Fl fragrant, in whorls at the ends of the shoots, tubular, two-lipped, to 5cm long and about 2·5cm wide, pale yellow flushed with pink. Fl 6–7. Fr orange. Distinguished from the honeysuckle, L. periclymenum, by the upper lv being united. Native of Europe, possibly including southern England.

Lonicera chaetocarpa (BATALIN) REHDER

4.5. (L. hispida var chaetocarpa BATALIN) Deciduous shrub to 2m and more with bristly bts. Lv sessile, oblong-ovate, to 7cm long and half as wide, bristly, particularly below. Fl in stalked pairs, two pairs to the axil, each pair on a peduncle about 2cm long, subtended by two large leafy bracts about 2·5cm long. Fl tubular with spreading lobes, to 3cm long, primrose-yellow. Fl 5–6. Fr red. Related to the popular L. involucrata, but the bracts are not coloured. On the other hand the fl are larger and the fr more attractive. A shrub that might well be seen more often. Native of western China. Introduced by Wilson in 1904.

Lonicera chrysantha TURCZANINOW

4.5. Deciduous shrub to 4m. Bts hollow, somewhat hairy at first. Lv ovate to rhombic, to 11cm long and half as wide, downy on the mid-rib and along the main veins below, dark green above, paler below. Fl in pairs, two pairs from each axil, each pair on a hairy stalk to 2cm long, pale yellow deepening as they age, to 2cm long. Fl 5–6. Fr bright red. A very hardy and ornamental shrub. Native to Siberia, N China and Japan. Introduced about 1854 according to Rehder.

Lonicera ciliosa (PURSH) POIRET

4.5. Deciduous, twining shrub. Lv ovate, conjoined below the fl, very short-petioled, mid-green above, glaucous beneath, margins ciliate. Fl in 1–3 terminal whorls, slightly two-lipped, to 3cm long, orange or yellow. Fl 6. Fr translucent orange-red. Native of western N America. Introduced in 1825.

Lonicera etrusca SANTI

4.(5). Vigorous, deciduous or semi-evergreen twiner, with purple bts. Lv oval, shortly stalked below, then sessile and united into a cup below the fl; to 9cm long and 5cm wide, glaucous. Fl fragrant in numerous whorls the stems branching at the summit and each stem bearing a terminal whorl, two-lipped, yellowish, later suffused red, to 4·5cm long. Fl 7–8. Fr red, but rarely produced in the UK. A splendid plant, but it does not flower when young and is less hardy than its hybrid L. X americana. Native of the Mediter-ranean region.

Lonicera fragrantissima LINDLEY AND PAXTON

4. Evergreen shrub in mild localities, semi-evergreen or deciduous elsewhere to 3m. Lv oval, coriaceous, ciliate when young, later glabrous, dark green above, glaucous beneath. Fl to 5cm long in numerous pairs at the lv axils, creamy-white, fragrant, about 1·5cm long. Fl 12–3. Fr joined together, red. Fr 5–6. Useful for its very

early flowering, but not particularly showy. Introduced from China by Fortune in 1845.

L. X purpusii is a hybrid between this sp and the not dissimilar *L. standishii* (qv), growing somewhat taller and spreading more widely with ovate lv to 8cm long and 5cm wide and always deciduous. Fl 12–3.

Lonicera henryi HEMSLEY

4. Evergreen twiner of great vigour and rapid growth. Lv oblong-ovate, acuminate, to 10cm long and 4cm wide, dark green above, paler below. Fl in a terminal cluster of stalked pairs, two-lipped, 2cm wide and long, of a rather muddy purple. Fl 6–7. Fr black-purple with bluish bloom. Useful for forming an evergreen screen rapidly, but the least attractive among the *Nintooa* section. Both *L. alseuosmoides* and *L. japonica* are more decorative. Native of western China. Introduced by Wilson in 1908.

Lonicera involucrata

Lonicera involucrata (RICHARDSON) SPRENGEL

4.5. (Including *L. ledebourii* ESCHSCHOLZ) Deciduous, rather sprawling shrub, to 3m high and wide. Bts somewhat square, becoming rounded later. Lv ovate-oblong, to 10cm long and 4·5cm wide, dark green and glabrous above, lighter and downy beneath, on a petiole of 6mm. Fl in twin pairs at the end of a downy stalk to 3cm long, subtended by a pair of crimson bracts which expand after the flowers fade, eventually to 3cm long and conspicuous. The fl are tubular, to 2cm long, reddish outside, yellow within. Fl 5–6 and often again 8–9. Fr black. Native of southern Canada and western America. *L. ledebourii* is the most vigorous form and comes from California. *L. involucrata* introduced in 1824, *L. ledebourii* in 1838.

Lonicera japonica THUNBERG

4. Vigorous evergreen climber to 10m or more. Bts sometimes stained purple. Lv generally oval-elliptic, but sometimes lobed on vigorous plants, to 8cm long, varying from somewhat hairy to quite glabrous. Fl in pairs from the axils, two-lipped, to 4cm long, and usually as wide, fragrant, white fading to yellow; some forms are purple on the outside. The plant most usually seen in gardens is 'Halliana' with pure white, extra fragrant fl from June onwards. The original introduction, known as 'Repens', may have the lv tinged with purple below. 'Aureo-reticulata', introduced by Fortune from Japan in 1860, has the veins and midrib bright yellow, giving a netted effect. This plant is often damaged (although rarely killed) in severe winters. Native of Japan, China and Korea. Introduced from China in 1814.

Lonicera maackii (RUPRECHT) MAXIMOWICZ

4.5. Deciduous shrub, to 5m, of spreading habit, most marked in the most desirable form var *podocarpa* REHDER (*L. podocarpa* FRANCHET). Lv oval-elliptic or oval lanceolate, to 7cm long and 4cm wide, dark green and downy on both surfaces. Fl in twin pairs from upper axils, fragrant, two-lipped to 2cm long and wide, white fading to yellow. Fl 6. Fr dark red. A handsome shrub both in fl and fr. The type was introduced from Manchuria to St Petersburg in 1880, var *podocarpa* by Wilson from China in 1900.

Lonicera nitida WILSON

Evergreen shrub, to 4m, with abundant lv. Bts purplish and downy. Lv ovate or roundish, closely set along the twigs, to 1·5 cm long, dark glossy green above, pale green below. Fl very small, only to 6mm long, off-white and fragrant. Fl 4–5. Fr about 6mm across, translucent purple. The plant has no beauty of fl but makes a neat hedging plant.

L. pileata OLIVER is a dwarfer shrub of horizontal growth, rarely exceeding 1m high, but evidently closely allied. *L. nitida* 'Baggesen's

Lonicera japonica

Gold' has golden lv and a rather dwarf spreading habit. *L. nitida* was introduced by Wilson from western China in 1908. He also introduced *L. pileata* in 1900.

Lonicera periclymenum LINNAEUS Honeysuckle

4.5. Deciduous or semi-evergreen twining shrub to 7m. Lv ovate or obovate, to 6cm long and 3·5cm wide, dull green above, glaucous beneath, shortly petioled or sessile below the fl but never united in a cup as in *L. caprifolium*. Fl in a series of terminal whorls, very fragrant, two-lipped, to 5cm long, cream within, cream or red-flushed outside. Fl 7–8. Fr red, translucent. The Dutch Honeysuckle 'Belgica' is a less vigorous climber with redder fl which appear in June. 'Serotina' the late Dutch Honeysuckle, has apparently been lost. The plant sold under this name flowers from July to September, but looks very like 'Belgica'. Native of all of Europe, the Caucasus and western Asia.

Lonicera quinquelocularis HARDWICKE

4.5. Deciduous shrub, to 5m, with purplish downy bts. Lv oval or round, to 6cm long and 4cm wide, dull green and downy at first above, later glabrous, grey and hairy beneath. Fl in short-stalked pairs from the axils, two-lipped, about 2cm wide but only 6mm long, creamy-white fading to yellow. Fl 6. Fr white, translucent. Unique for its white fr. Native of the Himalaya and Afghanistan. Introduced, possibly by Falconer, before 1840.

Lonicera sempervirens LINNAEUS

4.(5). Semi-evergreen twining shrub with glaucous bts. Lv oval to 7cm long and 5cm wide, dark green above, glaucous and somewhat downy below, united below the fl. Fl in 3 or 4 whorls, each of about 6 blooms, tubular with 5 rather small, spreading lobes, usually bright scarlet outside, yellowish within, unscented, to 5cm long. Fl 6–8. Fr red, but rarely seen in the UK. Hardy on a wall in most districts. Valued for its scarlet fl and has proved hardier than originally thought. Native of the eastern USA. Introduced by the younger Tradescant about 1656.

L. X heckrottii is a hybrid, it is thought, between *L. sempervirens* and *L. X americana*, although this latter parent is not proven. The plant makes a sprawling, deciduous shrub, not climbing without support, with oblong-oval lv to 6cm long, nearly sessile and conjoined beneath the fl. These are 3·5cm long, deep pink outside, yellow inside, produced in numerous terminal whorls. Fl 7–9. Not, apparently, deliberately bred, and first noticed in 1895. It is very floriferous, but awkward to manage, as it has to be tied in.

Lonicera splendida BOISSIER

4.5. Evergreen climber of considerable vigour when happily established. Lv oval or oblong to 3·5cm long, glaucous, sessile, joined below the fl. Fl in numerous terminal whorls, two-lipped, fragrant, to 3·5cm long, reddish-purple without, yellow within. Fl 6–8. Fr red. A very attractive plant, with its glaucous lv, even when not in flower, but not easy to establish; probably best on a south-facing wall. Native of Spain. Introduced about 1880.

Lonicera standishii JACQUES

4.(5). Deciduous or semi-evergreen shrub to 2·5m. Closely allied to *L. fragrantissima*, from which it is distinguished by its more compact habit, bristly bts and the lv hairy beneath. The lv are also more pointed and the plant is more likely to be deciduous. It tends to start flowering earlier than *L. fragrantissima*, often in November. Fl white. Fr red, the two berries conjoined for most of their length. Native of China. Introduced by Fortune with *L. fragrantissima* in 1845.

Lonicera syringantha

Lonicera syringantha MAXIMOWICZ

4.5. Deciduous, rather spreading, shrub to 2m high. Lv sometimes in whorls of 3, oblong, to 2·5cm long and 1cm across, dull glaucous green. Fl in twin pairs, fragrant, on a stalk to 6mm,

131

each fl is 12mm long and wide, lilac-pink. Fl 5–6. Fr red. Tends to be rather shy-flowering. Native of China and Tibet. Introduced about 1890.

Lonicera tatarica LINNAEUS

4.5. Deciduous shrub of rapid, spreading growth to 3m or more. Lv oblong-ovate, rounded at the base, to 6cm long and 3cm wide on extension growths, about half this size on flowering shoots; glabrous, dark green above, glaucous below. Fl in twin pairs from axils, each pair on a stalk to 2·5cm long. The fl two-lipped, to 2·5cm across, white, pink or nearly red. Fl 5–6. Fr red. Named clones of good deep pink colour are 'Arnold Red' and 'Hack's Red'. A yellow-berried form has been in cultivation but is probably now lost. Fr are not always freely produced, but very showy when they are. Native from central Asia to S Russia. Introduced about 1752, probably through one of Collinson's Russian correspondents.

Lonicera thibetica BUREAU AND FRANCHET

4.5. Spreading, deciduous shrub, to about 2m high but more than 3m in diameter. Bts purplish and downy. Lv in pairs or whorls of 3, linear-oblong, to 2·5cm long and 8mm wide, dark green above, white-woolly below. Fl in pairs from lv axils, often 3 pairs produced, 12mm long and 8mm wide, lilac in colour and perfume. Fl 5–6. Fr red. Allied to *L. syringantha*, but distinct with the lv white-woolly below. Native of western China. Introduced about 1897.

Lonicera tragophylla HEMSLEY

4.5. Twining, deciduous shrub of some vigour. Lv oval-elliptic, glaucous, to 11cm long and 5cm wide, conjoined beneath the fl, often coloured bronze in full sun. Fl in a terminal head of up to 20 blooms, two-lipped, lacking fragrance, the tube to 9cm long, the lips to 2·5cm wide, bright yellow. Fl 6–7. Fr red. The showiest of the honeysuckles, said to have been introduced by Wilson in 1900, but a plant brought back by Potts for the Horticultural Society, depicted in the *Proceedings* as *L. longiflora*, looks very like *L. tragophylla*.

L. X tellmanniana SPAETH

4. A hybrid between *L. tragophylla* and *L. sempervirens*, raised in Budapest and put into commerce in 1927. It is a vigorous, deciduous climber. Lv ovate-elliptic, to 9cm long and 5cm wide. Fl in terminal heads of 6–12 fl. Each fl two-lipped, about 5cm long and 2·5cm wide, yellow flushed red on the outside. Fl 7–8. A number of perfectly hardy, but not very ornamental, shrubby loniceras which are available in commerce, such as *L. coerulea* and *L. pyrenaica*, have been omitted, mainly for reasons of space,

but also because of their comparatively limited garden value.

LUPINUS LINNAEUS *Leguminosae*

A fairly large genus of mainly American plants, but with some species in Europe and Asia. Most species are herbaceous.

Lupinus arboreus SIMS   Tree Lupin

4. Evergreen shrub of rapid growth, but short-lived, up to 3m high. Bts silky-hairy. Lv digitate with 7–11 leaflets, grey-green and hairy, each up to 5cm long, oblanceolate, downy beneath on a petiole about 6cm long; the complete lv more or less circular. Fl in erect, terminal racemes to 25cm long, composed of numerous fragrant fl, usually sulphur but occasionally deeper yellow or mauve, each floret about 2cm long, pea-shaped. Fl 5–8. Seed freely produced and the best method of propagation, but pods should be removed if seed not required as the plant tends to seed itself to death. The plants do best in rather poor soil and older plants usually succumb to severe frosts. However, near the coast it has naturalised itself in many localities. Native of California. Introduced before 1800.

LYCIUM LINNAEUS *Solanaceae*

A widespread genus of about ninety species from both hemispheres. It has alternate leaves, often in clusters, axillary flowers, usually funnel-form, and the fruit is a berry.

Lycium barbarum LINNAEUS
Duke of Argyll's Tea Tree

4.5. (Includes *L. halimifolium* MILLER and *L. chinense* MILLER) Deciduous shrub of very variable character; some forms are spiny, others unarmed and the brs may be erect, pendulous or prostrate. The lv also vary in size and shape, but are usually more or less elliptic, up to 6cm long. Fl in clusters of 2 or 3 or more at the axils, funnel-shaped, purple or pink, about 1cm long. Fl 5–7. Fr egg-shaped, about 2·5cm long, scarlet or orange. Best propagated by seed, but cuttings and layers will root. Native of China. Introduced in 1696 according to *Hortus Kewensis*.

LYONIA NUTTALL *Ericaceae*

A genus of some thirty species from N America, the West Indies and eastern Asia, formerly included in *Andromeda*. There are only two N American species in commerce. They require acid soil and rather moist conditions.

Lyonia lucida (LAMARCK) K. KOCH

4. Evergreen shrub, to 2m, with triangular

stems. Lv widely elliptic, coriaceous, acuminate, glossy green above, to 8cm long and half as wide. Fl in axillary clusters giving the effect of a terminal raceme, conical in shape, about 6–8mm long, white or pink. Fl 4–5. Native of the south-eastern USA. Introduced through John Cree in 1765.

Lyonia mariana (LINNAEUS) D. DON

4.6. Deciduous shrub, to 2m. Lv elliptic or oblong, to 7cm long, glabrous above, sometimes downy below, colouring red in autumn. Fl in numerous axillary clusters, giving a racemose effect at the ends of the previous year's growths; nodding, cylindrical, white or pale pink. Fl 5–7. Native of eastern N America. Sent by John Bartram to Collinson in 1736.

MAACKIA RUPRECHT AND MAXIMOWICZ Leguminosae

A genus of ten species of deciduous, slow-growing trees from eastern Asia, valuable for their late-flowering and for the beauty of the unfolding leaves. Propagated by seeds.

Maackia amurensis (RUPRECHT AND MAXIMOWICZ) K. KOCH

3.4. Slow-growing, small tree, to 15m in the wild but little more than 5m in cultivation and often grown as a bush. Lv pinnate, metallic-blue when unfurling, later dark green, with 7–11 leaflets and up to 30cm long. Leaflets, ovate, blunt at the apex, to 7cm long, dark green above, paler below and glabrous (downy in the Japanese var buergeri). Fl, white, in terminal, erect racemes, to 15cm long, each fl about 1cm long. Fl 7–8. Pods to 7cm long. Native of Manchuria. Introduced in 1864.

Maackia chinensis TAKEDA

3.4. Flat-headed tree, to 10m so far in cultivation, up to 17m in the wild. Lv covered with silvery-grey down when unfurling, this persisting on the underside of the leaflets. Lv resemble those of the last sp but are smaller in all respects, not exceeding 20cm long and the leaflets not longer than 6cm. Fl in a terminal panicle made up of several erect racemes, the whole panicle to 20cm long, 12cm wide; each fl about 1cm long, dull white. Fl 7–8. Native of western China. Introduced by Wilson in 1908.

MACHILUS NEES Lauraceae

A genus of about twenty species of evergreen, east Asian trees, of which little is known in this country. Requiring a moist, fertile soil. Some authorities divide the species between Persea and Neolitsea, the genus Machilus then becoming obsolete.

Machilus ichangensis REHDER AND WILSON

3.4.5. Small, semi-evergreen tree with glabrous bts. Lv lanceolate, acuminate, copper-coloured when young, later dark green, to 20cm long. Fl in axillary panicles to 5cm long, small, white. Fl 4–6. Fr a shining black berry. A plant that appears to be very little known although in commerce; not mentioned either by Bean, Rehder or the RHS Dictionary. Native of Hupeh and introduced by Wilson in 1901.

MACLURA NUTTALL Moraceae

A monotypic genus. Propagated by root cuttings or seeds.

Maclura pomifera (RAFINESQUE) SCHNEIDER

5. (Toxylon pomifera RAFINESQUE, Maclura aurantiaca NUTTALL) Deciduous, dioecious tree, to 15m, with spiny brs, the spines to 3cm long. Lv, alternate, ovate or oblong-lanceolate, to 10cm long and half as wide, acuminate, dark green, turning yellow before falling. Fl green, inconspicuous, but the female fl, if fertilised, swells up to form a large globular compound fr, about 10cm in diameter and yellowish-green. Much used for hedging in its native USA. Introduced in 1818.

MAGNOLIA LINNAEUS Magnoliaceae

A genus of around thirty-five species of trees and shrubs mainly from eastern Asia and North America with alternate leaves and solitary, terminal flowers. This is regarded as one of the more primitive families and petals and sepals are not clearly differentiated. In the centre of the flower is an elongated structure, known as the torus, on which the carpels are borne. After fertilisation the torus and carpels enlarge considerably, giving a cone-like impression. When ripe, the carpels open to disclose the seeds which are often brilliantly coloured. If propagation by seed is desired, they should be sown as soon as ripe, as they soon lose their viability if dried out. Even so they may be very slow to germinate; a wait of two years is not unusual, although not invariable. The roots are somewhat thick and fleshy and most authorities recommend transplanting in April or May, rather than in the autumn. Propagation is also possible by layers, air-layers and, with some species and hybrids, cuttings. Cultivars are either layered or grafted. Although a large number of species are hardy so far as winter cold is concerned, a number open their flowers very early in the year and these are frost tender, so that in districts where spring frosts are rife, it is best to concentrate on the later-flowering species as MM. sinensis, wilsonii, *virginiana, thompsoniana, hypoleuca,* etc. Most of the more tree-like species do not flower until sizeable plants. Few species will thrive on thin chalky soil, but most will tolerate some alkalinity, although they seem to do best on acid soil. They tend to be intolerant of prolonged drought.

Magnolia acuminata LINNAEUS   Cucumber Tree

4.5.7. Deciduous tree, to 30m, but most large trees in cultivation are around 20m. Lv more or less heart-shaped, to 25cm long and half as wide, green on both surfaces. Fl cup-shaped, about 7cm long and 5cm across, greenish-yellow, sometimes with blue markings. Fl 5–6. Fr red, somewhat cucumber-shaped, to 7cm long. The fl are inconspicuous and not produced on young plants, but the tree is impressive. Native of eastern N America. Introduced by Bartram in 1736 and first flowered 26 years later.

Magnolia campbellii

JOSEPH HOOKER AND THOMSON

4. Deciduous tree, to 20m, usually forming several trunks. The plant requires acid soil and shelter from wind. Owing to its early flowering, is really only satisfactory in southern or western areas of the UK. Lv broad-elliptic, to 25cm long, glabrous above, hairy below. Fl bowl-shaped, up to 25cm wide, with 12–16 tepals, deep pink, pale pink or, rarely, white. Fr cone-shaped to 20cm long. Var *mollicomata* is generally hardier and also comes more rapidly to flower from seed. Fl 2–4, but the clone 'Darjeeling', with deep pink fl, delays until late April and early May. One of the most magnificent flowering trees, but with rather brittle wood, so most successful in woodland situations. Var *mollicomata* should probably prove hardy in most parts of the UK, but would only be worth growing where the fl can be expected not to be frosted. Native of the Himalaya, eastwards to Yunnan. *M. campbellii* is said to have been introduced in 1865, but 1851 is more likely the correct date and Joseph Hooker the introducer. Var *mollicomata* introduced by Forrest in 1924.

Magnolia denudata DESROUSSEAUX   Yulan

4.7. (*M. conspicua* SALISBURY) Deciduous bush or small tree, to 10m. Lv obovate or oval, to 15cm long and 10cm wide, mucronate, green above, downy beneath. Fl before lv, goblet-shaped, about 7cm high and with about 9 tepals, pure white, although there exists also a var *purpurascens* with tepals tinged purple on the outside. Fl 3–5. Fr spindle-shaped, 12cm long. An exceptionally beautiful plant, but the fl often damaged by frost. Native of China. Obtained by Sir Joseph Banks from the East India Co at Canton in 1789. A parent of the popular *M. X soulangiana* (qv) but more elegant.

Magnolia fraseri WALTER

3.4.5.7. (*M. auriculata* W. BARTRAM) Deciduous tree, to 13m, of spreading habit. Lv in clusters at the ends of the brs, obovate, but with two distinct lobes (auricles) at the base, up to 40cm long, bronzy when unfurling. Fl up to 20cm across, saucer-shaped, pale yellow at first, fading to milky-white, scented but not particularly agreeably. Fl 5–6. Fr a pink cone up to 12cm long, splitting to reveal scarlet seeds. Acid soil seems to be essential. The plant flowers when quite young and is one of the best of the American tree magnolias for garden decoration. Native of the south-eastern USA. Introduced by Fraser in 1786.

Magnolia grandiflora LINNAEUS

4.(7). Evergreen tree, up to 12m in the UK but to 25m in districts with a hot summer. Lv oblong-obovate, to 25cm long and nearly half as wide, dark glossy green above, usually covered with rust-coloured felt below, but glabrous beneath in the clone known as 'Goliath'. Fl more or less globular, but later opening wide and then to 25cm across, cream-coloured and very fragrant. Fl 6–9. The fl open successively over a long period. Although hardy except in the most severe winters, the plants flower more freely trained against a wall. A number of named clones exist of which 'Exmouth', with rather lanceolate lv and a fastigiate habit, is probably one of the original 1734 introductions. 'Goliath' starts flowering earlier than most other cv and has larger fl. One of the few spp which can be propagated by cuttings. Native of the southern USA. Introduced in 1734 according to *Hortus Kewensis.*

M. X highdownensis   See *M. wilsonii*

Magnolia hypoleuca SIEBOLD AND ZUCCARINI

4.5.(7). (*M. obovata* THUNBERG) Deciduous, erect-growing tree, to 25m and more in the wild but only up to 15m in cultivation in the UK. Bts dark purple. Lv in terminal clusters, obovate, up to 45cm long, half as wide, coriaceous, glaucous above, blue-white beneath. Fl saucer-shaped, to 20cm wide, scented, creamy-white with a conspicuous mass of red stamens. Fl 6. Fr cone-shaped, to 20cm tall and 6cm wide, bright red. Slow-growing and rather gaunt when young. *M. officinalis* REHDER AND WILSON is closely allied and differs mainly in its yellowish-grey (not purplish) bts, its larger lv (up to 50cm long), and in its ovate, flat-topped fr. It is a much smaller tree in the wild. *M. hypoleuca* is native to Japan and was introduced in 1865 according to Rehder, 1884 according to Bean. *M. officinalis* is native to China and was introduced by Wilson in 1900.

Magnolia acuminata

Magnolia kobus DE CANDOLLE

4.5. Deciduous, fairly rapid-growing tree, to 13m, pyramidal at first, later round-headed. Lv obovate, often mucronate, bright green and rather thin, to 15cm long. Fl rather open and starry, about 10cm wide, pure white, before the lv. Fl 3–4. Fr sausage-shaped, to 15cm long, pink, later revealing bright red seeds. Although hardy and rapid growing most forms do not flower until mature, when they cover themselves with blossom, so a long wait is often necessary. Most gardeners may prefer the hybrid with *M. stellata* known as *M. X loebneri* (qv). Native of Japan. Introduced by Maries in 1879 (Rehder gives 1865).

Magnolia liliiflora DESROUSSEAUX

4. (*M. purpurea* CURTIS) Deciduous, straggling bush to 4m. Lv ovate or oblong, to 20cm long and 12cm wide, acuminate, dark green above, downy below. Fl before and with lv erect, rather constricted, to 7cm long, purple outside white within. Fl 4–6 and quite often odd fl are produced subsequently. 'Nigra' is a very dark purple. Native of China; obtained by the Duke of Portland in 1790. The plant is much cultivated in Japan and the original introduction is said to have been from Japan, but both *Hortus Kewensis* and Loudon give China as its provenance.

Magnolia X loebneri KACHE

4. A deciduous shrub or small tree, to 8m, spreading more widely and possibly eventually larger. This is a hybrid between *M. kobus* and *M. stellata* (qv) made originally by Max Loebner in 1910. Lv obovate or broad-elliptic, to 10cm long and 6cm wide, dark green. Fl composed of numerous strap-shaped petals, reflexing eventually, white, except in the cv 'Leonard Messel' which is flushed pink on the outside, appearing mostly before lv, about 12cm across. Fl 4–5. Usually the fl have 12 tepals. A very useful hybrid, it flowers when quite young and grows more rapidly than *M. stellata*.

Magnolia macrophylla MICHAUX

4.5. Deciduous tree, to about 12m in the UK. Lv very large, occasionally to 1m long and 30cm wide, oblong-obovate, bright green above, grey and downy beneath. Fl open, 6-tepalled, to 25cm (occasionally to 35cm) wide, creamy-white. Fl 6. Fr ovoid, pink. Remarkable for its enormous lv, which are easily damaged in high winds. The plant is immune to low winter temperatures but very sensitive to spring frosts. Acid soil is essential. Native to the south-eastern USA. Introduced by Lyon in 1800.

Magnolia salicifolia (SIEBOLD AND ZUCCARINI) MAXIMOWICZ

3.4.5. Deciduous shrub or small tree, to 13m. Lv lanceolate or narrow-oval, bronzy when young, to 10cm long and 3cm wide, but some forms have larger dimensions, green above glaucous below. Fl before lv with 6 strap-shaped, pure white petals, about 10cm wide. Fl 4. Fr sausage-shaped, to 7cm long, rosy pink, later revealing scarlet seeds. The bark of young shoots is lemon scented when bruised. The plant has been hybridised with *M. stellata* and the resultant hybrid is known as *M. X proctoriana*. *M. X* 'Kewensis' is a hybrid with *M. kobus*. Both make rather larger plants than *M. salicifolia* but are not markedly different in appearance. *M. salicifolia* is native to Japan. Introduced to the Arnold Arboretum in 1892, received in the UK about 1900.

Magnolia sargentiana REHDER AND WILSON

4.7. Although the type is in cultivation and commerce, the var *robusta* REHDER AND WILSON is vastly superior for garden work, and it is this plant which is described here. Bushy, deciduous tree to 15m, often with several trunks, usually starting about 1m from the ground. Lv oblong-ovate, to 20cm long and 7cm wide, often notched at the apex, dark and glossy above, greyish-hairy below. Fl very large, to 30cm in diameter, saucer-shaped with 10–16 tepals, purplish-pink without, paler within. Fl before the lv, 3–4. Fr cone-shaped to 20cm long, conspicuous when the scarlet seeds are revealed. The plant does not flower until quite sizeable. It appears to be perfectly winter hardy, but most plants are found in the southern half of the UK. The very early fl make it unsuitable for districts where spring frosts regularly occur. Native of Szechuan and Yunnan. Collected by Wilson in 1908.

Magnolia sieboldii K. KOCH

4.5. (*M. parviflora* SIEBOLD AND ZUCCARINI) Usually a spreading bush to 5m high and wide, deciduous. Lv obovate, abruptly acuminate, to 15cm long (usually much less) and half as wide, dark green above, glaucous beneath, on a petiole to 1cm. Fl pendant, about 10cm wide, cup-shaped, pure white with a conspicuous boss of crimson stamens. Fl 5–8. The largest display is 5–6 but sporadic flowers appear subsequently. Fr cone-shaped, carmine, about 5cm long. Native of Japan and Korea. Introduced by Maries in 1879.

Magnolia sinensis STAPF

4.5. (*M. globosa* var *sinensis* REHDER AND WILSON, *M. nicholsoniana* of gardens) Deciduous shrub, to 7m, of spreading habit. Bts brown-silky. Lv oval-oblong, mucronate, rounded at base, to

17cm long and 13cm wide, bright green above, velvety and hairy beneath at first, later glabrous. Fl nodding, saucer-shaped, to 12cm wide, pure white with a conspicuous centre of crimson stamens, fragrant. Fl 6. Some plants also flower again 8–9. Fr cylindrical, somewhat prickly, occasionally pink and attractive when the scarlet seeds are disclosed. Native of Szechuan. Introduced by Wilson in 1908 (but not reaching the UK until 1920). This is probably the best of the nodding-flowered magnolias and is very close to *M. wilsonii* (qv).

Magnolia X soulangiana SOULANGE-BODIN

4. The most popular of the genus; a hybrid between *M. denudata* and *M. liliiflora.* Deciduous tree, to 10m, or spreading bush. In the form most often seen, lv obovate or oval, to 15cm long, downy beneath at first. The lv often unfurl a somewhat unhealthy yellowish-green and colour up later in the season. Fl before lv, goblet-shaped, about the same size as *M. denudata,* white within, purple-stained outside. Fl 4. There are a large number of named cv, of which 'Brozzonii', with pure white tepals blotched purple at the base and making fl of up to 25cm across when expanded, is notable. 'Lennei' is very distinct and probably has a reversed parentage. The lv are broadly-obovate, to 20cm long and 12cm wide. The fl are shaped like an electric light bulb, are rosy-purple and open much later than most soulangianas, usually not until May, making this the best cv for cold areas. Usually a few secondary flowers are produced in the autumn, and these may be more or less white. 'Lennei' seeds freely and 'Rustica rubra' is probably one of its seedlings. 'Lennei Alba' is quite distinct from 'Lennei' and barely distinguishable from *M. denudata.* The hybrid first flowered in the garden of M. Soulange-Bodin in 1826.

Magnolia stellata (SIEBOLD AND ZUCCARINI) MAXIMOWICZ

4. Twiggy deciduous shrub of rather rounded habit, slow-growing, to 4–5m tall and half as wide. Bts silky. Lv to 10cm long and 4cm wide, narrow-oblong, dark green. Fl composed of numerous (up to 18) strap-shaped tepals, which are 5cm long; the fl are tubular at first, later reflexed. Fl 3–4. 'Rosea' has the fl just tinged pink before opening, but this cv sets seed whereas the usual commercial form of *M. stellata* does not. This flowers as a small plant and, provided the blooms are not frosted, presents a most charming sight in early spring. This species is now known to be a dwarf mutant; 50 per cent of plants raised from seed develop into typical *M. kobus.* Native of Japan. Introduced in 1877.

Magnolia X thompsoniana DE VOS

4. (*M. glauca* var *thompsoniana* LOUDON) Probably a hybrid between *M. virginiana* and *M. tripetala,* noticed by a nurseryman Thomson in 1808. Sprawling, deciduous shrub of up to about 7m, making long growths each year. Lv oblong-oval, to 25cm long and about half as wide, bright green above, glaucous beneath. Fl creamy-white, more or less tubular, to 10cm long, very fragrant, but lasting only about 48 hours. Fl 6–8. The plant never has a large display but continues in bloom over a long season and starts flowering when very young. It is much easier to establish than *M. virginiana,* but that sp is otherwise preferable.

Magnolia tripetala LINNAEUS Umbrella Tree

4.5. Deciduous tree, to 12m, often with several trunks. Lv obovate, up to 50cm long and 25cm across, bright green above, downy below when young, later glabrous. Fl tubular, fetid, with 6–9 tepals, to 12cm long. Fl 5–6. Fr cone-shaped, up to 10cm long, bright pink, seeds scarlet. The plant is grown mainly for its magnificent lv. The fl are inconspicuous, but the fr, which are freely produced on mature plants, are striking. Native of the eastern USA. Introduced by Bartram to Collinson in 1752.

Magnolia X veitchii BEAN

4.7. This is *M. denudata* pollinated by *M. campbellii.* Deciduous tree, to 27m or more, with purplish bts. Lv obovate, sharply acuminate, up to 30cm long and 17cm wide, purplish when young, later dark green, veins beneath downy. Fl goblet-shaped, before lv, up to 15cm long. Fl 4. This perfectly hardy hybrid has rather brittle wood and so needs protection when young as it is a vigorous grower and can be damaged in severe winds. Fl much like those of *M. soulangiana* but larger and of a better pink. The plant was raised by Peter Veitch in 1907 and first flowered 10 years later.

Magnolia virginiana LINNAEUS Sweet Bay

4.(5). (*M. glauca* LINNAEUS) Deciduous or semi-evergreen shrub or small tree, but more usually a spreading bush, to 10m. Lv oval or obovate, mid-green above, glaucous bluish-white below, downy when young; to 12cm long and about half as wide. Fl globular, creamy-white, intensely fragrant, about 7cm in diameter, produced over a very long period. Fl 6–9. Fr cone-shaped and bright red, but not produced with any freedom in the UK. Does not resent alkaline soil and seems to thrive best in the eastern part of the UK. Very slow to establish, but a charming plant when well grown. The first magnolia to be cultivated in Europe. Native of the eastern USA. Introduced by Banister and in cultivation in 1688.

Magnolia virginiana

Magnolia wilsonii REHDER

4.5. (Includes *M. nicholsoniana* REHDER AND WILSON and *M. taliensis* W. W. SMITH) Deciduous shrub or small tree to 8m. Bts brown-hairy at first, later purplish-brown (as opposed to greyish in *M. sinensis*). Lv ovate-lanceolate, acuminate, to 15cm long and about 4–6cm wide, dull green above, brown-woolly below (glabrous in some forms). Fl pendulous, fragrant, cup-shaped, to 10cm wide, white with a central boss of carmine stamens. Fl 5–6. Fr cylindric, purplish pink, seeds scarlet. A more upright plant than *M. sinensis* and with narrower lv but evidently closely allied. The similar *M. X highdownensis* is considered to be a hybrid between *MM. sinensis* and *wilsonii*. Native of Yunnan and Szechuan. Introduced by Wilson in 1908.

MAHONIA NUTTALL *Berberidaceae*

A genus of seventy evergreen shrubs with yellow wood, pinnate, spiny leaves and, usually, an inflorescence consisting of clusters of spike-like racemes. The fruit is a berry, usually dark blue. Most of the species in cultivation flower in winter or very early in the year. The Asiatic species are somewhat slow to branch out, but must be left to do this in their own good time; stopping seems to have no effect. A few species on the border-line of hardiness are omitted here, but the majority of species are not in cultivation at all. Propagation by seeds, by division in the sucker-ing species or by cuttings.

Mahonia aquifolium
(PURSH) NUTTALL Oregon Grape

4.5. Evergreen shrub, to 2m but usually 1m, spreading widely by underground suckers. Lv pinnate with 5–9 leaflets, usually broadly ovate, the whole lv to 30cm long but usually less; often turning reddish or (in the cv 'Atropurpurea') purplish in the winter. Fl in a cluster of erect racemes to 7cm long, crowded with golden-yellow fl. Fl 2–5. Fr black with violet bloom. Native of western N America. Introduced in 1823.

Mahonia japonica (THUNBERG) DE CANDOLLE

4. (*Ilex japonica* THUNBERG; including *M. bealei* FORTUNE) Evergreen shrub, to 4m, with erect, rather sparsely branched stems. Lv pinnate, dark green, purplish when young, with up to 19 leaflets which are spiny, up to 10cm long. Fl in a cluster of pendulous racemes (erect in *M. bealei*), to 25cm long, primrose-yellow, smelling of lily of the valley. Fl 11–4. Easily one of the best winter-flowering shrubs. When the buds first appear in October they are frost tender and early autumn frosts can damage them, but once fully formed they will stand the lowest temperatures; the fl themselves are rarely damaged by frost. *M. bealei* was introduced from China by Fortune in 1849. *M. japonica* has long been cultivated in Japan, but is apparently not native there and its exact wild locality is not known.

Mahonia X media BRICKELL

3.4. The collective name for hybrids between the last sp and the slightly tender *M. lomariifolia*. As known so far it makes a rather gaunt shrub to 5m. Lv purplish on unfurling, as large as those of *M. japonica* with up to 21 leaflets, which are ovate-lanceolate to 10cm long and 3cm wide, spiny-toothed. Fl in up to 20 terminal racemes, usually erect and up to 30cm long. In some forms these racemes are branched. Fl varying from lemon to quite a deep yellow, fragrant. Fl 11–1. Fr a bluish berry. The original hybrid seems to have been raised about 1950. A number of named cv are available, of which 'Buckland', 'Charity' and 'Winter Sun' are outstanding, but any plant from this cross and seedlings taken therefrom all seem to be excellent, particularly valuable for their brilliant flowers at the deadest time of the year. Again the emerging buds are frost-tender, but once fully expanded take no harm.

Mahonia pinnata of gardens

4. The true *M. pinnata* LAGASCA (*M. fascicularis* DE CANDOLLE) is a somewhat tender shrub which is probably not in cultivation, the plants in commerce under that name being hybrids of *M. pinnata* with *M. aquifolium* and perhaps *M.*

repens. These are quite spreading shrubs to 2m, lv generally much like those of *M. aquifolium.* Fl in erect racemes, not only from the top of the shoots but also from lower axils, to give a very large inflorescence. 'Undulata' is a particularly fine form with lv with wavy margins. Fl bright yellow. Fl 3–5. Fr blue-black. *M. pinnata* itself comes from California and Mexico and was introduced to Madrid in 1791, reaching Great Britain in 1818. The first hybrid occurred about 1840 in Messrs. Rivers' nursery. The hybrids are quite hardy.

Mahonia repens (LINDLEY) GEORGE DON

4.5. Really too low a plant to be included here, but the form known as var *rotundifolia* can reach nearly to 2m. The usual form rarely exceeds 30cm in height and spreads widely by underground runners. Lv composed of 3–7 leaflets, which are ovate, to 6cm long, dull bluish-green above usually but sea-green in var *rotundifolia.* Racemes to 7cm long, usually deep yellow but one form of *rotundifolia* is a rather pale yellow. Fl 4–5. Fr black with a blue bloom. Native of western N America. Discovered by the Lewis and Clarke expedition of 1804–6 but not introduced to cultivation until 1822.

All *Mahonias*, like *Berberis*, grow very slowly in the first two or three years from seed, after which they quickly accelerate and are then quite rapid growers. *Mahonia aquifolium* has been hybridised with three spp of *Berberis* to create the hybrid *X Mahoberberis*, but they are not always very satisfactory garden shrubs.

MALUS MILLER *Rosaceae*

A genus of thirty-five species of deciduous trees and shrubs spread over the temperate parts of the northern hemisphere and generally known as crab apples, although the apple of orchards is evolved from one or more species. The leaves are simple, occasionally lobed, alternate. The flowers are in umbel-like clusters, terminal and axillary while the fruit is a pome, usually with the calyx persisting at the apex. The plants hybridise readily, so that seed is not a reliable method of propagation unless only one species is grown. Cuttings are possible, but plants are usually grafted on to apple stocks.

Linnaeus included *Malus* in *Pyrus*, so that, when *Malus* was finally separated, new authorities for the names appeared. When an authority appears in brackets, as for example *Malus baccata* (LINNAEUS) BORKHEIM, it may be assumed that the plant was previously known as *Pyrus baccata* LINNAEUS and these synonyms will not be repeated.

Malus angustifolia (AITON) MICHAUX

4. One of a series of three very similar N American crabs, the other two being *M. coronaria* and *M. ioensis,* described below. Small tree, to 7m, semi-evergreen in mild seasons. Lv more or less lanceolate, to 7cm long and 5cm wide on extension growths, only to 3cm on flowering shoots. Fl patulate, about 3cm wide, smelling of violets, pink or white, usually in clusters of 4, each on a slender pedicel to 3cm long. Fl 6. Fr, greenish, fragrant. Native of the south-eastern USA. Possibly a Bartram introduction, grown by the nurseryman Christopher Gray in 1750.

Malus baccata (LINNAEUS) BORKHEIM

4.5.7. Round-headed tree, usually about 7m high but capable of reaching 15m. Lv to 9cm long and half as wide, ovate, acuminate, finely toothed, bright green. Fl in umbels, each fl about 3cm wide, white. Fl 4. Fr globular, about 1cm in diameter, red (occasionally yellow) and lacking calyx teeth. The plant has a wide distribution from eastern Siberia to Korea and also in the Himalaya and SW China (var *himalaica* MAXIMOWICZ). Var *mandshurica* MAXIMOWICZ from Manchuria flowers slightly later and has slightly larger fr. Introduced before 1784, possibly by Pallas. Apparently the true species is rare in gardens; most plants sold under this name being *M. X robusta,* described below.

Malus baccata

Malus coronaria (LINNAEUS) MILLER

4.6. Deciduous tree or large bush with a spreading head and downy bts. Lv ovate, sometimes 3-lobed, up to 10cm long and 6cm wide, downy at first, later glabrous, margins toothed; often colouring well in the autumn. Fl up to 5cm wide, shell-pink, violet-scented, in clusters of up to 6. Fl 5–6. Fr to 3cm across, greenish-yellow.

Malus coronaria

'Charlottae' has semi-double fl, like a miniature rose. Native of eastern N America from New York southwards. Possibly a Mark Catesby introduction; grown by the nurseryman Robert Furber, who took many of Catesby's plants, in 1724. 'Charlottae' discovered in the wild in 1902.

Malus florentina (ZUCCAGNI) SCHNEIDER

5.(6). (Crataegus florentina ZUCCAGNI) Small tree or large bush of rounded habit, to 7m, with woolly bts. Lv resembling a hawthorn, to 6cm long and 4·5cm wide, with a number of lobes, the margins toothed; usually turning orange-scarlet in the autumn. Fl about 2cm wide, pure white on pink pedicels, in clusters of up to 7. Fl 6. Fr oval, 1cm long, yellowish turning red, without calyx teeth. It has been suggested that this oddly-leaved Malus is a bigeneric hybrid between the wild crab apple, M. sylvestris, and the service tree, Sorbus torminalis; presumably an amphi-diploid as the plants come true from selfed seed. Native of N Italy, but only in cultivation since about 1877.

Malus floribunda SIEBOLD EX VAN HOUTTE

4.5.(7). Tree, to 10m, with a rounded head of often greater diameter. Bts downy at first; lv usually ovate-elliptic, to 7cm long and half as wide but on vigorous new growths they are sometimes 3- or 5-lobed and up to 11cm long. Fl in clusters of up to 7, deep red in bud, pale pink when open, to 3cm wide. Fl 4–5. Fr round, without calyx teeth, yellow, 2cm in diameter. Thought not to be a true sp, but a hybrid between M. sieboldii, which also has lobed lv, and M. prunifolia. Introduced from Japan by Siebold in 1862.

Malus florentina

Malus halliana KOEHNE

4. A small tree, to 5m, with purple bts. Lv ovate, to 7cm long and half as wide, dark green, sometimes with a purple tint. Fl in clusters of up to 7 fl, up to 3·5cm across, often semi-double, deep pink. Fl 4–5. Fr very small, purple. Long cultivated in China and Japan, but only known in the wild in a white-flowered form from Japan (var. spontanea KOIDZUMI). Introduced from Japan by Dr G. R. Hall in 1863. Malus X atrosanguinea (SPAETHE) SCHNEIDER is intermediate between M. floribunda and M. halliana, with deep pink fl but occasionally lobed lv.

Malus hupehensis (PAMPANINI) REHDER

4.7. (Malus theifera REHDER) Somewhat fastigiate tree, to 15m, with white downy bts. Lv oval, acuminate, to 10cm long and 6cm wide, purplish at first, later dark green and glabrous. Fl in clusters of up to 7, up to 3·5cm across, fragrant, pale pink fading to white. Fl 4. Fr inconspicuous, about 8mm in diameter, yellow tinged red. One of the most gorgeous of flowering trees. Native of China, introduced by Wilson in 1900. He considered it the finest flowering tree that he ever introduced. The sp is a triploid and produces fertile seed without pollination, so always comes true from seed and never hybridises.

Malus ioensis (WOOD) BRITTON

4. Bush or small tree allied to M. coronaria but distinguished by the persistent down on the bts and underside of the lv and by the fact that the side brs are often spine-tipped. Lv to 10cm long and half as wide. Fl to 5cm wide, in clusters of 4–6, white or pale pink, smelling of violets. Fl 5–6. Fr greenish-yellow, about 3cm in diameter. 'Plena' has very attractive double pink fl to 6cm across, but is, unfortunately, a poor doer. Native of the central USA. Introduced only in 1885.

Malus kansuensis (BATALIN) SCHNEIDER

4.5.6. Large shrub or small tree to 8m, with downy bts. Lv ovate or 3-lobed (sometimes 5-lobed), to 9cm long and 6cm across, downy at first, later glabrous and usually colouring well in the autumn. Fl in large clusters of up to 10, only to 1·8cm across, white. Fl 5. Fr scarlet, on stalks to 5cm long, ovoid, to 1cm long. Introduced by Wilson in 1904 and 1910 from western China.

Malus niedzwetzkyana DIECK

4.5. Small tree, to 7m with reddish-purple bts. Lv ovate, downy below at first, to 12cm long and half as wide, petiole and midrib red, blade reddish at first, later dark green and later still purple. Fl in clusters of up to 6·3cm across, reddish-purple. Fl 5. Fr conical, up to 5cm long, claret coloured. Not a very satisfactory garden plant, and possibly little more than a colour variant of one of the *M. sylvestris* group of wild crabs. It is found wild in central Asia.

It was introduced to cultivation about 1891 and was at once used to hybridisation. Most of the hybrids are included in *M. X purpurea* (BARBIER) REHDER, based mainly on hybrids between this plant and *M. floribunda*, *M. halliana* and *M. X atrosanguinea*. These are all small trees with purple lv, purple-red fl and deep red fr. In this group are the plants known as 'Aldenhamensis', 'Eleyi' and 'Lemoinei'. 'Hopa' is a hybrid between this sp and *M. baccata*, while 'Red Tip' is a cross between this sp and *M. ioensis*, with bright red young lv which later turn green, dark purple fl and red-flushed fr. 'Profusion' is a hybrid between *'Lemoinei'* and *M. sieboldii*, with reddish young growths, claret-coloured fl and small, dark red fr.

Malus prattii (HEMSLEY) SCHNEIDER

4.5.6.7. Deciduous tree, to 10m. Bts white-hairy at first, later glabrous. Lv large, often red-veined, ovate, to 14cm long and 7cm wide, usually colouring well in the autumn. Fl in large clusters of up to 12, each about 2·5cm wide, white. Fl 5. Fr ovoid, 12mm diameter, red with white dots; calyx persistent. Native of Szechuan. Introduced by Wilson in 1904. A handsome tree akin to *M. yunnanensis*.

Malus prunifolia (WILLENDOW) BORKHEIM

4.5. Tree, to 8m, of rounded habit, with downy bts. Lv ovate, toothed, to 10cm long and half as wide, downy below. Fl in umbels of 6–10, pink before opening, white when open, up to 3cm wide, fragrant. Fl 4. Fr round, 2·5cm in diameter, red or yellow, calyx persistent. Var *rinki* (KOIDZUMI) REHDER has pink fl and very handsome yellow fr. The plant has never been found in the wild, although cultivated for its edible fr in China and Japan. The plant was grown by Miller in 1758 and may have come from one of Collinson's Siberian correspondents as the plant was said to come from Siberia. Var *rinki* (*Malus ringo* SIEBOLD) was obtained from Japan by Siebold about 1850.

Malus X robusta

(CARRIÈRE) REHDER Siberian Crab

4.5. Very ornamental fruiting trees from the hybrid between *M. baccata* and *M. prunifolia*, distinguished from these spp by their larger fr up to 3cm wide and generally with persistent calyx. Usually the lv are somewhat downy beneath. Fl white, sometimes flushed pink. Fl 4–5. Fr red or yellow. The first record of this hybrid is from seeds from Siberia received at Cambridge Botanic Garden in 1814. The fr closely resemble cherries.

Malus sargentii REHDER

4.5. Shrub of spreading habit, to 3m but usually less than 2m, with downy bts. Lv ovate-lanceolate, to 7cm long and 5cm wide, sometimes 3-lobed, woolly at first, later glabrous. Fl in clusters of 5–6, pure white (pink in the bud in the cv 'Rosea'), 2·5cm across. Fl 4–5. Fr bright red but small, only about 8mm wide, produced with great freedom. Discovered by Professor Sargent in a salt marsh in Japan in 1892, this is probably a form of *M. sieboldii* (qv). The bushy habit is only maintained with grafted plants; selfed seedlings make trees up to 7m.

Malus X scheideckeri ZABEL

4.5.(7). Tree, to 10m, somewhat fastigiate at first, with downy bts, later becoming glabrous. This is the name for hybrids between *M. floribunda* and *M. prunifolia* or *M. baccata*. Lv elliptic-ovate, shining green above, paler and downy at first below, to 7cm long and half as wide (but to 11cm long on vigorous extension shoots). Fl often semi-double, pale pink or white, to 3cm wide, in clusters of 6–10 and produced with great profusion. Fl 5. Fr round, 1·5cm wide with persistent calyx. The original hybrid is of rather poor constitution and is usually replaced by 'Hillieri'. Other clones in this group are 'Arnoldiana' and 'Excellenz Thiel', which has a very pendulous habit. The original *M. X scheideckeri* was in commerce in 1888.

Malus sieboldii (REGEL) REHDER

4. (*M. toringo* SIEBOLD) Small tree or large shrub, to 5m, with arching or pendulous brs. Bts downy. Lv often 3-lobed but also narrowly-oval or intermediate, to about 6cm long and a dull green. Fl in clusters of 3–6, each on a thread-like pedicel, pale or deep pink, to 1cm wide. Fl 4. Fr small, about the size of a pea, without persistent calyx, red or brown. Var *zumi* (MATSUMURA) ASAMI (*M. X zumi* REHDER), has oblong lv which are rarely lobed. Fl pink in bud, white on opening, up to 3cm wide and the fr red, 1cm wide. 'Calocarpa' has lv often lobed, lv and fl somewhat smaller, but red fr to 12mm wide, persisting on the tree for a long time. *M. sieboldii* was obtained by Siebold from Japan in 1856 var *zumi* by Sargent in 1892, but the seeds of 'Calocarpa' had been received from a Japanese correspondent of the Arnold Arboretum in 1890.

Malus sikkimensis (J. HOOKER) KOEHNE

4.5. Small tree to 7m, with a short trunk which is festooned with short branching spurs – a unique feature in the genus. Lv elliptic or ovate, woolly below less so above, to 11cm long and 5cm wide. Fl in clusters of 4–9, pink in bud, white when open, 2·5cm across, on slender pedicels to 5cm. Fl 5. Fr pear-shaped, 1.5cm long, dark red with pale dots, calyx not persistent. Possibly a geographic form of *M. baccata*. Rare in cultivation but a good flowering and fruiting tree. Native of the Himalaya. Introduced by Joseph Hooker about 1849.

Malus spectabilis (AITON) BORKHEIM

4.5.(7). Tree, to 10m, with a rounded head and downy bts. Lv elliptic or ovate-acuminate, to 9cm long and 5cm wide, glossy green above, downy beneath at first, later glabrous. Fl red in bud and quite a deep pink when open, in umbels of 6–8, each fl 5cm wide. Fl 4–5. Fr round, to 2·5cm wide, yellow with persistent calyx. 'Riversii' has semi-double, very deep, pink fl and occurred in Rivers' nursery in 1864. The plant is presumably Chinese, but only known in cultivation there. Obtained by Dr Fothergill, who died in 1780, so introduced some time before then.

Malus sylvestris MILLER Wild Crab

Tree of up to 10m or large shrub. Lv elliptic or ovate, about 4cm long, dark green. Fl in clusters of up to 6, white flushed pink. Fr round, greenish-yellow with red flush, about 2cm wide. Our native crab, although attractive in the wild, is not sufficiently showy for gardens, but either this plant or its derivative the apple *(M. domestica)*, when hybridised with such spp as *MM. baccata, prunifolia* and *sieboldii*, have given rise to trees with apple-like flowers and very attractive fruits up to 4cm long, such as 'John Downie', with conical red fr, 'Golden Hornet', with long-persisting yellow fr, and 'Veitch's Scarlet' ('King of the Pippins' X *M.* X *robusta*), with large crimson fr.

Malus toringoides (REHDER) HUGHES

4.5.6. (*M. transitoria* var *toringoides* REHDER) Graceful tree, to 8m, with slender bts, covered with grey down at first. Lv usually deeply lobed, although basically ovate, to 9cm long and 5cm wide, slightly downy at first, glabrous above later, colouring in autumn. Fl in umbels of 6–8, up to 2·5cm wide, white. Fl 5. Fr round, to 1·5cm diameter, yellow flushed scarlet. *M. transitoria* (BATALIN) SCHNEIDER is very similar, but with smaller, more downy lv (to 5cm long), which are more deeply lobed, and the fr are also smaller, being not more than 1cm diameter. Both spp are native to western China. *M. toringoides* introduced by Wilson in 1904; *M. transitoria* by Purdom in 1911.

Malus trilobata (LABILLARDIÈRE) SCHNEIDER

5.(6). (*Crataegus trilobata* LABILLARDIÈRE) Somewhat fastigiate tree, to 12m, bts very downy. Lv unique in the genus, basically trilobed but the 3 lobes are often lobed themselves to give

an impression of a 7-lobed lv. The lv are up to 10cm wide and about 9cm long, dark green and shining above, downy below, often colouring red and yellow in the autumn. Fl in few-flowered umbels, white, each fl to 3·5cm wide, the petals contracted at the base in a manner not found elsewhere in the genus. Fl 4–5. Fr rarely produced, round or pyriform, calyx persistent, red or yellow, to 2cm across. Rare both in the wild and in cultivation, and quite distinct from any other *Malus*. Native of Asia Minor and Thrace. In cultivation in 1877.

Malus tschonoskii (MAXIMOWICZ) SCHNEIDER

3.4.6.(7). Tree, to 15m, fastigiate at first, later somewhat pyramidal. Bts greyish-downy at first. Lv ovate, acuminate, covered with silvery hairs at first, later glabrous above and grey-hairy below, to 12cm long and 7cm wide but usually less, turning very brilliant colours of bronze, red and yellow before falling. Fl in clusters of 4–6, white flushed pink, up to 3cm wide. Fl 4–5. Fr rarely produced, yellowish with purple flush. Although the fl are inconspicuous against the silver lv, this is one of the most ornamental of garden trees and particularly sumptuous in the autumn. Would probably prove an admirable street tree. Native of Japan. Introduced by Dr Sargent in 1892.

Malus yunnanensis (FRANCHET) SCHNEIDER

4.5.6.(7). Tree, to 13m, with bts at first pubescent, later glabrous and purplish-brown. Lv basically ovate, but quite often lobed especially in the var *veitchii* REHDER, which is the form most usually seen. The lv are up to 11cm long and 7cm across, dull green above, brown tomentose beneath, turning scarlet and orange in the autumn. Fl in clusters of about 6, 1·5cm wide, white or pink-flushed. Fl 5. Fr red with white dots, round, about 12mm diameter, calyx persisting. Var *veitchii* is more fastigiate in habit and has slightly larger fr. Both the type and the var were introduced from western China by Wilson: var *veitchii* in 1900 and the type in 1908.

MELIOSMA BLUME *Sabiaceae*

A genus of deciduous (so far as hardy species are concerned) trees and shrubs of rather elusive characteristics. The leaves are alternate, but either simple or pinnate. The flowers are small, five-petalled, three petals being much larger than the other two, in large, terminal panicles. The fruit is in the form of a berry-like drupe. Although a number of species are undoubtedly hardy in southern England, we do not hear much of their being grown in the midlands and north, although there seems no reason why they should not prove hardy there. Propagation appears to be mainly by seed.

Malus tschonoskii

Meliosma cuneifolia FRANCHET

4.5. Deciduous shrub, to 7m, with erect brs. Lv simple, wedge-shaped, mucronate, to 17cm long and 7cm wide, upper surface hispid, rusty-pubescent below at first. Fl fragrant, cream at first, later white, in pyramidal panicles to 25cm long and almost as wide. Fl 7. Fr about 6mm across, black. Native of western China. Introduced by Wilson in 1901.

Meliosma myriantha SIEBOLD AND ZUCCARINI

4.5. Deciduous shrub of about 3m in cultivation but spreading more widely, to 7m, in the wild. Lv elliptic-obovate, to 20cm long and 7cm wide, much like the lv of a sweet chestnut, toothed; veins beneath brown-hairy. Fl very small but very fragrant, in pyramidal panicles about 15cm long. Fl 6–7. Fr about 6mm in diameter, dark red. Young plants are often tender, but apparently quite hardy when well established. Native of Japan. Introduced by Maries in 1879.

Meliosma veitchiorum HEMSLEY

4.5.(6).7. Deciduous tree to 16m with stout brs, usually somewhat fastigiate. Lv pinnate, with red petioles and 9–11 leaflets, the whole lv to 60cm long, the individual leaflets ovate or oblong, to 17cm long and half as wide, often colouring gold before falling. Fl in panicles to 45cm long and 30cm wide, the fl more widely spaced than in the other spp described but larger, to 6mm across; creamy-white, or pale yellow. Fl 5. Fr round, 1·5cm across, rich violet. Like all the genus, rather slow-growing, but a striking tree with a multitude of attractions and one that might well be seen more often. It is very suitable for small gardens. Native of China. Introduced by Wilson in 1901.

MENISPERMUM LINNAEUS Mensipermaceae

The exotically named moonseed gets its name from the shape of the seed which is like a crescent moon. Only two species have been described – one N American, the other Asian – neither being very distinct.

Menispermum canadense Moonseed

5. Deciduous twiner, to 5m. Lv peltate, basically cordate but with from 3–7 lobes, up to 15cm long and wide on slender petioles to 10cm. Fl in axillary racemes to 6cm long, greenish, inconspicuous. Fr black, much resembling a black-currant. The plant is usually dioecious, but apparently monoecious plants occur occasionally. The plant spreads rapidly by underground suckers and is only suitable for the wilder parts of the garden. Native of eastern N America from Quebec to Georgia. Introduced in the seventeenth century.

MENZIESIA J. E. SMITH Ericaceae

A small genus of about seven species of deciduous shrubs, most of which are too dwarf for inclusion here. They require acid soil and ample sunshine. Propagated by seed and by cuttings.

Menziesia ciliicalyx (MIQUEL) MAXIMOWICZ

4. (Andromeda ciliicalyx MIQUEL) Slow-growing shrub, to 1m. Lv elliptic-oval, margins hairy, otherwise glabrous, to 7cm long and 3cm wide. Fl in terminal umbels at the tips of the previous year's shoots, pendent, more or less urn-shaped, creamy or purple. The type is rarely seen in gardens, its place being taken by var purpurea MAKINO (M. purpurea of gardens) with buds almost blue in colour and the opened fl rosy-purple to clear pink. The fl are about 1·5cm long and the pedicels tend to have glandular hairs. Fl 5. Native of Japan. Introduced about 1914 or 1915.

Two N American spp, M. ferruginea and M. pilosa, are occasionally offered, but neither are outstandingly attractive with whitish or yellowish fl.

MESPILUS LINNAEUS Rosaceae

A monotypic genus.

Mespilus germanica LINNAEUS Medlar

4. An attractively gnarled, deciduous tree, to 7m, with very hairy bts. In wild plants the main brs are often spiny with spines to 2·5cm long. Lv sessile, oval-lanceolate, to 12cm long, downy. Fl like a wild rose, solitary, terminal, to 3cm across, white (rarely very pale pink). Fl 5–6. Fr brown, edible, to 3cm across. Native to northern Europe (possibly including the UK).

METASEQUOIA MIKI Taxodiaceae

The genus was named from fossil material in 1941. In 1945 a living exemplar was found in Hupeh, China. Seeds were first collected in 1947 and distributed the following year.

Metasequoia glyptostroboides HU AND CHENG

6.7. Rapid-growing, deciduous tree, to 35m in the wild but possibly more in cultivation although this is not yet proven. Besides lv the brs produce opposite shoots up to 5cm long which fall off after the first year. Lv opposite, linear, about 12mm long and 2mm wide, an attractive soft green, turning pink or russet before falling. Cones apparently cylindrical, dark brown, to 2·5cm long, ripening the first year. The plant grows most rapidly in a deep, moist soil, when it may average an extension of 75cm per year; some plants started in 1949 were up to 17m high 20 years later. The plants propagate easily from

Metasequoia glyptostroboides

half-ripe or hardwood cuttings. Cones have been seen, but no fertile seed has been set in the UK. The plants are perfectly winter hardy, but occasionally damaged by late spring frosts.

MORUS LINNAEUS *Moraceae*

A genus of about ten species of deciduous shrubs and trees, both monoecious and dioecious. The mulberry, *M. nigra*, is the best known of the genus so far as gardens are concerned. The flowers are of no interest, being inconspicuous catkins, and the fruit, although palatable, is not decorative; only the habit of the trees is picturesque. They are easily propagated by hardwood cuttings or layers.

Morus alba

Morus alba LINNAEUS

7. Deciduous tree, to 15m, with a rounded head. Bts downy at first, later glabrous. Lv more or less heart-shaped, often 3-lobed, light green and slightly hispid above, downy below, to 20cm long and 15cm wide. The plant is usually dioecious. Fr pale pink, edible but insipid. There are some aberrant forms, such as 'Laciniata' with deeply-lobed lv, 'Macrophylla', with extra large lv, and 'Pendula', an attractive weeping form which requires the leader supporting until a strong erect trunk is formed. This is the mulberry used for feeding silkworms. Native of China but cultivated in Europe for at least four centuries.

Morus australis POIRET

(*M. acidosa* GRIFFITH, *M. alba* var *stylosa* BUREAU) Deciduous tree, to 8m, more often seen as a shrub to 5m. Lv either basically cordate or deeply 3–5-lobed, up to 15cm long and wide, but very variable both in size and in shape. The plant is dioecious. Fr dark red and juicy. Native to Assam, China and Japan. In cultivation as *M. alba* var *stylosa* some years before Wilson brought it from China in 1907.

Morus nigra LINNAEUS Mulberry

7. Slow-growing, deciduous tree of up to 10m, bts downy with a milky fluid inside. The bark is attractively fissured. Lv more or less cordate, rarely 2–5-lobed, deep green above and hispid, paler and pubescent below. Lv up to 15cm or more on extension growths, not more than 10cm on fruiting shoots. The plant is both dioecious and monoecious. Fr up to 2·5cm long, dark red and very palatable. The common mulberry has been cultivated for so long that its native country is not known.

MYRICA LINNAEUS *Myricaceae*

A genus of some five species of evergreen and deciduous shrubs of no floral beauty, but with aromatic leaves and reasonably attractive fruit. The species in cultivation require acid soil and most prefer damp or even boggy conditions. The plants are both monoecious and dioecious.

Myrica cerifera LINNAEUS

5. (*M. carolinensis* MILLER) Deciduous or semi-evergreen shrub, to 3m. with reddish downy bts. Lv usually oblanceolate but very variable in size and shape, normally to 7cm long and 2cm across; dark green and glabrous above, dotted with yellow resin-glands below. The plant is dioecious. Fr round, 3mm across, coated with white wax. *M. pensylvanica* LOISELEUR is similar, but lv downy above, more oval in shape, long persisting. Fr somewhat larger, to 4mm in diameter,

Myrica cerifera

and the plant has no objection to quite dry conditions. In the USA it is known as the bayberry. *M. cerifera* was being grown in 1699 and may be a Banister sending from the south-eastern USA. *M. pensylvanica* has a more northerly distribution, but was introduced in 1727, probably by Catesby from Carolina.

Myrica gale LINNAEUS Sweet Gale

Deciduous shrub, to 1m 30cm, with fragrant lv and wood. Lv oblanceolate, toothed at the apex, to 6cm long and 2cm wide, dark green and glossy above, paler and downy below. The plants are both monoecious and dioecious, the tiny catkins appearing before the lv. Native of the northern parts of the northern hemisphere, including the UK.

MYRICARIA DESVAUX *Tamaricaceae*

A small genus of about ten species of deciduous shrubs, distinguishable from *Tamarix* only in the parts of the flower being always in fives or multiples thereof and the stamens being united at the base.

Myricaria germanica DESVAUX

4. (*Tamarix germanica* LINNAEUS) Deciduous shrub, to 3m, with rather glaucous bts. Lv scale-

like, linear, not more than 4mm long, blue-green. Fl in terminal racemes on the various bts, each fl only about 6mm long, pink or white tinged pink. Fl 5–8. Native of southern Europe and western Asia as far east as the Himalaya, often growing in gullies which are flooded in winter and dry out in summer. 1582 is the date given for its introduction, but on what grounds is unknown.

NANDINA THUNBERG *Berberidaceae*

A monotypic genus.

Nandina domestica THUNBERG

3.4.(5).6. Evergreen shrub, to 3m, with erect, unbranched stems. Lv pinnate or bipinnate, tinged red when emerging, to 30cm long or occasionally even more; leaflets linear-lanceolate, to 10cm long, turning purplish in the autumn. Fl in a terminal panicle, up to 35cm long, each fl only to 1cm wide, white, with conspicuous yellow anthers. Fl 6–7. Fr a round 2-seeded berry, red or white but rarely produced in the UK. The plant will survive in most districts of the UK but rarely looks happy outside the Gulf Stream areas. Native of China, Japan and India. Introduced from China by Kerr in 1804.

NEILLIA D. DON *Rosaceae*

A small genus of deciduous shrubs, of which only one species is in general cultivation.

Neillia longiracemosa HEMSLEY

4. Deciduous shrub of 1–2m with arching br, spreading by means of sucker growths which can be detached for propagation. Lv ovate, usually 3-lobed and much resembling currant lv, acuminate, to 8cm long; dull green, somewhat downy. Fl in terminal racemes to 15cm long, tubular, rosy-pink, with sepals of the same colour, reminiscent of the american currant, *Ribes sanguineum*, but more graceful. Fl 5–6. Native of western China. Introduced in 1904 by Wilson. The plant will thrive in any soil, but likes ample light.

NEVIUSIA ASA GRAY *Rosaceae*

A monotypic genus

Neviusia alabamensis A. GRAY

4. Deciduous shrub, to 2m but usually spreading wider. Bts downy at first. Lv oblong-ovate, to 8cm long, slightly lobed on vigorous new growths. Fl in clusters at the ends of short laterals, lacking petals but with a very conspicuous bunch of white stamens. Fl 4–5. Very attractive when suited, but uncertain in its flowering habits in the UK. Confined to a few localities in Alabama. Discovered by the Rev R. D. Nevius in 1858 and introduced about 1860.

NOTHOFAGUS BLUME *Fagaceae*

A genus of about seventeen species of evergreen and deciduous trees, very distinct from the beech of the northern hemisphere in appearance, but closely similar in flower and fruit. However the male flowers are usually solitary, while those of *Fagus* are in clusters; also the fruit usually contain three nuts as opposed to the pair in *Fagus*. The genus ranges from S America to New Zealand and Australia. A number of species are hardy in southern England, but only three species can be regarded as safe in all parts of the UK. The plants grow very rapidly, but some appear to be short-lived, the oldest surviving plants having been started in 1902. They will not grow in chalky soil, although mildly alkaline soil is acceptable. Most species can be propagated by layers as well as by seed.

Nothofagus antarctica (FORSTER) OERSTEDT

(6).7. (*Fagus antarctica* FORSTER) Deciduous tree, to 35m in the wild but not more than 20m in cultivation; often with twisted trunk and main boughs. Lv ovate to cordate, produced in great profusion along the downy bts, up to 3cm long but usually less and about as wide, giving a somewhat puckered appearance; dark green, often turning a good clear yellow before falling. In young trees growths 1m long in the season are not infrequent. Native of Tierra del Fuego and southern Chile. Introduced in 1830.

Nothofagus betuloides (MIRBEL) BLUME

7. Evergreen tree, to 35m in the wild and to about 17m in cultivation, with sticky bts. Lv wedge-shaped or ovate, to 2·5cm long and 2cm wide, shining green above, paler below. From much the same regions as *N. antarctica* and originally introduced at the same time. The hardiest of the evergreen spp.

Nothofagus obliqua (MIRBEL) BLUME

7. Deciduous tree, to 35m in the wild and about 20m in cultivation; of very rapid growth when young. Lv ovate-oblong, to 7cm long and 3cm across, dark green above, paler below. Fr containing 4 nuts. Native of Chile. Introduced by W. Lobb in 1849.

No plants of any of the original introductions survive, and the largest surviving trees come from seed collected by H. J. Elwes in 1902.

NYSSA LINNAEUS *Nyssaceae*

Formerly included in the *Cornaceae*. A genus of about six species of deciduous trees or large shrubs, either monoecious or dioecious, but neither flowers nor fruit are at all attractive and it is in the leaves, particularly in the autumn, that the attraction of the plant lies. The plants require acid soil, so far as is known, although *N. sinensis* tolerates alkaline conditions providing plenty of humus is present. They resent root disturbance and only young plants should be moved. The plants are not very rapid growers.

Nyssa sinensis OLIVER

3.6. Apparently a deciduous tree, to 15m, although few specimens have reached that height as yet. Bts downy. Young lv red. Lv narrowly ovate, almost spatulate, to 15cm long, and 5cm across, dull green above, changing to various shades of red and crimson in the autumn. A rare tree both in the wild and in commerce. Native of central China. Introduced by Wilson in 1902.

Nyssa sylvatica MARSHALL Tupelo

6.(7). Deciduous tree, to 27m, of more or less columnar habit, flat-topped when mature. Lv more or less oval, to 15cm long and half as wide, usually considerably smaller. The plant is monoecious and the inconspicuous heads open in June. The lv turn very brilliant reds and yellows in the autumn. Native of the eastern USA from Maine southwards, where it grows most usually in swampy ground. Probably introduced by Bartram in 1735, but there was considerable confusion between this sp and the not dissimilar *N. aquatica*.

OLEARIA DE CANDOLLE *Compositae*

A genus of evergreen shrubs occasionally attaining tree-like proportions in their native Australasia. Many species are hardy near the coast, even in northern regions, but most species are not sufficiently hardy for inclusion here. They have alternate, entire leaves and heads of daisy-like flowers. Propagated by seed or by half-ripe cuttings.

Olearia avicenniifolia J. HOOKER

4. Evergreen shrub, to 4m, with oval, acuminate lv to 3cm long, dark green above, white or buff tomentose below. Fl in axillary cymes at the ends of the brs, forming a flat-headed corymb, white, fragrant, about 1cm across. Fl 8–9. Useful for its late-flowering and tolerant of atmospheric pollution. Native of New Zealand.

Olearia haastii J. HOOKER

4. Thought to be a natural hybrid between the last sp and *O. moschata*. Evergreen shrub, to 3m, with white tomentose bts. Lv oval, to 2·5cm long and half as wide, shining dark green above, white tomentose below. Fl in a series of axillary cymes to give a flat-headed corymb to 7cm across, each fl about 8mm wide; fragrant, white with yellow centre. Fl 7–8. Native of New Zealand. Introduced by Messrs Veitch in 1858.

Olearia macrodonta BAKER

4. (*O. dentata* J. HOOKER) Evergreen shrub, to 3m in cultivation, but a small tree to 7m or more in the wild. Lv shaped much like a holly, basically narrowly ovate, to 12cm long and 5cm across, glossy green above, silvery tomentose below. Fl in terminal corymbs to 15cm across; each fl about 1cm across, white with reddish centre. Fl 6–7. Native of New Zealand. Introduced before 1895.

Olearia nummulariifolia J. HOOKER

4. A medium-sized evergreen shrub, to 2m rarely more, with numerous roundish, sessile, yellowish-green lv, which are coriaceous and only about 8mm in diameter. Fl solitary in upper lv axils, white, fragrant. Fl 7. Native of New Zealand. Introduced in 1889.

ORIXA THUNBERG *Rutaceae*

A monotypic genus.

Orixa japonica THUNBERG

6. A deciduous, dioecious shrub, to 3m. Lv scented, alternate, oblong-obovate, bright green above, to 12cm long and 5cm wide, turning practically white before falling. Fl inconspicuous, opening in June. The plant has a graceful fountain-like appearance, but its appeal is mainly in contrast with bright autumn colourers. A variegated form is known, but probably not yet in commerce. Native of Japan and China. Introduced 1870.

OSMANTHUS LOUREIRO *Oleaceae*

A small genus of about fifteen species of evergreen shrubs and trees with opposite leaves, smallish fragrant white flowers and the fruit a small drupe, which is colourful but rarely produced in the UK. Some species are dioecious. There are two species from the southern USA which are not hardy, the remainder come from eastern Asia. Propagated by cuttings of half-ripe young wood.

Osmanthus armatus DIELS

4. Evergreen shrub, to 5m, with greyish-white bts. Lv oblanceolate, entire, to 15cm long (occasionally even more) and 3cm wide, coriaceous, with coarse, spine-tipped teeth, dark green and dull. Fl in axillary clusters, tubular, about 6mm long, very fragrant, creamy-white. Fl 8–10. Fr egg-shaped, to 2cm long, dark violet, rarely produced. Native of western China. Introduced by Wilson in 1902.

Osmanthus delavayi FRANCHET

4. Slow-growing shrub, to 3m but usually not more than 2, with stiff, spreading brs. Lv oval-elliptic, to 2·5cm long and half as wide, on a short petiole; dark shining green above, with tiny black spots beneath. Fl in axillary and terminal clusters of 4–8, tubular, with 4 reflexed lobes, about 12mm long, very fragrant and pure white. Fl 4. Fr blue-black, roundish. A delightful shrub, but its hybrid with *Phillyrea decora* (see below X *Osmarea*) seems a better doer. Native of China. Introduced by Père Delavay in 1890, although only one seed germinated from his sendings.

Osmanthus X fortunei CARRIÈRE

4. A hybrid between *O. heterophyllus* and the tender *O. fragrans*. Evergreen, rounded shrub, dioecious and only the male form is common. Usually not more than 2m high but in sheltered districts it can reach 5–7m. Lv leathery, somewhat holly-like, to 10cm long and 7cm wide, some of the lower lv lack the spiny tips, dark green. Fl axillary, in clusters of 4–6, extremely strongly perfumed, about 8mm across, white. Fl 8–11. Although winter-hardy it does not flower with much freedom except in warm localities. The hybrid is of Japanese origin and was brought from Japan in 1862 by Fortune. The introduction by T. Lobb in 1856 probably in fact refers to the next sp.

Osmanthus heterophyllus P. S. GREEN

4. (*O. aquifolium* SIEBOLD AND ZUCCARINI, *O. ilicifolia* HASSKARL) Rounded, evergreen shrub, to 3m or more in mild districts. Lv holly-like, basically oval, spine-tipped, to 6cm long and 3·5cm wide, dark glossy green above, paler below. Fl in axillary clusters, small, white, fragrant, only about 4mm across. Fl 9–10. Fr 1·5cm long, blue, rarely seen. There are var with white or yellow margins to the lv and 'Purpureus', with the young lv very dark purple, making this a striking plant. Useful for its late fl, which are unspectacular but very fragrant. Native of Japan. Introduced by T. Lobb in 1856.

Osmanthus yunnanensis P. S. GREEN

4. (*O. forrestii* REHDER) Evergreen shrub, to 8m in the wild. Lv very variable in shape and texture, lanceolate to oblong-lanceolate, undulate or not, margins spine-toothed or entire, all forms sometimes being found on the same plant, dark green, to 20cm long. Fl in axillary clusters on slender pedicels to 1cm long, each fl only 5mm long, but the reflexed lobes occasionally 1cm across, fragrant, ivory. Fl 10–12. A handsome foliage shrub, useful for its late flowering. Native of western China. Introduced by Forrest in 1923.

X OSMAREA BURKWOOD

X Osmarea burkwoodii BURKWOOD

4. A bigeneric hybrid between *Phillyrea decora* and *Osmanthus delavayi*. Evergreen, rather slow-growing shrub, to 3m but tending to spread rather than ascend. Lv elliptic-ovate, to 4cm long and half as wide, dark green, saw-toothed. Fl in axillary and terminal clusters of 5–7, tubular, the fl about 5mm long and nearly twice as wide; fragrant, white. Fl 4–5. A better plant for most gardens than *O. delavayi*. Raised by Burkwood and Skipwith about 1928.

Osmaronia cerasiformis

OSMARONIA GREENE *Rosaceae*

A monotypic genus, so far as is known. Also known as *Nuttallia* TORREY AND GRAY, but not the *Nuttallia* of Barton. Now classified as *Oemleria* REICHENBACH.

Osmaronia cerasiformis GREENE

4.(5). Deciduous suckering shrubs, to 3m or more, usually dioecious, but monoecious plants have been in cultivation. Lv alternate, lanceolate, to 8cm long and 3cm across; a brilliant sea green above, greyish below. Fl in axillary

racemes to 6cm long, each raceme conspicuously bracted; the fl tubular-campanulate, about 6mm wide, greenish-white and almond scented. Fl 2–4. Fr plum-like, egg-shaped, 2cm long, brown at first but purple when ripe, ripening about June. Useful for its early fl and lv but not showy. Native of California. Introduced in 1848.

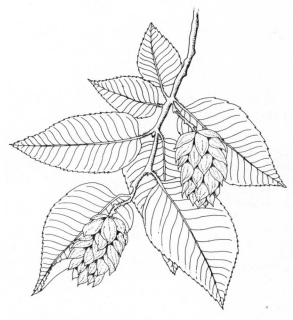

Ostrya carpinifolia

OSTRYA SCOPOLI *Carpinaceae*

A small genus of deciduous trees, with a scattered distribution throughout the northern hemisphere, which do not differ much in appearance. They are very close to the hornbeams, *Carpinus*, differing mainly in the curious bladder-like fruit which have given them the popular name of hop hornbeams. The plants are monoecious, the male flowers in pendent catkins, female flowers in smaller ones, each subtended by a leafy involucre, which closes after fertilisation to give a bag-like effect. The species in cultivation are all hardy and will thrive in most soils.

Ostrya carpinifolia SCOPOLI

4.5.6.7. (*O. vulgaris* WILLDENOW) Deciduous tree up to 20m eventually, with a round head. Bts sparsely hairy. Lv oval, acuminate, to 10cm long or slightly more and half as wide, double-toothed; dark green, turning a good clear yellow in the autumn. Male catkins to 7·5cm long, female to 5cm. Fl before lv, 3–4. Native of southern Europe and Asia minor. Grown by Furber in 1724.

Ostrya virginica WILLENDOW Hop Hornbeam

4.5.6.(7). Deciduous tree, usually to about 10m in cultivation, differing from the last sp in the bts being furnished with glandular hairs, the shorter male catkins (only to 5cm long), and the slightly larger lv which are more lanceolate in shape. Native of eastern America from Canada to north Mexico. Grown by Compton in 1692, so probably a Banister introduction.

OXYDENDRUM DE CANDOLLE *Ericaceae*

A monotypic genus, requiring acid soil.

Oxydendrum arboreum DE CANDOLLE
Sorrel Tree

4.6. Deciduous tree, to 10m in cultivation but often only a large, pyramidal bush. Lv alternate, oblong-lanceolate, acuminate, to 15cm long and 6cm wide; dark green, usually turning brilliant red in the autumn. Fl in panicles, composed of terminal and axillary racemes, the whole panicle to 25cm long; each fl urceolate, only 6mm long, milky-white. Fl 7–8. The lv taste of sorrel, hence its popular name. A very beautiful, but rather slow-growing, tree which seems to do best as a young plant in shade from which the top can emerge into the light. Native of eastern N America. Introduced by Bartram in 1747 according to Rehder. Miller was growing it in 1752.

OZOTHAMNUS ROBERT BROWN *Compositae*

A genus of Australasian evergreen shrubs, included by some in the vast genus *Helichrysum.* Most of the species are tender, but *O. ledifolius* appears to be reasonably hardy. Propagated by seed and by cuttings.

Ozothamnus ledifolius JOSEPH HOOKER

3.4. Rounded bush to 1·6m. Bts bright yellow and rather sticky. Lv almost scale-like, thickly set along the twigs, to 1cm long and only about 2mm wide; very dark green above, yellow beneath. The lv are semi-erect so that the yellow underside is apparent. Fl in terminal clusters, each fl to 2·5cm across, daisy-like, white, reddish in bud, the petal-like bracts of papery consistency. Fl 6–7. Native of Tasmania. Introduced by Harold Comber in 1930.

PAEONIA LINNAEUS *Paeoniaceae*

Some authorities keep this in the *Ranunculaceae.* A genus of mainly tuberous perennials, chiefly in Europe and Asia with one species in California and one in Morocco. The shrubby section is confined to the Sino-Himalaya. Propagation is mainly by seed, but cuttings are possible although

not easy, while cultivars of *P. suffruticosa* are usually grafted on to *P. lactiflora* – the common Chinese peony of gardens. Seeds usually take two years to germinate and do not make very rapid growth, so a period of about seven years may elapse between seed sowing and seeing the first flowers. The plants flourish in most soils.

Paeonia delavayi FRANCHET

4. Rather gaunt deciduous shrub, to 2m. Some forms appear to spread by suckers but this may indicate hybridisation with the dwarf, suckering *P. potaninii*, or possibly some clones are stoloniferous and others are not. Lv bipinnatifid, purplish when unfurling, divided up into numerous segments, to 25cm long and about 16cm wide. Fl in a terminal cluster, each fl to 10cm across, maroon. Fl 5–6. Fr in 2 follicles. This sp comes very readily from seed. It hybridises with *P. lutea* if the two are grown in proximity and the resultant offspring are not pleasing, but occasionally attractive. Native of western China. Introduced in 1908.

Paeonia ludlowii

Paeonia lutea FRANCHET

4. A variable plant, rarely over 1m in the originally introduced form but up to 3m in the var *ludlowii* STERN AND TAYLOR, which is, indeed, so distinct as to merit specific rank. Lv basically ternate, but deeply pinnatifid, so that the main outline is hard to discern; sometimes purplish when young, grey-green when mature (bright green in var *ludlowii*, which also has much larger, less incised lv). Fl cup-shaped, with a varying number of tepals, some forms being semi-double; buttercup yellow, sometimes with a crimson stain at the base, about 6cm across, often hidden beneath the lv or barely free, but quite distinct, larger and pure yellow in var *ludlowii*. Fl 5. Native of western China. Introduced by Farges in 1886. Var *ludlowii* native of Tibet. Introduced by Ward and by Ludlow and Sherriff in 1937.

Paeonia suffruticosa ANDREWS Tree Peony

4. (*P. moutan* SIMS *P. arborea* DONN) Deciduous shrub, very rarely to 2m, spreading quite widely when happily established. The bts die back to about half their length after the autumn, so that extension is slow. Lv bipinnate or biternate with pinnatifid segments, often reddish-purple when expanding, with red petioles and main veins persisting. The lv vary from 20 to 45cm long. Fl solitary, terminal, up to 30cm across on occasion but usually from 15 to 20cm. The wild forms, rarely seen, are either rose-pink or, in Joseph Rock's form, white with a crimson blotch at the base of the petals. The cv range in colour from white to magenta, mainly pink and red. The fl are fragrant. Fl 5-6.

Hybrids between *P. suffruticosa* and *P. lutea* are known as *P. X lemoinei*, and may be recommended for districts where the true tree peonies are likely to be damaged by late frosts, as they start later into growth. *P. suffruticosa* is quite hardy so far as winter frost is concerned, but starts very early into growth and the bud is free of lv early in April so that late frosts can easily damage both lv and fl. *PP. lutea* and *delavayi* come later into lv and so are less liable to be damaged. The plant is native to China where it has been cultivated probably for 2,000 years. First obtained in a double red form by Joseph Banks in 1789. Not discovered in the wild until about 1913, when it was seen in Szechuan and Kansu.

PALIURUS MILLER *Rhamnaceae*

A small genus of about six species of deciduous shrubs and trees with alternate leaves. Only one species is in general cultivation.

Paliurus spina-christi MILLER Christ's Thorn

4.5. Deciduous shrub or small tree, to 7m, heavily armed with a pair of spines with each lv. Lv ovate, to 3cm long and more than half as wide, medium green, often turning yellow before falling. Fl in axillary umbels, greenish-yellow, very small but produced very plentifully. Fl 7-8. Fr shaped like a cardinal's hat, greenish, up to 2·5cm across. One of the contenders for the supplying of Christ's crown of thorns. Native to southern Europe, but perfectly hardy; requiring full exposure to sunlight, but indifferent as to soil. Not a showy plant but the fl are produced with such abandon that it is attractive enough in bloom and the fr are very curious.

PARASYRINGA W. W. SMITH *Oleaceae*

A monotypic genus about half-way between *Ligustrum* and *Syringa* and requiring similar treatment.

Parasyringa sempervirens W. W. SMITH

4. (*Ligustrum sempervirens*. LINGELSHEIM, *Syringa sempervirens*. FRANCHET) Evergreen shrub to 2m. Lv roundish or broad-elliptic, to 4cm long and nearly as wide, dark shining green, rather leathery. Fl in dense, terminal panicles made up of several terminal and axillary racemes each to 7cm long, creamy-white. Fl 8-9. Fr fleshy at first, but later becoming a dry capsule. Native of western China. Introduced by Forrest in 1913.

PARROTIA C. A. MEYER *Hamamelidaceae*

A monotypic genus, propagated by layers, seeds and cuttings, although the last method is not easy.

Parrotia persica C. A. MEYER

4.6.(7). Deciduous tree, to 13m, of graceful spreading habit, with exfoliating bark, much like the plane. The brs tend to extend horizontally and a leader should be trained vertically in the early stages. Lv ovate, much like those of the hazel, to 12cm long and half as wide, colouring very gorgeously gold and crimson in the autumn. Fl before the lv, lacking petals but with a conspicuous head of red stamens, backed by brown bracts. Fl 3. Native of Iran and the Caucasus. Introduced about 1840.

PARROTIOPSIS SCHNEIDER *Hamamelidaceae*

A monotypic genus; the solitary species was originally included in *Parrotia*. Cuttings root more readily than those of *Parrotia*. The plant prefers acid soil, but will tolerate alkalinity.

Parrotiopsis jacquemontiana (DECAISNE) REHDER

4. (*Parrotia jacquemontiana* DECAISNE, *Parrotiopsis involucrata* SCHNEIDER) Usually seen as a small bush to 2m, but occasionally a small deciduous tree to 6m. Lv hazel-like, to 7cm long and wide, turning yellow in the autumn. Fl terminal, in a head about 1·5cm wide of yellow stamens sub-

Parrotiopsis jacquemontiana

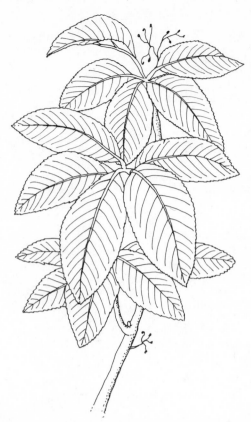

Parthenocissus henryana

tended by 4–6 petal-like bracts, which are a milky white, giving the impression of a fl about 4cm across; much like *Cornus florida*, but less attractive. Fl 4–5. A few odd fl may be produced at other times during the summer. Native of the Himalaya. Introduced in 1879.

PARTHENOCISSUS   PLANCHON   *Vitidaceae*

A genus of climbing shrubs, usually supporting themselves by means of adhesive pads at the tips of the tendrils. The leaves are alternate, usually three-lobed. The flowers are inconspicuous, in compound cymes, sometimes crowded together at the ends of the shoots. The fruit is a blue or blue-black berry. Most species will thrive in any soil. They are very suitable for clothing walls rapidly, although their attraction is mainly in the autumn colour of the leaves. The genus was formerly included in *Vitis*.

Parthenocissus henryana
(HEMSLEY) DIELS AND GILG

3.6. Deciduous climber of some vigour, clinging by adhesive disks. Lv digitate, composed of 3–5 leaflets which are a velvety dark green with the midrib and main veins silvery white and turn red in the autumn. The lv are on petioles up to 10cm long, and the leaflets are obovate or narrowly oval to 10cm long (though more usually 5–7cm) and about a third as wide. The fl come in terminal inflorescences to give the appearance

of a panicle and the fr, which are not often seen, are dark blue. The plant preserves its variegation best if placed on a wall facing north or north-west, where too much direct sunlight is not received. Plants are sometimes slightly tender when young in exceptionally severe winters, but usually prove hardy. Native of central China. Introduced by Wilson in 1900.

Parthenocissus himalayana   PLANCHET

6. Vigorous, deciduous climber with adhesive pads. Lv trifoliolate, each leaflet with a short stalk from a common petiole to 12cm long. The central leaflet is ovate or obovate, the two laterals are ovate, but, characteristically their midribs are not in the centre of the lamina. All leaflets acuminate, dark green, to 15cm long on vigorous specimens, turning scarlet or crimson in the autumn. Fr blue-black. **3.** Var *rubrifolia* GAGNEPAIN has the young lv purple at first, and these are somewhat smaller, when mature, than in the type. A slightly tender plant, but quite safe against a wall. Native of the Himalaya. Introduced about 1894. Var *rubrifolia*, from western China, was introduced in 1907.

Parthenocissus inserta   K. FRITSCH

6. (*P. vitacea* HITCHCOCK, *Cissus quinquefolia* of Bot Mag) Easily distinguished from other spp in cultivation by the absence of adhesive pads at the end of the tendrils, so more suitable for training over shrubs or trellis-work than for clothing a wall. Lv with 5 leaflets, which are saw-toothed, elliptic, to 12cm long and slightly more than half as wide; dark shining green, turning red in the autumn. Fl in axillary cymes. Fr blue-black with a bluish bloom. Native of the eastern USA from Maine to Florida. Probably introduced about 1800 but confused with the next sp.

Parthenocissus quinquefolia
(LINNAEUS) PLANCHON

6. (*Hedera quinquefolia* LINNAEUS, *Vitis hederacea* EHRHART) This is the true Virginian creeper but its name has been usurped by *P. tricuspidata*. Deciduous climber, clinging by adhesive pads. Lv with 5 leaflets on a petiole to 10cm long; leaflets oval or obovate, to 10cm long and 6cm across, tapered at both ends, toothed; dull green above, almost glaucous below, turning orange and scarlet in the autumn. Fr blue-black. Native of the eastern USA from New England to Mexico. Introduced 1622 according to Rehder; certainly in cultivation in 1629.

Parthenocissus thomsonii PLANCHON

3.6. Deciduous climber, clinging by adhesive pads. Young lv and bts claret purple at first, later the lv turn greenish-purple and crimson-purple in the autumn. Lv with 5 leaflets, to 10cm long and 4cm across, toothed in the upper half and tapered at both ends. Fr black. Related to *P. henryana* but hardier and equally attractive, and should be seen more often. Native of the Himalaya and China, whence it was introduced by Wilson in 1900.

Parthenocissus tricuspidata PLANCHON

6. (*Vitis inconstans* MIQUEL, *Ampelopsis veitchii* of gardens) The best-known member of the genus, universally, but incorrectly, known as Virginia creeper; it is known in the USA as Boston ivy. Vigorous, deciduous climber, clinging by adhesive pads. Lv usually deeply 3-lobed, but practically unlobed lv and trifoliolate ones have also been recorded, usually on young plants, while the 3-lobed form is usually found on mature specimens. These lv can be anything from 5 to 20cm wide and are a shining green. In the cv 'Veitchii' the young lv are purplish. In the autumn the lv turn brilliant crimson. Native of Japan, Korea and China. Introduced from Japan by J. G. Veitch in 1862.

PASSIFLORA LINNAEUS *Passifloraceae*
A genus of mainly tropical climbers.

Passiflora coerulea LINNAEUS Passion Flower

4. Vigorous, semi-evergreen climber, ascending by means of axillary tendrils. Lv palmate, 5–7-lobed, the lobes with rounded ends and quite deep, dark green above, somewhat glaucous beneath, to 15cm across but usually about 12cm. Fl singly from upper lv axils, patulate, of very characteristic shape, the 5 petals and 5 sepals opening flat like a saucer with a number of thread-like growths, known as the corona, forming an inner ring. Petals and sepals off-white, the corona blue or bluish-purple, to 10cm across. Fl 6–9. Fr rarely produced except after very hot summers, egg-shaped, to 4cm long, orange. 'Constance Elliott' has ivory-white fl and corona. The plant requires the protection of a south or west-facing wall and may be damaged in exceptionally severe winters, but is rarely killed. The plant should be somewhat starved, as otherwise it grows to excess and produces few fl. Cuttings of firm, young wood root easily and it also comes readily from seed. Native of central and western S America. Apparently not in cultivation before 1699, although illustrated in late sixteenth-century books.

PAULOWNIA SIEBOLD AND ZUCCARINI
Scrophulariaceae
A small genus of about ten species of deciduous trees from east Asia. They require deep soil, but appear indifferent as to whether the reaction is acid or alkaline. The two species in commerce are both perfectly hardy so far as winter cold is concerned, but they form their flower buds in the autumn and these can be damaged in severe winters. Propagated by seed and by root cuttings.

Paulownia fargesii FRANCHET

4. Tree, to 20m, with sticky bts which remain green for the first year, turning brown thereafter. Lv opposite, ovate-cordate, acuminate to 30cm long and 17cm wide; dull green, downy below. Fl in terminal pyramidal panicles to 45cm long and 30cm wide; each fl tubular with 5 recurved lobes, 7cm long and 6cm wide; pale lavender with a yellowish base to the tube. Fl 5. Fr an ovoid capsule, brown, to 5cm long and half as wide. Apparently better suited to the climate of the UK than the next sp, and flowers as a comparatively young plant (in 10–15 years from seed). Native of Szechuan. Introduced by Père Farges in 1895.

Paulownia tomentosa (THUNBERG) STEUDEL

4. (*P. imperialis* SIEBOLD AND ZUCCARINI) Round-headed tree, to 15m, with stout brs. Lv opposite, usually 3–5-lobed, the lobes being rather shallow. Lv very large on young trees, on adult trees to 25cm long and wide, dark green and hairy above, grey tomentose below. Fl in terminal

Paulownia tomentosa

panicles to 30cm long. Fl like a foxglove, blue-purple, to 5cm long and wide. Fl 5. Capsules to 5cm long. The plant is sometimes grown for its foliage alone, when it is cut down to the base each year and only one of the emerging sucker growths allowed to develop. Under these circumstances one can get growths of up to 3m or more, bearing lv 60–100cm wide. Native of China. Long cultivated in Japan whence it was obtained in 1834.

Paulownia tomentosa

PERIPLOCA LINNAEUS *Asclepiadaceae*

A small genus of about twelve species of which only one is in general cultivation. Usually propagated by division.

Periploca graeca LINNAEUS Silk Vine

4. Deciduous or semi-evergreen twining shrub, to 10m or more. Lv opposite, ovate, to 10cm long and 5cm wide on petioles about 1cm long, dark green and glossy above. Fl in cymes terminating short laterals, the cymes with 8–12 fl; each fl about 2·5cm across, greenish-yellow outside, chocolate-coloured inside, composed of 5 narrow petals, giving a somewhat star-like effect. Seeds in follicles up to 12cm long but only 7mm wide, filled with silk-tufted seeds. The fl are fragrant, although the heavy odour is not attractive to everyone. Fl 7–8. An easy, but not very exciting, climber. Native of the south-eastern Mediterranean region; in cultivation since 1597 and probably long before. Requires full sun, but will thrive in any soil.

PERNETTYA GAUDICHAUD *Ericaceae*

A genus of low-growing, evergreen shrubs with a curious distribution from Mexico, through S America to New Zealand and Tasmania, with alternate leaves, axillary flowers and berried fruits. Among the hardy species only one is large enough to figure here. It requires a well-lit situation, acid soil, and is intolerant of drought.

Pernettya mucronata GAUDICHAUD

4.5. Evergreen shrub, rarely over 1m high but occasionally to nearly 2m, spreading often by means of suckers. Lv cordate-acuminate, spiny at the apex, toothed, rigid, lustrous green, about 2cm long and 6mm wide. Fl solitary, axillary, from the top axils of the shoots, pendent, urn-shaped, about 6mm long, with 5 lobes at the mouth. Fl 5–6. Fr a round berry, to 12mm across, in colours ranging from white to pink, red, purple and violet. Fr 9–10. Most birds do not attack the fr which may persist until February. The fl are usually perfect but behave as though they were dioecious, and one known male should be planted among 3 or more of the plants selected for berry colour. 'Thymifolia' is a very floriferous male clone. 'Bell's Seedling' is a hermaphrodite clone with dark red fr. Native of southern Chile and the Argentine. Introduced in 1828.

PETTERIA PRESL *Leguminosae*

A monotypic genus; propagated by seed.

Petteria ramentacea PRESL

4. (*Cytisus weldenii* VISIANI) Deciduous shrub,

Pernettya mucronata

Phellodendron amurense RUPRECHT

1.6.7. Deciduous tree, to 15m, with conspicuous, grey fissured bark in mature specimens; this bark is corky. Bts orange or yellowish-grey. Lv pinnate, to 37cm long, with 5–11 leaflets which are ovate-lanceolate, acuminate, to 10cm long; dull green above and glabrous, turning gold in the autumn. In the var *japonicum* OHWI (*P. japonicum* MAXIMOWICZ) the lv are grey tomentose below. Fl in erect panicles to 7cm long. Fr black. As in all the spp the leaves are aromatic when crushed. Native of northern China and Manchuria. Winter-hardy, but liable to damage by spring frosts, a danger which var *japonicum* does not seem to share. Introduced about 1856 from St Petersburg. Var *japonicum* introduced 1863.

Phellodendron chinense SCHNEIDER

6.7. Similar to *P. amurense* var *japonicum* but bark less corky. Lv with 7–13 leaflets which are oblong-lanceolate, to 12cm long and 4cm wide. Underside less tomentose than *P. amurense* var *japonicum*. Most easily distinguished by the larger, closely-packed fr. Native of Hupeh. Introduced by Wilson in 1907.

to 2m or slightly more. Lv trifoliolate on a petiole to 3cm long. Each leaflet oval or obovate, to 5cm long and half as wide, glabrous. Fl in erect, terminal racemes to 7cm long. Fl fragrant, dense, with a tubular calyx much resembling a *Cytisus* fl, about 2cm long, bright yellow. Fl 5–6. Pods shortly-stalked, to 5cm long. A curious shrub about midway between *Laburnum* and *Cytisus*. Native only to the eastern Adriatic. Introduced in 1837.

PHELLODENDRON RUPRECHT *Rutaceae*

A genus of ten species of deciduous trees with handsome large pinnate leaves which turn yellow before falling. The plants are dioecious, but the flowers are of no beauty, although the fruit is not unattractive. *Euodia* is separated from *Phellodendron* by the fact that the buds of the former are not enclosed by the base of the petiole, while in the latter they are. Propagated by seeds or by firm cuttings of young wood.

Petteria ramentacea

PHILADELPHUS LINNAEUS *Philadelphaceae*

A genus of seventy-five species of deciduous shrubs with opposite leaves and white flowers in racemes or, more rarely, solitary, often strongly scented. The flowers are more or less patulate with four petals (as opposed to the five of *Deutzia*). The genus contains about forty species distributed throughout the northern hemisphere from Mexico to China. The plants have been so often hybridised that identification of the species is difficult, so many so-called species not being true. The plants like full light, but will tolerate partial shade and grow in almost any soil. Easily propagated by hard wood cuttings in autumn.

Philadelphus argyrocalyx WOOTON

4. Deciduous shrub, to about 130cm, with slender bts. Lv elliptic, to 4cm long, silky below, dull green above. Fl usually solitary, about 4cm across, subtended by 4 silvery tomentose sepals. Fl 7–8. Evidently related to the more common *P. microphyllus* (qv) but distinct by its silvery calyx and later flowering. Native of New Mexico, USA. Introduced in 1916.

Philadelphus brachybotrys (KOEHNE) KOEHNE

4. (*P. pekinensis* var *brachybotrys* RUPRECHT) Deciduous shrub, to nearly 3m, with exfoliating bark. Lv ovate, toothed, acuminate, to 9cm long and 5cm wide; dull green, petiole and midrib purplish. Fl in racemes, usually about 5-flowered, about 3cm across, cream rather than white. Fl 5–6. Native of China whence it was obtained by Vilmorin in 1892.

Philadelphus californicus BENTHAM

4. Deciduous shrub, to 3m, with somewhat pendulous brs. Lv ovate, to 8cm long and 5cm wide, toothed or entire. Fl in racemes or panicles of up to 20 fl each one about 2·5cm across. Notable for its many-flowered panicles. Native of California. Introduced in 1858, possibly through W. Lobb.

Philadelphus coronarius LINNAEUS
Mock Orange, Syringa

4. Deciduous shrub, to 4m, with erect stems. Lv ovate, toothed, to 10cm long and half as wide, smooth on both surfaces but with a few inconspicuous hairs. Fl in terminal racemes of 5–9 blooms, each about 2·5cm in diameter and heavily perfumed, white with a touch of cream. Fl 6. 'Aureus' has the emerging lv bright yellow, which fades somewhat after June. 'Variegatus' has the lv with a cream margin. Double flowered forms existed formerly, but have been dropped from cultivation in favour of the double flowered *Lemoinei* hybrids, which will be mentioned under *P. microphyllus*. Probably native to SE Europe but so long in cultivation that its exact wild habitat is uncertain.

Philadelphus delavayi LOUIS HENRY

4. A rather leggy shrub, to 3m, with purplish glabrous bts. Lv ovate, rounded at base to 8cm long and 4cm wide, slightly pubescent above, grey tomentose below. Fl in clusters of 7–11, each fl subtended by a dark purple calyx (this is apparently not invariable, the dark-caliced forms are often referred to var *calvescens* f. *melanocalyx* REHDER, which also has purple calices and has the lv nearly glabrous below). Fl about 3cm across, white and fragrant. Fl 5–6. *P. purpurascens* REHDER (*P. brachybotrys* var *purpurascens* KOEHNE) is slightly shorter with hairy bts and less hairy lv than *P. delavayi*. Fl in racemes of 5–9, with purple calyx and smaller fl to 3cm across. It is most distinct in its habit, with arching brs as opposed to the erect ones of *P. delavayi*. Both plants are very attractive with their deep purple calices, which enhance the whiteness of the fl. *P. purpurascens* has a slightly better habit but smaller and fewer fl. Both plants are native to western China. *P. delavayi* sent by Delavay in 1888, *P. purpurascens* sent back by Wilson in 1904.

Philadelphus grandiflorus WILLDENOW

4. This sp seems to have dropped out of cultivation, but since it has entered largely into hybrids a short description is given. Shrub, to 5m; lv ovate, to 12cm long and 6cm wide, glabrous except for tufts of hair along the midrib on the underside. Fl either singly or in threes, scentless, to 5cm across. Fl 6–7. Later flowering than most spp. Introduced from the south-eastern USA in 1811.

Philadelphus incanus KOEHNE

4. Shrub, to 3m, with hairy bts. Lv oval, rounded at base, slightly downy above, grey-hairy below, to 10cm long and 5·5cm wide ·on non-flowering shoots, only to 5cm long on flowering ones. Fl in racemes of 5–9 fl, each about 2·5cm wide, with a hawthorn-like scent. Fl 7. The last to flower in the genus and so valuable. *P. subcanus* is sometimes supplied by mistake as it looks very similar, but it flowers in June and so is not particularly desirable. Native of western China. Introduced by Wilson in 1904.

Philadelphus X insignis CARRIÈRE

4. A hybrid of uncertain origin. Rehder suggests *pubescens* X *californicus*; Bean states 'a hybrid in whose origin *P. grandiflorus* has shared'. Shrub, to 4m, bts glabrous. Lv ovate or cordate, to 9cm long and 6cm wide, glossy green above, hairy beneath. Fl cupped, in terminal racemes of up to 20 blooms, about 2·5cm in diameter. Fl

6–7. An attractive shrub, which is not as often seen as its floriferousness and late flowering warrant. Bred before 1870.

Philadelphus lewisii PURSH

4. Shrub, to 4m, with arching brs. Lv ovate, wedge-shaped at base, dentate or entire, to 10cm long and 6cm wide, slightly hairy. Fl in racemes of 5–9, scentless, about 3cm across. Fl 6–8. One of the more attractive sp, allied to *P. californicus* but with less dense inflorescence. Native to western N America. Introduced apparently in 1823.

Philadelphus maculatus HU

4. (*P. coulteri* of gardens, *P. mexicanus* var *coulteri* BEAN) This sp is not of much importance in itself as, being a native of Mexico, it is somewhat tender and even with protection does not flower very freely. It is noteworthy for its large fl, up to 5cm across, and the purple blotch at the base of the petals. Crossed with *P. X lemoinei* it has given rise to a race of hybrids known collectively as *P. X purpureo-maculatus* LEMOINE, of which named clones are 'Beauclerc', 'Etoile Rose' and 'Sybille', all of which are rather low shrubs with purple or carmine bases to the white petals. The fl are fragrant and open in mid-June.

Philadelphus microphyllus GRAY

4. A rounded bush a little over 1m high with downy bts. Lv ovate, entire, to 2cm long and 8mm wide, bright green above, grey-hairy below, almost sessile. Fl smelling of pineapples, singly, at the end of short lateral twigs, about 2·5cm across. Fl 6. A very attractive, compact shrub and perfectly hardy in spite of its being native to Colorado and Arizona. Introduced through Professor Sargent in 1883.

It was immediately used by Lemoine as a parent in hybrids. *P. X lemoinei* is *microphyllus X coronarius*, of which 'Avalanche' and the double 'Boule de Neige' are typical. However, *P. X lemoinei* was further hybridised with *P. grandiflorus*, to give such plants as 'Voie lactée', and possibly with *insignis* and *X nivalis*, to give such plants as the polyanthus group which includes 'Gerbe de neige' and the *Virginalis* group which have double fl and includes that great favourite 'Virginal'. The crosses with *P. maculatus* have already been referred to.

Philadelphus pubescens LOISELEUR

4. The form in commerce is var *intectus* A. H. MOORE, (*P. intectus* BEADLE), which is described here. Vigorous shrub, to 4m. Lv ovate to elliptic, to 10cm long and half as wide, slightly toothed or entire, dark green above, nearly glabrous below. (In typical *P. pubescens* the lv are grey tomentose below.) Fl scentless, in racemes of 5–9 fl, about 4cm across. Fl 6–7. Crossed with *P. coronarius*, the resultant hybrids were called *P. X nivalis* JACQUES, of which the double form is thought to be the pollen parent in the *Virginalis* group of hybrids. Native of the south-eastern USA. Introduced about 1800, although var *intectus* was not recognised before about 1880.

Philadelphus satsumanus MIQUEL

4. Erect shrub, to 2·5m, with glabrous bts. Lv ovate, long-acuminate, to 15cm long and half as wide on extension growths, smaller on flowering wood, slightly toothed or entire. Fl in erect racemes of 5–9 flowers, slightly scented, about 3cm across. Fl 6. Native of Japan. Introduced in 1851.

Philadelphus schrenkii RUPRECHT

4. Shrub, to 3m, of vigorous erect habit. Bts somewhat hairy. Lv ovate, to 12cm long, slightly toothed, dark green. Fl in 5–7-flowered racemes, each fl to 3·5cm across, strongly scented. Fl 6. Possibly only a form of *P. coronarius*. Native of north-eastern Asia from Siberia to Korea. Introduced about 1874.

Philadelphus tomentosus WALLICH

4. (*P. coronarius* var *tomentosus* HOOKER AND THOMSON) Shrub, to 3m, with glabrous or slightly hairy bts. Lv oval, acuminate, dentate, dark green above and slightly hairy, densely grey tomentose beneath, to 10cm long and half as wide. Fl in 5–7-flowered racemes, each blossom white, fragrant, about 3cm across. Fl 6. Similar in appearance to *P. coronarius* but very distinct in its grey tomentose leaves. Native of the Himalaya. Introduced, presumably through Wallich, in 1822.

PHILLYREA LINNAEUS *Oleaceae*

A small genus of four species of evergreen shrubs or small trees with opposite leaves and small whitish flowers which are dioecious or hermaphrodite. Propagated by seed or by cuttings of half-ripe wood. At one time the most popular evergreen for British gardens from the sixteenth century until the nineteenth. Now rarely seen, but still good for hedges.

Phillyrea angustifolia LINNAEUS

4. Evergreen shrub, to 3m, often spreading more widely. Lv linear-elliptic, to 6cm long and 1cm across, coriaceous, dark green above and matt, paler below. Fl tubular, about 1cm long and wide, in axillary clusters, a rather dirty white but fragrant. Fl 5–6. Fr, if produced, a small, round, blue-black drupe. Native of central and western Mediterranean regions. In cultivation since the sixteenth century.

Phillyrea decora BOISSIER AND BALANSA

4. (*P. vilmoriniana* BOISSIER) A dome-shaped bush of up to 3m, often wider, with warted bts. Lv oblong-elliptic, to 12cm long and 4·5cm across, dark shining green above, paler below, usually with entire margins, occasionally sparsely toothed. Fl a clear white, about 6mm across, in dense axillary clusters. Fl 4. Fr reddish at first, later dark purple. The seed parent of *X Osmarea* but also a plant that might be seen more often. Native of Turkey around the Black Sea. Discovered by Balansa in 1866, who sent seeds the same year to Vilmorin.

Phillyrea latifolia LINNAEUS

4. Spreading shrub or small tree, usually to 5m, occasionally twice as high. Lv variable, generally ovate or elliptic-ovate, to 6cm long and half as wide, sometimes rounded at the base, usually sharply serrate. Fl dull white, in axillary clusters, each fl about 5mm wide, fragrant. Fl 5–6. Fr blue-black, round, about 6mm in diameter. 'Spinosa' *(ilicifolia)* has dentate lv with a slight suggestion of holly lv. *P. media* LINNAEUS is now generally regarded as a smaller-leaved form of *P. latifolia.* Native of the whole Mediterranean region. In cultivation since the sixteenth century.

PHOTINIA LINDLEY *Rosaceae*

A genus of deciduous and evergreen shrubs and small trees from south and east Asia, of which about forty species have been named. They are akin to *Crataegus,* but with unlobed leaves, no thorns and the fruit is a true pome, not a pome-like drupe as in *Crataegus.* The evergreen species have very handsome young leaves but are susceptible to very low temperatures, although quite resilient to spring frosts. Propagation by seed, grafting or by semi-hard stem cuttings with a heel in late summer.

Photinia beauverdiana SCHNEIDER

4.5.6. Deciduous tree, to 7m, with purplish bts. Lv lanceolate, acuminate, rounded at base, serrate, to 12cm long and 4·5cm wide, with very conspicuous raised veins on the underside usually colouring well in the autumn. Fl in terminal corymbs on lateral twigs, each corymb about 5cm across, the white fl being individually about 12mm across. Fl 5–6. Fr deep red, about 6mm wide. If it can be obtained, the var *notabilis* REHDER AND WILSON is preferable with its broader lv, inflorescences to 10cm across and orange fr. Native of western China. Introduced by Wilson in 1900; var *notabilis* from Hupeh in 1908.

Photinia X fraseri DRESS

3.4.(5). The collective name for hybrids between *P. glabra* and *P. serrulata,* which may be expected to make a fairly large evergreen shrub, or perhaps a small tree to 7m. Lv oblong, acuminate, coppery or crimson when young, later dark green, obovate, sharply toothed. Fl white in largish corymbs. Fl 5. Probably requiring shelter in most districts, but both parents will usually regenerate if damaged by frost. 'Red Robin' has almost scarlet young lv.

Photinia glabra (THUNBERG) MAXIMOWICZ

3.4.5. Evergreen shrub, to 3m, with lv elliptic to obovate, bronze when young (but almost scarlet in the cv 'Rubens'), to 8cm long and about half as wide, minutely toothed. Fl in corymbs to 10cm across, white, about 1cm in diameter. Fl 5–6. Fr bright red, only 5mm in diameter. The hardiest of the evergreen spp. Native of Japan. In cultivation in 1903.

Photinia serrulata LINDLEY

3.4.5. Evergreen shrub or tree, to 12m in sheltered districts. Lv coppery-red when young, and the plant has a long growing season so that this coppery colour is prevalent for most of the season, oblong, acuminate, rounded at base, coriaceous, serrate, to 20cm long (usually 10–15) and to 9cm wide, glabrous, but the petiole is white-hairy. Fl in terminal corymbs to 15cm across, each fl white to 1cm across. Fl 4–5. Fr red, the size of haws. Damaged in exceptionally severe winters, but the young growths seem to tolerate spring frosts without much damage. Native of China. Introduced by Captain Kirkpatrick in 1804.

Photinia villosa DE CANDOLLE

4.5.(6). A rather slow-growing, deciduous shrub, occasionally a small tree to 5m. Bts pubescent. Lv obovate-lanceolate to oblong, long-acuminate, tapered at base, finely serrate, glabrous above, villous below. In most districts the lv colour red or yellow in the autumn. Fl in small corymbs to 4cm across, each fl slightly over 1cm across. Fl 5. Fr bright red. Var *sinica* (REHDER AND WILSON) makes a larger plant and the fr tend to be pendulous. The type is native to northern China, Korea and Japan, whence it was introduced about 1865. Var *sinica* was introduced from western China by Wilson in 1901.

PHYSOCARPUS MAXIMOWICZ *Rosaceae*

A genus of about thirteen species of deciduous shrubs, which have, in their time, been included both in *Neillia* and in *Spiraea.* All but one of the species come from N America. They are of easy growth with alternate leaves and flowers in terminal umbel-like racemes. The leaves are attractive but the plants are not among the most showy. Propagated by cuttings of half-ripe wood.

Physocarpus capitatus (PURSH) KUNTZE

4. Deciduous shrub, to 3m or slightly more. Lv 3-lobed, broadly ovate, to 10cm long and wide, glabrous above, hairy beneath. Fl in a corymb, white. Fl 6–7. Fr an inflated pod. Native of western N America. Introduced 1827 but not, apparently, by Douglas. In cultivation barely distinct from *P. opulifolius*, but apparently in the wild up to 7m high with a climbing habit.

Physocarpus malvaceus (GREENE) KUNTZE

4. Shrub, to 2m or less, with erect stems, pubescent when young. Lv basically almost orbicular, but 3–5-lobed, to 7cm long and wide, usually glabrous above and downy below. Fl in corymbs to 4cm across, white. Fl 6. Native of western N America from British Columbia to Utah. Introduced in 1896.

Physocarpus opulifolius (LINNAEUS) MAXIMOWICZ

4. Deciduous shrub of spreading habit, to 3m tall but occasionally 10m in width. Lv basically broadly obovate, but 3-lobed, toothed, to 7cm long and nearly as wide. Fl in a rounded corymb at the end of lateral twigs, white with a pinkish tinge. Fl 6. 'Luteus' has the young lv a bright golden yellow, but this colour soon fades. *P. amurensis* is very similar, but larger in all its parts (although no taller), the lv tend to be 5-lobed and they are downy below. *P. opulifolius* is native to eastern N America and was introduced by Banister before 1687. *P. amurensis* is native to Manchuria and Korea and was introduced between 1854 and 1860 according to Rehder.

PICEA A. DIETRICH Pinaceae Spruce

A genus of evergreen trees of pyramidal habit, with the branches radiating in whorls. The leaves are either quadrangular in section or flattened, attached to the branches by peg-like projections known as pulvini, which persist and are one of the main means of distinguishing *Picea* from *Abies*. Another distinguishing feature is provided by the pendulous cones (erect in *Abies*) which persist for a long time on the tree, although the seeds are shed the first autumn. The plants are monoecious and both male and female flowers are usually axillary. The male flower is catkin-like, the female flower usually violet or purple and quite showy. The flowers appear in spring any time from February to May. Spruces need ample water and are intolerant of drought, although they will often thrive in cold, wet and unpromising situations. They are very intolerant of atmospheric pollution and will usually not thrive in town gardens. The genus, which contains about forty species throughout the northern temperate zone, has been divided into three sections: *Eupicea*, in which the leaves are quadrangular with stomata on all surfaces; *Casicta*, in which the leaves are unequally quadrangular with stomata only at the top and bottom; and *Omorika*, with flat leaves with stomata only on one surface. In *Omorika* the stomata appear to be on the lower surface, but in point of fact they are on the upper surface and the leaf is twisted so as to invert the surfaces.

Picea abies (LINNAEUS) KARST Eupicea
Norway Spruce

7. (*P. excelsa* LINK) The typical Christmas tree. Tree, to 40m, with reddish bts. Lv spirally arranged, those on the upper side pointing forward, those below radiating somewhat, hard-pointed, dark green, to 2·5cm long. Cones cylindrical, pendulous, from 10–15cm long, falling in the second year. A very large number of cv have been introduced which are propagated by cuttings. Some, such as 'Clanbrasiliana', make a dense rounded bush not more than 2m high; 'Inversa' has very pendulous brs which adhere closely to the main trunk; 'Pyramidata' is a fastigiate form, while 'Virgata' has very few brs, which have very few side shoots but are densely clothed with lv. Native of most of Europe, apart from the Mediterranean region.

Picea asperata MASTERS Eupicea

7. Tree, to 30m, very similar to *P. abies*. Bts yellowish-brown, smooth. Bark grey. Lv very stiff and prickly, not more than 2cm long and thickly spread all round the stem. Cones to 12cm long, fawn-grey at first, later dark brown. Native to much of western China, where it tends to be the dominant conifer. Introduced by Wilson in 1910.

Picea bicolor (MAXIMOWICZ) MAYR Eupicea

7. (*Picea alcockiana* CARRIÈRE) Tree, to 25m in the wild but so far much less in cultivation. Bts whitish the first year, then light brown. Lv to 2cm long, with conspicuous white stomata in lines, otherwise glossy green. A preferable tree is var *acicularis* SHIRASAWA AND KOYAMA, with longer lv which are attractively glaucous. Cones reddish-purple while growing, later brown, to 10cm long and 3cm across. Native of Japan. Introduced by J. G. Veitch in 1861.

Picea brachytyla (FRANCHET) PRITZEL Omorika

7. (*P. sargentiana* REHDER AND WILSON) Tree, from 10 to 25m in the wild, pyramidal or round-headed. Bts pendulous, buff-coloured. Lv rigid, sometimes rather yellowish-green above, vivid blue-white beneath. Cones green with a purple flush while developing, brown when ripe, to 9cm long. Cone-scales of varying shapes, which have been considered sufficient to give varietal differences. Native of Hupeh and Szechuan. Introduced by Wilson in 1901.

Picea breweriana WATSON *Omorika*

7. One of the most attractive of all conifers, although somewhat slow-growing. Tree, to 40m in the wild, with grey flaky bark. Bts of young trees stiff and horizontal, in mature trees very pendulous and often extremely long and slender, to 2m or more. In mature trees the lower brs are somewhat decumbent, the upper ones curve upwards. The lv are flat, convex on both surfaces, dark green, to 3cm long. Cones oblong, purple before ripening, later russet brown, to 12cm long and 2·5cm wide. The first plant sent to Kew had reached a height of 10m in 50 years, although other later importations have grown more rapidly. A mature specimen with the extraordinary slender pendulous brs is a most attractive sight and probably well worth the long wait which seems essential, as, apparently, moderate-sized specimens resent movement. A very local plant in the wild, confined to a few populations in the Siskyou Mountains of northern California and Oregon. First described in 1884 and in cultivation in 1893.

Picea engelmannii (PARRY) ENGELMANN *Casicta*

7. Tree, to 50m in the wild and about 30m in cultivation, forming a dense pyramid with slightly ascending brs, densely clothed with soft needles of an attractive blue-green colour (more pronounced in the form 'Glauca'). When bruised the lv have a very unpleasant smell and are up to 2·5cm long. The lv of *P. glauca* (qv) also have an unpleasant scent, but they are horny at their tips, not soft like this sp. Cones more or less cylindrical, from 3 to 7cm long; green tinged with crimson when fully developed, turning brown when ripe. Apparently the tree is somewhat rare in cultivation, *P. pungens* being often offered under this name. It is a mountain plant requiring rather severe winter conditions and may be damaged by spring frosts. It is likely to do best in the northern parts of the UK and is a good conifer for mountain slopes. Native of western N America from Alberta south to New Mexico. Introduced 1864.

Picea glauca (MOENCH) VOSS *Eupicea*

7. (*P. alba* LINK, *P. canadensis* BRITTON) Tree, to 30m or somewhat less, with brs at first descending and then turning up at their ends. Lv unpleasantly scented when bruised, pale green or glaucous, only 1cm long, with a horny point. Cones cylindrical, small, from 2·5 to 6cm long, pale brown. An arctic tree, not thriving very well in the UK except, possibly, in the extreme north. Native of northern N America. Grown by Bishop Compton in 1700.

Picea glehnii (F. SCHMIDT) MASTERS *Eupicea*

7. Tree, to 30m in the wild but not apparently long-lived in the UK. Easily distinguished from all other spp by its chocolate (or reddish-brown) bark, which divides into thin flakes before falling. The tree is short-branched so that only a narrow crown is produced. Bts reddish, with dense hairs. Lv to 3cm long, with a horny point. Cones cylindrical, to 6cm long and 2·5cm across, shining brown. Native of Saghalien and Hokkaido in Japan. Introduced by Maries in 1877.

Picea jezoensis
(SIEBOLD AND ZUCCARINI) CARRIÈRE *Casicta*

7. (*P. ajanensis* FISCHER) The form best known in cultivation is the var *hondoensis* (MAYR) REHDER, which is distinguished from the type by its reddish rather than yellowish bts and by its curved, shorter lv. It is a much better tree in cultivation, although otherwise not noticeably distinct. Tree, to 25m or more, with brownish bts and grey bark. Lv curved, to 2·5cm long, dull green above, shining blue-white beneath. Cones bright crimson when young, brown when ripe, to 7cm long and 2·5cm wide. A very attractive, spire-like tree with its vivid blue-white underleaves and its crimson cones. Native of Japan and NE Asia. Introduced by J. G. Veitch in 1861; the seed being mixed with *P. bicolor* and causing great confusion.

Picea koyamai SHIRASAWA *Eupicea*

7. Moderate-sized, pyramidal tree, to 20m. Bts reddish-brown, sometimes with glandular hairs. Lv crowded, dark green or slightly glaucous, to 12mm long. Cones to 11cm long, pale brown. Not one of the more attractive spp perhaps, but worth planting, as it exists (or existed) in the wild in only one small grove of about 100 trees on one mountain in Hokkaido and should be preserved through cultivation. Discovered in 1911 by a Mr Koyama.

Picea likiangensis (FRANCHET) PRITZEL *Casicta*

7. (Including *P. balfouriana* REHDER AND WILSON and *P. purpurea* MASTERS) Tree, to 30m, with thick, deeply-furrowed bark on mature trees. Bts of varying colours and usually somewhat bristly. Lv dense, pointing forwards on top of the shoot, spreading from the lower surface, to 2cm long (more crowded but only 1cm long in var *purpurea*), glaucous grey-green. Cones pinkish or violet in colour, to 7·5cm long.

Native of western China. Introduced by Wilson in 1910.

Picea mariana
(MILLER) BRITTON, STERNS AND POGGENBERG
Eupicea Black Spruce

7. (*P. nigra* (AITON) LINK) Tree, to 20m in the wild but usually only about 10m in cultivation, with reddish-brown bark. Lv short, stiff, glaucous blue-green, about 12mm long. Cones purple or greenish-purple while developing, then turning reddish-brown and persisting for many years. Probably requires acid soil. Native of much of eastern N America from Labrador to Wisconsin. Introduced by Banister for Bishop Compton before 1700.

Picea morrisonicola HAYATA, from Mt Morrison on Taiwan, is barely to be distinguished from *P. glehnii*, while *P. obovata* LEDEBOUR is a Siberian tree, barely to be distinguished from *P. abies*, and not thriving in the UK.

Picea omorika (PANCIC) PURKYNE *Omorika*

7. A tree of up to 30m, with rather short brs giving an elegant, slender, spire-like tree. Lower brs descending at first, later turning upwards; upper brs horizontal or ascending. Bark reddish-brown, exfoliating in plate-like layers. Lv to 2cm long with a white underside. Cones small, bluish-black when young, later dark brown, to 5cm long. 'Pendula' has drooping bts. One of the best spruces for alkaline soils, for dry conditions and for town gardens. It will also thrive in rather wet soils and alkaline conditions are not essential, although it is found on limestone in the wild. Confined to the valley of the Drina in Yugoslavia, where it was first discovered by Dr Pancic in 1875.

Picea orientalis (LINNAEUS) CARRIÈRE *Eupicea*

7. Tree of over 30m of pyramidal habit, with brown bark and pale brown, hairy bts. Lv dark green, glossy, very short, not more than 12mm long, bluntish at the apex. Immature cones purple and very attractive, brown when ripe; narrower than most cones in the genus, being up to 10cm long but not more than 2cm wide. This is the best spruce to plant in dry districts and it also seems to tolerate a certain amount of atmospheric pollution. Native of the Caucasus and the mountains of western Asia. Introduced in 1839.

Picea polita (SIEBOLD AND ZUCCARINI) CARRIÈRE
Eupicea

7. A tree of up to 40m in the wild but has proved very slow-growing in cultivation and its ultimate height is not yet known. It makes a very attractive pyramidal tree of somewhat stiff habit. Bark pale grey, bts yellowish-brown, glabrous.

Lv somewhat spiny, sickle-shaped, to 2·5cm long, dark glossy green. Cones cinnamon-brown when ripe, to 10cm long and 4cm across. Native of Japan. Introduced by J. G. Veitch in 1861.

Picea pungens ENGELMANN *Casicta*
Blue Spruce

7. Tree, to 30m, pyramidal at first. Bts glaucous, later orange-brown. Lv rather rigid and very prickly, to 3cm long, dull green in the type but blue-grey in the more usual garden form, 'Glauca' ('Moerheimii' is even more blue). Cones cylindrical, to 10cm long and 3cm across, pale brown. One of the most handsome of trees, particularly when young; older plants are apt to become somewhat untidy in appearance. The plants also have an annoying habit of suddenly collapsing when about 4m high. It is thought that aphis infection may be one cause, so spraying directly any infection is detected is essential. Once the lv begin to fall, the harm is done. Native to the western USA from Wyoming to Colorado. Introduced by Anthony Waterer in 1877.

Picea sitchensis (BONGARD) CARRIÈRE *Casicta*
Sitka Spruce

7. Tree, to 40m or more, with dark purple or reddish-brown bark and glabrous, pale brown bts. Lv with hard points, bluish-green above, silvery below, to 2cm long. Cones to 10cm long and 3cm across, pale brown. The plant thrives in moist and boggy situations, where it may grow with great rapidity making growths of more than 1m per year. It would appear to prefer acid soil. It is much used in forestry. Native to western N America from Alaska to California. Introduced by Douglas in 1831.

Picea smithiana (WALLICH) BOISSIER *Eupicea*

7. (*P. morinda* LINK, *Abies khutrow* LOUDON) Tree, to over 60m in the wild and up to 40m in cultivation, making a pyramidal tree with very pendulous brs. Bts pale brown, glabrous. Lv long and slender, dark green, prickly, to 3·5cm long. Cones up to 17cm long and 5 cm across, brown. A very graceful tree, but less so than the similar *P. breweriana*, although the dark green lv give it a rather sombre appearance. Perfectly hardy, although young shoots can be damaged by late spring frosts.

A plant that is sometimes confused with this sp is *P. spinulosa* (GRIFFITH) HENRY (*P. morindoides* REHDER), which has the same pendulous habit but belongs to the *Omorika* section and has lv which are glaucous beneath. It is found in the eastern Himalaya, while *P. smithiana* is found in the western part of the range. *P. spinulosa* appears to be somewhat tender in the UK. *P. smithiana* was introduced in 1818, when cones were sent to Lord Hopetoun. He gave them to Dr Govan, whose gardener was named Smith and it is in his honour that the sp is named.

PICRASMA BLUME *Simaroubaceae*

A genus of about eight species only one of which is hardy.

Picrasma ailanthoides PLANCHON

2.6.7. (*Picrasma quassioides* BENNETT) Slender, deciduous tree, to 13m. Bts red-brown with conspicuous yellow lenticels. Lv pinnate with 9–13 leaflets, up to 36cm long overall, each leaflet ovate acuminate, to 10cm long and half as wide, turning orange and scarlet in the autumn. Fl in axillary branched corymbs to 20cm long and wide. Fr a red berry. The fl have no beauty but the fr are attractive, although usually rather sparingly produced. Native of Japan, Korea, N China and the Himalaya. Introduced in 1890 from Japan.

PIERIS D. DON *Ericaceae*

One of the genera created when the all-embracing *Andromeda* was studied in depth. A genus of evergreen shrubs with, usually, alternate leaves and flowers in terminal panicles. The flowers are urceolate, usually white and somewhat resemble lily of the valley. The buds are actually produced in the autumn and pass through the winter in a dormant state, opening in early spring. Most of the asiatic species have very attractive young growth, but this is easily damaged by spring frosts and it is the prevalence of these, rather than low winter temperatures, which will decide whether the plants succeed in gardens or not. Like most ericaceous plants they require acid soil and ample humus. Layering is the easiest method to propagate good forms, but semi-hard stem cuttings with a heel are possible, although often slow to root. The plants flower within 3 years from seed. The genus is separated from *Lyonia* only by the presence of bristle-like awns on the anthers and magnification is necessary to observe these.

Pieris floribunda (PURSH) BENTHAM AND HOOKER

4. Slow-growing, evergreen shrub, to 2m, forming a mound-shaped bush with bristly bts. Lv elliptic-ovate, to 7cm long and 2·5cm across, dark glossy green above, paler and matt below, sparsely black-hairy on both surfaces. Fl in erect panicles to 12cm long, the panicles consisting of several separate racemes grouped together. Fl 3–4. 'Elongata' has longer panicles and flowers 4–5. Native of the south-eastern USA. Introduced by Lyon in 1800.

Pieris formosa D. DON

3.4. Large, evergreen shrub, to 7m but usually around 4m, spreading more widely. Young growths copper-coloured. Lv elliptic-lanceolate, to 15cm long and 5cm wide, leathery, dark glossy green. Fl in terminal panicles which droop, up to 15cm long and wide, white. Each fl to 1cm long. Fl 5. An attractive shrub, but it has now been largely superseded by **3.4.** var *forrestii* AIRY-SHAW, (*P. forrestii* HARROW). This is of slightly more erect growth, but is distinguished by the very brilliant red or crimson young growths which are more spectacular than the fl. These latter are similar to *P. formosa* but open about a fortnight earlier. Crossed with *P. japonica*, the resultant hybrid has been called 'Forest Flame'. This has the young growths red at first, but they fade to pink and almost white before turning green. It is said to be hardier than var *forrestii*, but the new growths are not quite as brilliant. The plant known as *P. japonica* 'Bert Chandler' seems very similar. The young growths start to emerge as the fl open and both are susceptible to spring frosts, so they should be planted where they are sheltered from an easterly air-stream. Good clones of var *forrestii* are 'Jermyns' and 'Wakehurst'. *P. formosa* is native to the eastern Himalaya and was in cultivation in 1858. Var *forrestii* was first introduced by Forrest from China in 1910. It is also found in Burma. 'Forest Flame' was introduced to commerce in 1957.

Pieris japonica (THUNBERG) D. DON

3.4. Usually a rather dwarf, mound-shaped shrub, but capable of reaching 3m eventually. Bts usually glabrous. Lv elliptic-obovate, to 9cm long and 2cm across, serrate, glabrous. Young growths copper-coloured. Fl in pendulous panicles to 15cm long. They are usually white but some pink forms exist, of which 'Blush' is the most easily obtainable. 'Variegata' has the lv variegated creamy-white, which shows pink on young lv. It is very slow-growing. Fl 3–4. The fl are often damaged by late frosts, but the lv unfurl considerably later and are usually unhurt. Native of Japan. In cultivation by 1870.

Pieris taiwanensis HAYATA

3.4. Shrub, to 3m, with bronzy young growth. Lv oval-elliptic, to 12cm long and 2·5cm across, glossy green above. Fl pure white, in terminal panicles which are more or less erect, which distinguishes it most easily from *P. japonica*. The panicles are up to 15cm long. Fl 3–4. Native of Formosa, but appears quite hardy. Introduced by Wilson in 1918.

PILEOSTEGIA JOSEPH HOOKER AND THOMSON
Hydrangeaceae

A small genus of climbing shrubs, of which only one is in general cultivation. Propagated by cuttings. Included by some in *Schizophragma*.

Pileostegia viburnoides HOOKER AND THOMSON

4. Evergreen climber attaching itself by means of aerial roots, up to 6m tall eventually. Lv opposite, leathery, oblong or ovate, tapered at both ends, to 15cm long and 6cm wide, dull green. Fl small, about 1cm across, in dense terminal panicles to 15cm long and wide, cream-coloured. Fl 9–10. Useful for its evergreen habit and late flowering; appears to thrive best on a wall. Native of India, China and Formosa. Introduced by Wilson from China in 1908.

PINUS LINNAEUS *Pinaceae* Pine

A large genus of evergreen trees and shrubs found from the Arctic to the Equator but not extending to the southern hemisphere. At first the trees tend to show the pyramidal form of so many conifers, with a whorl of branches radiating horizontally yearly. In older plants the lower branches tend to drop off and the tree becomes more or less flat-topped with a long trunk that is of much the same diameter throughout its length. The pines have two sorts of leaves; the scale leaves are found at the base of the current year's growth, are often fringed and soon fall, whereas the typical needles persist for two or more years. These needles are in bundles, typically of two, three or five, and the number of needles per bundle is a helpful diagnostic point in determining the species. The plants are monoecious; the male flowers appear in small clusters at the base of the year's growth, the female, usually at the end but sometimes clustered in a more or less haphazard way along the previous year's growth. They appear in late spring and early summer.

Pollination is effected by the wind, and once this has taken place the scales of the female flower close, but actual fertilisation does not take place until early summer of the next year. Once fertilised, the cone starts to swell, but it may take a further year or more to ripen by which time the branch has made from two to three years' growth, so that the cones are no longer terminal. Once ripe, the majority of cones open their scales and release the seeds, which are usually winged, but some species never open under normal conditions and distribution is either effected by animals, such as squirrels or birds, or must wait until the heat of a forest fire dries and opens the scales. The seeds are nut-like and some pines are grown for their edible seeds.

The majority of pines are montane plants and usually it is a pine that is found at the upper tree limit, but they are also found at sea level in such areas as the Mediterranean region and can be found on both alkaline and acid soils. Taking the genus as a whole, they are not usually very rapid growers, but are extremely long-lived if suited in soil and situation. They are generally intolerant of atmospheric pollution and most species require well-drained soil, although there are a few species which inhabit bogs in the wild. Generally it may be assumed that they require full light and a well-drained soil. Most species are usually tolerant of drought, but a few, of which *P. banksiana* is the most often seen, will do badly if frequently made to endure such conditions. Seed is much the most satisfactory method of propagation but cuttings will occasionally root while cv are usually grafted on to their type plants.

Pinus aristata ENGELMANN Bristle Cone Pine

A slow-growing small tree of up to 12m. Bts yellowish with reddish hairs. Lv in 5s to 3·5cm long, covered with white resinous exudations which gives the plant an unhealthy appearance. Cones to 9cm long, with a slender spine at the end of each scale. The longest-lived plant, trees in the wild are known to be 4,000 years old. *P. balfouriana* JEFFREY is similar, but the lv lack the resinous exudations and the cones are much larger – up to 12cm long. They have not, however, often been produced in the UK, if ever. *P. aristata* comes from the Rocky Mountains and was introduced in 1863. *P. balfouriana* is confined to two stations in California and was introduced by Jeffrey in 1852.

Pinus attenuata LEMMON

7. (*P. tuberculata* GORDON) A small tree, to 15m, sometimes with several trunks, with glabrous, light brown bts. Lv in 3s, to 18cm long (more usually about 10cm), grey-green in colour. Cones usually produced in whorls of 3 or more, usually narrowly conical, to 12cm long and 5cm across at the base. The scales on the upper side of the base of the cone develop small spine-tipped knobs. The cones are very loath to open and shed their seeds, and they will persist on the tree for up to 40 years. When first ripe they are tawny-yellow in colour. Native to most of the Californian mountains. Introduced by Hartweg in 1847.

Pinus ayacahuite EHRENBERG

7. Tree, to 30m, with thin smooth bark. Bts brown or greyish with orange hairs. Lv in 5s, grey-green, to 20cm long, usually persisting for 3 years. Cones from 15 to 45cm long and 6cm across before expanding; cylindrical in shape.

The forms with the smaller cones are said to be hardier. It seems generally to be hardy in most parts of the UK, although it is a native of Mexico where it is found at great heights. It was introduced by Hartweg in 1840.

Pinus banksiana LAMBERT

7. A tree to about 15m in cultivation but sometimes only a large bush. Young plants tend to have a rounded head rather than the pyramidal form of most pines, owing to the branches turning upwards in a marked manner. Lv in pairs, olive-green, slightly curved, to 3cm long. Cones somewhat curved and distorted, to 6cm long and 2·5cm across, tawny, remaining closed for many years and releasing the seeds gradually.

This tree requires acid soil, but is fairly distinct with its crooked brs and comparatively short needles. Native of much of eastern N America from the Arctic Circle to New York. In cultivation before 1785.

Pinus bungeana ZUCCARINI

(1).7. A tree, to 30m in the wild but little more than 15m in cultivation where it makes a handsome, pyramidal tree. Bark dull grey on trees under 50 years old, after which it is said to turn chalk white and be extremely effective. Lv in 3s, scattered rather sparsely, rigid and pointed, to 7cm long; dark green and smelling of turpentine when bruised. Cones rounded or egg-shaped, to 6cm long and wide with a short spine on each scale. It may well require rather mild conditions. Native of China. First introduced by Fortune in 1843.

Pinus cembra LINNAEUS Arolla Pine

7. A tree rarely exceeding 35m in cultivation, although taller in its native Alps. In this country it tends to make a rather narrowly-pyramidal tree, clothed to the ground. Bts covered with shaggy orange-brown wool, only found otherwise in *P. koraiensis* from which it differs in minor characteristics and which, at the moment, does not seem to be available commercially. Lv in 5s, very dense on the brs, rather rigid, bright green, to 8cm long. Cones erect, ovoid, purplish-brown, opening only as the result of a forest fire. Native of the Alps and of Siberia. Introduced in 1746 for the Duke of Argyll.

Pinus cembroides ZUCCARINI

A curiously variable small tree, rarely more than 7m high, with a rounded head. In the many var it can have its leaves singly (var *monophylla* TORREY AND FREMONT) or in 2s or 3s (var *edulis* ENGELMANN), occasionally in 4s or 5s, although the type usually has its needles in 3s. These needles are closely arranged, somewhat incurved, to 5cm long, dark green. Cones ovoid, to 6cm

long and wide, yellowish or reddish-brown. Seeds edible. Native of Arizona, California and Mexico. Introduced by Hartweg in 1839.

Pinus contorta DOUGLAS

7. The type is rather rare and is usually replaced by the var *latifolia* WATSON (*P. murrayana* BALFOUR), which is described here. Tree to 25m or more with reddish bark and short, twisted brs which are very characteristic. Needles in pairs, yellowish-green, rather twisted, to 7cm long. Cones to 6cm long, usually somewhat less; sometimes opening as soon as ripe, sometimes remaining closed for many years. This pine will not thrive in alkaline soils, but will grow in very sandy conditions and is sometimes used for stabilising sand dunes, although these are usually alkaline in reaction. It will also thrive in very dry conditions. It is a rather slow grower. Native of western N America. Var *latifolia* introduced by Jeffrey in 1853; the type probably received in 1855.

Pinus densiflora SIEBOLD AND ZUCCARINI

7. Tree, to 40m, with a reddish trunk that is often somewhat twisted. Bts glaucous and glabrous. Needles in pairs, dull green, to 10cm long, lasting about 4 years. Cones rather small, to 5cm long and 2·5cm wide, grey. Not easily distinguished from *P. sylvestris*. A favourite subject for Bonsai treatment. It requires acid or neutral soil. Native of Japan. Obtained by Siebold in 1854.

Pinus flexilis JAMES

7. An attractive tree, from 13 to 20m, with long pendulous brs on older specimens and extremely flexible young wood. Needles in 5s, persisting for some 7 years, crowded, forward-pointing, to 7cm long. Cones to 10cm long and 3·5cm across before opening, buff. Probably not suitable for alkaline soils. A rather rare tree in cultivation and slow-growing, but eventually very attractive. Native of the eastern slopes of the Rockies. Introduced by Jeffrey in 1851.

Pinus halepensis MILLER

7. A tree to rarely more than 45m in this country, with ashy grey bark on the brs and young trunks, but these later become reddish-brown. Bts glaucous grey and glabrous. Needles in pairs (but occasionally in 3s), slender, curved, to 10cm long. Cones pointing downwards or backwards, reddish, to 11cm long, sometimes remaining closed for many years. Var *brutia* (TENORE) ELWES AND HENRY (*P. brutia* TENORE) has longer needles, to 15cm, green bts and the cones point forwards and are sometimes borne in whorls. The plants are somewhat tender when young, but older trees are perfectly hardy. They

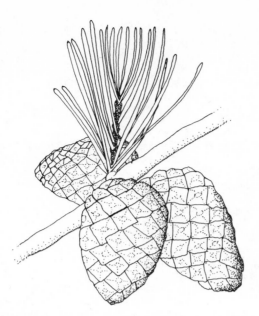

Pinus halepensis

will thrive on calcareous soils and in districts with low rainfall where drought may be expected. Native of the Mediterranean region and Portugal. First grown by Bishop Compton in 1683.

Pinus jeffreyi MURRAY

See below under *P. ponderosa*.

Pinus lambertiana DOUGLAS

7. A tree of up to 80m in the wild and up to 35m in the UK. Needles in 5s, bluish-green, spirally twisted at the base, to 11cm long. Cones at first erect, later pendent, to 45cm long and 7cm across before expanding. These enormous cones are not produced with great freedom even in the wild and only on mature trees; in cultivation cones are rather exceptional. The tree is shallow rooting but thrives best in rather mild and moist conditions; it tends to do best in the western parts of the UK, although it does fairly well in the midlands. Native of western N America, whence it was introduced by Douglas in 1827.

Pinus massoniana LAMBERT

7. A tree from 10 to 25m high, with reddish bark like that of *P. sylvestris*. Needles in pairs, light or dark green, to 20cm long. Cones to 6cm long, brown, not persisting for long. Some strains appear to be tender, others appear quite hardy. Native of south-east China. Introduced in 1824.

Pinus montezumae LAMBERT

7. A remarkably lovely tree, but of rather dubious hardiness, although many quite old specimens exist. Bark reddish-brown as are the

Pinus lambertiana

bts, which are glabrous. Needles usually in 5s, but all numbers from 3 to 8 have been noted, and in var *hartwegii* (LINDLEY) ENGELMANN (*P. hartwegii* LINDLEY), which is the hardiest form, they are usually in 4s. They are up to 25cm long on the type, about 15cm long in var *hartwegii*. Cones of var *hartwegii* are bluish when immature, later dark brown or almost black, to 6cm long. In the type the cones may be as long as 20cm. Although extreme winter cold is sometimes damaging, it is spring frosts that do most damage, making the tree unsuitable for places where these are frequent. Where it can be expected to survive it is well worth growing as one of the most attractive of evergreens. Native of Mexico. Introduced by Hartweg in 1839.

Pinus monticola DOUGLAS

7. A rather slow-growing, long-lived tree, to at least 30m in cultivation and up to 55m in the wild. Bark grey-brown. Bts with reddish down. Needles in 5s, glaucous, stiff, dense, persisting 3–4 years, to 10cm long. Cones erect at first, later pendulous, green or purple before ripening, finally buff, to 20cm long and 3cm across, sometimes curved at the tip. The cone opens as soon as it is ripe. The plant requires acid soil and is closely allied to *P. strobus*. It is not suitable for dry districts. Native of the western slopes of the Rockies. Introduced by Douglas in 1831.

Pinus mugo TURRA

(*P. montana* MILLER) A plant of the most varying habits, from sprawling shrubs to tall trees (var *rostrata* HOOPES, sometimes given specific rank as *P. uncinata* RAMOND). Bark blackish-grey. Needles in pairs, dark green, curved, very rigid and prickly, to 7cm long. Cones light brown, to 5cm long. The most usually-seen form is a sprawling shrub, to 3m (var *mughus* or var *pumilio*), which has a number of erect stems from which lateral whorls radiate and which spread sideways rather than extending upwards. The plants grow in the most unpromising soil, but are not among the most ornamental pines. Native of the Alps and Pyrenees and eastwards to Yugoslavia.

Pinus nigra ARNOLD   Corsican Pine

7. (*P. laricio* POIRET) A very variable tree, to 40m, of which two forms are commonly grown as the austrian pine and the corsican pine. The austrian pine (forma *austriaca* (HOESS) ASCHERS) makes a tree to 40m, pyramidal when young, later flat-headed. The bts are yellowish-brown. The whorls of the brs are densely produced and in their turn produce lateral whorls. Needles in pairs, to 15cm long, very dark green, rigid, usually straight, with a horny point. Cones pale brown, either solitary or in clusters, to 7cm long and 3cm across.

163

The corsican pine, var *maritima (calabrica)*, is characterised by its pale brown bark, its more erect habit, its more widely spaced whorls of brs and its fewer lateral whorls. The lv are also less rigid and less dense on the brs.

Although rather sombre in appearance, *P. nigra* is useful for its tolerance not only of chalky soils but also of very sandy soil and its ability to withstand sea spray. It is very useful as a plant for shelter belts, but should be put in its permanent position as a very small tree as large specimens will not move successfully. The allied *P. leucodermis* ANTOINE, with glaucous bts and slightly more glaucous needles, is perhaps to be preferred if it can be obtained. *P. nigra* is found from Spain to the Caucasus. Introduced about 1814.

Pinus parviflora SIEBOLD AND ZUCCARINI

7. Tree, to 16m, with thin greyish bark and greyish, faintly downy bts. Needles in 5s, with silvery lines on the inner surface, slender and curved, to 7cm long, persisting 3–4 years. In the var *glauca* BEISSNER the bts are pale and shining, while the lv are stiffer and more glaucous. Cones erect, egg-shaped, often in whorls, to 6cm long and 3cm across, soon opening but long persistent. Probably happier in acid soil. A very suitable pine for small gardens as it never gets very large and is fairly slow-growing. Young trees are pyramidal, but mature trees develop a wide, flat head. Native of Japan. Introduced by J. G. Veitch in 1861.

Pinus pinaster AITON

7. (*P. maritima* POIRET) A tree, to 30m or more, with a long, bare trunk in old specimens. Bark dark red-brown, deeply fissured in mature trees. Bts pale brown and glabrous. Needles in pairs, very stout and rigid, slightly curved, to 15cm long with a hard, horny apex. Cones often in clusters, from 12 to 18cm long, shining brown, often remaining several years before opening. An excellent tree for light and sandy soils, often used for stabilising dunes but not successful on heavy land or on clay. It is also not particularly hardy and does best in the UK near the coast, where it thrives admirably. Native of the Mediterranean region.

Pinus pinea LINNAEUS

Umbrella Pine, Stone Pine

7. A very attractive tree, pyramidal at first but soon developing a rounded head of characteristic umbrella shape. Bark reddish-grey with deep fissures on older trees. Bts grey-green at first, glabrous, later pale brown. Needles in pairs, dark lustrous green, slightly twisted, to 15cm long. Cones erect, ovoid, to 15cm long and 10cm across, shining brown, ripening in the third

year. The seeds are the pine kernels of the delicatessen trade. As with the corsican pine, large plants do not transplant well and young plants should be moved every two years until they are placed in their final position. Severe frosts injure the plant, even in the wild. Native of the Mediterranean region and Portugal.

Pinus ponderosa DOUGLAS

7. A tree to 35m and more (70m in the wild), with yellowish or dark brown bark. Brs drooping at first but ascending at the extremities, to give a columnar appearance. Bts orange-brown at first, later nearly black, with a fragrance of oranges when bruised. Needles in 3s, dense on the brs, rigid and curved, to 25cm long, dark green. Cones very variable in size, from 7 to 20cm long and from 6 to 10cm across, light reddish-brown, with a short prickle on the scales. *P. jeffreyi* MURRAY is similar in appearance but differs in having lighter red bark, glaucous bts, needles bluish-green, cones to 25cm long and 11cm across. Both are natives of western N America. *P. ponderosa* was introduced by Douglas in 1827; *P. jeffreyi* by Jeffrey in 1853.

Pinus radiata D. DON Monterey Pine

7. Tree, to 35m. Bark dark brown and fissured in old specimens. Bts yellowish-brown, glabrous. Needles in 3s, rich grass-green, slender and soft, set very densely and persisting 3–4 years, to 15cm long. Cones solitary or in whorls, asymmetrically ovoid, 7–15cm long and 6–8cm wide, bright brown, not opening for several years as a rule unless seared by a forest fire, but sometimes opening naturally after 2 years. The plant seems to do best on acid soil and near the coast in the south and west of the UK, although good specimens can be seen inland. In places where it is suited it grows with great rapidity – as much as 1m per year. Although sea winds appear to do the plant no harm at all, inland it can be browned by freezing winds. Like so many of this genus, it should be planted out when about 50cm high. It is a plant that has been preserved by introduction to cultivation. It is confined in the wild to a small area near Monterey, California, where it is only just holding its own. As a forest tree it has been much planted in many countries, notably Australia, New Zealand and S Africa, so there are many more trees in cultivation than exist in the wild. Introduced by Douglas in 1833.

Pinus strobus LINNAEUS Weymouth Pine

7. Trees of rarely more than 27m in cultivation but up to 50m in the wild. Bark greyish, fissured in old trees. Bts with tufts of down below the leaf bundles, otherwise glabrous. Needles in 5s, to 12cm long, bluish-green, slender, lasting 2–3 years. Cones pendulous, cylindric, often curved, to 15cm long and 2·5cm across. An attractive tree, but not particularly easy, requiring open acid soil with no possibility of even temporary waterlogging. Unlike the last sp, it will tolerate cold winds inland, but not winds off the sea. If conditions are unsatisfactory it is liable to be infested by various insect pests. Native of Canada and the western USA. Introduced about 1705.

Pinus sylvestris LINNAEUS Scots Pine

1.7. Tree, to 35m, pyramidal when young but later branching only at the top of the trunk and flat-headed. Bark reddish at the top of the trunk, greyish-brown and fissured into plates at the base. Bts green and glabrous. Needles in pairs, stiff, twisted, grey-green, 3–10cm long, persisting for about 3 years. Cones, ovoid, greyish, to 7cm long. 'Argentea' has markedly glaucous lv, while the slow-growing 'Aurea' has lv which turn yellow during the winter and back to grey-green in the summer. The tree does best on fairly light soil but is not hard to please, although it is less resistant to extreme wind than *P. nigra*. Small plants get away much more rapidly than larger specimens. Native to most of Europe, including Great Britain, eastwards to Siberia and the Amur river.

Pinus tabulaeformis CARRIÈRE

7. (*P. sinensis* MAYR but not of LAMBERT) A tree of varying habit, sometimes pyramidal to 25m, in other instances a low gnarled tree with a flat head. Bark on the trunk grey, but reddish on the main brs and pale orange on laterals. Bts glaucous and glabrous. Needles in pairs or in 3s, sometimes both counts are found on the same tree; erect or slightly spreading, somewhat glaucous, to 15cm long. Cones egg-shaped, to 5cm long, tawny-yellow at first, later dark brown, persisting for several years. The attractive var *yunnanensis* DALLIMORE (*P. yunnanensis* FRANCHET) is very distinct with its lv always in 3s, drooping, to 25cm long and cones to 8cm long. This is the longest-needled pine that is hardy in all places. The type is native to much of China and Korea, var *yunnanensis* is confined to western China and Tibet. The type was introduced about 1862; var *yunnanensis* by Wilson in 1909.

Pinus thunbergii PARLATORE

7. A tree, to 35m in the wild, with greyish-brown, deeply-fissured bark on the trunk, orange-red on the brs. Bts light brown and glabrous. The winter buds are a very conspicuous ash-white. The brs are of unequal length, sometimes slightly pendulous, so that the tree has often a rather irregular appearance, although basically it is pyramidal. Needles in pairs, crowded, rigid, bright green, to 10cm long. Cones sometimes solitary, sometimes in immense clusters of 40

or more, conical, nut-brown, up to 6cm long. A good plant for light soils and even for pure sand. Native of Japan. Introduced by J. G. Veitch in 1861.

Pinus virginiana MILLER

(7). At its best a tree to 15m, but sometimes only a scrubby bush. Bts purple, with a waxy bloom which later disappears, glabrous. Needles in pairs, rigid and slightly twisted, to 6cm long, persisting for 3 years. Cones conical, to 6cm long and 3cm across, with minute prickles at the apex of the scales. Unique in its purple bts but otherwise little valued as a garden ornament. Native of eastern N America from New York to Alabama. Introduced by John Bartram in 1739.

Pinus wallichiana A. B. JACKSON

7. (*P. excelsa* WALLICH, *P. griffithii* MCCLELLAND) Tree, from 15 to 50m, of elegant habit with the lower brs horizontal, the upper ones ascending somewhat. Bark smooth and grey-brown. Branchlets glaucous and glabrous. Needles in 5s, persisting 3–4 years, erect at first, later drooping, 12–20cm long, grey-green. Cones erect the first year, pendulous the second, cylindrical, to 25cm long and 5cm across, on stalks to 5cm long, light brown. One of the best spp for gardens, making rapid growth of up to 1m a year in suitable conditions, which are a good sandy loam and shelter from wind. Like so many pines, it should be put in its permanent position when a young plant not more than 60cm high. Native of the Himalaya from Afghanistan to Nepal. Sent by Wallich to A. B. Lambert in 1823.

PIPTANTHUS DON *Leguminosae*

A small genus of about six species of evergreen and deciduous shrubs, native to the Himalalya and eastern Asia.

Piptanthus laburnifolius STAPF

4. (*P. nepalensis* SWEET) Evergreen or semi-evergreen shrub, to 4m or more if grown against a wall. Lv trifoliate, alternate, each leaflet to 15cm long and 5cm wide, lanceolate, silky when young, later dark green and glabrous, set on a petiole to 5cm long. Fl in erect, terminal racemes to 7cm long and wide. Each fl pea-shaped, bright yellow, to 3·5cm long. Fl 5. Fr a pod to 12cm long. Requires the protection of a south or west-facing wall in most districts, where it may survive for some years. It seems naturally to be rather short-lived. Easily propagated by seeds, but they should be sowed singly and the young plants put early in their final position as they are somewhat resentful of root disturbance. Native of the Himalaya. Introduced through Wallich in 1821.

165

Piptanthus laburnifolius

PISTACIA LINNAEUS *Anacardiaceae*

A small genus with a very peculiar distribution, the majority of species being around the Mediterranean, but there are also species in China, Mexico and Texas. The plants have no beauty of flower and, although the fruits may be attractive, the plants are dioecious and therefore the fruits are only produced where both sexes are present. However, the emerging leaves are usually attractively coloured, while the one reliably hardy species also has brilliant autumn colour in most districts.

Pistacia chinensis BUNGE

3.6.(7). Tree, to 25m in the wild, usually a large shrub to 7m in the UK. Lv peach-coloured when young, pinnate, to 22cm long with 10–12 leaflets; the presence of a terminal leaflet is occasional. Each leaflet is obliquely ovate-lanceolate, to 8cm long and 1·5cm wide, often colouring crimson before falling. Fl, lacking petals, in terminal panicles; male panicles to 7cm long, female to 22cm long. Fl 4. Fr a small berry, red at first, then blue-purple. Native of China. Received at Kew in 1897, but probably in cultivation some few years before.

PLANERA GMELIN *Ulmaceae*

A monotypic genus.

Planera aquatica (WALTER) GMELIN

Small deciduous tree, to 12m, with spreading brs. Bts somewhat pubescent. Lv alternate, oval, to 7cm long and half as wide, toothed, hispid, somewhat tomentose below at first. Fl monoecious, inconspicuous, axillary, in small clusters. Fr a small nut with warty processes on the shell, about 8cm across. A swamp plant in the wild and therefore useful for planting in wet situations, but otherwise not outstanding. Native of the south-eastern USA. Introduced in 1816.

PLATANUS LINNAEUS *Platanaceae*

A small genus of deciduous trees with exfoliating bark, alternate leaves and flowers in globose heads, which are monoecious. Very tolerant of a polluted atmosphere and easily propagated by cuttings or layers.

Platanus X hispanica MUENCHAUSEN

London Plane

7. (*P. X acerifolia* WILLDENOW) A hybrid between *P. orientalis* and *P. occidentalis*, this makes a tree of up to 35m with a rounded head. The bark peels off yearly in plates to disclose a smooth surface to the trunk. Bts and young lv brown tomentose at first. Lv basically cordate but 5-lobed, the lobes up to half as long as the lamina; lv to 25cm across, slightly less in length. Fl in balls, from 2–6 on a stalk, to 10cm long; each inflorescence about 3cm in diameter. A small percentage of the seeds are fertile and seedlings show considerable variation in leaf shape. 'Suttneri' has the lv variegated creamy-white and is somewhat slow-growing. 'Pyramidalis' is a fastigiate form. It has been suggested that the hybrid most likely originated in the Tradescants' famous garden at Lambeth and was thence sent to Oxford by Elias Ashmole. It seems to have been first noticed there about 1663. We know that the Tradescants grew both the putative parents and so it is not improbable. Other authorities consider that it arose in France or Spain about 1650.

Platanus occidentalis LINNAEUS

Although a tree to 50m in its native USA, this is a very unsatisfactory plant in British gardens. it is distinguished from *P. X hispanica* and *P. orientalis* by its shallowly lobed lv and the fact that there is usually only one inflorescence on each stalk, occasionally two. Native of the eastern USA. Introduced probably by the younger Tradescant, in 1636.

Platanus orientalis LINNAEUS

7. Tree, to 35m, with the trunk occasionally 6m in diameter and a wide, spreading head. Bts brown tomentose at first, later glabrous. Lv

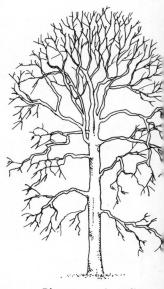

Platanus orientalis (profile)

silky tomentose at first, later smooth, palmate, to 25cm wide and long with 5–7 lobes, to about half the length of the blade. Inflorescences 2–6 per stalk. This is much slower-growing than the hybrid plant, but otherwise distinct in its more deeply lobed lv and its different silhouette. A very long-lived tree, there are traditions of plants up to 2,000 years old. Native of the eastern Mediterranean region; certainly cultivated since the sixteenth century.

POLIOTHYRSIS OLIVER *Flacourtiaceae*
A monotypic genus.

Poliothyrsis sinensis OLIVER
4.(7). Slender, deciduous tree, to 15m in the wild. Lv ovate, long-acuminate, rounded at base, to 15cm long and 12cm across, downy below. Fl in terminal panicles, monoecious, but both sexes on the same panicle, lacking petals; greenish-white at first, later yellow. Fl 7. Fr a dry capsule. Native of China. Introduced by Wilson in 1908.

POLYGONUM LINNAEUS *Polygonaceae*
A large genus of mainly herbaceous plants with a fairly cosmopolitan distribution. The only species to interest us are two deciduous climbers, by some put in a separate genus – *Bilderdykia*. Of easiest cultivation; propagated by seed, cuttings or by layers.

Polygonum aubertii LOUIS HENRY
4. (*Bilderdykia aubertii*) Vigorous, deciduous climber, to 15m. Lv hastate, alternate, to 9cm long and 5cm across, reddish when young, later bright green. Fl in dense, terminal panicles from lateral shoots, white or greenish-white, becoming pinkish when fading. The stems of the panicle slightly rough to the touch. Fl 7–9. Native of China. Introduced in 1899. Often supplied in place of the next species.

Polygonum baldschuanicum REGAL
Russian Vine
4. (*Bilderdykia baldschuanicum*) Differs from the last sp in its paler, slightly larger lv, in its pink fl and in the stems of the panicle being smooth to the touch. Both spp ascend by twining and may make as much as 7m growth in a single season. The individual fl are tiny but produced in abundance so that the general effect is spectacular. Native of SE Russia, notably the Bokhara region. Introduced from St Petersburg in 1894, probably introduced to St Petersburg by its discoverer Regel in 1883.

PONCIRUS RAFINESQUE *Rutaceae*
A monotypic genus.

Poncirus trifoliata (LINNAEUS) RAFINESQUE
4.(5). (*Aegle sepiaria* DE CANDOLLE, *Citrus trifoliata* LINNAEUS) Deciduous shrub, to 4m but usually little more than 2m, with very spiny brs. Lv rather sparse, trifoliate (occasionally with 5 leaflets), each leaflet obovate, the centre 1–5cm long, the two laterals half as long, dark glossy green. Fl solitary from the spine axils, white, patulate, fragrant, to 5cm across. Fl 5. Fr like a small orange, to 5cm diameter, green with yellow shading. Interesting as being the hardiest member of the orange family and both fl and fr are handsome, but rather sparsely produced. Native of northern China and long cultivated in Japan. Introduced in 1850.

POPULUS LINNAEUS *Salicaceae* Poplar
A genus of around thirty-five species of deciduous trees, usually rapid growing, with alternate leaves. They are usually dioecious, the flowers coming before the leaves in the form of catkins and hybridisation, either chance or deliberate, is a common phenomenon. Many of the species are useful for their tolerance of waterlogged situations. They are shallow-rooted and the roots will travel for long distances and are very persistent in their search for water, so that the plants should not be planted near houses, where the roots are liable to penetrate drainage and other underground pipes. Generally, poplars come very easily from hardwood cuttings, which are inserted in the open ground in autumn. Some of the aspens are less likely to respond so well to this treatment and half-ripe cuttings are usually more successful. The poplars are generally divided into four or five sections.

The balsam poplars, *Tacamahaca* SPACH section, are characterised by furrowed bark, large, viscid, fragrant buds and young leaves, whitish beneath but glabrous; these are the first to come into leaf.

The white poplars, *Leuce* DUBY section, include the aspens, which are sometimes put into a separate section. The *Leuce* section has smooth bark, although in old trees it may be rough at the base of the trunk. The leaves of the aspens have flattened petioles. The leaves are generally tomentose on the underside. The white poplars can also be increased by detaching sucker growths, which they tend to produce in large numbers. The *Leucoides* SPACH section differs from the above in their rough, scaly bark and less hairy leaves. The black poplars, *Aegeiros* DUBY section, are the last to come into leaf, the young leaves are often copper coloured and the catkins are usually large and handsome. They have a furrowed bark and viscid winter buds and the leaves are green on both surfaces and usually glabrous. These revel in damp conditions and they will not thrive in dry, sandy or chalky soils.

Populus alba LINNAEUS *Leuce* White Poplar

2.7. Tree, to 20m and occasionally more, but larger trees are more likely to be *P. canescens* (qv), suckering freely. Bts white tomentose, as are the young lv, the mature lv remain white tomentose below until they fall. Lv variable in shape, some 3–5-lobed like a maple, usually more or less heart-shaped; as is usual in most poplars, the lv on leading shoots are larger than those on secondary growths. The lv often turn yellow before falling (and, according to Bean, 'fiery red' occasionally). The large lv are up to 12cm long, those on the secondary growths about 5cm long. A handsome tree, particularly when the lv are disturbed by wind to reveal their white undersides. Quite happy on chalk. Native of most of N Europe, but possibly not England, where it is replaced by *P. canescens*.

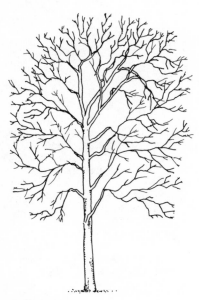

Populus alba (profile)

Populus balsamifera LINNAEUS *Tacamahaca*
Balsam Poplar

7. (*P. tacamahaca* MILLER) Tree, to about 17m in cultivation, suckering freely. Winter buds sticky and balsamic, while the unfolding lv diffuse an agreeable odour around them. Brs erect. Lv cordate-acuminate, dark shining green above, whitish and conspicuously net-veined beneath, usually glabrous but if somewhat hairy they are often referred to as var *michauxii* FARWELL. Male and female catkins to 7cm long. *P. candicans* AITON, which is only known as a female tree, is thought to be a hybrid between this sp and *P. deltoides*. It is distinguished by its more spreading habit, the bts may be slightly angled, not circular, and are always downy, whereas those of *P. balsamifera* are glabrous. The lv are generally longer, up to 16cm as opposed to the 12cm of *P. balsamifera*. 'Aurora' has lv variegated cream in spring and early summer. *P. balsamifera* is native to eastern N America and was in cultivation in 1696. *P. candicans*, according to *Hortus Kewensis*, was brought from Canada by Dr John Hope in 1772.

Populus canescens SMITH *Leuce*

(6).7. Suckering tree, to 30m, with an attractive smooth grey trunk. Very close to *P. alba* but bts and undersides of lv grey, not white, and the tomentum has usually dropped before the lv do; lv occasionally turn red before falling. The lv are never lobed as in *P. alba*, but roundish or ovate, to 10cm long on strong shoots and half that on laterals, all round-toothed. Male catkins are reddish and up to 10cm long. 'Macrophylla' has lv to 15cm long. Native of northern Europe, including southern Britain.

Populus deltoides MARSHALL *Aegeiros*
Cottonwood

7. (*P. monilifera* AITON) A tree that is now rare in cultivation, having been replaced by its hybrids with *P. nigra*, which are known as *P. X canadensis* MOENCH, or as hybrid black poplars. The true *P. deltoides* is a tree to 30m with erect, spreading brs. Bts either slightly angled or round, winter buds sticky. Lv almost triangular (deltoid), acuminate, coarsely toothed, to 12cm long and broad, bright green on both surfaces. Male catkins to 10cm long, female to 20cm. Like all the black poplars female plants cover the ground with cottony tufts in summer.

P. angulata AITON has markedly ribbed bts and large heart-shaped lv to 17cm long and 12cm across, but does not seem to differ very greatly otherwise from the southern form of *P. deltoides* (var *missouriensis* HENRY). *P. X canadensis* MOENCH much resembles *P. nigra* (qv), but usually more vigorous. Some, such as 'Eugenei', have attractive copper-coloured young lv. *P. deltoides* is native to the eastern side of N America and was introduced from Canada by Dr Hope in 1772, but probably had arrived in France before then as the first form of *P. X canadensis* is thought to have originated in France about 1750. *P. angulata* was grown by Miller before 1738 and may well be a Bartram sending. It is, of course, possible that the first *P. X canadensis* was *P. nigra* X *P. angulata*.

Populus koreana REHDER *Tacamahaca*

7. Tree, to 25m in the wild, with pale brown bts. Lv elliptic-ovate, with a twisted point, dark green and wrinkled above, whitish beneath with a conspicuous red midrib, coming into lv very early in the spring. Male catkins to 5cm long, female to 14cm. An attractive tree, but possibly liable to damage by late spring frosts. Native of S Korea. Introduced by Wilson in 1918.

Populus lasiocarpa OLIVER *Leucoides*

7. Round-headed tree, to 20m. Bts angled somewhat, tomentose at first. Lv cordate, acuminate, to 25cm long and 20cm wide (occasionally on young plants lv up to 35cm long and 22cm wide have been noted), downy on both surfaces at first, later glabrous above and bright green, lighter below and always slightly pubescent. Petiole and midrib a rich red; the petiole to 10cm long. Male catkins to 9cm long, female to 24cm and very striking. A remarkable tree with its huge lv with their conspicuous red midribs, but not a very rapid grower. Native of central and western China. Introduced by Wilson in 1900.

Populus lasiocarpa

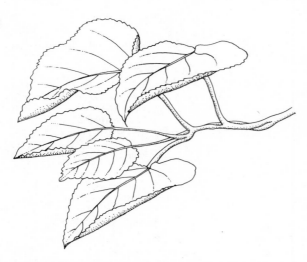

Populus nigra (profile)

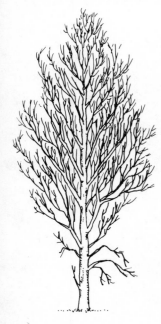

Populus laurifolia LEDEBOUR *Tacamahaca*

7. Tree, to about 20m, with pendulous brs and angled bts, which are grey pubescent at first. Lv lanceolate or elliptic-lanceolate, acuminate, serrate, dark green and glabrous above, grey and slightly tomentose beneath with conspicuous net veins, to 12cm long and 5cm across. Male catkins erect at first, to 5cm long. Native of Siberia and the Altai mountains. Introduced about 1830.

Populus nigra LINNAEUS *Aegeiros*
Black Poplar   Lombardy Poplar

7. Rapid-growing tree, to 35m, with wide-spreading brs. Trunk very rugged, often with large burrs on the surface. Bts glabrous, rounded and orange in colour, sometimes quite conspicuous in winter. (In var *betulifolia* TORREY the bts, as well as petioles and young lv, are pubescent.) Lv variable in shape, some being rhombic, some almost triangular, others ovate, to

11cm long and sometimes much wider; the young lv are usually copper coloured. The mature lv are green and glabrous on both surfaces with toothed margins. Male catkins with deep red anthers to 7cm long. 'Italica' is a fastigiate form known as the lombardy poplar, which can reach over 40m. The true 'Italica' is a male plant, but there is also a female form which is not quite as slender as the male. 'Plantierensis' is another fastigiate form, with pubescent bts, which seems slightly more vigorous in this country and is tending to replace the true lombardy poplar. It is difficult to distinguish between the true *P. nigra* and plants of the *P. X canadensis* group. The only sure differences are the absence of marginal hairs and basal glands on the lv. Plants of the *Canadensis* group have one or both of these characters. *P. nigra* is native to northern Europe including the UK.

Populus szechuanica SCHNEIDER *Tacamahaca*

3.7. Tree, to 30m or more in the wild, slightly angled, glabrous bts (pubescent in var *tibetica* SCHNEIDER), purplish-brown at first, later yellowish-brown. Young lv reddish in colour. Mature lv cordate, acuminate, to 22cm long and 12cm across, bright green above, pale grey below, often with crimson midrib. Another very large-leafed chinese poplar, which is quick growing but liable to damage by late spring frosts. Native of western China. Introduced by Wilson in 1907.

Populus tremula LINNAEUS *Leuce* Aspen

7. Tree, to about 17m, often suckering and doing best in very damp, almost swampy, conditions. Lv tomentose when young, slowly becoming glabrous, often turning yellow in late autumn. Lv ovate or orbicular, grey-green, to 10cm across on most brs but up to twice as long on vigorous growths. Petiole slender but flattened, so as to be responsive to the slightest breeze. Male catkins grey, to 10cm long. Native of Europe, western Asia and N Africa.

Populus trichocarpa WILLIAM HOOKER
Tacamahaca

7. Pyramidal tree, to 60m in the wild but probably to only 30m or more in the UK. Unlike most of the section, the bark, particularly in young trees, is smooth and peels off yearly. It is yellowish-grey in colour. Bts slightly angled, pubescent at first, but soon glabrous. Lv ovate or cordate, acuminate, serrate, up to 25cm long on vigorous growths, but only to 5cm long on short twigs. Dark green above, shining white (occasionally rust-coloured) beneath. The lv usually turn a good yellow in the autumn. Catkins to 6cm long.

The plant grows very rapidly, often increasing

in height at an average of 60cm per year, but is prone to canker in unfavourable districts and is perhaps well replaced by *P. X generosa* HENRY. This is a hybrid between *P. angulata* (see under *P. deltoides*) and *P. trichocarpa*, raised at Kew in 1912. This is an exceptionally vigorous tree; growths of 2m per year are not uncommon and Bean records growths of 4m in a year. The tree retains the balsamic odour of the *Tacamahaca* group; has glabrous, grey-green, very slightly angled bts. Lv triangular-ovate, pale green above, grey beneath, up to 30cm long and 25cm wide on vigorous growths, about 10cm long and 8cm wide on less vigorous growths. They usually turn a clear yellow before falling. Male catkins with reddish anthers, to 12cm long, appearing in April. *P. trichocarpa* is native to western N America and Mexico and was only introduced to cultivation in 1892.

Populus violascens DODE *Leucoides*

7. Tree, to 20m, closely related to *P. lasiocarpa* but with more vigorous growth and smaller, oblong-ovate or elliptic-ovate lv to 15cm long, green above, but somewhat white hairy below, particularly on the veins. The petiole and midrib are violet in colour. Native of China. Introduced in 1921.

Populus wilsonii SCHNEIDER *Leucoides*

7. Tree, to 25m in the wild, of pyramidal shape. Bts olive-brown at first, later purplish. Lv cordate, serrate, to 22cm long and 17cm wide, blue-green above, at first rusty tomentose below, later pale grey and nearly glabrous. Only the female plant seems to be in cultivation and this has catkins to 15cm long, with extremely woolly ovaries at first. Native of western and central China. Introduced by Wilson in 1907.

Populus yunnanensis DODE *Tacamahaca*

7. Tree, of up to about 15–20m as far as is known, with strongly angled bts which are green at first, but later turn brown. Lv elliptic-ovate or obovate, to 15cm long and half as wide, vivid green above, almost white beneath, glabrous. The short petiole (usually less than 2cm) and the midrib are often red, suggesting a kinship to *P. lasiocarpa*, which is, in fact, erroneous. Native of Yunnan. Sent by Père Ducloux to Dode before 1905.

POTENTILLA LINNAEUS *Rosaceae*

A genus of five species throughout the northern hemisphere, of which only one or two species are shrubby. The main suffruticose species, *P. fruticosa*, has such an extensive distribution that it was formerly divided up into numerous species, partly dependent upon flower colour and partly upon geographical distribution. These have now been reduced, by most authorities, to varietal rank. Nevertheless, the rather dwarf plants, characterised by brown stipules at the base of the petioles, are often placed as forms of *P. arbuscula* D. DON. These are mainly Himalayan in origin and too dwarf for inclusion here, although they have been hybridised with forms of *P. fruticosa*; 'Elizabeth' is the best-known of these hybrids. The attractive-sounding *P. salesoviana*, with cymes of white, pink-tinted flowers, is not, so far as I can discover, still in cultivation. *P. fruticosa* is easily propagated by cuttings or by seed.

Potentilla fruticosa LINNAEUS
Shrubby Cinquefoil

4. A very variable, deciduous shrub, usually making a rounded bush which can attain 1·5m but is usually somewhat less. Lv pinnate, but appearing digitate, with 3–7 leaflets, 5 being the most usual count. Leaflets lanceolate, to 2·5cm long and 6mm wide, grey-green above, grey-silky below. Fl at ends of lateral twigs, usually solitary, like a small wild rose, bright yellow, pale yellow or white. Two rather dwarf cv, 'Sunset' and 'Tangerine', have coppery or orange fl. 'Friedrichsenii' is a very vigorous yellow form, sometimes reaching 2m. Almost as vigorous is 'Vilmoriniana', with cream fl and very silvery lv, – arguably the most attractive of the taller cv. Fl 5–9. Native to northern parts of Europe, Asia and America. Requires full light and resents drought, but otherwise remarkably trouble free and with a very long flowering season. The main display is usually about June.

PRINSEPIA ROYLE *Rosaceae*

A small genus of deciduous shrubs, the branches armed with spines and with lamellate pith, which is the chief distinction between this genus and *Prunus*. The leaves are alternate. They are not particularly conspicuous in their flowers, but these open very early in the year and so may be regarded as valuable. The fruits are also ornamental, but very rarely produced in the UK. Propagation is by seed or by cuttings of half-ripe wood. Three species are in cultivation, but *P. utilis* is rather too tender for inclusion.

Prinsepia sinensis OLIVER

4.(5). (*Plagiospermum sinensis* OLIVER) Deciduous, spreading shrub, to 2m, with stiff, short spines just above the lv. Lv oblong-lanceolate, to 7cm long but only 1cm across, produced singly on the current year's growth, in clusters of 2–4 on older wood. Fl produced from the axils as the lv unfurl, usually singly, 5-petalled, much like a small plum blossom, bright yellow, about 2cm across. Fl 3–4. Fr red, about 15mm in diameter. Native of northern China and

Manchuria. In cultivation in 1896 according to Rehder.

Prinsepia uniflora BATALIN

4.(5). Deciduous, spreading shrub, to 2m, with grey bts. Lv linear, to 5cm long but only 8mm across, pointed and sparsely toothed at the base; dark green above, paler beneath. Fl from axils of year-old wood, sometimes singly, occasionally in clusters of 3–4, white, about 1·5cm across. Fl 4–5. Fr globular, red at first, later dark purple, 8mm in diameter. Native of northern China. Introduced by Purdom in 1911.

PRUNUS LINNAEUS *Rosaceae*

A large genus of some 430 species of both evergreen and deciduous trees and shrubs with alternate leaves, with stipules at their base, flowers with five petals and a one-seeded drupe as the fruit. In most of the species the fruit have the stone surrounded by a fleshy layer, but in the case of the almond, *P. dulcis*, this becomes dry when the fruit is ripe and splits open. All the species flower early in the season and the flowers are usually either white or pink, occasionally the pink is so deep as to be more correctly described as red. A number of hybrids, particularly of japanese cherries, and cultivars swell the list of available garden ornaments, but most of these will only be briefly alluded to in the following pages. They can be propagated by seed, by half-ripe cuttings or by grafting. Most species appreciate an alkaline soil and require full exposure to the sun. In many districts birds may damage the flower buds before they can expand, but where this does not happen the various species and hybrids are among the most floriferous and conspicuous of all spring trees, while many of the deciduous species also have gay autumn tints.

The genus is divided for purposes of identification into five subgenera:

1 *Prunophora* FOCKE, the plums, characterised by the absence of a terminal bud and axillary flowers which are either solitary or in small clusters. The fruit is often bloomy and the stone is furrowed. The flowers appear before the leaves.
2 *Amygdalus* (LINNAEUS) FOCKE, peaches and almonds. In this section the flowers emerge before the leaves, the skin of the fruit is downy (except in the case of the nectarine), and the branches have a terminal bud.
3 *Cerasus* PERSOON, the cherries. The flowers appear before or with the leaves in clusters, or occasionally cymes or racemes, from axils of year-old wood, with a long peduncle, while the flowers of the previous two subgenera are nearly sessile.
4 *Padus* (MOENCH) KOEHNE, the bird cherries, have the flower in racemes which are leafy at the base and formed on the current year's growth. The flowers appear after the leaves.
5 *Laurocerasus* KOEHNE, the cherry laurels, differ from Padus only in their evergreen leaves and the racemes arising from year-old wood.

Prunus americana MARSHALL *Prunophora*

4. Deciduous tree, to 7m occasionally 10m, but tending to send up numerous sucker growths and form a thicket. The brs are somewhat pendulous. Lv oval or obovate, acuminate, to 10cm long and slightly less than half as wide, toothed, practically glabrous, petiole to 2cm long. Fl white, about 2·5cm across in clusters of 2–5. Fl 4. Fr yellow, later red. The fr are said to be very handsome, but are rarely produced in the UK. Native of much of the USA to the eastern slopes of the Rockies. Most authorities give 1768 as the date of introduction, but it is not mentioned either by *Hortus Kewensis* or by Loudon.

Prunus amygdalus
See *P. dulcis*

Prunus armeniaca LINNAEUS *Prunophora*
Apricot

4. The wild ancestor of the apricot is a round-headed tree, of up to 10m. Lv broad-ovate, to 9cm long and 5cm across, deep green above and below. Fl singly from year-old wood, sometimes clusters on short spurs, white or pale pink, 2·5cm across. Fl 3–4. Fr yellow with red flush, not usually seen on trees in the open, about 3cm across. Cultivated apricots are, of course, larger. Var *ansu* MAXIMOWICZ has purplish bts and deep pink fl, while its double form is often known in gardens as *P. mume* 'Rosea plena'. Its fl are up to 3cm across. *P. armeniaca* is probably native to northern China and other districts in N Asia. Var *ansu* is native to northern China and was introduced in 1880.

Prunus avium LINNAEUS *Cerasus* Bird Cherry

4.6.7. Deciduous tree, to 20m, with attractive reddish peeling bark when mature. Younger plants have greyish bark. Lv oblong-ovate, acuminate, to 12cm long and 5cm across, toothed, usually turning crimson in the autumn; petiole to 4cm long with two reddish glands beneath the lamina. Fl in clusters, on pedicels to 4cm long and about 2·5cm across, pure white. Fl 4–5. Fr small, red-black, about 18mm in diameter. 'Decumana' has lv up to 25cm long, 'Flore Pleno', with numerous double fl, is extremely showy. It flourishes on the chalk. Native of Europe including the UK.

Prunus canescens BOIS *Cerasus*

4. Deciduous shrub with spreading brs, to 2m, with pubescent bts. Lv lanceolate, acuminate, grey hairy above and grey tomentose below, to 6cm long and 2·5cm across. Fl fugacious, in clusters of 3–5, each on a pedicel to 8mm long, pale pink, to 1cm across. Fl 4. Fr edible, red, 1cm across. Curious with its grey hairy lv but only sparingly ornamental. The lv sometimes turn purple in the autumn and the bark eventually becomes smooth and polished. Native of Szechuan, whence it was sent to Vilmorin in 1898.

Prunus cerasifera EHRHART *Prunophora*
Cherry Plum Myrobalan

4. Round-headed tree, to 10m, with glabrous bts. Lv ovate or obovate, dull green, usually glabrous, occasionally a few tufts of hairs beneath. Fl singly from axils, or clustered on spurs, white, to 2·5cm across. Fl 3. Fr reddish, about 3cm in diameter. A number of var are known, of which 'Lindsayae' has bright pink fl, 'Nigra' has very dark lv and bts and bright pink fl, while the most well-known is 'Pissardii', with dark red lv which age to purple and fl pink in the bud but white when open. This was hybridised with *P. mume* (qv) to give rise to *P. X blireiana*, with coppery lv and double pink fl. *P. cerasifera* is thought to be native to the Caucasus, but has been a very long time in cultivation. 'Pissardii' was brought from Iran by the Shah's gardener, M. Pissart, about 1880; *P. X blireiana* dates from 1895.

Prunus cerasus LINNAEUS *Cerasus*

4.(5). (Including *P. acida* EHRHART) The parent of the morello and similar sour cherries. Deciduous bush or small tree, occasionally to 10m, suckering from the root. Brs slender and pendulous. Lv oval or ovate, to 7cm long and 5cm wide, dark green, doubly toothed with glands on the petiole. Fl with lv in axillary clusters, white, to 2cm across. Fl 4–5. Fr red. 'Rhexii' has double fl. 'Semperflorens' is a curious anomaly known as the All Saints cherry, in which the fl are produced on the current year's growth from June onwards and very few if any fl are produced at the normal time. Native of much of Europe, including the UK.

Prunus concinna KOEHNE *Cerasus*

3.4. A shrub, to 2m or slightly more. The unfurling lv are purple in colour, later dull green above, greyish below, narrowly ovate, to 7cm long and 2cm wide, slightly hairy on both sides. Fl in clusters on pedicels to 6mm long, pale pink or white. Fl 3–4. A useful dwarf shrub with its early fl. Native of Hupeh. Introduced by Wilson in 1907 (Hillier gives 1900 for the year of introduction).

Prunus cerasifera

Prunus conradinae KOEHNE *Cerasus*

4. A graceful tree, to 7 or 8m. Lv oval-lanceolate, acuminate, toothed, to 11cm long and 5·5cm wide, serrate, usually glabrous above, but with a few hairs below. Fl before the lv, either solitary or in small clusters of up to 4, about 2·5cm across; fragrant pale pink or white, or, in 'Maliflora', quite a deep pink. Fl 2–3. Fr egg-shaped, red, small. One of the earliest plants to flower, so it will appreciate some shelter although the plant itself is not damaged by frost. Native of China. Introduced by Wilson in 1907.

Prunus cornuta (WALLICH) STEUDEL *Padus*

4.5. Deciduous tree, to 20m in the wild. Lv oblong-ovate, to 15cm long and 5cm across, dull green above, paler below and somewhat downy at first. Fl in racemes to 15cm long and 2·5cm wide, each white bloom being about 8mm across. Fl 5. Fr red at first, later reddish-brown. Distinguished from *P. padus* mainly by its larger lv and reddish rather than black fr. Native of the Himalaya. Cultivated in 1860.

Prunus cyclamina KOEHNE *Cerasus*

3.4. A rather slow-growing tree, which can eventually reach 7m but is more usually seen as a bush. Young lv copper coloured, mature lv oblong or ovate, acuminate, serrate, to 15cm long and 6cm across, dark green above, lighter below, both surfaces glabrous. Fl before the lv in clusters, deep pink, with the sepals very characteristically reflexed, suggesting the petals of the cyclamen; the fl are about 2·5cm across and slightly campanulate, ends of the petals notched. Fl 4. *P. dielsiana* SCHNEIDER is less tall, has larger lv, which are downy below, attractive mahogany red bark and white or pale pink fl with the same reflexed calyx. It is evidently closely allied. Both spp are native to Hupeh and were introduced by Wilson in 1907.

Prunus davidiana FRANCHET *Amygdalus*

4. Slender, deciduous tree, to 10m. Lv ovate-lanceolate, willow-like, acuminate, to 12cm long and 3cm across, finely toothed, light green and glabrous. Fl usually singly from axils of the previous year's growth, 2·5cm across, patulate, white (or pink in 'Rubra'). Fl 2–3. Fr, rarely seen, yellow and downy, 3cm across. Notable for its very early flowering, otherwise much like an almond. Native of northern China. Introduced to France by Père David in 1865.

Prunus dulcis WEBB *Amygdalus* Almond

4. (*P. amygdalus* BATSCH, *P. communis* (LINNAEUS) ARCANGELI, *Amygdalus dulcis* MILLER) Deciduous, rather slender tree, to 10m. Lv lanceolate, sometimes slightly glaucous, to 12cm long and 3cm wide, glabrous. Fl usually in pairs before lv in axils, to 5cm across, white or, more usually, pink. Fl 2–4. Fr downy and without pulpy flesh. The almond of commerce is the kernel of the stone. 'Macrocarpa' has large fl and edible fr. There is also a white and a double-flowered form. Apparently wild plants exist in western Asia and N Africa, but the plant has been so long in cultivation that its native habitat is doubtful. One of the most popular small trees for early spring flowers. *P. fenzliana* FRITSCH, from the Caucasus, is clearly related, but never makes more than a large shrub with rather deeper pink fl and narrower blue-green lv. It was introduced shortly before 1890.

Prunus fruticosa PALLAS *Cerasus*

4. Naturally a low, spreading shrub, to 1m, but sometimes grafted on to standards of *P. avium* to make a small, mop-headed tree, with the lower brs pendulous (such plants are sometimes called 'Pendula' without much excuse; any grafted plant of this origin is pendulous). Lv elliptic, to 5cm long and 2cm wide, glossy dark green and glabrous. Fl 2–4, with lv, on pedicels to 2·5cm long, white, about 2cm across. Fl 5. Fr small, reddish-purple. There is a rather poor form with variegated lv. Native of central and eastern Europe, east to Siberia. Cultivated since 1587.

Prunus glandulosa THUNBERG *Cerasus*

4.(5). (*P. japonica* THUNBERG, *P. sinensis* PERSOON) A rounded bush, to 1·5m. Lv ovate-lanceolate, acuminate, to 6cm long and 2·5cm across. Fl about 1cm in diameter, white or pink. Fl 4. Fr also 1cm in diameter, red and sometimes borne in sufficient numbers to be ornamental. The type is rarely seen, but two double-flowered forms, 'Albiplena' with white fl and 'Sinensis' ('Roseoplena') with quite deep pink fl, have long been popular. The fl are very double, up to 3cm across and opening in May rather than April. The lv are also longer, up to 10cm. The plants require a rather sheltered situation, otherwise the fl can be damaged. The plant is native to northern China and, perhaps, Japan, where it has long been cultivated. The type seems to have been received about 1810, but the double pink form was grown by Kennedy and Lee in 1774 and may conceivably have been in cultivation since 1687. Loudon gives this date, but Sweet claims that this was a different plant. See *P. tenella*.

Prunus grayana MAXIMOWICZ *Padus*

4. A small tree, to 10m, and very similar to *P. padus* itself, from which it is distinguished by the more finely toothed lv and the absence of glands on the short petioles. Fl in erect racemes. Fl 6. Fr black. Native of Japan. In cultivation in 1900.

Prunus incana (PALLAS) BATSCH *Cerasus*

4. Rather sprawling shrub, to 2m or slightly more, with downy bts. Lv lanceolate, to 7cm long and slightly over 2cm across, dark green above, densely white tomentose below. Fl singly or in pairs, from the axils with the lv, only about 8mm in diameter, deep pink. Fl 4. Fr cherry-like, red, about 8mm across. Superficially the plant resembles *P. tenella*, but it can easily be distinguished by the grey tomentum on the lv and by its cherry-like, not almond-like, fr. Native of SE Europe and Asia Minor. Introduced in 1815.

Prunus incisa THUNBERG *Cerasus*

4. Large shrub or small tree, to 10m. Lv reddish on emergence, later dull green, sometimes colouring in the autumn. They are ovate, slightly pubescent, sharply toothed, to 6cm long and half as wide. Fl with deep red calices which persist after the fugacious petals have dropped. Fl about 2cm across, white or pale pink. Fl 3–4. Fr small, black. This is a very graceful cherry, which makes a brave show in spite of the short-lived fl owing to the coloured calyx. It is native to Japan and only seems to have reached cultivation in 1910.

4.6. *P. X. hillieri*, a tree to 10m, is a hybrid between this sp and *P. sargentii* (qv), with soft pink fl in April and brilliant red colours in the autumn. 'Spire' is a fine fastigiate form.

Prunus jacquemontii JOSEPH HOOKER *Cerasus*

4. (*Amygdalus humilis* EDGEWORTH) Shrub, to 4m, of rounded habit with smooth, slender bts. Lv ovate-elliptic, to 6cm long and 2·5cm wide, with jagged stipules at the base of the petiole. Fl in clusters of 1–3, about 1cm across, bright pink. Fl 4. Fr, rarely produced, 1·5cm in diameter, red. Related to *P. humilis* which has downy bts and entire stipules. Native to Afghanistan. Introduced by Aitchison in 1879.

Prunus kurilensis MIYABE *Cerasus*

4. (*P. nipponica* var *kurilensis* WILSON) Slow-growing, bushy shrub or small tree, to 6m in the wild. Lv with rusty down when young, finally more or less glabrous, ovate, to 9cm long and half as wide, dull green. Fl before lv in clusters of 1–3, about 2·5cm across, white or pale pink (a deeper pink in the cv 'Ruby'). Fl 4. Fr dark purple. Probably only a large-flowered form of *P. nipponica*, as Wilson suggested, but this is in commerce while *P. nipponica* is not. Native of the Kurile Islands and Japan. Introduced in 1905.

Prunus laurocerasus

Prunus laurocerasus LINNAEUS *Laurocerasus*
Cherry Laurel

4.5. This is the laurel of seventeenth and eighteenth-century gardens. Evergreen shrub of quick growth, to 7m high and wide, with lv usually oblong or oblanceolate, but varying much in both shape and size from 'Magnolifolia', with lv to 30cm long and 11cm across, to the willow-like lv of 'Schipkaensis' and 'Zabeliana', which are 10cm long and 3cm across. Lv deep glossy green and glabrous. Fl in axillary racemes to 12cm long, each fl about 8mm across, white. Fr conical, red at first, later dark purple, about 1cm in diameter. The plants thrive happily under trees and where dripping may be expected. The plant can be damaged in exceptionally hard winters, but is never killed. Indeed it is not affected by as much as ten degrees of frost and is generally very hardy. Native of eastern Europe. Probably in cultivation since the sixteenth century, but it does not seem to be recorded before Parkinson's *Paradisus* of 1629.

Prunus lusitanica LINNAEUS *Laurocerasus*
Portugal Laurel

4. Evergreen, usually a bushy shrub to 6m, but it can make a tree to 17m; bts glabrous and very dark. Lv ovate, to 12cm long and 5cm wide, dark green above, lighter below, shallowly toothed. Fl in axillary and, occasionally, terminal racemes, to 25cm long, each floret white and 1cm in diameter. Fl 6. Fr very dark purple, 8mm long. Var *azorica* NICHOLSON has the largest lv. There is also a variegated form. Even hardier than *P. laurocerasus*. Native of the Iberian peninsula, the Canaries and Azores. Introduced in 1648 according to *Hortus Kewensis*. Two Californian members of the section, *PP. ilicifolia* and *lyonii*, are too tender for inclusion here.

Prunus maackii RUPRECHT *Padus*

1.4. Somewhat intermediate between this section and *Laurocerasus* as the fl come on the year-old wood. A tree to 15m, with conspicuous brown-yellow bark, which exfoliates like a birch, and downy bts. Lv elliptic-ovate, to 10cm long and half as wide, dull green. Fl white, in short racemes to 7cm long, leaflets at the base. Fl 4–5. The trunk makes this a very ornamental plant, the shining bark being unusually coloured, but neither fl nor fr are at all showy. Native of Manchuria and Korea. Introduced from St Petersburg in 1910, but in cultivation in 1878 according to Rehder.

Prunus mahaleb LINNAEUS *Cerasus*
St Lucie Cherry

4. Large bush or small, rapid-growing tree, to 13m. Lv roundish, to 6cm long and 5cm across, glossy green, slightly hairy along the midrib below, otherwise glabrous. Fl in small racemes from axils of year-old wood. The racemes are about 4cm long, but each of the 10–12 fl is on a pedicel about 1cm long, while the individual, white, fragrant fl may be 2cm across. Fl 4–5. Fr ovoid, black, about 6mm long. Young trees are somewhat reluctant to come to the flowering stage. Native of central Europe. Introduced in 1714.

Prunus mandshurica KOEHNE *Prunophora*

4. A small tree, to about 5m, with spreading, pendulous brs. Lv ovate or widely elliptic, to 12cm long, sharply toothed and dull green. Fl before lv, solitary, from the axils, deep pink in bud, pale pink and 3cm wide when expanded. Fl 2–3. Fr yellow, about 2·5cm in diameter. Native of Manchuria and Korea. In cultivation in 1900, probably introduced through St Petersburg.

Prunus maritima MARSHALL *Prunophora*

4. A straggling shrub, occasionally to 2m and usually extending wider horizontally. Bts grey pubescent. Lv oval, grey downy beneath at first, serrate, to 7cm long and 3cm wide. Fl in clusters of 2–3, white, about 1·5cm wide, produced with great freedom and later than most plums. Fl 5. Fr about 2·5cm across, red, purple or yellow. Native of the eastern USA from Maine to Virginia, usually near the coast. Introduced by Fraser in 1800.

Prunus maximowiczii RUPRECHT *Cerasus*

4.(6). Tree, to 16m in the wild and about 12m in cultivation, with downy bts. Lv obovate-elliptic, to 8cm long and 3cm wide, doubly toothed, bright green above, sparsely hairy below. In some districts the lv turn scarlet before falling. Fl just after lv in erect, corymbose racemes of 6–10 fl. The racemes are furnished with leaf-like bracts. Each fl on the racemes is on a pedicel to 2cm long, is creamy-white and about 1cm across. Fl 5. Fr first red, later black, only 4mm across. The plant is interesting as bridging the gap between the *Cerasus* and the *Padus* sections, but not otherwise outstanding. Native of Japan, Korea and Manchuria. Introduced by Sargent in 1892.

Prunus mume SIEBOLD AND ZUCCARINI
Prunophora Japanese Apricot

4. Large shrub or round-headed tree of up to 10m. Lv broad-ovate and long-acuminate, to 10cm long and 6cm wide, sparsely hairy at first, later glabrous, conspicuously toothed. Fl 1–2 before lv, white or pink; a number of double and semi-double cv exist. Fl 2–4 according to season. Native of China, whence it was intro-

duced by Fortune in 1844. Long cultivated in Japan, where most of the cv originated.

Prunus padus LINNAEUS *Padus* Bird Cherry

4. Tree of up to 15m although usually less. Lv oval or obovate, to 12cm long, dull green above, a few tufts of down on the lower midrib. Fl fragrant, on racemes to 15cm long, each fl white, to 1cm across. Fl 5. Fr black. A number of cv are in cultivation. 'Plena' has semi-double fl, 'Watereri' has racemes up to 20cm long and is the most spectacular. **3.** 'Colorata' has purplish young lv and a pale pink fl. Var *commutata* DIPPEL starts to flower in mid-April and is sometimes damaged by late frosts. All the forms are very hardy. The plant is native to most of Europe eastwards through N Asia to Japan; var *commutata* comes from Manchuria.

Prunus padus (fruit and flowers)

Prunus persica (LINNAEUS) BATSCH *Prunophora* Peach

4. Tree of up to 7m. Lv lanceolate, to 15cm long and 3cm across, long acuminate, finely toothed. Fl solitary or in pairs before the lv, to 3·5cm wide, bright pink. Fr downy, to 7cm in diameter (larger in some orchard forms), yellow suffused red. Fl 4. A large number of cv are in cultivation, of which the most popular is 'Klara Meyer' with large double fl. There are also cv with white and with crimson fl, while 'Foliis Rubris' has the young lv purplish-red. There is a pendulous form, and 'Pyramidalis', which may no longer be in cultivation, is fastigiate. The plant is probably native to China, but has been so long cultivated that it is not possible to be sure.

Prunus pilioscula KOEHNE *Cerasus*

4. Usually a large shrub, but capable of making

a tree of 12m. Lv oval, long acuminate, heart-shaped at base, sharply toothed, to 10cm long and half as wide, slightly bristly on both surfaces. Fl with lv in 2–4-flowered umbels, on pedicels to 2·5cm long, white or very pale pink. Fl 4. Fr ovoid, about 8mm long, red. Native of Hupeh. Introduced by Wilson in 1907.

Prunus pseudocerasus LINDLEY *Cerasus*

4. (*P. cantabrigiensis* STAPF) A very mysterious tree which was received by a Mr Samuel Brooks of Ball's Pond Road, London, in 1819. It makes a small tree, to about 5m, with slightly hairy bts. Lv elliptic-ovate, to 10cm long and 6cm wide, long acuminate, somewhat hairy on both sides. Fl before lv in an umbel-like raceme of usually 4 blooms, pale pink, about 2·5cm across. Fl 2–3. Fr, apparently, red, edible about 1cm across. Easily the earliest cherry to flower and so often damaged by frosts. The *P. pseudocerasus* cultivated in China (the plant has never been found wild) has white fl.

Prunus pubigera KOEHNE *Padus*

4. A tree of up to 20m in the wild but probably considerably less in cultivation. Lv obovate, to 12cm long and half as wide, with a short point, dull green above, whitish beneath, glabrous on both surfaces. Fl in racemes to 14cm long, creamy-white, each fl about 1cm in diameter. Fl 5. Fr black. Native of western China. Introduced by Wilson in 1908.

Prunus pumila LINNAEUS *Cerasus*

4.(6). Often a low shrub of 60cm, but occasionally to nearly 3m, spreading widely. Lv obovate but narrow, to 5cm long and 1·8cm across, grey-green, often turning red in the autumn. Fl in umbels of 2–4 before lv, about 1cm wide, produced in profusion, white but rather a dull white in some forms. Fl 5. Fr black or red, 1cm across. Native to the north-eastern USA. In cultivation in 1756, possibly a Bartram sending. *P. pumila* X *cerasifera* 'Pissardii', a red-leaved, white-flowered shrub to 2m, is known as 'Cistena'.

Prunus rufa JOSEPH HOOKER *Cerasus*

4. Small tree, to 7m, with rusty tomentose bts, a unique feature in the genus. Lv elliptic-oblong, to 10cm long and about half as wide, toothed and each tooth tipped with a gland. Fl 1–3, about 1cm wide, pink. Fl 5. Fr red. Native of the Himalayas. Introduced about 1897.

Prunus salicina LINDLEY *Prunophora*

4.6. (*P. triflora* ROXBURGH) A small tree, to 10m, often a large shrub, with attractive reddish-brown, smooth bark. Lv ovate or obovate, long acuminate, to 11cm long and half as wide, glabrous above, slightly downy below, turning red in the autumn. Fl before lv, usually in fascicles of 3, white, about 2cm across. Fl 4. Fr about 5cm in diameter, edible, red, orange or yellow, but not produced freely. Native of China cultivated for fruit in Japan. Introduced about 1870.

Prunus sargentii REHDER *Cerasus*

4.6. A vigorous pyramidal tree, to 25m, with attractive smooth brown bark. Lv reddish when unfurling, later ovate, long acuminate, to 10cm long and half as wide, sharply toothed, colouring brilliantly in early autumn. Fl before lv in 2–4-flowered umbels, each fl to 4cm across, pink, on pedicels to 3cm long. Fl 4. Fr small, black. Native of Japan. Sent by the Reverend Bigelow to the Arnold Arboretum in 1890. Doubts have been cast on its true specific identity and some consider it of hybrid origin. In any case it is one of the most satisfactory of Japanese cherries with two distinct seasons of attraction.

Prunus serotina EHRHART *Padus*

4. In the wild a tree to 33m, but rarely more than 5m in the UK. The bark is dark brown and somewhat aromatic. Lv ovate to lanceolate, somewhat elliptic, to 14cm long and 4cm across, glabrous and glossy above, paler beneath, with a few hairs on the midrib. The lv usually turn yellow before falling. Fl in racemes to 15cm long, each fl 8mm in diameter, white. Fl 5–6. Fr black. Var *asplenifolia* has the lv deeply incised, while var *salicifolia* KOEHNE (*P. salicifolia* KUNTHE) has pendulous brs, with dark, very narrow lv. Keeps its lv until November or occasionally later. One of the most attractive of the bird cherries. Native of most of N America from Nova Scotia to Florida and west to Arizona. Var *salicifolia* is native from Mexico to Peru, high in the mountains. In cultivation in 1629.

Prunus serrula FRANCHET *Cerasus*

1.4. (*P. tibetica* of gardens) A tree, to about 10m, with shining brown bark, like polished mahogany, which peels at intervals. Lv lanceolate, willow-like, to 10cm long and 3cm across, finely toothed. Fl a rather dull white, in clusters of 1–4, about 1·5cm across. Fl 4. Fr red, about 1cm in diameter. Worth growing for its shining trunk, but the fl are inconspicuous. Some nurserymen graft forms of the next sp on to trunks of this one. Native of western China. Introduced by Wilson in 1908. This plant was described as var *tibetica* by Koehne, but appears to be the same as Franchet's type.

Prunus serrulata LINDLEY *Cerasus*
Japanese Cherry

4.(6). It is convenient to group all the japanese cherries under this name, although Wilson considered that they also included *P. lannesiana* WILSON (*P. speciosa* INGRAM), some being forms of either of these two spp, others being hybrids between them. They have been cultivated so long that it is probably impossible to draw any proven conclusions. Wilson considered that *P. lannesiana* had grey bark and fragrant fl, while *P. serrulata* had brown bark and fl with no scent. The emerging lv of *P. serrulata* are usually reddish, while those of *P. lannesiana* are green or bronzy. Some forms of var *pubescens* and var *spontanea* of *P. serrulata* have vivid autumn tints, but in general these are lacking in most of the cv.

Small tree, sometimes with spreading brs, sometimes fastigiate. Lv often reddish when unfurling, elliptic-ovate, to 15cm long and 7cm wide, toothed, bright green. Fl before or with lv in corymbs of 2–5, white pink or pale yellow, single and double, to 5cm across. Fl 4–5. Lindley's type plant, sometimes called *alba plena*, which arrived from Canton in 1822, had double white fl about 2·5cm in diameter. The various large double cv started to arrive towards the end of the nineteenth century and the bulk arrived at the start of the twentieth. Wilson introduced two wild forms from China, var *hupehensis* in 1900 and var *pubescens* in 1907.

Few flowering trees give such a massive display as the japanese cherries, while the buds are seldom damaged by birds, as are those of so many of the earlier-flowering spp. They appear to thrive in any soil, while their moderate dimensions mean that they will grace a small garden. Moreover such cv as 'Asagi' and 'Ukon' introduce a pale yellow colour which is not found elsewhere in the genus.

Prunus spinosa LINNAEUS *Prunophora*
Blackthorn, Sloe

4. A spiny, suckering shrub, to 4m, which can be trained as a small tree. Lv ovate or obovate, to 4·5cm long and 1·8cm wide, dark green, slightly downy on the lower veins at first. Fl before lv, singly or in pairs, about 2cm across, white. Fl 3–4. Fr round, 12mm across, black with blue bloom. **3.** 'Purpurea' has bright red young lv, later turning purple, and pink fl. 'Plena' has double white fl. Native of Europe including the UK.

Prunus subhirtella MIQUEL *Cerasus*

4. A variable plant, probably including some hybrids. Small tree, to 10m, with very twiggy brs. Bts hairy at first. Lv ovate-elliptic, to 7cm long and about half as wide, toothed, glabrous above, downy on veins below. Fl before lv in clusters of 2–5, about 18mm wide, pink or white. Fl 3–4. Fr rarely produced, black, 8mm in diameter.

The wild form is thought to be var *ascendens*

WILSON, with erect brs. 'Pendula', 'Pendula rosea' and 'Pendula rubra' are forms with very pendulous brs. They come true from seed and were considered to be a distinct sp – *P. pendula* – by Maximowicz. The plant usually offered as *P. pendula*, with deep pink buds and paler fl, should correctly be known as 'Pendula Rosea'. There are a couple of double forms, one with white and one with reddish fl ('Flore Pleno' and 'Fukubana'), while 'Autumnalis' starts to flower in October and continues off and on until April, opening fl whenever the weather is mild enough. Frost will damage the open fl but not the buds.

P. subhirtella was introduced from Japan in 1894, 'Autumnalis' about 1910. *P. yedoensis* MATSUMURA is now thought to be a hybrid between *P. lannesiana* and *P. subhirtella*. It makes a sizeable spreading tree, to 15m, with fragrant white or pink fl which appear before or with the lv in March and April. The lv are ovate, to 11cm long and 6cm wide, glabrous above, more or less downy below. One of the most attractive flowering cherries.

Prunus tangutica (BATALIN) KOEHNE
Prunophora

4. (*P. dehiscens* KOEHNE) Shrub, to 4 or 5m, with spiny spreading brs. Bts grey, sometimes pubescent, later brown and glabrous. Lv oblanceolate, to 5cm long and 1cm across, usually in clusters, dark green above, paler below. Fl before lv, singly, 2·5cm across, bright rose pink. Fl 3. Fr downy, not fleshy, splitting when ripe, about 2·5cm across. A curious bushy almond. Introduced from Szechuan by Wilson in 1910.

Prunus tenella BATSCH *Prunophora*
Dwarf Almond

4. (*Amygdalus nana* LINNAEUS) Low suckering shrub, occasionally to 1m 60cm high (up to 2m in var *georgica*). Lv obovate, to 8cm long and 2·5cm wide. Fl with lv in clusters of 3, a fairly deep red, about 2cm across. Fr, rarely seen, like a small almond, 2·5cm long. Native of the Balkans and Russia east to Siberia. Introduced by James Sutherland before 1683. A double-flowered form seems to have been known at the same time, but this has now been lost.

Prunus triloba LINDLEY *Prunophora*

4. Shrub or small tree, to 5m. Lv ovate-elliptic, to 6cm long and half as wide, sometimes 3-lobed at the apex. Fl in clusters of 1–3, pink, about 2·5cm wide. Fl 3–4. Fr said to be red. The single form is rarely seen, the most usual form and the original introduction being double and a deeper pink, about 3cm across. This is sometimes known as 'Multiplex'. The plant does best with wall or evergreen protection and should be pruned hard back as soon as flowering is complete. Native of China; brought thence by Fortune in 1845. The single form was introduced in 1884.

Prunus virginiana LINNAEUS *Padus*

4. Shrub to 5m or tree to 10m. Lv broadly ovate, to 12cm long and 8cm wide, mucronate, shining dark green above, paler below with tufts of down. Fl in racemes to 15cm long, white, each about ·8mm wide. Fl 5. Fr dark red, about 8mm in diameter. Allied to *P. serotina*, but distinct with its red fr. Native to eastern N America. Said to have been introduced in 1724, but I can find no mention of a date before 1830. It was, apparently, known as the cornish cherry in the eighteenth century, and thought by some to be a form of *P. padus*.

PSEUDOLARIX GORDON *Pinaceae*
A monotypic genus, very similar to the larch.

Pseudolarix amabilis (NELSON) REHDER

6.(7). (*P. kaempferi* GORDON, *P. fortunei* MAYR) Slow-growing, deciduous tree, to 40m in some climes but rarely exceeding 15m in the UK. It differs from the larches in its broader lv, in the male catkins being clustered (those of *larix* are solitary) and in the cones being composed of thick woody scales which fall off after the seeds have dispersed, whereas the cones of the true larch remain intact. The lv are yellowish-green in the spring and turn a good clear yellow before falling. The plant needs a moist, fertile, neutral to acid soil. Native of China. Introduced by Fortune in 1853.

PSEUDOTSUGA CARRIÈRE *Pinaceae*
A small genus of evergreen trees from western N America and east Asia, of which only one species, the Douglas fir, is in general cultivation. They are distinguished from *Abies* by their pendulous cones, and from *Picea* by the absence of leaf-cushions

Pseudotsuga menziesii FRANCO Douglas Fir

7. Evergreen tree of the largest size, to 80m in the UK and occasionally to 100m in the wild. On old trees the bark becomes corky and deeply fissured, it is smooth on younger plants. Bts pale orange at first, later darkening to greyish-brown. The tree makes a pyramidal shape and the bts are extremely pendulous, particularly with young trees. The lv, although spirally arranged, fall into two ranks, are linear, to 3cm long and 2mm wide, with whitish bands of stomata below while above they may be dark green, grey-green or blue-green (var *glauca* (MAYR) FRANCO). Male fl axillary and cylindrical. Cones pendulous, ovoid,

Pseudotsuga menziesii

to 6cm long and 3cm across, green at first, later brown, with conspicuous bracts protruding between the scales. The plant may be met with as *Abies douglasii* LINDLEY, *P. douglasii* CARRIÈRE or *P. taxifolia* BRITTON. The plant needs moisture-retentive, fertile soil, preferably neutral or acid, although the glaucous-leaved forms appear more lime-tolerant, and resents prolonged drought. Much used in forestry. Native of western N America from British Columbia to Mexico. Introduced by Douglas in 1827.

PTELEA LINNAEUS *Rutaceae*
A small genus of deciduous monoecious shrubs or small trees native to N America.

Ptelea trifoliolata LINNAEUS Hop Tree

4.5. Shrub or small spreading tree, to 7m; bts reddish-brown, pubescent at first. Lv aromatic, trifoliolate, the leaflets ovate or elliptic, the central one to 15cm long, the two laterals smaller and with the midrib not in the centre, all on a petiole to 10cm long. Fl in corymbs, with both sexes present, the corymbs about 7cm across. The fl greenish-white, to 1cm in diameter, patulate, not showy but fragrant. Fl 6–7. The plant is well worth growing for its fragrance alone. Fr in clusters, a flat round disc to 2·5cm wide, conspicuous when green. 'Aurea' has attractive soft yellow lv. Native to eastern N America from Canada to Florida. Introduced by Banister before 1704. One of the few plants attributed to him in *Hortus Kewensis*. According to Miller most of the 1704 plants were lost in a severe winter, but further seeds were sent over by Catesby in 1724.

PTEROCARYA KUNTH *Juglandaceae*

A small genus of about eight species of deciduous trees, one from the Caucasus, the others from eastern Asia. The pith is lamellate, as in *Carya*, and the small nuts, which are produced on slender spikes, are winged, unlike either *Juglans* or *Carya*. The leaves are alternate. The flowers are monoecious, the female catkins being much the longer. Propagation by seed, although sucker growths can often be detached. Cuttings are possible but not easy.

Pterocarya fraxinifolia (LAMARCK) SPACH

7. (*Juglans pterocarya* MICHAUX, *P. caucasica* MEYER) A deciduous tree, to 30m but usually about half that height, with a spreading head, starting to branch very low down, with deeply furrowed bark. Lv pinnate, to 45cm long and with from 7 to 27 leaflets. These are oblong-lanceolate, serrate, to 10cm long and 4·5cm across (occasionally much larger on vigorous shoots). Male catkins to 12cm long, but female catkins from 30 to 50cm long. Nuts, rarely formed in the UK, about 2cm in diameter. Usually produces suckers. Var *dumosa* SCHNEIDER remains always shrubby. The plant requires abundant moisture and grows in or near swamps in the wild. Native of the Caucasus and Iran. Introduced to France by Michaux in 1782, but did not reach the UK until 1828 according to Sweet.

Pterocarya stenoptera DE CANDOLLE

7. Deciduous tree, to 30m but rarely more than 20m in cultivation. Lv from 20 to 37cm long, with the rachis conspicuously winged between the leaflets. There are from 1·1 to 21 leaflets, elliptic, to 12cm long and 5cm across. Male catkins to 6cm long, female to 20cm, nuts with two wings, to 2cm long. Native of China. Introduced about 1860.

PTEROSTYRAX SIEBOLD AND ZUCCARINI
Styracaceae

A small genus of east Asian deciduous shrubs or trees of rapid growth and easy cultivation, although unsuitable for shallow soils.

Pterostyrax corymbosa SIEBOLD AND ZUCCARINI

4. Large shrub or small tree to 6m. Lv elliptic to ovate, to 12cm long, alternate, margins serrate with bristles attached to the teeth. Fl in nodding corymbose axillary panicles to 12cm long. The fl white, fragrant, 5-petalled. Fl 5–6. Fr markedly winged. A rather rare plant and less attractive than the next sp but more compact. Native of Japan and China. Introduced in 1850.

Pterostyrax hispida SIEBOLD AND ZUCCARINI

4. Large shrub or tree, to 15m, of vigorous,

Pterostyrax hispida

rapid growth and rather spreading habit. Lv oval or oblong-oval, acuminate, toothed, dark green above, greyish below with a whitish pubescence at first to 15cm long and half as wide. Fl in pendulous panicles to 20cm long, composed of numerous fragrant white tubular fl, each about 8mm long. Fl 6–7. Fr not winged, 12mm long. A rapid grower but only starts to flower when quite a sizeable plant. Native of China and Japan. Introduced in 1875.

PYRACANTHA ROEMER *Rosaceae*

A small genus of ten species of evergreen shrubs, usually with thorny branches, alternate leaves and white flowers in corymbs with a very showy berry-like pome. They are mainly found in Sino-Himalaya, but one species extends as far west as Spain. At various times they have been included in *Cotoneaster* and in *Crataegus*. They require full light and do not care for wet soils. They are often trained against walls, although most are completely hardy. Propagation is by seeds or semi-hard stem cuttings with a heel in late summer.

Pyracantha angustifolia (FRANCHET) SCHNEIDER

4.5. Evergreen shrub, to 4m but more inclined, if not supported, to be nearly prostrate. Bts grey tomentose. Lv narrow-oblong, mucronate, larger lv obscurely serrate, most lv entire, to 5cm long and 12mm wide, dark green above, grey tomentose below. Fl in corymbs 5cm across, each fl about 6mm wide, rose-shaped, white. Fl 6. Fr orange-yellow, grey tomentose before ripening, about 1cm across; persisting until March on occasion. The most tender member of the genus and best against a wall. The fl are unattractive, but the long-persisting fr are very showy. Native of western China. Introduced by a Lieutenant Jones in 1899.

Pyracantha atalantioides (HANCE) STAPF

4.5. (*P. gibbsii* JACKSON) Vigorous shrub, to 7m, of pyramidal habit often unarmed. Bts downy at first, later glabrous and bright brown. Lv elliptic, sometimes oblong-lanceolate, to 7cm long and 3cm wide, dark shining green above, pale and matt beneath. Fl in corymbs from the ends of lateral twigs, about 5cm across, each fl to 1cm across. Fl 5–6. Fr scarlet to 6mm wide. 'Aurea' has yellow fr. The most vigorous sp and the fr will persist for a long time. Native of western China. Introduced by Wilson in 1907.

Pyracantha coccinea ROEMER Fire Thorn

4.5. Dense evergreen shrub which can be trained as a small tree to 5m. Bts grey-pubescent. Lv narrowly elliptic, to 6cm long and 2cm wide, dark glossy green above, paler below. Fl in corymbs terminating lateral twigs about 4–5cm wide, each fl about 8mm across. Fl 6. Fr coral-red, about 6mm across. 'Lalandei' is a particularly vigorous form with larger lv, fl and fr, which are orange-red in colour. Native of southern Europe from NE Spain eastwards to Asia Minor. In cultivation before 1629.

Pyracantha crenatoserrata REHDER

4.5. (*P. yunnanensis* CHITTENDEN) Evergreen shrub, to 4m or more, with reddish pubescent bts. Lv elliptic to oblanceolate, to 7cm long and 2·5cm across, dark shining green above, paler below. Corymbs of fl to 5cm across, each fl to 1cm. Fl 6. Fr coral-red, about 7mm across. A floriferous and fructiferous plant with long-persisting fr. This sp, *P. atalantioides* and *P. rogersiana* are barely distinct botanically, although reasonably distinct in the garden. Native of Yunnan. Introduced by Père Ducloux in 1906.

Pyracantha rogersiana CHITTENDEN

4.5. (*P. crenulata* var *rogersiana* Jackson) Erect, spiny tree, to 3m, pyramidal in habit. Bts pale pubescent, later pale brown. Lv oblanceolate, shallowly toothed and the teeth gland-tipped, to 3cm long and 1cm across, far smaller than the lv of other spp. Fl in corymbs to 3cm across, each fl 6–7mm in diameter. Fl 6. Fr orange or ('Flava') yellow 6mm across. An attractive, rather dainty shrub. Native of Yunnan. Introduced by Forrest in 1911.

PYRUS LINNAEUS *Rosaceae*

Although a number of wild pears are in commerce, it is only *P. salicifolia* that is at all commonly cultivated. They are all deciduous trees or shrubs with alternate leaves and white flowers in umbels, either before or with the leaves. The fruit is a pear-shaped, oval, or globular pome. Linnaeus's treatment of the genus included the genera *Aronia*, *Malus* and *Sorbus*, to which *Chaenomeles* was later added. This unscientific grouping was confirmed by Bentham and Hooker in their *Genera Plantarum*. Propagation is usually by grafts on pear stock, but seeds of the species germinate fairly rapidly if sown as soon as ripe.

Pyrus betulifolia BUNGE

3.4. A rapid-growing, slender tree of up to 10m, with grey tomentose bts. Lv grey downy at first, later dark green and shining, ovate, long-acuminate, to 8cm long and half as wide, petiole grey tomentose. Fl in an umbel-like corymb of 8–10, each fl up to 2·5cm across. Fl 4. Fr very small, only about 1·5cm in diameter. Native of northern China. Bretschneider sent seeds to Kew in 1882, but, according to Rehder, it had previously been introduced about 1865.

Pyrus nivalis JACQUIN

3.4. A small tree, to 10m, of rather fastigiate habit; bts and young lv densely covered with white tomentum, most of which has gone by the end of the season. Mature lv ovate, to 7cm long and 3cm wide. Fl pure white in clusters of 6–10, each fl to 3·5cm across, abundantly borne with the young lv. Fl 4. Fr 3cm or more across; edible when overripe. *P. eleagnifolia* PALLAS has greyer lv and is usually thorny, while *P. kotschyana* BOISSIER is intermediate between the two forms. *P. canescens* SPACH is thought to be a hybrid between *P. nivalis* and *P. salicifolia*, with tomentose lv which are narrowly oval and twisted. All these plants are native to eastern Europe and Asia Minor and were introduced in 1800.

Pyracantha angustifolia

Pyrus pashia D. DON

4. (*P. variolosa* WALLICH) Round-headed tree, to 7m. Lv ovate, but apex is either long-acuminate or obtuse, to 10cm long and half as wide, finely toothed, glabrous on both surfaces. Fl in close-set corymbs about 5cm across, each fl 2cm across, pale pink at first, later white. Fl 4. Fr round, 2·5cm across. Unusual in its close-set corymbs, which suggest a *Crataegus* rather than a *Pyrus*, and in its pale pink fl. Native to the Himalaya and western China. Introduced, presumably through Wallich, in 1825.

Pyrus pyrifolia (BURMAN) NAKAI

4.(6). (*P. serotina* REHDER, *P. sinensis* auct) Tree of up to 12m, with bts hairy at first, later turning more or less purple. Lv covered with a grey cobweb-like down at first, later glabrous, ovate, mucronate, to 10cm long and 6cm wide, often colouring well in the autumn in shades of bronze and crimson. Fl in clusters of 6–8, each fl to 3·5cm across. Fl 3–4. Fr round, about 2·5cm across in the wild form, but pear-shaped and up to 7cm long in some cultivated forms. Native of China and cultivated there and in Japan. The cultivated forms reached the USA before 1850. The wild form was introduced about 1909.

Pyrus salicifolia PALLAS

3.4. Tree, to 8m, of pendulous habit; bts covered with white down. Lv narrow-lanceolate, tapering at both ends, to 8cm long and 16mm wide, silver tomentose on both surfaces at first, later most of this falls from the upper side leaving it glossy green. Fl in dense corymbs about 2cm across, each fl about 2cm across, white. Fl 4. Fr pear-shaped, 3cm long and wide. 'Pendula' is the form usually offered, but apparently all forms are pendulous. One of the most attractive of all small trees both for foliage and for fl. Native of the Caucasus, south-east Europe and western Asia. Introduced by Pallas in 1780.

Pyrus ussuriensis MAXIMOWICZ

4.6. (*P. simonii* CARRIÈRE, *P. sinensis* DECAISNE) Tree, to 12m, with yellowish-grey young wood. Brs forking at very long intervals to give the tree a very gaunt appearance. Lv roundish, but pointed at the apex, to 10cm long and wide, bristle-toothed, turning bronze and crimson in the autumn. Fl in clusters of 6–8, each fl to 3·5cm across. Fl 3–4. Fr conical, juicy, to 3·5cm long and wide. Native of N China and Korea. Introduced 1855.

QUERCUS LINNAEUS *Fagaceae* Oaks

A large genus of about 450 species of deciduous or evergreen trees or shrubs with alternate leaves and monoecious flowers. The male flower is a catkin, which appears as the leaves start to unfurl, the females are sessile and inconspicuous. The most easily identifiable character of the genus is the fruit, which is the acorn, a nut of ovoid or conical shape with the base enclosed in a cup, the scales on which are used to separate the genus into various sections or subgenera. Oaks require moisture-retentive and fertile soil, and some of the American species require this to be acid. They are best propagated by seed, although they are rather slow growers and should be put in their final positions as early as possible. If this is not possible they should be transplanted every two years, as once a large root system is developed the plant may die if it is damaged.

Quercus acuta THUNBERG

An evergreen shrub or small tree, to 13m in the wild but rarely more than 7m in cultivation, of slow growth. Bts and young lv covered with brown tomentum at first, soon glabrous. Lv coriaceous, oval, tapered at both ends (in young plants the lv tend to be rounded at the base) with entire, undulate margins, dark glossy green above, dull and yellowish below. Acorns with a downy cup, several on a short spike. Native of Japan. Introduced by Maries in 1878.

Quercus acutissima CARRUTHERS

7. (*Q serrata* of Siebold, but not of Thunberg) Deciduous tree to 17m. Bts downy at first, soon glabrous. Lv oblong, rounded or tapered at base, mucronate, to 17cm long and 5·5cm wide, bristle toothed, shining green above, paler and with tufts of down below. Acorns small, cups with spreading, recurving scales. Native of China, Japan, Korea and the Himalaya. Introduced by Oldham from Japan 1862.

Quercus bicolor WILLDENOW

7. Deciduous tree, to 20m in the UK, and the only moderately satisfactory tree of the American white oaks. The bark is loose and scaly, light grey-brown. Lv obovate or oblong-obovate, with shallow lobes on each side, tapered at the base, to 18cm long and 10cm wide, dark shining green above, pale grey tomentose below. Acorns in pairs, about 2·5cm long. Native of eastern N America. Introduced in 1800, presumably by Lyon or Fraser.

Quercus canariensis WILLDENOW

7. (*Q. mirbeckii* DURIE) Deciduous tree, very rapid-growing for an oak, to 25m. The lv usually persist until December, sometimes even later. Lv oval or obovate, lobed or coarsely toothed, rounded or auricled at the base, to 17cm long and 9cm across on young trees, somewhat smaller on mature specimens; dark green above, glaucous beneath, usually glabrous, although brown tomentum on the underside may persist for some time. Acorns in clusters of 2–3, about 2·5cm long, cup with flattened, downy scales. Native of N Africa, the Canaries and the Iberian peninsula. Introduced to France in 1844 by General Pelissier and to England a year later by King Louis Philippe.

Quercus castaneifolia MEYER

7. Deciduous, somewhat pyramidal tree, to 33m in the wild. Lv narrow-oblong, remarkably like sweet chestnut, lv coarsely toothed, to 19cm long and 7cm wide, dark shining green above, grey and puberulent below. Acorns to 3cm long, the cup with long, reflexed downy scales. Var *incana* BATTANDIER (var *algeriensis* BEAN) has smaller lv and a fastigiate habit. Native of the Caucasus and Iran. Introduced about 1840; var *incana,* from N Africa, introduced about 1869.

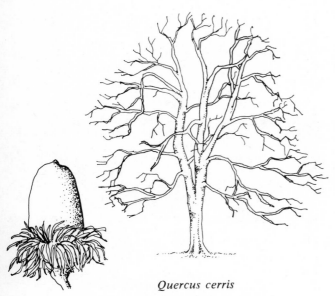

Quercus cerris

Quercus cerris LINNAEUS Turkey Oak

7. Rapid-growing tree, to 40m, bts grey-downy. Lv oval to oblong, coarsely toothed or shallowly lobed, about 12cm long and 7cm wide, dark green and rough to the touch above, greyish below, both surfaces with grey pubescence which eventually disappears. Acorns 1–2, about 3cm long, cups with a mossy appearance. 'Variegata' has the lv with a wide, white margin. Native of southern Europe and western Asia. Introduced in 1735.

Quercus chrysolepis LIEBMANN

7. Slow-growing evergreen tree or large shrub, to 15m in the wild. Lv round to ovate, spine-toothed, to 5cm long and wide; on older trees the lv are entire. Dark green with starry down above at first, grey or yellowish tomentose beneath, this tomentum only persists for a year. Acorns almost sessile, to 5cm long, cup covered with yellowish tomentum. Apparently a splendid plant in the wild with markedly pendulous brs, but usually only shrubby in the UK. Native of south-western America and Mexico. Introduced 1877.

Quercus coccinea MÜNCHAUSEN Scarlet Oak

6.7. Deciduous tree, to 25m, with warted reddish bts. Lv basically ovate or obovate, but deeply lobed on both sides, the lobes being more or less triangular and 7–9 in number, to 15cm long and 11cm wide. The lv turn scarlet in October and may remain on the tree until December. The vividness of the colour varies considerably from tree to tree and is also affected by soil and weather. The acorns take 2 years to ripen, are about 2·5cm long and the cup is almost smooth. Although a less vigorous grower than *Q. rubra* (see below), this is one of the most ornamental oaks, but it does require acid or neutral soil. 'Splendens' is a clone with particularly good autumn colour. Native of eastern America. Introduced (by Banister?) in 1691.

Quercus frainetto TENORE Hungarian Oak

7. (*Q. conferta* KITAIBEL) A rapid-growing tree, to 33m or slightly more, with fissured bark. Lv basically obovate, but deeply lobed 6–10 times, the lobes often being 5cm deep. Dark green and soon glabrous above, pubescent and greyish below, to 20cm long and 11cm wide. Acorns nearly sessile in clusters of 2–4, 2cm long. Native of south-eastern Europe. Introduced about 1837.

Quercus X hispanica LAMARCK

7. This name covers hybrids between the turkey and cork oaks, *QQ. cerris* and *suber*, the latter being tender in most of the UK. Both the Lucombe oak and the Fulham oak have this parentage. The hybrids themselves are fertile, and probably most of the plants available are not the original clones. *Q. X hispanica* makes a large tree, to 30m, of pyramidal form; the bark may be corky or not, corrugated, or more or less smooth. Lv basically ovate with 7–9 sharp teeth, somewhat leathery and dark green above, grey or almost white tomentose below; lv to 12cm long and 5cm across, usually long-persisting until January or even February. Acorns to 2·5cm long in a scaly cup, taking 2 years to ripen. The form most commonly in cultivation is Loudon's var *crispa*, with a compact habit, a rather spreading head and lv which persist throughout the winter, dark green above, almost white beneath, and corky, fissured bark. The cross has occurred in the wild, but it was first noticed at Lucombe's nursery at Exeter in 1765 or thereabouts. 'Fulhamensis', the Fulham oak, was raised at Osborne's nursery, Fulham, slightly earlier.

Quercus ilex LINNAEUS
Evergreen Oak, Holm Oak

3.(7). Evergreen tree, to 25m or sometimes a very sizeable bush, with smooth or corrugated bark, often scaly. Bts and young lv covered with pale grey down which soon falls away but looks striking as the new lv emerge, particularly when combined with yellow catkins. Sucker growths often occur, which afford a means of propagation. Lv variable in shape, but usually ovate, sometimes lanceolate, toothed on young plants, often entire on older ones, leathery, dark green and glossy above, grey tomentose below, up to 7cm long and 2·5cm across. Acorns 1–3, about 2cm long, cup with thin, appressed scales. An impressive tree when well grown and admirable in coastal areas, where the sea spray will cause no harm. Generally hardy, but might prove unsatisfactory in very cold districts as severe winters can cause defoliation. Native of the Mediterranean region. In cultivation certainly since 1580, probably long before.

Quercus libani OLIVIER

7. An elegant, small, deciduous tree of up to 10m. Bts slightly downy at first, soon glabrous. Lv oblong-lanceolate, acuminate, to 10cm long and 2·5cm wide, triangular, bristle-tipped, toothed; dark glossy green above, paler beneath with a few hairs on the veins. Acorns 1–2 on a short woody peduncle, about 2·5cm long, taking 2 years to ripen, almost enclosed by their cups. Native of Lebanon, Syria and Asia Minor. Introduced in 1855.

Quercus macranthera FISCHER AND MEYER

7. Deciduous tree, to 20m, with stout bts covered in grey down, which later darkens but persists. Lv to 15cm long and 10cm wide, basically obovate, but deeply 7–11-lobed, the lobes being 2·5cm deep; dark green and sparsely hairy above, grey tomentose beneath. Acorns to 2·5cm long, the cup with downy scales. Native of the Caucasus and Iran. Introduced before 1783 according to Rehder.

Quercus mongolica TURCZANINOW

7. Tall, deciduous tree, to 30m, of rather irregular form. Lv clustered together at ends of brs, with a practically invisible petiole. Lv to 22cm long and 14cm wide, obovate, with each margin furnished with large triangular teeth; dark green above, paler below, glabrous except for a few tufts of down on the main veins. Acorns about 2cm long in a fringed cup. In regions with hot summers this is a very vigorous and rapid-growing tree, but is less spectacular in the UK. It requires acid soil. Native of eastern Asia and Japan. Introduced in 1879.

Quercus muhlenbergii ENGELMANN

6.7. (*Quercus castanea* WILLDENOW) Deciduous tree, usually to 20m but, according to Rehder, occasionally to 50m. Bts hairy at first. Lv oblong-lanceolate, acuminate, with 8–13 pairs of acute teeth, to 16cm long and 5cm across; yellowish-green above, downy white beneath, colouring in the autumn. Acorns to 2cm long. Requires acid or neutral soil. Native of eastern N America from Vermont to Mexico. Introduced in 1822.

Quercus myrsinifolia BLUME

3. (*Q. vibrayeana* FRANCHET, *Q. bambusifolia* FORTUNE) Evergreen tree, to 15m in the wild but a large bush in cultivation in the UK. Lv lanceolate, acuminate, toothed in the upper half, to 10cm long and 3cm across, purplish-red when unfurling, later pale green above and glaucous beneath. Acorns not produced in the UK. Striking with the contrast between the purplish-red young lv and the pale green of the mature lv. Native of China and Japan. Introduced by Fortune in 1854.

Quercus palustris MUNCHAUSEN

6.7. Deciduous tree, to 25m, occasionally more, with slender, rather pendulous brs. Bts reddish-brown. Lv basically obovate, to 15cm long and wide, deeply 5–7-lobed, glossy-green on both surfaces, but with a few tufts of greyish down in vein axils below; petiole slender, to 5cm long. The lv often turn red or scarlet in the autumn. Acorns small, not more than 1cm long, but requiring 2 years to ripen. Native of the eastern USA. Introduced by Fraser in 1800.

Quercus petraea LIEBLEIN

7. (*Q. sessiliflora* SALISBURY) One of our two English oaks, the other being *Q. robur*, described below. Deciduous tree, to 25m or more, somewhat less open in its head than *Q. robur*. Lv basically oval or obovate, but deeply lobed, to 12cm long and 7cm wide on a petiole to 2·5cm long; glossy green above, greyish beneath and somewhat pubescent. Acorns to 3cm long, 1–3, sessile or very shortly stalked. A few deviant clones are in existence, of which 'Laciniata', with lv to 15cm long, pinnatifidly lobed, is handsome, while 'Mespilifolia' has very long, narrow elliptic lv, to 20cm long and 5cm wide. 'Purpurea' has the young lv red, later turning dull purple. This latter plant is a very slow grower. Native of most of Europe and western Asia, inhabiting damper places than *Q. robur*.

Quercus phellos LINNAEUS Willow Oak

6.7. Deciduous tree, to 30m, with slender reddish bts. The tree is round-headed at first, but later becomes almost columnar. Lv elliptic, sometimes lobed on young trees but usually entire, to 14cm long and 2·5cm wide; pale green, slightly pubescent below at first. Lv turn orange and yellow in the autumn. Acorns rarely seen but very small, only about 1cm long. Requires acid soil. Native of eastern N America. Introduced, probably by Catesby, in 1723.

Quercus phillyreoides ASA GRAY

Large evergreen shrub or small tree, to 10m, with pubescent bts. Lv leathery, obovate or oval, to 6cm long and 3cm across, rounded at base, slightly tapering at apex, blunt-toothed, dark green and shining above, paler but glabrous below. Acorn to 2cm long, rarely produced. The only evergreen oak without spine-topped teeth on the lv. Native of Japan. Introduced by Oldham in 1861.

Quercus pontica KOCH

6. A large shrub or small deciduous tree, to 7m. Lv obovate to elliptic, tapered to the base but almost mucronate at the apex, to 15cm long and half as wide, smooth green above, glaucous and slightly hairy below, petiole 1cm long, midrib petiole yellow. The lv turn golden in the autumn. The main veins give the lv a strongly ribbed appearance. Native of Armenia and the Caucasus, requiring acid soil. Introduced in 1885.

Quercus prinus LINNAEUS

6.7. Deciduous tree, to 20m, very similar to *Q. muehlenbergii* with lv turning yellow in the autumn and with the midrib and petiole yellow. Most readily distinguished by the acorns being on a short stalk, whereas those of *Q. muehlenbergii* are practically sessile. It also requires acid soil. Native of eastern N America. Introduced about 1730 and several times subsequently by Bartram.

Q. montana WILLDENOW differs only in its larger lv, to 18cm long, which are nearly glabrous below. Rehder gives the introductory date for this as 1688; Loudon and Sweet both give 1800.

Quercus pyrenaica WILLDENOW

7. (*Q. toza* DE CANDOLLE) Deciduous tree, to 20m, also suckering, with slender, often pendulous, brs (the more pendulous forms often sold as 'Pendula'). Bts grey tomentose. Lv variable in size and shape, from 7 to 22cm long and 3 to 11cm wide, usually very deeply lobed, basically oblong, the lobes in 4–7 pairs; dark green above with some stellate hairs, grey tomentose below.

The long, yellow male catkins are conspicuous and attractive. Native of south-western Europe and northern Italy. Introduced in 1822.

Quercus robur LINNAEUS English Oak

7. (*Q. pedunculata* EHRHART) Deciduous tree of 45m and usually taller than *Q. petraea*, from which it is also distinguished by the lv being either sessile or very shortly petioled, by the two small lobes (auricles) at the base of the lv and by the lv not being pubescent beneath. In addition, the acorns are borne on a peduncle which may be 12cm long, as opposed to the sessile acorns of *Q. petraea*. However the two spp often hybridise in the wild and intermediate forms are not infrequent. The lv of *Q. robur* are also smaller, usually not exceeding 10cm in length. A number of deviant clones have been isolated, of which 'Atropurpurea', with claret-coloured young lv, and 'Concordia', with golden-yellow young lv, are attractive, but extremely slow-growing. Fastigiate, pendulous and variegated-leaved forms also exist. A very long-lived, but rather slow-growing tree.

Quercus robur

Quercus rubra DU ROI

6.7. (*Q. borealis maxima* ASHE) It seems to be far from certain which plant Linnaeus intended for his *Q. rubra*. Du Roi has chosen this plant, otherwise known as *Q. borealis maxima*, while others think it was *Q. falcata* of Michaux. Deciduous tree of up to 30m in the UK, rapid-growing when young with glabrous, warted, dark red bts. Lv basically ovate but markedly lobed, to 22cm long and 15cm wide; dark green and glabrous above, grey-green below with tufts of brownish tomentum in vein axils, on a yellowish petiole to 5cm long. In the autumn the lv colour, usually a rather dull red but occasion-

Quercus rubra (borealis)

ally russet, yellow or quite a bright red. The acorns, which may be 3cm long and broad and take 2 years to mature, are enclosed in a very shallow, saucer-like cup, which is one of the easiest ways of distinguishing this plant from *Q. coccinea* or *Q. palustris.* Other distinguishing features are the larger lv, which are less deeply lobed and a less shining green. 'Aurea' has the young lv yellow and is slow growing. Native of eastern N America. Introduced by Bartram about 1739. I can find no authority for Rehder's date of 1724, suggesting a Catesby sending.

Quercus shumardii BUCKLEY

6.7. (*Q. schneckii* BRITTON) A tree of up to 40m in the wild. It appears to be midway between *Q. coccinea* and *Q. rubra,* the lv resembling the former, the acorns the latter. The bts are glabrous. Lv basically obovate, but 5–9-lobed, to 20cm long and half as wide; dark glossy green above, grey pubescent below at first, but later almost glabrous and shining, turning red or golden brown in the autumn. Acorns up to 3cm long in a saucer-like cup. Native of central and south-eastern USA. Introduced, probably as *Q. texana,* in 1897. The true *Q. texana* of Buckley is not in cultivation.

Quercus stellata WANGENHEIM

7. (*Q. obtusiloba* MICHAUX) Deciduous tree, to 20m, with reddish-brown fissured bark and brown tomentose bts. Lv lyre-shaped, but deeply lobed, to 20cm long and 12cm across, very dark green above and rough to the touch, covered below with grey or brown stellate tomentum. Acorns in pairs, to 2·5cm long, in a cup which covers

one third of the nut. Native of much of the USA. Introduced by Fraser in 1800.

Quercus variabilis BLUME

7. (*Q. chinensis* BUNGE) Deciduous tree, to 25m, with yellowish-grey, corky, deeply furrowed bark; bts hairy at first. Lv oblong, much like a sweet chestnut, to 15cm long and 5cm wide, pointed, with bristle-tipped teeth, dark matt-green above, grey tomentose below. Acorn to 2cm long, almost entirely enclosed in the mossy cup. Native of China, Korea and Japan. Introduced by Fortune in 1861.

Quercus velutina LAMARCK

(6).7. (*Q. tinctoria* MICHAUX) Deciduous tree, to about 30m. Bts brown tomentose. Lv basically oval or obovate, but deeply 5–7-lobed, dark green shining and eventually glabrous above, brown pubescent beneath, but nearly glabrous by the end of the season, to 30cm long and 20cm wide (or, in var *rubifolia,* to 40cm long), on a petiole to 6cm long. The lv often turn dull red or orange-brown in the autumn. Acorns solitary, almost sessile, to 2cm long and half enclosed in the cup. Native of eastern and central USA. Introduced by Fraser in 1800.

Raphiolepis umbellata

RAPHIOLEPIS LINDLEY *Rosaceae*

A small genus of three or four species of ever-green shrubs with alternate, short-stalked leaves

185

and small flowers in terminal panicles and fleshy fruit. Propagated by seeds or by cuttings of half-ripe shoots.

Raphiolepis umbellata (THUNBERG) MAKINO

4. (*R. japonica* SIEBOLD AND ZUCCARINI) Slow-growing evergreen shrub, to 2m usually but up to 3 or 4 against a wall. Lv coriaceous, oval, usually toothed towards the apex, covered with grey down when first emerging, later glabrous on both surfaces, to 7cm long and 5cm wide. Fl fragrant, 5-petalled, to 2cm across, white, in a stiff terminal raceme to 10cm long. Fl 6. Fr pyriform, blue-black. *R. X delacourii* ANDRÉ is a hybrid between this sp and the tender *R. indica*, raised at the end of the nineteenth century. It seldom reaches 2m in height, has slightly longer and narrower lv than *R. umbellata* (to 9cm long and 3·5cm across) and the fl are an attractive rosy-pink. It seems to be able to flower at any time of the year. Both the sp and the hybrid are normally hardy, but do better with some wall protection and may be damaged by exceptional frosts. *R. umbellata* is native of Japan and Korea and was introduced about 1862.

REHDERODENDRON HU *Styracaceae*

A little-known genus of deciduous trees of about eight species all native to southern and western China, of which only one is in cultivation. This requires lime-free soil and dislikes drought. Propagation by cuttings is not easy, but seed is satisfactory, although slow. The genus was established as recently as 1930.

Rehderodendron macrocarpum HU

4.5.(6). Deciduous tree, to 9m. Bts glabrous. Lv elliptic to oblong-ovate, finely toothed glabrous above, with a fine starry down below at first on the veins, often colouring well before falling, to 10cm long and half as wide. Fl in lax axillary racemes before or with the lv, the racemes 6–7-flowered, each fl tubular, to 12mm long, white, with conspicuous yellow anthers. Fl 4–5. Fr oblong, ribbed, bright red. Native of western China (Mt Omei). Introduced by Hu in 1934.

RHAMNUS LINNAEUS *Rhamnaceae*

A large genus of 160 species mainly deciduous shrubs (rarely trees) with very few definitive characters. The leaves are usually alternate, but sometimes opposite. The flowers are perfect, monoecious or dioecious, and are always small and greenish. The fruit is a drupe with two to four seeds. Propagated by seeds or layers; cuttings are possible but often slow and reluctant to root. Few species are of much ornamental value.

Cascara Sagrada is obtained from the bark of *R. purshiana*.

Rhamnus alaternus LINNAEUS

Evergreen shrub, to 4m, of rounded, bushy habit; bts pubescent. Lv alternate, oval to oblong, to 5cm long and half as wide, sometimes mucronate, dark glossy green above, yellowish-green below. Fl on short umbel-like racemes, greenish-yellow, monoecious or dioecious. Fr black. Var *angustifolia* (MILLER) DUMONT DE COURSET is somewhat dwarfer with lv to 5cm long but only 1·5cm wide. 'Argenteovariegata', with slightly distorted lv with a cream margin, is interesting as being the first popular variegated evergreen in gardens. All this group root readily from cuttings. Native of SW Europe. Introduced early in the seventeenth century, but not satisfactory in very cold regions.

Rhamnus californica ESCHSCHOLZ

5. Evergreen shrub, to 5m, with pubescent bts. Lv alternate, oval, to 10cm long and half as wide (larger and tomentose beneath in var *crassifolia* WOLF). Fl greenish in short-stalked umbels, perfect. Fr 8mm across, red at first, later dark purple. Native of the western USA from Oregon to California. Introduced in either 1858 or 1871.

Rhamnus frangula LINNAEUS
Buckthorn, Alder Buckthorn

5.6. Deciduous shrub, to 6m, which can be trained to make a small tree; bts downy. Lv obovate, alternate, to 7cm long and 3cm across; dark green above, paler below and slightly pubescent, turning a clear yellow before falling. Fl in small, axillary clusters. Fr red at first, eventually nearly black. 'Asplenifolia' has the lv threadlike, not more than 5mm wide. Native of Europe including the UK.

Rhamnus imeretina KIRCHNER

6. The most attractive sp owing to its handsome foliage. Deciduous shrub, to 3m, with markedly sturdy, slightly pubescent bts. Lv alternate, elliptic-oblong or oblong, to 25cm long and 10cm wide, dark green above but slightly rugose, paler and downy below. The lv turn a dull purple before falling. Fl green in axillary clusters. Fr black. Requires a moist situation and has no objection to shady conditions. Native of the Caucasus region of western Asia. Introduced slightly before 1858.

Rhamnus infectoria LINNAEUS

Spreading, deciduous shrub, to 2m high but considerably wider, with spine-tipped laterals. Lv opposite, elliptic-ovate, serrate, to 3cm long and half as wide, dark green above, sometimes pubescent below. Fl green, fr black. The seeds

Rhamnus imeretina

were formerly used for dyeing. Native of south-western Europe. It makes quite an attractive gnarled bush.

Rhamnus japonica MAXIMOWICZ

Deciduous shrub, to 3m, with lateral brs often spine-tipped and short and spur-like. Lv opposite, obovate, always tapered at the base, rounded or acuminate at the apex, crowded at the apices of the bts; pale green to 7cm long and 2·5cm wide. Fl greenish, in dense clusters, fragrant, mono-ecious or dioecious. Fl 5. Fr black. The fragrance is faint, although pleasant. Native of Japan. Introduced in 1888.

Rhamnus utilis DECAISNE

Deciduous shrub, to 3m, Laterals occasionally spine-tipped but usually unarmed. Lv opposite, oblong or obovate, mucronate, to 12cm long and 5cm across, yellowish-green on both surfaces. Fl yellow-green. Fr black. Native of central and eastern China, used in dyeing. Introduced about 1870.

RHODODENDRON LINNAEUS *Ericaceae*

A very large genus of about 600 species of shrubs or trees, of which about half are hardy in many parts of the UK. In addition to this basic rich-ness of material, hundreds of hybrids also exist, so that any treatment must be rather superficial in a work of this character. Some space may be saved by listing characters that are common to the majority. These are evergreen leaves, which are basically elliptic in shape, alternate, (but the internodes are often so short that the leaves appear whorled). The flowers are in terminal, umbel-like racemes, known as trusses; the flowers are large, funnel-shaped, rotate, or campanulate, often asymmetric (zygomorphic). Numerous exceptions will be found in the following descrip-tions, but where no details are given, it may be assumed that these characters obtain.

The hardy rhododendrons can be conveniently divided initially in two sections, defined by whether the underside of the leaf is scaly (lepidote) or lacking scales (elepidote), and it is practically impossible to hybridise between these two categories. All the species need acid soil and resent prolonged drought; although in the wild many species are found on limestone formations, they all appear to require acid soil in cultivation. The dwarf species are usually happy in direct sunlight, but the larger-leaved plants need more or less shady conditions, the amount of shade seemingly correlated to the size of leaf, although dappled shade will suit the majority.

The hybrids cannot be dealt with here, but, although usually lacking the grace of the true species, they may well be more reliable in flower-ing, some of the species showing a tendency to biennial flowering. If the trusses are not removed as soon as flowering is complete, there is a great risk that the plants may weaken themselves by overproduction of seed. This removal is known as dead-heading. Propagation is most effective by layering; the layers being left for two seasons before being detached. Seed is a ready means of getting large numbers, but the plants are often rather variable from seed and the best forms can only be propagated vegetatively. Semi-hard stem cuttings with a heel and some bottom heat root fairly readily for plants with small or medium leaves, but the larger-leaved species are difficult to root. Formerly much propagation was done by grafting, usually on *R. ponticum* rootstock, but this practice is to be deprecated.

Rhododendrons have very fine roots which do not descend very deep, so that quite sizeable specimens can be moved without injury, although they usually take three or four years to restart making vigorous growth and it is preferable to move smaller plants. The shrubby species will start to flower in four to seven years from seed; the arborescent species take longer. The flower buds are formed in the autumn before flowering and are roughly conical with numerous imbricate scales, which are often diagnostic. In many species the young leaves are densely coated with indumentum, and in some this persists on the underside. It has already been said that the species are very variable from seed, and with some species it is advisable to get a named clone.

The species have been described with some accuracy in Part I of the *Rhododendron Handbook*, and only such plants as have been given the greatest hardiness rating are included here.

In order to give some organisation to so vast a number of species, the late Sir Isaac Bayley Balfour divided them up into a number of series, the members of which had sufficient characters in common with each other and distinct from others to make their affinity recognisable. Often these series were further divided into sub-series, and later experience has found that some of these sub-series should themselves constitute series, but no authoritative reclassification has been done. With a few exceptions, however, it is not possible to give a brief key to recognise the different series. Most rhododendrons have ten or more stamens, but the *Azalea* series has five or ten, which, together with their asymmetric flowers (and often their deciduous habit), makes them one of the easiest series to recognise. Similarly the *Triflorum* series, with the flowers in threes and, often, the presence of more than one terminal bud and occasionally axillary ones, is also readily distinct. Otherwise one has to rely on a microscopic examination of the hairs on the leaves and on a number of badly defined characters. I mention the series(s) and sub-series(ss) in my descriptions, but, in most cases, they will not be of much help. Most plants with very large leaves will belong to the *Falconeri* series; the other large-leafed series, the *Grande*, not being sufficiently hardy for inclusion. Many of the *Barbatum* series have the branchlets and petioles covered with glandular bristles, but there are exceptions.

Unless described as deciduous, all the plants below may be assumed to be evergreen.

During the early years of this century, there was an enormous influx of Chinese and Tibetan species, and in many cases it is not possible to say whether Forrest or Kingdon Ward was the original introducer; nor is the matter of much importance as each sending may have produced superior forms.

Rhododendron aberconwayi COWEN *Irroratum*

4. Rather spreading shrub, to about 3m. Lv very hard and brittle, leathery, dark green above, pale below and eventually nearly glabrous. Fl patulate, to 7cm diameter, white or pink, base spotted to a greater or lesser degree. Fl 5–6. Native of Yunnan and easily recognised by its lv which break if bent.

Rhododendron adenopodum FRANCHET
Caucasicum[1]

3.4. Often rather slow-growing shrub, to 3m, with bts and undersides of lv densely covered with whitish indumentum. The lv are held almost erect, so that this indumentum is conspicuous and makes the young lv very attractive. Lv oblong-lanceolate, to 15cm long and 3·5cm across, somewhat cupped. Fl funnel-campanulate in a loose, elongated truss, each fl to 7cm across, 5-lobed, pale pink. Fl 4–5. This attractive, but uncertain, plant seems to be best in full light. Native of Hupeh and Szechuan. Introduced by Farges in 1901.

Rhododendron albrechtii MAXIMOWICZ
Azalea Canadense

(3).4. The ss is distinguished by the growth buds not being included among the scales of the fl bud, but separate, below. Deciduous shrub, to 3m occasionally but usually not more than 2m. Lv obovate, in whorl-like clusters of 5 at the end of the twigs, purple-tinged when young. Fl before lv, rotate-patulate, with 10 stamens and a very small calyx, in clusters of 3–4, about 5cm across, rosy-purple. Fl 4–5. A very attractive plant that is quite hardy so far as winter cold is concerned, but may be damaged by late spring frosts. Native of Japan. Introduced 1914 by Wilson.

Rhododendron amagianum MAKINO
Azalea, Schlippenbachii

4. Deciduous shrub, to 4m. Lv in whorls of 3 at the ends of the brs, ovate or diamond-shaped, to 6cm long and nearly as wide. Fl asymmetric, funnel-shaped with expanded mouth to 3cm long, about twice as wide, in clusters of 3–4, brick-red. Fl 6–7. Useful for its late flowering. Native of Japan.

Rhododendron ambiguum HEMSLEY *Triflorum*

4. Shrub, to about 2m, with bts covered with glistening yellow scales. Lv oval, to 7cm long and 3cm broad, dark green above, paler below and scaly on both surfaces, densely so below. Three to four fl terminal, funnel-shaped asymmetric, about 3cm long and as much across at the mouth, greenish-yellow or yellow with green spots. Fl 4–5. The greenish fl are unusual but not markedly attractive. Native of western China. Introduced by Wilson in 1904.

Rhododendron arborescens TORREY
Azalea, Luteum

4.(6). This ss is similar to *Canadense*, but the fl have 5 stamens not 10. Deciduous shrub, to around 3m, occasionally a small tree to 6m in the wild. Lv to 9cm long and 3–4cm across, shining green above, glaucous below, sometimes colouring in the autumn. Fl in clusters of 3–6,

[1] I am regarding here the ss *Caucasicum* of the *Ponticum* series and the ss *Argyrophyllum* of the *Arboreum* series, as series in their own right.

tubular, with expanded limb to 3cm long and 6cm wide; white, more or less pink-tinged, extremely fragrant, the red stamens and style protruding. Sometimes the fl are somewhat hidden by the young lv. Fl 6–7. Native of the eastern USA. Introduced in 1818.

Rhododendron argyrophyllum FRANCHET
Argyrophyllum

3.4. Somewhat slow-growing shrub, to 7m eventually. Bts and young lv covered with silvery tomentum, which persists on the underside of the lv as a thin, white felt. Lv oblong-lanceolate, to 13cm long and 3cm across, medium green. Fl in a loose truss of 6–12, campanulate, to 3·5cm long with 12–14 stamens; white to pink, sometimes spotted or blotched. Fl 5. One of the more attractive spp. Native of Szechuan. Introduced by Wilson in 1904.

Rhododendron atlanticum REHDER
Azalea, Luteum

4. Deciduous, stoloniferous shrub, rarely exceeding 1m. Lv obovate, bright green above, somewhat glaucous below. Fl with lv in clusters of 4–10, fragrant, funnel-shaped, tubular, about 3cm across and 2·5cm long; white, flushed pink, sometimes with yellow blotch. Fl 5. Native to coastal regions of the eastern USA. Confused with *R. viscosum* (qv), and not consciously introduced before about 1916.

Rhododendron augustinii HEMSLEY
Triflorum, Augustinii

4. (includes *R. chasmanthum* DIELS) Evergreen or, in cold districts, semi-evergreen shrub, to 5m. Lv elliptic, purple-flushed when young, to 12cm long and 3cm wide. Fl usually in 3s, asymmetric, widely funnel-shaped, to 5cm long and 6cm across, varying in colour from almost a gentian blue to lavender and mauve, often with greenish markings in the throat. The intensity of the blue varies from year to year, so is presumably controlled by the weather of the preceding season and also seems to depend to a certain extent on the soil. Fl 4–5. The best blue forms have the reputation of being slightly tender, but this does not seem to always be the case. Native to western China and Tibet. Introduced to Vilmorin in 1899.

Rhododendron auriculatum HEMSLEY
Auriculatum

4. Large shrub or small spreading tree to 10m. Lv obovate, mucronate, with two small lobes (auricles) at the base, to 30cm long, 10cm wide, dark green above, pale green below. Fl in loose trusses of 7–15, open funnel-shaped, to 10cm long and slightly less wide, white (rarely pale pink) fragrant. Fl 8. Unique for its late flowering;

only the unobtainable *R. serotinum* flowers later, and it is distinct when not in flower by its long, pointed fl buds. Does not flower as a young plant and lv often turn an unhealthy-looking pale yellow-green. The young growths are furnished with conspicuous red scales, appearing more or less with the fl. Native of western China. Introduced by Wilson in 1900.

Rhododendron barbatum WALLICH *Barbatum*

1.4. Large shrub or small tree to 10m, with smooth, reddish-purple bark in mature specimens, exfoliating. Lv and fl buds very sticky. Bts and petioles usually densely set with glandular bristles, which may or may not persist for more than a year. Lv to 20cm long and 7cm wide, somewhat wrinkled above, some ephemeral indumentum below (in the closely related *R. smithii* NUTTALL AND HOOKER the indumentum below is persistent and the plant does not exceed 6m), dark green. Fl in rounded, compact trusses of 10–16 blooms, each tubular-campanulate with 5 lobes, to 5cm long, with 5 dark crimson nectar pouches at the base. Fl 3.
R. imberbe HUTCHINSON is a shrub, to nearly 3m, with lv not more than 12cm long and devoid of bristles, otherwise similar. Delightful for its early deep red fl, which may be damaged by frost. Native of the Himalaya. Obtained by Messrs Loddiges about 1829.

Rhododendron bodinieri FRANCHET
Triflorum, Yunnanense

4. Shrub, to 2·5m, only to be distinguished from *R. yunnanense* (qv) by its smaller dimensions, its earlier flowering season and, most particularly, by the lanceolate, long-acuminate lv. Fl pink with purple spots. Fl 3–4. Native of Yunnan.

Rhododendron brachycarpum G. AND D. DON
Caucasicum

3.4. Shrub, to 3m, with white tomentose bts and young lv. Mature lv oblong, to 12cm long and half as wide, dark green above, and with a fawn indumentum below. Fl in an elongated truss of 10–20 fl, funnel shaped, 5-lobed, to 4cm long and 5cm wide, white (rarely pale yellow), flushed pink and with green spots, stamens 10, style very short. Fl 6–7. Almost without exception Caucasicum rhododendrons from Japan are attractive, hardy plants, and this sp has the additional advantage of late flowering. Introduced 1861, according to Rehder.

Rhododendron bureavii FRANCHET
Taliense, Adenogynum

3.4. A shrub, to little more than 2m, with the bts and young lv deeply covered in brilliant rust-red indumentum, which persists on the underside of the lv. Lv thick, coriaceous, to 12cm long and 5cm across, eventually glabrous and dark green above. (*R. bureavioides* I. BALFOUR is identical but slightly larger in all its parts, with lv to 14cm.) Fl tubular-campanulate, 5-lobed, in a compact truss of 10–15 fl, each fl to 5cm long, white or pink with crimson markings. Fl 4–5. Like all the *Taliense* series, this tends to take a long time to arrive at a flowering stage and then flowers irregularly, but the foliage is outstanding. Native of western China. The first introduction I can trace is Wilson in 1904.

Rhododendron calendulaceum
(MICHAUX) TORREY   *Azalea, Luteum*

4.6. Deciduous shrub, to 5m, with bristly bts. Lv obovate, to 10cm long and 3cm across, turning orange and red in autumn. Fl before lv in clusters of 5–7; the fl funnel-shaped, asymmetric, about 1cm long and 5cm across, yellow, orange, salmon, red or scarlet. Fl 5–6. Although extensively used in hybrid azaleas, the sp is rarely seen, but is extremely ornamental both in fl and again in autumn. Native of eastern N America. Introduced by Fraser in 1806.

Rhododendron callimorphum
I. BALFOUR AND W. W. SMITH
Thomsonii, Campylocarpum

4. (*R. cyclium* BALFOUR AND FORREST) Shrub of up to 3m, forming a rounded bush. Lv rounded, to 5cm long and only slightly less wide, glossy green above, glaucous beneath. Fl in trusses of 5–8, wide-campanulate, to 5cm long and wide; rose-pink, stamens 10. Fl 4–6. A very attractive, small shrub, not very free-flowering. Native of Yunnan. Introduced by Forrest in 1912.

Rhododendron calophytum   FRANCHET
Fortunei, Calophytum

4. Large shrub or tree to 10m. Lv obovate, glabrous on both surfaces (slightly tomentose along midrib when young), to 30cm or more long and 10cm wide. Fl in large trusses of 15–30 fl on long pedicels to 7cm long, widely campanulate, to 6cm long and wide, 5–8-lobed; rosy-white, pink or pale lilac, stamens 15–20. Fl 3–4. A magnificent plant with its huge lv; not very easily obtained and not flowering until quite sizeable, unlike the similar-looking *R. sutchuense*, but well worth the wait. Requires fairly deep shade. Native of western China. Introduced by Wilson in 1904.

Rhododendron caloxanthum
I. BALFOUR AND FARRER
Thomsonii, Campylocarpum

4. Shrub of up to 2m. Lv rounded, to 7cm long and nearly as much wide, dark green above, glaucous beneath. Fl in trusses of 4–9, broadly campanulate, to 4cm long and wide; orange-scarlet in bud, yellow when open, either pale, or quite dark, stamens 10. Fl 4–5. Native of Burma, Tibet and Yunnan. Introduced Farrer and Cox in 1919.

Rhododendron campanulatum   D. DON
Campanulatum

4. Although often tree-like in the wild, it rarely exceeds 6m in cultivation. Lv coriaceous, broad-elliptic, tomentose on both surfaces at first, later glabrous above, rusty-brown felted below, to 15cm long and 6cm across, petiole often reddish. In some forms the scales between the expanding lv are bright crimson. Fl in trusses of 6–12, widely campanulate, to 5cm long and broad, varying from white to pale pink, purple and almost blue; stamens 10. Fl 4–5.
3. var *aeruginosum* NICHOLSON has the young lv of a very striking metallic blue-green with a hint of silver. It is compact and slow growing. The best blue forms are very attractive, but all take rather a long time to arrive at flowering. Native of the Himalaya. Introduced by Wallich in 1825.

Rhododendron campylocarpum   J. HOOKER
Thomsonii, Campylocarpum

4. Shrub, to 4m (var *elatum*) although usually about 2m. Lv ovate, to 10cm long and half as wide, shining green above, glaucous beneath. Fl in trusses of 6–10, campanulate, about 4cm long and wide; usually pale yellow, with or without a crimson blotch, occasionally pale pink or ivory, usually orange in bud; stamens 10. Fl 4–5. Once it has arrived at flowering size, extremely free-flowering. Some forms may be slightly tender, but normally sturdy enough. Native of the Himalaya. Introduced by Joseph Hooker in 1849–51.

Rhododendron carolinianum   REHDER
Carolinianum

4. (*R. punctatum* var *carolinianum* KER) Shrub growing to little over 1m, rarely to 2m. Lv to 7cm long and half as wide, leathery, dark green and with a netted appearance above. Fl in trusses of 4–10, tubular with expanded mouth, about 2·5cm long and 3cm broad, purplish pink or (in var *album* REHDER) white with a yellow blotch (also more pointed lv). Stamens 10. Fl 5–6. Requires light soil and perfect drainage. Native of the southern USA. Introduced by Fraser in 1812.

Rhododendron catawbiense   MICHAUX
Ponticum

4. Spreading shrub, to 5m, but more horizontally, often layering itself. Lv to 15cm long and

5cm across, glabrous on both surfaces. Fl in pyramidal truss of 15–20, funnel-campanulate, blooms to 3cm long and 6cm across; normally lilac-purple, occasionally white or purple-pink; stamens 10. Fl 6. Distinguished from *R. ponticum* by the base of the lv being broad, not tapered to the petiole. Although one of the main parents of the earlier hardy hybrids (it has survived −20°C), the true sp is not often seen in gardens nowadays. Native of the Alleghenny Mountains. Introduced by Fraser in 1809.

Rhododendron caucasicum PALLAS
Caucasicum

4. Shrub, occasionally to 3m but usually less and somewhat spreading, slow-growing. Lv to 10cm long and 3cm across, dull green above, fawn or pale-rusty tomentose below. Fl in a pyramidal truss, broadly campanulate, to 3·5cm long and 5cm wide, cream, rose-flushed or yellow; stamens 10. Fl 4–6. Native of the Caucasus region. Introduced by Mussin-Puschkin in 1803.

Rhododendron cerasinum TAGG
Thomsonii, Cerasinum

4. Shrub, to 4m but usually considerably less. Lv to 10cm long and half as wide, shining green above, somewhat glaucous below. Fl in trusses of 6–7, pendulous, bell-shaped, to 5cm long and slightly wider; scarlet, cherry-red or (from KW 6923) cream with a broad red band around the mouth. Fl 5. Shy-flowering when young, and often many of the fl are hidden beneath the lv, but good forms are enchanting. Native of Burma, Tibet and Assam. First sent by Kingdon Ward from his 1924–5 expedition under number 5830.

Rhododendron charitopes BALFOUR AND FARRER
Glaucophyllum

4. Shrub of little more than 1m high and quite often considerably less. Lv obovate, to 7cm long and 3cm across, glossy green above glaucous and densely scaly below. Fl usually in 3s, occasionally up to 6, spreading campanulate, 2·5cm long and wide; apple-blossom-pink with crimson spots. Fl 4–5. Usually a few fl are also produced in the autumn. Native of northern Burma and Yunnan. Introduced by Farrer, according to Bean, but the sp does not appear in the Rhododendron Society's list of his sendings.

Rhododendron ciliatum JOSEPH HOOKER
Maddenii, Ciliicalyx

4. Most plants in this series need cool, greenhouse treatment, but this sp is usually hardy, although slow-growing, in colder districts. Spreading shrub to 2m, usually less with peeling bark; bts covered with bristly hairs. Lv to 10cm

Rhododendron cinnabarinum

long and 4cm across, fringed around the margin and slightly bristly above. Fl rose-coloured in bud, opening pink and fading to white, campanulate and nodding, in clusters of 2–4, to 5cm long and wide. Fl 3–4. About 1855 Mr Isaac Davies crossed this with *R. dauricum* (qv) to produce *R. X praecox*, with rosy-purple fl 5cm across. Fl 2–3. Native of Sikkim and Bhutan. Introduced by Hooker in 1851.

Rhododendron cinnabarinum JOSEPH HOOKER
Cinnabarinum

(3).4. This series is immediately recognisable by the pendent, tubular fl resembling a fuchsia or a lapageria, quite unlike the fl of any other rhododendron. Shrub from 3–5m, often with purplish bts. Lv often blue-green when young, to 8cm long and 4·5cm across, grey-green or (in var *roylei*, particularly) glaucous above, always glaucous below and scaly. Fl in trusses of about 5, tubular, with expanded lobes to 5cm long, nodding; variable in colour from cinnabar red to rose-purple and pale apricot, often yellow within. Fl 4–6 (var *aestivale*, which does not appear to be in commerce, fl 7). Var *roylei*, with attractive lv and plum-crimson fl slightly shorter and more open than the type, is the most attractive form. Although capable of surviving very low temperatures, spring frosts may damage the fl in the buds before they open. Introduced from Sikkim by Joseph Hooker in 1849.

Rhododendron concatenans HUTCHINSON
Cinnabarinum

3.4. Shrub, to slightly under 3m, with reddish-brown bts. Lv glaucous, almost blue when young, to 6cm long and 3cm across, slightly purple-tinged below. Fl in trusses of 7–8, tubular-campanulate, 5-lobed, to 5cm long and wide; orange to apricot, sometimes stained purple or yellow, with marked veins. Fl 4–5. Closely allied to *R. cinnabarinum*, but with more bell-shaped fl. Native of Tibet. Discovered and introduced by Kingdon Ward in his 1924–5 expedition.

Rhododendron concinnum HEMSLEY
Triflorum, Yunnanense

4. (*R. yanthinum* BUREAU AND FRANCHET, *R. pseudoyanthinum* I. BALFOUR) Shrub, to 3m. Lv to 7cm long and 2cm wide, dark green above, greyer below, scaly on both surfaces. Fl in clusters of 3 or 6, to 3·5cm long and 5cm across, asymmetric, widely funnel-shaped; purple or magenta (in var *pseudoyanthinum* DAVIDIAN, which is the form most usually seen). Fl 4–5. The sp varies much in colour, but usually a bright purple. Native of Szechuan. Introduced by Wilson in 1901.

Rhododendron coryanum TAGG AND FORREST
Argyrophyllum

4. A shrub, to 7m, with grey-hairy bts. Lv to 17cm long and 4cm across, rather leathery, light green above, with a suede-like grey or fawn indumentum below. Fl in trusses of 20–30, funnel-campanulate, to 3cm long, 5-lobed, creamy-white with crimson spots; stamens 10–12. Fl 4–5. Notable among this series for the very large number of fl in the truss. Native of the Yunnan–Tibetan border. Introduced by Forrest in 1921.

Rhododendron crinigerum FRANCHET
Barbatum, Crinigerum

3.4. Shrub, to 4m, with very sticky, bristly bts, the bristles persisting for several years. Lv to 18cm long and 5cm across, woolly and white when young, later dark green and glossy above, somewhat puckered, white or buff indumentum persisting below. Fl in trusses of about 12, campanulate, with 5 lobes, about 4cm long and wide; cream flushed pink or pale pink with a deep crimson blotch at the base; stamens 10. Fl 4–5. Native of Yunnan and south-eastern Tibet. Introduced by Forrest in 1914.

Rhododendron cuneatum W. W. SMITH
Lapponicum

4. Shrub, usually to 2m but occasionally to 3m. Lv to 3cm long and 2cm across, dark glossy green above, scaly below. Fl in clusters of 3–6, widely funnel-shaped, to 2·5cm long and wide, varying from deep rose to rose-purple. Fl 4. Native of Yunnan. Introduced by Forrest in 1913.

Rhododendron cyanocarpum
(FRANCHET) W. W. SMITH
Thomsonii

3.4. Shrub or small tree, to 6m, with glaucous bts and young lv. Mature lv rounded, to 11cm long and 7cm across, dark green above and glaucous beneath. Fl in trusses of 8–10, fragrant, widely funnel-campanulate, to 6cm long and 8cm across, 5-lobed; white, flushed pink or soft pink; stamens 10, calyx large, about 12mm long. Fl 3–4. Fr purple. Very close indeed to *R. thomsonii* (qv) but with larger lv and fl and with different coloured fl, which are also fragrant. Native of Yunnan. Introduced by Forrest in 1910.

Rhododendron dauricum LINNAEUS
Dauricum

4. Somewhat leggy semi-evergreen or evergreen shrub, to 2m and occasionally to 3m. Lv elliptic, to 3cm long and 12mm wide, dark green and shining above. The plant produces a cluster of terminal buds, each of which produces a single fl, widely funnel-shaped, almost patulate, to 3cm wide and 2cm long, magenta-purple; stamens 10. Fl 1–3. Very reliable for its early flowering, but slow-growing. Individual fl may be damaged by frost, but those still in bud will remain unharmed. Native of northern Asia. Introduced, probably by Pallas, in 1780.

Rhododendron davidsonianum
REHDER AND WILSON *Triflorum, Yunnanense*

4. (*R. charianthum* HUTCHINSON) Leggy shrub, to 3m, purplish bts. Lv slightly inclined along the midrib, so that a horizontal section is V-shaped, scaly on both surfaces but densely below, to 6cm long and 2cm wide; dark glossy green above, brownish below. Fl in terminal and axillary trusses of 3 or 6, to 4cm long and 5cm across, widely funnel-shaped, a clear pink in the best forms, but varying from almost white to purplish; 5-lobed, stamens 10. Fl 4–5. Excellent in its best forms. Native of Szechuan. Introduced by Wilson in 1908.

Rhododendron decorum FRANCHET *Fortunei*

4. Large shrub or small tree to 7m. Lv to 15cm long and half as wide, oblong-obovate, mid-green and waxy above, somewhat glaucous below. Fl in trusses of 8–14, open funnel-shaped, to 7cm long and wide, 6–8 lobed with 12–16 stamens, fragrant, white or pale pink, sometimes green or pink-spotted. Fl 5–6. A plant of wide distribution, varying in size and in hardiness, but perfectly hardy in most forms. Comes readily from seed and usually flowers when quite small, after 5 years or even less. Native to western China. Said to have been introduced by Delavay about 1889, but this seems to have been the allied, late-flowering *R. serotinum*, and the first introduction of the true species should be credited to Wilson in 1904.

Rhododendron desquamatum
I. BALFOUR AND FORREST *Heliolepis*

4. Large shrub or small tree to 8m. Lv to 9cm long and 3cm across, dark green above, densely brown-scaly below. Fl in lax trusses of 4–6, almost patulate but somewhat funnel-shaped, to 5cm across, stamens 10; mauve to reddish purple. Fl 3–4. Native of Burma, Yunnan and Tibet. Introduced by Forrest in 1924.

Rhododendron dichroanthum DIELS
Neriiflorum, Sanguineum

4. (Includes *R. apodectum, herpesticum* and *scyphocalyx*, which are reduced to varieties of this variable sp). Shrub from less than 1m to 2m; bts with thin, whitish indumentum. Lv oblong-obovate or oblanceolate to 10cm long and 4cm across, slightly wrinkled above and glabrous, a thin greyish indumentum below. Fl in lax trusses of 4–8, tubular campanulate, 5-lobed, the calyx the same colour as the petals, some shade of orange from almost yellow to nearly salmon. The most conspicuous is the coppery-orange of var *scyphocalyx*. Var *herpesticum* is a very dwarf shrub. Fl 5–6. First introduced by Forrest in 1910; var *scyphocalyx* introduced by Forrest in 1919, var *herpesticum* by Kingdon Ward in 1914. Native of Burma and Yunnan.

Rhododendron discolor FRANCHET *Fortunei*

4. A fairly rapid-growing shrub or small tree, to 7m, with leathery lv, glabrous on both surfaces. Lv to 20cm long and 7cm across, dark green. Fl in a loose truss of about 10 blooms, each funnel-campanulate, 7-lobed, to 9cm long and 10cm wide; fragrant, pale pink fading to white. The new growths tend to elongate as the fl open. Fl 6–7. A splendid shrub both for its attractive fl and for its late season, but somewhat slow to attain a flowering rhythm. Native of central and western China. Introduced by Wilson in 1900.

Rhododendron dryophyllum
BALFOUR AND FORREST *Lacteum*

3.4. A shrub of up to 3m in the wild but occasionally to 8m in cultivation. Bts and young lv covered with buff indumentum. Lv to 7cm long and 5cm across, glossy green above, covered below with a thin, suede-like indumentum vary-ing in colour from beige to cinnamon. Fl in trusses of 8–16 blooms, funnel-campanulate or campanulate, 5-lobed, to 4cm long and 6cm across, varying in colour from white to pinkish-purple, sometimes with crimson spots, occasionally with a crimson blotch at the base. Fl 4–5. A very variable sp. Like most of the series, does not flower as a young plant. Native of Yunnan, Burma, Bhutan and Tibet. Introduced by Forrest about 1917.

Rhododendron erubescens HUTCHINSON
Fortunei, Oreodoxa

4. Shrub, to 3m, with smooth, purple bark. Lv to 15cm long and 5cm wide, dark green above, yellowish-green below. Fl in trusses of up to 8, open campanulate, 5cm long and 4cm wide, 7-lobed, 12–14 stamens; carmine or deep pink outside, white inside. Fl 4. Native of China. Introduced by Wilson in 1902.

Rhododendron fargesii FRANCHET
Fortunei, Oreodoxa

4. Shrub, to 6m, closely allied to the last sp but with lv only to 8cm long and 5cm across and with the veins below slightly raised (slightly sunken in *R. erubescens*). Fl in trusses of 6–10, rose-lilac, pink or white, spotted or unspotted, 5–7-lobed, with 14 stamens. Fl 3–4. Although this sp *R. erubescens* and *R. oreodoxa* (qv) appear sufficiently distinct when the various characters are described, examples are so often slightly atypical that they are easily confused. Once it starts flowering *R. fargesii* is extremely floriferous and must then be deadheaded regularly to keep the shrub in condition. Native of Szechuan. Introduced by Wilson in 1901.

Rhododendron fastigiatum FRANCHET
Lapponicum

4. Erect shrub not exceeding 1m. Lv from 8–16mm long, greyish, scaly on both surfaces. Fl funnel-shaped, in clusters of 4–5, about 1cm long and 2·5cm across, from light-purple to deep purple-blue. Fl 4–5. A charming and reliable dwarf shrub. Native of Yunnan. Introduced by Forrest in 1911.

Rhododendron fauriei FRANCHET *Caucasicum*

4. Shrub from 2–3m with loose white indumentum on the bts, which soon falls away. Lv to 12cm long and 4cm broad, dark green above and soon glabrous on both surfaces. Fl funnel-campanulate, about 2·5cm long and wide, 5-lobed with 10 stamens, in a truss of 12–15 white or pink-flushed fl, green-spotted. Fl 6. Possibly only a form of *R. brachycarpum* DON, which has larger lv with a felt-like indumentum below. Native of Japan.

Rhododendron ferrugineum LINNAEUS
Ferrugineum Alpen Rose

4. Dwarf shrub, sometimes reaching 1m 30cm with oblanceolate lv to 3cm long, densely rusty-scaly below, light green above. Fl in small trusses, tubular, with 5 lobes and about 18mm long, crimson or, rarely, white; stamens 10. Fl 6. Native of the Pyrenees and Alps. Said not to have been introduced before 1752, but Parkinson depicts either this or *R. hirsutum* in his *Paradisus* of 1629.

Rhododendron fictolacteum I. BALFOUR
Falconeri

3.4. Tree, to 13m, with bts and young lv covered with cinnamon tomentum. Lv oblong-obovate, to 30cm long and 10cm wide, eventually glabrous and dark green above, often slightly quilted, with a buff or rusty-brown indumentum below. Fl in a truss of 10–25 fl, campanulate, to 5cm long and 7cm across, creamy-white or pink-flushed with a deep crimson blotch at the base, 7–8-lobed with 14–16 stamens. Fl 4–5. Together with *R. rex* (qv), the hardiest of the large-leaved tree rhododendrons, but they all require quite dense shade when small and protection from winds, if they are to appear presentable. They do not flower until quite large, but are worth growing for their foliage alone. *R. fictolacteum* has an extensive distribution in China, and forms vary considerably from different localities. First introduced by Delavay to Vilmorin in the 1880s.

Rhododendron floribundum FRANCHET
Argyrophyllum

3.4. Shrub or small tree, from 3–5m, with bts covered with white indumentum. Lv to 15cm long and 5cm across, dark green and bullate above, with a white persistent tomentum below. Fl in trusses of 5–12, widely campanulate, to 4cm long and 6–7cm across, 5-lobed with 10 stamens. Almost magenta at first with a dark crimson blotch at the base and numerous crimson spots; some forms are rose or paler pink and all fade to a lighter colour after a day or so. Fl 4. Native of China. Introduced by Wilson in 1903.

Rhododendron fortunei LINDLEY Fortunei

4. Usually a bush to 4m but occasionally tree-like and up to 10m. Lv to 20cm long and 8cm across, glabrous on both surfaces, dark green above, glaucous below. Fl in a truss of 6–12, funnel-campanulate, almost patulate, to 5cm long and 9cm wide, 7-lobed (rarely 8-lobed) with 14 stamens; calyx very small, lilac-pink, very fragrant. Fl 5. A delightful plant, which, although offered in most catalogues, is apparently very rarely unhybridised so that the true sp is very scarce. It has been also extensively used as a parent. Native of China. Introduced by Fortune in 1855.

Rhododendron fulgens JOSEPH HOOKER
Campanulatum

3.4. A shrub, to 4m, rounded in habit, with conspicuous red bracts between the young lv. Lv to 12cm long and 7cm across, oval, dark green above, with a thick tawny indumentum below. Fl in a tight truss of 10–12 fl, tubular-campanulate, rather fleshy, to 3cm long and 5cm wide, 5-lobed with 10 stamens, blood-red. Fl 3–4. Like all the series, somewhat slow in coming to flower, but then very welcome for its brilliant display so early in the year. Native of the Himalaya. Introduced by J. Hooker in 1851.

Rhododendron fulvum
I. BALFOUR AND W. W. SMITH Fulvum

3.4. (Including *R. fulvoides* TAGG AND FORREST) Straggling tree, to 7m, with bts and young lv covered with tawny or, occasionally, grey indumentum. Lv oblong-obovate, to 20 (rarely 25) cm long and 7cm wide, shining dark green above when mature, covered below with a dense indumentum, which is a rich cinnamon in the best forms but may be yellowish or tawny. Fl in a loose, rounded truss of about 18 fl, funnel-campanulate, 5–6-lobed, to 3cm long, slightly wider, stamens 10; pale pink to deep rose, often with a crimson blotch at the base. The sp varies greatly in the quality of the fl and in the colour of the indumentum. Native from Assam to Yunnan. Introduced by Forrest in 1912.

Rhododendron glischrum
I. BALFOUR AND W. W. SMITH
Barbatum, Glischrum

4. Tree, to 8m in the wild but, so far, only a large shrub to 4m in cultivation, bts covered with long, glandular bristles. Lv to 25cm long and 6cm wide, green above and eventually glabrous, sticky and bristly beneath. Fl in trusses of about 10 fl, tubular-campanulate, about 4cm long, 5-lobed, stamens 10; usually nearly magenta, but occasionally white or pink, with a crimson blotch at the base. Fl 4–5. Native of Yunnan and Burma. Introduced by Forrest in 1914.

Rhododendron griersonianum
I. BALFOUR AND FORREST Griersonianum

4. A rather gaunt, straggling shrub, to 3m, with glandular-hairy bts. Lv lanceolate, dull green above and nearly glabrous, with a loose white or buff woolly tomentum below, to 20cm long and 5cm across. Fl in loose trusses of 5–12 funnel-campanulate fl, to 9cm long and 10cm across, 5-lobed, geranium scarlet with a silvery sheen on the exterior and darker spots within; stamens 10. Fl 6. So far unique in the genus for its brilliant scarlet fl, unlike any other scarlet. The long, tapered flower buds recall those of *R. auriculatum*, although otherwise the plants are very distinct. Young plants are apt to prove tender and should be put in sheltered situations. Native of Yunnan and northern Burma. Introduced by Forrest in 1917.

Rhododendron haematodes FRANCHET
Neriiflorum, Haematodes

3.4. A rounded bush, often less than 1m high, but occasionally attaining 3m, with bts and young lv rusty tomentose. Lv obovate, to 8cm long and 4cm wide, dark green, slightly wrinkled, covered with a thick, rusty, woolly tomentum below. Fl in trusses of 6–8, tubular-campanulate, 5–6-lobed, enclosed in a sizeable red calyx. The fl are fleshy, scarlet crimson; stamens 10–12. Fl 5–6. Slow growing and not flowering freely when young, but a very attractive plant both in habit and flower. Native of the Tali range in Yunnan. Introduced by Forrest in 1910.

Rhododendron heliolepis FRANCHET
Heliolepis

4. Shrub of 3–4m with aromatic lv, which are up to 10cm long and 3cm wide, mucronate, netted above, scaly below. Fl in a lax truss of 4–6, widely funnel-shaped, 5-lobed fl, to 3cm long and wide, scaly outside, rosy-purple to old rose and white; stamens 10. Fl 5–6. Native of Yunnan. Introduced by Forrest in 1912.

Rhododendron hemitrichotum
BALFOUR AND FORREST *Scabrifolium*

4. In this series the fl are not terminal but come from axillary buds towards the ends of the twigs. Low shrubs, to 1m 30cm, with oblanceolate lv to 2·5cm long and half as wide, dull green and slightly hairy above, glaucous and scaly below. Fl usually in pairs but giving the appearance of a cluster, widely funnel-shaped (almost patulate), 5-lobed, to 2cm across, reddish in bud, white or pale pink with darker margin; stamens 8–10. Fl 4. Fl in 3–4 years from seed. Native of Szechuan. Introduced by Forrest in 1919.

Rhododendron hippophaeoides
BALFOUR AND FORREST *Lapponicum*

4. Shrub to 1m 60cm. Lv greyish, oblanceolate, to 3cm long and 8mm across, scaly on both surfaces, densely below. Fl in a close truss of 6–8, almost patulate, 5-lobed fl to 2·5cm across: lavender-blue in the best forms, also lilac and pink. Fl 3–4. A very attractive dwarf shrub, often found growing in bogs in the wild. Native of Yunnan. Introduced by Forrest from his 1912–14 expedition.

Rhododendron hirsutum LINNAEUS
Ferrugineum

4. Very similar to *R. ferrugineum* but distinguished by the bristly bts and margins to lv,

which are green rather than rusty beneath. Grows on limestone formations in the Alps, but always in humus-rich soil. Introduced in 1656 according to *Hortus Kewensis*, possibly earlier.

Rhododendron hodgsonii J. HOOKER
Falconeri

1.3.4. A small tree to 6m with smooth reddish-brown bark which exfoliates yearly; bts and young lv with grey or buff indumentum. Lv to 30cm long and 12cm across, slightly wrinkled above and dark green with shining spots, and a grey or fawn indumentum below. Fl in a rounded truss, tubular-campanulate, to 5cm long and wide, 7–8-lobed, more or less magenta, fading somewhat to magenta-lilac; stamens 15–18. Fl 4. Needs the same treatment as *R. fictolacteum*. Native of the Himalaya from Nepal to Bhutan. Introduced by Joseph Hooker 1849–51.

Rhododendron hormophorum
BALFOUR AND FORREST *Triflorum, Yunnanense*

4. (*R. chartophyllum* var *praecox*) Distinguished from *R. yunnanense* (see below) only in being deciduous.

Rhododendron houlstonii HEMSLEY AND WILSON
Fortunei

4. Shrub, to 4m in the wild but up to 6m and tree-like in cultivation. Lv to 15cm long and 5cm across, glabrous on both surfaces with a purple petiole, dark green above, paler below. Fl in a truss of 6–10 funnel-campanulate, 7-lobed, soft lilac or pale pink fl, to 6cm long and 7cm across; stamens 14. Fl 5. A very attractive shrub closely related to *R. fortunei*. Native of western China. Introduced by Wilson in 1900.

Rhododendron hunnewellianum
REHDER AND WILSON *Argyrophyllum*

(3).4. Shrub to about 5m, rather slow-growing, with grey felty bts and young lv. Lv narrow-elliptic, to 15cm long but only 2·5cm across, eventually glabrous above, somewhat wrinkled, dark green above but with silvery indumentum below. Fl in a truss of 5–7, widely campanulate, 5-lobed fl, white flushed pink (deep rose in bud), to 5cm long and 6cm wide, often pink-spotted within; stamens 10. Attractive with its narrow lv. Introduced from Szechuan by Wilson in 1908.

Rhododendron insigne HEMSLEY AND WILSON
Argyrophyllum

4. Shrub to 4m, rarely to 5m, slow-growing, with ash-grey bts. Lv leathery, oblong-lanceolate, to 12cm long and 5cm across, dark green and glabrous above, covered below with a skin-like indumentum which is grey with a coppery sheen. Fl in a truss of about 8 widely campanulate, 5-lobed fl to 4cm long and 6cm wide, soft pink with deeper stripes down the centre of each petal and crimson spots within; stamens 10–14. Fl 5–6. A very lovely sp introduced from Szechuan by Wilson in 1908.

Rhododendron irroratum FRANCHET *Irroratum*

4. Shrub or small tree to 8m in the wild but usually only about 4m in cultivation. Bts tomentose only for a short time. Lv to 12cm long and 3cm wide with a rather wavy margin, slightly woolly at first but later glabrous on both surfaces, light green above, very pale green below. Fl in a truss of up to 15 tubular-campanulate fl, to 5cm long and wide, 5-lobed, white or cream, more or less heavily marked with spots and often pink-flushed; stamens 10. Fl 3–5. Native of Yunnan. Discovered and probably introduced by Delavay in 1886.

Rhododendron japonicum SURINGAR
Azalea, Luteum

4. (*R. molle* of Siebold not of G. Don; *R. sinense* of Maximowicz, not of Sweet) Deciduous shrub, to 3m, with obovate lv to 10cm long and 3cm wide, dull green above, paler below, with a fringe of hairs. Fl before lv in trusses of 6–12, broad funnel-shaped fl to 6cm across, 5-lobed, orange-red, salmon-red or brick-red; stamens 5. Fl 5. Much confused with *R. molle* of G. Don, which differs in its larger lv, to 15cm long and 6cm across, with greyish pubescence beneath and golden-yellow fl with a green blotch. *R. japonicum* is native of Japan and was introduced in 1861; *R. molle* native of eastern China and introduced in 1824. Neither spp are often seen nowadays, but form the main parents in the Molle azalea hybrids.

Rhododendron kaempferi PLANCHON
Azalea, Obtusum

4. (*R. obtusum* var *kaempferi* WILSON) Deciduous or semi-evergreen shrub of up to 3m. Bts bristly. Lv to 7cm long and 2·5cm across, bristly on both surfaces, dark green above, paler below. Fl in clusters of up to 4, widely funnel-shaped, to 6cm long and wide; salmon-red to rosy-scarlet and purple, sometimes white; stamens 5. Fl 5–7. Probably a parent of the Kurume azaleas with *R. kiusianum*, a much dwarfer plant with smaller, purple fl. Native of Japan. Introduced by Dr Sargent in 1892.

Rhododendron lanigerum TAGG *Arboreum*

3.4. (*R. silvaticum*) Shrub or small tree, to 7m; bts grey tomentose at first. Lv to 22cm long and 7cm wide, dark green above, with white, grey or brown indumentum below. Fl buds covered with russet indumentum. Fl in trusses of up to 25, campanulate, 5-lobed, rose-purple to dark magenta, to 5cm long and slightly wider;

stamens 10. Fl 3–4. A variable plant, the best forms very attractive. Native of Assam and south-eastern Tibet. Introduced by Kingdon Ward in his 1924–5 expedition.

Rhododendron lutescens FRANCHET *Triflorum*

3.4. Somewhat gaunt shrub, to 3 or 4m, with reddish bts and coppery young lv. Lv lanceolate, green above, paler and scaly below. Fl in terminal and axillary heads of 1–6, patulate, to 5cm wide, primrose yellow, asymmetric; stamens 10. Fl 2–4. Some forms are rather tender, and its hybrid 'Bo-peep' is a more reliable plant and equally attractive both in young lv and fl. Native of western China. Introduced by Wilson in 1904.

Rhododendron luteum SWEET *Azalea, Luteum*

4.6. (*R. flavum* DON, *Azalea pontica* LINNAEUS) A deciduous shrub, to 4m, spreading widely. Lv oblong-lanceolate, to 10cm long and 3·5cm across, margin slightly toothed and hairy, with a slight grey pubescence at first, later nearly glabrous, green above, glaucous beneath, turning crimson and orange in the autumn. Fl very fragrant, before lv, in trusses of 7–12, funnel-shaped, about 1cm long and 5cm wide, bright yellow; stamens 5. Fl 5. Native of eastern Europe and the Caucasus. Introduced by Pallas, reaching the UK through Anthony Hove in 1793.

Rhododendron makinoi TAGG *Caucasicum*

3.4. Rounded shrub of up to 2·5m. Bts and young lv clothed with white, later tawny, tomentum and not appearing until August or September. Lv narrow-lanceolate, to 17cm long and only 2·5cm wide, but appearing even narrower as the margins are recurved, slightly puckered above and dark green, with a thick, woolly, tawny tomentum below. Fl in a truss of about 6, open, funnel-campanulate fl, 5-lobed, to 4cm long and wide; usually a soft pink, sometimes more lilac, with or without crimson dots; stamens 10. Fl 5–6. A very attractive shrub both for fl and foliage, and the very late young growths make it additionally attractive. It would seem from the Rhododendron Society's rating of 3–4 that some forms may be slightly tender, but in my experience it is very hardy. Native of Japan. At one time known as *R. metternichii* var *angustifolia* and later considered a form of *R. degronianum*.

Rhododendron mallotum BALFOUR AND WARD
Neriiflorum, Haematodes

3.4. (*R. aemulorum* BALFOUR) Shrub or small tree of 5–6m; bts with grey or cinnamon indumentum, which also covers the young lv. Mature lv to 17cm long and 7cm across, thick, dark green and wrinkled above, with a thick, woolly cinnamon indumentum below. Fl in a close truss of up to 15 tubular-campanulate, 5-lobed, dark crimson fl, to 4cm long and 5cm across; stamens 10. Fl 3–4. Rather slow to arrive at flowering stage, but then very rewarding, although like all these early-flowering spp not to be recommended in districts where spring frosts are a feature. Native of Yunnan and Burma. Introduced by Forrest in 1919.

Rhododendron maximum LINNAEUS
Ponticum

4. Often a tree in the wild, but in cultivation a shrub of 3m, spreading widely. Bts hairy at first. Lv leathery, to 30cm long and 7cm across, dark green above, with a film-like indumentum below which soon disappears. Fl in trusses of 15–20 broadly funnel-shaped, 5-lobed fl, to 3cm long and 4cm across, pale pink or purplish, rarely white, with greenish spots; stamens 8–12, usually 10. Fl 7. The first large-leaved evergreen sp to reach cultivation, now rarely seen, although useful for its late flowering and tolerance of unfavourable conditions. It will flower happily in deep shade. Native of eastern N America. Introduced by Bartram in 1736.

Rhododendron metternichii
SIEBOLD AND ZUCCARINI *Caucasicum*

4. Shrub, to nearly 3m, with lv held semi-erect. Lv coriaceous, to 15cm long and 4cm across, with a slightly recurved margin, covered with a cinnamon pubescence at first, later glossy green above, with a thin, felty rust-coloured indumentum below. Fl in a truss of up to 15 campanulate, 7-lobed, rose or rosy-purple fl, paling as they age, to 5cm long and 6cm wide; stamens 14. Fl 4–5. Unique in the series for its 7 lobes and 14 stamens. Formerly very rare in cultivation. Native of Japan. Introduced in 1860 both by Fortune and by Siebold.

Rhododendron micranthum TURCZANINOW
Micranthum

4. Straggling shrub, to 2·5m. Lv oblanceolate-elliptic, to 4cm long and 1cm across, dull green above, with brown scales beneath. Fl in many-flowered trusses, with 5 starry lobes, about 1cm across, with a tube about 8mm long, milky-white; stamens 10. Fl 5–7. With its very small fl it resembles a ledum rather than a rhododendron. Native of much of China. Introduced by Wilson in 1901.

Rhododendron morii HAYATA
Barbatum, Maculiferum

4. Shrub or tree, to 8m in the wild. Lv to 13cm long and 5cm across, dark green above, paler below and glabrous or nearly so on both surfaces. Petiole slightly hairy. Fl in a truss of 12–15 widely campanulate fl, to 6cm long and slightly

wider, 5-lobed, white, sometimes suffused rose and spotted within with crimson, often merging into a blotch; stamens 10–14. Fl 4–5. A very attractive plant in fl. Sometimes damaged by very low temperatures. Native of Taiwan. Introduced by Wilson in 1919, although this may not have been the first introduction.

Rhododendron moupinense FRANCHET
Moupinense

3.4. Spreading shrub rarely exceeding 1m with bristly bts. Young lv reddish in colour, mature lv to 3cm long and 2·5cm across, rather thick, glabrous and medium green above, scaly below, fringed at first along the margin. Fl widely funnel-shaped, to 5cm long and wide, fragrant, 5-lobed, ranging from white to pink and rosy-purple, sometimes spotted red; stamens 10. Fl 2–3. Perfectly hardy so far as winter cold is concerned, but the early fl may be damaged by frost, so should be sheltered from the easterly air stream. Native of Tibet, Szechuan. Introduced by Wilson in 1909.

Rhododendron mucronulatum TURCZANINOW
Dauricum

4. Deciduous shrub to 2·5m. Lv to 7cm long and 3cm across, bright green and scaly above and below. Fl in a series of single-flowered buds clustered at the ends of the stems, before lv, the bud scales persisting (soon falling in the not dissimilar *R. dauricum*). Each fl is widely funnel-shaped, almost patulate, about 4cm across, almost magenta; stamens 10. Fl 1–2. In spite of its very early flowering, this plant is little affected by frost, and although flowers may be cut, those still in the buds are not, so that some fl may always be expected. The plant grows very slowly. Native of NE Asia and Japan. Introduced in 1907.

Rhododendron neriiflorum FRANCHET
Neriiflorum

4. (Includes *R. euchaites* BALFOUR AND FORREST and *R. phaedropum* BALFOUR AND FARRER as subspecies) A very variable plant. Typical *R. neriiflorum* makes a spreading shrub up to 3m; ssp *euchaites* makes a small tree to 6m; ssp *phaedropum* makes a tall shrub to 5m. Lv to 10cm long and 3·5cm across, dark green and glabrous above, white and waxy below (glaucous in ssp *euchaites*, with traces of rusty indumentum in ssp *phaedropum*). Fl in a truss of 5–12 tubular-campanulate fl, to 4·5cm long, 5-lobed, varying in colour from deep pink to scarlet. Ssp *euchaites* has slightly larger, crimson-scarlet fl, while ssp *phaedropum* may have the fl straw-coloured. The large calyx is coloured the same as the petals, but persists longer; stamens 10. Fl 4–5. Native of Yunnan, India and Burma.

R. neriiflorum introduced by Forrest in 1906 and 1910. Ssp *euchaites* by Forrest in 1913; ssp *phaedropum* by Cox and Farrer in 1919.

Rhododendron niveum JOSEPH HOOKER
Arboreum

3.4. Large shrub or small tree, to 5m, with glistening white bts and young lv. Mature lv to 15cm long and 6cm across, dull green above and eventually glabrous, covered below with a thick, felty white tomentum, later becoming greyish-brown. Fl in a truss of 15–20 tubular-campanulate, 5-lobed fl, about 5cm long and wide, dull purple to magenta, sometimes a smoky-blue; stamens 10. Fl 4–5. Native of the Himalaya. Introduced by J. Hooker in 1849.

Rhododendron nudiflorum (LINNAEUS) TORREY
Azalea, Luteum

4. Deciduous shrub, to 3m, bts sometimes bristly. Lv to 8cm long and 3cm across, rather thin, about the same shade of dull green above and below but slightly bristly on the under part. Fl before lv in trusses of 6–12, barely scented, about 2cm long and 4cm across, most frequently pale pink but varying from white to crimson; stamens 5. In the nineteenth century double forms were observed. Fl 5. Native of eastern N America. Sent by Bartram to Collinson in 1734.

Rhododendron obtusum PLANCHON
Azalea, Obtusum

4. (Includes *R. amoenum* LINDLEY) Low-growing, sometimes prostrate, evergreen or semi-evergreen shrub, not exceeding 1m. Bts covered with brown hairs. Lv to 3cm long in different shapes; those produced in spring elliptic-ovate, those during the summer more leathery and obovate; dark green above, paler below and sparsely hairy on both surfaces. Fl in trusses of 1–3, funnel-shaped, about 2·5cm across, varying in colour from magenta to salmon, almost scarlet, crimson and white; stamens 5. Fl 5. There are a number of evergreen azaleas from Japan which are very close to each other and this sp can easily be confused with *R. indicum*, *R. kaempferi* and *R. mucronatum*, with larger, fragrant white fl. The plant is said to be native of N Japan, but has long been cultivated and var *amoenum* was introduced by Fortune from China in 1844. A probable parent of the famous Kurume azaleas.

Rhododendron occidentale ASA GRAY
Azalea, Luteum

4.6. Deciduous shrub, to 3m. Lv to 8cm long and 3cm wide, glossy-green and slightly downy above, glaucous and somewhat hairy below. They turn scarlet and yellow in the autumn. Fl with or after lv, in trusses of 6–12, widely funnel-shaped, to 5cm long and 7cm across; fragrant,

white or pale pink, with a yellow blotch; stamens 5. Fl 6–7. A beautiful plant, much used for breeding late-flowering hybrids, but deserving to be planted more frequently in its own right. Native of western N America. Introduced from California by W. Lobb in 1851.

Rhododendron orbiculare DECAISNE
Fortunei, Orbiculare

4. A rounded shrub, to 3m, usually somewhat less in height and wider in diameter. Lv rounded, to 10cm long and 8cm across, matt-green above, glaucous below. Petiole often purplish. Fl in a loose truss of 7–10, open-campanulate, 7-lobed, rose-pink with an odd bluish tinge which makes the plants difficult to combine with other pinks; each fl to 4cm long and 7cm across. Fl 3–5. The plant will thrive in permanently wet, almost marshy, soil, but such conditions are not necessary. Native of western China. Introduced by David in 1873, but these probably lost and the main introduction was by Wilson in 1904.

Rhododendron oreodoxa FRANCHET
Fortunei, Oreodoxa

4. Shrub or small tree, to 7m. Bts greyish-pubescent at first, but soon nearly glabrous. Scarcely to be distinguished from *R. fargesii* (qv) but with longer (to 10cm) and narrower lv. Fl in a truss of 10–12 (6–10 in *R. fargesii*), 7–8-lobed (5–7-lobed in *fargesii*), pale pink, spotted or unspotted. Fl 3–4. Does not flower as a young plant. Native of western China. Introduced by Wilson in 1904.

Rhododendron oreotrephes W. W. SMITH
Triflorum, Yunnanense

4. (Includes *RR. exquisitum*, *artosquameum* and *timeteum*) Shrub, to 7m, usually evergreen but some forms deciduous in cold districts. Bts glaucous. Lv more or less rounded, to 5cm long and 4cm across, sometimes oblong to 7cm long and 3cm across, grey-green above, glaucous and scaly below. Fl in terminal or in terminal and axillary trusses; the whole inflorescence 5–8-flowered, usually widely campanulate, sometimes narrowly so, to 4cm long and 6cm across, 5-lobed, varying in colour from purple to mauve and pink, sometimes spotted, sometimes not, stamens 10. Fl 4–5. One of the most delightful of garden shrubs in its best forms. Starts flowering as a young plant, but improves as it increases in size. Native of Yunnan, Szechuan, Burma and Tibet. Introduced by Forrest in 1906 and 1913.

Rhododendron pachytrichum FRANCHET
Barbatum, Maculiferum

4. Shrub, to 6m; bts densely clothed with long brown hairs. Lv to 13cm long and 4cm wide, with reflexed margin, somewhat wrinkled and bright green above, pale green and glabrous below, apart from tufts of hairs along midrib. Petiole about 1·5cm long, shaggy brown and hairy. Fl in a truss of 7–10 campanulate fl, to 5cm long and wide, 5-lobed, white through pink to magenta, usually with a purple blotch at the base; stamens 10. Fl 3–4. Handsome both in foliage and in fl. Native of western China. Introduced by Wilson in 1903.

Rhododendron pentaphyllum MAXIMOWICZ
Azalea, Canadense

4.6. Deciduous shrub, to 3m. Lv in whorls of 5, to 6cm long and 3cm across, turning orange and crimson in the autumn. Fl before lv. One to two fl per head, more or less patulate (rotate-campanulate), to 5cm across, bright rose-pink. Fl 3–4. A very attractive shrub, not always easy to obtain. Can be confused, when not in flower, with *R. quinquefolium* (qv). Native of Japan. Introduced by Wilson in 1914.

Rhododendron polylepis FRANCHET *Triflorum*

4. Shrub, to 4m. Lv to 10cm long and 4cm across, dull green above, densely scaly below. Fl in clusters of 3–5, widely funnel-shaped, about 4cm long and wide, 5-lobed, various shades of purple from pale to dark and violet-purple; stamens 10. Fl 4. Native of Szechuan. Introduced by Wilson in 1904.

Rhododendron ponticum LINNAEUS *Ponticum*

4. Shrub, to 5m, spreading widely by means of stoloniferous growths. Lv glabrous on both surfaces, to 20cm long and 7cm across, dark green above, paler below. Fl in a truss of 10–15 campanulate, 5-lobed fl, to 5cm long and wide, lilac-purple or pinkish-purple with greenish spots; stamens 10. Fl 6. Although the plant is very widespread and semi-naturalised in many places, the true sp is scarce in cultivation; most of the plants being hybridised with other spp and hybrids. Native of the Black Sea region, with an outlying colony in Spain and Portugal, whence came the original introduction in 1763.

Rhododendron pseudochrysanthum HAYATA
Barbatum, Maculiferum

3.4. A variable shrub of which the AM clone is the best to obtain. Shrub, to 3m, with bts sparsely hairy. Young lv covered with grey-blue indumentum, later more or less glabrous on both surfaces, rather thick and rigid, glossy dark green above, pale below, to 7cm long and 3cm across, crowded. Fl in a truss of about 9 camp-anulate fl, to 4cm across and slightly wider, 5-lobed, white or pink with a darker line along the centre of each petal exteriorly, spotted crimson within; stamens 10. Fl 4. Native of Taiwan. Collected by Wilson in 1919, but possibly not the first introduction.

Rhododendron pulchrum SWEET
Azalea, Obtusum

4. Evergreen shrub, to 2m, with grey-brown hairy bts. Lv elliptic or oblanceolate, to 5cm long and 2cm across, at first rusty hairy on both surfaces, later glabrous above. Fl 1–3, widely funnel-shaped, to 7cm across, purple or magenta; stamens 10. Fl 5. Of garden origin, perhaps a hybrid between *R. scabrum*, which is tender, and *R. mucronatum*. Many forms cultivated in China and Japan and first sent by Reeves to the Horticultural Society about 1826. Not suited for cold districts.

Rhododendron quinquefolium
BISSET AND MOORE *Azalea, Schlippenbachii*

3.4.6. Deciduous shrub or small tree ranging from 1–8m. Lv in whorls of 4 or 5, to 5cm long and 3cm wide, elliptic to obovate, margined red-purple at first, later bright green above, somewhat hairy below, colouring well in the autumn. Fl 1–3, pendulous, rotate-campanulate, 5cm across, white with green spots; stamens 10. Fl 4–5. Perfectly hardy so far as cold winters are concerned, but coming early into growth, so unsuitable for districts where spring frosts are frequent. A shy-flowerer at first and by no means easy to establish, but extremely rewarding. Native of Japan. Introduced by Lord Redesdale about 1896.

Rhododendron racemosum FRANCHET
Scabrifolium

4. In both this series and the *Virgatum*, in which this plant was previously included, the inflorescences are axillary, not terminal. Shrub, to 2m; bts sometimes reddish. Lv dull green above, glaucous and scaly below, obovate, to 3cm long and half as wide. Fl in axillary clusters of 3–6, giving a racemose appearance, funnel-shaped, 5-lobed, about 2·5cm long and 3cm wide; pale or deep pink, rarely white; stamens 10. Fl 4–5. A very reliable plant, flowering when young. Native of Yunnan. Introduced by Delavay about 1889.

Rhododendron reticulatum D. DON
Azalea, Schlippenbachii

3.4.6. (*R. rhombicum* MIQUEL). Deciduous shrub, usually about 2m in cultivation but capable of reaching 5m, with yellowish-brown, hairy bts. Lv purplish when young, in pairs or 3s, more or less diamond-shaped (rhombic), to 7cm long and 6cm across, hairy at first, later glabrous above, paler and conspicuously net-veined below; lv turn claret-colour or nearly black in autumn. Fl before lv, usually 1–2, rarely 3 or 4, rotate-campanulate, 5-lobed, to 5cm across, purple; stamens 10 (5 in var *pentamerum*). Fl 4–5. Native of Japan. Introduced 1865.

Rhododendron rex LÉVEILLÉ *Falconeri*

3.4. Large shrub or tree, to 15m, barely to be differentiated from *R. fictolacteum* except that the indumentum on the bts is grey-white not cinnamon, and the indumentum on the underside of mature lv is grey or pale buff, not rusty. Usually the lv are somewhat larger. Fl somewhat larger than *R. fictolacteum* and slightly more in a truss. In cultivation it appears to be more satisfactory than *R. fictolacteum*, growing more rapidly and making a more shapely tree. Native of Szechuan. Earlier sendings were probably confused with *R. fictolacteum*, but KW 4509 from Ward's 1921 expedition is certainly *R. rex*, and may well be the first introduction.

Rhododendron rigidum FRANCHET
Triflorum, Yunnanense

4. (*R. caeruleum* LÉVEILLÉ). Shrub, to 2m, of dense twiggy habit. Lv to 5cm long and 2cm wide, dark green and glabrous above, glaucous and scaly below. The margins bearing a few bristles at the base of the lv and at the top of the petiole. Fl in terminal and axillary trusses of 2–6, widely funnel-shaped, 5-lobed, asymmetric; pink, lavender or white spotted, to 2cm long and 3cm across; stamens 10. Fl 3–5. Native of Yunnan and Szechuan. Introduced by Forrest in 1910, it is not known whether this was the first introduction.

Rhododendron ririei HEMSLEY AND WILSON
Argyrophyllum

3.4. Shrub, to 6m, with whitish bts and silvery young lv. Mature lv to 15cm long and 5cm across, bright green above, silvery-white below. Fl in trusses of about 10 campanulate, 5-lobed fl, to 5cm long and wide; dull purple or smokey-blue; stamens 10. Fl 2–3. Attractive both in foliage and fl, although flowering so early it requires a sheltered situation. Native of Szechuan. Introduced by Wilson in 1904.

Rhododendron roseum (LOISELEUR) REHDER
Azalea, Luteum

4. Shrub, with whorled brs, usually about 2m, occasionally to 5m; bts slightly bristly. Lv to 7cm long and 6cm across, slightly pubescent above, with grey hairs below, bluish-green. Fl with the lv in trusses of 5–9 funnel-shaped fl, which are about 2cm long and 3·5cm across, clove-scented; deep pink to violet-red, with a reddish-brown blotch; stamens 5. Fl 5. Probably originally confused with the very similar *R. nudiflorum*, from which it is distinguished by rather small characters. Native of the eastern USA. Introduced in 1812, probably earlier among sendings of *R. nudiflorum*.

Rhododendron roxieanum FORREST
Taliense, Roxieanum

3.4. A very slow-growing shrub from 1–3m, with densely woolly bts, which retain the bud scales for many years. Lv linear, covered with rusty indumentum on both surfaces when young, later glabrous above, shining, slightly wrinkled, with a dense rust-coloured indumentum below, to 10cm long and only 4cm wide. The plant has very short internodes and makes very little growth each year, so the lv are very congested on the shoots, giving a characteristic and very unrhododendron-like appearance. Fl in a truss of 10–15 campanulate, 5-lobed fl, creamy-white, sometimes flushed pink, sometimes with crimson spots within; stamens 10. Fl 4–5. Like most of the *Taliense* series, this takes a long time to attain flowering size and is grown principally for its foliage. Native of Yunnan, Szechuan and Tibet. Introduced by Forrest in 1913.

Rhododendron rubiginosum FRANCHET
Heliolepis

4. Shrub, occasionally tree-like, to 10m but usually about 3m in gardens, with purplish bts. Lv to 6cm long and 2·5cm across, dull green above, densely covered with rust-coloured scales below. Fl in a truss of 4–8 funnel-shaped, 5-lobed, fl, to 3cm long and 4–5cm across; rosy-lilac, pink or deep pink; stamens 10. Fl 4–5. Usually a very floriferous and ornamental plant. Native of Yunnan. Introduced by Delavay in 1889.

Rhododendron rude TAGG AND FORREST
Barbatum, Glischrum

4. Shrub, to 3m, with bristly bts and bud-scales persisting for 2 years. Lv to 20cm long and 7cm across, dark green and bristly above, with many curled hairs below. Fl in a truss of up to 10, tubular-campanulate, 5-lobed, purplish-crimson, to 3·5cm long and slightly less across; stamens 10. Fl 4–6. A striking looking plant with unusual lv. Native of Yunnan. Introduced by Forrest in 1924–5.

Rhododendron russatum
I. BALFOUR AND FORREST *Lapponicum*

4. (Includes *R. cantabile* BALFOUR). A dwarf shrub rarely exceeding 1m, the bts covered with reddish scales. Lv very close, oval, to 4cm long and 2cm across, dull green above, rusty-yellow below, scaly on both surfaces. Fl in a truss of 4–6, open funnel-shaped, vivid blue-purple and white-throated, to 2cm long and 2·5cm across; stamens 10. Fl 4–5. One of the best of the dwarf blue-flowered *Lapponicum* series. Native to Yunnan and Szechuan. Introduced by Forrest in 1913.

Rhododendron sanguineum FRANCHET
Neriiflorum, Sanguineum

4. A very variable sp, formerly split up into several spp which are now reduced to subspecific level. A low shrub, not exceeding 1m in height and often less; bts with a thin, white indumentum. Lv leathery, to 6cm long and 2·5cm across, dark green and glabrous above, grey-white below with a thin, skin-like indumentum. Fl in a loose truss of 3–6, fleshy, tubular-campanulate, 5-lobed, blood-red; stamens 10. Fl 5. Ssp *haemaleum* has almost black fl, as does ssp *didymum* (*R. didymum* [BALFOUR] FORREST) which is a very dwarf plant. Ssp *roseotinctum* has pink or yellowish-red fl. Attractive but shy-flowering shrubs. Native of Yunnan, Tibet and upper Burma. Introduced by Forrest in 1914.

Rhododendron schlippenbachii MAXIMOWICZ
Azalea, Schlippenbachii

3.4.(6). Deciduous shrub to 5m. Lv in whorls of 5, obovate, purplish when young, to 8cm long and 7cm across, dark green and slightly downy at first, later glabrous, paler below, sometimes colouring well in the autumn, but not invariably. Fl before lv, in a truss of 3–6, nearly patulate, 5-lobed, pale or deep pink, to 8cm across; stamens 10. Fl 4–5. Considered by many to be one of the most beautiful plants in cultivation. Native of Korea, Japan and Manchuria. Introduced by Sir J. H. Veitch in 1893.

Rhododendron searsiae REHDER AND WILSON
Triflorum, Yunnanense

4. Shrub, to 4m, with lv to 7cm long and 2cm across; dark green above, scaly at first, later smooth, glaucous beneath with yellow and brown scales. Fl both terminal and axillary in clusters of 3–4 from each bud, 5-lobed, funnel-shaped, to 4cm long and 5cm across; pale lavender, white or pink or purplish-mauve; stamens 10. Fl 4–5. Native of Szechuan. Introduced by Wilson in 1908.

Rhododendron smirnowii TRAUTVETTER
Caucasicum

3.4. Shrub, to 3m, with bts and young lv densely covered with white felty tomentum. Lv oblong with recurved margin, to 15cm long and 3cm across, at first with white tomentum above, later glabrous and with a pale buff tomentum below. Fl in a truss of 10–12, funnel-campanulate, 5-lobed, rosy-purple, to 4cm long and 6cm across; stamens 10. Fl 5–6. An exceptionally hardy shrub. Native of the Caucasus, discovered and introduced by Baron Ungern-Sternberg in 1885. *R. ungernii* (qv) discovered at the same time.

Rhododendron souliei FRANCHET
Thomsonii, Souliei

4. Shrub, from 2–4m, bts glaucous or purple. Lv almost orbicular, to 7·5cm long and 5cm across, dark green, sometimes slightly glaucous above, glaucous below. Fl in a truss of 5–8, patulate, 5-lobed, to 5cm across, rosy-pink; stamens 10. Fl 5. *R. puralbum* W. SMITH AND I. BALFOUR is distinguished only by its white fl. One of the most charming sp and one which appears to thrive better in drier districts. Native of Szechuan and Tatsienlu. Discovered and introduced by Père Soulié, but the first large introduction was by Wilson in 1905.

Rhododendron stewartianum DIELS Thomsonii

4. Shrub to 2–3m. Lv leathery, obovate or elliptic, to 12cm long and 7cm across. Bright green sometimes glaucous above, with a thin creamy-yellow indumentum below, which soon disappears. Fl in trusses of 3–7, tubular-campanulate 5-lobed, 4·5cm long and wide; in a great variety of colour – white, yellow, pink, rose and crimson; stamens 10. Fl 2–4. Although winter hardy, its early flowering means that a sheltered situation is required. Widespread in Upper Burma, Yunnan and south-eastern Tibet. Although discovered by Forrest in 1904, the first introduction I can find is Kingdon Ward's 3096 in 1919.

Rhododendron strigillosum FRANCHET
Barbatum, Maculiferum

4. Usually a bush to 3m, but capable of reaching 7m in the wild. Bts and young lv densely clad with stiff, pale, glandular bristles. Lv oblanceolate, to 17cm long and 5cm across, dull green and eventually glabrous above, underneath sparsely covered with curled hairs. Fl in a truss of 8–12, tubular-campanulate, 5-lobed, to 6cm long and wide; crimson, or crimson-scarlet so far as plants in cultivation are concerned, sometimes white and pink in the wild; stamens 10. Fl 2–4. Striking both in its foliage and in its fl, but young plants are somewhat tender. Native of Szechuan. Introduced by Wilson in 1904.

Rhododendron sutchuenense FRANCHET
Fortunei, Davidii

4. Tree or shrub to 6m, often only a shrub to 3m, with lv to 25cm long and 7cm across, dark green and matt above when mature, paler below with a loose woolly tomentum along the midrib. Fl in a truss of about 10, widely campanulate, 5-lobed (rarely 6-lobed), pink, unblotched, to 7·5cm long and wide; stamens 13–15. Fl 3. *R. praevernum* HUTCHINSON is closely allied but distinguished by its midrib below being glabrous, lv to 18cm long and 6cm wide and fl to 6cm long and wide, white or pink with a deep wine-red blotch. Stamens 15. *R. sutchuenense* var *geraldii* is thought to be a natural hybrid between these two plants, having the dimensions of *R. sutchuenense* but blotched fl. *R. sutchuenense* from Szechuan and Hupeh. Introduced by Wilson in 1901. *R. praevernum* from Hupeh. Introduced by Wilson in 1907, although *R. sutchuenense* var *geraldii* had been introduced by him in 1900.

Rhododendron telopeum
I. BALFOUR AND FORREST
Thomsonii, Campylocarpum

4. Shrub from 1–3m. Lv leathery, rounded to obovate, to 5cm long and 3cm across, glabrous above and dark green, glaucous below. Fl in a truss of 4–5, openly campanulate, 5-lobed, to 4cm long and slightly wider, bright yellow sometimes with a crimson blotch; stamens 10. Fl 5. Native of south-eastern Tibet and Yunnan. Discovered by Forrest in 1919 but introduced considerably later.

Rhododendron tephropeplum
I. BALFOUR AND FARRER
Boothii, Tephropeplum

4. (*R. deleiense* HUTCHINSON AND WARD). Dwarfish shrub, sometimes to 2m, usually little more than 1m 30cm. Lv oblong-obovate, to 6cm long and 2·5cm across, dark green with scattered black scales above, glaucous and black-scaly below. Young lv are purplish and quite attractive. Fl in trusses of 3–9, tubular-campanulate, 5-lobed; pink, carmine-rose or purplish; calyx large, stamens 10. Fl 4–5. A very attractive sp but some forms are somewhat delicate; usually it is quite hardy enough, although not always easy to cultivate successfully. Found from Assam through Burma and Tibet to Yunnan. First introduced by Forrest in 1921–2. The forms introduced by Ward in 1927–8 as *R. deleiense* have larger, better-coloured fl.

Rhododendron thomsonii J. HOOKER
Thomsonii

1.3.4. Shrub or tree, to 7m, with smooth plum-coloured peeling bark and markedly glaucous bts and young lv. Lv nearly orbicular, to 8cm long and 6cm across, glaucous above at first, later dark green and glabrous, whitish or pale glaucous green below. Fl in a loose truss of 6–8, campanulate, waxy, 5-lobed; crimson or blood-red, to 6cm long and 7·5cm across; stamens 10, calyx large, sometimes red. Fl 4. One of the most magnificent of all flowering plants with its brilliant fl, attractive lv and attractive bark. It does not flower as a small plant, but once it starts, it flowers with such abundance that deadheading

is immediately necessary. It is very intolerant of prolonged drought. Some forms have rather muddy pink fl and should be eliminated. Native of the Himalaya. Introduced by Joseph Hooker in 1849–51.

Rhododendron tosaense MAKINO
Azalea Obtusum

4.6. Deciduous or semi-evergreen, very twiggy shrub from 1–2m. Lv lanceolate, crowded at ends of twigs, to 3cm long and 1cm across, with scattered grey hairs on both surfaces and turning purplish-crimson in the autumn. Fl in a truss of 1–6, funnel-shaped, about 3cm long and wide, lilac-purple or (in 'Barbara') clear pink; stamens 5–10. Fl 4–5. Only moderately hardy and not suitable for very cold areas. Native of Tosa in Japan. Introduced by Wilson in 1914.

Rhododendron triflorum J. HOOKER *Triflorum*

4. Shrub, to 3m, with attractive smooth, red, peeling bark. Lv to 7cm long and 3cm wide, bright green and glabrous above, glaucous and scaly below. Fl usually in 3s, but sometimes 2 or 4, widely funnel-shaped, 5-lobed, pale yellow, green-spotted, to 4cm long and 5cm wide; stamens 10. Fl after the young growth has started, 5–6. Var *mahogani* is suffused with a mahogany colour to a greater or lesser degree. Native of the Himalaya. Introduced by J. Hooker in 1849–52. Var *mahogani* by Ward in 1924–5.

Rhododendron ungernii TRAUTVETTER
Caucasicum

3.4. Shrub or tree, to 6m, with white tomentose bts and young lv. Mature lv leathery, oblanceolate, to 20cm long and 6cm across, dark green and glabrous above, with a grey or fawn woolly indumentum below, later becoming skin-like. Fl in a truss of 20–30, funnel-campanulate, 5-lobed, to 3·5cm long and 5cm across, pale pink or white, faintly spotted; stamens 10. The fl sometimes rather hidden by the new growth. Fl 7. Native of the Caucasus, discovered and introduced by Count Ungern-Sternberg in 1885; received at Kew a year later.

Rhododendron uvariifolium DIELS *Fulvum*

3.4. (*R. niphargum* BALFOUR AND WARD). Shrub or small tree, to 10m, with silvery bts and young lv. Mature lv oblanceolate, to 23cm long and 6cm across, glabrous and dark green above, below with white, pale grey or fawn tomentum. Fl in a tight truss of up to 18 (but often considerably less), funnel-campanulate, to 4cm long and wide, in varying shades from white to deep pink, sometimes spotted and sometimes with a crimson blotch; stamens 10. Fl 3–4. Very handsome foliage shrub, but the fl are usually nothing out of the ordinary. Native of Yunnan, Szechuan and Tibet. Probably first introduced by Forrest in 1913 (F 10292).

Rhododendron vaseyi ASA GRAY
Azalea, Canadense

4.(6). Deciduous shrub, to 5m. Lv bristly at first, sometimes reddish when emerging, to 10cm long and 4cm across, soon smooth both above and below. The lv frequently turn red before falling, although not invariably. Fl before lv, in clusters of 4–8, widely funnel-campanulate, 2-lipped, like an enormous honeysuckle flower but 5-lobed, to 5cm long and wide, pale pink; stamens 5–7. Fl 4–5. The best pink forms are among the loveliest in the *Azalea* series. Discovered, somewhat incredibly, as late as 1878, by Mr G. R. Vasey in N Carolina.

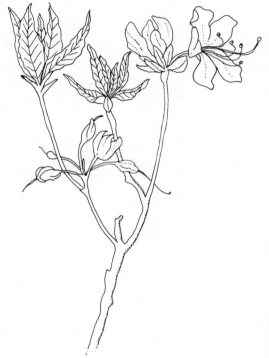

Rhododendron vaseyi

Rhododendron violaceum REHDER AND WILSON
Lapponicum

4. Small shrub, rarely exceeding 1m and growing slowly. Lv very scaly on both surfaces, to 8mm long and half as wide. Fl in cluster of 1–3, open funnel-shaped, to 12mm long and slightly wider, 5-lobed, deep violet-purple; stamens 10. Fl 4–5. Unusual in its deep violet fl. Native of Szechuan. Introduced by Wilson in 1910–11.

Rhododendron viscosum (LINNAEUS) TORREY
Swamp Honeysuckle   *Azalea, Luteum*

4. Much-branched deciduous shrub, occasion-ally to 4m but usually considerably less, bts hairy. Lv in tufts of 5–6, to 5cm long and 2cm across, dark, light or glaucous green above and nearly glabrous, slightly bristly below. Fl after lv in a loose truss of 4–9 fl, funnel-shaped, very sticky, 5-lobed to 5cm long, 4cm wide; very fragrant, white to pink; stamens 5. Fl 6–7. Valuable for its late flowering, its great fragrance and its tolerance of marshy conditions. Native of the eastern USA where it inhabits swamps. Introduced by Bartram in 1734.

Rhododendron wallichii J. HOOKER
Campanulatum

4. Probably should be regarded simply as a form of *R. campanulatum* (qv) from which it only differs in the indumentum of the lower surface of the lv being dotted rather than continuous, as in *R. campanulatum*. In the type specimens the lv are smaller and the fl slightly larger than in *R. campanulatum*, but with so variable a genus little can be made of this. Native of the Himalaya. Presumably introduced by Hooker in 1849–51.

Rhododendron wardii W. W. SMITH
Thomsonii, Souliei

4. (Includes *R. croceum* BALFOUR AND SMITH). A shrub of 7m eventually, with slightly sticky bts. Lv roundish, to 10cm long and half as wide, dark green and glabrous when mature, glaucous beneath and eventually glabrous. Fl in a loose truss of 7–14, cup-shaped, 5-lobed, to 5cm across; yellow, sometimes with a crimson blotch; stamens 10. Fl 5–6. If it can be obtained, the similar *R. litiense* BALFOUR AND FORREST has slightly smaller fl but the advantage of blue-green young growths. Less tender and a somewhat deeper yellow than *R. campylocarpum*, also flowering a month later and highly desirable. Native to Yunnan, Szechuan and Tibet. Introduced by Kingdon Ward in 1913.

Rhododendron weyrichii MAXIMOWICZ
Azalea, Schlippenbachii

4. Deciduous shrub, from 1–5m in the wild but usually about 2m in cultivation. Lv 2–3 at ends of branches, whorled, covered at first with reddish-brown hairs, obovate to 9cm long and 6cm across, eventually glabrous on both surfaces. Fl before lv in clusters of 2–4, widely campanu-late, almost patulate, to 5·5cm across; bright brick-red, often with a deep purple blotch; stamens 6–10. Fl 4–5. The brick red colour is very unusual, but the plant is somewhat grace-less. Native of Japan. Introduced by Wilson in 1914.

Rhododendron williamsianum

REHDER AND WILSON *Thomsonii, Williamsianum*

3.4. Eventually a dome-shaped shrub that may reach as high as 1m 60cm, but more or less prostrate at first. Lv more or less heart-shaped, copper-coloured when young, eventually glabrous and dark green above, glaucous beneath with scattered hairs, to 4cm long and 3cm wide. Fl in a loose truss, usually of 2–3 fl, rarely 5, widely campanulate, 5-lobed, to 5cm long and wide, shell-pink; stamens 10. Fl 4. One of the most charming sp with its large fl and attractive young foliage. Usually free-flowering. Native of Szechuan. Introduced by Wilson in 1908.

Rhododendron xanthocodon HUTCHINSON
Cinnabarinum

3.4. Shrub, to 5m, with bts covered in golden scales and very glaucous young lv. Mature lv to 7cm long and 5cm across, dull green and scaly above, glaucous green and scaly below. Fl pendulous, in a truss of 5–10, waxy, bell-shaped, to 4cm long and slightly less wide, cream to yellow; stamens 10. Fl 5. Closely allied to *R. cinnabarinum,* but with yellow fl. The buds are somewhat susceptible to spring frosts, so a sheltered situation is advisable. Native of Bhutan and Tibet. KW 6026 from Ward's 1924–5 expedition is probably the first introduction.

Rhododendron yakushimanum NAKAI
Caucasicum

3.4. Also spelt *yakusimanum.* In cultivation a rounded shrub, to 1m 30cm, with bts and young lv covered with brownish indumentum. This persists to a greater or lesser degree on the upper surface of mature lv, which are to 9cm long and 3cm across, with recurved margins, densely brown tomentose below. Fl in a compact truss of up to 10, campanulate, 5-lobed, to 4cm long and 5cm across. deep pink in bud, opening pale pink and fading to nearly white; stamens 10. Fl 5. An attractive dwarf shrub, particularly ornamental in winter for its foliage; somewhat slow-growing and seeming to thrive best in full light. Native of the island of Yakusima in Japan, where it is apparently very variable: the dome-shaped plants in cultivation coming from the higher elevations. Introduced in 1934 and now much used to breed dwarf large-flowered hybrids.

Rhododendron yunnanense FRANCHET
Triflorum, Yunnanense

4. A very variable plant, which now includes *RR. aechmophyllum, chartophyllum, pleistanthum* and *suberosum.* Shrub, to 4m, usually evergreen, but in very cold districts may lose many of its lv in the winter. Lv to 7cm long and 3cm across, with a hairy margin and scattered

Rhododendron yunnanense

hairs above, much of which are shed during the summer, scaly below. Fl both terminal and axillary, in trusses of 3–5, widely funnel-shaped, 5-lobed, to 3cm long and 5cm wide, asymmetric, varying in colour from white to lavender and pink, usually with crimson spots; stamens 10. Fl 5–6. One of the most reliable of all spp, flowering profusely every year and growing reasonably rapidly. Deadheading is a tiresome operation but is well worth doing. Native of Yunnan, Szechuan, Burma and Tibet. First introduced by Delavay in 1889.

RHODOTYPOS SIEBOLD AND ZUCCARINI

A monotypic genus, easily propagated by seed or by cuttings of half-ripe wood.

Rhodotypos scandens (THUNBERG) MAKINO

4.(5). (*R. kerrioides* SIEBOLD AND ZUCCARINI). Deciduous, erect shrub, to about 2m. Lv opposite, ovate-acuminate, to 10cm long and 5cm across, dark green and glabrous above, paler and hairy below. Fl solitary, at the ends of lateral twigs, 4-petalled, pure white, like a wild rose. Fl 5–7. Fr like a very large blackberry and quite ornamental. Native of China and Japan. Introduced in 1866.

RHUS LINNAEUS *Anacardiaceae*

A genus of some 150 species of deciduous or evergreen shrubs or trees, sometimes climbing, and usually dioecious. The flowers are usually of little interest, the fruits are often conspicuous, but the plants are usually grown for their handsome pinnate leaves and vivid autumn tints. Many species produce sucker growths, otherwise root cuttings are the best method of propagation.

Rhus aromatica AITON

4.5. (*R. canadensis* MARSHALL). Deciduous, low-spreading shrub, rarely exceeding 1m. Lv trifoliolate, the leaflets sessile, the centre one obovate to 7cm long and wide, the two lateral ones about half as large, fragrant when crushed, toothed, dark green and smooth above, downy below. Fl before lv in a cluster of spikes, giving the effect of a terminal panicle, only about 2cm across, yellow. Fl 4. Fr red, about the size of red currants, hairy. Native of the eastern USA. Introduced by Bartram in 1759 (1772 sec HK).

Rhus chinensis MILLER

4.(6). (*R. osbeckii* STEUDEL, *R. javanica* THUNBERG, not LINNAEUS). Deciduous tree to 6m or more, with yellowish, downy bts. Lv pinnate, with 7–13 leaflets, the rachis between them being conspicuously winged, from 20 to 37cm long; the leaflets are toothed, oval, to 10cm long and half as wide, colouring brilliantly in the autumn in some districts. Fl, perfect, in a large pyramidal terminal panicle of small yellowish-white fl, the panicle to 25cm long. Fl 8. Fr rarely seen in the UK orange-red and downy. Useful for its late flowering, but the growths are often not sufficiently ripened in the autumn to prevent some from dying back. The plant has a wide range in the wild from Manchuria and Japan, through China south to Malaysia, and their hardiness varies according to their provenance. Miller received a plant from Paris in 1737 but lost it in 1740; presumably this was from seeds sent back by d'Incarville. Reintroduced by David Nelson from Macao in 1780.

Rhus copallina LINNAEUS

5.6. Dwarf deciduous shrub, to 1m 30cm, with reddish downy bts. Lv pinnate with a winged common stalk and 9–15 leaflets, which are lanceolate, to 6cm long and 3cm wide, usually untoothed, glossy green above, paler and downy below. The lv tend to turn attractively reddish-purple in the autumn. Fl unisexual, in crowded, pyramidal panicles from 10–15cm long and 7–10cm wide; the female inflorescences being the smaller, greenish-yellow. Fl 7–8. Fr hairy and bright red. Native of the eastern USA. Grown by Bishop Compton in 1688, so probably a Banister sending.

Rhus glabra LINNAEUS

4.5.6. Deciduous shrub, to 2m, with glabrous bts. Lv pinnate, from 30 to 45cm long with 15–25 leaflets, which are lanceolate, toothed, to 10cm long and 2cm wide, turning red in the autumn. 'Laciniata' has the leaflets deeply incised, so that they almost appear pinnate themselves. Fl in a dense, pyramidal panicle from 10 to 25cm long, the fl concealed by red down. Fl 7–8. Fr covered by crimson hairs and very ornamental. Native of eastern N America. Cultivated in 1620.

Rhus sylvestris SIEBOLD AND ZUCCARINI

6. Deciduous tree, to 10m, usually less, with downy bts. Lv pinnate, with 7–13 leaflets which are ovate, to 10cm long and half as wide, downy or glabrous above, usually downy below but sometimes only along the main veins. The lv colour red or scarlet in autumn. Fl in lax panicles to 18cm long, brownish. Fl 6. Fr brownish-yellow. Native of China, Japan and Korea. Introduced 1881.

Rhus typhina LINNAEUS Stag's Horn Sumach

5.6. Shrub or small tree, to 8m, with reddish-hairy bts. Lv pinnate, from 30–60cm long with 13–27 leaflets which are oblong-lanceolate, to 10cm long and 2·5cm across, toothed, brown-hairy at first, later smooth, colouring very brilliantly in the autumn. Fl dioecious, in pyramidal, hairy panicles to 20cm long for the females and slightly larger for the males. Fl 6–7. Fr closely covered with crimson hairs. Very similar to *R. glabra*, but distinguished by its larger growth, its hairy bts and its earlier flowering. The two spp hybridise freely, the resultant plant being known as *R. X pulvinata* GREENE. There is also a laciniate-leaved form. Native of eastern N America and probably introduced at the same time as *R. glabra*. Grown by Parkinson before 1629.

Rhus verniciflua STOKES Lacquer Tree

(*R. vernicifera* DE CANDOLLE). Deciduous tree, to 20m in the wild. Lv pinnate, to 60cm long, with 7–13 broad-ovate leaflets to 15cm long and half as wide, glabrous above, somewhat downy below. Fl dioecious, small, yellowish-white, in axillary panicles to 25cm long and 15cm wide. Fl 7. Fr yellowish, about the size of a pea. Grown mainly for its large and handsome lv. Although the sap is used in the East for producing lacquer, it is poisonous and may cause a rash if applied to the skin. Native of Japan, China and the Himalaya. Introduced originally from Japan about 1861, but most trees in cultivation derive from Wilson collectings in 1908.

RIBES LINNAEUS *Grossulariaceae*

A genus of about 150 species of rather small shrubs, usually deciduous but occasionally evergreen, usually with perfect fl, although sometimes dioecious. Black and red currants are the best-known of the genus. The leaves are alternate, the flowers have parts, usually in fives and occasionally in fours, the coloured calyx being larger than the small petals so that the flower resembles a small fuchsia; the calyx is tubular with expanded lobes. The fruit is a many-seeded berry. Cuttings both of hard wood and of half-ripe wood usually root readily. The plants range through the temperate zones of the northern hemisphere and down the Andes to Patagonia. A number of rather unattractive species, such as *R. alpinum* and *R. americanum*, persist in commerce but are not described here. On the other hand the attractive *R. cereum* now seems to be lost.

Ribes gayanum STEUDEL

4. A suckering, evergreen shrub, from 1–2m high, with villous bts and petioles. Lv greyish, basically ovate but 3-lobed, to 5cm long and wide, downy on both surfaces. Fl in erect racemes to 5cm long, yellow, fragrant, campanulate, dioecious. Fl 6. Fr round, about the size of a pea, purplish-black, hairy. Male and female fl both appear to be perfect, but in male fl the ovules are sterile and in female fl the pollen is sterile. Native of Chile. Introduced about 1858.

Ribes laurifolium JANCZEWSKI

4. (*R. vicarii* Hort). Evergreen shrub, to 1·5m. Bts brown or red. Lv ovate, leathery, unlobed, to 12cm long and 6cm across, dull green above. Fl in racemes, pendent in male plants, more erect in females, to 6cm long in female plants, some-what shorter in males, greenish-yellow. Fl 2–3. Fr black. Useful for its very early flowering. The fl seem little affected by frost, although very cold weather may delay their emergence. The plant is not a rapid grower and remains a dwarf shrub for many years. Native of western China. Introduced by Wilson in 1908.

Ribes menziesii PURSH

4.(5). Deciduous, spiny shrub, to 2m, with bristly bts. Lv basically roundish, but deeply 3 or 5-lobed, usually glabrous above, pubescent and glandular below. Fl axillary, singly or in pairs, calyx reddish-purple to 8mm long, petals white, small. Fr globular, bristly about 1cm across. There are a number of western American gooseberries with fl with red or purple calyx and white petals, of which this and *R. roezlii* are most easily obtained. Native to western America from Oregon to central California. Introduced by Douglas in 1827.

Ribes odoratum WENDLAND

4. This is apparently the earlier name for the plant known in gardens as *R. aureum* PURSH. A deciduous shrub, to 2m (occasionally more), with arching stems. Lv usually 3-lobed and toothed, basically kidney-shaped, to 5cm long and wide, pale green on both surfaces and soon glabrous, long-petioled. Fl in more or less pendulous racemes to 5cm long, each fl about 1cm long, golden-yellow and very fragrant, perfect. Fl, with lv, 4. Fr purplish black, about 8mm across. Native of central USA. Introduced in 1812 by Nuttall.

Ribes sanguineum PURSH
American Currant, Flowering Currant

4. Spreading, deciduous bush, to 2m 60cm and often spreading more widely. Lv basically cordate, but 3 or 5-lobed, to 10cm across and 8cm long, with a strong odour when crushed, smooth above, downy below. Fl in drooping or semi-erect racemes to 10cm long, each fl to 1cm long and wide, varying in colour from white, through pink to rosy crimson in the cv 'Splendens'. Fl 3–4. Fr black with bluish bloom. There is a slight mystery about the introduction of this western N American shrub. It is always regarded as one of Douglas's most important introductions in 1826, but Sweet's *Hortus Britannicus* gives the introductory date of 1820, while Loudon gives 1817.

Ribes X *gordonianum* BEATON is a hybrid between this sp and *R. odoratum* raised about 1837 by a famous gardener Donald Beaton. It is curiously intermediate between the two parents with smaller lv than those of *R. sanguineum* and fl red without, yellow within. Fl 4.

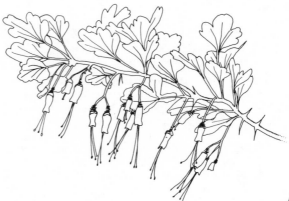

Ribes speciosum

Ribes speciosum PURSH

4. Deciduous, spiny shrub, to 2m in the open and up to 4m with wall protection. Lv basically roundish, 3 or 5-lobed, usually glabrous, to 3cm long and wide. Fl in axillary clusters of 2–5, the tubular calyx to 1cm long, with 4 spreading lobes, so about 2cm across, petals 4, both calyx and petals deep red, as are also the stamens which project about 2cm. Fl 4–5. Fr bristly, red, to 12mm long and wide but rarely seen in the UK. A very striking shrub when well-flowered, like a miniature fuchsia and unusual in the genus in having the parts in 4s, not 5s. Native of

California. Introduced by Collie in 1828 and shortly after by Douglas.

ROBINIA LINNAEUS *Leguminosae*

A small genus of about twenty species of deciduous trees or shrubs, usually spiny. The leaves are opposite, pinnate, with pea-shaped flowers in pendulous axillary racemes. In some of the more attractive species the wood is very brittle and snaps easily in strong winds, so shelter from wind is advisable. Most species in cultivation are perfectly hardy so far as winter cold is concerned.

Robinia X ambigua POIRET

4. A garden hybrid between the common *R. pseudoacacia* and the less frequently seen *R. viscosa*, both of which are described below. A deciduous tree, to 20m, with pinnate lv and 21 leaflets, which are oval, to 3cm long and nearly half as wide. Bts slightly sticky. Fl in pendulous racemes of pink fl, the racemes to 10cm long. Fl 6. 'Bella rosa' has small, elegant lv and rather sticky bts; 'Decaisneana' is a more vigorous form with larger lv and racemes to 12cm, The original hybrid was first noted about 1812. 'Decaisneana' dates from about 1862.

Robinia hispida

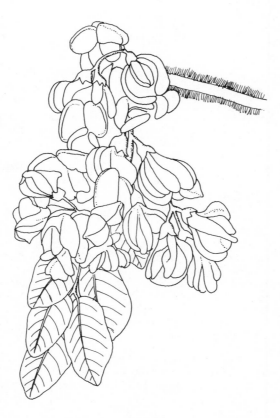

Robinia hispida LINNAEUS

4. Suckering shrub, to 2m, unarmed, with bristly bts. Lv pinnate, to 25cm long, composed of 7–17 leaflets which are ovate, to 5cm long and 3·5cm wide, dark green. Fl in racemes to 7cm long, each fl large, pea-shaped, to 3cm long, very deep pink. Fl 5–6. The plant is very shy of producing pods. It is often grafted on to a standard of *R. pseudoacacia*, to make a low, bushy-topped tree, when the wood proves very brittle. *RR. boyntonii, fertilis* and *elliottii* are all very close to *R. hispida*. Native of eastern N America. Introduced by Bartram in 1743.

Robinia kelseyi HUTCHINSON

4.5. Shrub or small tree, to 3m, with glabrous bts. Lv to 15cm long, composed of 9–11 ovate leaflets to 4cm long and 1·5cm across which are pointed. Fl in small axillary racemes, usually of 3–6 fl, which are 2·5cm long and bright rose pink. Fl 6. Pods covered with glandular red hairs and ornamental. Native of N Carolina. Introduced in 1901.

Robinia luxurians SCHNEIDER

4. (*R. neomexicana* auct). A large shrub or small tree, to 12m, bts downy. Lv to 30cm long, with 15–25 leaflets to 4cm long and 1.5cm across, bristle-tipped and spiny at the base. Fl in racemes to 7cm long, each fl about 2·5cm long, pale pink. Fl 6 and often a second time in 8. Pods hairy, to 10cm long and 8mm wide. Native of the southwestern USA from Colorado to Arizona and Utah. Introduced to the UK in 1887.

Robina pseudoacacia LINNAEUS False Acacia

4.7. Tree of up to 25m with very furrowed bark. Lv to 30cm long, composed of 11–23 leaflets, which are oval, sometimes to 5cm long and half as wide, often with silvery hairs at first, later glabrous and usually turning a clear yellow before falling. Young trees and sucker growths with spines to 2·5cm long. Fl fragrant, in racemes to 12cm long, each fl white with a yellow blotch on the standard petal, about 2cm long. Fl 6. Pods to 9cm long and 1cm wide. A number of cv exist, of which 'Frisia', with golden lv, is very attractive, 'Pyramidalis' is a fastigiate form while 'Rozynskyana' is partly pendulous, and 'Microphylla' has very small, fern-like lv. Native of the eastern USA and one of the first trees to be introduced from there, arriving in France about 1601.

Robinia viscosa VENTENAT

4.(7). Deciduous tree, to 12m, the trunk often furnished with burrs; bts very sticky. Lv 7–25cm long with 11–21 leaflets which are oval, to 5cm long and 2cm across, dark green above paler beneath. Racemes to 8cm long, about 2cm of this being bare stem, bearing 10–15 fl which emerge from a dark red, hairy calyx; they are about 2cm long, pale pink with a yellow blotch on the standard. Fl 6–7. Pods to 8cm long, sticky. A very uncommon tree in the wild, but arguably the best sp for gardens. Native of Carolina and Alabama. Introduced to France by Michaux in 1791.

ROSA LINNAEUS *Rose*

This genus of 250 species represents the most popular garden plant in the world; it was cultivated in Minoan Crete and also in China long before the Christian era. Besides the species, the number of hybrids and cultivars must run into many thousands, although more have been lost than survive. The plants are usually deciduous shrubs with alternate pinnate leaves, the stems usually armed with prickles. The flowers are patulate, five-petalled (except for *R. sericea*), while the fruit is a swollen receptacle, referred to as a hip or hep, which is often very ornamental. The flowers are terminal and may be solitary or in many-flowered corymbs. In the wild they range through temperate regions in the northern hemisphere, extending beyond the Equator only in the Philippines. They are generally of the easiest culture, but it seems that the species do much better on their own roots than budded on to other stocks, as is often done commercially. Thus *R. hugonis* has a reputation for suddenly dying off, although most growers find that if this is on its own roots it grows more satisfactorily. Cuttings of hard wood taken in the autumn and put in trenches out of doors usually root fairly well and the same may be said of cuttings of half-ripe wood taken about July and, preferably, rooted in a propagating frame. Some species spread with numerous sucker growths and these can usually be detached and rooted. Seed takes one to two years before germinating, unless stratified or frozen, and plants take about two to four years thereafter to flower. To give some semblance of order to the numerous species they have been divided into ten sections, of which the *Banksianae*, *Laevigatae* and *Bracteatae* each contain only a single species. The others are as follows:

1 *Pimpinellifoliae* Stems with straight prickles, or, sometimes, bristles. Flowers solitary. Leaflets small, 7–9. Sepals persisting on the heps. Heps usually black or brown.
2 *Gallicanae* Low shrubs with hooked prickles on stems. Leaflets 3–5. Flowers solitary, pink or red. Hep brick red. Probably only contains one species, which

has been used in numerous hybrids.
3 *Caninae* Upright or arching stems with numerous hooked prickles. Flowers corymbose. Leaflets 5–11. Fruit red.
4 *Carolinae* Usually low shrubs with straight prickles or unarmed, corymbs few-flowered. Heps reddish. Sepals not persistent on heps. Plants often suckering.
5 *Cinnamomeae* Erect shrubs with straight prickles, usually in pairs between the leaves. Corymbs many-flowered. Leaflets 5–11. Sepals persistent on the red heps.
6 *Synstylae* Usually climbing plants with hooked prickles. Flowers in many-flowered corymbs, styles united in a column. Sepals soon falling from the red heps.
7 *Indicae* Normally climbing plants, but *R. chinensis* better known in a shrubby, repeat-flowering, mutation. Leaflets 3–5. Flowers in corymbs, with free styles. Sepals more or less persistent on the greenish-red heps. Prickles hooked, but rather sparse.

Most of the sections are reasonably distinct, but the *Caninae* are not very clearly defined, being separated from the *Cinnamomeae* mainly by having hooked as opposed to straight prickles.

Bearing these characters in mind, it is hoped that the extremely brief descriptions will suffice. Although a few plants thought to be hybrids are included below, the list is mainly confined to species.

Rosa acicularis LINDLEY *Cinnamomeae*

4.5. Shrub of 1–2m, with bristly bts. Lv with 5–9 leaflets, the whole lv to 12cm long, blue-green above, downy below. Fl usually solitary, occasionally 2 or 3, deep pink, 6cm across. Fl 6. Heps pear-shaped, bright red, about 2·5cm long. Native of northern Europe, Siberia, Japan, Alaska and further south in N America under various varietal names. Introduced from Siberia in 1805 according to Rehder.

Rosa X alba LINNAEUS *Gallicanae*

4. Regarded as originally a hybrid of some form of *R. canina* with *R. damascena*, which is itself thought to be *gallica X phoenicea*. Shrub to 2 or rarely 3m, with more or less hooked prickles. Lv greyish, 5–7 leaflets, which are oval, toothed, to 5cm long. Fl singly, about 7cm across, white or very pale pink. Fl 6. Fr red, about 2cm long. The parent of many cv. Cultivated since classical times.

Rosa banksiae AITON *Banksianae*

4. Climbing evergreen or semi-evergreen shrub, to 6m, occasionally twice this, with unarmed wood. Lv with 3–5 leaflets, somewhat glossy. Fl in umbels, numerous, about 3cm across, white or yellow, single or double, smelling of violets. Fl 5–6. Fr (only from single fl) red, pea-shaped. Requires a warm, sunlit wall for successful cultivation in the UK, and since it flowers from the old wood, should be pruned only very rarely. Native of China. Apparently the single white form was introduced privately by an East Indiaman, Robert Drummond, in 1796, but the first known introduction was a double white form brought back by William Kerr in 1807.

Rosa banksiopsis BAKER *Cinnamomeae*

4.5. Shrub, to 4m. Stems usually unarmed. Lv with 7–9 leaflets, the whole lv being up to 15cm long. Fl in few-flowered corymbs, 3–4cm across, bright pink. Fl 6. Heps flask-shaped with erect, persistent sepals, coral-red, to 2·5cm long. Distinguished from *R. caudata* BAKER only by the downy underside to the lv (glaucous in *R. caudata*). Native of Hupeh. Introduced by Wilson in 1907.

Rosa bella REHDER AND WILSON *Cinnamomeae*

4.5. Spreading shrub, to 3m, with straight prickles. Lv with 7–9 leaflets, each elliptic to 2·5cm long, the whole lv being about 10cm long, dull green above, glaucous below. Fl in heads of 1–3, to 5cm across, bright pink. Fl 6. Fr elliptic, to 2cm long, scarlet. Native of north China. Introduced 1910.

Rosa blanda AITON *Cinnamomeae*

4.5. Shrub, to 2m, with unarmed stems, sometimes a few prickles present. Lv with 5–7 leaflets, the whole lv to 12cm long, each leaflet to 6cm long, glabrous and toothed. Fl solitary or in clusters of up to 7, to 8cm across, rosy-pink. Fl 5–6. Fr globular, about 1cm in diameter, with erect, persistent sepals.

R. arkansana PORTER is closely allied, but a dwarf shrub, usually under 1m, with bristly stems, lv with 5–11 leaflets and smaller, paler fl. *R. nutkana* PRESL is also not dissimilar, but with hooked prickles in pairs and fl usually solitary. *R. blanda* is native over much of N America and was being grown by Gordon in 1773. *R. arkansana* comes from the central and western USA and does not seem to have reached cultivation before 1917, while *R. nutkana* is native to western N America from Alaska to California and was introduced about 1876.

Rosa brunonii LINDLEY *Synstylae*

4.5. Vigorous climber, to 6m or more, with large, hooked prickles. Lv to 20cm long, made up of 5–9 leaflets which are oval-lanceolate and up to 7cm long, either bright green or greyish. Fl in large corymbs up to 15cm across, each fl to 3cm across, pale yellow on opening, soon fading to white. Fl 6–7. Fr red, elliptic, without sepals, about 8mm wide. Some forms are rather tender, but the clone known as 'La Mortola' is not only hardier but also more vigorous. Sometimes offered as *R. moschata* qv which is quite different. Native of the Himalaya. Introduced in 1820, presumably through Wallich.

Rosa californica CHAMISSO AND SCHLECHTENDAL *Cinnamomeae*

4. Shrub to 3m, usually little more than 2m, spreading by means of suckers with stout, hooked prickles. Lv to 12cm long with 5–7 leaflets more or less glabrous above, slightly downy below. Fl in clusters of up to 12, about 4cm across, pink, fading to purple. Fl 6. Fr more or less globular up to 1cm across, contracted at the top, sepals persisting, red. Usually found in a semi-double form 'Plena'. Native of western N America from British Columbia to California. Introduced about 1878.

Rosa carolina LINNAEUS *Carolinae*

4. Low suckering shrub to 1m. Stems with slender prickles, usually in pairs and usually straight, but occasionally hooked. Lv to 10cm long, made up of 5–7 leaflets which are finely toothed, obovate, to 5cm long and 1·6cm wide, dull green above grey below. Fl in clusters or solitary and flowering one at a time, very fragrant, deep pink tending to purple. Fl 6–8. Fr round, devoid of sepals, red, 8mm in diameter. Native of eastern N America. Introduced probably by Catesby, in 1726.

Rosa chinensis JACQUIN Monthly Rose
Indicae

4. (*R. indica* LINDLEY). The true wild sp is a climbing rose and not in cultivation, but a number of early garden forms are. Shrub, from 1–3m, often with copper-coloured young lv. Lv with 3–5 leaflets, which are up to 7cm long, ovate, toothed, shining green above, paler and matt below. Fl in clusters, usually semi-double, about 5cm across, crimson, pink or (rarely) white. Fl 6–10 or even later. Fr red, top-shaped, about 2cm long. 'Mutabilis' has single fl, orange in the bud, opening buff and fading to crimson. The essential ingredient in all the modern hybrid roses with their continuous flowering season. It would seem that the gene which causes the elongation of the stems for climbing has mutated to a gene that continues to produce flower spikes. Native of China. Appears in a painting by Bronzino in the sixteenth century and said to have been grown by Miller, although not described by him. The first authenticated introduction was in 1771.

Rosa damascena MILLER   Damask Rose
Gallicanae

4. There appear to be two hybrid roses under this name. According to Dr Hurst, the ordinary damask is *R. gallica* X *R. phoenicea* while the autumn damask, which may flower twice a year, was *R. gallica* X *R. moschata*. Shrub to 3m, usually with hooked spines, sometimes these are reduced to mere bristles. Lv usually with 5 leaflets, which are ovate, to 6cm long and half as wide. Fl in large clusters, very fragrant, to 5cm across, often double, pale pink to crimson. Best known in cultivation by the form 'Trigintipetala', a loosely double, pale pink rose, much grown in the east for making attar. 'Versicolor' is partly double and has white fl with pink blotches. Fl 6. Fr flask-shaped, about 2·5cm long, red and bristly. Probably in cultivation before the Christian era and an important parent in rose hybrids.

Rosa davidii CRÉPIN   *Cinnamomeae*

4.5. A spreading shrub to 3m high and wide. Stems erect and then arching, prickles reddish, usually straight. Lv to 15cm long, composed of 5–11 (but usually 7–9) leaflets, which are oval, toothed, to 5cm long and half as wide, dark green above and markedly veined, glaucous below. Fl in corymbs, up to 5cm across, mallow-pink. Fl 6–7. Fr pendulous, flask-shaped, bright red, about 2cm long, sepals persistent. *R. corymbulosa* ROLFE is similar, but smaller in all its parts, usually nearly thornless, with lv to 12cm long, fl 2·5cm across, and globose fr. Fl 7. Both spp are to be welcomed for their late flowering and copious, showy heps. Both spp are native to western China and were introduced by Wilson – *R. davidii* in 1903 and 1908, *R. corymbulosa* in 1907.

Rosa ecae AITCHISON   *Pimpinellifoliae*

4. Although it can reach 2m, this is usually a low shrub to 1m or little more. The bts are reddish and so are the dense, straight prickles. Lv very small, not more than 3cm long, made up of, usually, 7 leaflets, which are roundish, to 6mm long and wide. Fl solitary, about 2·5cm across, buttercup yellow. Fl 5–6. Heps round, dull red, with persistent sepals about 8mm wide. Requires a warm, sunny position. Native of Afghanistan. Discovered and introduced by Dr Aitchison (the initials of his wife, Mrs E. C. Aitchison, making up the name) in 1880.

Rosa farreri STAPF   Threepenny Bit Rose
Cinnamomeae

4. The type is not in cultivation, only the var *persetosa*. Shrub to 2m, often spreading more widely, with stems densely set with bristles which may be reddish, as may be the young lv. Lv to 6cm long made up of 7–9 leaflets, which are oval, to 1·5cm long, greyish. Fl solitary, coral-red in bud, salmon pink when expanded, about 2cm across. Fl 5–6. Fr egg-shaped, about 8mm long, scarlet with persistent sepals. Occasionally the lv colour slightly in the autumn. Native of Kansu. Introduced by Farrer in 1915.

Rosa fedtschenkoana REGEL   *Cinnamomeae*

4.5. Shrub, to 3m high and about 2m wide, with grey bts covered with pinkish, bristly thorns. Lv to 12cm long, made up of 7–9 handsomely grey-green leaflets. Fl 1–4, about 2·5cm across, white. Fl 6–9. Fr pear-shaped, bristly, orange-red, about 2cm long. Useful for its attractive grey foliage and its very long flowering season. Native of Turkestan. Introduced about 1876.

Rosa filipes REHDER AND WILSON   *Synstylae*

4.5. Vigorous climber to 7m or more, with coppery young lv. Mature lv to 18cm long, made up of 5–7 leaflets, light green. Fl in very large corymbs of sometimes 100 blooms, each on a very thin stem, creamy-white, fragrant, to 2·5cm across. Fl 7. Fr bright red. The clone in cultivation is called 'Kiftsgate' and is magnificent, although sometimes slow to get away. Native of western China. Introduced by Wilson in 1907.

Rosa foetida HERRMANN   Austrian Briar
Pimpinellifoliae

4. (*R. lutea*, MILLER). Shrub from 1–2m with brown stems and grey straight prickles. Lv about 7cm long with 5–9 oval leaflets, each to 4cm long, doubly toothed, dull dark green above, greyish and downy beneath. Fl usually solitary, up to 7cm across, deep yellow in the type but in the form known as 'Bicolor', the Austrian Copper, the petals are yellow exteriorly and a dazzling orange-scarlet within. 'Persiana' is a double form. Fl 6. Fr globular and red, but very rarely produced. Although very striking, by no means the easiest rose to cultivate. 'Bicolor' often carries a few typical yellow fl as well. 'Persiana' is the parent of many garden hybrids including the yellow Hybrid Tea roses, while 'Bicolor' has also been much used to give coppery effects. Native of western Asia. In cultivation since the sixteenth century, although 'Persiana' did not arrive before 1838.

Rosa foliolosa NUTTALL   *Carolinae*

4.(6). Low-growing, suckering shrub, rarely exceeding 1m, often devoid of prickles. Lv to 7cm long, made up of 7–9 (occasionally 11) rather forward-pointing leaflets, which are up to 5cm long, but only about 1·5cm wide, bright green, often colouring red in the autumn. Fl usually solitary, about 6cm across, deep pink, extremely fragrant. Fl 7–9. Fr round, sparingly bristly, red with sepals soon falling. Useful for its late flowering and for its intense fragrance. Native from Arkansas and Oklahoma to Texas. Apparently not in cultivation until 1888.

Rosa forrestiana BOULENGER *Cinnamomeae*

4.5. Spreading shrub, to 2m, with arching stems armed with straight thorns. Lv to 7cm long, made up of 5–7 oval leaflets, to 2m long. Fl in tight heads of 4–5, about 4cm across, deep carmine pink. Fl 6–7. Fr flask-shaped, hairy sepals persistent, bright red to 2cm long. Native of western China. Introduced by Forrest in 1918.

Rosa gallica LINNAEUS *Gallicanae*

4. Low suckering shrub to 1m or little more, with erect stems with small, curved, slender prickles. Lv variable in length, composed of 3–7 leaflets which may be up to 7cm long and half as wide, or only 2·5cm long, dark green and glabrous above, paler and downy below. Fl usually solitary, occasionally up to 3, to 6cm across, very fragrant, deep pink to crimson. Fl 6. Fr roundish, without sepals, to 12mm across. 'Officinalis', or the Provins rose, has semi-double fl of a very heavy fragrance, which is retained when the petals are dried. 'Versicolor', or 'Rosa Mundi', has semi-double fl which are red with white flecks and stripes. Probably the oldest rose in European cultivation. Native to central and southern Europe, getting as far north as Belgium.

Rosa helenae REHDER AND WILSON *Synstylae*

4.5. Very vigorous climber, to 7m or more, with very large hooked prickles. Lv to 17cm long, made up of 7–9 ovate leaflets, to 6cm long and half as wide, slightly downy below on the veins, otherwise glabrous on both surfaces. Fl in large corymbs to 15cm across, each bloom being up to 3cm across, white and fragrant. Fl 6–7. Fr possibly even more spectacular, brilliant red, without sepals, egg-shaped, about 1cm long. In my opinion the best of the spp which include *brunonii*, *filipes*, *longicuspis* and *rubus*, the autumn display being extraordinary. Native of western China. Introduced by Wilson in 1907.

Rosa hugonis HEMSLEY *Pimpinellifoliae*

4. Rounded bush, to nearly 3m high and wide in very good specimens, but more usually 2m in each direction. Prickles straight. Lv to 10cm long, of 5–11 leaflets, oval to 2cm long, deep green, rather sparsely set on the brs. Fl solitary, 5cm across, bright yellow. Fl 5–6. Fr globular, blackish, with persistent sepals. One of the earliest roses to flower. The plant has a reputation for dying off suddenly without warning, although this seems mainly to happen when the plants are budded on to other spp; plants on their own roots seem more satisfactory. Plants have

been crossed with *R. pimpinellifolia*, to give 'Canary Bird' and 'Headleyensis', and with *R. sericea*, to give 'Cantabrigiensis' and 'Earldomensis'. All of these are attractive, floriferous shrubs with yellow fl, usually showing hybrid vigour. *R. hugonis* is a native of western China, where it was collected by Father Hugh Scallan in 1899.

Rosa longicuspis BERTOLONI *Synstylae*

4.5. (Includes *R. lucens* ROLFE but not *R. sinowilsonii* HEMSLEY). Vigorous climber, often described as semi-evergreen but not so in my experience. Young lv and young stems coppery, with large hooked thorns. Lv to 20cm long, leathery, glossy and dark green, with 5–7 leaflets. Fl in very large corymbs, occasionally with 150 blooms with a fragrance of bananas, cream in bud, opening white, up to 5cm across. Fl 7. Fr orange-red, to 1·5cm long. Usually the last of this group to flower, although *R. filipes* may be as late. The fr are less decorative than those of either *R. filipes* or *R. helenae*. Received as *R. lucens* at Kew in 1899 and sent back by Wilson in 1902.

Rosa 'Macrantha' DESFONTAINES *Caninae*

4.5. A hybrid of the dog rose, *R. canina*, apparently found wild originally in France in 1823, according to W. J. Bean. This makes a spreading, arching shrub, occasionally to 2m, with small prickles. Lv with 5–7 leaflets, about 5cm long and half as wide. Fl fragrant, in clusters of 3–5, large, up to 10cm across, pale pink fading to white. Fl 6. Heps red, flask-shaped to 2cm long. A very attractive and comparatively compact shrub.

Rosa macrophylla LINDLEY *Cinnamomeae*

4.5. A very vigorous, spreading bush, up to 5m high and wide with pruinose bts. The stems may be unarmed or with straight prickles. Lv to 20cm long, usually with 7–9 leaflets, which are oval and up to 6cm long, smooth above, downy below. Fl either singly or in small clusters, to 7cm across, bright pink. Fl 6. Fr slightly bristly, pear-shaped, bright red to 3·5cm long. 'Glaucescens', collected by Forrest in his 1917–19 expedition (F 14958), has very glaucous lv and rosy-purple fl. 'Rubricaulis' (F 15309) is slightly tender, but has the stems red and covered with a purple bloom. Native to the Himalaya and western China. Introduced in 1818 by Roxburgh or Wallich.

Rosa moschata HERRMANN *Synstylae*

4. A moderate climber, from 2–4m, with short, hooked prickles. Lv of 5–7 rather oval leaflets, dark green, glabrous above, slightly downy below, as are the petioles and stems of the inflorescence. Fl in corymbs, about 5cm across, creamy, with a very individual fragrance of musk, often becoming semi-double. Fl 8–10. A very old plant, which was nearly lost to cultivation and has only recently been restored. Unique in its autumnal flowering and formerly used extensively in hybridising. Recently *R. brunonii* or some hybrid thereof used to be sent out as *R. moschata*. Native country not certainly known, possibly Iran.

Rosa moyesii HEMSLEY AND WILSON
Cinnamomeae

4.5. (Includes *R. holodonta* STAPF). A rather gaunt, tall shrub, to 4m, with large, triangular, straight prickles. Lv to 15cm long with 7–13 leaflets, which are a slightly bluish-green, oval, to 3cm long. Fl usually solitary, to 7cm across, an extraordinary shade of ruby crimson. Fl 6. Fr to 5cm long, flask-shaped, brilliant scarlet. Var *fargesii* ROLFE has brilliant carmine fl and is tetraploid, so of more use in hybridising than the hexaploid type. Var *holodonta* STAPF has deep pink fl and is more widespread than the type. Seedlings of *R. moyesii* are said often to revert to this form. Both in flower colour and in its conspicuous fr this is one of the most distinctive and decorative of rose species. Native of western China. The main introduction was by Wilson in 1903, but apparently its original discoverer, A. E. Pratt, brought back some seeds in 1894.

Rosa multibracteata HEMSLEY AND WILSON
Cinnamomeae

4. Bush, to 2m high and wide, with slender straight prickles, usually in pairs. Lv to 6cm long, with 7–9 leaflets, which are oval to only 1·5cm long and nearly as wide, grey-green above, grey below. Fl in sizeable clusters, each fl to 3cm across and subtended by leafy bracts, lilac-pink. Fl 7–8. Fr round, with persistent sepals, about 8mm in diameter, bright red. Graceful, with its small ferny lv, and useful for its late flowering. Native of Szechuan. Introduced by Wilson in 1908.

Rosa multiflora THUNBERG *Synstylae*

4.5. (*R. polyantha* SIEBOLD). Large, arching shrub or rambling climber, capable of ascending 7m into trees or making an impenetrable thicket, so often used as an edging to motorways in the US. Like many rambler roses, of which it is the main parent, it throws up fresh growths each year, which should, ideally, be removed after they have flowered in the second year. Brs with small, curved prickles. Lv to 15cm long (considerably larger on var *platyphylla*), usually with 9 leaflets, which are slightly downy when young. The stipules at the

base of the petioles are very jagged, which forms a diagnostic feature. Fl in large panicles, each about 2cm across, cream fading to white, with a heavy fragrance. Fr about 6mm wide, bright red without sepals. Although known as long ago as 1696, the first introduction seems to have been a double pink form in 1804, which was followed by the seven sisters rose, var *platyphylla,* which arrived in 1817. This form has much larger double fl which open cerise and fade to mauve, and is probably an early Chinese or Japanese garden hybrid. The white form is thought not to have arrived before 1862, but Sweet mentions a *R. multiflora albiflora* arriving in 1825, while Loudon gives 1810. Native to northern China, Korea and Japan.

Rosa nutkana PRESL *Cinnamomeae*

4.5. Vigorous shrub, to 3m, with prickles either straight or hooked. Lv to 12cm long with 5–9 leaflets, oval, to 5cm long, downy beneath. Fl 1–3, to 6cm across, deep pink. Fl 6–7. Fr round, with persistent sepals, bright red, 1·5cm in diameter, hanging until the new year. Native of western N America from Alaska to California. Introduced only in 1876, although detected by Archibald Menzies.

Rosa pendulina LINNAEUS *Cinnamomeae*

4.5. (*R. alpina* LINNAEUS). A shrub, to nearly 3m, usually unarmed. Lv to 15cm long with 5–9 leaflets, ovate, to 5cm long, with tiny prickles on the midrib, otherwise glabrous and light green. Fl usually solitary, occasionally up to 5, to 5cm across, bright pink with a touch of purple, very fragrant. Fl 5–6. Fr bright red, pear-shaped, to 2·5cm long. Var *pyrenaica* is extremely dwarf, rarely exceeding 30cm. Not all forms are without prickles, but the majority are. Native of the Alps, Pyrenees, some Spanish mountains and the Caucasus.

Rosa pimpinellifolia LINNAEUS Burnet Rose
Pimpinellifoliae

4. (*R. spinosissima* LINNAEUS). Usually a suckering shrub rarely exceeding 1m, but in var *altaica* (WILLDENOW) REHDER, a vigorous shrub to 2m. Intermediate forms are common. Stems covered with slender, straight spines, intermixed with bristles. Lv to 6cm long, with 5–9 leaflets which are more or less round, to 1cm long, deep green. Fl solitary, to 5cm across (7·5cm across in var *altaica*), usually cream, sometimes white, pink or yellow. Fl 5–6. Fr with persistent sepals, globose, about 2cm across, brownish-black. The yellow forms are probably early hybrids with *R. foetida*. Found from Iceland to eastern Siberia, and south to Spain. Native of the UK.

Rosa pisocarpa ASA GRAY *Cinnamomeae*

4.5. Shrub from 1–2m, sometimes thornless, sometimes with a few prickles which point upwards. Lv to 7cm long, with 5–7 leaflets, glabrous above, downy below, ovate, to 2·5cm long. Fl up to 3cm across, fragrant, rosy-pink or lilac-pink, usually in corymbs of 4–5, the fl opening successively. Fl 6–8. Fr globose, about the size of a pea (as the name *pisocarpa* suggests), bright red. Interesting with its minute fr and with a long flowering season. Native of western N America from British Columbia southwards.

Rosa prattii HEMSLEY *Cinnamomeae*

4. Shrub to 2m with, usually, both prickles and bristles. Lv to 7cm long with 7–15 ovate leaflets to 15mm long, grey-green. Fl usually in clusters, sometimes solitary, to 3cm across, deep pink. Fl 7. Fr flask-shaped, to 1cm long, scarlet. Useful for its late flowering. Native of western China. Introduced by Wilson in 1903 and 1908.

Rosa primula BOULENGER Incense Rose
Pimpinellifoliae

4. Upright shrub, to 2m, with reddish bts with numerous straight prickles. Lv aromatic, smelling of incense when crushed, up to 12cm long, made up of 9–15 elliptic leaflets to 2cm long, grey, slightly glaucous green. Fl solitary, to 4cm wide, primrose yellow. Fl 5–6. Fr rounded, dull red, soon falling. Useful for its early flowering. Native of Asia from Turkestan to northern China. Introduced 1910.

Rosa roxburghii TRATTINICK Chestnut Rose

4.5. The sole representative of the subgenus *Platyrhodon*. (*R. microphylla* of ROXBURGH, not DECAISNE). A rather stiff bush, as wide as high (usually around 2m), with grey peeling bark and stiff straight prickles in pairs. Lv to 10cm long, made up of 9–15 leaflets, elliptic, to 2cm long, dark green and glabrous above, downy below. Fl usually solitary, to 6cm across, white to quite a deep pink, very fragrant. Fl 6. Fr greenish-yellow, about 3cm across, densely covered with prickles to resemble a chestnut burr. The first form to be introduced was a double form which was deep pink. Native of China. The double form sent over by Roxburgh from Calcutta about 1820; the wild single form introduced by Wilson in 1908.

Rosa rubiginosa LINNAEUS Sweet Briar
Caninae

4.5. Erect bush, to 3m, with scattered, hooked prickles. Lv fragrant, to 15cm long, with 5–9 leaflets which are roundish, to 3cm long and wide, dark green above, slightly downy below. Fl 1–7, about 3cm across, bright or pale pink. Fl 6. Fr bright red, ovoid, about 2cm across.

Excellent for hedges, which should be trimmed in spring before growth starts. Native of most of Europe including the UK.

Rosa rubrifolia VILLARS *Caninae*

(4).5. Almost the only sp which is grown mainly for the effect of its foliage. An upright shrub, to 2m and more, sparingly armed, with violet-purple bts which age to red-brown. Lv to 12cm long, made up of 5–7 oval leaflets to 3cm long. In full light these lv are coppery mauve, in shade they are glaucous with a hint of mauve. Fl in clusters, to 3cm across, usually pink, but red and white forms are known, not very showy, although the white form is attractive. Fl 6. Fr ovoid, about 15mm across, red. Native to the mountains of central and southern Europe. Introduced in 1814 according to Loudon.

Rosa rubus LÉVEILLÉ AND VANIOT *Synstylae*

4.5. (*R. ernestii* STAPF). Very vigorous climber, to 9m, and closely allied to *R. helenae* but more vigorous. Lv to 22cm long, made up, usually, of 5 leaflets which may be 10cm long. Fl in large corymbs, often pink in bud, opening deep cream and fading to white, about 3cm across. Fl 6–7. Fr dark scarlet. All these Chinese synstylae climbers are hard to distinguish, but they are all desirable shrubs provided a large amount of room is available. They do excellently trained into sizeable trees. Native of central and western China. Introduced by Wilson in 1907.

Rosa rugosa THUNBERG *Cinnamomeae*

4.5. Vigorous, suckering shrub, to 2m, with stout prickly stems, which are downy. Lv to 15cm long, with 5–9 leaflets which are to 5cm long, with a wrinkled appearance above, downy below. Fl 1–4, to 9cm across, rose-purple to white, very fragrant. Fl 6–8. Fr round, bright red, to 3cm across. In some districts the lv colour well in the autumn. Some forms are a rather unpleasing magenta. The white forms are a very pure white. Native of China, Japan and Korea. Received from Japan, through Siebold, about 1845.

Rosa sericea LINDLEY *Pimpinellifoliae*

4.5. (Including *R. omeiensis* ROLFE). Authorities differ as to whether we have 1 or 2 species which are unique in the genus for having 4, not 5, petals to the fl, although occasionally 5-petalled fl do occur. The differences are rather insignificant and it is probably best to look at the various forms as manifestations of a single variable species. The differences regarded as specific are leaflets of *R. omeiensis*, usually 11–13, those of *R. sericea*, 7–11, lv of *R. omeiensis*, glabrous below, and those of *R. sericea*, silky below. Fr of *R. omeiensis* are borne on a thickened yellow stalk, those of *R. sericea* on a slender green stalk.

Shrub, to 3m high and wide, with upright stems usually set with flat, wide based prickles (which in var *pteracantha* are a beautiful translucent red and 2·5cm wide at the base). Lv ferny in appearance, leaflets obovate, to 2·5cm long and 1cm across, the whole lv being about 10cm long. Fl solitary, white or pale yellow, to 5cm across. Fl 4–5. Fr red, pear-shaped to 2·5cm. Var *chrysocarpa* has yellow fr. Var *pteracantha* is the only rose grown mainly for the sake of its prickles, which are ornamental at all times; most so, perhaps, in the winter. One of the first roses to flower. *R. sericea* is native to the Himalaya, *R. omeiensis* to western China. *R. sericea* introduced in 1822, presumably through Wallich; *R. omeiensis* by Wilson in 1901.

Rosa setigera MICHAUX Prairie Rose
Synstylae

4. (*R. rubifolia* R. BROWN). A shrub, to 5m, which usually sprawls but which can be trained into small trees as a climber. Lv usually trifoliate, each leaflet up to 7cm long and 5cm across, deep green above, pale and downy below. Fl in corymbs that may be 15cm or more across, each fl to 6cm across, mallow-pink fading to magenta. Fl 6–8. Fr small, 8mm across, dull red. Useful for its late flowering. Apparently it is quite variable in the wild, with fl from white to crimson, so it is unfortunate that the cultivated form is a disappointing muddy colour. Native of eastern N America. Introduced by Francis Masson in 1800.

Rosa setipoda HEMSLEY AND WILSON
Cinnamomeae

4.5. Vigorous shrub, to 3m, sometimes nearly unarmed, sometimes with large flat prickles, which are fairly sparse. Lv to 17cm long, made up of 7–9 leaflets which are up to 6cm long and about half as wide, dark green above, glaucous below; the lv with a faint fragrance, as in the sweet briar. Fl in corymbs of from 6 to 20 or more, each fl on a purple, bristly stem and the calyx is also purple. Fl to 5cm across, pink fading to white in the centre; some forms are rosy-purple. Fl 6. Fr pendulous, flask-shaped, deep red, rather hairy, about 2·5cm long. One of the very best sp for fl and fr. Native of western China. Introduced to Vilmorin (by Farges?) in 1895 and later by Wilson.

Rosa soulieana CRÉPIN *Synstylae*

4.5. An extremely vigorous bush, to 4m high and somewhat wider, with quite excessively prickly brs which can be up to 3m long in a single season. Lv to 10cm long, made up of 7–9 leaflets which are a very attractive pale grey-green; the leaflets to 2·5cm long. Fl in large clusters, to 15cm across, ivory in bud, opening white, each fl to 3cm across. Fl 6–7. Fr ovoid, 1·2cm long, 8mm wide, orange. A very fine shrub, but requiring ample space. The orange fr are particularly striking. Native of western China. Introduced by Père Soulié to Vilmorin in 1896.

Rosa stellata WOOTON

4. One of the 2 (or 3) species in the subgenus *Hesperhodon*. The true *R. stellata* rarely exceeds 60cm, but the var *mirifica* (GREENE) COCKERELL can sometimes reach to 2m, so can be included here. A suckering shrub, with prickles in pairs at the base of the lv. Bts of true *stellata* with stellate pubescence, which is lacking in var *mirifica*. Lv to 3cm long, with 3 or 5 leaflets to 1cm long, slightly downy on both surfaces. The shrub is somewhat reminiscent of a gooseberry bush. Fl solitary, about 5cm across, pinkish-purple, not unlike *Cistus villosus*. Fl 7–8. Fr egg-shaped, prickly, dull red, about 1cm across. Curious rather than beautiful. Native of the Sacramento mountains in New Mexico. Introduced by Rehder in 1916. *R. stellata* from west Texas to Arizona; introduced in 1902.

Rosa sweginzowii KOEHNE *Cinnamomeae*

4.5. Large shrub, to 4m high and wide, with very prickly brs. Very close to *R. moyesii*, but with bright pink fl, slightly smaller, and with less bristly heps. It makes a less gaunt shrub than *R. moyesii* and is somewhat more vigorous. Fl 6. Native of north-west China. Introduced about 1909.

Rosa villosa LINNAEUS *Caninae*

4.5. (*R. pomifera* HERRMANN). Large shrub, to 2m high, spreading rather more widely. Lv to 17cm long, with 5–7 leaflets to 6cm long and 3·5cm wide, grey-green, somewhat downy on both surfaces. Fl in clusters of 3–6, each on a bristly pedicel, to 6cm across, deep pink. Fr rounded red, bristly, with persistent sepals, orange-red at first, later plum coloured, to 3cm long and 2·5cm across. 'Duplex', Wolley-Dod's rose, is a hybrid between this sp and a garden rose, and is semi-double. Native of central Europe and western Asia. Naturalised in the UK.

Rosa virginiana MILLER *Carolinae*

4.5.(6). (*R. lucida* EHRHART). Suckering shrub, to 2m, with either straight or hooked prickles at the base of the lv and prickly bristles on the bts, which turn reddish-brown by the autumn. Lv to 12cm long, made up of 7–9 leaflets which are markedly glossy on the upper surface and glabrous, or nearly so, below, narrowly oval, to 5cm long. The lv usually colour first dull red and later orange before falling. Fl 1–3, to 6cm across, cerise. Fl 7–8. Fr to 1·5cm across, red, sepals soon falling. Native of eastern N America. Probably introduced by Catesby about 1726. Known to Miller, but confused with *R. carolina* in *Hortus Kewensis*. *R. virginiana* 'alba' is probably a hybrid of *R. virginiana* with *R. carolina*.

Rosa wardii MULLIGAN *Cinnamomeae*

4.5. Apparently the typical form is not in cultivation, being replaced by Kingdon Ward's 6101, although it is not clear how this differs from true *R. wardii*. It is given the cv name 'Culta'. A shrub, to 2m high and wide, with arching brs. Lv similar to those of *R. moyesii*, although rather smaller. Fl 1–4, creamy-white, with a conspicuous red disk in the centre, to 6cm across. Fl 6. Fr flask-shaped, scarlet about 2·5cm long. Sometimes referred to as the white *moyesii*. Native of south-eastern Tibet. Introduced by Kingdon Ward in 1924.

Rosa webbiana ROYLE *Cinnamomeae*

4.(5). A graceful shrub, to 2m high and wide, with arching brs, often blue-white at first, with straight spines in pairs. Lv to 7cm long, made up of 5–9 almost round leaflets, which are up to 1·5cm long, rather greyish-green. Fl solitary, lilac-pink or clear pink, to 5cm across. Fl 5–6. Fr bottle-shaped, about 2cm long, bright scarlet with persistent sepals. A very graceful shrub; the heps are sometimes very ornamental, but not always produced as freely as the fl. Native of the western Himalaya. Introduced 1879.

Rosa wichuraiana CRÉPIN *Synstylae*

5. (Including *R. luciae* FRANCHET AND ROCHEBRUNE, which has priority over *wichuraiana*). Evergreen or semi-evergreen shrub, normally prostrate and rooting as it goes; the climbing form is known as *R. luciae*, and can ascend to 5m. Large, curved prickles. Lv to 7cm long, made up of 7–9 leaflets (those of *R. luciae*, narrower, usually with 7 leaflets), dark glossy green above, paler below; the leaflets almost round, up to 2cm long. Fl in panicles of 6–10 fl, each to 5cm across, fragrant and pure white. Fl 7–9. Fr round, 8mm in diameter, reddish, without sepals. An important parent for many rambling and climbing roses, but well worth growing on its own account. Admirable for ground cover. *R. luciae* is slightly tender. Native of eastern China, Korea and Japan. Introduced before 1891, when it was received at Kew from America.

Rosa willmottiae HEMSLEY *Cinnamomeae*

4. Graceful, spreading bush to 2m high, rather more in width; bts covered with pinkish thorns. Lv to 5cm long, made up of 7–9 nearly round leaflets, up to 1cm long, greyish and glabrous.

Fl solitary, lilac-pink or purplish, to 3cm across. Fl 5–6. Fr small, round, orange-red, without sepals, which is unusual in the *Cinnamomeae*. Very close to *R. webbiana* but smaller in lv, fl and fr. Native of western China. Introduced by Wilson in 1904.

Rosa woodsii LINDLEY *Cinnamomeae*

4.5. The var *fendleri* (CRÉPIN) REHDER is the best form to obtain, the type being rather insignificant. Shrub of up to 1·5m, with straight prickles. Lv glaucous grey, to about 10cm long, with 5–7 obovate leaflets which are shortly stalked, to 3cm long. Fl in clusters of up to 6, to 5cm across, lilac-pink. Fl 5–6. Fr rounded, about 1cm in diameter, sealing-wax red, usually pulling the branch down by its weight to hang vertically like giant red currants. Native of western N America from British Columbia to Arizona. *R. woodsii* itself introduced in 1815, var *fendleri* in cultivation in 1888.

Rosa xanthina LINDLEY *Pimpinellifoliae*

4. Although described and diagnosed by Lindley as long ago as 1820 from a Chinese painting, the plant has only comparatively recently come into cultivation. The name was given to a double-flowered rose, so the wild, single original is known as var *spontanea* REHDER. Shrub, to 3m high and wide, with stout prickles. Lv to 7cm long, with 7–13 leaflets which are rounded, up to 1cm in diameter and a fresh green downy below. Fl about 4cm across, golden yellow. Fl 5–6. Fr dull red, round, about 1cm across with persistent sepals. 'Canary Bird', sometimes offered as a cv of *R. xanthina*, is almost certainly of hybrid origin; possibly *R. hugonis* is the other parent. Native of China. The double form introduced by F. N. Meyer in 1906; the single form arrived at the same time, although it had been found by David sometime earlier.

ROSMARINUS LINNAEUS *Labiatae*
Rosemary

A very small genus, monotypic according to some botanists; others have regarded the prostrate form as specifically distinct. Propagated readily by mature stem cuttings.

Rosmarinus officinalis LINNAEUS

4. Evergreen shrub, to 2m high and wide but usually less. Lv opposite, linear, densely crowded so as to appear whorled, sessile, to 5cm long and 3mm wide, dark glossy green above, white tomentose below, very aromatic. Fl in small, axillary racemes of 2–3, two-lipped, about 1–5cm long, calyx purplish, pale or dark blue. Fl 4–5. The variegated forms, so much admired in Tudor times, appear to have been lost, but there are a number of clones of fastigiate form, notably 'Fastigiatus' and 'Pyramidalis', and selected deep colour forms, which are usually rather more tender than the paler forms. In any case, being a Mediterranean shrub, it is liable to damage in very severe winters, old plants being more susceptible, so it is as well always to have a few rooted cuttings under cover.

RUBUS LINNAEUS

This large genus of 250 species and at least 300 microspecies and forms, including the raspberries and blackberries, is a complicated one. Moreover, it contains comparatively few plants of much garden value. Although woody, many, including all those in the subgenus *Idaeobatus*, have stems of biennial duration only and these have to be cut out after the second year, otherwise the plants become unsightly. The blackberries and many in the subgenus *Malachobatus* root at the tips and can easily be propagated in this way. Other species can be propagated by division, by cuttings or by layers. The subgenera with which we will be concerned are:

Malachobatus FOCKE Composed of evergreen and deciduous, prickly, climbing or trailing shrubs. Lv simple or digitately compound; the stipules below the leaves soon falling.

Anoplobatus FOCKE Upright stems with peeling bark, simple leaves and large flowers.

Idaeobatus FOCKE Raspberries. Biennial, erect stems, usually prickly, compound leaves.

Eubatus FOCKE Blackberries. Usually biennial, trailing angled stems, usually very prickly, and compound leaves. Fruit usually blackish.

The fruit, composed of a number of drupelets gathered on a conical base called the torus, is the most regular feature of the genus, and whether the ripe fruit separates from the torus (as in the raspberry) or whether the torus comes away with the fruit (as in the blackberry) may be diagnostic.

Rubus amabilis FOCKE *Idaeobatus*

4. Deciduous shrub, to 2m occasionally but usually little more than 1m, armed with small prickles. Lv to 20cm long, pinnate, with 7–11 leaflets which are shortly stalked, ovate, pointed, toothed, to 5cm long and half as wide. Stems presumably biennial. Fl solitary, terminating lateral twigs, white, to 5cm across. Fl 6–7. Fr conical, red, 1·5cm long, edible but not very freely produced. Native of Szechuan. Introduced by Wilson in 1908.

Rubus biflorus BUCHANAN-HAMILTON *Idaeobatus*

1. Vigorous, deciduous shrub with erect, biennial, branching stems to 3m, covered with a thick, white, waxy coat, which makes them very striking in winter. Lv pinnate with 3 or 5 leaflets, to 25cm long, the leaflets to 10cm long, ovate, dark green above, white tomentose below. Fl in terminal clusters of 2–5, white; fl 2cm across, but inconspicuous. Fl 5–6. Fr roundish, yellow, edible, about 2cm across. One of a number of attractive, white-barked raspberries, and the first to reach cultivation. Native of the Himalaya. Introduced through Wallich in 1818.

Rubus cockburnianus HEMSLEY *Idaeobatus*

1. (*R. giraldianus* FOCKE). Vigorous, deciduous shrub, to 3m, with erect, biennial stems which branch freely at the top, the side brs being somewhat pendulous. The stems are covered with a waxy, white covering and are sparingly spiny. Lv pinnate, to 20cm long, usually with 9 leaflets which are rhombic, to 6cm long and 3cm wide, smooth above, white tomentose below. Fl in terminal panicles up to 12cm long, small, purple and inconspicuous. Fl 6. Fr blackish. Native of north and central China. Introduced from Szechuan by Wilson in 1907.

Rubus deliciosus TORREY *Anoplobatus*

4. Deciduous shrub, to 3m, with spreading, slightly pendulous brs and brown peeling bark. Lv basically triangular but 3 or 5-lobed, much resembling a black-currant leaf, to 7cm long and rather wider. Fl solitary, about 5cm across, much like a wild rose, pure white. Fl 5–6. Fr about 1cm across, blackish, sparingly produced. *R. trilobus* TORREY, with slightly larger lv and fl, is rarely in cultivation, but the hybrid between the two spp, 'Tridel', a more vigorous plant than either of its parents, is available and is one of the loveliest flowering shrubs, reaching sometimes 4m with white fl to 7cm across. *R. deliciosus* is native of the Rocky Mountains in Colorado and was introduced in 1870. 'Tridel' was raised by Collingwood Ingram in 1950.

Rubus flagelliflorus FOCKE *Malachobatus*

A very vigorous evergreen climber with growths of up to 2m in a single season. Bts covered with white tomentum. Lv simple, more or less heart-shaped, to 15cm long and 10cm across, toothed or very shallowly lobed, dark green above, with a yellowish tomentum below. Fl in axillary clusters with purple sepals and white petals which soon fall. Fl 6. Fr black, 1cm across, edible. Grown solely for its foliage and elegant habit, but it requires support, like all these evergreen *rubi*, otherwise it trails over the ground. Native of central and western China. Introduced by Wilson in 1901.

216

Rubus henryi HEMSLEY Malachobatus

(Including *R. bambusarum* FOCKE). Vigorous, evergreen climber to 7m, sometimes making growths to 4m in a single season. Stems slender, prickly, with a white cobweb-like tomentum at first. Lv dark green, leathery, basically heart-shaped but deeply 3- (rarely 5) lobed, with a white felty tomentum below, to 15cm long. Fl in terminal and axillary racemes to 8cm long, each fl to 2cm across, pink, petals soon falling. Fl 6. Fr black. Var *bambusarum* (FOCKE) REHDER has the lv divided into 3 separate leaflets, to 12cm long and 2cm across. Again these plants are grown for their foliage alone. Both the type and the var were introduced by Wilson in 1900.

Rubus leucodermis TORREY AND GRAY
Idaeobatus

1. Erect shrub, to 2·5m, with biennial stems armed with stout prickles, and an effective glaucous blue-white in colour. Lv usually with 3 leaflets, occasionally 5, ovate, to 7cm long, dull green above, white-tomentose below. Fl in terminal clusters of a few white fl. Fl 6. Fr round, purplish-black, edible. Less attractive than the Asian, white-stemmed spp. Native of western N America. Introduced by Douglas in 1829.

Rubus linkianus SERINGE Eubatus

4. (*R. thyrsoideus plenus* WIMMER). Deciduous shrub with arching, ribbed biennial stems, downy at first but soon glabrous and with many straight prickles. Lv of 5 leaflets, which are ovate, dull green above, with a dull white tomentum below. Fl in erect panicles to 18cm long, each fl about 2·5cm across, white and double. Fl 7–8. The plant is not known in the wild and does not agree entirely either with *R. candicans* or with *R. thyrsoideus*. It does well in semi-shade and can be persuaded to penetrate a hedge.

Rubus odoratus LINNAEUS Anoplobatus

4. Vigorous deciduous shrub, to nearly 3m, with erect, very pale brown, unarmed stems with peeling bark. Lv simple, 5-lobed, much like a vine leaf, to 30cm wide, slightly less long, hairy on both surfaces. Fl in short, many-flowered panicles, each fl to 5cm across, purple, fragrant, with pedicels and calyx densely hairy. Fl 7–9. Fr red, rarely produced. A very vigorous plant, soon making a thicket and scarcely suitable for a restricted space, but useful in its late flowering and also because it thrives best in semi-shade. Native of eastern N America. According to Aiton in cultivation in 1700, suggesting a Banister introduction. Rehder give 1635 as the date of introduction.

Rubus phoenicolasius MAXIMOWICZ Wineberry
Idaeobatus

4.5. Deciduous shrub, to 3m, with biennial stems, densely and ornamentally covered with red bristles when young. Lv to 17cm long, made up of 3 leaflets, of which the terminal one is up to 10cm long with a distinct petiolule. Fl in terminal racemes, very small, pink, but hidden in the distinctive red, bristly calyx. Fl 6–7. Fr roundish, yellow at first, later red and quite ornamental; edible but somewhat insipid. Fr 8–10. The young growths are attractive enough, but the attraction of the fr is rather mild. Native of Japan and China. Introduced about 1876.

Rubus spectabilis PURSH Idaeobatus

4.5. Vigorous suckering raspberry with biennial stems, to 2m, prickly at their base. Lv to 15cm long, made up of 3 leaflets which are ovate, the largest to 10cm long. Fl singly or in a small cluster, about 3cm across, purple verging on magenta, fragrant. Fl 4–5. Fr orange and large, but sparingly produced. The earliest-flowering rubus and a very rampant grower. Native of western N America. Introduced by Douglas in 1827.

Rubus thibetanus FRANCHET Idaeobatus

1. (*R. veitchii* ROLFE). Yet another of the Asiatic raspberries with attractive stems. Shrub, to 2m, with biennial stems which are purplish-brown and covered with a blue-white bloom, rarely branching. Lv pinnate, to 22cm long, with 7–13 leaflets, the largest to 5cm long, dark green above, white tomentose below. Fl solitary, axillary and in a few-flowered, terminal panicle, to 1·5cm across, purple. Fl 6. Fr black with bluish bloom about 1·5cm across. All these attractive-stemmed *rubi* tend to be rather vigorous and spread widely. Native of western China. Introduced by Wilson in 1904.

Rubus ulmifolius SCHOTT Eubatus

4. The type is one of the British wild brambles and is not cultivated deliberately, but the double form, known as 'Bellidiflorus', is a handsome shrub. Stems arching, usually biennial, slightly downy at the apex of new growths, thickly armed with usually straight prickles. Lv semi-evergreen, made up of 3–5 leaflets, each stalked, broadly ovate, to 8cm long and more than half as wide, slightly downy and dark green above, white tomentose below. Fl rose-pink, in long slender panicles, each fl about 1·2cm across, very double, so no fr is set. Fl 7–8. Too rampant for most situations but admirable in a hedge or trained against a fence. Young plants sometimes take a year or so to come to flowering, in which case the stems perennate, fading away once a flowering rhythm is attained.

RUSCUS LINNAEUS *Liliaceae*

A small genus of suckering evergreen shrubs, of which only one is large enough to be included here. Although ostensibly evergreen, in truth the plants have no leaves whatever, their place being taken by flattened branches known as cladodes. Normally the plants are dioecious, but hermaphrodite forms do exist and, since the fruit is the only attractive feature of the plants, these should be sought after. Propagation by seed or by division.

Ruscus aculeatus LINNAEUS Butcher's Broom

5. Suckering evergreen shrub to 1m, the erect stems branching near their summits and renewing themselves by yearly sucker growths. Cladodes alternate or whorled, broadly ovate, to 3cm long and 2cm wide, very dark green and glabrous, terminating in a stiff spine. Fl small, greenish-white, in centre of cladode, 6mm across, usually solitary. Fl 3–4. Fr a round, bright red berry to 1·5cm in diameter. The plant grows quite happily in deep shade, which has its uses. Native of much of Europe including southern England.

RUTA LINNAEUS *Rutaceae*

A small genus of seven species of herbs and shrubs with alternate leaves and yellow flowers; only one or two are in general cultivation. Propagated by cuttings.

Ruta graveolens LINNAEUS Rue

4. Evergreen shrub, to 1m, with markedly glaucous lv which are bipinnate to 12cm long, the divisions being obovate to 1cm long. Fl in terminal cymes, to 10cm across, each fl being dull yellow, cup-shaped, the 4 (rarely 5) petals being fringed on the margins. Fl 6–8. Fr a dry capsule. 'Jackman's Blue' has lv of a very attractive blue-green colour. 'Variegata' has creamy variegation. The lv have a strong acrid scent and the plant has long been grown as a herb. Native probably of the Balkans, but widely naturalised around the Mediterranean.

SALIX LINNAEUS *Salicaceae* Willow

A very confusing genus of some 500 species of shrubs and trees, mainly deciduous. They are dioecious, the flowers in the form of catkins, usually coming before the leaves, so that if flowers are available the leaves may not be. In addition, natural and artificial hybrids occur abundantly, so that they are not only difficult to identify, but may well be forms that have not hitherto been recorded. Although the flowers of some species, such as the sallow, are ornamental, they are usually grown either for their grace of habit or for their foliage or brightly coloured young wood. In these cases they are often pollarded regularly, so as to encourage a large number of young shoots, but, although there may be less coloured wood, they still appear attractive if allowed to develop into trees. Hardwood cuttings, inserted in the open ground during the winter, usually root readily, but willows are intolerant of root disturbance and should be put in their permanent positions as soon as possible. Most species require ample supplies of water and many will grow in quite marshy conditions. The leaves are alternate.

Salix adenophylla WILLIAM HOOKER

2.3. Straggling shrub, to nearly 3m, with densely silky, hairy bts, which are pale grey. Lv very densely set, more or less heart-shaped, toothed, to 5cm long and 3cm across, with white hairs on both surfaces. Female catkins to 7cm long before lv. The male plant may not be available in commerce. Native of N America from Labrador southwards and westwards. Not apparently cultivated before 1900.

Salix alba

218

Salix alba LINNAEUS

(2).7. (2) applies to certain forms described below with very brilliant year-old wood, which is conspicuous in winter. Deciduous tree, to 25m, the bts pendulous and grey tomentose at first. Lv elliptic-lanceolate, to 7 or 8cm long, 1·5cm across, covered with silvery, silky down below, nearly glabrous above. In the form known as 'Sericea' or 'Argentea', which is a less vigorous plant, the lv are a brilliant silver below and also have less silver silky hairs above. Catkins to 5cm long, appearing in early May with the lv. 'Chermesina' ('Britzensis') has the year-old wood a brilliant orange scarlet, which glows in winter. 'Vitellina', a male clone, has the year-old wood brilliant yellow. A rapid-growing, moisture-loving tree from most of Europe, including the UK.

Salix babylonica LINNAEUS   Weeping Willow

7. A tree, to 15m, with long, pendulous, brown bts. Lv lanceolate, to 10cm long and 1cm wide, dark green above, glaucous beneath, glabrous on both surfaces when mature. Catkins to 5cm long, slender, appearing in April. The true weeping willow is quite scarce nowadays, its place being taken by *S. X chrysocoma*, a hybrid between this plant and *S. alba* 'Vitellina', with the weeping habit of *S. babylonica* but yellow bts. Unfortun-

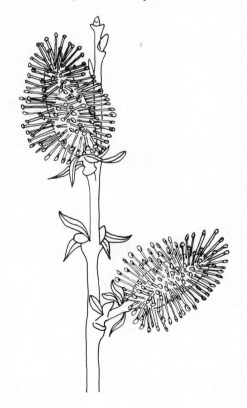

Salix caprea

ately the hybrid appears vulnerable to scab and to canker, and the true sp is more reliable. Native to western China. Early introduced to the Near East and, according to Collinson, first brought to England in 1730 by a Mr Vernon, a merchant of Aleppo. It had previously been brought to France by Tournefort. (*Hortus Kewensis*, quoting Plukenet, says it was in cultivation at Hampton Court in 1692.)

Salix caprea LINNAEUS   Palm Sallow

4. Shrub or small tree, occasionally to 7m, with grey downy bts at first. Lv oval to nearly lanceolate, to 10cm long and 5·5cm across, grey-green and wrinkled above, grey tomentose below. Catkins before lv. The males grey-silver at first, bright yellow when the stamens emerge, conical, about 2·5cm long. The females silvery-green, to 5cm or more. Fl 3–4. Native of most of Europe, including the UK. *S. cinerea* LINNAEUS is very similar, but smaller and with narrower lv, the grey down persisting on the bts for about 18 months. There is a rather unattractive variegated form known as 'Tricolor'.

Salix daphnoides VILLARS

2.4.(7). Rapid-growing tree, to 13m, or large shrub with bts of an attractive violet with a whitish bloom. Lv elliptic-lanceolate, to 10cm long and 2·5cm wide, dark green above, glaucous beneath. Catkins much like those of *S. caprea*, the males to 4cm long, the females to 6cm. Fl 3. The males tend to make rather spreading trees, the females are more pyramidal. *S. acutifolia* WILLDENOW is barely distinct, but with narrower lv which are white below. It is native to the Caucasus and Turkestan, while *S. daphnoides* is found in most of Europe, eastwards to the Himalaya. An extremely attractive tree, often pollarded every other year to encourage the violet bts.

Salix elaeagnos SCOPOLI

(*S. incana* SCHRANK, *S. rosmarinifolia* HORT). A bushy shrub, to 4m, bts grey tomentose at first, later glabrous. Lv linear, elliptic, to 12cm long and 5mm wide, but with recurved margins so appearing narrower, dark green above, glaucous beneath. Catkins with lv erect, to 3cm long. Fl 4–5. Native of central Europe and Asia Minor. Introduced about 1820.

Salix exigua NUTTALL

Shrub or small tree to 5m. Lv linear, to 10cm long, finely toothed, yellowish-green above, silky and silvery below. Catkins with lv slender, to 5cm long. Native of western N America. Introduced in 1921.

Salix fargesii BURKILL

A spreading shrub, to nearly 3m, with bright red winter buds. Lv elliptic, to 17cm long and 8cm wide, wrinkled and shining dark green above, dull green and rather silky hairy below. Catkins erect before or with lv, the males to 12cm long, the females to 16cm. It is much confused with the closely allied *S. moupinensis* FRANCHET from which it is barely distinguishable. The lv of the latter are glabrous on both surfaces and bts become red-brown rather than dark brown. Lv only to 12cm long and catkins to 9cm for the males, 14cm for females. Both spp are native to western China and were introduced by Wilson in 1911.

Salix gracilistyla MIQUEL

4. Vigorous shrub, to 3m, with grey downy bts, which become smooth the second year. Lv narrowly elliptic, silky at first, later glabrous; to 10cm long and 3cm across, grey-green. Male catkins before lv, silvery-grey, later reddish as the red anthers become visible, later still yellow when the anthers dehisce, to 3·5cm long. Female catkins, to 7·5cm long, rarely seen in cultivation, 3–4. Var *melanostachys* (*S. melanostachys* MAKINO), only the male form in cultivation. Bts glabrous not silky, catkins not silky, nearly black with red anthers dehiscing to yellow, making it a striking object in early spring. Probably of hybrid origin, with *S. gracilistyla* as one parent. Native of Japan, Korea, Manchuria and northern China. Introduced, according to Bean, about 1895.

Salix irrorata E. ANDERSON

2.(4). A vigorous shrub, to 3m, with purple (rarely yellowish) bts densely covered with silvery, waxy bloom and singularly attractive. Lv linear-lanceolate, to 10cm long and 1cm across, bright green above, somewhat glaucous below. Catkins before lv to 2·5cm long. The males with red anthers, later turning yellow. Very attractive for winter ornament. Native of the western USA. Introduced in 1898.

Salix lucida MUEHLENBERG

Large shrub or tree, to 8m, with shining yellowish-brown bts. Lv lanceolate, long-acuminate, rounded at base, to 12cm long and 3cm across, glossy green above, paler below. Catkins with lv, the males erect to 6cm long, the females more slender and drooping to 5cm. Fl 4–5. Native of N America from Newfoundland to the Rockies. In cultivation in 1830.

Salix magnifica HEMSLEY

4. Large shrub or small tree, to 6m, with purple bts and winter buds. Lv oval or obovate, mucronate, to 20cm long and 12cm wide, petiole to 3cm, the lamina grey-green, slightly pruinose above, glaucous below, petiole tinged with purple. Catkins with lv, males to 17cm, females to 30cm. A very unusual willow with its enormous catkins and magnolia-like lv. Although hardy, it usually proves somewhat short-lived in cultivation. Native of western China. Introduced by Wilson in 1909.

Salix matsudana KOIDZUMI

7. Tree of pyramidal habit, to 16m, bts yellowish and downy at first, later glabrous, brownish-grey. Lv linear-elliptic, to 10cm long and 1·5cm across, bright green above, glaucous beneath, much like those of *S. babylonica*. Only the female is in cultivation and the catkins for this appear with lv and are about 2·5cm long. 'Pendula' is a very attractive and reliable weeping willow. 'Tortuosa' is a mutant plant with contorted brs which look very curious. It is still a vigorous grower. Native of northern China, Korea and Manchuria. Introduced from Korea to the USA in 1905.

Salix pentandra LINNAEUS

Large shrub or tree, to 15m, with smooth brownish bts and yellow winter buds. Lv ovate, to 11cm long and 5cm across, bright shining green above, dull pale green below, glabrous on both surfaces, midrib yellow. Catkins after lv, the males cylindrical to 3cm long, the females longer. Fl 5. The lv are aromatic when crushed and have been used as a substitute for bay leaves. Native of northern Europe, including the UK, and northern Asia.

Salix purpurea LINNAEUS

2. Spreading bush or small tree, to 6m, with long thin bts, usually purple, particularly when growing in full light, yellowish in shade. Lv often opposite as well as alternate, narrowly elliptic, to 7cm long and 8mm wide, glossy green above, glaucous blue below. Catkins before lv, erect, to 2·5cm long. Fl 3–4. 'Eugenei' has attractive silver-pink male catkins. 'Pendula' (*S. americana pendula* of gardens) makes a graceful pendulous plant, best grafted on to a standard of *S. alba*. An attractive, medium-sized tree, found in the wild in situations with a very high water table and so useful for such positions. Native of Europe, including the UK.

Salix sachalinensis F. SCHMIDT

A large shrub or small tree, to 10m, with purplish bts which are slightly downy at first. Lv lanceolate, to 14cm long and 2·5cm wide, dark green above, glaucous and faintly pubescent below. Catkins about 2·5cm long. The type may not be in cultivation but there exists a peculiar cv known as 'Sekka' or 'Setsuka' in which the bts are flattened, fasciated and contorted, which is highly thought of by some flower arrangers. Native of Japan and Sakhalin. Introduced 1905.

Salix triandra LINNAEUS

(Includes *S. amygdalina* LINNAEUS). Shrub or small tree, to 10m, with angled bts. Lv lanceolate, to 10cm long and 2·5cm across, glabrous on both surfaces and nearly the same green colour. Catkins with lv, males erect to 6cm long, females more or less pendent. Fl 4–5. Native of Europe, including the UK and northern Asia.

Salix viminalis LINNAEUS Osier

Erect shrub or small tree, to 6m, bts greypubescent at first, later glabrous and yellowish. Lv held somewhat vertically, linear, to 15cm long and 1cm across, dull dark green above, with a silvery pubescence below. Catkins before lv, to 2·5cm long and 2cm across. Fl 3–4. The willow that was most extensively used for basket making. A large number of hybrids between this and other spp exist, but no very outstanding plants have resulted. Native of most of Europe, including the UK, and Asia from Siberia to the Himalaya; usually growing on the banks of streams.

SAMBUCUS LINNAEUS *Caprifoliaceae* Elder

A small genus of about twenty species of herbs, shrubs and small trees, which are deciduous with opposite, pinnate leaves, flowers in large, terminal compound corymbs and the fruit, a drupe, invariably referred to as a berry. Only three species are in general cultivation but these are all somewhat variable. Propagation by both hard wood and half-ripe cuttings is usually easy and seeds germinate readily.

Sambucus canadensis LINNAEUS

4.5. Deciduous shrub, to 4m. Lv pinnate with 5–11 (usually 7) leaflets, which are ovateacuminate, the largest to 15cm long and 6cm across. Fl in convex heads to 20cm across. Berries very dark purple. The form most usually grown is 'Maxima', which is very vigorous, with lv to 45cm long and flower heads as much across, while the pedicels are an attractive rosy purple. Fl 7. 'Rubra' has red fr, while 'Aurea' has red fr and yellow lv. Probably both are of hybrid origin. Native of the eastern USA. Introduced by Bartram about 1760.

Sambucus nigra LINNAEUS Common Elder

4.5. Shrub or tree from 6 to 10m. Lv 10–30cm long, usually with 5 leaflets, occasionally 3 or 7, which are ovate, to 12cm long and 5cm across, fetid, very dark green. Fl in umbel-like corymbs to 20cm across. Fl 6. Fr black and shining. The type is too invasive for cultivation, but a number of attractive cv exist. These include 'Albovariegata' and 'Aureomarginata', with white and yellow-margined leaflets, while the whole leaflet is mottled white in 'Pulverulenta'. 'Aurea' is a very lovely golden-leafed form. 'Laciniata' has the leaflets deeply dissected, while in 'Heterophylla' the blades have almost disappeared to leave the leaflets thread-like. There is a double form, and at one time a double pink-flowered form was known, but this seems to have been lost. Finally 'Fructu luteo' has yellow fr.

Sambucus racemosa LINNAEUS

5. Quick-growing shrub to 3m high and wide. Lv to 22cm long, made up of 5 leaflets which are ovate, coarsely toothed, to 10cm long and 5cm across. Fl in pyramidal panicles, greeny-white, rather inconspicuous. Fl 4. Fr brilliant red and very showy. Fr 7–9. 'Plumosa Aurea' has the leaflets deeply dissected and a golden yellow which persists throughout the season. 'Tenuifolia' is a dwarf form with the leaflets themselves pinnately divided. It is very slow-growing. Native of most of Europe, eastwards to Siberia and northern China.

Sassafras albidum

221

SASSAFRAS NEES *Lauraceae*

A small genus of about three species, only one of which is in cultivation.

Sassafras albidum NEES

(6).7. Deciduous tree, to 30m in the wild but rarely more than 16m in cultivation. Lv alternate, oval, obovate or orbicular, often with 2 or 3 lobes at the apex, to 17cm long and 10cm across; dark green above, somewhat glaucous below, both surfaces downy when young, later glabrous; turning a clear yellow in the autumn. Fl either perfect or monoecious, although the unisexual fl appear to have both stamens and pistils, but one or other does not function. Fl petalless, with greenish-yellow calyx, in racemes to 5cm long. Fl 5. Fr a dark blue, round drupe, to 1cm long on a red stalk. An attractive foliage tree, difficult to propagate and best raised from seed. It requires acid soil. It is sometimes met with as *S. officinale* and Linnaeus called it *Laurus sassafras*. Native of the eastern USA. Cultivated in 1633.

SAXEGOTHAEA LINDLEY *Podocarpaceae*

A monotypic genus, apparently linking *Podocarus* with *Araucaria*.

Saxegothaea conspicua LINDLEY

Evergreen tree, to 14m, with whorled brs, slow-growing and liable to damage in exceptionally hard frosts. Lv linear, to 2·5cm long and 2mm wide, dark green above, glaucous beneath, but much resembling a yew in general appearance. Male and female fl on the same plant, the males axillary, the females terminal, both small and inconspicuous. Fr a leafy cone, only 1cm across, the scales spine-tipped. A plant of considerable interest, but not particularly decorative. Native of Chile. Introduced by W. Lobb in 1847.

SCHINUS LINNAEUS *Anacardiaceae*

A comparatively small genus of evergreen shrubs and trees in which only one species is both hardy and in cultivation. At one time plants with simple leaves (most species have compound pinnate leaves), were put in the genus *Duvaua* KUNTHE. *S. dependens* is fairly readily propagated by cuttings of half-ripe wood.

Schinus dependens ORTEGA

4.5. Evergreen shrub with spine-tipped twigs to 5m. Lv alternate, obovate, to 2·5cm long and nearly as wide, dark green. Fl minute but numerous in axillary racemes about 1cm long, greenish-yellow. Fl 5. Fr a dry capsule, looking like a berry, deep purple, the size of a peppercorn.

Schinus dependens

Most *schinus* are dioecious, but this sp appears to have perfect fl. Liable to damage in very severe winters, but regenerates. Native of Chile. Obtained by Banks in 1790; one would have thought through Archibald Menzies, but *Hortus Kewensis* only attributes *S. dentata* to him.

SCHISANDRA MICHAUX *Schisandraceae*

Often spelt *Schizandra*. A genus of evergreen and deciduous twining shrubs, which are dioecious. The fruit is a spike of berries. *Schisandraceae* was regarded as a branch of the *Magnoliaceae* by the older botanists, and, like the members of that family, sepals and petals are not clearly differentiated and flowers may have any number of these from seven to twelve. The fruit are very ornamental, but can only be produced when plants of both sexes are present, and it is rare that nurserymen can differentiate the sexes as plants are mainly propagated by seed and do not flower until a reasonable size. Apart from seed, propagation is not easy, layering being the most satisfactory method. Cuttings of semi-hard lateral stems with a heel are said by Bean to root readily if given some bottom heat, but not everyone would agree. They are among the most delightful of climbing plants.

Schisandra chinensis BAILLON

4.(5). Deciduous, twining shrub, to 10m, with reddish bts. Lv elliptic, to 10cm long, slightly toothed. Fl in axillary clusters of 2–3, each on a pedicel to 2·5cm long, pale pink, fragrant, cup-shaped, to 2cm across. Fl 4–5. Fruiting spike to 15cm long, berries scarlet. Native of China and Japan. Introduced in 1860.

Schisandra grandiflora
var *rubiflora*

Schisandra grandiflora HOOKER AND THOMSON

4.(5). The plant originally diagnosed by Hooker and Thomson from the Himalaya is probably not in cultivation; its place being taken by two varieties – *cathayensis* SCHNEIDER and *rubriflora* SCHNEIDER (*S. rubriflora* REHDER AND WILSON). Slender, twining shrub, to 7m or more, with reddish-brown bts. Lv obovate, to 12cm long and 6cm across in var *rubriflora*, less in var *cathayensis*. Fl in axillary clusters of 2–6, solitary, on pedicels which are reddish, to 4cm long. Fl cup-shaped, to 2cm across in var *cathayensis* and rose-pink, to 3cm across in var *rubriflora* and ruby red, seeming to glow. Fl 5–6. Fr in pendulous spikes, each fr about the size of a pea, the stalk to 15cm long, of which half is occupied by the scarlet berries. The two culti-vated var were introduced by Wilson from western China in 1907.

Schisandra propinqua HOOKER AND THOMSON

4.(5). The typical form, although introduced in 1828 from the Himalaya, is not reliably hardy, its place in gardens being taken by the Chinese var *sinensis* OLIVER. Climber, to 7m, with angled bts. Lv lanceolate, long-acuminate, to 10cm long. Fl short-stalked, about 1·5cm across, orange-yellow. Fl 7–9. Fr on a stem to 15cm

long, bright scarlet. Useful for its late flowering, but this may militate against fr being set. Var *sinensis* introduced by Wilson in 1907. *S. henryi* and *S. glaucescens* with white fl, and *S. sphenanthera* with orange-red fl in May and June, are occasionally offered and are all desirable climbers.

SCHIZOPHRAGMA SIEBOLD AND ZUCCARINI
Hydrangeaceae

A small genus of eight species of deciduous shrubs, climbing by means of aerial rootlets, very similar in appearance to *Hydrangea petiolaris*, from which it is distinguished by having floral bracts around the flower cluster, while the hydrangea has large sterile florets. The leaves are opposite and the flowers are in terminal cymes. Easily propagated by cuttings or by layers and tolerant of most soils, if not too poor.

Schizophragma hydrangeoides
SIEBOLD AND ZUCCARINI

4. Climbing shrub, to 13m, with reddish-brown bts. Lv ovate to cordate, coarsely toothed, to 15cm long and 10cm across, dark green above, somewhat glaucous and silky-hairy below, on a petiole to 5cm. Fl in terminal cymes to 25cm across, slightly fragrant, the fertile fl very small, but each branch of the cyme terminated by a large ovate bract to 4cm long. The colour is usually ivory, but 'Roseum' has a faint pink flush. Fl 7. Native of Japan. Apparently not in cultivation before 1880.

Schizophragma integrifolium
(FRANCHET) OLIVER

4. Climbing to 13m, distinguished from *S. hydrangeoides* by its larger lv (to 17cm long,

Schizophragma integrifolium

11cm across) which have either an entire margin or one that is very finely toothed, while that of *S. hydrangeoides* is coarsely toothed. The petiole is slightly hairy at first. Fl in cymes to 30cm across, the sterile bract to 9cm long and 4·5cm across and pure white. Fl 7. A better plant than *S. hydrangeoides*, but not always easy to obtain. Native of central China. Introduced by Wilson in 1901.

SCIADOPITYS SIEBOLD AND ZUCCARINI
Pinaceae

A monotypic genus requiring lime-free soil and ample patience.

Sciadopitys verticillata SIEBOLD AND ZUCCARINI

7. A slow-growing, pyramidal tree, eventually to 30m or more in the wild. Brs in whorls, spreading horizontally, but slightly pendulous at the ends. Lv dimorphic, one kind scattered along the brs, small and scale-like, the others are like the spokes of an umbrella at the ends of the brs (hence the name umbrella pine given to this sp among others). These consist of two fused needles, or possibly they are modified bts and should be regarded as cladodes. These are rigid, linear, to 12cm long, dark glossy green with two bands of whitish stomata beneath. Male fl in a terminal raceme, 2·5cm long. Cones to 7cm long and 5cm across, ripening in the second year. When trees get large enough to display the trunk, it is seen that the bark peels yearly to disclose attractive, reddish-brown new bark beneath. Restricted in the wild to two regions of Honshu

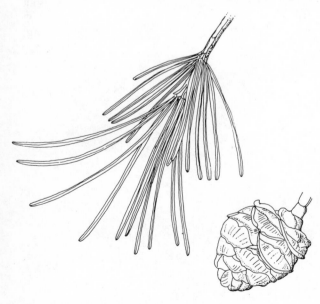

Sciadopitys verticillata

in Japan. Sent by Siebold to Java before 1830, whence Thomas Lobb sent a single plant to Veitch in 1853. Introduced in quantity by Fortune and J. G. Veitch in 1861. Although so slow-growing, it makes an attractive specimen when quite small. It has no objection to shade in its youth.

SENECIO LINNAEUS *Compositae*
This enormous genus of over 2,000 species comprises more herbs than shrubs and many of these are not hardy. There exists, however, a group of New Zealand shrubs which are admirable for planting near the coast, although they may prove somewhat tender inland. Easily propagated by cuttings or by seed. The species described below are generally hardy, but may suffer in very severe winters. They are all evergreen.

Senecio elaeagnifolius JOSEPH HOOKER
Evergreen shrub, to 3m, with bts covered with buff tomentum. Lv leathery, obovate, tapered at the end, rounded at the apex, to 12cm long and 9cm wide, dark glossy green above, buff tomentose below. Fl in a terminal panicle, pyramidal, to 15cm, each fl to 1cm across without ray florets, yellow. Fl 7. Of no floral beauty. Native of both islands of New Zealand.

Senecio greyi of gardens
4. The true *S. greyi* of Joseph Hooker is a somewhat tender shrub, but the plant sold by nurserymen under this name is reasonably hardy. Evergreen shrub, to 1m high, spreading more widely. Bts, undersides of lv and petioles covered with a soft white, felty tomentum. Lv silvery grey above at first, later dull grey-green, ovate, to 7cm long and 3cm wide. Fl in flattish panicles to 15cm tall and 10cm across, composed of yellow daisies each about 2·5cm across. Fl 6–7. Presumably a hybrid between the true *S. greyi* (or perhaps *S. laxifolius* BUCHANAN) and some more hardy sp.

Senecio monroi JOSEPH HOOKER
Evergreen, dome-shaped, shrub, to 2m in the wild but rarely more than 1m in cultivation. Bts petioles, pedicels and under surface of lv densely covered with white tomentum. Lv oblong, with a very undulate margin, dull green and glabrous above to 3cm long, half as wide. Fl in large, pyramidal panicles to 15cm across, composed of numerous yellow daisies about 2cm across. Fl 6–7. Somewhat tender away from the coast. Native of S Island, New Zealand.

Senecio reinoldii ENDLICHER
(*S. rotundifolius* JOSEPH HOOKER). Shrub or small tree, to 9m in the wild but usually not more

Senecio greyi

than 3m in cultivation. Bts, petioles, pedicels and underside of lv covered with white tomentum. Lv rounded, dark shining green, the largest to 12cm long and wide, but more usually to half that figure. Fl heads in a cluster of terminal corymbs to 20cm across, devoid of ray florets and rather fetid, yellow, each head to 8mm across. Fl 6–7. The lv are attractive and the plant is quite impervious to sea spray. Native of S Island, New Zealand.

SEQUOIA ENDLICHER *Taxodiaceae*

A monotypic genus. The plant once known as *S. gigantea* is now *Sequoiadendron:*

Sequoia sempervirens ENDLICHER Redwood

7. Very long-lived, evergreen tree to 100m or more, of slender, pyramidal habit, occasionally sending up sucker growths. The bark is thick, furrowed and reddish-brown. Lv of two kinds; those on the extension growths scale-like and disposed all round the stem, those on laterals needle-like, in 2 ranks, linear, to 2·2cm long, dark green above with 2 stripes of white stomata below. Male fl terminal and axillary in small catkins. Cones terminal, pendulous, egg-shaped to 3cm long. Requires a cool, moist climate. Native of California and Oregon. Introduced to St Petersburg in 1840; in 1843 Hartweg sent seeds to the Horticultural Society. 'Adpressa' ('Albospica') has the shoots tipped with white at first.

Sequoia sempervirens

SEQUOIADENDRON BUCHHOLZ
Taxodiaceae

(*Wellingtonia* LINDLEY). A monotypic genus.

Sequoiadendron giganteum BUCHHOLZ

Big Tree

7. Evergreen tree of pyramidal habit up to 80m or more in the wild and already 50m in cultivation, with spongy bark that may be 50cm thick. Brs somewhat pendulous. Lv somewhat glaucous, triangular, pointing forward and overlapping, to 1cm long. Male fl terminal on lateral twigs, cones terminal at first, but not ripening until the second year and persisting for some years thereafter, so appearing axillary; very woody, ovoid, to 7cm long and 5cm across. In sheltered conditions it can make up to 60cm growth in a year, but it does not thrive for long in very exposed conditions, although low temperatures in themselves seem to cause little damage. Native of the Sierra Nevada, California. Introduced in 1853 by W. Lobb and by a Mr J. D. Matthews.

SIBIRAEA MAXIMOWICZ *Rosaceae*

A small genus of two species removed from *Spiraea* on rather small botanical differences, but requiring similar treatment.

Sibiraea laevigata (LINNAEUS) MAXIMOWICZ

4. (*Spiraea laevigatas* LINNAEUS). Deciduous shrub of bushy habit, to 1·5m, with smooth brown bts. Lv alternate, entire, sessile, obovate, sometimes mucronate, tapering at the base, to 11cm long and 2cm wide, glaucous green. Fl in a terminal panicle composed of axillary and terminal racemes, to 12cm long, each fl small, white, 5-petalled. Fl 4–6. The plant spreads more widely than it rises. Native of Siberia. Obtained by Solander in 1774.

SINOFRANCHETIA HEMSLEY
Lardizabalaceae

A monotypic genus.

Sinofranchetia chinensis HEMSLEY

(5). Deciduous twining shrub to 10m, or more, the young bts with purplish bloom. Lv trifoliolate on a long, purple petiole to 22cm long. Leaflets shortly stalked, the central and largest one obovate, to 15cm long, the two laterals elliptic to 11cm long, glabrous and dark green above, glaucous below. Fl unisexual, sometimes monoecious, more usually dioecious, in racemes terminating lateral shoots, about 10cm long, dull white and inconspicuous. Fl 5. After flowering the fruiting racemes elongate, bearing round, blue-purple fr each about the size of a grape and ornamental. Native of central and western China. Introduced by Wilson in 1907.

SINOMENIUM DIELS *Menispermaceae*

A monotypic genus from China

Sinomenium acutum

(THUNBERG) REHDER AND WILSON

7. (*Menispermum acutum* THUNBERG). A vigorous, deciduous twiner, dioecious, mainly of interest on account of the diverse shape of the lv. These may be heart-shaped, kidney-shaped, entire or shallowly or deeply 3 or 5-lobed, to 15cm long and 11cm wide, bright green and glabrous in the type, in var *cinereum* the lv are slightly pubescent above and thickly grey-pubescent below, and this is the form usually obtainable. Fl in slender panicles to 20cm long or more, yellow, about 3mm wide. Fr black with blue bloom about the size of a small pea, but both sexes must be present for this to form. Fl 6. Native of China. Introduced by Wilson in 1901; var *cinereum* in 1907.

SKIMMIA THUNBERG *Rutaceae*

A small genus of evergreen shrubs, usually dioecious and all native to eastern Asia. The leaves are alternate, the flowers are in terminal panicles, fragrant, and the fruit is a berry-like drupe, long-persisting and very ornamental. Propagation by seed or by cuttings. With the dioecious *S. japonica* it is recommended to put a male plant among up to six females.

Skimmia japonica THUNBERG

4.5. (*S. oblata* MOORE). A low evergreen shrub, to 1·3m, spreading more widely. Lv clustered at the ends of the shoots, aromatic when crushed, obovate, to 10cm long and 3cm wide, pale green, speckled beneath with transparent glands. Fl in terminal panicles to 7cm long, each fl 4–5-petalled, about 8mm across, dull white. Fl 4–5. Fr round, bright red. 'Fragrans' is a male form with very perfumed fl. 'Foremanii' is a very vigorous female clone, probably a hybrid with the next sp, with both round and pear-shaped fr.

Skimmia reevesiana FORTUNE

4.5. (*S. fortunei* MASTERS). A dwarf shrub, usually not exceeding 60cm. Lv elliptic, dark green, to 10cm long and 2·5cm across. Fl perfect, in terminal panicles to 7cm, a purer white than *S. japonica*. Fr pear-shaped, dull red. Although the fl are perfect, a better set of fruit is obtained if more than one plant is available. Fl 5. *S. X rogersii* is apparently a hybrid between *S. japonica* and this sp, with a rather dwarf habit, perfect fl but round fr. *S. reevesiana* requires acid soil, whereas *S. japonica* thrives on all soils. Native of China. Introduced by Fortune in 1849. *Skimmia laureola* SIEBOLD AND ZUCCARINI, a native of the Himalayas, is in cultivation but rather unsatisfactory in bearing fruit.

SOLANUM LINNAEUS *Solanaceae*

A very large genus of 1,700 species. Two climbing species are commonly grown in the UK, neither is completely hardy. Both are propagated by means of summer cuttings.

Solanum crispum RUIZ AND PAVON

4. A rambling, scandent, semi-evergreen shrub to 8m. Lv ovate, long-acuminate, from 6–12cm long and nearly half as wide, faintly downy on both surfaces. Fl in large, axillary corymbs from the current year's growth. Each flower starry with a prominent yellow beak in the centre, about 3cm across, purple-blue. The small yellowish berries are rarely set in the UK. Fl 7–9. 'Glasnevin' is a selected clone flowering 6–10. The plant thrives in all soils, but needs a south or west-facing wall in cold districts. Native of Chile. Introduced about 1830.

Solanum jasminoides PAXTON

4. Distinguished from the last sp by its twining stems, which can reach 9m, and its generally more slender habit. Lv ovate-acuminate, to 10cm long, rather thin in texture. Fl smaller than *S. crispum*, not more than 2cm across. The form most usually seen is the white var *album*; those of the type being pale blue. The plant is said to be more tender than *S. crispum*, but does well on south and west-facing walls, and once established will regenerate if badly frosted. Native of Brazil. Introduced in 1838.

Solanum jasminoides

SOPHORA LINNAEUS *Leguminosae*

A genus of about fifty species of deciduous and evergreen shrubs, trees and herbaceous plants with pinnate leaves and flowers pea-shaped in *Sophora* proper, tubular in the subgenus *Edwardsia*. None of these latter are fully hardy in the UK without wall protection, except in western parts of the UK, but they are admirable shrubs for such a situation with elegant ferny evergreen leaves and large tubular flowers. Both *S. tetraptera* and *S. microphylla* should be considered for such situations. The hardy species are best propagated by seed and like all large leguminous shrubs or trees should be put in their final situation straight from pots as young plants.

Sophora japonica LINNAEUS

4.7. An elegant, spreading, round-headed

deciduous tree to 25m. Lv to 25cm long, made up of 9–15 leaflets, glossy green, ovate, to 5cm long and 2·5cm wide, faintly hairy below. Fl in terminal pyramidal panicles to 20cm long and wide, each bloom pea-shaped, about 1cm long, creamy-white or lilac ('Violacea'). Fl 8–9. Owing to its late flowering, seeds are seldom ripened in the UK. A pendulous form exists, but is hard to obtain and only starts to flower when mature. Native of China. Grown by Gordon in 1753, so probably obtained by Collinson from one of his Chinese correspondents. Rehder gives 1747 as the date of the original introduction, probably by D'Incarville.

Sophora viciifolia HANCE

4. (*S. davidii* KOMAROV). Deciduous shrub, to 2·5m, of rounded habit; bts grey-pubescent and spiny. Lv pinnate, to 7cm long, with 7–10 pairs of leaflets which are up to 9mm long and 3mm across, greyish above, grey-silky below. Fl in racemes terminal on lateral twigs; the racemes to 6cm long, each bloom to 2cm long, bluish-white. Pods to 6cm long with up to 4 seeds, the pods constricted between them. The calyx of the fl is blue in colour. Fl 6. Requires a light soil and full sunshine. Native of western China. Introduced, presumably by one of the French missionaries, in 1897.

SORBARIA ALEXANDER BRAUN *Rosaceae*

A genus of about ten species of deciduous shrubs with pinnate alternate leaves from eastern Asia. Included in *Spiraea* by some authorities and mainly differentiated from this genus by their compound leaves, although the terminal panicles are larger than those of most spiraeas. The year-old branches are reddish and not unattractive. Propagation by seed or by cuttings. The distinctions between the different species are sometimes rather small.

Sorbaria aitchisonii HEMSLEY

4. Deciduous, spreading shrub, to 3m high and as wide, with red bts. Lv to 36cm long, made up of 11–23 leaflets which are lanceolate-acuminate, to 10cm long and 1·5cm across. Fl in terminal, pyramidal panicles, occasionally to 45cm long and 36cm wide, usually less but always sizeable: each fl only 8mm across, creamy-white. Capsules reddish. Fl 7–8. Old flowering stems are best pruned hard in early spring. Native of Afghanistan. Introduced by J. F. Duthie in 1895.

Sorbaria arborea SCHNEIDER

4. A spreading shrub, to 6m in cultivation and apparently in the wild a tree to 10m. Lv to 45cm long with 13–19 leaflets which are lanceolate-acuminate, to 10cm long and 3cm across, toothed, with marked parallel veins, glabrous above, somewhat downy below. Fl in large panicles, to 45cm long and 30cm wide, each individual bloom about 1cm across, ivory. Seed capsules often pendulous. Fl 7–9. Native to central and western China and barely distinct from *S. tomentosa* (see below), but a more satisfactory plant in the garden. Introduced by Wilson in 1908.

Sorbaria assurgens VILMORIN AND BOIS

4. Shrub, to 3m, with rather erect brs. Lv to 30cm long, with 11–17 leaflets, lanceolate-acuminate (often curved at the ends), to 8cm long and 2·5cm across, toothed, glabrous on both surfaces or with a little down on the veins below. Fl in rather narrow panicles from 15–30cm long; the blooms white, about 1cm across. Fl 7–8. Obtained by Messrs Vilmorin in 1896, probably from one of their Chinese correspondents, but its wild locality is not certainly known.

Sorbaria sorbifolia (LINNAEUS) A. BRAUN

4. Suckering shrub, occasionally to 2m, but usually about 1m high with erect stems. Lv from 20 to 30cm long with 13–25 leaflets which are lanceolate, to 9cm long and 2·5cm across, toothed and green on both surfaces and glabrous (var *stellipila* MAXIMOWICZ has the lv starry-hairy below). Fl in an erect raceme to 25cm, each bloom to 8mm across, white. Fl 7–8. Native of northern Asia and Japan. Introduced from Siberia, probably to Collinson before 1759, when Miller was able to describe the plant in the seventh edition of the *Gardeners' Dictionary*.

Sorbaria tomentosa (LINDLEY) REHDER

4. (*Spiraea tomentosa* LINDLEY, *S. lindleyana* WALLICH). A shrub of spreading habit, to 6m. Lv to 45cm long, with 11–23 leaflets, lanceolate, long-acuminate, growing to 11cm long and 4cm wide, toothed, glabrous above, sparsely hairy below. Fl in branching, pyramidal panicles, to 45cm long and 30cm wide, ivory, each bloom to 6mm wide. Seed capsules downy. Fl 7–9. Somewhat less hardy than other spp although generally reliable. Native of the Himalaya. In cultivation in 1840. Probably introduced through Royle.

SORBUS LINNAEUS *Rosaceae*

A genus of eighty or more species of deciduous shrubs and trees with alternate leaves, flowers in large, flat corymbs, usually white, and the fruit a pome, usually berry-like and showy. They will thrive on most soils, although if these are shallow they may not prove very long-lived, and are propagated best by seed, although growth in the early stages is slow. They can also be grafted on to stocks of *P. aria* or *P. aucuparia* if deviant forms require to be perpetuated. Bentham and Hooker included *Sorbus* in *Pyrus*, which became a very unwieldy and meaningless genus in the nineteenth century. *Sorbus* itself is divided into three sections:

Aria Leaves simple; fruit with persistent calices.
Micromeles Leaves simple; fruit without persistent calices.
Aucuparia Leaves pinnate.

The flowers, although agreeable enough, are not outstanding in the way of ornament and the main interest in the *Aucuparia* section is the fruit and also the attractive foliage, which in many species colours well in the autumn. However, in districts with a large bird population it is doubtful if they are worth the space they take up; in towns and other places where birds are not a menace they are among the most magnificent fruiting trees. The interest in the other two sections lies mainly in the foliage. Unless statements to the contrary are made below, it may be assumed that the flowers are either white or cream and open in May-June. Names in parenthesis before the authority may be assumed to mean that the first authority diagnosed the plant as a *Pyrus* species.

Sorbus alnifolia
(SIEBOLD AND ZUCCARINI) K. KOCH *Micromeles*

4.5.6. A slender tree, eventually to 20m. Bts greyish-pubescent at first, later becoming purplish. Lv ovate, pointed, toothed, to 7cm long and 3·5cm wide, glabrous above, silky hairy below (more markedly so in the var *submollis*, which also has larger lv). The lv usually colour red and orange in the autumn. Fl in corymbs to 7cm across, each fl 1cm across. Fr to 1cm long, bright red. Native of Japan and Korea. Introduced by Späth in 1892.

Sorbus americana MARSHALL *Aucuparia*

4.5.(6). A small, round-headed tree, to 8m, with glabrous bts. Lv to 30cm long, made up of 11–17 leaflets, to 7cm long and 2cm across, toothed, glabrous except when first unfurling. Often colouring well in the autumn. Fl in corymbs to 12cm across. Fr bright red, only 6mm across. Very close to our own *S. aucuparia*, but with larger lv. Native of eastern N America. Introduced in 1782.

Sorbus aria CRANTZ *Aria* Whitebeam

3.4.(5). Tree, to 15m, occasionally more, with bts covered with white down, also both surfaces of lv at first, later the upper side becomes glabrous while the underside remains silvery, so

Sorbus aria

that plants in a wind are very decorative. Lv ovate, toothed, to 10cm long and 5–6cm broad. Fl about 1cm across, scented, in corymbs to 7cm across. Fr dull red with brown dots to 1cm across. 'Lutescens' has the upper surface of the lv silvery for most of the season. 'Decaisneana' is a very large form, probably the best to obtain. Lv up to 17cm long and 10cm across, slightly larger fl and fr, sometimes known as 'Majestica'.

S. hybrida LINNAEUS and *S. intermedia* PERSOON appear to have established themselves as spp but may have originated as hybrids between *S. aria* and *S. aucuparia*, as they have lv like those of *S. aria* but pinnately lobed. Both are not uncommon in Scandinavia. 'Wilfred Fox' is a hybrid between *S. aria* and the large-leafed but tender *S. cuspidata*. It makes a columnar tree of up to 12m with lv like *S. aria* but up to 20cm long and 10cm wide, elliptic, on a longish petiole, to 4cm. Fr up to 2cm across but grey-brown. *S. aria* is native of much of Europe, including the UK where it is a typical plant of chalk downs.

Sorbus aucuparia LINNAEUS *Aucuparia*
Rowan, Mountain Ash

4.5. A tree, sometimes to 20m but usually less, with a slender trunk and a spreading head; bts downy at first. Lv to 22cm long with 13–15 leaflets which are ovate-oblong, to 5cm long, grey-green above, tomentose below at first, later nearly glabrous. Fl to 8mm across in corymbs to 12cm across. Fr to 1cm across, scarlet-red. 'Edulis' has larger lv, fl and fr. It is also known as 'Dulcis' and 'Moravica'. **2.** 'Beissneri' has coral-red bts and the petioles are also reddish, while the trunk eventually becomes russet; the lv are yellowish when young. 'Aspleniifolia' has the leaflets pinnately lobed. 'Xanthocarpa' has yellow fr. Native to most of Europe, including the UK.

Sorbus caloneura REHDER *Micromeles*

4. Large shrub, or small tree, to 6m, with erect stems. Lv oval-elliptic, to 9cm long and half as wide, hairy at first, later glabrous, with a few hairs remaining on the veins below. Fl in rounded, not flattened, corymbs, to 7cm across, each bloom about 1cm across. Fr pyriform, 8mm long. Native of western China. Introduced by Wilson in 1904.

Sorbus cashmiriana HEDLUND *Aucuparia*

4.5. Small tree, probably to 4–5m, with reddish bts. Lv to 5cm long with 17–19 more or less round leaflets, with fine teeth, about 1cm in diameter. Fl pink, in corymbs to 7cm across. Fr pendulous, white, about 2·5cm in diameter, very showy. An unusual sp with its pink fl and large, pendulous white fr. Presumably native to Kashmir and only fairly recently introduced to cultivation.

Sorbus chamaemespilus CRANTZ *Aria*

4.5. A dwarf shrub, eventually to 2m, bts grey-cobwebby at first. Lv ovate, to 7cm long and half as wide, finely toothed on a short petiole to 1cm, green and glabrous on both surfaces. Fl in a tight corymb to 3cm across, pink, the petals remaining upright, never spreading as in most sp. Fr 1cm long, red. Native to the mountains of central and southern Europe from the Pyrenees to Bulgaria. Introduced in 1683 according to *Hortus Kewensis*.

Sorbus commixta HEDLUND *Aucuparia*

3.4.5.6. Tree to about 10m, of narrow columnar habit when young, later with a more spreading head; winter buds sticky. Lv copper-coloured at first, pinnate to 17cm long, with 11–13 leaflets which are lanceolate, to 7cm long and 1·8cm wide,. dark green above, glaucous below, usually colouring red in the autumn. Fl in flat corymbs to 12cm wide, each bloom about 6mm across. Fr small, orange-red, to 6mm across.

S. rufoferruginea SCHNEIDER differs only in its somewhat woolly winter buds and the underside of the lv being covered with reddish down, mainly along the midrib and principal veins. *S. commixta* is a very valuable garden shrub with its columnar habit and range of interesting features. Both spp are native to Japan. *S. commixta* in cultivation in 1880, according to Rehder; introduced via Germany in 1906 according to Bean. *S. rufoferruginea* introduced about 1913, according to Bean, in 1915 according to Rehder. *S. serotina* KOEHNE is barely distinct.

Sorbus decora (SARGENT) SCHNEIDER
Aucuparia

4.5. (*S. americana* var *decora* SARGENT). Allied to *S. americana*, a shrub or tree, to 10m. Lv to 30cm long, with 11–17 leaflets, elliptic, to 7cm long and 2·5cm wide, sea-green above, paler below and downy at first. Fl in corymbs to 12cm across, each fl to 1cm wide. Fr to 1cm across, orange at first, later bright red. Native to north and eastern N America. Cultivated in 1636 according to Rehder. Often confused with *S. americana*.

Sorbus discolor (MAXIMOWICZ) HEDLUND
Aucuparia

4.5.6. (*S. pekinensis* KOEHNE). Tree, to 11m. Bts (and petioles) purplish. Lv to 25cm long with 11–17 leaflets, oblong-acuminate, to 7cm long and 1cm wide, toothed, dark green above, grey beneath, turning brilliant red in autumn. Fl in a loose corymb to 15cm across, each fl 6mm wide. Fr creamy-white, about 6mm across, on purple pedicels and therefore striking. *S. discolor* of gardens is now known as 'Embley', and seems to be a form or hybrid of *S. commixta*. Our plant is native to northern China (although doubt has been cast on whether it is the true plant of Maximowicz) and was introduced to the Arnold Arboretum about 1883.

Sorbus domestica LINNAEUS *Aucuparia*
Service Tree

4. Tree to 17m (rarely to 21m) with a scaly bark; bts silky at first, later glabrous, winter buds sticky. Lv to 22cm long with 13–21 leaflets, ovate, to 6cm long and 1cm wide, smooth above, downy beneath, usually glabrous by the autumn. Fl about 1cm across, in a more or less pyramidal panicle to 10cm across. Fr to 3cm long, green or brown with red flush, edible when overripe. Native to southern Europe and N Africa. Long cultivated for its fr.

Sorbus esserteauiana KOEHNE *Aucuparia*

4.5. (*S. conradinae* KOEHNE). Tree, to 11m, with greyish downy bts. Petioles grey-downy at first, later purplish. Lv to 25cm long with 7–13 leaflets which are ovate-lanceolate, acuminate, toothed, to 8cm long and 2·5cm across, dark green above, grey (rarely white) tomentose below. Lv sometimes colour well in the autumn. Fl 1cm across, in a rounded corymb to 10cm or more wide. Fr scarlet, 5mm across. 'Flava' has pale yellow fr. Native of Szechuan. Introduced by Wilson in 1908.

Sorbus folgneri (SCHNEIDER) REHDER
Micromeles

2.4.5.6. A variable plant, but usually a tree to 10m with spreading and arching brs; bts silver tomentose at first, eventually glabrous. Lv elliptic, to 8cm long and 3cm wide, dark green above, with a dense white tomentum below, often colouring brilliantly in the autumn. Fl about

8–10mm wide, in somewhat elongated corymbs to 10cm across. Fr ovoid, 1cm in diameter, red. 'Lemon Drop' has yellow fr. In its best forms, a singularly attractive tree, but plants vary in the amount of white tomentum on the bts and the underside of the lv. Native of Hupeh. Introduced by Wilson in 1901.

Sorbus gracilis (SIEBOLD AND ZUCCARINI) KOCH Aucuparia

4.5. A shrub, to 2m, with slender bts. Lv to 15cm with 7–9 leaflets, elliptic, to 8cm long at the apex and only 1·5cm long at the base, matt green above, slightly pubescent below. Fl in corymbs only 4cm across, with few fl to 8mm wide. Fr pyriform, to 1·5cm long, orange-red. Native of Japan. In cultivation in 1934.

Sorbus hupehensis SCHNEIDER Aucuparia

4.5.(6). Tree to 13m; bts hairy at first, later glabrous and purplish-brown. Lv to 25cm with 11–17 leaflets which are elliptic, finely-toothed, up to 6cm long and 2·2cm wide, glaucous above, almost white below. The lv often colour brilliantly in the autumn. Fl about 1cm across, in a corymb to 12cm across. Fr round, 6mm across, white or pale pink, drooping. Var *aperta* SCHNEIDER has smaller lv with 9–11 leaflets and white fr. With its attractive, glaucous lv and unusual fr, one of the very best sp. Native of Hupeh. Introduced by Wilson in 1910.

Sorbus 'Joseph Rock' Aucuparia

4.5.6. A plant sent back by the famous explorer and collector Joseph Rock. Its status has never yet been diagnosed; botanists varying between thinking it a natural hybrid, with *S. serotina* as a parent, or regarding it as a distinct sp. In any case, it is an excellent garden plant. Tree, to 9m, with a somewhat erect habit. Lv to 25cm long, made up of 15–19 leaflets, oblong-lanceolate, toothed, to 3cm long, colouring very brilliantly in the autumn. Fl in corymbs to 12cm across. Fl 5–6. Fr amber-yellow. Only a proportion of the seedlings have yellow fr, others are scarlet, but they are all characterised by slightly glaucous lv and brilliant autumn tints. Discovered in northern Yunnan.

Sorbus koehneana SCHNEIDER Aucuparia

4.5. A small tree, to 4m or slightly more, with very dark bts. Lv to 15cm long, usually less, with 17–25 small round leaflets, to 3cm long but more usually around 1·5cm, dark green above, grey-green below. Fl in corymbs to 7cm wide, each bloom about 1cm across. The pedicels are grey-downy at flowering time but later they become reddish, while the fr, which is about 6mm in diameter, is white. One of a group of small trees with attractive, ferny foliage, of which *S.*

vilmorinii is the best known. This sp is unique in its white fr. Native to western China. Introduced by Wilson in 1907 and again in 1910.

Sorbus latifolia PERSOON Aria

4. This is thought to be a natural hybrid between the wild service, *S. torminalis* (qv), and the whitebeam, *S. aria*; discovered originally in the forest of Fontainebleau about 1750. It makes a largish tree, to 16m, with shaggy, peeling bark; bts downy at first, later glabrous. Lv basically ovate, to 10cm long and nearly as wide, but with the margins more or less sharply lobed and toothed; dark green above, grey tomentose beneath. Fl in corymbs to 8cm across, each fl being 1·5cm wide. Fr brownish-red, 1cm across. The plant apparently sets seed without any fertilisation and so comes true from seed.

Sorbus matsumurana (MAKINO) KOEHNE Aucuparia

4.5.6. Small tree, to 5m, with glabrous, reddish bts. Lv to 20cm long, with 9–13 leaflets which are oblong, pointed, to 7cm long and 2·5cm across; usually colouring brilliantly in the autumn. Fl each about 1cm across, in a corymb to 10cm across. Fr ovoid, to 1cm long, scarlet. Native of Japan. Introduced in 1912.

Sorbus megalocarpa REHDER Aria

4.(6). Shrub or small tree, to 8m, of rather spreading habit; bts stout, reddish at first, later dull purple, with large, sticky winter buds which show conspicuous red scales as they unfurl. Lv ovate, up to 22cm long and 11cm wide, glabrous on both surfaces eventually, some down on underside at first; often turning a good crimson in the autumn. Fl before lv in corymbs to 15cm across and to 10cm tall, each fl to 1cm across, creamy. Fl 3–4. Fr russet, egg-shaped, to 3cm long. Unique in its early flowering. Liable to be damaged by spring frosts, but said otherwise to be perfectly hardy, although it is a very uncommon plant in gardens. Native of Szechuan. Introduced by Wilson in 1903.

Sorbus meliosmifolia REHDER Micromeles

3.4. Small tree, to 11m, with purplish-brown bts. Lv copper-coloured when young and among the first of all trees to come into leaf; the young lv apparently quite untouched by the severest frosts. Mature lv ovate-elliptic, to 17cm long and half as wide, toothed, dull green above and below with a few tufts of down along the main veins below. Fl about 1cm across in flat corymbs to 10cm across, white. Fl 4. Fr russet. An attractive tree in the spring with its early copper-coloured lv and early fl. Disappointing later. Native of western China. Introduced by Wilson in 1910.

Sorbus pohuashanensis HEDLUND *Aucuparia*

4.5. (*S. conradinae* of gardens not of Koehne). Tree, to 10m, with bts downy at first, later glabrous but always grey. Lv to 22cm long made up of 11–15 leaflets which are oblong-ovate, acuminate, finely toothed, to 6cm long, dark green and glabrous above, greyish tomentose below. Fl in flat corymbs, to 12cm across. Fl 5–6. Fr orange-red, to 8mm in diameter. One of the showiest fruiting trees in the *Aucuparia* section; the brs often almost bowed down by the weight of the fr. Native of western China. Introduced to France in 1883.

Sorbus poteriifolia HANDEL-MAZZETTI

Aucuparia

4.5. A somewhat uncommon plant in the *vilmorinii* group. Small tree, to 5m, with erect, purplish bts. Lv to 15cm long, made up of 15–19 small, ovate leaflets, dark green above, downy below, up to 3cm long, sharply toothed. Fl in corymbs to 8cm wide, each fl to 8mm wide. Fr rosy-pink, to 1cm across. Attractive with its graceful lv and unusually coloured fr. Native of China. Certainly collected by Forrest, but probably in cultivation before.

Sorbus prattii KOEHNE *Aucuparia*

4.5. (*S. munda* GIBBS). Shrub or small tree, to 6m. Lv to 14cm long, with 21–27 leaflets which are ovate, to 2cm long, dull green above, slightly paler below (or, in var *subarachnoidea*, covered with a rusty, cobwebby down on the underside). Fl in corymbs to 8cm across, each fl to 1cm wide. Fr pearly-white, about 6mm in diameter. A very graceful tree, difficult to distinguish from *S. koehneana* but the fr lack the red pedicels of that sp. Native of China. Introduced by Wilson in 1904, var *subarachnoidea* in 1910.

Sorbus sargentiana KOEHNE *Aucuparia*

4.5.6. Somewhat slow-growing tree, to 10m, with spreading brs, very stocky bts, which are villous at first, and winter buds large and sticky like a horse chestnut. Lv to 30cm long, made up of 9–11 lanceolate-acuminate leaflets, to 14cm long and 3·5cm wide, smooth above, villous below at first, later smooth; turning crimson in the autumn. Fl in dome-shaped corymbs to 15cm wide, each creamy fl about 6mm across. Fr bright red, 5mm across. The largest-leaved *sorbus* that is generally hardy (the tender *S. harrowiana* has even larger lv) and a notable plant for autumn colour. The fr are surprisingly small but are borne in large, dense clusters. Native of western China. Introduced by Wilson in 1908.

Sorbus scalaris KOEHNE *Aucuparia*

4.5.(6). Small tree, to 10m, with bts, petioles and pedicels all covered with grey tomentum. Lv to 20cm long, made up of 21–35 leaflets, each ovate, to 3cm long and 7mm wide, glossy green above, grey tomentose below, sometimes colouring brilliantly in the autumn. Fl in flattish corymbs, to 12cm across, each fl dull white, about 6mm across. Fr bright red, 5mm wide. A brilliant plant and the birds appear to like the fr less than those of most of the *aucuparias*. Native of western China. Introduced by Wilson in 1904.

Sorbus scopulina GREENE *Aucuparia*

4.5.(6). (*S. americana nana*; *S. decora nana* HORT). A slow-growing, fastigiate shrub, to 4 or 5m. Lv to 25cm long with 11–15 leaflets up to 7cm long and 2·5cm across, dark green above, slightly paler below, sometimes colouring well in the autumn. Fl in corymbs, to 15cm across, creamy-white, each fl about 6mm wide. Fr bright scarlet, to 12mm across. A very useful small tree with exceptionally brilliant fr. Native of western N America; possibly of hybrid origin, although it is not easy to envisage potential parents. Apparently not introduced until 1917 according to Rehder, but probably in cultivation before.

Sorbus torminalis CRANTZ *Aria*
Wild Service Tree

4.6.7. A round-headed tree, to 13m usually but occasionally to 20m; bts villous at first, later glabrous. Bark scaly. Lv basically triangular, to 12cm long and wide, lobed about half way to the midrib 6–8 times; lustrous dark green above, paler below and downy at first, turning gold or crimson in the autumn. Fl in corymbs to 10cm across, each fl about 1cm in diameter. Fl 6. Fr round, russet, edible, about 1cm long. Native of most of Europe including the UK.

Sorbus vilmorinii SCHNEIDER *Aucuparia*

4.5. Shrub or small tree, to 6m, bts rufous-tomentose at first. Lv to 14cm long, with 13–29 leaflets, which are oval, to 2cm long and 6mm wide, dull green on both surfaces. Fl in corymbs to 10cm across, each fl to 6mm wide. Fl 6. Fr pendulous, about 8mm in diameter; rose-pink fading to nearly white. Very attractive with its ferny lv and attractive fr. Native of China. Introduced by Delavay in 1889 to Messrs Vilmorin.

There are a number of hybrid clones of various *aria* and *aucuparias* which cannot be mentioned here but which contain many attractive plants.

SPARTIUM LINNAEUS *Leguminosae*

Now a monotypic genus. Easily propagated by seed, but, like all brooms, they should be put in their final positions immediately as breaking the tap-root causes the death of the plant. In any case the plants are not very long-lived, and are best replaced every seven years.

Spartium junceum LINNAEUS Spanish Broom

4. Tall, rather gaunt, deciduous shrub, to 3m. Stems erect, rush-like, green and serving as lv. Lv themselves small, linear, fugacious, to 2cm long. Fl in terminal racemes, sometimes to 45cm long. Fl pea-shaped, bright yellow, fragrant, to 3cm long and wide. Fl 6–9. Fr a pod to 8cm long. Requires full exposure and is useful for its late flowering. Native of the Mediterranean region; somewhat commoner in the east, in spite of its popular name. In cultivation since 1548.

Spartium junceum

SPIRAEA LINNAEUS *Rosaceae*

A rather confusing genus of some eighty or more species of deciduous shrubs distributed throughout the northern temperate zone. The leaves are alternate and simple. The flowers are perfect, in umbels, racemes or panicles with five petals and sepals. The fruit is a dry capsule with numerous minute seeds. The genus has been divided into three sections depending on the inflorescence.

Chamaedryon White flowers in a fascicle or umbel on short lateral branches from the year-old growths.
Calospira White or purple flowers in flat corymbs on laterals from year-old shoots.
Spiraria Flowers in pyramidal panicles, often terminal to the current year's growth, white or purple.

Numerous hybrids have been bred. Many of the species are suckering shrubs, which provides an easy means of increase; with others cuttings of half-ripe shoots in July and August will usually root readily. Seed germinates readily, but is apt to be of a hybrid nature if more than one species is present. Most species will grow in any soil and any exceptions will be noted. Spring-flowering species should be pruned as soon as flowering is complete. The summer and autumn flowering species should be pruned hard back in March.

Spiraea albiflora ZABEL *Calospira*

4. (*S. japonica alba* HORT). A dwarf shrub, usually under 1m, with angled stems. Lv lanceolate, acuminate, to 7cm long and 2·5cm wide, dark green above, glaucous below. Fl in dense, flat corymbs to 25cm across, white. Fl 7–8. *S. X bumalda* was produced by hybridisation with *S. japonica* (qv). It is a shrub about 1m high, with lv often variegated with cream and corymbs of magenta or crimson fl, about 25cm across. 'Anthony Waterer' is probably the best-known clone. *S. albiflora* has long been cultivated in Japan and was introduced before 1868. *S. X bumalda* first raised about 1880.

Spiraea X arguta ZABEL *Chamaedryon*

4. A hybrid between *S. thunbergii* (qv) and *S. X multiflora*, which is itself a hybrid between *S. crenata* and *S. hypericifolia*. A shrub of spreading habit, to 3m high and wide, with slender twiggy brs. Bts downy. Lv lanceolate, to 3cm long and 1cm wide, entire or lightly toothed, bright green above, slightly downy below. Fl before and with lv in clusters of about 4, scattered thickly along the ends of year-old shoots. Fl 4–5. One of the most effective of spring-flowering shrubs. It appears to have been raised shortly before 1884.

Spiraea bella SIMS *Calospira*

4. (*S. expansa* WALLICH). Small shrub, to 1m, with spreading brs which are angular and slightly villous when young. Lv ovate, acuminate, toothed, to 5·5cm long on large shoots, smaller on flowering ones, about half as wide; dull green above, whitish and downy below. Fl in corymbs to 4cm across, bright pink. Fl 6. Best on acid soils. Native of the Himalaya. Introduced by Wallich in 1818 or 1820.

Spiraea canescens D. DON *Calospira*

4. A rapid-growing shrub, sometimes to 5m but usually to 3m, with long, arching whippy brs, sometimes 1m long in each season. Bts angled, downy. Lv oval, to 2·5cm long and 1·5cm wide, grey-green above, dull grey and tomentose below. Fl in corymbs, to 5cm across, at the end of lateral twigs, creamy-white, very abundantly produced. Fl 6–7. *S. X brachybotrys* LANGE is a hybrid between this sp and *S. douglasii* (qv), with much the same habit as *S. canescens* but with bright pink fl. *S. canescens* is native of the Himalaya. Introduced in 1837. *S. X brachybotrys* in cultivation before 1867.

Spiraea cantoniensis LOUREIRO *Chamaedryon*

4. (*S. reevesiana* LINDLEY). Shrub, to 2m, with arching brs. Lv diamond-shaped, to 6cm long and 2cm wide, deeply toothed, glabrous on both surfaces and more or less glaucous. Fl in sessile umbels, 5cm across, each fl about 8mm in diameter, white. Fl 6. There is a double form with more lanceolate lv. Native of China. Introduced by Reeves to the Horticultural Society in 1824.

Spiraea chamaedrifolia LINNAEUS *Chamaedryon*

4. Suckering shrub, to 2m, with yellowish, glabrous bts. Brs often arching. Lv elliptic-ovate, to 7cm long and 3cm wide, toothed; dark green above, glaucous and slightly downy below. Fl in a racemose umbel, to 5cm long, each fl about 1cm in diameter, white. Fl 5–6. Usually seen in var *ulmifolia* MAXIMOWICZ, with broader lv and a more racemose inflorescence. Native of mountains of central Europe, eastwards to Siberia. Introduced in 1789.

Spiraea douglasii W. J. HOOKER *Spiraria*

4. Suckering shrub, to 2m, with reddish bts, tomentose at first. Lv narrow-oblong, to 10cm long and 2·5cm wide, coarsely toothed, dark green above, grey tomentose below. Fl in a terminal, pyramidal panicle to 20cm long, rosy-purple. Fl 6–7. A very vigorous shrub requiring acid soil, and then soon making a thicket. Native of western N America. Introduced by Dr Tolmie about 1840.

Spiraea gemmata ZABEL *Chamaedryon*

4. Shrub, to 3m but usually rather less, with slender, arching glabrous stems and unusually long, slender leaf buds. Lv narrowly elliptic or oblong, to 2·5cm long and 8mm wide, glabrous on both surfaces, often entire, sometimes sparingly toothed. Fl in umbels to 2·5cm across, white. Fl

5. *S. arcuata* J. HOOKER is distinguished only by its angled, slightly pubescent bts, while the lv are always entire and are slightly pubescent. *S. gemmata* is native to northern China and Mongolia. In cultivation in 1886. *S. arcuata*, from the Indian Himalaya, was introduced about 1908.

Spiraea henryi HEMSLEY *Calospira*

4. Spreading shrub, to 3m high and more in width, with reddish-brown bts which tend to be slightly hairy at first. Lv oblanceolate, to 9cm long and 3cm wide on extension shoots, to 4cm long on flowering shoots, toothed, grey-green above, with grey tomentum below. Fl in flattish corymbs to 5cm across, white. Fl 6. An attractive sp but requiring ample room. Native of central China. Introduced by Wilson in 1900.

Spiraea hypericifolia LINNAEUS *Chamaedryon*

4. Shrub, to 2m, with brs erect and arching; bts brown at first, later grey and pubescent. Lv obovate, to 3cm long and 1cm wide, grey-green on both surfaces and slightly downy below. Fl in sessile umbels to 5cm across, often much less, pure white. Fl 5. Native of south-eastern Europe and across much of Asia. In cultivation in 1640.

Spiraea japonica CHARLES LINNAEUS *Calospira*

4. (*S. callosa* THUNBERG). A shrub, to 1·5m high, with erect brs. Lv lanceolate, toothed, to 11cm long and 4cm wide, dark green above, glaucous below, eventually glabrous on both surfaces. Fl in a number of small corymbs to form a large, flattish inflorescence to 30cm across, pink to crimson. Fl 6–8. The first form to be introduced was var *fortunei* REHDER, differing only in its larger lv.

3. 'Atrosanguinea' has red young growths and deep crimson fl, while 'Macrophylla' turns reddish in the autumn. 'Bullata' and 'Alpina' are dwarf, compact forms. Native of China and Japan. Introduced by Fortune about 1850.

Spiraea media F. SCHMIDT *Chamaedryon*

4. (*S. confusa* REGEL). Erect shrub, to 2m, with smooth round bts, sometimes downy at first. Lv ovate, rounded at the base, coarsely toothed at the apex, to 5cm long and 2cm wide, dull green and glabrous above, hairy below (except in var *glabrescens*). Fl white, about 8mm in diameter, in longish racemes to 4cm wide and 10cm long, somewhat untypical for *Chamaedryon*. Fl 4–5. Allied to *S. chamaedrifolia*. Native to eastern Europe and eastwards through Siberia to Japan. Introduced 1789, according to Rehder, 1827 according to Sweet.

233

Spiraea menziesii W. HOOKER *Spiraria*

4. Suckering shrub, to 1·5m, very close to *S. douglasii* and possibly a hybrid between that sp and *S. salicifolia* (qv). Lv oval-lanceolate, to 9cm long and 4cm across, grey-green above, usually downy below. Fl in erect terminal panicles to 20cm long, rosy-purple. Fl 7–8. 'Triumphans' (*S. X billiardii* 'Triumphans') has very large panicles. Requires acid soil, but otherwise of easiest cultivation. Native of western N America. Introduced in 1838.

Spiraea mollifolia REHDER *Chamaedryon*

4. Shrub to 2m with arching brs; bts hairy at first, later glabrous and purplish; winter buds long and slender. Lv oval-elliptic, to 2cm long and 1cm wide, grey-hairy on both surfaces. Fl about 8mm wide in umbels about 2·5cm across, white. Fl 6–7. Attractive with its silky grey lv. Native of western China. Introduced by Wilson in 1904.

Spiraea nipponica MAXIMOWICZ *Chamaedryon*

4. (*S. bracteata* ZABEL). A shrub, to 2·5m, with reddish bts. Lv almost orbicular, to 3cm long and 2cm wide, dark green above, bluish below, with a few teeth at the apex. Fl in fascicles to 3cm wide, pure white. Fl 6. Native of Japan. Introduced as *S. rotundifolia* by Siebold in 1830.

Spiraea prunifolia SIEBOLD AND ZUCCARINI *Chamaedryon*

4. Known in gardens only in a double-flowered form grown in Japan in the nineteenth century. A shrub, to 2m or more, spreading widely with arching bts, which are downy at first. Lv elliptic, to 4cm long and 2cm wide at the end of petioles 5mm long, green and glabrous above, somewhat downy below. Fl in fascicles of up to 6, about 1cm across, pure white and extremely double. Fl 4–5, before or just with the lv. Native of China, but obtained from Japan by Siebold in 1845.

Spiraea salicifolia LINNAEUS *Spiraria*

4. Vigorous suckering shrub, to 2m. Lv lanceolate, to 7cm long and 2·5cm wide, acuminate, toothed, glabrous on both surfaces. Fl in pyramidal panicles to 10cm long and 5cm wide. Fl 6–7. *S. alba* DU ROI has the panicles to 30cm long, while *S. latifolia* BORKHEIM has panicles to 20cm long and broader lv. In *S. salicifolia* the fl are pink, but in the two American spp (if they really are distinct and not just geographic forms) the fl are white or a pale pink. All these plants do best on acid or neutral soil.

S. salicifolia is found throughout Europe and northern Asia to Japan, and is naturalised in some parts of Britain. *S. latifolia* is found in the eastern parts of N America, while *S. alba* goes farther west. It is, however, improbable that either ever meets *S. menziesii* in the wild, so that its hypothetical hybrid origin sounds unlikely. *S. salicifolia* grown in 1586; *S. alba* and *S. latifolia* probably introduced by Bartram.

Spiraea thunbergii SIEBOLD *Chamaedryon*

4. A spreading shrub, to 1·5m, but often spreading more widely, with slender twiggy brs; bts downy and angled. Lv linear-lanceolate, acuminate, to 4cm long and 6mm wide, a lively pale green. Fl in fascicles of 2–5, each fl about 8mm across, pure white. Fl 3–4. Often used for forcing. Requires a hot summer to ripen its wood adequately and so rather unsatisfactory in wet districts. Native of China, but long cultivated in Japan, whence it was introduced in 1863.

Spiraea tomentosa LINNAEUS *Spiraria*

4. Suckering shrub, to 1·5m, with angled brs. Really only to be distinguished from *S. douglasii* by the thick yellow or grey indumentum on the underside of the lv. The lv are also somewhat smaller and the ovaries, which are glabrous in *S. douglasii*, are hairy in this sp. It also flowers rather later. Native of the eastern USA. Introduced by Bartram in 1736.

Spiraea trichocarpa NAKAI *Chamaedryon*

4. Shrub, to 2m, with arching brs and angled bts. Lv elliptic, acuminate, either entire or with a few teeth near the apex, to 6cm long and 2·5cm wide; bright green above, pale glaucous below, glabrous on both surfaces. Fl in umbels to 5cm across, each fl 8mm wide, pure white, petals notched. Fl 6. Close to *S. nipponica*, but slightly preferable in gardens. Native of Taiwan. Introduced by Wilson in 1917.

Spiraea trilobata LINNAEUS *Chamaedryon*

4. A shrub of little more than 1m in height, spreading more widely. Lv nearly orbicular, sometimes slightly 3 or 5-lobed, more usually coarsely toothed, to 3cm long and wide, somewhat glaucous. Fl in umbels to 3·5cm wide, white. Fl 6. Similar, but a better plant, is *S. X vanhouttei* (*S. trilobata* X *S. cantoniensis*), reaching to 2m high with arching stems. Lv, obovate, sometimes 3-lobed, to 4cm long and 3cm wide, dark green above and glaucous beneath. Fl in umbels to 7cm across produced in great profusion. Fl 6. Raised about 1862. *S. trilobata* native to northern Asia; obtained from Siberia by Joseph Banks in 1801.

Spiraea veitchii HEMSLEY *Calospira*

4. A vigorous shrub, to 4m, with shoots erect at first, later arching, bts reddish, downy at first. Lv obovate, entire, to 5cm long and 2cm wide, glabrous on both surfaces, sometimes slightly pubescent below at first. Fl in corymbs to 6cm across, pure white. Fl 6–7. *S. wilsonii* DUTHIE is similar but smaller, never more than 2·5m high, with lv somewhat hairy below and corymbs to 5cm wide. Both spp native to central and western China. Introduced by Wilson in 1900.

Spiraea yunnanensis FRANCHET *Chamaedryon*

4. (*S. sinobrahaica*, W. SMITH). Shrub with arching brs, to 1·8m tall, bts yellowish tomentose at first. Lv more or less rounded, to 2cm long and wide, entire, toothed, or shallowly lobed; slightly downy and dull green above, with a dense white or grey tomentum below. Fl in umbels to 2cm across. Fl 5–6. Native of western China. Introduced by Forrest in 1923.

STACHYURUS SIEBOLD AND ZUCCARINI
Stachyuraceae

The family contains only the single genus, of which two species are hardy. The leaves are alternate, the flowers appear in pendulous racemes and the fruit is berry-like. Propagated by semi-hard stem cuttings, with a heel.

Stachyurus praecox

Stachyurus chinensis FRANCHET

4. Spreading, deciduous shrub, perhaps to 4m eventually but the horizontal spread is wider than the vertical; bts greenish or dull brown. Lv ovate, long acuminate, finely toothed, to 14cm long and half as wide. Fl in axillary racemes to 14cm long, opening before the lv, each fl cup-shaped, pale yellow, to 8mm long. The

inflorescence is catkin-like in appearance. Fl 2–4. The racemes emerge in autumn before the lv fall. Like the buds of mahonia, they are frost tender when emerging but later unmoved by the worst weather, until when the fl start to open, when they are again liable to frost damage. Fr about 6mm across, green, red-flushed. Native of China. Introduced by Wilson in 1908.

Stachyurus praecox SIEBOLD AND ZUCCARINI

4.(6). Similar to the last sp but less vigorous, usually not more than 1·5m high. The lv slightly larger and sometimes colouring red in the autumn. Bts red-brown. Fl in racemes to 8cm long. Fr to 8mm across. Some forms are monoecious. Starts to flower about a fortnight before *S. chinensis*. Unsuitable for very alkaline soils. Native of Japan. Introduced about 1863.

STAPHYLEA LINNAEUS *Staphyleaceae*
Bladder Nut

A small genus of about ten species of deciduous shrubs or small trees, with smooth bark, opposite leaves, which are trifoliolate or pinnate, and flowers in terminal panicles, tubular, sepals and petals usually concolorous. The fruit is an inflated capsule of very characteristic appearance. Propagation is by seed or by semi-hard stem cuttings with a heel. Tolerant of all soils and usually of fairly rapid growth.

Staphylea colchica STEVEN

4.5. Deciduous shrub, to 4m, with erect brs. Lv trifoliolate, occasionally in 5s, ovate-oblong, to 9cm long, finely toothed; glabrous and shining on both surfaces. Fl in terminal panicles to 12cm long and wide, each fl to 2cm long, white, the sepals very pale green, almost white. Fl 5–6. Fr an inflated capsule to 10cm long, half as wide, pointed. 'Coulombieri' is a more vigorous clone with larger lv, the terminal one occasionally to 15cm long, and smaller fr. Native of the Caucasus. Introduced in 1850.

Staphylea holocarpa HEMSLEY

4. Large shrub or small tree, to 10m. Lv trifoliolate, the leaflets lanceolate, the two laterals sessile, the terminal one stalked and to 10cm long, toothed and slightly downy below. Fl in corymbs to 10cm long, usually axillary, on the year-old brs, but also terminal. Each fl to 1cm long, pink in the bud, white when open. Fl 4–5. **3.** 'Rosea' has pink fl and bronzy young lv. Rather slow growing and an admirable plant for chalky soil. Native of China. Introduced by Wilson in 1908.

Staphylea pinnata LINNAEUS Bladder Nut

4.5. Deciduous shrub of up to 5m. Lv usually

pinnate, with 5 leaflets, occasionally trifoliolate; leaflets ovate, to 10cm long, dull green above and pale dull green below. Fl in drooping, terminal panicles to 10cm long, each fl about 1cm long, white. Fl 5–6. Fr to 4cm long and wide. Distinguished from *S. colchica* by the dull underside of the lv and the panicles drooping, not erect. *S. X elegans* ZABEL is a hybrid between this sp and *S. colchica*, with the larger inflorescence of *S. colchica* but the panicles nodding. 'Hessei' has pinkish fl. Native of most of Europe. In cultivation since 1596, probably before.

STEPHANANDRA SIEBOLD AND ZUCCARINI
Rosaceae

A small genus of only four species of deciduous shrubs, related to *Spiraea,* with alternate leaves and small flowers in terminal panicles. They are grown for their attractive foliage and the attractively coloured year-old branches. The leaves may colour orange or purplish in the autumn in some districts. They can be propagated by division, by cuttings of young shoots or by root cuttings. Two-year-old wood may be pruned quite hard to encourage the production of fresh cane-like shoots from the base.

Stephanandra incisa (THUNBERG) ZABEL

1. Suckering shrub, to 2·5m, with zigzag, brown brs. Lv basically triangular, to 8cm long and slightly less wide, the margins deeply lobed to give a ferny appearance. Fl in panicles terminating lateral twigs, the panicles to 7cm long, the individual fl very small, greenish-white. Fl 6. Native of Japan and Korea. Introduced to St Petersburg before 1872.

Stephanandra tanakae FRANCHET AND SAVATIER

1.6. Shrub, to about 2m, with arching, bright brown br. Lv basically triangular, to 12cm long and 8cm wide, slightly lobed and conspicuously toothed, turning orange or yellow in the autumn. Fl in branching panicles to 10cm long, yellowish-white. Fl 6–7. Native of Japan. Introduced in 1893.

STEWARTIA LINNAEUS *Theaceae*

(*Stuartia* L'HÉRITIER). A small genus of extremely valuable garden trees, requiring acid soil; they are all characterised by late flowering. Many species eventually develop attractive bark and most species have good autumn colour. The leaves are alternate and deciduous and the flowers are usually axillary and single. They resent root disturbance and are best moved as young plants and put in their final positions. Apart from seed, propagation is difficult, but cuttings will occasionally root if taken when semi-hard and with a heel.

Stewartia gemmata CHIEN AND CHENG

4.6. So far as is known, a small tree of up to about 7m, but possibly considerably more, with hairy bts. Lv elliptic, acuminate, to 6cm long, often colouring well in the autumn. Fl solitary, axillary, white, fragrant, to 5cm wide. Fl 8. Native of China and only recently introduced.

Stewartia koreana REHDER

1.4.6. Deciduous tree, to 15m, with flaky reddish-brown bark. Lv elliptic, acuminate, to 10cm long and 8cm wide, slightly hairy at first, later glabrous, often colouring brilliantly in the autumn. Fl axillary and also terminating small lateral twigs, white, with a conspicuous boss of yellow anthers, about 8cm across. Fl 6–7. The first sp to flower. Native of Korea. Introduced by Wilson in 1917.

Stewartia malachodendron LINNAEUS

4. Large shrub or small tree, to 6m, with downy bts. Lv ovate-elliptic, acuminate, to 10cm long and half as wide, hairy below, margins toothed. Fl solitary, axillary, to 10cm wide, white with a conspicuous centre of purple stamens. Fl 7–8. The loveliest-flowered of the genus, but a difficult plant and apparently very short-lived. Native of the south-eastern USA. Flowered for Catesby in 1742 and probably introduced by him in 1728, but possibly sent later by Bartram.

Stewartia monadelpha SIEBOLD AND ZUCCARINI

4.6. A tree of up to 25m in the wild with flaking bark and hairy bts. Lv elliptic, to 6cm long and half as wide, somewhat downy below, colouring well in the autumn. Fl to 4cm across, solitary, axillary, stamens with purple anthers. Fl 7. Native of Japan. In cultivation in 1903.

Stewartia ovata (CAVANILLES) WEATHERBY

3.4.6. (*S. pentagyna* L'HÉRITIER). Large shrub or small tree to 5m with bts, petioles and young lv tinged with red. Lv ovate to ovate-elliptic, acuminate to 12cm long and 6cm wide, dull green above, grey-green and slightly hairy below, turning orange and scarlet in the autumn. Fl axillary, solitary, to 10cm across, with conspicuous yellow anthers (or in var *grandiflora* WEATHERBY with purple anthers and larger fl). Fl 7–8. One of the most attractive sp. Native of the south-eastern USA. Introduced before 1785 according to *Hortus Kewensis*.

Stewartia pseudo-camellia MAXIMOWICZ

1.4.6. Tree, to 20m in the wild, so far less in cultivation with attractive, flaking, pinkish bark when sufficiently large. Lv ovate-elliptic, to 9cm long and half as wide, finely toothed, shining green above, margins slightly crenate, glabrous or sparsely hairy below, colouring yellow and red in the autumn. Fl axillary, solitary, cup-shaped, white, about 6cm across. Fl 7–8. The cup-shaped fl make this less showy than the former spp with open fl. Native of Japan. Introduced about 1874.

Stewartia sinensis REHDER AND WILSON

1.4.6. A tree, to 10m, with brown, flaking bark; bts either slightly hairy or glabrous. Lv oval, acuminate, to 10cm long and 4·5cm wide, hairy on both surfaces at first, later glabrous or nearly so, colouring brilliantly in the autumn. Fl cup-shaped, to 5cm across, white, fragrant. Fl 7. Native of China. Introduced by Wilson in 1901.

STRANVAESIA LINDLEY *Rosaceae*

A small genus of ten species of vigorous ever-green shrubs from China and the Himalaya, of which one variable species is in cultivation. Formerly the varieties were given specific names, but they differ only in habit and minor leaf characters. Propagated by semi-hard stem with a heel or by seed.

Stranvaesia davidiana DECAISNE

4.5.(6). Vigorous evergreen shrub to 8m high, but usually less, and more in width. Bts downy, sometimes reddish. Lv alternate, rather leathery, lanceolate, to 10cm long and 3cm wide, bright green above, paler beneath, with wavy margin in var *undulata*. The lv often turn orange or scarlet before falling, so a number of 'autumn tints' are visible during most months of the year. Fl 6. Fl in terminal corymbs to 8cm across, each fl about 1cm wide with 5 petals, dull white. Fr a globose, berry-like pome, about 6mm wide, bright red (but yellow in var *undulata* 'Fructu Luteo'). Var *salicifolia* is an upright form, scarcely to be

Stranvaesia davidiana

distinguished from the type, except that the latter has slightly larger lv. Var *undulata* has a more spreading habit. Native of China. The typical form introduced by Forrest in 1917, var *undulata* and var *salicifolia* introduced by Wilson in 1901 and 1907.

STYRAX LINNAEUS *Styracaceae*

A genus of some 130 species of shrubs and trees, all those in cultivation being deciduous. They are distributed throughout the northern hemisphere, with a preponderance in eastern Asia. The leaves are alternate, the flowers white, campanulate, sometimes in terminal racemes, sometimes solitary and axillary. The fruit is a large, elongated, persistent drupe, usually dry but fleshy in some tropical species. Apart from the very tender European *S. officinalis*, acid soil seems essential for the cultivated species. Propagation seems best by seed, although cuttings can be rooted with some difficulty. Mature plants seem hardy enough, but young plants are slightly tender and may be protected with advantage. Most of the species do not flower until quite sizeable. They are not very rapid growers, but neither are they excessively slow.

Styrax hemsleyanum DIELS

4. A tree, to 10m, with bts downy at first. Lv obovate, to 14cm long and 9cm wide, tapered at both ends, distantly toothed, pale green and glabrous above, sparsely downy below, petiole to 1·5cm long. Fl in terminal, erect racemes to 15cm long, occasionally the racemes are branched. Each fl pure white, bell-shaped with 5 deep lobes, about 2cm long and 2·5cm wide, calyx reddish. Fl 6. Native of China. Introduced by Wilson in 1900.

Styrax japonica SIEBOLD AND ZUCCARINI

4. Tree, to 10m, with very slender brs; bts sparsely downy at first. Lv oval-elliptic, to 9cm long and 2·5cm wide, minutely toothed, glossy green and rather dark above, paler below, glabrous on both surfaces. Fl in clusters of 3–6 on short lateral twigs, nodding, pure white, each on a pedicel to 3cm long and about 2cm long and wide, corolla 5-lobed. Fl 6. The sp most frequently seen and extremely attractive, but should be grown on a sufficiently tall trunk for the fl to be viewed from below. Native of China (where a more vigorous form, var *fargesii*, is found), Korea and Japan. Introduced by Oldham in 1862.

Styrax obassia SIEBOLD AND ZUCCARINI

4. Tree, to 10m, with hairy bts. Lv nearly orbiculate, to 20cm long and from 14–20cm wide, deep green above, densely downy beneath. Fl fragrant in terminal drooping racemes, to 20cm long, each fl about 2·5cm long, pure white. Fl 6. The large lv tend to hide the fl somewhat. Native of Japan. Introduced by Maries in 1879.

Styrax shiraiana MAKINO

4. Large shrub or small tree to 7m; bts tomentose at first. Lv obovate to orbicular, to 10cm long and 7cm wide, coarsely toothed or shallowly lobed in the upper half, dull green above, downy below. Fl in few-flowered racemes terminating short lateral twigs; the racemes to 6cm long. Each fl funnel shaped, to 2cm long, the tube twice as long as the 5-lobed limb. Fl 6. Apparently unique in the genus in the shape of the fl with their long tube; the lv are also unusual. Native of Japan. Introduced to USA in 1915.

Styrax wilsonii REHDER

4. Deciduous twiggy shrub of from 1–3m with downy bts. Lv ovate, to 2·5cm long and 1·5cm wide, downy on both sides at first, the upper surface becoming glabrous eventually, the lower side sometimes tomentose and always slightly downy, sparingly toothed in the upper half. Fl pendulous, axillary and terminal, solitary or in clusters of up to 5, campanulate, about 2cm wide. Fl 6. The plant starts to flower when only a few inches high, unlike the majority of spp, and is almost invariably shrubby in character. Young plants somewhat tender. Native of China. Introduced by Wilson in 1908.

SYCOPSIS OLIVER *Hamamelidaceae*

A small genus of seven species, only one of which is in general cultivation.

Sycopsis sinensis OLIVER

4. An evergreen shrub, to 7m high in the wild but so far less in cultivation. Lv alternate, leathery, ovate-lanceolate, usually entire, but sometimes with a few teeth at the apex, to 10cm long and 5–7cm wide, dark green above, paler below, smooth on both surfaces. Fl monoecious, lacking petals, in small heads enclosed in chocolate-coloured bracts whence emerge reddish stamens and pistils. Fl 2–3. Fr a dry, egg-shaped capsule. Useful for cut floral decoration, but otherwise not very showy. Native to China. Introduced by Wilson in 1901.

SYMPHORICARPOS DUHAMEL DE MONCEAU
Caprifoliaceae

A small genus of rather low-growing, suckering, deciduous shrubs, mainly native to N America. The best known species is the common snowberry. The genus has opposite leaves, small flowers in axillary or terminal clusters and conspicuous berry-like fruits which are actually drupes. They will thrive in most soils and have no objection to shade. Propagation is by seed or by removing sucker growths.

Symphoricarpos microphyllus KUNTH

5. Shrub of up to 3m. Lv ovate, to 3cm long and half as wide, dull green above, bluish and slightly downy below. Fl in axillary and terminal clusters, pinkish, tubular, about 1cm long. Fl 8–9. Fr pale pink, sometimes almost white. The plant a native of Mexico and introduced in 1829, is probably no longer in cultivation, but it is one parent of *S. X chenaultii* REHDER, which is *microphyllus* X *orbiculatus*. This plant much resembles *S. microphyllus* in habit, but the fl are somewhat smaller, open 6–7 and are usually in spikes. The lv are downy below and the fr is reddish on the exposed side, pale pink on the other. This, in turn, has been crossed with *S. rivularis* to give *S. X doorenbosii*, of which a number of named clones exist with fr in clusters varying from white, through pale pink to rose-pink and rose-lilac.

Symphoricarpos orbiculatus MOENCH
Coral Berry

5. (*S. vulgaris* MICHAUX). Shrub, to 2m, with very downy bts. Lv ovate, to 3cm long and 2cm wide, dull green above, hairy below. Fl in axillary clusters each fl only about 3mm long, dull white. Fl 7–8. Fr roundish, 4mm in diameter, purplish-red. 'Variegatus' has the lv margined with yellow. Only liable to fruit satisfactorily after hot summers, when the lv may also turn crimson. Native to the eastern USA. Probably introduced by Catesby in 1727.

Symphoricarpos rivularis SUKSDORF
Snowberry

5. (*S. racemosus* HORT, *S. albus* var *laevigatus* FERNALD). Suckering shrub to 3m with shredding bark. Lv orbicular, sometimes lobed, to 7cm long and half as wide, but usually about 2cm long and wide, glabrous on both surfaces. Fl in terminal and axillary spikes, pink, about 1cm long. Fl 6–7. Fr round, white, to 1·5cm across. *S. albus* BLAKE (*S. racemosus* MICHAUX) is only distinguished by the lv being downy below and the whole plant not exceeding 1m. Native of the eastern and western USA. Introduced in 1817 (1812 according to Sweet).

SYMPLOCOS JACQUIN *Symplocaceae*

A genus of only this single family which contains a number of species only two of which are hardy; one of these having dropped out of cultivation. Propagated by seeds which usually take two years to germinate.

Symplocos paniculata (THUNBERG) MIQUEL

4.5. (*S. crataegoides* DAVID DON). Deciduous shrub or small tree, to 10m, with downy bts. Lv oval or obovate, elliptic, to 9cm long and 4cm across, slightly hairy on both surfaces, with more along the veins below, petiole to 8mm long and downy. Fl in a compound inflorescence of terminal and axillary corymbs to 6cm long; each bloom only 8mm across, white and fragrant. Fl 5–6. Fr a berry-like drupe, topaz-blue and very striking. In order to get a good set of the remarkable fr cross fertilisation seems to be necessary, although the fl are perfect and at least two plants should be close together. Even so, the fr are very attractive to birds so some protection is necessary. Native to the Himalaya, China and Japan, whence it was introduced to the USA in 1871.

SYRINGA LINNAEUS *Oleaceae*

A genus of thirty species of deciduous shrubs or small trees, native mainly to Asia but with a few species in Europe. The leaves are opposite and in one section, *Vulgares*, the shoots lack a terminal bud, which is present in the *Villosae*. The leaves are simple with one exception and the inflorescence is panicular. In the *Vulgares*, of which the common lilac is the best known, the inflorescence is on the leafless, lateral twig, in the *Villosae* the inflorescences are generally terminal and have leaves below the flowers. There is a small subgenus known as *Ligustrina*, which tends to be intermediate between *Syringa* and *Ligustrum* and which looks rather privet-like It is distinguished by the flowers being barely longer than the calyx and in the stamens protruding beyond the petals. The flowers are tubular with four lobes, and the fruit is a dry, flattened capsule. Propagation is by cuttings or by seed, while cultivars are often grafted on to *S. vulgaris*. A large amount of hybridisation has taken place, which can only be briefly alluded to here. The plants like full light but seem to thrive on most soils, so long as they are not waterlogged.

Syringa amurensis RUPRECHT *Ligustrina*

4. Shrub or small tree, to 6m, in the wild but usually only about half as high in cultivation, with either spreading or erect brs. Lv ovate, long acuminate, to 10cm long and about half as wide, bright green above, glaucous below and conspicuously net-veined, sometimes slightly downy. Fl in a loose panicle to 15cm long and 10cm wide, rather fetid. Fl 6. Liable to start too early into growth and be damaged by spring frosts. Native of Manchuria and northern China. Introduced about 1855 according to Rehder, but Bean says it was not discovered before 1857.

Syringa emodi GEORGE DON *Villosae*

4. A vigorous shrub, to 5m, with olive-green bts spotted with lenticels. Lv oval or obovate, pointed, to 20cm long and half as wide, dull green above, nearly white below. Fl in a terminal head of simple and branched racemes to 15cm long, scented but not agreeably, each fl to 1cm long and wide, pale lilac fading to white. Fl 6. A golden-leaved form and a golden variegated form have been in cultivation. Native to the Himalaya. Introduced about 1840.

Syringa josikaea JACQUIN *Villosae*
Hungarian Lilac

4. Shrub, to 4m, with rather stout bts which are downy at first. Lv more or less elliptic or ovate-acuminate, to 12cm long and about half as wide, dark green and shining above, glaucous-white below, glabrous or slightly hairy below. Fl in one or more terminal panicles to 20cm long and half as wide, lilac-violet, fragrant, each bloom to 12mm long and 6mm wide. Fl 6. Crossed with *S. villosa* the resulting hybrids are called *S. X henryi*, making a rather large spreading shrub with large fragrant panicles in June. 'Lutèce' is the best known cv, with violet fl. *S. X josiflexa* is *S. josikaea* hybridised with *S. reflexa*, with very large panicles (up to 30cm long) of rose-pink fl in the cv 'Bellicent'. *S. josikaea* is native to Hungary and Galicia and was introduced about 1830.

Syringa meyeri SCHNEIDER *Vulgares*

4. A dwarf, slow-growing shrub, to nearly 2m; bts downy and more or less square. Lv oval, to 4·5cm long and half as wide, more or less glabrous on both surfaces. Fl in panicles terminating leafless, lateral twigs, to 10cm long and 6cm wide, violet-purple. Fl 5–6 and often again in the autumn. Plants start to flower when only 25cm high. Native of China, where it is only known as a cultivated plant. Introduced by F. Meyer in 1908.

Syringa microphylla DIELS *Vulgares*

4. Spreading shrub, to 1·8m high, with ovate lv to 5cm long and 3cm wide, pointed at the apex; dark green above, greyish beneath, glabrous or downy. Fl in pairs of panicles to 10cm long, half as wide, very fragrant, lilac, about 9mm long and 6mm wide. Fl 6 and often again 9. Native of China. Introduced by Purdom in 1910.

Syringa oblata LINDLEY *Vulgares*

4. In this country more important as a parent than for its own sake. A shrub or small tree, to 4m, with stout glabrous bts. Young lv bronzy. Lv broadly heart-shaped to 7cm long and 10cm across, glabrous on both surfaces. Fl in pairs of broad panicles to 12cm long and about as wide, pale lilac to dark purple (var *giraldii*). Fl 4–5. Comes early into growth and is liable to damage by late frosts. Hybridised with *S. vulgaris* (*S. X hyacinthiflora* LEMOINE) many of the cultivated lilacs originated, and it is not easy now to determine which are selected forms of *S. vulgaris* and which are *S. X hyacinthiflora*. The presence of a bronze flush to the young lv will indicate *S. oblata* blood and generally the hybrids flower rather earlier than *S. vulgaris*. *S. oblata* is native to China and was introduced by Fortune in 1856. Apparently in the USA the lv turn claret-coloured in the autumn, but this has not been reported from the UK so far as I know.

Syringa pekinensis RUPRECHT *Ligustrina*

4. Large spreading shrub or small pendulous tree, to 6m, with bts reddish-brown at first and glabrous. Lv elliptic or ovate-acuminate, to 10cm long and half as wide, glabrous on both surfaces, dark green above, greyish below. Fl in lax panicles to 15cm long, yellowish-white. Fl 6. Native of northern China. Introduced by Bretschneider in 1881.

Syringa persica LINNAEUS *Vulgares*
Persian Lilac

4. Although the plant has been in cultivation for at least 400 years there still seems doubt as to whether this is a true species or a hybrid between *S. laciniata* MILLER (perhaps *S. afghanica* SCHNEIDER) and *S. vulgaris*. The confusion seems to arise because forms with entire lv and with laciniated lv exist. It is not easy to see where the crossing can have taken place. A shrub to 2m of rather bushy growth with slender bts. Lv elliptic-lanceolate or deeply 5–7-lobed, to 6cm long but only 1cm wide, medium green and glabrous on both surfaces. Fl in small terminal and axillary panicles, sometimes to 7cm long and wide, usually less, very fragrant, lilac or white. Fl 5. *S. X chinensis*, the Rouen lilac, is a hybrid between *S. persica* and *S. vulgaris*, making a rounded bush, to 5m, with ovate lv to 6cm long and 3cm wide and large drooping panicles in pairs up to 15cm long. Fl 5. Known in lavender, white, and reddish forms. *S. persica* was introduced to England about 1614 by the elder Tradescant, but had been in cultivation in the near East for much longer.

Syringa pinnatifolia HEMSLEY *Pinnatifoliae*

4. A distinctive plant which has a series all of its own. Shrub, to 3m. Lv pinnate, to 9cm long, made up of 7–11 leaflets which are ovate-lanceolate, to 3cm long and 1cm wide, pointed at the apex, usually rounded at the base, dull green and glabrous on both surfaces. The brs

have a terminal bud, but the fl spring from pairs of lateral racemes which are axillary, much as in *S. persica*. The racemes are up to 7cm long, white with a lavender tinge. Fl 5. Unique among lilacs with its pinnate lv but not particularly ornamental. Native of western China. Introduced by Wilson in 1904.

Syringa reflexa SCHNEIDER *Villosae*

4. Vigorous shrub, to 4m, with stout angular bts which are somewhat warty. Lv oval or obovate, acuminate and sometimes tapered at the base, to 20cm long and half as wide, dark green above, paler and slightly hairy below. Fl in nodding, cylindrical racemes to 20cm long and half as wide, purple-pink outside, whitish inside, unscented. Fl 6. Notable for its cylindrical, drooping inflorescences. Crossed with *S. villosa* (qv) a remarkable race of so-called Canadian lilacs (*S. X prestoniae* MCKELVEY) has been raised, making vigorous shrubs of up to 4m with erect or pendulous, narrowly pyramidal inflorescences with red-purple or deep pink fl. A number of named clones exist. Fl 5–6. *S. reflexa* was introduced from Hupeh in 1910 by Wilson.

Syringa reticulata HARA *Ligustrina*

4. (*S. japonica* DECAISNE, *S. amurensis* var *japonica* MAXIMOWICZ). Large shrub or small tree, to 10m, with bts marked with pale dots. Lv ovate, long-acuminate, rounded at the base, to 20cm long and 10cm wide, glabrous above, netted and at first downy below. Fl in broad, pyramidal panicles, usually in pairs, to 30cm long and 20cm wide, creamy-white. Fl 6–7. Although evidently very close to *S. amurensis*, it is a much more satisfactory garden plant. Native of Japan. Introduced to the USA in 1876.

Syringa tomentella BUREAU AND FRANCHET
Villosae

4. (*S. wilsonii* SCHNEIDER). Shrub, to 5m, with warty bts. Lv ovate, acuminate, to 15cm long and half as wide, faintly downy above, densely so below, although the degree of pubescence varies from plant to plant. Fl in erect, terminal, pyramidal panicles to 20cm long and 12cm wide, with the same scent as *S. vulgaris*, pale lilac-pink without, whitish within. Fl 6–7. Useful for its late flowering. Native of China. Introduced by Wilson in 1904 from western China.

Syringa velutina KOMAROW *Vulgares*

4. Probably better known under its synonym of *S. palibiniana* NAKAI. A slow-growing, rather dwarf shrub, eventually to 3m, of dense compact habit; bts purplish both glabrous and downy. Lv oval, acuminate, to 9cm long and 5cm wide but usually less, dull green and glabrous above, downy to some extent below. Fl in pairs of panicles, rather lax, to 15cm long, fragrant, lilac without, whitish within. The blooms small, only 8mm long. Fl 5–6 and often again in autumn. The plant starts to flower when very small, when it is suitable for the alpine garden, although it will eventually get too large. Native to northern China and Korea. In cultivation in 1902.

Syringa villosa VAHL *Villosae*

4. (*S. bretschneideri* LEMOINE). A vigorous shrub, to 3m, with stout, lenticellate bts. Lv oval or oval-lanceolate, acuminate, to 15cm long and 6cm wide, dark green and glabrous above, thinly hairy (villous) below. Fl in terminal and axillary panicles, to 25cm long (occasionally more) and two-thirds as wide, lilac-pink. Fl 5–6. *S. sweginowzii* KOEHNE is closely related but with smaller lv and inflorescences and fl which are almost flesh-pink. *S. villosa* introduced by Bretschneider about 1882 and *S. sweginowzii* by Potanin in 1894. Both natives of China; *villosa* from the north, *sweginowzii* from the west.

Syringa vulgaris LINNAEUS *Vulgares* Lilac

4. Usually a suckering shrub, but in some forms a small tree to 6m. Lv more or less cordate, to 15cm long and 12cm wide, glabrous on both surfaces on a petiole to 3cm long. Fl in pyramidal panicles, often in pairs, to 20cm long but up to 45cm long in cv and hybrids; very fragrant, purple, lilac or white. Fl 5. One of the most popular of all garden shrubs with an immense number of cv, some of which may well be hybrids with *S. oblata*. Native of eastern Europe. In cultivation since the sixteenth century.

Syringa wolfii SCHNEIDER *Villosae*

4. (*S. robusta* NAKAI). A very vigorous shrub, to 6m, with conspicuous grey brs. Lv elliptic-oblong, to 17cm long and 8cm wide, dark green above, paler below and sometimes slightly pubescent. Fl in terminal panicles, up to 30cm long and nearly half as wide, lilac-purple, fragrant. Fl 6. Akin to *S. josikaea* but a much better garden plant. Native of Manchuria and Korea. Introduced about 1909 according to W. J. Bean, in 1904 according to H. G. Hillier.

TAMARIX LINNAEUS *Tamaricaceae*
Tamarisk

A genus of about fifty-four species of deciduous shrubs from western Europe to China, most of the cultivated species being native to the Mediterranean region. They have very slender branches which are covered with minute, scale-like sheathing leaves, which are reminiscent of some *Cupressaceae*. The flowers are individually small but collected either in racemes or in dense panicles and are often very decorative. Many of the species are found wild near the sea-shore and they are admirable for seaside gardens, but they will usually thrive equally happily inland. Cuttings of ripened wood, taken in late autumn, usually root readily in the open ground and the plants are fairly rapid growing.

Tamarix gallica LINNAEUS

4. (Includes *T. anglica* WEBB). Shrub to 4m or small tree, of rather spreading habit, capable of reaching 10m in the Mediterranean. Bts with purplish bark. Lv scale-like, bright green or glaucous. Fl in cylindrical racemes all along the bts, about 5cm long, pink or white tinged pink. Fl 7–10. Native of SW Europe; more or less all round the Mediterranean.

Tamarix juniperina BUNGE

4. (*T. chinensis* SIEBOLD, *T. japonica* and *T. plumosa* of gardens). A large shrub or small tree, to 5m, with very distinct and attractive, feathery, pale green lv on thread-like brs. Fl on year-old wood in axillary racemes about 4cm long, deep pink in bud, paler on opening. Fl 5. A very attractive plant, particularly when young; it tends to get rather gaunt with age. It is, however, rather a shy flowerer and is damaged (although not killed) in very severe winters, although why it should be, given its provenance, is hard to understand. Native of northern China and Manchuria. Introduced about 1877.

Tamarix parviflora DE CANDOLLE

2.4. (*T. tetrandra purpurea* of gardens). Shrub, to 5m, with arching dark purple bts and very thin twigs. Fl on year-old wood in numerous axillary racemes, each to 4cm long, but so densely set as to give the impression of huge panicles; deep pink. Fl 5. **4.** *T. tetrandra* PALLAS is very similar but the bts are almost black, not reddish-purple, and the fl are a much paler pink. Both plants are native to SE Europe (*T. tetrandra* also in western Asia). *T. parviflora* seems to have reached cultivation about 1853, while *T. tetrandra* was cultivated in 1821.

Tamarix pentandra PALLAS

4. A shrub or small tree, to 5m and more, with feathery brs densely covered with scale-like glaucous or very pale green lv. Fl in numerous racemes terminating the current year's growths, sometimes to give the effect of a panicle up to 60cm long; the individual racemes up to 12cm long, sometimes branching. Fl rose-pink. Fl 8–9. The best of the autumn-flowering spp, appreciating hard pruning in the winter. Native of SE Europe and western Asia. Apparently not introduced before 1883.

Tamarix ramosissima LEDEBOUR

(2).4. (*T. odessana* STEVEN). Shrub, to 2m, with rather upright, reddish-brown bts and sea-green scale-like lv. Fl in numerous racemes, each about 3cm long, crowding the ends of the current year's growth, pink. Fl 7–9. More compact than the other autumnal spp. Native around the Caspian. Introduced about 1885.

TAXODIUM RICHARD *Taxodiaceae*

A small genus of American trees with light brown, furrowed and scaly bark and branchlets of two kinds. Those near the apex of the branches are persistent, have axillary buds and the leaves radially arranged. Those on the lower part of the shoot have the leaves arranged in two ranks to resemble à pinnate leaf, and the branchlet drops off in the autumn with the leaf. Propagation is usually by seed, although cuttings are possible. In the wild the plants tend to grow in very marshy and waterlogged situations and they will also do this in cultivation, although such conditions are not essential. When in very moist conditions the roots throw up so-called 'knees', which protrude from the ground and are stated to help conduct oxygen to the water-logged roots. Male and female flowers appear on the same plant. The fruit is a short-stalked cone, more or less globular, with two seeds to each scale, ripening the first year. Not suitable for chalky soils.

Taxodium distichum (LINNAEUS) RICHARD
Swamp Cypress

6.7. (*Cupressus disticha* LINNAEUS). A large, deciduous tree of up to 50m, pyramidal at first, later with a more spreading head. Lv awl-shaped, to 1·5cm long, of an exquisite yellow-green when first emerging, darkening later and turning russet before falling. An exceptionally beautiful tree. Cones about 2·5cm wide. **6.7.** *T. ascendens* BRONGNIART differs in its lesser dimensions, never more than 25m high, while lv do not exceed 1cm in length and the autumnal colour is a darker brown. The form in cultivation, 'Nutans', has bts nodding at first; a better plant for small gardens. Both spp are native to the south-eastern United States; *T. distichum* was introduced by the younger Tradescant about 1637, while *T. ascendens*, although not distinguished as a separate sp until late in the nineteenth century, was in cultivation in 1789.

TAXUS LINNAEUS *Taxaceae* Yew

A small genus of ten species of evergreen trees or shrubs of rather slow growth, with reddish scaly bark and flowers usually dioecious. The flowers are axillary, the males in small-stalked petalless heads, the females eventually making a sort of cone enclosed in a red, cup-shaped, fleshy container. Excellent for chalky soils. Propagation is by stem cuttings with a heel taken in July and August or by seed.

Taxus baccata LINNAEUS English Yew

(1).(7). A pyramidal bush or a tree, to 12m (occasionally to 20m), making eventually an extremely thick trunk, which, if scrubbed yearly, looks very ornamental with its reddish-brown colour. Lv arranged spirally but twisted so as to appear in two opposite ranks, to 3cm long and not more than 2mm wide, very dark green above, paler below, sometimes greyish or yellowish. Fl in spring and the female plants bear their attractive red fr in the autumn. An enormous number of cv have arisen, some with yellow lv, ('Elegantissima' 'Semperaurea'), while 'Glauca' has glaucous young lv, some of columnar habit ('Erecta', Fastigiata'), while 'Dovastoniana' has a tabular habit much like a cedar, but with the bts pendulous, a most attractive form. 'Lutea' ('Fructuluteo') has yellow fr. Native of Europe, including the UK, and N Africa and western Asia.

Taxus cuspidata SIEBOLD AND ZUCCARINI
Japanese Yew

Although in the wild this can reach 15m it grows to much less in cultivation, and is usually seen as a spreading shrub to 3m. Lv to 2·5cm long and 3mm wide, dark green above, yellowish below. A number of dwarf, compact cv exist. Much used in the northern USA where *T. baccata* suffers in the severe winters. Equally hardy and a larger plant is *T. X media* REHDER, hybrids between *T. baccata* and *T. cuspidata* with a number of named clones mostly of upright, columnar habit, but 'Thayerae' and 'Nidiformis' make spreading, cup-shaped trees or shrubs. *T. cuspidata* is native to Japan, but was brought from China by Fortune in 1855.

Taxodium distichum

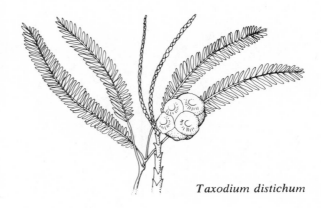

Taxodium distichum

TETRACENTRON OLIVER *Tetracentraceae*
A monotypic genus.

Tetracentron sinense OLIVER

4.7. A deciduous tree, to 20m or more in the wild, with glabrous lenticular bts. Lv alternate, ovate or cordate, to 8cm long and 5cm wide, the margins bluntly toothed, the apex long-acuminate. Fl minute, in catkin-like racemes to 15cm long, pale yellow. Fl 6–7. Liable to damage by late spring frosts, but otherwise hardy. Native of western China and northern Burma. Introduced by Wilson in 1901.

THUJA LINNAEUS *Cupressaceae* Arbor-Vitae
A small genus of some five species of pyramidal, evergreen trees, very similar to *Chamaecyparis*. mainly distinguished by the shape of the cones which are egg-shaped in *Thuja* with a few overlapping thin scales, while those of *Chamaecyparis* are globose with shield-shaped scales which do not overlap. The leaves are often aromatic. Propagated by seeds or by cuttings.

Thuja koraiensis NAKAI

A curious sp with two distinct habits of growth; usually it is a low shrub, under 1m high but spreading widely, but occasionally it makes a pyramidal tree to 8m with chocolate-coloured bark. The bts are flattened and the frond-like sprays are sea green above and markedly glaucous white below. The foliage is aromatic when crushed. Cones ellipsoid, about 8mm long. Native of Korea. Introduced by Wilson in 1917.

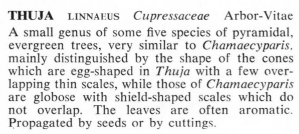

Thuja occidentalis

Thuja occidentalis LINNAEUS

7. Pyramidal, evergreen tree, to about 10m in cultivation usually but twice as high in the wild; somewhat slow-growing for the genus. Lv yellowish-green above, grey-green below, with a somewhat acrid odour when crushed. Cones egg-shaped, 8mm long. A large number of variants have been isolated, such as 'Aurea' with golden-yellow lv, 'Beaufort' with lv variegated white, 'Ericoides' which maintains its juvenile needle-like lv as opposed to the scale-like ones of mature plants, and a number of dwarf forms. Native of eastern N America and one of the first trees to be introduced thence; 1534 being the accepted date of its introduction.

Thuja orientalis LINNAEUS

7. A pyramidal evergreen, to 12m, with very erect brs, either narrowly pyramidal or more broadly so with a number of leaders rather than a single trunk. Lv scale-like, yellowish-green on both surfaces. Cones purplish, ovoid, to 2cm long, each scale with a small hooked boss at the apex. There are rather less variants of this plant but 'Conspicua' and 'Elegantissima' are yellow-leaved forms, while 'Juniperoides' has juvenile foliage. There are also a number of dwarf forms. Native of northern and western China. Introduced to Paris by missionaries in the early years of the eighteenth century.

Thuja plicata D. DON

7. (*T. lobbii* of gardens). A fast-growing tree, to 60m in the wild and already over 35m in cultivation. It is of pyramidal habit with the brs descending at first and then curving upwards at the ends. Once the lower brs have completed their growth the handsome, cinnamon, shredding bark is disclosed. Lv scale-like, dark green above, dark green with glaucous patches below. Cones ovoid to 1cm long. Apart from its larger size, recognisable by the glaucous patches on the underside of the lv.

A number of yellow-leaved cv are known ('Aurea', 'Semperaurescens'), one with the lv variegated yellow and green ('Zebrina') and a narrowly fastigiate form known either as 'Stricta' or as 'Fastigiata'. The plant is much used for hedging. Native of western N. America from British Columbia to N California. Introduced by W. Lobb in 1853.

Thuja standishii (GORDON) CARRIÈRE

7. (*T. japonica* MAXIMOWICZ, *Thujopsis standishii* GORDON). Tree, only to about 8m in the UK but up to 18m in the wild, with reddish peeling bark. Very slow-growing for the genus, although rapid compared to some trees. The brs curve upwards at the ends, while the scale-like lv

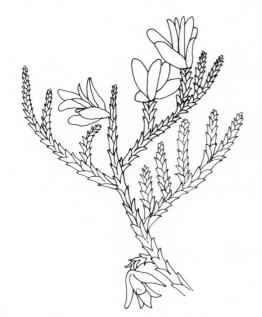

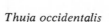

Thuja occidentalis

243

are pale yellowish-green above, glaucous below and lemon-scented when crushed. Mature plants are of more open habit than other *thujas*. Cones to 8mm long. Native of central Japan. Introduced by Fortune in 1860.

THUJOPSIS SIEBOLD AND ZUCCARINI
Cupressaceae

A monotypic genus akin to *Thuja*, but cones with woody scales that overlap and opposite leaves, while the branchlets are much thicker than those of *Thuja*.

Thujopsis dolabrata
(LINNAEUS THE YOUNGER) SIEBOLD

7. Evergreen tree or large bush, to 12m and more, of pyramidal form with horizontal brs, pendulous at the ends, the bts opposite each other. Lv scale-like, rigid, but to 6mm long; dark shining green above, with conspicuous glaucous patches below. Cones more or less globular, to 2cm in diameter, with about 8 overlapping woody scales with a horn-like protrusion at the apex. 'Aurea' has golden lv, 'Variegata' has the lv variegated with cream, but is liable to revert. Native of Japan. Introduced to Java by Siebold about 1830, whence Thomas Lobb sent a plant back to Veitch in 1853. Large importations by Fortune and J. G. Veitch in 1860.

Thujopsis dolabrata

TILIA LINNAEUS *Tiliaceae* Lime, Linden

The limes form a fairly homogeneous group of deciduous trees, comprising some fifty species from N America, Europe and eastern Asia. They have alternate, cordate leaves and fragrant flowers in drooping cymes, subtended by a large, oblong, leaf-like bract, usually yellowish or whitish. The flowers have five sepals and five petals, usually concolorous, and the fruit is a dry, round, nutlike capsule, usually single-seeded. Propagation is by seed or by layers; cuttings are not easy. Cultivars are grafted on to stocks of their species. Many species are hosts for numerous aphids and drip honey-dew during the late summer. The common lime is, surprisingly, a natural hybrid, although it appears to come true from seed.

Tilia americana LINNAEUS

4.(7). A tree, to 20m in the wild but seldom thriving for long in the UK as, although impervious to winter cold, it requires a hot summer to ripen the wood thoroughly. Lv cordate, acuminate, toothed, to 20cm long and 15cm wide (occasionally to 37cm long and 25cm across); dark dull green above, paler and shining below. Fl rarely produced but in a pendulous cyme, subtended by a large oblong bract to 12cm long and 3cm wide on a stalk to 10cm long; each fl yellowish-white, 2cm across. Fl 7. Remarkable for its huge lv. Native of eastern N America. Introduced by Bartram probably before 1752, when Miller recorded it.

Tilia chinensis MAXIMOWICZ

4. Small tree, to 15m, with glabrous, glossy bts and flaking bark. Lv ovate, cordate at the base, to 10cm long and nearly as wide, with a long slender point, sharply toothed, glabrous above, thinly pubescent beneath with rust-coloured tufts along the midrib. Fl in quite large clusters, up to 15, pendulous, subtended by a bract 10cm long. Fl 7. Native of China; introduced in 1925.

Tilia cordata MILLER

4.7. (*T. parvifolia* EHRHART). A tree, to 20m, with a rounded head. Lv heart-shaped, to 7cm long and wide, dark green and glabrous above, paler below with tufts of rusty down in vein axils on petioles to 5cm long. Fl in few-flowered cymes, whitish-yellow, subtended by a bract to 9cm long and 2cm wide. Fl 7. Easily recognised by its small lv. Native of most of Europe including the UK. Confused by Linnaeus with *T.* X *vulgaris* and included in his *T. europaea*, which is a confused name.

Tilia dasystyla STEVEN

4.7. (*T. caucasica* RUPRECHT). A tree, to 30m, with smooth red bts. Lv round, cordate at the base, with bristle-like teeth, to 14cm long and wide; dark green above, bright green below with tufts of whitish hairs between the veins. Fl in cymes of 3–7. Fl 7. Native of the Caucasus and Crimea. Not known in cultivation before 1880.

Tilia X euchlora KOCH

4.7. (Sometimes sold as *T. dasystyla*). A plant of uncertain origin, thought to be a hybrid between *T. cordata* and *T. dasystyla*, but in cultivation in 1860, while, as we have seen, *T. dasystyla* was not known in cultivation until 20 years later. The two spp could conceivably meet in the wild and hybridise there, but no such wild hybrids are mentioned in *Flora Europaea*. A tree to 20m, with brs becoming pendulous; bts green glabrous. Lv heart-shaped, to 10cm long and wide, shining green above, paler beneath with reddish tufts in the vein axils. Fl yellowish, in cymes of 3–7 fl; floral bract to 7cm long and 1·5cm wide. Fl 7. The best lime for street planting, as aphids appear to shun it.

Tilia henryana SZYSZYLOWICZ

4.7. Tree, to 15m, with bts covered with starry down at first. Lv ovate, sometimes cordate at base, long acuminate, with hair-like teeth, to 12cm long and 7cm wide, slightly downy above, covered with brownish down below. Fl in cymes of up to 20 fl, whitish; the floral bract to 15cm long and 2cm wide. Fl 7. Only *T. japonica* (qv) has a more brilliant floral display. Native of China. Introduced by Wilson in 1901.

Tilia heterophylla VENTENAT

4.7. It is doubtful if the true plant is in cultivation, being usually represented by var *michauxii* SARGENT (*T. michauxii* NUTTALL), which some authorities consider to be a hybrid between *T. heterophylla* and *T. americana*. Tree of up to 25m in the wild, with reddish glabrous bts. Lv large, usually to 20cm long and 15cm broad, but Bean records some to 42cm long and 30cm wide; dark green and smooth above, grey-downy below, coarsely toothed. Fl yellowish, in cymes of 10–20, the floral bract to 15cm long and 2cm wide. Fl 7. Like *T. americana* it is liable to die back and grow irregularly. Native of the eastern USA. Probably introduced by Fraser in 1800. *T. heterophylla* was introduced by Bartram about 1755 and his sendings may have included var *michauxii*.

Tilia insularis NAKAI

4.7. Tree of up to 15m with either glabrous or slightly hairy bts. Lv reniform (kidney-shaped), to 9cm long and usually slightly wider, glabrous on both surfaces, apart from tufts of grey down below in the vein axils. Fl 20 or more per cyme, yellowish, the floral bract to 6cm long. Fl 7. Native of Korea. Introduced by Wilson in 1917.

Tilia japonica (MIQUEL) SIMONKAI

4.7. Tree, to 20m, much resembling *T. cordata* in appearance; bts pubescent at first. Lv cordate, to 8cm long and wide, abruptly acuminate, somewhat glaucous beneath and downy at first. Fl in cymes with up to 40 fl, subtended by a bract 15cm long and 3cm wide. Fl 7. The most floriferous of the lindens, but rare in cultivation. Native of Japan. Introduced in 1875.

Tilia maximowicziana SHIRASAWA

4.7. Tree, to 30m in the wild but the dimensions in cultivation are not yet known; bts downy. Lv heart-shaped to 15cm long and 13cm wide, coarsely toothed, dark green and downy above, grey-downy below. Fl 10–18 in a cyme, the floral bract to 10cm long. Fl 6. Flowering a month earlier than most spp. Native of Japan. Introduced to USA in 1880 and to Kew 10 years later.

Tilia miqueliana MAXIMOWICZ

4.7. Moderate tree, to 15m, with grey tomentose bts. Lv ovate, long-acuminate, cordate at the base, to 12cm long and 9cm wide, dark glossy green above, grey tomentose below; the petioles also are grey pubescent. Fl small, in cymes of 10–20, the floral bract to 10cm long and 2cm wide. Fl 8. Native to eastern China, but much grown in Japan, particularly around temples. Introduced from Japan about 1900. The lv tend to persist until November.

Tilia mongolica MAXIMOWICZ

(3).4.7. Small tree, to 10m, with reddish glabrous bts. Lv reddish when unfurling, almost triangular, but 3–5-lobed, much resembling an ivy, to 7cm long and wide, coarsely toothed, shining green above, rather glaucous below, glabrous on both surfaces, with a few tufts of down in the vein axils below; petiole about 2·5cm long, reddish. Fl whitish, in cymes of 6–20, the floral bract to 8cm long and 1cm wide. Fl 7. Unique in the genus for its lobed lv which are most frequent on young plants. Arguably the best sp for small gardens. Native of northern China and Mongolia. Introduced to Paris in 1880.

Tilia oliveri SZYSZYLOWICZ

4.7. Tree of up to 15m with glabrous, reddish bts. Lv cordate, to 10cm long and wide, dark green and shining above, silvery tomentose below; petiole to 5cm. Fl in cymes of 7–20, whitish, floral bract about 7cm long. Very similar to *T. tomentosa* (qv) but with glabrous bts. Native of China. Introduced by Wilson in 1900.

Tilia petiolaris DE CANDOLLE

4.7. (*T. americana pendula* of gardens). A

remarkably beautiful tree which is best regarded as a form of *T. tomentosa*. See below.

Tilia platyphyllos SCOPOLI

4.7. A tree to 30m or more, often producing suckers, with a rounded head and downy bts. Lv heart-shaped, to 12cm long and wide, sharply toothed; dark green above and pubescent, paler and tomentose below, particularly by the main veins. Fl yellowish-white in 3–6 flowered cymes, the bract to 10cm long. Fl 6–7. Variants with laciniate lv ('Aspleniifolia' and 'Laciniata') are known and also forms with yellow or red bts ('Aurea' and 'Rubra'). Native of most of Europe, possibly including the UK.

Tilia tomentosa MOENCH Silver Lime

4.7. A somewhat variable tree, to 30m, of pyramidal habit; bts tomentose. Lv cordate, to 12cm long and wide, sometimes faintly lobed, dark green above and eventually glabrous, silvery tomentose below. Petioles to 3·5cm long. Fl in cymes of 3–10 fl, whitish, bract to 8cm long. Fl 7–8. *T. petiolaris* differs in its rather smaller lv, in its long petioles to 6cm long and in its graceful, pendulous habit. Moreover its seeds are very rarely produced, so it might have *T. cordata* blood in it. The plant is particularly attractive on windy summer days when the silver undersides to the lv flash in the sun. Native to eastern, central and south-eastern Europe, also western Asia. Offered by James Gordon in 1757, which suggests a Collinson introduction. *T. petiolaris* introduced about 1740.

T. X moltkei SPÄTH is a hybrid between *T. tomentosa* (or *petiolaris*) and *T. americana*, making a vigorous, rather pendulous tree with the large lv of *T. americana* and a grey tomentum on the underside. It is considerably hardier than *T. americana*, but less attractive than the other parent.

Tilia X vulgaris HAYNE

4.7. (*T. europaea* LINNAEUS in part). A large tree, sometimes to 40m, often with curious burrs on the trunk from which numerous shoots emerge. It is also prone to throw up suckers. Lv heart-shaped, to 10cm long and broad, on a petiole to 5cm; dark green and glabrous above, paler with tufts of whitish hair in vein axils below. Fl in cymes of 3–8 fl, yellowish, the floral bract to 11cm long. Fl 7. A hybrid between *T. cordata* and *T. platyphyllos*, often occurring in the wild. Fertile seed is not often set but seems to reproduce fairly exactly when it is obtained. Much planted in public, but inferior to *T. X euchlora* for this purpose.

TORREYA ARNOTT *Taxaceae*

A small genus of about six species of evergreen shrubs or trees with opposite branches and leaves arranged spirally, although on lateral branches they are twisted so as to lie in two ranks. The flowers are usually dioecious, although monoecious forms turn up from time to time. The fruit is drupe-like with a fleshy coat, which takes two years to ripen. Two species are in commerce, but *T. californica* requires very mild conditions. Propagation is by seed or by cuttings.

Torreya nucifera SIEBOLD AND ZUCCARINI

7. In the wild a tree to 25m, but in cultivation in the UK a bushy shrub to 4m. Lv linear, to 3cm long, with a rigid tip, dark glossy green above with 2 glaucous bands below. Fr green flushed purple. Native to Japan. Introduced by Captain Thomas Cornwall in 1764.

TRACHYCARPUS WENDLAND *Palmae*

The species described below is interesting as being the only palm that is reliably hardy in the UK, plants having survived temperatures of −18°C. The plants are usually dioecious, but can only be propagated by seed.

Trachycarpus fortunei WENDLAND

(*Chamaerops excelsa* of Martius, not of Thunberg). A palm, to 10m in sheltered districts but only to about 4m in less clement regions. Lv evergreen, fan-shaped, divided into innumerable linear segments about 5cm wide; the whole lv may measure 75cm long and 160cm wide. The petiole is narrow, two-edged, and may be a metre long but only 2·5cm wide. Small yellow fl in nodding panicles; the panicles may be 60cm long. Fr a blue-black drupe about the size of a

Trachycarpus fortunei

damson. Like the majority of palms, the plant has only a single trunk (although var *surculosa* HENRY will produce suckers). Plants should be protected from severe winds, which can damage them. They are very slow growing in the open, particularly when young, and there is much to be said for growing them under glass until they are fairly sizeable. Very severe winters may damage the lv but will not kill the plant. Introduced by Siebold in 1830 from Japan, but a native of China, whence it was introduced by Fortune in 1849.

TRIPETALEIA SIEBOLD AND ZUCCARINI
Ericaceae

A genus of only two species of deciduous shrubs from Japan. Like most of the *Ericaceae* they require acid soil. The leaves are alternate, the flowers in terminal racemes or panicles, usually three-petalled, but calyx five-lobed.

Tripetaleia bracteata MAXIMOWICZ

4. Deciduous shrub, to 2m, with glabrous pale brown bts. Lv obovate-elliptic, to 5cm long and half as wide, glabrous on both surfaces. Fl in erect, terminal racemes, to 15cm long. Fl solitary on pedicels to 1cm long, springing from a leafy bract 6mm long. The individual fl only 1cm long, white, tinged pink. Fl 7–8. Native of Japan. According to Bean, writing in 1933, it had been in intermittent cultivation for the last 40 years and was growing in the Arnold Arboretum in 1910. Rehder, on the other hand, gives 1915 as the date of introduction.

Tripetaleia paniculata SIEBOLD AND ZUCCARINI

4. Differs from the last sp in its lv which are lanceolate, sparingly pubescent above and with large tufts of white hairs in the vein axils below. Fl in a panicle, not a raceme, but otherwise not markedly different. Fl 7–9. Native of Japan. Introduced by Maries in 1879 according to Bean, but in 1892 according to Rehder.

TRIPTERYGIUM JOSEPH HOOKER
Celastraceae

A small genus of four or five species of deciduous clambering shrubs from E Asia. The leaves are alternate; the flowers in terminal panicles; the fruit is three-winged. Only one species is reliably hardy in the UK.

Tripterygium regelii SPRAGUE AND TAKEDA

4. Rambling shrub, to 6m if trained through a tree, with showy, angular warty, reddish-brown brs; bts downy. Lv ovate, rounded at base, long acuminate to 15cm long and 10cm wide, dark green above and finally glabrous, slightly pubes-

cent below, particularly along the veins. Fl fragrant, in terminal and axillary panicles to give a compound inflorescence to 20cm long and 8cm wide, yellowish-white. Fl 7–8. Fr greenish, three-winged, much like a wych elm. Native of Japan, Korea, and Manchuria. Introduced in 1905.

TROCHODENDRON SIEBOLD AND ZUCCARINI
Trochodendraceae

A monotypic genus.

Trochodendron aralioides
SIEBOLD AND ZUCCARINI

(4). In the wild a small, evergreen tree, but usually a bush to 3m in cultivation. Lv very similar to those of *Rhododendron ponticum*, lanceolate-elliptic, somewhat leathery, occasionally shallowly toothed towards the apex; shining dark green above, paler beneath, glabrous on both surfaces. Fl lacking petals in erect, terminal racemes to 10cm long, each fl on a pedicel to 2·5cm long comprising a vivid green disk from which the stamens and stigma emerge. Fl 4–6. Requires acid or neutral soil. Native of Japan. Possibly introduced by Maries; flowered for the first time in Veitch's nursery in 1894.

TSUGA CARRIÈRE *Pinaceae* Hemlock Spruce

A comparatively small genus of evergreen trees with the leaves set on cushion-like projections as in *Picea*, but the cones of *Tsuga* are very small, rarely more than 2·5cm long. The leaves are short, arranged in two ranks; the branchlets are very slender. They thrive best in regions with ample rainfall, where they make very elegant pyramidal trees of fairly rapid growth. They do best on acid soil. Propagated by seed or by cuttings.

Tsuga canadensis CARRIÈRE Hemlock Spruce

7. Tree, to 33m, the trunk usually dividing near the base, with reddish bark and grey hairy bts. Lv linear-lanceolate to 1·5cm long, dark green above with two bands of whitish stomata below. Cones to 2·5cm long, pendulous. persisting for 2 years, although ripe the first season. There is a pendulous form, 'Pendula', a slow-growing form with white growing tips, 'Albospica', and a large number of dwarf forms. Will tolerate limey conditions but not shallow, chalky soils. Native of eastern N America. Introduced by Bartram in 1736.

Tsuga diversifolia MASTERS

(7). A tree, to 25m in the wild but in cultivation usually only a pyramidal bush to 5m, with downy bts. Lv linear, to 1·5cm long, attractively yellowish-green when young, when mature dark

Tsuga heterophylla

glossy green above, with two well-defined white lines below. Cones ovoid to 2cm long. Native of Japan. Introduced by J. G. Veitch in 1861.

Tsuga heterophylla SARGENT

7. (*T. albertiana* SÉNÉCLAUZE). A tree, to 60m in the wild and over 40m in cultivation, of rapid growth, with reddish-brown bark and pendulous brs. Bts very slender, hairy, the hairs persisting. Lv to 2·5cm long, dark green above, greyish below. Cones to 2·5cm long. A very attractive tree. Native to western N America. Introduced by Jeffrey in 1851–2.

Tsuga mertensiana CARRIÈRE

7. (*T. pattoniana* SÉNÉCLAUZE). Tree, to 30m, with downy bts. Lv set all round the brs not in 2 ranks as in other spp, slightly curved, to 2·5cm long, with stomata (inconspicuous) on both surfaces. Lv grey-green or glaucous blue ('Glauca'). Cones purplish when young, cylindric, to 8cm long. Native of western N America. Introduced by Jeffrey in 1851–2; at the same time he introduced *T. X jeffreyi*, which is thought to be a natural hybrid between *T. heterophylla* and *T. mertensiana*, but no wild tree has been found. This is slow-growing with green lv only 12mm long.

Tsuga sieboldii CARRIÈRE

7. Although a tree to 30m in Japan, this only makes a large pyramidal bush to 6m in the UK. Bts glabrous, making this a distinguishing feature. Lv linear, to 2·5cm long, notched at the apex, glossy green above, with 2 conspicuous white lines below. Cones to 2·5cm long. Native of Japan. Obtained by Siebold about 1850.

ULEX LINNAEUS *Leguminosae*

A genus of twenty species, confined to western Europe and N Africa. The leaves are alternate, trifoliolate, only present on seedling plants, later transformed to spiny phyllodes. Fl axillary, usually solitary, pea-shaped, yellow.

Ulex europaeus LINNAEUS Gorse, Furze

4. A spiny shrub, rarely reaching 2m and more often from 1m to 1m 50cm, extremely spiny. Brs hairy. Fl yellow, about 2cm long and 1·5cm wide, fragrant, produced throughout the year. The plant needs full sun and rather poor soil. 'Plenus' has the stamens transformed into petals and, since it does not produce seed, is probably preferable for garden work. It is propagated by cuttings taken in August. 'Strictus' is a fastigiate form with rather soft prickles, which is very shy flowering and not very desirable, except as a hedging plant. Native of much of western Europe, particularly the UK. The double form first noted about 1828.

Tsuga heterophylla

ULMUS LINNAEUS *Ulmaceae* Elm

A genus of about forty-five species of deciduous trees, ranging from eastern N America to China and Japan, but lacking in western Asia and in western N America. The leaves are alternate, toothed, short-petioled. The flowers usually appear before the leaves and are inconspicuous. Some species throw sucker growths but otherwise propagation is mainly by seed, although cultivars may be grafted on to stocks of their own species. The fruit is a samara, usually disk-like, with the seed in the centre. Although rapid-growing, elms have an unfortunate habit of shedding limbs without warning and are also liable to be killed by dutch elm disease, so they are not the best of garden trees, although some of the golden-leaved cultivars are attractive enough. Elms seem to hybridise almost indefinitely. The Dutch elm is thought to contain the blood of three species. With a few exceptions, the flowers are in axillary clusters; they lack petals but have reddish anthers, which are slightly colourful. The leaves of many species turn a good clear yellow before falling. The taxonomy of the elms is very involved; many slight deviants being given specific rank. Here I am following *Flora Europaea*, so far as European elms are concerned.

Ulmus alata MICHAUX

7. Moderate-sized tree of up to 15m; bts smooth at first but later developing a very conspicuous pair of corky wings. Lv ovate-oblong, to 6cm long and half as wide, doubly toothed, glabrous above, with tufts of hair in the leaf axils below. Fr 8mm long. Native of the southeastern USA. Introduced in 1820.

Ulmus americana LINNAEUS

7. Tree, to 40m in the wild, with ash-grey, scaly, fissured bark; bts usually downy at first. Lv ovate, acuminate, doubly toothed, 15cm long and half as wide, slightly hairy above, downy below. Fr oval, about 1cm long. Native of most of America east of the Rockies. Introduced by Bartram about 1752.

Ulmus crassifolia NUTTALL

A tree of up to 25m in the wild, but in the UK very slow-growing and rarely more than 10m; bts pubescent. Lv hispid, ovate, toothed, rounded at the apex, downy below, to 5cm long and 3cm wide. Unusually the fl appear in axillary clusters in August. *U. serotina* SARGENT was for long confused with this sp. It differs in its larger, acuminate, thinner lv and in its racemose inflorescence and fr. Both are native to the southeastern USA. Introduced in 1876 and 1903.

Ulmus fulva MICHAUX Slippery Elm

7. (*U. rubra* MICHAUX THE YOUNGER, *U. elliptica* KOEHNE not KOCH). Tree, to 20m, with downy bts. Lv oblong-ovate, to 20cm long and half as wide, mucronate, doubly toothed, hispid above, hairy below. Fr with tufts of red-brown hairs over the seed, orbicular, to 2cm in diameter. Native of the eastern USA from Quebec to Florida. Probably among Bartram's sendings as *U. americana rubra*.

Ulmus glabra HUDSON Wych Elm

5.7. (*U. montana* WITHERING, *U. scabra* MILLER, *U. glabra* of Miller is also his *U. minor* (qv)). A tree to 40m with downy young shoots, not suckering. Lv obovate, slender-acuminate, to 17cm long and 10cm wide, coarsely toothed, dull green and somewhat wrinkled above, downy below. Fr thickly clustered along the twigs, oval, to 2·5cm long, with the seed in the centre, and conspicuous before ripening. A number of different forms have been selected of which 'Pendula', with a flat head of brs, pendulous at the ends, is remarkably ornamental; 'Camperdownii' is also pendulous but makes a dome-shaped tree. 'Exoniensis' ('Fastigiata', 'Pyramidalis') is a fastigiate form, while in 'Lutescens' the young lv are creamy-yellow, fading later to yellowish-green. Native of most of Europe, including the UK.

Ulmus X hollandica MILLER Dutch Elm

7. According to some authorities, a hybrid between *U. minor, U. glabra* and *U. plottii,* but *Flora Europaea* merges *U. minor* and *U. plottii.* A vigorous tree, to 40m, often with pendulous brs and slightly hairy bts. Lv oval or ovate, slender-acuminate, asymmetric at the base, to 12cm long and 7cm wide; shining green above, bright green below and glabrous except for some pubescence along the main veins. Fr to 2·5cm long, oval. A number of somewhat unremarkable clones have been named. More attractive are 'Dampieri', a fastigiate form making a narrow cone, and its sport 'Wredei', with the same habit but yellow lv. 'Serpentina' has brs both pendulous and contorted. *U. X sarniensis* is a hybrid between the dutch elms and the var *angustifolia* of *U. minor*, and has two attractive forms; 'Dicksonii', with golden-yellow lv, and 'Purpurea' (*U. glabra purpurea* and *U. procera purpurea*), which has the bts and young lv purple, later fading to dark green. Native of north-western Europe.

Ulmus minor MILLER

7. (Includes *U. plottii* DRUCE and *U. angustifolia* WESTON [*U. carpinifolia* SUCKOW, *U. nitens* MOENCH, *U. campestris* LINNAEUS in part]). A tree to 30m, suckering freely, the older brs often bearing 4 corky ridges; bts more or less glabrous. The habit varies from conical to widely spreading and pendulous. Lv more or less oval, acuminate, unequal at the base, to 10cm long and half as wide (smaller and narrower in var *angustifolia*), glossy green above, glabrous on both surfaces, except for a little pubescence in vein axils. Fr oval to 1·5cm long. A form with lv to 6cm long, and 3·5cm wide, downy below, was named *U. plottii* by Druce, and this, crossed with the more widespread form, has given *U. X viminalis*, of which 'Aurea' has golden young lv, 'Marginata' has greyish-white margins, while *U. minor* 'Variegata' has the lv densely mottled white. *U. X vegeta* is *U. minor X U. glabra*, known as the Huntingdon elm. The Cornish elm is a fastigiate form of var *angustifolia*. Native of most of Europe including the UK.

Ulmus parvifolia JACQUIN

7. (*U. chinensis* PERSOON, *U. sieboldii* DAVEAU). A small tree, to 15m, with a rounded head and very slender bts, which are covered with grey pubescence. Lv leathery, oval or elliptic, acuminate, toothed, lustrous green above, slightly downy in the vein axils below, otherwise glabrous and pale green, persisting until the New Year. Fl 9–10. Fr ovate, only 8mm long. One of the most attractive spp for gardens and seemingly immune to Dutch elm disease. Native of China and Japan. Introduced in 1794.

Ulmus procera SALISBURY   English Elm

7. (*U. campestris* LINNAEUS in part). Suckering

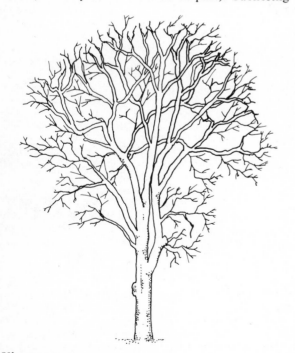

Ulmus procera

tree, to 50m, with hairy bts. Lv round-ovate, acuminate, asymmetric at base, doubly toothed, to 9cm long and 5cm wide, dark green and hispid above, paler below and downy. Fr round, 1cm in diameter. 'Louis van Houtte' has golden-yellow lv which retain their colour, 'Argenteo-variegata' has the lv variegated silvery-grey. The plant very rarely sets seed. Native of southern England; reported also from other countries in western and southern Europe, but always with some doubt as to its being genuinely native to these countries.

Ulmus pumila LINNAEUS

Shrub or small tree, to 10m, with rough bark. Lv elliptic, to 5·5cm long and 2·5cm wide, dark green and glabrous on both surfaces. Fr circular, 1cm in diameter, with the seed in the middle. Native of Siberia and northern China. Introduced by M. Richard in 1771. 'Arborea' (pinnato-ramosa) has the bts in opposite rows and the lv are arranged pinnately on these. Introduced in 1894.

UMBELLULARIA   NUTTALL   *Lauraceae*

A monotypic genus.

Umbellularia californica NUTTALL

An evergreen tree, to 25m in its native California but, unless trained against a wall, rarely more than 7m in the UK. Lv alternate, leathery, elliptic, to 12cm long and 4cm wide, dark green and glossy above, glaucous below, glabrous on both surfaces at maturity, aromatic when crushed. Fl in terminal and axillary umbels, 2cm across; each bloom to 6mm wide, yellowish-green. Fr a pear-shaped drupe to 2·5cm long, green with purple flush. Fl 4. Requires a sunny position; damaged in severe winters but not killed. Native of California. Introduced by Douglas in 1829.

VACCINIUM   LINNAEUS   *Ericaceae*

A large and confusing genus ranging from the arctic to the tropics, of evergreen and deciduous shrubs, many of them too low-growing for inclusion here. The leaves are alternate, short-petioled, often colouring brilliantly in the autumn. The flowers are small, nodding, urceolate or campanulate with four or five lobes. The fruit is a many-seeded berry, often edible. Like so many ericaceous plants they require acid soil. They are propagated by seed or by cuttings of half-ripe wood, which probably require some heat. Some species spread by means of sucker growths and these can be detached. Some of the more attractive species, such as *V. floribundum* (*mortinia*), are on the borderline of hardiness and have been omitted.

Vaccinium arboreum MARSHALL

4.5.6. In the wild both deciduous and ever-green forms are known, but it is the deciduous form that is found in cultivation. In cultivation a shrub, to 3m, with oval lv to 5cm long and half as wide with the margins slightly recurved, coriaceous, dark glossy green above, paler and downy below, colouring shades of red in the autumn. Fl solitary, axillary and in short termi-nal racemes, campanulate, white, about 6mm long. Fl 7–8. Fr black, 6mm in diameter. Native of the south-eastern USA from Virginia south-wards. Introduced by John Cree in 1765.

Vaccinium arctostaphylos LINNAEUS

2.4.6. Rather slow-growing, deciduous shrub, eventually to 3m, with reddish bts. Lv ovate-oblong, acuminate, finely toothed, to 10cm long, dark green above and downy along the veins, paler and more downy below colouring well in the autumn and persisting until December. Fl in axillary racemes to 5cm long, each fl campanulate, 8mm long, greenish-white with a pink tinge. Fl 6. Fr black, 8mm in diameter. *V. padifolium* SMITH is fairly like *V. arctostaphylos*, with downy bts and smaller lv, while the fl are greenish-yellow. The lv do not colour but persist until January. Fr blue. *V. arctostaphylos* is native to the Caucasus. Introduced, probably through Bieberstein, in 1800. *V. padifolium* is native to Madeira. Introduced by Masson in 1777.

Vaccinium bracteatum THUNBERG

3.4.5. Evergreen shrub to 2m. The young lv are copper-coloured, later they become elliptic, to 7cm long and 2·5cm wide, dark green and glabrous. Fl in axillary racemes, to 5cm long, furnished with linear-lanceolate leafy bracts, from the axils of which a single white, cylindrical fl, to 6mm long, emerges; the whole raceme may carry up to 12 fl. Fl 7–9. Fr red, 6mm wide. Native of China, Japan and Korea. Introduced by Reeves to Loddiges in 1829.

Vaccinium corymbosum LINNAEUS   Blueberry

4.5.6. A very variable, deciduous shrub, to 4m, forming a dense thicket with bts either pubescent or glabrous. Lv elliptic, to 9cm long and half as wide, slightly downy below along the main veins, turning red before falling. Fl in terminal and axillary fascicles, before lv, cylindrical, to 1cm long, pink or white. Fl 5. Fr black with blue bloom, edible. Ornamental but also grown com-mercially for its fr, which need to be protected from birds. *V. atrococcum* HELLER is closely related, but with lv tomentose beneath and black fr without any bloom. Native of eastern N America where it often grows in swamps. Intro-duced by Cree and Bartram in the 1760s.

Vaccinium corymbosum

Vaccinium glaucoalbum JOSEPH HOOKER

4.5. Evergreen, suckering shrub to 1·5m. Lv rigid, ovate, to 6cm long and half as wide, very finely toothed, dull green above, glaucous blue-white beneath. Fl in axillary racemes to 7cm long, furnished with large blue-white bracts, from the axils of which emerge the pale pink, cylindrical fl, 6mm long. Fr 8mm in diameter, black with blue-white bloom. Although generally hardy is often damaged in severe winters, although not killed. Native of the Himalaya. Introduced 1931.

Vaccinium ovatum PURSH

3.4. Evergreen shrub, to 4m, of bushy habit; bts purple and downy. Lv coppery when unfurl-ing, later ovate, coriaceous, toothed, to 4cm long and 2cm wide, glossy green above, paler below, glabrous on both surfaces. Fl in short axillary racemes of up to 6 urceolate white fl to 8mm long. Fl 5–6. Fr black, about 8mm in diameter, edible but rarely formed. Native of western N America. Introduced by Douglas in 1826.

VIBURNUM LINNAEUS *Caprifoliaceae*

A genus of at least 200 species of evergreen and deciduous shrubs found throughout the northern hemisphere (although confined to N Africa in that continent) with a few in Malaysia. The leaves are opposite and the flowers in terminal compound inflorescences, usually cymes or panicles but occasionally in simple racemes or umbels. The fruit is a one-seeded drupe, often very ornamental. Some species resemble the *Hydrangeaceae* in having large sterile flowers in their inflorescences, and some cultivars consist entirely of sterile flowers; the popular snowball tree being a well-known example. The flowers are usually perfect but *V. davidii* tends to be dioecious, and since it is mainly grown for its blue fruit it is important to obtain both sexes. However, even where the flowers are perfect, a better set of fruit seems to be obtained when more than one plant is present, so that in those species, such as *V. betulifolium*, it is sound policy to have more than one plant (and this should be quite distinct; not a rooted cutting of your existing plant). Most species seem tolerant of all soils, but a few seem to require acid conditions. Propagation is by seed, by cuttings and by layers.

Viburnum acerifolium LINNAEUS

4.5.6. Deciduous bush, to 2m; bts downy at first. Lv 3-lobed, basically more or less round but giving the effect of a maple leaf to 10cm long and wide, heart-shaped at base, slightly downy and dull green above, more downy and with black dots beneath, turning crimson in the autumn. Fl in terminal cymes to 7cm in diameter, the fl small, yellowish-white. Fl 6. Fr oval, 8mm long, red at first, later dark purple. Native of eastern N America. Introduced by Bartram in 1736.

Viburnum alnifolium MARSHALL

4.5.6. Shrub, to 3m, of spreading growth, requiring acid, shady conditions; bts covered with scurfy tomentum. Lv roundish, up to 20cm long and wide, dark green above and pubescent at first, more pubescent below, particularly along the veins, turning deep red in the autumn. Fl in cymes to 12cm across, the outer fl sterile and up to 2·5cm across, the inner ones perfect and very small, white. Fl 5–6. Fr red at first, finally black-purple. *Viburnum furcatum* BLUME is distinct only in its more erect habit and in its shorter stamens and is equally desirable. Both spp appear to be intolerant of prolonged drought and neither is particularly easy in gardens. They probably require woodland conditions. *V. alnifolium* is native to eastern N America and was introduced in 1820. *V. furcatum* is native to Japan and Korea and was introduced in 1892.

Viburnum atrocyaneum CLARKE

3.4.5. (*V. wardii* of gardens). Evergreen shrub, to 4m, of densely bushy habit. Lv copper-coloured when emerging, ovate, dark green, to 5cm long and half as wide. Fl in cymes to 5cm across, dull white. Fl 5–6. Fr blue. Native of the Himalaya. Introduced by Kingdon Ward.

Viburnum betulifolium BATALIN

4.5. Large shrub or small tree, to 4m, with purplish-brown bts. Lv ovate or rhomboid, coarsely toothed in the upper half, dark green above, paler below, glabrous on both surfaces. Fl

Viburnum betulifolium

dull white in corymbs to 10cm across. Fl 6. Fr brilliant red, round, about 6mm in diameter. One of the most attractive of fruiting shrubs, but it is necessary to have more than one plant to get a satisfactory display and plants do not fruit freely until mature, so some patience is necessary. Native of western China. Introduced by Wilson in 1901.

Viburnum bitchiuense MAKINO

4. A straggling shrub, to 3m, with bts covered with starry down. Lv ovate to 9cm long and 6cm wide, finely toothed, downy on both surfaces. Fl in a rounded corymb to 6cm across, opening pale pink and fading to white, extremely fragrant. Fl 4–5. Fr black, rarely seen. Much like *V. carlesii* (qv) but a larger shrub, although the fl are inferior. Native of Bitchiu, Japan. Introduced in 1911.

Viburnum carlesii HEMSLEY

4. A somewhat dwarf, rounded shrub, rarely exceeding 1m, with pubescent bts. Lv broadly-ovate, toothed, usually cuneate at base, to 9cm long and 6cm wide, dull green above, greyish below and pubescent on both surfaces. Fl with the emerging lv in rounded corymbs to 8cm across; each bloom to 12mm wide, pale pink fading to white. The fl are outstandingly fragrant. Fl 4–5. Fr black, rarely set. The plant has been much used in hybridisation.

V. X burkwoodii is said to be *V. utile* (qv) X *V. carlesii*, although owing to its straggling habit one would have thought that *V. bitchiuense* were a more likely parent. This is a tall, straggling evergreen shrub with bright green, somewhat wrinkled lv to 10cm long and 5cm wide, with pale brown pubescence below. Fl very similar

252

to *V. carlesii*. 'Anne Russell' and 'Park Farm' belong here. Raised in 1924.

V. X juddii is *V. carlesii* X *V. bitchiuense*, and makes a larger shrub than *V. carlesii* but with a better habit than *V. bitchiuense*. Raised in 1920. *V. X carlcephalum* is *V. carlesii* crossed with the large-flowered, rather tender *V. macrocephalum*, and makes a rather stiff shrub, to about 2m, with large corymbs, to 15cm across, of greeny-white fl (sometimes pink in bud) which are less fragrant than *V. carlesii* but still agreeably scented. *V. macrocephalum* is only known in cultivation in a cv with all sterile fl, but presumably these must contain some stamens. *V. carlesii* is native to Korea and was collected in 1885 by a Mr Unger for a Japanese nursery, who introduced the plant to Europe in 1902.

Viburnum cassinoides LINNAEUS

4.5.(6). Deciduous, rounded bush, to 3m, with scurfy bts, needing acid conditions. Lv ovate, acuminate, to 11cm long and 5·5cm across, slightly toothed or with an undulate margin, dark green above, scurfy below. The lv sometimes colour well in the autumn. Fl yellowish-white in cymes to 10cm across. Fl 6. Fr blue-black. *V. nudum* LINNAEUS is only distinguished by the bts, petioles and pedicels lacking any scurf and by the lv being shining green, not dull green, above and only slightly scurfy, if at all, below. The lv colour rather more reliably. Both spp are native to eastern N America and were introduced by Bartram. *V. nudum* was in cultivation in 1750, *V. cassinoides* about 10 years later.

Viburnum cinnamomifolium REHDER

4.5. Evergreen shrub of up to 6m. Lv leathery, elliptic, to 14cm long and 5cm wide, conspicuously 3-nerved; dark green above, paler below, glabrous or nearly so on both surfaces. Fl in cymes to 7cm in diameter, dull white. Fl 6. Fr blue-black, egg-shaped, only 4mm long. Much like a large form of the dwarf *V. davidii*, but the fr are smaller and not the turquoise-blue colour of the dwarf plant. It would be interesting to try crossing the two. Should be planted where protected from winds. Native of western China. Introduced by Wilson in 1904.

Viburnum dasyanthum REHDER

4.5. Deciduous shrub, to 2·5m, with bts glabrous, becoming purplish-brown. Lv ovate, long-acuminate, distantly toothed, dark green above, paler below. Fl in corymbs to 10cm across, white. Fl 6–7. Fr egg-shaped, 8mm long, bright red. Tends to be rather shy fruiting, otherwise admirable, although the allied *V. hupehense* (qv) is probably preferable. Native to western China. Introduced by Wilson in 1907.

Viburnum dilatatum THUNBERG

4.5. Shrub, to 3m, with erect stems and pubescent bts. Lv more or less obovate, to 12cm long and half as wide, acuminate, hairy on both surfaces. Fl very numerous, from lateral twigs as well as from main brs, in cymes to 12cm across, long-stalked, pure white. Fl 6. Fr bright red, ovoid, 8mm long. 'Xanthocarpum' has yellow fr. One of the most attractive spp, apparently fruiting best in eastern counties of the UK and so presumably requiring rather dry conditions. Elsewhere, although it flowers freely, fruiting is not abundant. Native of Japan and China. Introduced before 1845 according to Rehder, but first flowered in the UK in 1875. *V. wrightii* MIQUEL is distinct only in its glabrous bts and lv.

Viburnum erubescens WALLICH

4. Shrub, to 4m or occasionally more. Lv elliptic or ovate, to 10cm long and half as wide, glabrous or nearly so, long-petioled (to 2·5cm). Fl in pendulous panicles to 12cm long, white with a pinkish tinge. Fl 6. Fr to 6mm long, red at first, later black, rarely produced. The Chinese form, var *gracilipes* REHDER, is considerably hardier than the plant from the Indian Himalaya and slightly more floriferous, therefore a more attractive plant. Unique in its pendulous inflorescence. No one knows when the Himalayan plant was introduced, but var *gracilipes* arrived in 1910.

Viburnum farreri STEARN

4. Much better known under its synonym *V. fragrans* BUNGE. Suckering shrub, to 3m high and spreading more widely. Lv obovate or oval, tapered at the base, toothed, to 10cm long and 7cm wide, glabrous on both surfaces except for a few tufts of down in the leaf axils below. Fl theoretically after lv fall, but usually some fl are open before this. Fl in terminal corymbs to 5cm across, pinkish in bud, usually opening white, sometimes pinkish, fragrant; each fl about 1·5cm across. Fl 10–3. Fr red, rarely produced. *V. X bodnantense* is a hybrid between this sp and the allied *V. grandiflorum* (see below), and makes a tall, rather stiff, rapid-growing shrub to 4m. The fl are slightly larger than those of *V. farreri* and are produced when the plant is comparatively young, whereas *V. farreri* has to become quite sizeable before it starts to flower. The fl are usually quite a deep pink. *V. farreri* is native to China. Originally introduced by Purdom in 1910, and subsequently by Purdom and Farrer in 1915.

Viburnum foetidum WALLICH

4.5. (*V. ceanothoides* WRIGHT). Evergreen or semi-evergreen shrub, to 3m, with downy bts. Lv elliptic, sometimes sparsely toothed, to 6cm long and 3cm wide, dark green above, greyish and slightly pubescent below. Fl in corymbs to 5cm across, white with conspicuous purple anthers. Fl 6–7. Fr crimson. A good fruiting plant where room allows for 2 or 3 plants to be grown. Native of India and China, whence it was introduced by Wilson in 1901.

Viburnum grandiflorum WALLICH

4. (*V. nervosum* of J. HOOKER not of D. DON). Slow-growing, rather stiff deciduous shrub, rarely more than 2m in cultivation but, apparently, a small tree occasionally in the wild. Bts downy at first. Lv elliptic, to 10cm long and half as wide, dull green and glabrous above, grey-pubescent below; petiole purplish. Fl before lv in a cluster of corymbs, to 7cm wide, bright pink in bud, barely opening but whitish eventually. Fl 2–3. Fr red at first, later very dark purple, but very rarely set in the UK. Evidently akin to *V. farreri* but a less satisfactory garden plant, although starting to flower when quite small. The fl rarely open simultaneously, but one after the other, so that the buds are more conspicuous than the fl themselves. Native of the Himalaya. Introduced from Bhutan by R. E. Cooper in 1914.

Viburnum harryanum REHDER

4. Evergreen, very bushy, shrub to 3m; bts brown-pubescent. Lv more or less orbicular, mucronate, tapered at the base, 5cm long and wide, dark green above, paler below, glabrous on both surfaces. On strong extension growths the lv are not in pairs but in threes. Fl in an umbel to 4cm across, white. Fl 5–6. Fr shining black. Unusual in its small privet-like lv. Native of China. Introduced by Wilson in 1904.

Viburnum henryi HEMSLEY

4.5. Evergreen shrub or small tree, to 3m, with very stiff brs. Lv narrowly oval, to 12cm long and 4cm wide; dark green and shining above, paler below, glabrous on both surfaces. Fl in stiff, pyramidal panicles to 10cm long and wide, the individual fl pure white. Fl 6–7. Fr red at first, later black. The pyramidal inflorescence is unusual. Native of China. Introduced by Wilson in 1901.

Viburnum hupehense REHDER

4.5.6. Deciduous shrub, to 2·5m, with pubescent bts, later turning glabrous and purplish-brown. Lv broad-ovate, long-acuminate, toothed, to 7cm long and 5·5cm wide; dark green and pubescent above, paler and more downy below; petiole very downy. The lv usually colour well in early autumn. Fl in corymbs to 5cm across. Fl 5–6. Fr ovoid, to 1cm long, yellow at first,

later red. A member of a confusing group including *VV. betulifolium, dilatatum* and *lobophyllum*, all of which have handsome fr. Native of China. Introduced by Wilson in 1908.

Viburnum ichangense REHDER

4.5. (*V. erosum* var *ichangense* HEMSLEY). Deciduous shrub of erect habit, to 2m. Lv ovate-lanceolate, to 6cm long and 2cm wide, rather scurfy above, pubescent below. Fl in cymes to 4cm across, white. Fl 5. Fr red, 6mm long. Closely related to the unsatisfactory *V. erosum* and slightly more reliable in setting fruit. Native of Hupeh. Introduced by Wilson in 1901.

Viburnum japonicum SPRENGEL

4.5. (*V. macrophyllum* BLUME). A slow-growing, evergreen bush to 2m in the UK but apparently larger in warm areas or if grown against a wall. Lv leathery, variable in shape from orbicular to broad-ovate, to 15cm long and from 8–15cm wide, mucronate or acuminate; dark glossy green above, paler below with many tiny black dots. Fl in rounded cymes to 12cm across, white, extremely fragrant. Fl 6. Fr 8mm long, red. Is slow in coming to flowering size and probably unsuitable for very cold districts. Native of Japan. Introduced by Maries in 1879, although Rehder gives 1859; this date may possibly be a misprint.

Viburnum kansuense BATALIN

4.5. Deciduous shrub, to 3m, with greyish bts. Lv basically ovate, but 3 or 5-lobed, to 5cm long and wide, somewhat like a maple leaf; dark green and sparsely hairy above, paler and more hairy below. Fl pinkish-white, in corymbs to 4cm wide. Fl 6–7. Fr red, roundish, to 1cm long. Requires acid soil and shady conditions. Native of western China. Introduced by Wilson in 1908.

Viburnum lentago LINNAEUS

4.5.6. Strong-growing, deciduous shrub or small tree to 10m; bts covered with red scurf. Lv ovate, long-acuminate, toothed, to 10cm long and 5cm wide, dark shining green above, paler below, petioles winged to 2·5cm long, colouring red and yellow in the autumn. Fl fragrant, creamy-white in cymes to 11cm wide. Fl 5–6. Fr oval, blue-black with blue bloom to 1·5cm long. A handsome large shrub, although slightly reluctant to set fruit freely. Native of eastern N America. Introduced by Bartram before 1761, when Gordon listed it.

Viburnum lobophyllum GRAEBNER

4.5. Deciduous shrub, to 5m, with dark reddish-brown young wood. Lv ovate, acuminate or mucronate, toothed, to 10cm long and 8cm wide. Fl in cymes to 10cm across, white with protruding yellow anthers. Fl 6–7. Fr round, red, 8mm long. On paper this should be the best of the red-fruited group, but in practice *V. betulifolium* seems better. Native of western China. First introduced by Wilson in 1901.

Viburnum opulus LINNAEUS Guelder Rose

4.5.(6). Vigorous suckering shrub, to 5m. Lv basically orbicular but 3–5-lobed, much like a maple, to 10cm long and wide, dark green and glabrous above, downy below; petiole to 2·5cm long. In most districts the lv colour brilliantly in the autumn. Fl in cymes to 8cm across, edged with a border of large, sterile fl to 2cm wide; inner fl perfect, with yellow anthers. Fl 6. Fr translucent, red (or yellow in 'Fructuluteo' and 'Xanthocarpum'). 'Sterile', the snowball tree, has all the fl sterile and collected into a ball-shaped inflorescence about 6cm wide. *V. sargentii* KOEHNE is very little different, but with larger lv, the fl have purple, not yellow, anthers, and the bark becomes corky. The fr is smaller and less freely produced. *V. trilobum* MARSHALL is also closely related. *V. opulus* native to most of Europe, including the UK where it is often found in waterlogged conditions. *V. sargentii* from northern China, introduced in 1892; *V. trilobum* from northern N America, introduced in 1812, presumably by Nuttall.

Viburnum plicatum THUNBERG

4.(5).(6). This name, unfortunately, has priority over the better-known name of *V. tomentosum* THUNBERG. Deciduous shrub of tabular form, to 3m, the brs emerging horizontally. Bts covered at first with fine, starry, grey down. Lv ovate, acuminate, to 10cm long and 6cm wide, toothed, dull dark green and sparsely hairy above, grey-downy below. Fl in corymbs terminating short lateral twigs along the main brs; the corymbs flat, to 10cm across, with a ring of sterile fl to 3cm wide on the outside of the umbel, pure white. Fl 5–6. Fr rarely set in much profusion, coral-red darkening to blue-black. In some seasons lv colour well in the autumn, but this is not invariable.

This plant should correctly be known as *V. plicatum* var *tomentosum* REHDER. A number of named clones exist, of which 'Lanarth' and 'Mariesii' are the best known. Thunberg gave the name *plicatum* to a form with all the fl sterile, much like our own snowball tree, although the individual florets are larger. The plant seems slightly less vigorous than var *tomentosum* and less tabular in habit than 'Mariesii'. Native of China and Japan, *V. plicatum* was introduced by Fortune, from China, in 1844 and var *tomentosum* about 1865.

Viburnum propinquum HEMSLEY

4.5. Evergreen shrub of bushy habit, to 3m or slightly more, with reddish-brown, shining, young wood. Lv elliptic, to 9cm long and 3cm wide, dark glossy green above, paler below, glabrous on both surfaces. Fl in cymes to 8cm across, greenish-white. Fl 6. Fr blue-black. Not the most attractive of the genus. Native of China. Introduced by Wilson in 1901.

Viburnum rhytidophyllum

Viburnum rhytidophyllum HEMSLEY

4.5. A rapid-growing evergreen shrub, to 3m high and wide, with the bts covered with grey, stellate, down. Lv ovate-oblong, to 18cm long and 6cm wide, glossy grey-green and much wrinkled above, grey-tomentose below. The petioles to 3cm long. Fl in large, umbel-like trusses to 20cm across, creamy-white. Fl 5–6. Fr oval, 8mm long, red at first, finally shining black. One of the best large-leaved evergreens for chalky districts, although the lv are liable to be damaged by gales. Fr are only produced when more than one plant is present, but are very showy in their red stage. The plant has been hybridised with *V. utile* ('Pragense'), *buddleifolium* (X *rhytidocarpum*) and *lantana* (X *rhytidophylloides*), all of which have given rise to vigorous, large-leaved evergreens. 'Pragense', with fl a better white than the type, is probably the best of these hybrids. Native of western and central China. Introduced by Wilson in 1900.

Viburnum tinus LINNAEUS *Laurustinus*

4.(5). Evergreen shrub of rounded form, 2–3m high and often more in width. Bts either glabrous or slightly hairy. Lv ovate-elliptic, to 10cm long and 3cm wide; very dark, glossy green above, paler beneath, glabrous on both surfaces apart from the odd tuft of down in the lower vein axils. Fl in corymbs to 10cm across, pink in bud, white or pinkish when open. Fl 11–4. Fr ovoid, 6mm long, dark blue, finally black. Var *lucidum* AITON has larger lv and inflorescences but is slightly less hardy. Although such a popular evergreen, it can be damaged in very severe winters. It is excellent for maritime districts. Native of the Mediterranean region, where it tends to be rather a dwarf shrub. In cultivation since the sixteenth century.

Viburnum utile HEMSLEY

4.5. Evergreen shrub, to 2m, with rather thin brs, which are downy at first. Lv elliptic to ovate-oblong, to 8cm long and 3cm wide, smooth and dark glossy green above, grey tomentose below. Fl in terminal, rounded corymbs to 8cm wide, white and fragrant. Fl 5. Fr blue-black. An attractive small evergreen. Native of China. Introduced in 1901 by Wilson.

VITIS LINNAEUS *Vitidaceae* Vines

A genus of at least sixty species of shrubs, climbing by means of tendrils and mainly deciduous. The leaves are alternate, usually lobed, toothed. The flowers appear in panicles, opposite the leaves, on the current year's growth; they are of little beauty, with the parts in fives. The petals are joined together to form a sort of cup, which falls away when the anthers are ripe. In some species they are attractively fragrant. The fruit is a large, pulpy berry, containing two to four pear-shaped seeds. Although the fruits are sometimes ornamental, the plants are grown mainly for their foliage which is liable to colour brilliantly in the autumn. Propagation is easiest by 'eyes', single buds from one-year-old stems, started into growth in early spring, but *V. coignetiae* is slow at reproducing in this way and seeds or layers are a better method.

Vitis amurensis RUPRECHT

6. Vigorous, deciduous climber, with reddish, floccose bts. Lv 3-lobed, usually quite deeply, basically cordate, to 20cm long and wide; glabrous above, somewhat downy below, colouring crimson and purple in the autumn. Fl 6. Fr about 8mm in diameter, black. Native of the Amur region of Manchuria. Introduced about 1854.

Vitis betulifolia DIELS AND GILG

6. A vigorous, high-climbing vine with floccose bts and young lv. Lv usually unlobed, broad-ovate, remaining downy below but becoming glabrous above, to 10cm long, nearly as wide, colouring richly in the autumn. Panicle slender, to 10cm long. Fl 6. Fr black. *V. wilsonae*, which

seems to be no longer in commerce, is very similar but with larger lv. Native of central and western China. Introduced by Wilson in 1907.

Vitis coignetiae PLANCHON

6. An extremely vigorous climber, with bts greyish-floccose at first. Most vines produce a tendril at every joint, but in this sp the tendril is lacking every third joint. Lv basically orbicular, shallowly 3–5-lobed, dark dull green and nearly glabrous above, rusty tomentose below, to 25cm long and 20cm broad (sometimes more), turning brilliant crimson in the autumn. Panicle rather short. Fl 6–7. Fr about 1cm wide, black with a purple bloom. The plant will run up a tree with ease, but is rather too vigorous for most walls. Native of Japan and Korea. Introduced by Madame Coignet to France in 1875 but possibly received earlier by Anthony Waterer.

Vitis davidii FOEX

6. (*V. armata* DIELS; *Spinovitis davidii* ROMANET). A vigorous climber, the bts covered with spiny, hooked, gland-tipped bristles. Lv cordate, dark lustrous green above, glaucous below and glabrous, apart from glandular bristles along the main veins; turning brilliant crimson in the autumn. Fl in panicles to 25cm. Fl 6–7. Fr black about 1·5cm wide. Var *cyanocarpa* SARGENT (var *veitchii* VEITCH) is less prickly, has larger lv and fr with a blue bloom. Native of China. In cultivation in 1885. Var *cyanocarpa* introduced by Wilson in 1900.

Vitis flexuosa THUNBERG

3. Slender-stemmed vine of moderate growth. The form in commerce is var *parvifolia* GAGNE-PAIN, in which the young lv are bronzy above, purple below. The bts are covered with a rusty tomentum at first. The lv, when mature, are roundish-ovate, usually unlobed, to 7cm long and wide. Panicle to 15cm. Fl 6. Fr black about the size of a pea. The var *parvifolia* introduced from central China by Wilson in 1900.

Vitis labrusca LINNAEUS Fox Grape

6. Vigorous climber with a tendril or inflorescence opposite each lv. Bts densely floccose. Lv rather thick, cordate-orbicular, unlobed or 3-lobed, dark green and eventually glabrous above, rusty tomentose below. Panicles to 10cm. Fl 6. Fr 1·5cm across, dark purple, edible, with a 'foxy' aroma. Important commercially as a parent of many American-raised grapes, but not outstandingly ornamental. Native of the eastern USA, the Tradescants were growing it in 1656, so it was brought back by the younger Tradescant in 1642 or 1654.

Vitis piasezkii MAXIMOWICZ

6. (*V. pagnuccii* ROMANET, *Parthenocissus sinensis* DIELS AND GILG). A slender-stemmed vine of moderate growth with bts (and petioles) covered with rusty down and glandular bristles. Remarkable for the various-shaped lv which may occur on the same branch. Some are ovate, unlobed or quite deeply lobed, to 10cm long and wide, others are composed of 3–5 leaflets, which are ovate, the central one stalked, the others sessile. the simple lv is up to 10cm long and wide; in the compound lv, the lv are up to 12cm long and 4cm wide, glabrous above, rusty tomentose below. They turn a brilliant crimson in the autumn. Panicle to 15cm long and nearly as wide. Fl 5–6. Fr black with a purple bloom, about 1cm across. *V. pagnuccii* is now reduced to a var of *V. piasezkii*, distinguished only by its glabrous bts and lv. *V. pagnuccii* was in cultivation in France in 1885. *V. piasezkii* introduced by Wilson in 1900. Rehder says it was introduced in 1807, but this seems unlikely.

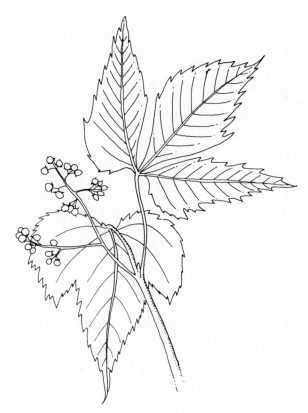

Vitis piasezkii

Vitis riparia MICHAUX

4.(5). (*V. vulpina* of gardens but not of LINNAEUS, *V. odoratissima* D. DON). Vigorous climber with smooth bts, lacking a tendril every third joint. Lv basically heart-shaped, shallowly or deeply 3-lobed, rather thin in texture, shining green on both surfaces, to 20cm wide and slightly longer. Fl in panicles to 20cm long, with a strong scent of mignonette. Fl 6. Fr round, 8mm in diameter, very dark purple with blue bloom. Worth growing for its attractive lv as well as its fragrant fl. It also sets fr fairly regularly. Native of much of N America from Nova Scotia southwards to Texas and westwards to Colorado. Introduced by the younger Tradescant either in 1642 or in 1654.

Vitis vinifera LINNAEUS   Grape Vine

(5).6. Vigorous climber, to 20m, with bts either glabrous or floccose. Lv basically orbicular, 3–5-lobed, with the lobes tending to overlap, more or less smooth above, downy below, up to 15cm long and wide. Some cv colour well in the autumn. Fl 6. Fr black with a bluish bloom. A number of cv exist, of which 'Apiifolia' has the lv very deeply incised, 'Incana' has greyish lv covered with a light grey cobwebby down, and in 'Purpurea' the lv are claret coloured, turning lurid purple in the autumn. 'Brant' is a hybrid between 'Clinton', which was *V. labrusca X riparia*, and a fruiting cv of *V. vinifera*, 'Black St Peters'. It fruits freely with purple-black fr while the lv turn dark red and purple in the autumn. Possibly native to Asia Minor or the Caucasus, but so long cultivated that its original habitat is lost.

WEIGELA THUNBERG *Caprifoliaceae*

(At one time included in *Diervilla*.) A small genus of about twelve species of deciduous shrubs from eastern Asia with showy funnel-shaped flowers. The leaves are opposite, serrate, short-petioled. The flowers have five lobes and five stamens, the fruit is a dry capsule, usually shaped like a beak. There are a number of hybrids, mainly based on *WW. coraensis*, *japonica* and *florida*. The flowers are on the second year's wood, which can be hard pruned when flowering is over. Propagation by seed is easy, but for the hybrids and cultivars cuttings of half-ripe wood root readily. They appear happy in all soils.

Weigela coraensis THUNBERG

4. (*W. grandiflora* SIEBOLD AND ZUCCARINI). Shrub, to 5m occasionally but more usually to 3m, with glabrous bts. Lv ovate, acuminate, to 12cm long and 7cm wide, glabrous or nearly so above, slightly hairy along veins below; petiole bristly. Fl usually in threes, funnel-shaped, to 3cm long and 2cm wide, pale pink deepening as the bloom ages. Fl 6. Native of Japan, not of Korea. In cultivation in 1850.

Weigela floribunda SIEBOLD AND ZUCCARINI

4. Differs from *W. coraensis* in its slender brs, which are usually faintly hairy at first, in the lv being downy on both surfaces and in the downy, not glabrous, ovary. The fl are sessile, usually a dark crimson although var *versicolor* is greenish-white on emergence, fading to pale crimson. Fl 6. The true plant is rare in cultivation, although the main parent of the dark crimson-flowered hybrids, such as 'Eva Rathke'. Native of Japan. Introduced about 1860.

Weigela florida

Weigla florida SIEBOLD AND ZUCCARINI

4. (*Weigela rosea* LINDLEY, *W. amabilis* of gardens). A shrub, to 2m, with arching brs; bts with 2 lines of short hairs. Lv oval-lanceolate, long-acuminate, toothed in the upper half, glabrous above, slightly tomentose along the midrib below, to 11cm long and 4cm wide. Fl in threes or fours, to 3cm long, deep pink outside, paler inside. Fl 5–6. Forms with white fl and with variegated lv exist. Native of China. Introduced by Fortune in 1845.

Weigela japonica THUNBERG

4. Shrub, to 3m, with bts either glabrous or with 2 rows of hairs. Lv ovate, long-acuminate, to 10cm long and 5cm wide, slightly hairy above, grey tomentose below. Fl in terminal and axillary clusters of 3, to give a leafy panicle. Fl to 3cm long, pale pink deepening with age. Fl 5–6. *W. hortensis* SIEBOLD AND ZUCCARINI is very similar but with the lv densely white tomentose beneath. It is only known in cultivation nowadays by the white-flowered 'Nivea'. *W. decora* NAKAI has the lv glabrous and glossy above, slightly hairy below. Fl white fading to pink. *W. hortensis* 'Nivea' was the first to reach western gardens in 1864; the rather tender pink form arrived in 1870. *W. japonica* arrived in 1892 and *W. decora* not until 1933.

Weigela maximowiczii REHDER

4. A low shrub not exceeding 1·5m; the bts with 2 rows of hairs. Lv elliptic-ovate, to 12cm long and half as wide, with a few scattered hairs above and on the veins below, nearly sessile. Fl in twos, about 3·5cm long, greenish-yellow. Fl 4–5. Like the next sp, this requires a rather sheltered position. Native of Japan. Introduced in 1915.

Weigela middendorfiana K. KOCH

4. Low-growing shrub, to 1·5m, the bts with 2 downy ridges. Lv ovate, to 8cm long and half as wide, acuminate, toothed, wrinkled, more or less glabrous when mature, sessile. Fl in twos or threes, to 3cm long, sulphur-yellow with orange markings on the lower lobes. Calyx markedly two-lipped. Fl 4–5. Liable to damage by late spring frosts, but interesting for its yellow fl which are a better colour than the preceding sp. Native of northern China, Manchuria and Japan. Introduced in 1850.

Weigela praecox (LEMOINE) BAILEY

4. Shrub, to 2m, with both glabrous and hairy bts. Lv elliptic-ovate, to 12cm long and half as wide, toothed, hairy above, pubescent below. Fl in threes or fives, to 3·5cm long, pink with yellow throat. Fl 5. The earliest-flowering pink sp. Native of Japan, Korea and Manchuria. Received from Japan by Lemoine, who put it into commerce in 1894.

WISTERIA NUTTALL *Leguminosae*

A small genus of about nine species of twining, deciduous shrubs from eastern Asia and the eastern USA. Only three species are generally available. The leaves are alternate, pinnate; the flowers pea-shaped in long racemes. The fruit is a pod much like a runner bean. Propagation is generally by layers or grafts on seedlings of *W. sinensis*, as plants from seed are extremely variable and may well, after several years, prove to be unsatisfactory forms. *W. sinensis*, if continually pinched back, may be grown as a small standard tree. The species are generally hardy and seem to thrive on most soils. In some districts birds may destroy the buds before they open, as they tend to be formed in the autumn or early spring before the leaves emerge. It is a pity that the American *W. macrostachya,* which blooms June-August after the leaf, is not available for such districts.

Wisteria floribunda DE CANDOLLE

4. A tall climber, to 8m, twining clockwise. Lv pinnate with 13–19 leaflets, the whole lv sometimes to 35cm, leaflets ovate, downy when young, to 8cm long and about half as wide, light green. Fl in terminal racemes from lateral year-old growths, purplish-blue, to 12cm long, but in the form known as 'Macrobotrys' (*Wisteria multijuga* VAN HOUTTE), the racemes may be over 1m long and usually exceed 30cm. Each fl is about 2cm long, pale lilac with darker tips. Fl 5–6. There are forms of the typical plant with pinkish fl ('Rosea') and a double form in which the violet fl are rosette shaped, but this is a shy flowerer. There is also a white form. Native of Japan. The type introduced by Siebold in 1830; 'Macrobotrys' also introduced by Siebold in the early 1860s.

Wisteria sinensis SWEET

4. (*W. chinensis* DE CANDOLLE). A very vigorous twiner, anti-clockwise, to 20m or more. Lv pinnate, to 30cm long, usually with 11 leaflets but varying from 9–13; the leaflets downy at first, later green and smooth above, slightly hairy below, elliptic, to 10cm long and 3cm wide. Racemes to 30cm long on second year wood, opening with the lv in May. Each fl to 2·5cm long, lilac-mauve, fragrant. There exist white and dark purple forms, as well as an unsatisfactory double form. Native of China. Introduced to Sir Joseph Banks about 1816 and subsequently by Fortune.

Wisteria venusta REHDER AND WILSON

4. A vigorous climber, to 10m and more, with downy bts. Lv pinnate, to 40cm long, with 9–13 leaflets. Leaflets oval-acuminate, to 9cm long and 3·5cm wide, downy on both surfaces but more so below. Racemes to 15cm long, the fl up to 3cm long and 2·5cm wide, the largest in the genus; white with a yellow flush at the base of the standard. Fl 5–6. Only known as a Japanese garden plant. Introduced in 1912 according to Bean, before 1900 according to Rehder (possibly this was the so-called double form). The wild plant, known as f *violacea* REHDER, has rather smaller, bluish-violet fl and has only very recently been introduced.

XANTHOCERAS BUNGE *Sapindaceae*

A monotypic genus.

Xanthoceras sorbifolium

Xanthoceras sorbifolium BUNGE

4. Deciduous shrub or small tree, to 7m, with stout, upright, glabrous bts. Lv alternate, pinnate, to 20cm long, the leaflets borne on the upper two thirds of the rachis, 9–15 in number, lanceolate, toothed, to 6cm long and 1·5cm wide; dark green above, lighter beneath, smooth on both surfaces. Fl in terminal and axillary panicles on year-old wood; the terminal panicle up to 20cm long, the axillary ones only half as large. Each floret has 5 patulate petals, the whole floret to 2·5cm across, white with a yellow blotch at the base which turns carmine later. Fl 5. Fr a top-shaped capsule to 5cm wide at the top, tapering to the base. A very attractive tree but liable to be damaged by spring frosts, which may also encourage attacks by coral spot fungus. The lv persist for a long time in the autumn. Propagated by seed or by root cuttings. An excellent wall shrub. Native of China. Introduced by Père David in 1866.

YUCCA LINNAEUS *Liliaceae*

A genus of woody evergreens with long, sword-like leaves, which are arranged in dense rosettes, and tall panicles of drooping flowers looking like a huge lily of the valley. They are not produced on young plants and by no means every year, once flowering has started. Quite a number of these exotic-looking plants are hardy in most parts of the UK, but all but three species are rather too low for inclusion here. They require full sunshine. Propagated by offshoots, when these occur, otherwise rosettes can be detached and trimmed of the lower leaves when they will root. The plants are slow-growing.

Yucca glauca NUTTALL

4. (*Y. angustifolia* PURSH). The plant is either stemless or the trunk is prostrate, but the rosette is up to 1·3m wide. Lv narrow, to 75cm long and only 2cm wide, pointed, the margins white with detached·threads, the rest of the blade glaucous. Fl in erect racemes to 1·5m tall with numerous greenish-white campanulate fl to 7cm long. Fl 7–8. Although quite hardy, a shy flowerer. Native of the eastern USA from S Dakota to New Mexico. Introduced before 1696, but 1812 according to Sweet.

Yucca gloriosa LINNAEUS

4. Evergreen shrub, to 3m in the UK, the stem sometimes branched but only on old plants. Lv to 60cm long, spine-tipped, 7cm wide, glaucous when young, later grey-green. Fl in a conical panicle, to 1·5m tall and 30cm wide. The fl pendulous, creamy-white, sometimes with a purplish tinge outside, about 7cm long. Fl 7–9. Native of the eastern USA from S Carolina to Florida. Grown by Gerard in 1596.

Yucca recurvifolia SALISBURY

4. Shrub, to 2m or more, the stems usually branched. Lv to 1m or more long, 5·5cm wide, spine-tipped, glaucous at first, recurving after the first year. Fl in an erect, branched panicle to 1m (or more), each fl creamy-white, to 8cm wide. Fl 7–9. Forms with yellow margins to the lv, or with a yellow stripe in the centre, have occurred from time to time. The best sp for general cultivation, although the other spp are equally hardy but less floriferous. Native mainly of Georgia. Introduced in 1794.

ZANTHOXYLUM LINNAEUS *Rutaceae*

A genus of about thirty shrubs or trees, of which only very few are found in temperate regions. They normally have rather spiny branches and the leaves are somewhat aromatic when crushed. The leaves are alternate, pinnate or occasionally trifoliolate. The flowers are in panicles, dioecious usually, sometimes lacking petals, capsules much like those of *Celastrus*, eventually splitting to reveal the single seed within. Although the fruit is attractive, it is usually necessary to have plants of both sexes, although *Z. planispinum* tends to be monoecious. Even so it would seem to need a hot summer to set fruit satisfactorily. The plants seem easy-going as regards soil and seem to have no objection to partial shade. Propagation is by seed, by root cuttings and by cuttings of half-ripe wood.

Zanthoxylum piperitum DE CANDOLLE

(5).(6). Rounded, deciduous shrub, to about 3m in cultivation although a small tree in the wild. Bts pubescent at first, armed with a pair of flattish spines to 1cm long at each node. Lv pinnate, to 15cm long, with 11–23 leaflets, the rachis pubescent, slightly spiny and winged at the base. The leaflets sessile, ovate, to 4cm long and half as wide, dark green often turning a good yellow in the autumn. Fl in small corymbs to 5cm long, greenish. Fl 6. Fr reddish, small, the seeds black. The lv are very attractive. In Japan the seeds are ground for pepper. Native of Japan, Korea and northern China. In cultivation in 1877.

Zanthoxylum planispinum
SIEBOLD AND ZUCCARINI

(5). (*Z. alatum* ROXBURGH var *planispinum*). Spreading, deciduous shrub, to 4m, with spines to 2cm long, flattened at the base, in pairs. Lv usually trifoliolate occasionally pinnate, with 5 leaflets, the rachis winged and 2cm wide at the base, the whole lv to 25cm long, the largest, terminal leaflet to 12cm long, ovate-lanceolate, acuminate, serrate, persisting long into the autumn. Fl lacking petals, yellowish. Fl 5–6. Fr red, somewhat warty, handsome after hot summers. The true *Z. alatum*, which is not in cultivation, has 5–11 leaflets. Native of Japan, Korea, China. In cultivation in 1880.

Zanthoxylum schinifolium
SIEBOLD AND ZUCCARINI

(5). Deciduous shrub, to 4m, with solitary spines to 1cm long. Lv to 16cm long with 11–21 leaflets, the largest up to 4cm long, lanceolate, dark green above, paler beneath, rachis spiny. Fl on the current year's growth (the other spp flower on year-old wood) in a flattish cluster to 10cm across, the fl with green petals. Fr greenish, occasionally reddish, the seeds bluish. Fl 8. The fern-like lv are attractive. Native of Japan, N China and Korea. In cultivation in 1877.

Zanthoxylum simulans HANCE

(5). (*Z. bungei* PLANCHON). Deciduous, spreading bush, to 3m although occasionally a small tree to 7m; spines broad and flat to 2cm long. Lv aromatic, to 12cm long (occasionally to 20cm) with 7–11 leaflets which are roundish and up to 4cm long, often with a few spiny bristles on the upper surface, rachis prickly on both surfaces. Fl in a very short panicle, to 6cm wide, greenish-yellow, lacking petals. Fl 6–7. Fr reddish. The hardiest sp in cultivation, passing through the severest winters without damage. Native of China. Introduced in 1869, which rather suggests Père David as the introducer.

ZELKOVA SPACH *Ulmaceae*

A small genus of six or seven deciduous trees or shrubs with smooth, scaly bark, alternate leaves and monoecious flowers; the males clustered in the lower axils, the females solitary in the upper axils, both inconspicuous. The fruit is a small drupe with a dry surround. The plants are very similar to elms, but are distinguished by their monoecious flowers and the odd horned drupe. Propagation is mainly by seed. They resent drought, but otherwise will flourish in most soils.

Zelkova carpiniflora

Zelkova carpinifolia (PALLAS) K. KOCH

7. (*Z. crenata* SPACH, *Planera richardii* MICHAUX). Deciduous tree, to 30m, of slow growth and often with a number of trunks, with peeling bark and very downy bts. The tree makes an elegant, upright head. Lv ovate to elliptic, to 7cm long and 4cm wide, coarsely toothed, dark green and slightly hispid above, paler and somewhat downy below. Fl before lv. Fr about the size of a pea. *Z. verschaffeltii* NICHOLSON would appear to be a form of this plant, making a small tree or a large shrub with oval lv to 6cm long and 4cm wide. Fr similar to that of *Z. carpinifolia*. The plant has not been recorded in the wild, although known in gardens since 1886.

Z. carpinifolia itself is native to the Caucasus

and is said to have been introduced prior to 1760, however, this refers to a plant called *Ulmus nemoralis* in *Hortus Kewensis*, offered by Gordon in 1760 as coming from N America. Possibly it was obtained from one of Collinson's Russian correspondents and Gordon might have confused it with Bartram's sendings.

Zelkova serrata (THUNBERG) MAKINO

6.(7). (*Z. acuminata* PLANCHON, *Z. keaki* MAXIMOWICZ). A spreading, deciduous tree, rarely more than 10m in the UK although up to 40m in the wild. Bark smooth and grey. The trunk comparatively short and soon dividing into erect spreading brs; bts glabrous or glabrescent. Lv ovate, to 11cm long and 5cm wide, coarsely toothed, long-acuminate, slightly hispid above, paler and glabrous below. Often turning bronze or crimson in the autumn. Fr roundish, 3mm wide. Native to Japan and Korea. Introduced by J. G. Veitch in 1860.

ZENOBIA DAVID DON *Ericaceae*

A monotypic genus, requiring acid soil.

Zenobia pulverulenta (BARTRAM) POLLARD

3.4. (*Z. speciosa* D. DON, *Andromeda pulverulenta* BARTRAM). Deciduous or semi-evergreen, rather straggling, thin shrub, to 2m, glabrous in all its parts. Bts and young lv glaucous blue-green (but this is lacking in some forms, to which the varietal name *nuda* was given, but it appears to be a simple seminal variant). Later the glaucous bloom tends to fade. Lv ovate-elliptic, to 5·5cm long and 3cm wide. Fl in clusters of fours or fives, in the upper axils of year-old wood, to form a racemose inflorescence to 20cm long. The individual fl are much like a large lily of the valley, 1cm across, pure white with a scent of aniseed. Fl 6–7. This appears to thrive best in a semi-shaded position and resents prolonged drought. Propagated by seed and by cuttings of half-ripe young wood. Native of the south-eastern USA from N Carolina to Florida. Introduced by Fraser in 1801.

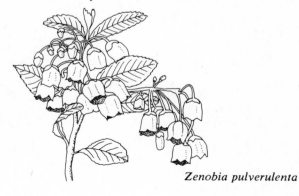

Zenobia pulverulenta

Glossary

ACICULAR Needle-shaped.

ACULEATE Prickly.

ACUMINATE Tapering to a point.

ANTHER The part of the stamen bearing the pollen.

ARIL A fleshy appendage to a seed.

ARISTATE Tipped with a bristle.

AUCT Auctorum (of authors); AUCT NON used to indicate a misapplied name.

AXIL The angle between a stem and a leaf.

AXILLARY Situated at the axil.

BRACT A modified leaf below a flower or the pedicel of a flower.

BRANCHLET The current year's growth of a woody plant.

BULLATE Puckered or quilted.

CALYX The outer, usually uncoloured, part of a flower.

CAMPANULATE Bell-shaped.

CAPSULE A dry fruit containing more than one seed and splitting when ripe.

CARPEL A single pistil.

CATKIN A spike of flowers, usually unisexual, with the flowers separated by scaly bracts.

CILIATE Fringed with hairs.

CORDATE Heart-shaped.

CORIACEOUS Leathery.

COROLLA The petals or tepals of a flower in their entirety.

CORYMB Basically a raceme with the pedicels of unequal length, so that the whole inflorescence has a flat top; the outer flowers open first.

CRENATE With scalloped edges.

CULTIVAR A plant varying in some details from the normal wild plant, which is known only as a result of cultivation.

CYME A branched inflorescence with the central flower opening first.

DELTOID Triangular.

DIGITATE Finger-like, with the members arising from a single point.

DIOECIOUS Bearing male and female flowers on separate plants.

DRUPE A fleshy fruit with a bony seed within.

EXFOLIATING Peeling off in strips.

FALCATE Sickle-shaped.

FASCICLE A cluster of flowers.

FASTIGIATE With branches erect and close together.

FERRUGINEOUS Rust-coloured.

FLOCCOSE Covered with tufts of wool.

FUSCOUS Grey-brown.

GLABROUS Lacking hairs.

GLAUCOUS Blue-white or blue-green.

HASTATE Shaped like a spear-head with the basal lobes pointing outwards.

HISPID With rigid hairs or bristles, giving a rough feel.

HORT Hortulanorum (of gardeners), denoting a name used in horticultural circles but having no botanical validity.

HYBRID The offspring of two different species.

IMBRICATE Overlapping, like tiles on a roof.

INVOLUCRE A whorl of bracts below an inflorescence.

LACINIATE Jagged, cut into narrow lobes.

LANCEOLATE Of a leaf about four times as long as wide, shaped like a lance.

LEAFLET Part of a compound leaf.

LEPIDOTE Scaly.

LOBE A division of a leaf, not into a separate leaflet.

MONOECIOUS With male and female flowers, but both on the same plant.

MONOTYPIC Refering to a genus which contains only one species.

MUCRO A small abrupt point at the apex of a leaf.

OB- A prefix signifying inversion, usually with the broader section of the leaf towards the apex, eg oblanceolate, obovate.

OBLIQUE Unequal-sided.

ORBICULAR Circular.

OVAL Round, about two thirds as wide as long.

OVATE Egg-shaped.

PALMATE Lobed or divided from a central point in a circle.

PANICLE A branched raceme.

PATULATE Spread out flat; flowers which open out in a plate-like fashion.

PEDICEL The stalk of a flower, particularly in a compound inflorescence.

PEDUNCLE The stalk of a flower cluster, or of a single flower.

PELTATE Shield-shaped, with the petiole attaching itself to the centre of the leaf.

PERIANTH The surroundings of stamens and pistil.

PETAL A separate, usually coloured, part of the corolla.

PETIOLE A leaf stalk.

PILOSE Covered with long, straight hairs.

PINNATE A compound leaf, with the leaflets placed on each side of the rachis. BIPINNATE when the leaflets are replaced by pinnate leaves.

PINNATIFID Pinnately lobed.

PINNATISECT Cut to the midrib in a pinnate fashion.

PISTIL The female organs of style, stigma and ovary.

PLICATE Pleated.

PROCUMBENT Trailing horizontally.

PRUINOSE Covered with bloom, as in grapes.

PUBESCENT Downy.

PYRIFORM Pear-shaped.

RACEME A spike of flowers.

RACHIS The central axis of a pinnate leaf. It can also be used of the central stem in a raceme.

RAY The petaloid parts of a composite flower.

RECURVED Curved outwards and downwards.

REFLEXED Bent backwards abruptly.

RENIFORM Kidney-shaped.

ROTATE Shaped like a wheel, circular; referring to flowers.

RUFOUS Red-brown.

RUGOSE Wrinkled.

SAGITTATE Shaped like an arrow-head.

SAMARA A flattened fruit, adapted for wind dispersal.

SCABROUS Rough to the touch.

SEPAL A leaf-like division of the calyx.

SESSILE Unstalked.

SETOSE Bristly.

SINUATE Wavy.

SPATULATE Spoon-shaped.

STIGMA The top of the style; the pollen-receiving receptacle.

STIPULE A leaf-like appendage at the base of the petiole.

STROBILE A small cone, as in *Chamaecyparis*.

STYLE The part of the pistil between the ovary and the stigma.

SYNCARP(S) Used of fruits that are formed from several carpels fused together eg *Magnolia*, *Rhododendron*, *Cistus*.

TEPAL A sepal acting as a petal (as in *Clematis*).

TERNATE With the parts in threes.

TETRAPLOID Plants with cells that have two sets of chromosomes – tiny structures that carry the units of heredity.

TOMENTUM A dense covering of matted hairs or down.

TRIFOLIATE With three leaflets, two arising below the middle one.

TRIFOLIOLATE With three leaflets all arising from the same point.

TURBINATE Top-shaped.

UMBEL A compound inflorescence with all the pedicels arising from the same point.

URCEOLATE Urn-shaped; ovoid and contracted at the mouth.

VARIETAS Abbreviated var; a race of plants evidently conspecific with the type, but differing consistently, even when raised from seed, in one or more details.

VILLOUS Bearing rather shaggy hairs, usually curved and long.

WHORL An arrangement of three or more organs in a circle around a central axis.

Bibliography

Aiton, W. *Hortus Kewensis*, 5 vols (1810–13)

Allan, Mea. *The Tradescants*

Bean, W. J. *Trees and Shrubs Hardy in the British Isles,* 3 vols (vol 1 1922, rev. Murray 1970; vol 2 1922, rev. Murray 1973; vol 3 1933)

Brett-James. *Life of Peter Collinson* (1926)

Dallimore, W. and Jackson, A. B. *Handbook of Coniferae and Ginkgoaceae* (1966)

Dillwyn. *Hortus Collinsonianus* (1843)

Flora Europaea (Cambridge, 1964–72)

Hillier, H. G. *Manual of Trees and Shrubs* (Newton Abbot, 1972)

Loudon, C. *Arboretum et Fruticetum Britannicum* (1838)

———. *Hortus Britannicus* (1839)

Miller, P. *The Gardeners' Dictionary*, (1768)

Rehder, A. *Manual of Cultivated Trees and Shrubs* (Macmillan, New York, 1949)

Sweet, Robert. *Hortus Britannicus* (1830)

RHS. *Dictionary of Gardening*, 4 vols (Oxford, 1956, suppl 1969)

———. *Journal*, Passim